Citroën Dispatch, Peugeot Expert & Fiat Scudo
Owners Workshop Manual

Martynn Randall

Models covered

(6412 - 320)

Citroën Dispatch, Peugeot Expert & Fiat Scudo vans with 1.6 litre (1560cc) & 2.0 litre (1997cc) turbo-diesel engines

Also covers most features of Toyota Proace vans

Does NOT cover petrol engined models, automatic transmission, or equipment specific to combi, refrigerated or crew vans
Does NOT cover new model ranges introduced during 2016

© Haynes Group Limited 2018

ABCDE
FGHIJ
KLMNO
PQRS

A book in the **Haynes Owners Workshop Manual Series**

ISBN **978 1 78521 412 7**

British Library Cataloguing in Publication Data
A catalogue record for this book is available from the British Library.

Printed in India

Haynes Group Limited
Sparkford, Yeovil, Somerset BA22 7JJ, England

Haynes North America, Inc
2801 Townsgate Road, Suite 340, Thousand Oaks, CA 91361

Disclaimer

There are risks associated with automotive repairs. The ability to make repairs depends on the individual's skill, experience and proper tools. Individuals should act with due care and acknowledge and assume the risk of performing automotive repairs.

The purpose of this manual is to provide comprehensive, useful and accessible automotive repair information, to help you get the best value from your vehicle. However, this manual is not a substitute for a professional certified technician or mechanic.

This repair manual is produced by a third party and is not associated with an individual vehicle manufacturer. If there is any doubt or discrepancy between this manual and the owner's manual or the factory service manual, please refer to the factory service manual or seek assistance from a professional certified technician or mechanic.

Even though we have prepared this manual with extreme care and every attempt is made to ensure that the information in this manual is correct, neither the publisher nor the author can accept responsibility for loss, damage or injury caused by any errors in, or omissions from, the information given.

Contents

LIVING WITH YOUR CITROËN DISPATCH/ PEUGEOT EXPERT /FIAT SCUDO

Roadside repairs

Weekly checks

Lubricants and fluids

Tyre pressures

MAINTENANCE

Routine maintenance and servicing

Contents

Designed as a joint venture between Citroën, Peugeot and Fiat; the Dispatch III, Expert III and Scudo (Mark II) were introduced into the UK in 2007 as purpose-built Vans. In 2013, Toyota joined the venture and launched the Proace. Although subtly different in external appearance, the vehicle are mechanically identical, and share the same range of diesel engines. Although 'Combi' MPV, Crew-cab and petrol engined versions were available, their specific features are not covered by this manual.

During the production run a variety of diesel engines have been offered according to model and year of production. These include 1.6 litre (1560cc) and 2.0 litre (1997cc) turbo diesel engines.

The engine is mounted transversely at the front of vehicle, with the transmission mounted on its left-hand end. All engines are fitted with a manual transmission as standard.

All models have fully independent front suspension, incorporating shock absorbers, coil springs and an anti-roll bar. The rear beam axle has a built-in anti-roll bar, with separate shock absorbers and coil springa. Rack-and-pinion steering gear is used with hydraulic or electro-hydraulic power assistance.

A wide range of standard and optional equipment is available within the range to suit most tastes, including power steering, central locking, engine immobiliser, electric windows, electric sunroof and airbags. An anti-lock braking system and air conditioning system are also available as options, or standard equipment.

Provided that regular servicing is carried out in accordance with the manufacturer's recommendations, the vehicle should prove reliable and very economical. The engine compartment is well-designed, and most of the items requiring frequent attention are easily accessible.

Your Owner's Manual

The aim of this manual is to help you get the best value from your vehicle. It can do so in several ways. It can help you decide what work must be done (even should you choose to get it done by a garage), provide information on routine maintenance and servicing, and give a logical course of action and diagnosis when random faults occur. However, it is hoped that you will use the manual by tackling the work yourself. On simpler jobs it may even be quicker than booking the vehicle into a garage and going there twice, to leave and collect it. Perhaps most important, a lot of money can be saved by avoiding the costs a garage must charge to cover its labour and overheads.

The manual has drawings and descriptions to show the function of the various components so that their layout can be understood. Tasks are described and photographed in a clear step-by-step sequence.

References to the 'left-hand' and 'right-hand' sides of the vehicle are always in the sense of when viewed by a person sat in the driver's seat, facing forwards.

Acknowledgements

Thanks are due to Draper Tools Limited, who provided some of the workshop tools, and to all those people at Sparkford who helped in the production of this Manual.

We take great pride in the accuracy of information given in this manual, but vehicle manufacturers make alterations and design changes during the production run of a particular vehicle of which they do not inform us. No liability can be accepted by the authors or publishers for loss, damage or injury caused by errors in, or omissions from, the information given.

Citroen Dispatch

Working on your car can be dangerous. This page shows just some of the potential risks and hazards, with the aim of creating a safety-conscious attitude.

General hazards

Scalding

• Don't remove the radiator or expansion tank cap while the engine is hot.
• Engine oil, transmission fluid or power steering fluid may also be dangerously hot if the engine has recently been running.

Burning

• Beware of burns from the exhaust system and from any part of the engine. Brake discs and drums can also be extremely hot immediately after use.

Crushing

• When working under or near a raised vehicle, always supplement the jack with axle stands, or use drive-on ramps. *Never venture under a car which is only supported by a jack.*

• Take care if loosening or tightening high-torque nuts when the vehicle is on stands. Initial loosening and final tightening should be done with the wheels on the ground.

Fire

• Fuel is highly flammable; fuel vapour is explosive.
• Don't let fuel spill onto a hot engine.
• Do not smoke or allow naked lights (including pilot lights) anywhere near a vehicle being worked on. Also beware of creating sparks (electrically or by use of tools).
• Fuel vapour is heavier than air, so don't work on the fuel system with the vehicle over an inspection pit.
• Another cause of fire is an electrical overload or short-circuit. Take care when repairing or modifying the vehicle wiring.
• Keep a fire extinguisher handy, of a type suitable for use on fuel and electrical fires.

Electric shock

• Ignition HT and Xenon headlight voltages can be dangerous, especially to people with heart problems or a pacemaker. Don't work on or near these systems with the engine running or the ignition switched on.

• Mains voltage is also dangerous. Make sure that any mains-operated equipment is correctly earthed. Mains power points should be protected by a residual current device (RCD) circuit breaker.

Fume or gas intoxication

• Exhaust fumes are poisonous; they can contain carbon monoxide, which is rapidly fatal if inhaled. Never run the engine in a confined space such as a garage with the doors shut.
• Fuel vapour is also poisonous, as are the vapours from some cleaning solvents and paint thinners.

Poisonous or irritant substances

• Avoid skin contact with battery acid and with any fuel, fluid or lubricant, especially antifreeze, brake hydraulic fluid and Diesel fuel. Don't syphon them by mouth. If such a substance is swallowed or gets into the eyes, seek medical advice.
• Prolonged contact with used engine oil can cause skin cancer. Wear gloves or use a barrier cream if necessary. Change out of oil-soaked clothes and do not keep oily rags in your pocket.
• Air conditioning refrigerant forms a poisonous gas if exposed to a naked flame (including a cigarette). It can also cause skin burns on contact.

Asbestos

• Asbestos dust can cause cancer if inhaled or swallowed. Asbestos may be found in gaskets and in brake and clutch linings. When dealing with such components it is safest to assume that they contain asbestos.

Special hazards

Hydrofluoric acid

• This extremely corrosive acid is formed when certain types of synthetic rubber, found in some O-rings, oil seals, fuel hoses etc, are exposed to temperatures above 4000C. The rubber changes into a charred or sticky substance containing the acid. *Once formed, the acid remains dangerous for years. If it gets onto the skin, it may be necessary to amputate the limb concerned.*
• When dealing with a vehicle which has suffered a fire, or with components salvaged from such a vehicle, wear protective gloves and discard them after use.

The battery

• Batteries contain sulphuric acid, which attacks clothing, eyes and skin. Take care when topping-up or carrying the battery.
• The hydrogen gas given off by the battery is highly explosive. Never cause a spark or allow a naked light nearby. Be careful when connecting and disconnecting battery chargers or jump leads.

Air bags

• Air bags can cause injury if they go off accidentally. Take care when removing the steering wheel and trim panels. Special storage instructions may apply.

Diesel injection equipment

• Diesel injection pumps supply fuel at very high pressure. Take care when working on the fuel injectors and fuel pipes.

⚠️ *Warning: Never expose the hands, face or any other part of the body to injector spray; the fuel can penetrate the skin with potentially fatal results.*

Remember...

DO

• Do use eye protection when using power tools, and when working under the vehicle.

• Do wear gloves or use barrier cream to protect your hands when necessary.

• Do get someone to check periodically that all is well when working alone on the vehicle.

• Do keep loose clothing and long hair well out of the way of moving mechanical parts.

• Do remove rings, wristwatch etc, before working on the vehicle – especially the electrical system.

• Do ensure that any lifting or jacking equipment has a safe working load rating adequate for the job.

DON'T

• Don't attempt to lift a heavy component which may be beyond your capability – get assistance.

• Don't rush to finish a job, or take unverified short cuts.

• Don't use ill-fitting tools which may slip and cause injury.

• Don't leave tools or parts lying around where someone can trip over them. Mop up oil and fuel spills at once.

• Don't allow children or pets to play in or near a vehicle being worked on.

The following pages are intended to help in dealing with common roadside emergencies and breakdowns. You will find more detailed fault finding information at the back of the manual, and repair information in the main chapters.

If your car won't start and the starter motor doesn't turn

☐ Open the bonnet and make sure that the battery terminals are clean and tight.
☐ Switch on the headlights and try to start the engine. If the headlights go very dim when you're trying to start, the battery is probably flat. Try jump starting using another car.

If your car won't start even though the starter motor turns as normal

☐ Is there fuel in the tank?
☐ Is there moisture on electrical components under the bonnet? Switch off the ignition, and then wipe off any obvious dampness with a dry cloth. Spray a water-repellent aerosol product (WD-40 or equivalent) on ignition and fuel system electrical connectors like those shown in the photos (Note that diesel engines do not normally suffer from damp).

A Pre-heater relay/control unit

B Airflow meter

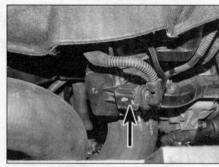

C Throttle body

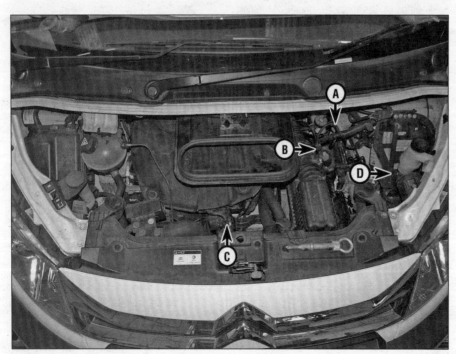

Check that electrical connections are secure (with the ignition switched off) and spray them with a water dispersant spray like WD-40 if you suspect a problem due to damp.

D Engine management ECU

Jump starting

 Jump starting will get you out of trouble, but you must correct whatever made the battery go flat in the first place. There are three possibilities:

1 *The battery has been drained by repeated attempts to start, or by leaving the lights on.*

2 *The charging system is not working properly (alternator drivebelt slack or broken, alternator wiring fault or alternator itself faulty).*

3 *The battery itself is at fault (electrolyte low, or battery worn out).*

When jump-starting a car using a booster battery, observe the following precautions:

Caution: Remove the key in case the central locking engages when the jump leads are connected.

✓ Before connecting the booster battery, make sure that the ignition is switched off.
✓ Ensure that all electrical equipment (lights, heater, wipers, etc) is switched off.
✓ Take note of any special precautions printed on the battery case.
✓ Make sure that the booster battery is the same voltage as the discharged one in the vehicle.

✓ If the battery is being jump-started from the battery in another vehicle, the two vehicles MUST NOT TOUCH each other.
✓ Make sure that the transmission is in neutral (or PARK, in the case of automatic transmission).

 Budget jump leads can be a false economy, as they often do not pass enough current to start large capacity or diesel engines. They can also get hot.

1 Open the drivers door, lift up the outer edge, and remove the battery cover. Connect the red jump lead to the positive (+) battery terminal.

2 Connect the other end of the red jump lead to the positive (+) terminal of the booster battery.

3 Connect one end of the black jump lead to the negative (-) terminal of the booster battery.

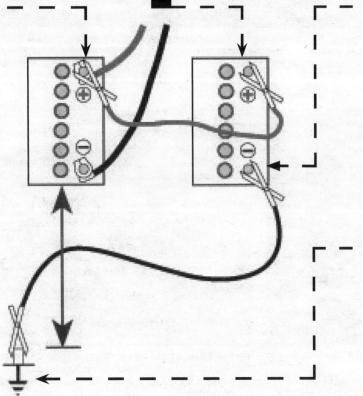

4 Connect the other end of the black jump lead to the drivers door striker on the pillar

5 Make sure that the jump leads will not come into contact with the fan, drive-belts or other moving parts of the engine.

6 Start the engine using the booster battery and run it at idle speed. Switch on the lights, rear window demister and heater blower motor, then disconnect the jump leads in the reverse order of connection. Turn off the lights etc.

Wheel changing

Warning: Do not change a wheel in a situation where you risk being hit by another vehicle. On busy roads, try to stop in a lay-by or a gateway. Be wary of passing traffic while changing the wheel – it is easy to become distracted by the job in hand.

Preparation

- [ ] When a puncture occurs, stop as soon as it is safe to do so.
- [ ] Park on firm level ground, if possible, and well out of the way of other traffic.
- [ ] Use hazard warning lights if necessary.
- [ ] If you have one, use a warning triangle to alert other drivers of your presence.
- [ ] Apply the handbrake and engage first or reverse gear.
- [ ] If the ground is soft, use a flat piece of wood to spread the load under the foot of the jack.
- [ ] Place a chock against the wheel diagonally opposite the wheel to be removed, or use a large stone (or similar) to stop the car rolling.
- [ ] The jack and tool kit are kept in a storage compartment under an access panel in the left-hand rear pillar.

1 The jack and tool kit is attached to the rear door pillar. Rotate the fastener anti-clockwise, then remove the jack and wheel brace

2 Using the wheel brace, rotate the security bolt anti-clockwise until the spare wheel carrier is fully lowered

3 Lift the carrier slightly, disengage the hook, then lower the carrier, and slide the spare wheel from place

4 Using one end of the towing eye, prise the wheel trim from the punctured wheel. The towing eye is clipped to the panel under the bonnet.

5 With the vehicle still on the ground, use the tool provided to slacken each wheel bolt by half a turn

6 Make sure the jack is located on firm ground, and engage the jack head correctly with the sill at the nearest jacking point. Ensure that the jack is vertical, then raise the jack until the wheel is raised clear of the ground.

7 Unscrew the wheel bolts and remove the wheel. Place the wheel under the vehicle sill in case the jack fails.

8 Fit the spare wheel and screw in the bolts. Lightly tighten the bolts with the wheel brace then lower the car to the ground.

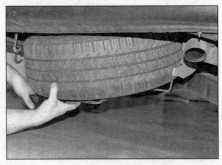

9 Securely tighten the wheel bolts in a diagonal sequence. Stow the punctured wheel on the carrier, then hook the carrier back onto the security bolt, and rotate the bolt clockwise until the carrier is fully raised. Stow the wheel trim and toolkit back in the vehicle.

Caution: If a temporary 'space-saver' spare wheel is fitted, do not exceed 50 mph (80 kmh), and take particular care when cornering.

Finally

- [ ] Remove the wheel chock.
- [ ] Check the tyre pressure on the wheel just fitted. If it is low, or if you don't have a pressure gauge with you, drive slowly to the next garage and inflate the tyre to the correct pressure.
- [ ] The wheel bolts should be slackened and retightened to the specified torque at the

earliest possible opportunity (see Chapter 1 Specifications).
- [ ] Have the damaged tyre or wheel repaired as soon as possible, or another puncture will leave you stranded.
- [ ] The spare wheel is not designed to be used over long distances. Have the punctured wheel repaired or replaced at the earliest opportunity.

Towing

When all else fails, you may find yourself having to get a tow home – or of course you may be helping somebody else. Long-distance recovery should only be done by a garage or breakdown service. For shorter distances, DIY towing using another car is easy enough, but observe the following points:

Caution: When towing a vehicle which has automatic transmission, do not tow the car at speeds in excess of 30 mph or for a distance greater than 30 miles. If towing speeds/distances are to exceed these limits, then the car must be towed with its front wheels off the ground.

- [ ] Use a proper tow-rope – they are not expensive. The vehicle being towed must display an ON TOW sign in its rear window.
- [ ] Always turn the ignition key to the 'on' position when the vehicle is being towed, so that the steering lock is released, and that the direction indicator and brake lights work.
- [ ] The towing eye is kept in the vehicle toolkit, located behind a panel in the rear, left-hand pillar, or clipped to the bonnet slam panel. To fit the eye, unclip the access cover from the relevant bumper and screw the eye firmly into position (see illustrations)
- [ ] Before being towed, release the handbrake and select neutral on the transmission.
- [ ] Note that greater-than-usual pedal pressure will be required to operate the brakes, since the vacuum servo unit is only operational with the engine running.
- [ ] The driver of the car being towed must keep the tow-rope taut at all times to avoid snatching.
- [ ] Make sure that both drivers know the route before setting off.
- [ ] Only drive at moderate speeds and keep the distance towed to a minimum. Drive smoothly and allow plenty of time for slowing down at junctions.

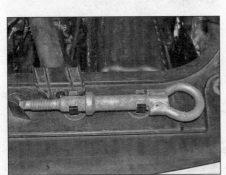

Unclip the towing eye from the bonnet slam panel

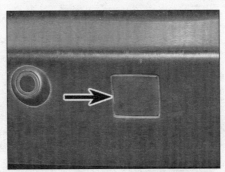

Prise open the towing socket cover using the flat end of the towing eye

Identifying leaks

Puddles on the garage floor or drive, or obvious wetness under the bonnet or underneath the car, suggest a leak that needs investigating. It can sometimes be difficult to decide where the leak is coming from, especially if an engine undershield is fitted. Leaking oil or fluid can also be blown rearwards by the passage of air under the car, giving a false impression of where the problem lies.

 Warning: Most automotive oils and fluids are poisonous. Wash them off skin, and change out of contaminated clothing, without delay.

HAYNES HiNT *The smell of a fluid leaking from the car may provide a clue to what's leaking. Some fluids are distinctively coloured. It may help to remove the engine undershield, clean the car carefully and to park it over some clean paper overnight as an aid to locating the source of the leak. Remember that some leaks may only occur while the engine is running.*

Sump oil

Engine oil may leak from the drain plug…

Oil from filter

…or from the base of the oil filter.

Gearbox oil

Gearbox oil can leak from the seals at the inboard ends of the driveshafts.

Antifreeze

Leaking antifreeze often leaves a crystalline deposit like this.

Brake fluid

A leak occurring at a wheel is almost certainly brake fluid.

Power steering fluid

Power steering fluid may leak from the pipe connectors on the steering rack.

Introduction

There are some very simple checks which need only take a few minutes to carry out, but which could save you a lot of inconvenience and expense.

These checks require no great skill or special tools, and the small amount of time they take to perform could prove to be very well spent, for example;

☐ Keeping an eye on tyre condition and pressures, will not only help to stop them wearing out prematurely, but could also save your life.

☐ Many breakdowns are caused by electrical problems. Battery-related faults are particularly common, and a quick check on a regular basis will often prevent the majority of these.

☐ If your car develops a brake fluid leak, the first time you might know about it is when your brakes don't work properly. Checking the level regularly will give advance warning of this kind of problem.

☐ If the oil or coolant levels run low, the cost of repairing any engine damage will be far greater than fixing the leak, for example.

Underbonnet check points

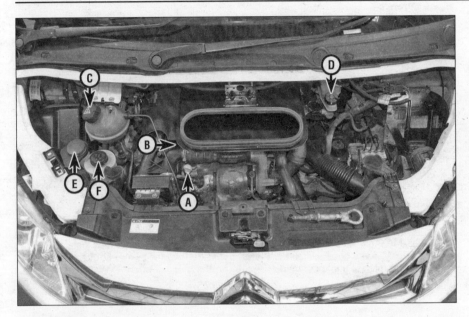

1.6 litre engine

A *Engine oil level dipstick*
B *Engine oil filler cap*
C *Coolant expansion tank/reservoir*
D *Brake (and clutch) fluid reservoir*
E *Screen washer fluid reservoir*
F *Power steering fluid reservoir*

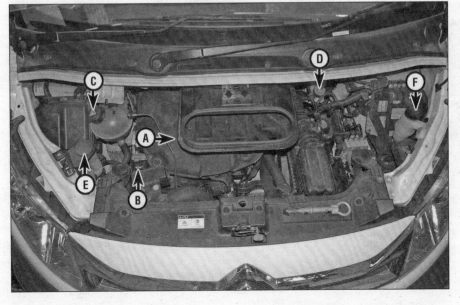

2.0 litre engine (Euro 5 engine shown – others similar)

A *Engine oil level dipstick*
B *Engine oil filler cap*
C *Coolant expansion tank/reservoir*
D *Brake (and clutch) fluid reservoir*
E *Screen washer fluid reservoir*
F *Power steering fluid reservoir*

Engine oil level

Before you start

✔ Make sure that your car is on level ground.
✔ Check the oil level before the car is driven, or at least 5 minutes after the engine has been switched off.

 If the oil is checked immediately after driving the vehicle, some of the oil will remain in the upper engine components, resulting in an inaccurate reading on the dipstick!

The correct oil

Modern engines place great demands on their oil. It is very important that the correct oil for your car is used (see *Lubricants and fluids*).

Car care

● If you have to add oil frequently, you should check whether you have any oil leaks. Place some clean paper under the car overnight, and check for stains in the morning. If there are no leaks, the engine may be burning oil.
● Always maintain the level between the upper and lower dipstick marks (see photo 3). If the level is too low severe engine damage may occur. Oil seal failure may result if the engine is overfilled by adding too much oil.

1 The dipstick is located at the front of the engine (see *Underbonnet check points*); the dipstick is often brightly coloured for identification. Withdraw the dipstick (2.0 litre engine shown).

2 Using a clean rag or paper towel, remove all oil from the dipstick. Insert the clean dipstick into the tube as far as it will go, then withdraw it again.

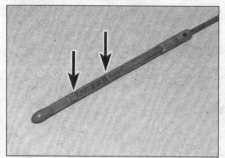

3 Note the oil level on the end of the dipstick, which should be between the upper (MAX) mark and lower (MIN) mark. Approximately 1.0 litre of oil will raise the level from the lower mark to the upper mark.

4 Oil is added through the filler cap aperture. Unscrew the cap and top-up the level; a funnel may help to reduce spillage. Add the oil slowly, checking the level on the dipstick often. Don't overfill (see *Car care*).

5 On 2.0 litre Euro 4 engines, unclip the oil filler spout from above the cabin air intake...

6 ...and fit it into the oil filler neck

Coolant level

 Warning: DO NOT attempt to remove the expansion tank pressure cap when the engine is hot, as there is a very great risk of scalding.

 Warning: Do not leave open containers of coolant about, as it is poisonous.

Car care

● Adding coolant should not be necessary on a regular basis. If frequent topping-up is required, it is likely there is a leak. Check the radiator, all hoses and joint faces for signs of staining or wetness, and rectify as necessary.

● It is important that antifreeze is used in the cooling system all year round, not just during the winter months. Don't top-up with water alone, as the antifreeze will become too diluted.

1 The coolant level must be checked with the engine cold; the coolant level should be between the MAX and MIN marks on the expansion tank.

2 If topping-up is necessary, remove the pressure cap (when engine is cold) from the expansion tank, which is located on the right-hand side of the engine compartment.

3 Add the pre-mixed coolant to the expansion tank until the level is between the MAX and MIN markings. Once the level is correct, securely refit the cap.

Brake (and clutch) fluid level

 Warning: Brake fluid can harm your eyes and damage painted surfaces, so use extreme caution when handling and pouring it.
Caution: Do not use fluid that has been standing open for some time, as it absorbs moisture from the air, which can cause a dangerous loss of braking effectiveness.

Before you start

✔ Make sure that your car is on level ground.

Safety first!

● If the reservoir requires repeated topping-up this is an indication of a fluid leak somewhere in the system, which should be investigated immediately.

● If a leak is suspected, the car should not be driven until the braking system has been checked. Never take any risks where brakes are concerned.

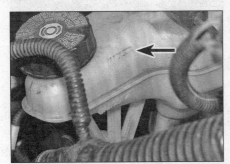

1 The upper (MAX) fluid level marking is on the side of the upper reservoir, which is located at the rear of the engine compartment.

2 If topping-up is necessary, first wipe clean the area around the filler cap with a clean cloth, then unscrew the cap and remove it along with the rubber diaphragm.

3 Carefully add fluid, avoiding spilling it on the surrounding paintwork. Use only the specified hydraulic fluid. After filling to the correct level, refit the diaphragm and cap, and tighten it securely. Wipe off any spilt fluid.

Power steering fluid level

Before you start
✔ Park the vehicle on level ground.
✔ Set the steering wheel straight-ahead.
✔ The engine should be cold and turned off.

Safety first!
● The need for frequent topping-up indicates a leak, which should be investigated immediately.

1 On models with an electro-pump assembly, the fluid reservoir is on the left-hand side of the engine compartment, behind the headlight.

2 On models with a belt driven pump assembly, the fluid reservoir is on the right-hand side of the engine compartment, on a bracket above the engine mounting. Unscrew the cap from the reservoir.

3 On models with an electro-pump assembly, check the fluid level is up to the upper (MAX) level indicated on the side of the reservoir.

4 On models with a belt driven pump assembly, check the fluid level is up to the upper (MX – MAX) level indicator inside the aperture of the reservoir.

5 Top-up the reservoir with the specified type of the fluid, using a funnel. Once the level is correct, securely refit the reservoir cap. Do not overfill the reservoir.

Bulbs and fuses

✔ Check all external lights and the horn. Refer to Chapter 12 Section 2 for details if any of the circuits are found to be inoperative.
✔ Visually check all accessible wiring connectors, harnesses and retaining clips for security, and for signs of chafing or damage.

HAYNES HiNT *If you need to check your brake lights and indicators unaided, back up to a wall or garage door and operate the lights. The reflected light should show if they are working properly.*

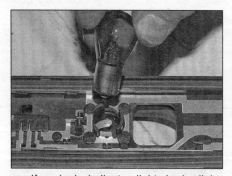

1 If a single indicator light, brake light, sidelight or headlight has failed, it is likely that a bulb has blown, and will need to be renewed. Refer to Chapter 12, Section 5 for details. If both brake lights have failed, it is possible that the switch has failed (see Chapter 9, Section 17).

2 If more than one indicator or tail light has failed, it is likely that either a fuse has blown or that there is a fault in the circuit. Fuses are located behind a panel on the drivers side of the facia, in a fusebox at the right-hand side of the engine compartment, and in the battery compartment.

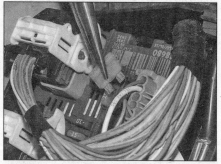

3 Additional fuses and relays are located in the fusebox on the right-hand side of the fusebox, and in the battery compartment. To renew a blown fuse, simply pull it out and fit a new fuse of the correct rating (see Wiring diagrams). If the fuse blows again, it is important that you find out why – a complete checking procedure is given in Chapter 12, Section 2.

Battery

Caution: Before carrying out any work on the vehicle battery, read the precautions given in 'Safety First!' at the start of this manual.

✔ Make sure that the battery tray is in good condition, and that the clamp is tight. Corrosion on the tray, retaining clamp and the battery itself can be removed with a solution of water and baking soda. Thoroughly rinse all cleaned areas with water. Any metal parts damaged by corrosion should be covered with a zinc-based primer, and then painted.

✔ Periodically (approximately every three months), check the charge condition of the battery, as described in Chapter 5A Section 3.

✔ If the battery is flat, and you need to jump start your vehicle, see Roadside repairs.

1 Open the drivers door, pull up the outer edge, then remove the cover to access the battery.

2 Check the battery lead clamps for tightness to ensure good electrical connections, and check the leads for signs of damage.

HAYNES HINT

Battery corrosion can be kept to a minimum by applying a layer of petroleum jelly to the clamps and terminals after they are reconnected.

3 If corrosion (white, fluffy deposits) is evident, remove the cables from the battery terminals, clean them with a small wire brush, then refit them. Automotive stores sell a tool for cleaning the battery post ...

4 ... as well as the battery cable clamps.

Wiper blades

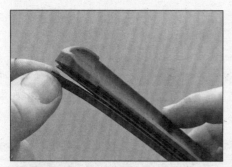

1 Check the condition of the wiper blades: if they are cracked or show signs of deterioration, or if the glass swept area is smeared, renew them. For maximum clarity of vision, wiper blades should be renewed annually.

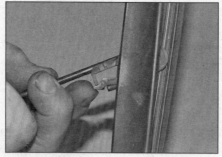

2 Lift the wiper from the screen. rotate it 90° and lift the retaining clip ...

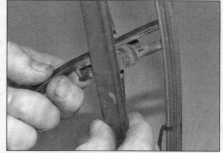

3 ...then disengage the blade by sliding it from the end of the wiper arm, taking care not to allow the wiper arm to spring back and damage the windscreen.

Screen washer fluid level

● Screenwash additives not only keep the windscreen clean during foul weather, they also prevent the washer system freezing in cold weather – which is when you are likely to need it most. Don't top-up using plain water as the screenwash will become too diluted, and will freeze during cold weather.

 Warning: On no account use coolant antifreeze in the washer system, as this may damage the paintwork.

1 The washer fluid reservoir is located in the right-hand front corner of the engine compartment. To check the fluid level, open the cap and look down the filler neck.

2 If topping-up is necessary, add water and a screenwash additive in the quantities recommended on the bottle.

Tyre condition and pressure

It is very important that tyres are in good condition, and at the correct pressure – having a tyre failure at any speed is highly dangerous. Tyre wear is influenced by driving style – harsh braking and acceleration, or fast cornering, will all produce more rapid tyre wear. As a general rule, the front tyres wear out faster the the rears. Interchanging the tyres from front to rear ("rotating" the tyres) may result in more even wear. However, if this is completely effective, you may have the expense of replacing all four tyres at once!

Remove any nails or stones embedded in the tread before they penetrate the tyre to cause deflation. If removal of a nail does reveal that the tyre has been punctured, refit the nail so that its point of penetration is marked. Then immediately change the wheel, and have the tyre repaired by a tyre dealer.

Regularly check the tyres for damage in the form of cuts or bulges, especially in the side walls. Periodically remove the wheels, and clean any dirt or mud from the inside and outside surfaces. Examine the wheel rims for signs of rusting, corrosion or other damage. Light alloy wheels are easily damaged by "kerbing" whilst parking; steel wheels may also become dented or buckled. A new wheel is very often the only way to overcome severe damage.

New tyres should be balanced when they are fitted, but it may become necessary to re-balance them as they ear, or if the balance weights fitted to the wheel rim should fall off. Unbalanced tyres will wear more quickly, as will the steering and suspension components. Wheel imbalance is normally signified by vibration, particularly at t certain speed (typically around 50 mph). If this vibration is felt only through the steering wheel, then it is likely that just the front wheels need balancing. If, however, the vibration is felt through the whole car, the rear wheels could be out of balance. Wheel balancing should be carried out by a tyre dealer or garage.

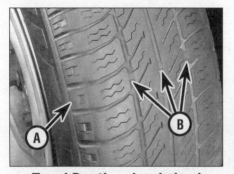

1 Tread Depth - visual check
The original tyres have tread wear safety bands (B), which will appear when the tread depth reaches approximately 1.6 mm. The band positions are indicated by a triangular mark on the tyre sidewall (A).

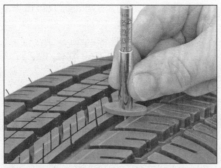

2 Tread Depth - manual check
Alternatively, tread wear can be monitored with a simple, inexpensive device known as a tread depth indicator gauge.

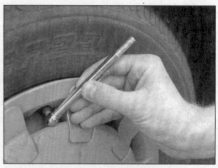

3 Tyre Pressure Check
Check the tyre pressures regularly with the tyres cold. Do not adjust the tyre pressures immediately after the vehicle has been used, or an inaccurate setting will result.

Tyre tread wear patterns

Shoulder Wear

Underinflation (wear on both sides)
Under-inflation will cause overheating of the tyre, because the tyre will flex too much, and the tread will not sit correctly on the road surface. This will cause a loss of grip and excessive wear, not to mention the danger of sudden tyre failure due to heat build-up.
Check and adjust pressures
Incorrect wheel camber (wear on one side)
Repair or renew suspension parts
Hard cornering
Reduce speed!

Centre Wear

Overinflation
Over-inflation will cause rapid wear of the centre part of the tyre tread, coupled with reduced grip, harsher ride, and the danger of shock damage occurring in the tyre casing.
Check and adjust pressures

If you sometimes have to inflate your car's tyres to the higher pressures specified for maximum load or sustained high speed, don't forget to reduce the pressures to normal afterwards.

Uneven Wear

Front tyres may wear unevenly as a result of wheel misalignment. Most tyre dealers and garages can check and adjust the wheel alignment (or "tracking") for a modest charge.
Incorrect camber or castor
Repair or renew suspension parts
Malfunctioning suspension
Repair or renew suspension parts
Unbalanced wheel
Balance tyres
Incorrect toe setting
Adjust front wheel alignment
Note: *The feathered edge of the tread which typifies toe wear is best checked by feel.*

Lubricants and fluids

Engine

Without particulate filter	Multigrade engine oil, viscosity SAE 0W/30, 5W/40 to ACEA B3 and API CD/CF specification*. EG. Total Quartz, Selina WR, Castrol edge.**
With particulate filter	Multigrade engine oil, viscosity SAE 5W/40 to ACEA B3 and API CD/CF specification*. EG. Total Quartz, Selina WR, Castrol Magnatec Stop-Start.**

Cooling system

All models.	Revkogel 2000, Glysantin G33, Paraflu UP**

Transmission

Manual transmission	ESSO EZL848, TOTAL H6965 or Tutela CAR MATRYX gear oil (SAE 75W-80W)

Braking and clutch system

All models.	Hydraulic fluid to DOT 4

Power steering system

Electro-pump assembly	Total Fluide DA, Tutela GI/R
Belt driven pump assembly	Total AT42, Tutela GI/E

Particulate filter additives (where applicable)

From DAM/RPO number 09492 – 12151 (green connector on the reservoir)	Eolys 176
From DAM/RPO number 12152 (blue connector on the reservoir)	Eolys Powerflex

Note: * *Due to the extended service intervals Peugeot/Citroen/Fiat specify, it is essential that semi-synthetic or fully-synthetic engine oil be used.*
Note: ** *Check with your dealer or parts specialist for the latest recommendations.*

Tyre pressures

Note: *The make of tyres, the sizes and the pressures for each vehicle are given on a label attached to the end of the driver's door.*

Note: *Pressures on the label apply to original-equipment tyres listed, and may vary if any other makes or type of tyre is fitted; check with the tyre manufacturer or supplier for correct pressures if necessary.*

Note: *Tyre pressures must always be checked with the tyres cold to ensure accuracy.*

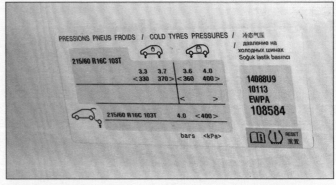

Label on driver's side door

Chapter 1
Routine maintenance and servicing

Contents

Degrees of difficulty

Easy, suitable for novice with little experience	**Fairly easy,** suitable for beginner with some experience	**Fairly difficult,** suitable for competent DIY mechanic	**Difficult,** suitable for experienced DIY mechanic	**Very difficult,** suitable for expert DIY or professional

1 Servicing specifications

Lubricants and fluids................................ Refer to *Lubricants, fluids and tyre pressures*

Capacities
Note: *All values are approximate.*

Engine oil
Including filter:
    1.6 litre models... 6.2 litres
    2.0 lite models .... 5.25 litres
Between dipstick MAX and MIN markings...................... 1.5 litres

Cooling system
1.6 litre models... 8.0 litres
2.0 litre models... 9.0 litres

Transmission
Manual transmission:
  Drain and refill:
    1.6 litre models....................................... 1.7 litres
    2.0 litre models....................................... 1.9 litres

Fuel tank
All models (when full) .... 80 litres
Reserve (warning light on) .... 8 litres

Cooling system
Antifreeze mixture: *
  50% antifreeze... Protection down to -37°C
  55% antifreeze... Protection down to -45°C
Note: * *Refer to antifreeze manufacturer for latest recommendations.*

Brakes
Brake pad friction material minimum thickness.................. 2.0 mm
Tyre pressures .... See *Lubricants, fluids and tyre pressures*

Remote control battery
Type CR1620
Volts 3V

Torque wrench settings	Nm	lbf ft
Engine oil drain plug:		
1.6 litre engine	25	18
2.0 litre engines	35	26
Manual transmission:		
Filler/level plug	22	16
Drain plug	35	26
Oil filter cap	25	18
Wheel bolts	100	74

2 Maintenance schedule

Note: *This maintenance schedule is a guide recommended by Haynes for servicing your own vehicle. Check with your local dealer for the manufacturer's maintenance schedule.*

1 The maintenance intervals in this manual are provided with the assumption that you will be carrying out the work yourself. These are the minimum maintenance intervals recommended by ourselves for vehicles driven daily, based on the schedule produced by the manufacturer. If you wish to keep your vehicle in peak condition at all times, you may wish to perform some of these procedures more often. We encourage frequent maintenance, because it enhances the efficiency, performance and resale value of your vehicle.

2 If the vehicle is driven in dusty areas, used to tow a trailer, or driven frequently at slow speeds (idling in traffic) or on short journeys, more frequent maintenance intervals are recommended.

3 When the vehicle is new, it should be serviced by a dealer service department (or other workshop recognised by the vehicle manufacturer as providing the same standard of service) in order to preserve the warranty. The vehicle manufacturer may reject warranty claims if you are unable to prove that servicing has been carried out as and when specified, using only original equipment parts or parts certified to be of equivalent quality.

4 All Citroën/Peugeot/Fiat models are equipped with a service indicator function incorporated into the mileage recorder, which will indicate the mileage until the next service is due. However, Citroën/Peugeot/Fiat point out that, 'due to the relationship between time and mileage, some operating conditions will make annual service more suitable'.

Every 250 miles or weekly
☐ Refer to *Weekly checks*

Every 10 000 miles or 12 months – whichever comes first
☐ Renew the engine oil and filter (Section 6)
☐ Check all underbonnet components for fluid leaks (Section 7)
☐ Check the steering and suspension components (Section 8)
☐ Check the condition of the driveshaft joints and rubber gaiters (Section 9)
☐ Lubricate all hinges and locks (Section 10)
☐ Drain the fuel filter (Section 11)
☐ Reset the service interval indicator (Section 12)

Every 20 000 miles or 2 years – whichever comes first
☐ Check the condition of the brake pads and discs (Section 13)
☐ Check the operation of the handbrake (Section 14)
☐ Check the seat belt condition (Section 15)
☐ Check the airbag system (Section 16)
☐ Carry out a road test (Section 17)
☐ Check the coolant antifreeze concentration (Section 18)
☐ Check the exhaust system (Section 19)
☐ Check the condition of the auxiliary drivebelt (Section 20)
☐ Check and renew the pollen filter (Section 21)
☐ Renew the brake fluid (Section 22).

Note: *The hydraulic clutch shares its fluid reservoir with the braking system, and will also need to be bled.*

Every 40 000 miles or 4 years – whichever comes first
☐ Renew the coolant (Section 23)
☐ Renew the air filter element (Section)
☐ Check the manual transmission oil level (Section 25)
☐ Renew the fuel filter (Section 11)
☐ Renew the remote control battery (Section 26)

Every 80 000 miles or 5 years – whichever comes first
☐ Timing belt renewal (Section 29)

Note: *The interval recommended by Peugeot/Citroën/Fiat is 120 000 miles or 5 years. However, It is strongly recommended that the interval be reduced on vehicles that are subjected to intensive use, ie, mainly short journeys or a lot of stop-start driving. The actual belt renewal interval is very much up to the individual owner, but bear in mind that severe engine damage will result if the belt breaks.*

Every 80 000 miles
☐ Check the particulate filter fluid (Section 27)

Every 120 000 miles
☐ Renew the particulate filter (Section 28)

3 Component location

Underbonnet view (Euro 5 2.0 litre model shown – others similar)

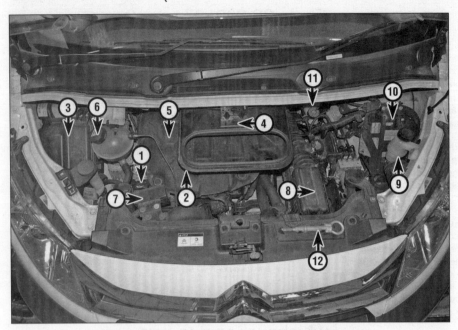

1 Engine oil filler cap
2 Engine oil level dipstick
3 Engine compartment fuse/relay box
4 Cabin air intake cowling
5 Engine cover
6 Coolant expansion tank
7 Relay box
8 Air cleaner housing
9 Power steering fluid reservoir
10 Engine management ECU
11 Brake/clutch fluid reservoir
12 Towing eye

Underbonnet view (Euro 5 1.6 litre model shown – others similar)

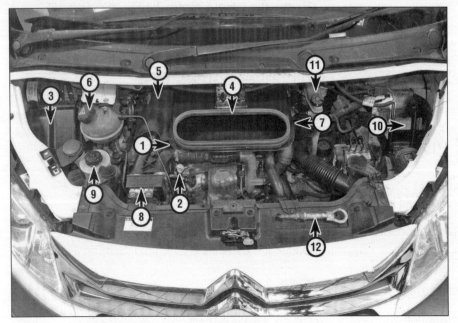

1 Engine oil filler cap (under cowling)
2 Engine oil level dipstick
3 Engine compartment fuse/relay box
4 Cabin air intake cowling
5 Engine cover
6 Coolant expansion tank
7 Air cleaner housing (under cowling)
8 Relay box
9 Power steering fluid reservoir
10 Engine management ECU
11 Brake/Clutch fluid reservoir
12 Towing eye

Front underbody view

1 Engine oil drain plug
2 Transmission drain plug
3 Driveshaft
4 Brake caliper
5 Track rod balljoint
6 Anti-roll bar
7 Air conditioning compressor
8 Radiator bottom hose
9 Catalytic converter (depending on model)
10 Auxiliary belt
11 Front lower suspension arm

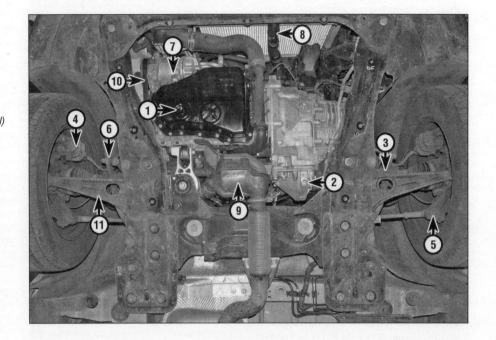

Rear underbody view

1 Beam axle
2 Handbrake cable
3 Brake caliper
4 Coil spring
5 Shock absorber
6 Exhaust rear silencer
7 Fuel filler neck
8 Panhard rod

4 General Information

1 This Chapter is designed to help the home mechanic maintain his/her vehicle for safety, economy, long life and peak performance.

2 The Chapter contains a master maintenance schedule, followed by Sections dealing specifically with each task in the schedule. Visual checks, adjustments, component renewal and other helpful items are included. Refer to the accompanying illustrations of the engine compartment and the underside of the vehicle for the locations of the various components.

3 Servicing your vehicle in accordance with the mileage/time maintenance schedule and the following Sections will provide a planned maintenance programme, which should result in a long and reliable service life. This is a comprehensive plan, so maintaining some items, but not others, at the specified service intervals will not produce the same results.

4 As you service your vehicle, you will discover that many of the procedures can – and should – be grouped together, because of the particular procedure being performed, or because of the close proximity of two otherwise-unrelated components to one another. For example, if the vehicle is raised for any reason, the exhaust system could be inspected at the same time as the suspension and steering components.

5 The first step in this maintenance programme is to prepare yourself before the actual work begins. Read through all the Sections relevant to the work to be carried out, then make a list and gather together all the parts and tools required. If a problem is encountered, seek advice from a parts specialist, or a dealer service department.

5 Routine Maintenance

1 If, from the time the vehicle is new, the routine maintenance schedule is followed closely, and frequent checks are made of fluid levels and high-wear items, as suggested throughout this manual, the engine will be kept in relatively good running condition, and the need for additional work will be minimised.

2 It is possible that there will be times when the engine is running poorly due to the lack of regular maintenance. This is even more likely if a used vehicle, which has not received regular and frequent maintenance checks, is purchased. In such cases, additional work may need to be carried out, outside of the regular maintenance intervals.

3 If engine wear is suspected, a compression test (Chapter 2A Section 2, Chapter 2B Section 2 or Chapter 2C Section 2) will provide valuable information regarding the overall performance of the main internal components. Such a test can be used as a basis to decide on the extent of the work to be carried out. If, for example, a compression test indicates serious internal engine wear, conventional maintenance as described in this Chapter will not greatly improve the performance of the engine, and may prove a waste of time and money, unless extensive overhaul work (Chapter 2D) is carried out first.

4 The following series of operations are those most often required to improve the performance of a generally poor-running engine:

Primary operations

a) *Clean, inspect and test the battery ('Weekly checks' and Chapter 5A)*
b) *Check all the engine-related fluids ('Weekly checks').*
c) *Check the condition and tension of the auxiliary drivebelt (Section 20).*
d) *Check the condition of the air filter element, and renew if necessary (Section).*
e) *Check the condition of all hoses, and check for fluid leaks (Section 7).*

5 If the above operations do not prove fully effective, carry out the following secondary operations:

Secondary operations

a) *Check the charging system (Chapter 5A Section 5).*
b) *Check the fuel system (Chapter 4A Section 1).*

6 Engine oil and filter renewal

1 Frequent oil changes are the most important preventative maintenance the DIY home mechanic can give the engine, because ageing oil becomes diluted and contaminated, which leads to premature engine wear.

2 Before starting this procedure, gather together all the necessary tools and materials. Also make sure that you have plenty of clean rags and newspapers handy, to mop-up any spills. Ideally, the engine oil should be warm, as it will drain better, and more built-up sludge will be removed with it. Take care, however, not to touch the exhaust or any other hot parts of the engine when working under the vehicle. To avoid any possibility of scalding, and to protect yourself from possible skin irritants and other harmful contaminants in used engine oils, it is advisable to wear gloves when carrying out this work.

3 Access to the filter and drain plug will be greatly improved if the front of the vehicle is raised and support securely on axle stands (see *Jacking and vehicle support*).

4 Undo the fasteners and remove the engine undershield **(see illustration)**.

5 Slacken the plug about half a turn **(see illustration)**. Position the draining container

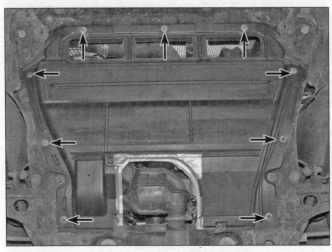

6.4 Engine undershield fasteners

6.5 Slacken the sump drain plug

HAYNES HINT

As the drain plug releases from the sump threads, move it away sharply, so the stream of oil issuing from the sump runs into the container, not up your sleeve.

6.7a Engine oil filter location – 1.6 litre engines

6.7b Engine oil filter location – 2.0 litre models

under the drain plug, then remove the plug completely – recover the sealing washer (see **Haynes Hint**).

6 Allow some time for the old oil to drain, noting that it may be necessary to reposition the container as the oil flow slows to a trickle.

7 The oil filter is of a separate disposable paper element contained under a plastic cap, which is screwed into a housing on the front of the cylinder block **(see illustrations)**.

1.6 litre engines

8 Remove the air intake hose from the front left-hand corner of the engine compartment to make easier access the oil filter cap **(see illustrations)**.

2.0 litre Euro 5 emissions level engines

9 Pull up and remove the right-hand edge of the sounding insulation material above the engine.

10 Unclip the oil filler assembly, then undo the 2 nuts and remove the alternator guard **(see illustrations)**.

6.8a Air intake hose retaining bolt – Euro 4 engines

6.8b Remove the air intake hose – Euro 5 engines

6.10a Depress the clip and slide the filler assembly upwards

6.10b Undo the nuts and remove the plastic guard above the alternator

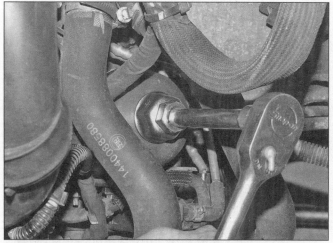

6.11a Slacken the oil filter cap

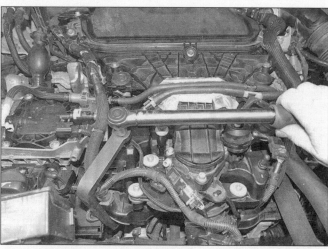

6.11b Using the special tool to slacken the oil filter cap – 2.0 litre Euro 5 engines

6.11c There's just enough clearance to use a short adjustable spanner – 2.0 litre Euro 5 engines

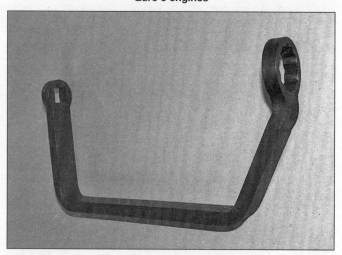

6.11d Special oil filter cap removal tool – 2.0 litre Euro 5 engines

All engines

11 Using a socket or spanner, slacken the oil filter plastic cap a couple of turns to allow the oil in the filter housing to drain into the sump **(see illustration)**. Do not completely remove at this stage. On 2.0 litre Euro 5 emissions level engines, access to the oil filter cap is extremely limited. It's advisable to use a special tool (Fiat no. 1.870.754.000 or equivalent) – a design of stepped tool with a 27 mm hexagon on one end, and a 1/2" drive on the other **(see illustration)**. In the absence of this tool, use a short 27 mm.

12 After all the oil has drained, wipe off the drain plug with a clean rag. Clean the area around the drain plug opening, and refit the plug with a new sealing washer **(see illustration)**. Tighten the plug to the specified torque.

13 The oil filter plastic cap can now be unscrewed the rest of the way by hand **(see illustration)**. Use a rag to catch any oil spillage as the filter is removed.

14 Lift the oil filter plastic cap away, depending on model the paper filter element may stay in the lower part of the housing or will stay in the cap as it is removed. Remove the paper element from the filter housing, if required **(see illustration)**.

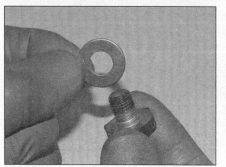

6.12 Renew the drain plug sealing washer

6.13 Unscrew the oil filter cap

6.14 Lift out the paper element

6.16a Renew the O-ring seal on the cap...

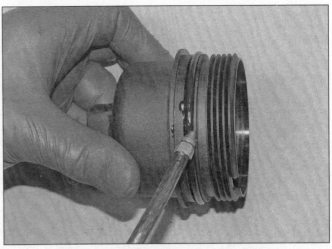

6.16b ... then apply a little clean oil to the seal

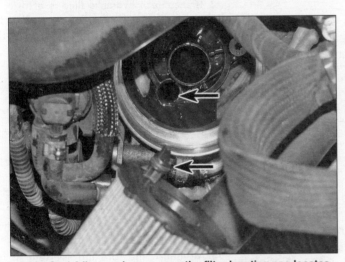

6.16c On 1.6 litre engines, ensure the filter locating peg locates into the corresponding hole in the housing

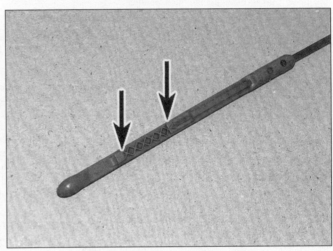

6.22 Upper and lower dipstick markings

15 Use a clean rag to remove all oil and dirt from inside the filter cap and housing, and then remove the O-ring seal from the cap. A new seal should be supplied with the new filter.

16 Fit a new O-ring seal to the cap. On 2.0 litre engines, fit the new paper element to the cap. On 1.6 litre engines, fit the element to the housing, ensuring the lug on the base of the element locates correctly in the corresponding hole in the housing. Lightly lubricate the O-ring seal with clean engine oil **(see illustrations)**.

17 Screw the cap into place by hand, and then tighten it to the specified torque.

1.6 litre engines

18 Refit the air intake hose.

2.0 litre Euro 5 emissions level engines

19 Refit the alternator guard, and tighten the retaining nuts securely.

20 Clip the oil filler assembly back into place, and refit the sound insulation material to the top of the engine.

All engines

21 Lower the vehicle to the ground, then remove the oil filler cap and withdraw the level dipstick from the tube.

22 Fill the engine, using the correct oil (see Lubricants and fluids 0 Section 6). An oil can spout or funnel may help to reduce spillage. Pour in half the specified quantity of oil first (see Specifications), and then wait a few minutes for the oil to run to the sump. Continue adding oil a small quantity at a time until the level is up to the lower mark on the dipstick. Adding a further 1.0 litre (approx.) will bring the level up to the upper mark on the dipstick **(see illustration)**. Insert the dipstick, and refit the filler cap when completed.

23 Start the engine and run it for a few minutes; check for leaks around the oil filter seal and the sump drain plug. Note that there may be a delay of a few seconds before the oil pressure warning light goes out when the engine is first started, as the oil circulates through the engine oil galleries and the new oil filter before the pressure builds-up.

24 Switch off the engine, and wait a few minutes for the oil to settle in the sump once more. With the new oil circulated and the filter completely full, recheck the level on the dipstick, and add more oil as necessary. When completed, jack up the vehicle and place it on axle stands, (see *Jacking and vehicle support*), then refit the engine undershield.

25 Dispose of the used engine oil safely, in accordance with the guidance given in *General repair procedures 13 Section 4*.

7 Hose and fluid leak check

Cooling system

⚠ **Warning: Refer to the safety information given in 'Safety first!' and Chapter 3 Section 1 before disturbing any of the cooling system components.**

A leak in the cooling system will usually show up as white- or antifreezecoloured deposits on the area adjoining the leak.

1 Carefully check the radiator and heater coolant hoses along their entire length. Renew any hose that is cracked, swollen or which shows signs of deterioration. Cracks will show up better if the hose is squeezed. Pay close attention to the clips that secure the hoses to the cooling system components. Hose clips that have been overtightened can pinch and puncture hoses, resulting in cooling system leaks.

2 Inspect all the cooling system components (hoses, joint faces, etc) for leaks. Where any problems of this nature are found on system components, renew the component or gasket with reference to Chapter 3 (see **Haynes hint**).

Fuel system

⚠ *Warning: Refer to the safety information given in 'Safety first!' and Chapter 4A Section 1 before disturbing any of the fuel system components.*

3 Diesel leaks are easier to spot than petrol, but can be difficult to pinpoint unless the leakage is significant and hence easily visible. Fuel tends to spread, especially in a hot engine bay. Small drips can spread before you get a chance to identify the point of leakage. If you suspect that there is a fuel leak from the area of the engine bay, leave the vehicle overnight then start the engine from cold, with the bonnet open. Metal components tend to shrink when they are cold, and rubber seals and hoses tend to harden, so any leaks will be more apparent whilst the engine is warming-up from a cold start.

4 Check all fuel lines at their connections to the fuel rail, fuel pressure regulator, fuel filter, fuel cooler and especially the return hoses on top of the injectors. Examine each rubber fuel hose along its length for splits or cracks. Check for leakage from the crimped joints between rubber and metal fuel lines. Examine the unions between the metal fuel lines and the fuel filter housing. Also check the area around the fuel injectors for signs of O-ring leakage.

5 To identify fuel leaks between the fuel tank and the engine bay, the vehicle should be raised and securely supported on axle stands (see *Jacking and vehicle support*). Inspect the fuel tank and filler neck for punctures, cracks and other damage. The connection between the filler neck and tank is especially critical. Sometimes a rubber filler neck or connecting hose will leak due to loose retaining clamps or deteriorated rubber.

6 Carefully check all rubber hoses and metal fuel lines leading away from the fuel tank. Check for loose connections, deteriorated hoses, kinked lines, and other damage. Pay particular attention to the vent pipes and hoses, which often loop up around the filler neck and can become blocked or kinked, making tank filling difficult. Follow the fuel supply and return lines to the front of the vehicle, carefully inspecting them all the way for signs of damage or corrosion. Renew damaged sections as necessary.

Engine oil

7 Inspect the area around the camshaft cover, cylinder head, oil filter and sump joint faces. Bear in mind that, over a period of time, some very slight seepage from these areas is to be expected – what you are really looking for is any indication of a serious leak caused by gasket failure. Engine oil seeping from the base of the timing belt cover or the transmission bellhousing may be an indication of crankshaft or transmission input shaft oil seal failure. Should a leak be found, renew the failed gasket or oil seal by referring to the appropriate Chapters in this manual.

Air conditioning refrigerant

⚠ *Warning: Refer to the safety information given in 'Safety first!' and Chapter 3 Section 11 regarding the dangers of disturbing any of the air conditioning system components.*

8 The air conditioning system is filled with a liquid refrigerant, which is retained under high pressure. If the air conditioning system is opened and depressurised without the aid of specialised equipment the refrigerant will immediately turn into gas and escape into the atmosphere. If the liquid comes into contact with your skin, it can cause severe frostbite. In addition, the refrigerant contains substances which are environmentally damaging; for this reason, it should not be allowed to escape into the atmosphere in an uncontrolled fashion.

9 Any suspected air conditioning system leaks should be immediately referred to a Citroën/Peugeot/Fiat dealer or air conditioning specialist. Leakage will be shown up as a steady drop in the level of refrigerant in the system.

10 Note that water may drip from the condenser drain pipe, underneath the car, immediately after the air conditioning system has been in use. This is normal, and should not be cause for concern.

Brake (and clutch) fluid

⚠ *Warning: Refer to the safety information given in 'Safety first!' and Chapter 9 regarding the dangers of handling brake fluid.*

11 With reference to Chapter 9, examine the area surrounding the brake/clutch pipe unions at the master cylinder for signs of leakage. Check the area around the base of fluid reservoir, for signs of leakage caused by seal failure. Also examine the brake pipe unions at the ABS hydraulic unit.

12 If fluid loss is evident, but the leak cannot be pinpointed in the engine bay, the brake calipers and underbody brake lines should be carefully checked with the vehicle raised and supported on axle stands (see *Jacking and vehicle support*). Leakage of fluid from the braking system is a serious fault that must be rectified immediately.

13 Brake/clutch hydraulic fluid is a toxic substance with a watery consistency. New fluid is almost colourless, but it becomes darker with age and use.

Unidentified fluid leaks

14 If there are signs that a fluid of some description is leaking from the vehicle, but you cannot identify the type of fluid or its exact origin, park the vehicle overnight and slide a large piece of card underneath it. Providing that the card is positioned in roughly the right location, even the smallest leak will show up on the card. Not only will this help you to pinpoint the exact location of the leak, it should be easier to identify the fluid from its colour. Bear in mind, though, that the leak may only be occurring when the engine is running!

Vacuum hoses

15 Although the braking system is hydraulically operated, the brake servo unit amplifies the effort applied at the brake pedal by making use of the vacuum supplied by the vacuum pump, driven by the engine. Vacuum is ported to the servo by means of a large-bore hose. Any leaks that develop in this hose will reduce the effectiveness of the braking system, and may affect the running of the engine.

16 In addition, a number of the underbonnet components, particularly the turbocharger control components, are driven by vacuum supplied from the vacuum pump via narrow-bore hoses. A leak in a vacuum hose means that air is being drawn into the hose (rather than escaping from it) and this makes leakage very difficult to detect. One method is to use an old length of vacuum hose as a kind of stethoscope – hold one end close to (but not in) your ear and use the other end to probe the area around the suspected leak. When the end of the hose is directly over a vacuum leak, a hissing sound will be heard clearly through the hose. Care must be taken to avoid contacting hot or moving components, as the engine must be running, when testing in this manner. Renew any vacuum hoses that are found to be defective.

8.2 Check the steering rack gaiters for signs of damage or deterioration

8.4 Check for wear in the hub bearings by grasping the wheel and trying to rock it ...

8.5 ... and checking for wear in the steering rack and balljoints

8   Steering and suspension components check

Front suspension and steering

1 Raise the front of the vehicle, and securely support it on axle stands (see *Jacking and vehicle support*).
2 Visually inspect the balljoint dust covers and the steering rack-and-pinion gaiters for splits **(see illustration)**, chafing or deterioration. Any wear of these components will cause loss of lubricant, together with dirt and water entry, resulting in rapid deterioration of the balljoints or steering gear.
3 Check the power steering fluid hoses for chafing or deterioration, and the pipe and hose unions for fluid leaks. Also check for signs of fluid leakage under pressure from the steering gear rubber gaiters, which would indicate failed fluid seals within the steering gear.
4 Grasp the roadwheel at the 12 o'clock and 6 o'clock positions, and try to rock it **(see illustration)**. Very slight free play may be felt, but if the movement is appreciable, further investigation is necessary to determine the source. Continue rocking the wheel while an assistant depresses the footbrake. If the movement is now eliminated or significantly reduced, it is likely that the hub bearings are at fault. If the free play is still evident with the footbrake depressed, then there is wear in the suspension joints or mountings.
5 Now grasp the wheel at the 9 o'clock and 3 o'clock positions, and try to rock it as before **(see illustration)**. Any movement felt now may again be caused by wear in the hub bearings or the steering track rod balljoints. If the outer balljoint is worn, the visual movement will be obvious. If the inner joint is suspect, it can be felt by placing a hand over the rack-and-pinion rubber gaiter and gripping the track rod. If the wheel is now rocked, movement will be felt at the inner joint if wear has taken place.
6 Using a large screwdriver or flat bar, check for wear in the suspension mounting bushes by levering between the relevant suspension component and its attachment point. Some movement is to be expected, as the mountings are made of rubber, but excessive wear should be obvious. Also check the condition of any visible rubber bushes, looking for splits, cracks or contamination of the rubber.
7 With the car standing on its wheels, have an assistant turn the steering wheel back-and-forth, about an eighth of a turn each way. There should be very little, if any, lost movement between the steering wheel and roadwheels. If this is not the case, closely observe the joints and mountings previously described. In addition, check the steering column universal joints for wear, and also check the rack-and-pinion steering gear itself.
8 The front suspension mountings should be checked for tightness.

Rear suspension

9 Chock the front wheels, then jack up the rear of the vehicle and support securely on axle stands (see *Jacking and vehicle support*).
10 Working as described previously for the front suspension, check the rear hub bearings, the suspension bushes and the strut or shock absorber mountings (as applicable) for wear.
11 The rear suspension mountings should be checked for tightness.

Shock absorber

12 Check for any signs of fluid leakage around the shock absorber bodies, or from the rubber gaiters around the piston rods. Should any fluid be noticed, the shock absorber is defective internally, or the rubber gaiter is split, and may need renewing. **Note:** *Shock absorbers should always be renewed in pairs on the same axle.*

9   Driveshaft joints and gaiters check

1 With the front of the vehicle raised and securely supported on stands, turn the steering onto full lock then slowly rotate the roadwheel. Inspect the condition of the outer constant velocity (CV) joint rubber gaiters while squeezing the gaiters to open out the folds **(see illustration)**. Check for signs of cracking, splits or deterioration of the rubber, which may allow the grease to escape and lead to water and grit entry into the joint. Also check the security and condition of the retaining clips. Repeat these checks on the inner CV joints. If any damage or deterioration is found, the gaiters should be renewed as described in Chapter 8 Section 3.
2 At the same time check the general condition of the CV joints themselves by first holding the driveshaft and attempting to rotate the wheel. Repeat this check by holding the inner joint and attempting to rotate the driveshaft. Any appreciable movement indicates wear in the joints, wear in the driveshaft splines or a loose driveshaft retaining nut.

10 Hinges and locks lubrication

1 Work around the vehicle and lubricate the hinges of the bonnet, doors and tailgate with a light machine oil.
2 Lightly lubricate the two bonnet release locks with a smear of grease.
3 Check carefully the security and operation of all hinges, latches and locks. Check that the central locking system operates correctly.
4 Check the condition and operation of the bonnet and tailgate/boot lid struts, renewing them if either is leaking or no longer able to support the bonnet/tailgate/boot lid.

9.1 Check the driveshaft gaiters for signs of damage or deterioration

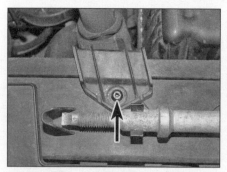

11.2a Drill out the rivet or undo the bolt securing the drain tube to the slam panel

11.2b Remove the nuts at the top of the air intake cowling...

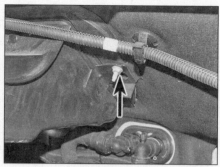

11.2c ...and slacken the nut each side

11.3 Undo the bolt and remove the air intake hose

11.4 Release the clamp at each end of the intake hose – turbocharger end shown

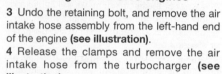

11 Fuel filter renewal

Renewal

1 Disconnect the battery negative lead as described in Chapter 5A Section 4.

2 Drill out the rivet/undo the bolt securing the drain tube to the bonnet slam panel, then undo the nuts and remove the cabin air intake cowling above the engine (see illustrations).

1.6 litre engines – DOHC engines

3 Undo the retaining bolt, and remove the air intake hose assembly from the left-hand end of the engine (see illustration).

4 Release the clamps and remove the air intake hose from the turbocharger (see illustration).

5 Place rags beneath the filter housing, then depress the release buttons and disconnect the fuel pipes from the fuel filter, noting their fitted positions (see illustration). Plug the openings to prevent contamination. Disconnect the wiring plug (where applicable) from the top of the filter housing.

6 Release the retaining clip and lift the filter from the bracket on the end of the cylinder head (see illustrations). As the filter is withdrawn, disconnect the wiring connector from the base of the fuel filter and disconnect the drain tube.

7 Release the clip and disconnect the heater from the side of the filter assembly (see illustrations).

11.5 Disconnect the fuel pipes from the rear of the filter housing

11.6a Release the clip and slide the filter upwards from the mounting bracket

11.6b Disconnect the wiring connector and the drain tube

11.7a Release the clip...

11.7b ...and slide the heater from the filter housing

11.10 Pull up the fasteners and remove the cover

11.11a Prise up the centre metal clip, then squeeze together the 'ears' of the retaining collar

11.11b Depress the release buttons to disconnect these pipes

11.13 Rotate the water drain control clockwise

11.14 Undo the screws and pull the filter upwards

11.15 Filter head retaining screws

8 Clip the fuel heater into place on the new filter. Fit the new filter into place, remove the plugs and reconnect the pipes, and the wiring plug.

9 The remainder of refitting is a reversal of removal.

1.6 litre engines – SOHC engines (Euro 5)

10 Pull up the fasteners and remove the sound insulation cover from the top of the engine (see illustration).

11 Place rags beneath the filter housing, then disconnect the fuel pipes from the fuel filter, noting their fitted positions (see illustrations). Plug the openings to prevent contamination.

12 Disconnect the wiring plug(s) from the top of the filter.

13 Rotate the water drain control clockwise (see illustration). This releases fuel and any water from the filter, through a tube at the back of the engine. Place a container under the rear of the engine to catch any fuel/ water.

14 Undo the 2 retaining screws, then pull the filter assembly upwards from place (see illustration).

15 Undo the 3 screws and separate the filter head from the body (see illustration).

16 Renew the rubber seal, locate the head on the new filter body, tighten the retaining screws securely, then rotate the water

drain control anti-clockwise to seal it (see illustration).

17 Refitting is a reversal of removal.

2.0 litre engines – Euro 4 emissions level engines

18 Thoroughly clean the area around the fuel pipe connectors, then disconnect the pipes and wiring connector (where applicable) at the top of the filter assembly (see illustration). Plug the openings to prevent contamination.

19 Using a 27 mm socket, unscrew the filter head.

20 Lift the filter head, and extract the filter element (see illustration). Discard the seal on the filter head – a new one must be fitted.

11.16 Renew the rubber seal on the filter

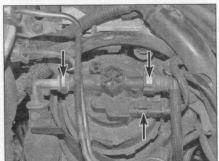

11.18 Depress the release buttons, disconnect the fuel pipes and the wiring plug

11.20 Lift out the filter element

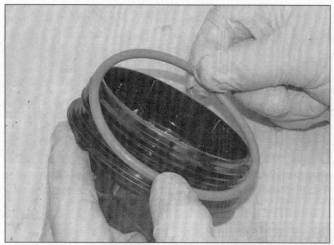

11.22a Renew the O-ring seal …

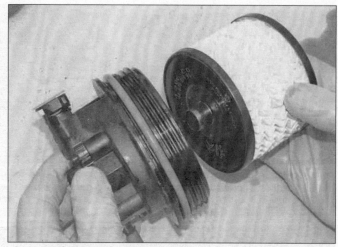

11.22b … insert the new filter element into the filter head …

11.23a … and then refit the fuel filter housing …

11.23b … tighten filter head until it reaches the stop

21 Thoroughly clean the filter housing chamber using clean, lint-free rags.

22 Fit the new seal and filter element into the filter head, and then lubricate the new seal using clean fuel, and fit it in place on the filter head (see illustrations).

23 Refit the filter head and tighten it until the filter head touches the stop (see illustrations).

24 Remove the protective plugs, and then reconnect the fuel pipes/wiring plug to the filter housing.

2.0 litre engines – Euro 5 emissions level engines

25 Pull up and remove the sound insulation cover from the top of the engine.

26 Ensure the engine is cold, then squeeze together the sides of the collar and disconnect the upper pipe from the coolant expansion tank (see illustration).

27 Place rags beneath the filter housing, then depress the release buttons and disconnect the fuel pipes from the fuel filter, noting their fitted positions (see illustrations). Plug the openings to prevent contamination.

11.26 Squeeze the sides of the collar and disconnect the pipe from the expansion tank

11.27a Depress the outside edges of the release buttons…

11.27b …and disconnect the fuel pipes

11.29a Undo the Torx screws...

11.29b ...and lift the filter

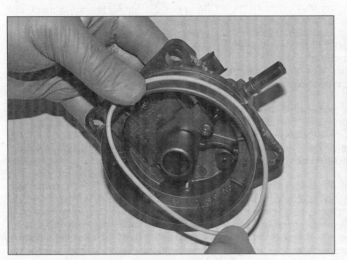

11.32a Fit a new O-ring seal...

11.32b ...and press the new element into the cover

28 Disconnect the wiring plugs from the top of the filter assembly.

29 Undo the 4 retaining screws and lift the filter from place **(see illustrations)**.

30 Pull the filter element from the cover, and remove the O-ring seal.

31 Take the opportunity to clean out the filter housing.

12.2 Service indicator trip/reset button

32 Fit the new O-ring seal to the cover, and press the new element into place **(see illustrations)**.

33 Refitting is a reversal of removal.

All engines

34 Reconnect the battery negative lead as described in Chapter 5A Section 4.

35 Bleed the fuel system as described in Chapter 4A Section 4.

12 Resetting the service indicator

1 The instrument cluster mileage recorder incorporates a service interval indicator. When the vehicle is started, the unit displays the mileage until the next service, or the mileage covered since the service was due. The service indicator is manually reset to zero after the vehicle has been serviced. The indicator can also be reset at any time using the Citroën/Peugeot diagnostic tool.

2 To manually reset the mileage to zero, carry out the following procedure:

a) Switch off the ignition and place the key in the steering lock "S" position.

b) Press and hold down the trip/reset button on the instrument panel **(see illustration)**

c) While the trip/reset button is held down, switch on the ignition.

d) Keep the trip/reset button pressed until zero appears and the maintenance symbol disappears.

e) Release the trip/reset button and switch off the ignition.

3 Switch on the ignition – the distance remaining until (or covered since) the next service is due will flash in the display.

13 Brake pad wear and disc check

1 The work described in this Section should be carried out at the specified intervals, or

13.3 Checking brake pad thickness through alloy wheels

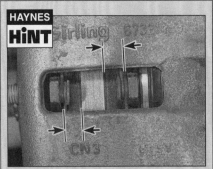

For a quick check, the thickness of the friction material on each brake pad can be measured through the aperture in the caliper body.

13.7 Check the thickness of the brake pad friction material

whenever a defect is suspected in the braking system. Any of the following symptoms could indicate a potential brake system defect:

a) *The vehicle pulls to one side when the brake pedal is depressed.*
b) *The brakes make squealing, scraping or dragging noises when applied.*
c) *Brake pedal travel is excessive, or pedal feel is poor.*
d) *The brake fluid requires repeated topping-up. Note that, because the hydraulic clutch shares the same fluid as the braking system, this problem could be due to a leak in the clutch system.*

Front disc brakes

2 Chock the rear wheels then loosen the front wheel bolts. Jack up the front of the vehicle, and support it on axle stands (see *Jacking and vehicle support*).
3 For better access to the brake calipers, remove the wheels **(see illustration)**.
4 Look through the inspection window in the caliper, and check that the thickness of the friction lining material on each of the pads is not less than the recommended minimum thickness given in the Specifications (see **Haynes hint**). Bear in mind that the lining material is normally bonded to a metal backing plate. To differentiate between the metal and the lining material, it is helpful to turn the disc slowly at first – the edge of the disc can then be identified, with the lining material on each pad either side of it, and the backing plates behind.
5 If it is difficult to determine the exact thickness of the pad linings, or if you are at all concerned about the condition of the pads, then remove them from the calipers for further inspection (refer to Chapter 9 Section 4).
6 Check the other caliper in the same way.
7 If any one of the brake pads has worn down to, or below, the specified limit, all four pads at that end of the car must be renewed as a set **(see illustration)**. If the pads on one side are significantly more worn than the other, this may indicate that the caliper pistons have partially seized – refer to the brake pad renewal procedure in Chapter 9 Section 4, and push the pistons back into the caliper to free them.
8 Measure the thickness of the discs with a micrometer, if available, to make sure that

they still have service life remaining. Do not be fooled by the lip of rust which often forms on the outer edge of the disc, which may make the disc appear thicker than it really is – scrape off the loose rust if necessary, without scoring the disc friction (shiny) surface.
9 If any disc is thinner than the specified minimum thickness, renew both (refer to Chapter 9 Section 7).
10 Check the general condition of the discs. Look for excessive scoring and discolouration caused by overheating. If these conditions exist, remove the relevant disc and have it resurfaced or renewed (refer to Chapter 9 Section 7).
11 Make sure that the transmission is in neutral. Spin the wheel, and check that the brake is not binding. Some drag is normal with a disc brake, but it should not require any great effort to turn the wheel – also, do not confuse brake drag with resistance from the transmission.
12 Before refitting the wheels, check all brake lines and hoses (refer to Chapter 9 Section 3). In particular, check the flexible hoses in the vicinity of the calipers, where they are subjected to most movement. Bend them between the fingers (but do not actually bend them double, or the casing may be damaged) and check that this does not reveal previously hidden cracks, cuts or splits.
13 On completion, refit the wheels and lower the car to the ground. Tighten the wheel bolts to the specified torque.

Rear disc brakes

14 Loosen the rear wheel bolts then chock the front wheels. Jack up the rear of the car, and support it on axle stands. Release the handbrake and remove the rear wheels.
15 The procedure for checking the rear brakes is much the same as described in paragraphs 2 to 13 above. Check that the rear brakes are not binding, noting that transmission resistance is not a factor on the rear wheels. Abnormal effort may indicate that the handbrake needs adjusting – see Chapter 9 Section 16.

14 Handbrake check and adjustment

1 To check the handbrake adjustment, pull the handbrake lever to the fully applied position, applying normal moderate pressure, counting the number of clicks emitted from the handbrake ratchet mechanism. If adjustment is correct, there should be 1 click before the brakes begins to apply, and the rear wheels locked from the 4th click onwards. If this is not the case, follow the handbrake adjustment procedure described in Chapter 9 Section 16.

15 Seat belt condition check

1 Working on each seat belt in turn, carefully examine the seat belt webbing for cuts, or for any signs of serious fraying or deterioration. Pull the belt all the way out, and examine the full extent of the webbing.
2 Fasten and unfasten the belt, ensuring that the locking mechanism holds securely, and releases properly when intended. Check also that the retracting mechanism operates correctly when the belt is released.
3 Check the security of all seat belt mountings and attachments, which are accessible from inside the vehicle without removing any trim or other components.
4 Check the function of the seat belt reminder lamp.

16 Airbag system check

1 The following work can be carried out by the home mechanic, however, if an electronic fault is apparent, it will be necessary to take the car to a Citroën/Peugeot/Fiat dealer or specialist who will have the necessary diagnostic equipment to extract fault codes from the system.
2 Turn the ignition switch to the drive position (ignition warning lights on), and check that the airbag warning light is illuminated for

approximately 6 seconds. After this period the light should go out, indicating that the system has been checked and is functioning correctly.

3 If the warning light remains on or refuses to light, have the system checked by a Citroën/Peugeot/Fiat dealer or specialist.

4 Visually examine the steering wheel centre pad, knee airbag and the passenger airbag modules for external damage. Also check the exterior of the front seats around the side airbag locations. If damage is evident, consult a Citroën/Peugeot/Fiat dealer or specialist.

5 In the interests of safety, make sure that there are no loose items inside the car, which could be thrown onto the airbag modules in the event of an accident.

17 Road test

Instruments and electrical equipment

1 Check the operation of all instruments and electrical equipment.

2 Make sure that all instruments read correctly, and switch on all electrical equipment in turn to check that it functions properly. Check the function of the heating, air conditioning and automatic climate control systems.

Steering and suspension

3 Check for any abnormalities in the steering, suspension, handling or road 'feel'.

4 Drive the vehicle, and check that there are no unusual vibrations or noises.

5 Check that the steering feels positive, with no excessive 'sloppiness', or roughness, and check for any suspension noises when cornering, or when driving over bumps. Check that the power steering system operates correctly.

Drivetrain

6 Check the performance of the engine, clutch, transmission and driveshafts.

7 Listen for any unusual noises from the engine, clutch and transmission.

8 Make sure that the engine runs smoothly when idling, and that there is no hesitation when accelerating.

9 Check that the clutch action is smooth and progressive, that the drive is taken up smoothly, and that the pedal travel is not excessive. Also listen for any noises when the clutch pedal is depressed. Check that all gears can be engaged smoothly, without noise, and that the gear lever action is smooth and not abnormally vague or 'notchy'.

10 Listen for a metallic clicking sound from the front of the vehicle, as the vehicle is driven slowly in a circle with the steering on full lock. Carry out this check in both directions. If a clicking noise is heard, this indicates wear in a driveshaft joint, in which case, refer to Chapter 8 Section 2.

Braking system

11 Make sure that the vehicle does not pull to one side when braking, and that the wheels do not lock when braking hard.

12 Check that there is no vibration through the steering when braking.

13 Check that the handbrake operates correctly, without excessive movement of the lever, and that it holds the vehicle stationary on a slope.

14 Test the operation of the brake servo unit as follows. With the engine off, depress the footbrake four or five times to exhaust the vacuum, and then start the engine while holding the brake pedal depressed. As the engine starts, there should be a noticeable 'give' in the brake pedal as vacuum builds-up. Allow the engine to run for at least two minutes, and then switch it off. If the brake pedal is now depressed again, it should be possible to detect a 'hiss' from the servo as the pedal is depressed. After about four or five applications, no further hissing should be heard, and the pedal should feel considerably harder.

18 Coolant antifreeze concentration check

1 The cooling system should be filled with the recommended antifreeze and corrosion protection fluid. Over a period of time, the concentration of fluid may be reduced due to topping-up (this can be avoided by topping-up with the correct antifreeze mixture) or fluid loss. If loss of coolant has

been evident, it is important to make the necessary repair before adding fresh fluid. The exact mixture of antifreeze-to-water that you should use depends on the relative weather conditions. The mixture should contain at least 40% antifreeze, but not more than 70%. Consult the mixture ratio chart on the antifreeze container before adding coolant. Use antifreeze, which meets the vehicle manufacturer's specifications.

2 With the engine cold, carefully remove the cap from the expansion tank. If the engine is not completely cold, place a cloth rag over the cap before removing it, and remove it slowly to allow any pressure to escape.

3 Antifreeze checkers are available from car accessory shops. Draw some coolant from the expansion tank and observe the concentration level **(see illustration)**. Follow the manufacturer's instructions.

4 If the concentration is incorrect, it will be necessary to either withdraw some coolant and add antifreeze, or alternatively drain the old coolant and add fresh coolant of the correct concentration.

19 Exhaust system check

1 With the engine cold, check the complete exhaust system, from its starting point at the engine to the end of the tailpipe. If necessary, raise the front and rear of the vehicle and support it on axle stands (see *Jacking and vehicle support*). Remove any engine undershields as necessary for full access to the exhaust system.

2 Check the exhaust pipes and connections for evidence of leaks, severe corrosion, and damage. Make sure that all brackets and mountings are in good condition and that all relevant nuts and bolts are tight **(see illustration)**. Leakage at any of the joints or in other parts of the system will usually show up as a black sooty stain in the vicinity of the leak.

3 Rattles and other noises can often be traced to the exhaust system, especially the brackets and rubber mountings. Try to move the pipes and silencers. If the components are able to come into contact with the body or suspension parts, secure the system with new mountings. Otherwise separate the joints (if possible) and twist the pipes as necessary to provide additional clearance.

20 Auxiliary drivebelt check and renewal

1 On all engines, a single, multi-grooved auxiliary drivebelt is used to transmit drive from the crankshaft pulley to the alternator, power steering pump (1.6 litre models) and the refrigerant compressor, depending on model. The drivebelt is tensioned automatically by

18.3 Check the antifreeze concentration with a hydrometer

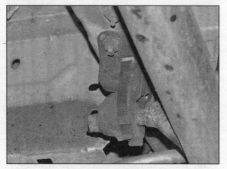

19.2 Check the condition of the exhaust rubber mountings

20.4 Check the condition of the auxiliary belt

20.8 The alignment lug must be between the two lines on the housing

20.9 Rotate the tensioner arm clockwise, then lock it in place by inserting a 4 mm drill into the hole (hidden behind spanner) in the tensioner body (arrowed)

a spring-loaded tensioner pulley. The layout of the belt routing will depend on whether there is air-conditioning and/or a belt driven power steering pump fitted. The following procedures show two different types of tensioner depending on model/engine type.

2 Due to their function and material make-up, drivebelts are prone to failure after a long period of time, and should therefore be inspected regularly.

Check

3 For better access to the drivebelt, chock the rear wheels then jack up the front of the car and support it on axle stands (see *Jacking and vehicle support*). Remove the right-hand front roadwheel, and then remove the plastic liner from under the right-hand wheel arch to expose the crankshaft pulley.

4 Using a suitable socket and extension bar fitted to the crankshaft pulley bolt, rotate the crankshaft so that the entire length of the drivebelt(s) can be examined. Examine the drivebelt for cracks, splitting, fraying, or other damage **(see illustration)**. Check also

for signs of glazing (shiny patches) and for separation of the belt plies.

5 If at any point the belt is to be removed and then refitted, mark its direction of normal rotation.

Renewal

1.6 litre engines

6 If not already done, proceed as described in paragraph 3.

7 If the belt is to be refitted, mark its direction of normal rotation with a pen.

8 The automatic tensioner has markings, which align with each other when the belt is in serviceable condition. If the small lug is outside these lines then the belt will need to be renewed **(see illustration)**.

9 Using an open-ended spanner, reach down and rotate the tensioner arm clockwise to release the belt tension. Insert a 4 mm drill bit or rod into the hole in the tensioner body, so that the tensioner arm rests against it, and locks it in this position **(see illustration)**. It is usefull to have a small mirror available to enable the alignment of the locking holes to be more easily seen in the limited space available.

10 Manoeuvre the belt from the pulleys **(see illustration)**. Take the opportunity to check the tensioner and idler pulleys spin freely, with no signs of roughness or slack.

11 Refit the belt around the pulleys, ensuring

that the ribs on the belt are correctly engaged with the grooves in the pulleys, and the drivebelt is correctly routed. If refitting a used belt, use the marks made on removal to ensure it is fitted the correct way around.

Caution: Do not allow the tensioner pulley to spring forcefully onto the belt as this could result in damage.

12 Using an open-ended spanner, hold the tensioner arm so that the locking drill bit/rod can be removed, then release the pressure on the spanner so that the automatic tensioner takes up the slack in the drivebelt.

13 Refit the wheel arch liner and roadwheel, and then lower the vehicle to the ground.

2.0 litre engines

14 If not already done, proceed as described in paragraphs 3.

15 If the belt is to be refitted, mark its direction of normal rotation with a pen.

16 Using a spanner on the centre bolt, rotate the tensioner pulley, and slacken the belt **(see illustration)**.

17 Lock the tensioner in this position using a 4.0 mm drill bit through the holes in the tensioner **(see illustration)**.

18 Manoeuvre the belt from the pulleys. Take the opportunity to check the tensioner and idler pulleys spin freely, with no signs of roughness or slack.

19 Begin refitting by placing the belt on

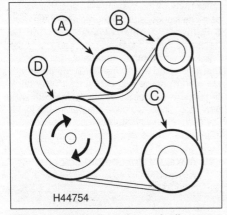

20.10 Auxiliary belt routing and adjustment (with air conditioning)

A Automatic tensioner
B Alternator pulley
C Air conditioning compressor pulley
D Crankshaft pulley

H44754

20.16 Rotate the tensioner clockwise – Euro 5 engine shown

20.17 Insert a 4 mm drill bit/rod through the holes in the tensioner – Euro 4 engine shown

20.19 Auxiliary belt routing and adjustment (with air conditioning)

1 Alternator pulley
2 Tensioner pulley bolt
3 Air conditioning compressor pulley
4 Crankshaft pulley

the pulleys, ensuring it's correctly located in grooves of the pulleys **(see illustration)**.
20 Hold the tensioner in place with the spanner, remove the locking drill bit, and slowly allow the tensioner pulley to rotate anti-clockwise and act against the belt. The belt is automatically tensioned by the spring-loaded tensioner.

21 Refit the wheel arch liner and roadwheel, and then lower the vehicle to the ground.

21 Pollen filter renewal

1 Drill out the rivet/undo the bolt securing the water drain pipe to the bonnet slam panel **(see illustration)**.
2 Undo the retaining nuts and remove the cabin air intake cowling **(see illustrations)**.
3 Unclip the pollen filter element, and manoeuvre it from place **(see illustrations)**.
4 If possible, wipe clean the inside of the housing and then fit the new element, making sure that it's correctly seated.
5 Refit the cabin air intake cowling and secure it with the nuts.
6 Secure the water drain pipe to the bonnet slam panel with a new rivet, or substitute a nut and bolt.

22 Brake fluid renewal

⚠️ *Warning: Brake hydraulic fluid can harm your eyes and damage painted surfaces, so use extreme caution when handling and pouring it. Do not use fluid that has been standing open for some time, as it absorbs moisture from the air. Excess moisture can cause a dangerous loss of braking effectiveness.*

Note: *A hydraulic clutch shares its fluid reservoir with the braking system, and will also need to be bled (see Chapter 6 Section 2).*
1 The procedure is similar to that for the bleeding of the hydraulic system as described in Chapter 9 Section 2, except that the brake fluid reservoir should be emptied by siphoning, using a clean ladle or similar before starting, and allowance should be made for the old fluid to be expelled when bleeding a section of the circuit.
2 Working as described in Chapter 9 Section 2, open the first bleed screw in the sequence, and pump the brake pedal gently until nearly all the old fluid has been emptied from the master cylinder reservoir.
3 Top-up to the MAX level with new fluid, and continue pumping until only the new fluid remains in the reservoir, and new fluid can be seen emerging from the bleed screw. Tighten the screw, and top the reservoir level up to the MAX level line.
4 Work through all the remaining bleed screws in the sequence until new fluid can be seen at all of them. Be careful to keep the master cylinder reservoir topped-up to above the DANGER level marking at all times, or air may enter the system and increase the length of the task.
5 When the operation is complete, check that all bleed screws are securely tightened, and that their dust caps are refitted **(see illustration)**. Wash off all traces of spilt fluid, and recheck the master cylinder reservoir fluid level.
6 Check the operation of the brakes before taking the car on the road.

(Lower belt photo)

21.1 Drill out the rivet or undo the bolt securing the pipe to the bonnet slam panel

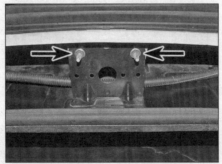

21.2a Undo the 2 nuts at the top…

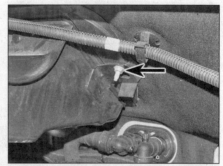

21.2b …slacken the nut each side and remove the cabin air intake cowling

21.3a Lift the filter element from the cowling

21.3b Note the arrow indicating airflow (upwards)

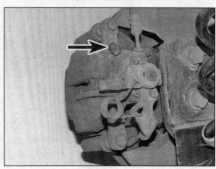

22.5 Make sure dust cap is refitted to bleed screw

23.4 Prise out the wire clip a little, and pull the hose from the radiator

23.5a Heater hose bleed caps at the bulkhead

23.5b Bleed cap on the thermostat housing

23 Coolant renewal

⚠️ *Warning: Do not allow antifreeze to come in contact with your skin or painted surfaces of the vehicle. Flush contaminated areas immediately with plenty of water. Don't store new coolant, or leave old coolant lying around, where it's accessible to children or pets – they're attracted by its sweet smell. Ingestion of even a small amount of coolant can be fatal. Wipe up garage-floor and drip pan spills immediately. Keep antifreeze containers covered, and repair cooling system leaks as soon as they're noticed.*

⚠️ *Warning: Never remove the expansion tank filler cap when the engine is running, or has just been switched off, as the cooling system will be hot, and the consequent escaping steam and scalding coolant could cause serious injury.*

⚠️ *Warning: Wait until the engine is cold before starting these procedures.*

Cooling system draining

1 With the engine completely cold, remove the expansion tank filler cap. Turn the cap anti-clockwise, wait until any pressure remaining in the system is released, then unscrew it and lift it off.

2 Chock the rear wheels, and then raise the front of the vehicle and support it on axle stands (see *Jacking and vehicle support*). Undo the retaining bolts/nuts and remove the engine undershield.

3 Position a suitable container beneath the radiator lower hose outlet at the lower centre of the radiator.

4 Prise out the wire clip a little, and pull the lower hose from the radiator **(see illustration)**. Be prepared for coolant spillage.

5 Open the bleed screws/caps; there maybe one, two or three bleed screws/caps. One or two on the heater hose at the bulkhead connection and one on the top of the thermostat housing at the left-hand side of the cylinder head **(see illustrations)**. **Note:** *On some models there is no bleed screw on the thermostat housing; the return pipe to the reservoir fits in its place.*

6 On 1.6 litre engines, to drain the cylinder block, pull out the clip and remove the plug

located in the coolant housing at the rear of the engine **(see illustration)**. The plug must be refitted with a new clip and O-ring. **Note:** *A cylinder block drain plug may not be fitted to all models.*

7 On 2.0 litre engines, a drain plug is located on the rear of the cylinder block adjacent to the flywheel **(see illustration)**. Access to the drain plug is extremely limited.

8 Once the coolant has finished draining, refit the plug, and reconnect the bottom hose. If the coolant has been drained for a reason other than renewal, then provided it is clean and less than two years old, it can be re-used, though this is not always recommended.

9 Refit the engine undershield, and then lower the vehicle to the ground.

Cooling system flushing

10 If coolant renewal has been neglected, or if the antifreeze mixture has become diluted, then in time, the cooling system may gradually lose efficiency, as the coolant passages become restricted due to rust, scale deposits, and other sediment. The cooling system efficiency can be restored by flushing the system clean.

11 The radiator should be flushed separately from the engine, to avoid excess contamination.

23.6 Prise out the retaining clip and pull out the coolant drain plug

23.7 Cylinder block drain plug – 2.0 litre engines

Radiator flushing

12 Disconnect the top and bottom hoses and any other relevant hoses from the radiator (see Chapter 3 Section 4).

13 Insert a garden hose into the radiator top inlet. Direct a flow of clean water through the radiator, and continue flushing until clean water emerges from the radiator bottom outlet.

14 If after a reasonable period, the water still does not run clear, the radiator can be flushed with a good proprietary cleaning agent. It is important that their manufacturer's instructions are followed carefully. If the contamination is particularly bad, insert the hose in the radiator bottom outlet, and reverse-flush the radiator.

Engine flushing

15 To flush the engine, remove the thermostat (see Chapter 3 Section 5). If the radiator top hose has been disconnected, temporarily reconnect the hose. **Note:** *This may not be possible on some models, as the thermostat may be part of the coolant housing on the end of the cylinder head.*

16 With the bottom hose disconnected from the radiator, insert a garden hose into the coolant housing. Direct a clean flow of water through the engine, and continue flushing until clean water emerges from the radiator bottom hose.

17 When flushing is complete, refit the thermostat and reconnect the hoses.

Cooling system filling

18 Before attempting to fill the cooling system, make sure that all hoses and clips are in good condition, and that the clips are tight. Note that an antifreeze mixture must be used all year round, to prevent corrosion of the engine components (see following sub-Section).

19 Make sure that the air conditioning (A/C) or automatic climate control (ACC) is switched off. This is to prevent the air conditioning system starting the radiator cooling fan before the engine is at normal temperature when refilling the system.

20 Remove the expansion tank filler cap and remove the cooling system bleed screws (see paragraph 5).

21 Slowly fill the system whilst observing the bleed holes. Coolant will emerge from each of the bleed holes in turn, starting with the heater matrix hose. As soon as coolant free from air bubbles emerges from the heater matrix hose outlet, securely refit the cap/screw (as applicable) then watch the bleed hole on the coolant housing. Once coolant free from air bubbles emerges from the housing hole, refit the bleed screw and sealing washer and tighten securely.

22 Continue to fill the cooling system until bubbles stop appearing in the expansion bottle. Help to bleed the air from the system by repeatedly squeezing the radiator bottom hose.

23 When no more bubbles appear, ensure the expansion tank is full then start the engine. Run the engine at a fast idle speed (do not exceed 2000 rpm) until the cooling fan cuts in and out TWICE, then when the fan has stopped for the second time, switch the engine off. Observe the coolant level in the expansion tank during this process. If the level drops below the base of the tank, stop the engine, carefully remove the cap and top up the tank.

Caution: The coolant will be hot. Take great care not to scald yourself.

24 Wash off any spilt coolant with cold water.

25 When the engine has cooled, check the coolant level with reference to *Weekly checks*. Top-up the level if necessary, and refit the expansion bottle cap.

Antifreeze mixture

26 The antifreeze should always be renewed at the specified intervals. This is necessary not only to maintain the antifreeze properties, but also to prevent corrosion, which would otherwise occur as the corrosion inhibitors become progressively less effective.

27 Always use an ethylene glycol based antifreeze, which is suitable for use in mixed-metal cooling systems.

28 Before adding antifreeze, the cooling system should be completely drained, preferably flushed, and all hoses checked for condition and security.

29 After filling with antifreeze, a label should be attached to the expansion tank, stating the type and concentration of antifreeze used, and the date installed. Any subsequent topping-up should be made with the same type and concentration of antifreeze.

Caution: Do not use engine antifreeze in the windscreen/tailgate washer system, as it will cause damage to the vehicle paintwork. A screen wash additive should be added to the washer system in the quantities stated on the bottle.

24 Air filter element renewal, diesel

1.6 litre engines

1 Drill out the rivet/undo the bolt securing the water drain pipe to the bonnet slam panel **(see illustration 11.2a)**.

2 Undo the 4 retaining nuts and remove the cabin air intake cowling **(see illustration 11.2a and 11.2b)**.

DOHC (Euro 4) engines

3 Disconnect and remove the air intake and outlet hoses from the air cleaner housing **(see illustration)**. Disconnect the airflow meter wiring plug.

4 Undo the bolts at the front edge, and open the filter casing **(see illustration)**.

24.3 Undo the bolt, release the clamps and remove the air hoses

24.4 Undo the bolts and lift open the filter casing

24.5 Lift out the filter element

24.10a Undo the retaining screws …

24.10b …and release the clip

24.11 Remove the air filter element

5 Note its fitted location, then lift the element from the casing **(see illustration)**.
6 Wipe clean the inner surfaces of the cover and main housing, then locate the new element in the housing, making sure that the sealing lip is correctly engaged with the edge of the housing.
7 Close the filter casing and securely tighten the retaining bolts.
8 Refit the intake and outlet hoses, then reconnect the airflow meter wiring plug.

SOHC (Euro 5) engines

9 Pull up the fasteners and remove the cover from the top of the engine **(see illustration 11.10)**.
10 Undo the air filter cleaner cover retaining screws, release the clip at the edge, and lift the cover from air filter housing **(see illustrations)**.
11 Lift the element from the housing **(see illustration)**.
12 Wipe clean the inner surfaces of the cover and main housing, then locate the new element in the housing, making sure that the sealing lip is correctly engaged with the edge of the housing.

All 1.6 litre engines

13 Refitting is a reversal of removal.

2.0 litre engines

14 Undo the 4 retaining screws, and lift the cover from place **(see illustration)**.
15 Lift the air filter element from place, noting which way around it's fitted **(see illustration)**.
16 Wipe clean the inner surfaces of the cover and main housing, then locate the new element in the housing, making sure that the sealing lip is correctly engaged with the edge of the housing.
17 Refit the cover, and secure it with the screws.

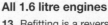

25 Manual transmission oil level check

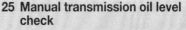

Note: *Some transmissions are described as 'Lubricated for life'. However, we consider it prudent to check the oil level, as a leak from the driveshaft oil seal or sealing washer could cause expensive damage.*
Note: *A suitable square-section wrench may be required to undo the transmission filler/ level plug on some models. These wrenches can be obtained from most motor factors or your Peugeot/Citroën dealer. A new sealing washer will be required for the transmission filler/level plug when refitting.*

1.6 litre models (BE4/5 transmissions)

1 Take the car on a short journey to warm the transmission up to normal operating temperature. Position the car over an inspection pit, or alternatively jack up the front and rear of the car and support on axle stands (see *Jacking and vehicle support*). Whichever method is used, make sure that the car is level for checking the fluid level later.
2 The oil level must be checked at least 5 minutes after the engine has been switched

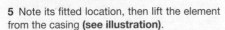

24.14 Undo the retaining screws, lift the cover...

24.15 … and withdraw the air filter element

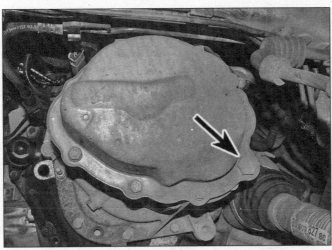

25.4 Fluid level/filler plug

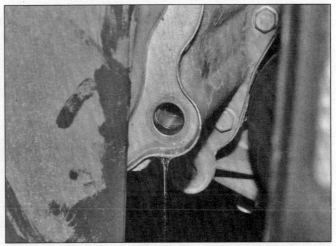

25.5 Add oil until a continuous trickle emerges from the plug hole

off. If the oil is checked immediately after driving the car, some of the oil will remain distributed around the transmission, resulting in an inaccurate level reading.

3 Remove the left-hand front wheel, and then release the fasteners and remove the wheel arch liner.

4 Wipe clean the area around the filler/level plug, which is on the left-hand end of the transmission. Unscrew the plug and clean it; discard the sealing washer **(see illustration)**.

5 The oil level should reach the lower edge of the filler/level hole. A certain amount of oil will have gathered behind the filler/level plug, and will trickle out when it is removed; this does not necessarily indicate that the level is correct. To ensure that a true level is established, wait until the initial trickle has stopped, then add oil as necessary until a trickle of new oil can be seen emerging **(see illustration)**. The level will be correct when the flow ceases; use only good-quality oil of the specified type (see Lubricants and fluids 0 Section 6).

6 Filling the transmission with oil is an extremely awkward operation; above all, allow plenty of time for the oil level to settle properly before checking it. If a large amount is added to the transmission, and a large amount flows out on checking the level, refit the filler/level plug and take the vehicle on a short journey so that the new oil is distributed fully around the transmission components, then recheck the level when it has settled again.

7 If the transmission has been overfilled so that oil flows out as soon as the filler/level plug is removed, Check that the car is completely level (front-to-rear and side-to-side), allow the surplus to drain off into a container.

8 When the level is correct, fit a new sealing washer to the filler/level plug. Refit the plug, tightening it to the specified torque setting. Wash off any spilt oil then refit the wheel arch liner, securing it in position with the

fasteners. Refit the roadwheel and tighten to the specified torque setting.

9 Frequent need for topping-up indicates a leak, which should be found and corrected before it becomes serious.

2.0 litre models (ML6C transmissions)

10 No level plug is fitted to these transmissions. If the level of the oil is suspected of being low, drain and refill the transmission as described in Chapter 7 Section 2.

26 Remote control battery renewal

1 Refer to Chapter 11 Section 18, for the renewal of the remote control battery.

27 Particulate filter fluid check

1 Eolys 176 and DPX42 fluid is an additive used on vehicles equipped with a particulate filter incorporated into the exhaust system. Over a period of time, the soot produced by

27.1 Particulate filter additive fluid tank

the engine will clog the filter. When the filter requires cleaning, the engine management system injects a small quantity of fuel into the combustion chamber after combustion has taken place. The unburnt fuel enters the exhaust system, where it ignites, and burns the soot deposits from the particulate filter. In order to lower the temperature at which the soot is burnt, Eolys fluid is added to the fuel in the tank. The fluid is stored in a separate tank in front of the fuel tank **(see illustration)**, and added to the main fuel tank. Every time the fuel tank is filled, the system computes how much Eolys fluid to add. Eventually the level of fluid will fall below a minimum level and a warning light will illuminate on the instrument cluster.

2 If the system runs out of fluid, the particulate filter will be unable to purge, causing its blockage, and premature failure. Unfortunately, the process of checking the level, replenishing the Eolys fluid tank and resetting the engine management values requires access to special diagnostic equipment, and therefore must be entrusted to a Peugeot/Citroën/Fiat dealer or suitably-equipped specialist. Failure to reset the ECM values will prevent the filter cleaning process from occurring.

28 Particulate filter renewal

1 Renewal of the particulate filter is described in Chapter 4A Section 18.

29 Timing belt renewal

1 Refer to Chapter 2A Section 7, Chapter 2B Section 7 or Chapter 2C Section 7 for timing belt renewal.

Chapter 2 Part A
1.6 litre SOHC engine in-car repair procedures

Contents

Degrees of difficulty

Easy, suitable for novice with little experience	Fairly easy, suitable for beginner with some experience	Fairly difficult, suitable for competent DIY mechanic	Difficult, suitable for experienced DIY mechanic	Very difficult, suitable for expert DIY or professional

Specifications

General

Designation	DV6DUM and DV6UC
Engine codes*	
DV6DUM...	9HH
DV6UC..	9HM, 9H07
Capacity	1560 cc
Bore	75.0 mm
Stroke	88.3 mm
Direction of crankshaft rotation	Clockwise (viewed from the right-hand side of vehicle)
No 1 cylinder location...............................	At the transmission end of block
Maximum power output.................................	66 kW (90 PS) @ 4000 rpm
Maximum torque output................................	180 Nm @ 1500 rpm
Compression ratio	18 : 1
Emissions level......................................	Euro 5

Note: * The engine code is stamped on a plate attached to the front of the cylinder block, next to the oil filter

Compression pressures (engine hot, at cranking speed)

Normal	20 ± 5 bar
Minimum	15 bar
Maximum difference between any two cylinders..........	5 bar

Cylinder head gasket

Gasket thickness:

1 notch	1.35 mm
2 notch	1.25 mm
3 notch	1.30 mm
4 notch	1.40 mm
5 notch	1.45 mm

Piston protrusion (gasket required):

0.685 to 0.734 mm	1 notch
0.533 to 0.634 mm	2 notch
0.635 to 0.684 mm	3 notch
0.735 to 0.784 mm	4 notch
0.785 to 0.886 mm	5 notch

Cylinder head bolts

Maximum length (measured under head)................... 149 mm

Camshaft

Drive .... Toothed belt from crankshaft
Length .... 410.10 ± 0.25 mm
Endfloat .... 0.195 to 0.300 mm

Lubrication system

Oil pump type.. Gear-type, driven directly by the right-hand end of the crankshaft, by two flats machined along the crankshaft journal.

Oil pressure at 110°C:
    1000 rpm .... 1.3 bar
    4000 rpm .... 3.5 bar

Torque wrench settings

	Nm	lbf ft
Ancillary drivebelt tensioner roller	20	15
Big-end bolts: *		
Stage 1	10	7
Stage 2	Slacken 180°	
Stage 3	30	22
Stage 4	Angle-tighten a further 140°	
Bolts	10	7
Camshaft housing-to-cylinder head bolts	30	22
Camshaft position sensor bolt	5	4
Camshaft sprocket bolt		
Stage 1	20	15
Stage 2	Angle-tighten a further 50°	
Coolant outlet housing bolts	8	6
Crankshaft position/speed sensor bolt	10	7
Crankshaft pulley/sprocket bolt: *		
Stage 1	35	26
Stage 2	Angle-tighten a further 190°	
Cylinder head bolts: *		
Stage 1	20	15
Stage 2	40	30
Stage 3	Angle-tighten a further 260°	
Cylinder head cover	10	7
Engine-to-transmission fixing bolts	47	35
Flywheel bolts: *		
Stage 1	30	22
Stage 2	Angle-tighten a further 90°	
Fuel pump sprocket	50	37
Left-hand engine/transmission mounting:		
Flexible mounting centre nut	65	48
Flexible mounting-to-bracket bolts	30	22
Mounting bracket-to-transmission bolts	60	44
Mounting bracket-to-vehicle body bolts	27	20
Main bearing ladder outer seam bolts:		
Stage 1	5	4
Stage 2	10	7
Main bearing ladder to cylinder block:		
Stage 1	10	7
Stage 2	Slacken 180°	
Stage 3	30	22
Stage 4	Angle-tighten a further 140°	
Piston oil jet spray tube bolt	20	15
Oil cooler retaining bolts	10	7
Oil filter cover	25	18
Oil pick-up pipe	10	7
Oil pressure switch	30	22
Oil pump to cylinder block:		
Stage 1	5	4
Stage 2	9	7
*Rear link rod:		
Link rod-to-cylinder block bracket bolt	58	43
Link rod-to-subframe bolt	87	64

Torque wrench settings (continued)

	Nm	lbf ft
Right-hand engine mounting:		
Flexible mounting-to-vehicle body bolts	30	22
Mounting bracket-to-engine bolts	60	44
Reaction rod mounting bracket-to-engine mounting bracket:		
Bolts	60	44
Nut	45	33
Reaction rod-to-vehicle body.	47	34
Reaction rod-to-mounting bracket bolt	47	34
Sump drain plug.	25	18
Sump bolts/nuts.	10	7
Timing belt idler pulley	37	27
Timing belt tensioner pulley	23	17

*Do not re-use

1 General Information

How to use this Chapter

1 This Part of Chapter 2 describes the repair procedures that can reasonably be carried out on the engine while it remains in the vehicle. If the engine has been removed from the vehicle and is being dismantled as described in Part D, any preliminary dismantling procedures can be ignored.

2 Note that, while it may be possible physically to overhaul items such as the piston/connecting rod assemblies while the engine is in the car, such tasks are not usually carried out as separate operations. Usually, several additional procedures are required (not to mention the cleaning of components and oilways); for this reason, all such tasks are classed as major overhaul procedures, and are described in Part D of this Chapter.

3 Part D describes the removal of the engine/transmission from the car, and the full overhaul procedures that can then be carried out.

DV series engines

4 The 1.6 litre DV series of engines are the result of development collaboration between Peugeot/Citroën and Ford. Originally specified as a double overhead camshaft (DOHC) 16-valve design, the latest version covered by this Chapter is a single overhead camshaft (SOHC), 8 valve variant. The direct injection, turbocharged, four-cylinder engine is mounted transversely, with the transmission mounted on the left-hand side.

5 A toothed timing belt drives the camshaft, high-pressure fuel pump and coolant pump. The camshaft operates the inlet and exhaust valves via rocker arms which are supported at their pivot ends by hydraulic self-adjusting tappets. The camshaft is supported by bearings machined directly in the cylinder head and camshaft bearing housing.

6 The high-pressure fuel pump supplies fuel to the fuel rail, and subsequently to the electronically-controlled injectors which inject the fuel direct into the combustion chambers. This design differs from the previous type where an injection pump supplies the fuel at high pressure to each injector. The earlier, conventional type injection pump required fine calibration and timing, and these functions are now completed by the high-pressure pump, electronic injectors and engine management ECM (Electronic Control Module).

7 The crankshaft runs in five main bearings of the usual shell type. Endfloat is controlled by thrustwashers either side of No 2 main bearing.

8 The pistons are selected to be of matching weight, and incorporate fully-floating gudgeon pins retained by circlips.

Repair operations precaution

9 The engine is a complex unit with numerous accessories and ancillary components. The design of the engine compartment is such that every conceivable space has been utilised, and access to virtually all of the engine components is extremely limited. In many cases, ancillary components will have to be removed, or moved to one side, and wiring, pipes and hoses will have to be disconnected or removed from various cable clips and support brackets.

10 When working on this engine, read through the entire procedure first, look at the car and engine at the same time, and establish whether you have the necessary tools, equipment, skill and patience to proceed. Allow considerable time for any operation, and be prepared for the unexpected.

11 Because of the limited access, many of the engine photographs appearing in this Chapter were, by necessity, taken with the engine removed from the vehicle.

⚠ **Warning: It is essential to observe strict precautions when working on the fuel system components of the engine, particularly the high-pressure side of the system. Before carrying out any engine operations that entail working on, or near, any part of the fuel system, refer to the special information given in Chapter 4A Section 1.**

12 Operations with engine in vehicle

a) Compression pressure – testing.
b) Cylinder head cover – removal and refitting.
c) Crankshaft pulley – removal and refitting.
d) Timing belt covers – removal and refitting.
e) Timing belt – removal, refitting and adjustment.
f) Timing belt tensioner and sprockets – removal and refitting.
g) Camshaft oil seal – renewal.
h) Camshaft, rocker arms and hydraulic tappets – removal, inspection and refitting.
i) Sump – removal and refitting.
j) Oil pump – removal and refitting.
k) Crankshaft oil seals – renewal.
l) Engine/transmission mountings – inspection and renewal.

2 Compression and leakdown tests – description and interpretation

Compression test

Note: A compression tester specifically designed for diesel engines must be used for this test.

1 When engine performance is down, or if misfiring occurs which cannot be attributed to the fuel system, a compression test can provide diagnostic clues as to the engine's condition. If the test is performed regularly, it can give warning of trouble before any other symptoms become apparent.

2 A compression tester specifically intended for diesel engines must be used, because of the higher pressures involved. The tester is connected to an adapter which screws into the glow plug or injector hole. On this engine, an adapter suitable for use in the glow plug holes will be required, so as not to disturb the fuel system components. It is unlikely to be worthwhile buying such a tester for occasional use, but it may be possible to borrow or hire one – if not, have the test performed by a garage.

3 Unless specific instructions to the contrary are supplied with the tester, observe the following points:

a) The battery must be in a good state of charge, the air filter must be clean, and the engine should be at normal operating temperature.
b) All the glow plugs should be removed as described in Chapter 5B Section 2 before starting the test.
c) Disconnect the fuel injector wiring plugs.

4 The compression pressures measured are not so important as the balance between cylinders. Values are given in the Specifications.

5 The cause of poor compression is less easy to establish on a diesel engine than on a petrol one. The effect of introducing oil into the cylinders ('wet' testing) is not conclusive, because there is a risk that the oil will sit in the swirl chamber or in the recess on the piston crown instead of passing to the rings. However, the following can be used as a rough guide to diagnosis.

6 All cylinders should produce very similar pressures; any difference greater than that specified indicates the existence of a fault. Note that the compression should build-up quickly in a healthy engine; low compression on the first stroke, followed by gradually-increasing pressure on successive strokes, indicates worn piston rings. A low compression reading on the first stroke, which does not build-up during successive strokes, indicates leaking valves or a blown head gasket (a cracked head could also be the cause). Deposits on the undersides of the valve heads can also cause low compression.

7 A low reading from two adjacent cylinders is almost certainly due to the head gasket having blown between them; the presence of coolant in the engine oil will confirm this.

8 If the compression reading is unusually high, the cylinder head surfaces, valves and pistons are probably coated with carbon deposits. If this is the case, the cylinder head should be removed and decarbonised. **Note:** *After performing this test, a fault code may be generated and stored in the ECM memory. Have the ECM self-diagnosis facility interrogated by a Peugeot/Citroen/Fiat/Toyota dealer or suitably-equipped specialist, and the fault code erased.*

Leakdown test

9 A leakdown test measures the rate at which compressed air fed into the cylinder is lost. It is an alternative to a compression test, and in many ways it is better, since the escaping air provides easy identification of where pressure loss is occurring (piston rings, valves or head gasket).

10 The equipment needed for leakdown testing is unlikely to be available to the home mechanic. If poor compression is suspected, have the test performed by a suitably-equipped garage.

3 Engine assembly/valve timing holes – general information and usage

Note: *Do not attempt to rotate the engine whilst the crankshaft and camshaft are locked in position. If the engine is to be left in this state for a long period of time, it is a good idea to place suitable warning notices inside the vehicle, and in the engine compartment. This will reduce the possibility of the engine being accidentally cranked on the starter motor, which is likely to cause damage with the locking pins in place.*

1 Timing holes or slots are located only in the crankshaft pulley flange and camshaft sprocket hub. The holes/slots are used to position the pistons halfway up the cylinder bores. This will ensure that the valve timing is maintained during operations that require removal and refitting of the timing belt. When the holes/slots are aligned with their corresponding holes in the cylinder block and cylinder head, suitable diameter bolts/pins can be inserted to lock the crankshaft and camshaft in position, preventing rotation.

2 Note that the fuel system used on these engines does not have a conventional diesel injection pump, but instead uses a high-pressure fuel pump. However, the fuel pump sprocket must be pegged in position in a similar fashion to the camshaft sprocket.

3 To align the engine assembly/valve timing holes, proceed as follows.

4 Slacken the right-hand front roadwheel bolts, apply the handbrake, then jack up the front of the vehicle and support it on axle stands (see *Jacking and vehicle support*). Remove the right-hand front roadwheel.

5 To gain access to the crankshaft pulley, to enable the engine to be turned, the wheel arch plastic liner must be removed. The liner is secured by several plastic expanding rivets/nut/bolts. To remove the rivets, push in the centre pins a little, then prise the clips from place. Remove the liner from under the front wing.

6 Remove the starter motor and remove the crankshaft pulley as described in Section 5.

7 Remove the upper and lower timing belt covers as described in Section 6.

8 Temporarily refit the crankshaft pulley bolt (without the crankshaft pulley) and then remove the crankshaft locking tool.

9 Turn the crankshaft until the timing hole in the crankshaft sprocket aligns with the hole in the oil pump casing (this is at the 12 o'clock position). Fit the special tool (No.303-732 (PSA) or 2.000.023.100 (Fiat)), or a suitable alternative and lock the crankshaft in position **(see illustration)**.

10 With the crankshaft locked in position fit the camshaft locking tool (No.303-735 (PSA), 2000.023.200 (Fiat) or similar). The hole in the camshaft sprocket should be at approximately the 1 o'clock position **(see illustration)**. If this is not the case remove the crankshaft locking pin and rotate the engine one revolution. Note that the crankshaft must always be turned in a clockwise direction (viewed from the right-hand side of vehicle).

11 When refitting the timing belt, insert special tool (No.303-732 (PSA or 2.000.23.000 (Fiat) or equivalent) through the slot in the fuel pump sprocket and into the corresponding hole in the fuel pump mounting bracket. In the absence of this tool use a 5 mm bolt or drill bit.

12 The crankshaft and camshaft are now locked in position, preventing unnecessary rotation.

3.9 Insert a 5.0 mm drill bit/bolt through the round hole in the sprocket flange into the hole in the oil pump housing (lower timing belt removed for clarity)

3.10 Insert an 8.0 mm bolt through the hole in the camshaft sprocket into the corresponding hole in the cylinder head

4.2a Drill out the rivet or undo the bolt securing the drain hose to the front panel

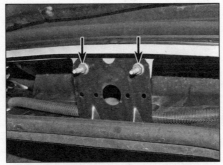

4.2b Undo the 2 nuts at the top…

4.2c …then slacken the nut each side and remove the air intake ducting

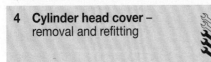

4 Cylinder head cover –
removal and refitting

Removal

1 Disconnect the battery negative lead as described in Chapter 5A Section 4.

2 Drill out the rivet/undo the bolt, release the water drain hose, then undo the retaining nuts and remove the cabin air intake ducting (see illustrations).

3 Pull up the fasteners and remove the cover from the top of the engine (see illustration).

4 Remove the air cleaner assembly as described in Chapter 4A Section 5.

5 Slacken the clamps securing the hoses to the plastic housing at the right-hand end of the cylinder head (see illustration).

6 Undo the 3 retaining bolts and remove the plastic housing (see illustration).

7 Undo the 4 bolts and remove the throttle body (see illustration). Disconnect any wiring plugs as the throttle body is withdrawn. Examine the throttle body seal and renew it if necessary.

8 Release the clips and remove the fuel return hose assembly from the top of the injectors and the manifold at the timing belt cover – refer to Chapter 4A Section 11 if necessary (see illustration).

9 Prise up the plastic fastener, release the clip, and undo the bolt securing the fuel manifold at the timing belt cover (see illustration).

10 Disconnect the wiring plugs at the front, right-hand end of the cylinder head, then

4.3 Pull up the fasteners and remove the cover

4.5 Slacken the clamps and disconnect the hoses

4.6 Undo the bolts and remove the housing

4.7 Note that one of the bolts is accessed from the rear

disconnect the wiring plugs from the fuel injectors and camshaft position sensor and then remove the breather hose from the valve cover. Release the wiring loom guide and fold the loom back over the engine.

11 Unbolt and then remove the timing belt upper cover as described in Section 6.

12 Remove the 9 bolts and then remove the valve cover (see illustration). Examine the rubber seal, and replace if necessary.

4.8 Pull up the green clips, then pull the return hose from the top of each injector

4.9 Use a trim removal tool to prise up the fastener

4.12 Remove the valve cover

4.13 Fit the seal correctly

5.3 Install the flywheel locking tool

5.4a Where fitted remove the cover

Refitting

13 Refitting is a reversal of removal, but ensure that the valve cover seal is correctly located in the valve cover **(see illustration)**.

| 5 | Crankshaft pulley – removal and refitting |

Removal

1 Remove the starter motor as described in Chapter 5A Section 10.

2 Remove the auxiliary drivebelt as described in Chapter 1 Section 20.

3 To lock the crankshaft, fit the manufacturers special tool (No.303-393 (PSA) or 2.000.022.500 (Fiat)) or suitable equivalent, to the flywheel ring gear **(see illustration)**.

4 Using a suitable socket and extension bar, unscrew the retaining bolt, remove the washer, then slide the pulley off the end of the crankshaft **(see illustrations)**. If the pulley is tight fit, it can be drawn off the crankshaft using a suitable puller. If a puller is being used, refit the pulley retaining bolt without the washer, to avoid damaging the crankshaft as the puller is tightened.

Caution: Do not touch the outer magnetic

5.4b Remove the bolt and...

5.4c ...then the pulley

sensor ring of the sprocket with your fingers, or allow metallic particles to come into contact with it.

Refitting

5 Refit the pulley to the end of the crankshaft.

6 Refit the crankshaft pulley. Fit a new bolt and retaining washer. Tighten the bolt to the specified torque, then through the specified angle.

7 Remove the locking tool and refit the starter motor

8 Refit and tension the auxiliary drivebelt as described in Chapter 1 Section 20.

9 Refit the remaining components in reverse order of removal.

| 6 | Timing belt covers – removal and refitting |

> **⚠ Warning:** *Refer to the precautionary information contained in Section 1 before proceeding.*

Removal

Upper cover

1 Remove the air cleaner housing as described in Chapter 4A Section 5.

2 Remove the throttle body as described in Chapter 4A Section 12.

3 Disconnect the fuel feed pipe from the connector **(see illustration)**, then undo the screw, prise out the plastic rivet, and move the pipe assembly to one side **(see illustration 4.9)**. Plug the openings to prevent contamination.

4 Release the fuel lines from the support bracket next to the cover and then unclip the wiring loom from the upper cover.

5 Undo the 4 bolts and remove the timing belt upper cover **(see illustration)**.

Lower cover

6 Remove the crankshaft pulley as described in Section 5.

7 Remove the timing belt upper cover as described previously in this Section.

6.3 Prise up the metal clip, then squeeze together the green 'ears' of the clip and disconnect the fuel pipe

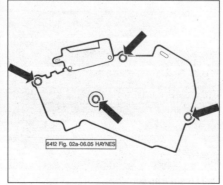

6.5 Upper cover retaining bolts

8 Undo the 6 bolts and remove the lower cover **(see illustration)**.

Refitting

9 Refitting of all the covers is a reversal of the relevant removal procedure, ensuring that each cover section is correctly located, and that the cover retaining bolts are securely tightened. Ensure that all disturbed hoses are reconnected and retained by their relevant clips.

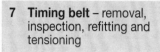

7 Timing belt – removal, inspection, refitting and tensioning

General

1 The timing belt drives the camshaft, high-pressure fuel pump, and coolant pump from a toothed sprocket on the end of the crankshaft. If the belt breaks or slips in service, the pistons are likely to hit the valve heads, resulting in expensive damage.

2 The timing belt should be renewed at the specified intervals, or earlier if it is contaminated with oil, or at all noisy in operation (a 'scraping' noise due to uneven wear).

3 If the timing belt is being removed, it is a wise precaution to renew the coolant pump at the same time. This may avoid the need to remove the timing belt again at a later stage, should the coolant pump fail. The timing belt tensioner should always be replaced when a new timing belt is fitted.

Removal

4 Apply the handbrake, then jack up the front of the vehicle and support it on axle stands (see *Jacking and vehicle support*). Remove the front right-hand roadwheel, wheelarch liner and the engine undershield.

5 Undo the nut, and move the coolant expansion tank to one side **(see illustration)**. There's no need to disconnect the hoses/pipes.

6 Support the engine with a trolley jack beneath the sump (use a block of wood on the jack head to prevent damage), then undo the bolts and remove the right-hand engine mounting assembly, as described in Section 17.

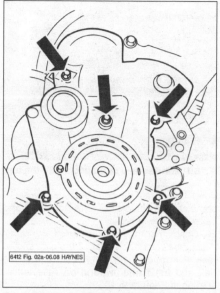

6.8 Lower cover retaining bolts

7 Remove the auxiliary drivebelt as described in Chapter 1 Section 20, then undo the retaining bolt and remove the auxiliary drivebelt tensioner **(see illustration)**.

8 Remove the upper and lower timing belt covers, as described in Section 6.

9 Undo the bolt and remove the crankshaft position sensor adjacent to the crankshaft sprocket flange, and move it to one side **(see illustration)**.

10 Undo the retaining bolt and remove the timing belt protection bracket, again, adjacent to the crankshaft sprocket flange **(see illustration)**.

11 Lock the crankshaft and camshaft in the correct position as described in Section 3. If necessary, temporarily refit the crankshaft pulley bolt to enable the crankshaft to be rotated.

12 Insert a hexagon key into the belt tensioner pulley centre, slacken the pulley bolt, and allow the tensioner to rotate, relieving the belt tension **(see illustration)**. With belt slack, temporarily tighten the pulley bolt.

13 Note its routing, then remove the timing belt from the sprockets.

7.5 Coolant expansion tank retaining nut

Inspection

14 Renew the belt as a matter of course, regardless of its apparent condition. The cost of a new belt is nothing compared with the cost of repairs should the belt break in service. If signs of oil contamination are found, trace the source of the oil leak and rectify it. Wash down the engine timing belt area and all related components, to remove all traces of oil. The tensioner must always be replaced. Check that the idler pulleys rotate freely without any sign of roughness, and also check that the coolant pump pulley rotates freely. It is highly recommended that both the coolant pump and the idler pulley are replaced at the same time as the timing belt and tensioner.

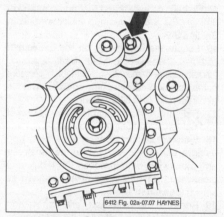

7.7 Auxiliary drivebelt tensioner retaining bolt

7.9 Undo the bolt and remove the crankshaft position sensor

7.10 Remove the timing belt protection bracket

7.12 Slacken the bolt and allow the tensioner to rotate, relieving the tension on the belt

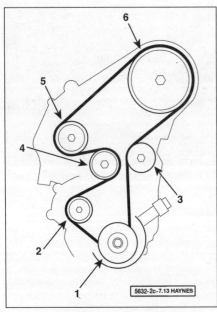

7.16 Timing belt routing

1 Crankshaft	4 Tensioner
2 Waterpump	5 Fuel pump
3 Idler	6 Camshaft

Refitting and tensioning

15 Commence refitting by ensuring that the crankshaft, camshaft and fuel pump sprocket timing pins are in position as described in Section 3.
16 Locate the timing belt on the crankshaft sprocket, then keeping it taut, locate it around the idler pulley, camshaft sprocket, high-pressure pump sprocket, coolant pump sprocket, and the tensioner roller **(see illustration)**.
17 Refit the timing belt protection bracket and tighten the retaining bolt securely.
18 Slacken the tensioner pulley bolt, and using a hexagonal key, rotate the tensioner anti-clockwise, which moves the index arm clockwise, until the index arm is aligned as shown **(see illustration)**.
19 Remove the camshaft, crankshaft and fuel pump sprocket (where applicable) timing pins and, using a socket on the crankshaft

7.18 The index arm must align with the lug

pulley bolt, rotate the crankshaft clockwise 10 complete revolutions. Refit the crankshaft and camshaft locking pins.
20 Check that the tensioner index arm is still aligned between the edges of the area shown **(see illustration 7.18)**. If it is not, remove the belt and begin the refitting process again, starting at Paragraph 15.
21 The remainder of refitting is a reversal of removal. Tighten all fasteners to the specified torque where given.

8 Timing belt sprockets and tensioner – removal and refitting

Camshaft sprocket

Removal

1 Remove the timing belt as described in Section 7.
2 Remove the locking tool from the camshaft sprocket/hub. Slacken the sprocket hub retaining bolt. To prevent the camshaft rotating as the bolt is slackened, a sprocket holding tool will be required. In the absence of the special manufacturers tool, an acceptable substitute can be fabricated at home (see **Tool Tip 1**). Do not attempt to use the engine assembly/valve timing locking tool to prevent the sprocket from rotating whilst the bolt is slackened.
3 Remove the sprocket hub retaining bolt, and slide the sprocket and hub off the end of the camshaft.
4 Clean the camshaft sprocket thoroughly,

A sprocket holding tool can be made from two lengths of steel strip bolted together to form a forked end. Drill holes and insert bolts in the ends of the fork to engage with the sprocket spokes.

and renew it if there are any signs of wear, damage or cracks.

Refitting

5 Refit the camshaft sprocket to the camshaft **(see illustration)**.
6 Refit the sprocket hub retaining bolt. Tighten the bolt to the specified torque, preventing the camshaft from turning as during removal.
7 Align the engine assembly/valve timing slot in the camshaft sprocket hub with the hole in the cylinder head and refit the timing pin to lock the camshaft in position.
8 Fit the timing belt around the pump sprocket and camshaft sprocket, and tension the timing belt as described in Section 7.

Crankshaft sprocket

Removal

9 Remove the timing belt as described in Section 7.
10 Check that the engine assembly/valve timing holes are still aligned as described in Section 3, and the camshaft sprocket and flywheel are locked in position.
11 Slide the sprocket off the end of the crankshaft and collect the Woodruff key **(see illustrations)**.
12 Examine the crankshaft oil seal for signs of oil leakage and, if necessary, renew it as described in Section 14.

8.5 Ensure the lug on the sprocket hub engages with the slot on the end of the camshaft

8.11a Slide the sprocket from the crankshaft...

8.11b ...and recover the Woodruff key

13 Clean the crankshaft sprocket thoroughly, and renew it if there are any signs of wear, damage or cracks. Recover the crankshaft locating key.

Refitting

14 Refit the key to the end of the crankshaft, then refit the crankshaft sprocket (with the flange facing the crankshaft pulley).
15 Fit the timing belt around the crankshaft sprocket, and tension the timing belt as described in Section 7.

Fuel pump sprocket

Removal

16 Remove the timing belt as described in Section 7.
17 Using a socket, undo the pump sprocket retaining nut. The sprocket can be held stationary by inserting a locking pin, drill or rod through the slot in the sprocket, and into the corresponding hole in the backplate, or by using a forked tool engaged with the holes in the sprocket (see **Tool Tip 1**).
18 The pump sprocket is a taper fit on the pump shaft and it will be necessary to make up another tool to release it from the taper (see **Tool Tip 2**).
19 Partially unscrew the sprocket retaining nut, fit the home-made tool, and secure it to the sprocket with two bolts. Prevent the sprocket from rotating as before, and unscrew the sprocket retaining nut. The nut will bear against the tool as it is undone, forcing the sprocket off the shaft taper. Once the taper is released, remove the tool, unscrew the nut fully, and remove the sprocket from the pump shaft.
20 Clean the sprocket thoroughly, and renew it if there are any signs of wear, damage or cracks.

Refitting

21 Refit the pump sprocket and retaining nut, and tighten the nut to the specified torque. Prevent the sprocket rotating as the nut is tightened using the sprocket holding tool.

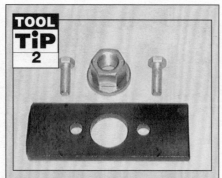

Make a sprocket releasing tool from a short strip of steel. Drill two holes in the strip to correspond with the two holes in the sprocket. Drill a third hole just large enough to accept the flats of the sprocket retaining nut.

22 Refit the timing belt as described in Section 7.

Coolant pump sprocket

23 The coolant pump sprocket is integral with the pump, and cannot be removed. Coolant pump removal is described in Chapter 3 Section 8.

Tensioner pulley

Removal

24 Remove the timing belt as described in Section 7.
25 Remove the tensioner pulley retaining bolt, and then remove the tensioner (see **illustration 7.12**).
26 Clean the tensioner pulley, but do not use any strong solvent which may enter the pulley bearings. Check that the pulley rotates freely, with no sign of stiffness or free play. The pulley should always be replaced when the timing belt is replaced.
27 Examine the pulley mounting stud for signs of damage and if necessary, renew it.

Refitting

28 Refitting is a reversal of removal.
29 Refit the timing belt as described in Section 7.

Idler pulley

Removal

30 Remove the timing belt as described in Section 7.
31 Undo the retaining bolt/nut and withdraw the idler pulley from the engine (see **illustration**).
32 Clean the idler pulley, but do not use any strong solvent which may enter the bearings. Check that the pulley rotates freely, with no sign of stiffness or free play. Renew the idler pulley if there is any doubt about its condition, or if there are any obvious signs of wear or damage.

Refitting

33 Locate the idler pulley on the engine, and fit the retaining bolt/nut. Tighten the bolt/nut to the specified torque.
34 Refit the timing belt as described in Section 7.

---

9 Camshaft, rocker arms and hydraulic tappets – removal, inspection and refitting

Removal

1 Remove the cylinder head cover as described in Section 4.
2 Remove the camshaft sprocket as described in Section 8.
3 Refit the right-hand engine mounting, but only tighten the bolts moderately; this will keep the engine supported during the camshaft removal.
4 Undo the bolts and remove the vacuum pump (see Chapter 9 Section 22). Recover the pump O-ring seals.
5 Disconnect the wiring plug from the camshaft position sensor (see illustration).

8.31 Timing belt idler pulley retaining nut

9.5 Remove the camshaft position sensor

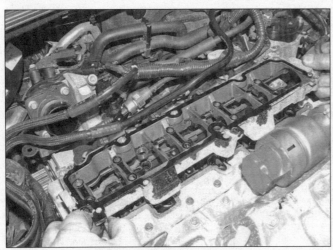

9.6 Remove the bearing ladder

9.7 Remove the camshaft

Unbolt and remove the sensor from the bearing ladder.

6 Working in reverse order to that shown **(see illustration 9.21)** remove the retaining bolts and then remove camshaft bearing cap ladder **(see illustration)**.

7 Lift out the camshaft **(see illustration)** and dispose of the oil seal. A new one will be required.

8 Obtain 8 small, clean plastic containers, and number them 1 to 4 inlet and 1 to 4 exhaust; alternatively, divide a larger container into 8 compartments.

9 Lift out each rocker arm. Place the rocker arms in their respective positions in the box or containers **(see illustration)**.

10 A compartmentalised container filled with engine oil is now required to retain the hydraulic tappets while they are removed from the cylinder head. Withdraw each hydraulic follower **(see illustration)** and place it in the container, keeping them each identified for correct refitting. The tappets must be totally submerged in the oil to prevent air entering them.

Inspection

11 Inspect the cam lobes and the camshaft bearing journals for scoring or other visible evidence of wear. Once the surface hardening of the cam lobes has been eroded, wear will occur at an accelerated rate. **Note:** *If these symptoms are visible on the tips of the camshaft lobes, check the corresponding rocker arm, as it will probably be worn as well.*

12 Examine the condition of the bearing surfaces in the cylinder head and camshaft bearing housing. If wear is evident, the cylinder head and bearing housing will both have to be renewed, as they are a matched assembly.

13 Inspect the rocker arms and tappets for scuffing, cracking or other damage and renew any components as necessary. Also check the condition of the tappet bores in the cylinder head. As with the camshafts, any wear in this area will necessitate cylinder head renewal.

Refitting

14 Thoroughly clean the sealant from the mating surfaces of the cylinder head and camshaft bearing housing. Use a suitable liquid gasket dissolving agent (available from the manufacturer) together with a soft putty knife; do not use a metal scraper or the faces will be damaged. As there is no conventional gasket used, the cleanliness of the mating faces is of the utmost importance.

15 Clean off any oil, dirt or grease from both components and dry with a clean lint-free cloth. Ensure that all the oilways are completely clean.

16 Liberally lubricate the hydraulic tappet bores in the cylinder head with clean engine oil.

17 Insert the hydraulic tappets into their original bores in the cylinder head unless they have been renewed.

18 Lubricate the rocker arms and place them over their respective tappets and valve stems. Lubricate the bearing surfaces **(see illustration)** and then refit the camshaft.

19 Apply a thin bead of appropriate silicone sealant to the mating surface of the camshaft cover/bearing ladder as shown **(see illustration)**.

9.9 Remove the rocker arms

9.10 Use long nose pliers to remove the hydraulic tappets

9.18 Lubricate the bearing surfaces

9.19 Apply sealant to the camshaft housing

20 Assembly the bearing ladder within 10 minutes of applying the sealant **(see illustration)**. A special tool to align the bearing ladder is used, however 2 suitable bolts (with their heads and threads cut off) can be used if the tool is not available.
21 Tighten the bolts to the specified torque in sequence **(see illustration)**.
22 Fit a new camshaft oil seal as described in Section 14.
23 Refit the camshaft sprocket, and tighten the retaining bolt.
24 Refit the timing belt and temporarily refit the crankshaft pulley bolt – use the old bolt. Rotate the engine at least 20 revolutions to allow the oil pump to deliver oil to the camshaft and associated components. Refit the timing belt cover.
25 Refit the remainder of the components in the reverse order of removal.

10 Cylinder head – removal and refitting

Removal

1 Apply the handbrake, then jack up the front of the vehicle and support it on axle stands (see *Jacking and vehicle support*). Remove the front right-hand roadwheel, the engine undershield, and the right-hand front wheel arch liner.
2 Disconnect the battery negative lead as described in Chapter 5A Section 4.
3 Drain the cooling system as described in Chapter 1 Section 23.
4 Remove the timing belt as described in Section 7.
5 Remove the cylinder head cover as described in Section 4.
6 Remove the EGR cooler as described in Chapter 4B Section 2.
7 Remove the engine oil level sensor as described in Section 15.
8 Remove the fuel injectors as described in Chapter 4A Section 11.
9 Remove the intake manifold as described in Chapter 4A Section 13.
10 Note its fitted position, then unclip and remove the fuel return manifold assembly.

10.18 Remove the coolant outlet housing from the left-hand end of the cylinder head

9.20 Refit the bearing ladder

11 Remove the vacuum pump as described in Chapter 9 Section 23.
12 Remove the turbocharger and exhaust manifold as described in Chapter 4A Section 14.
13 Working gradually, and evenly, from the outside in, slacken and remove the bolts securing the camshaft housing to the cylinder head. Lift the housing, complete with camshaft from place.
14 With reference to Section 9, remove the rocker arms and hydraulic tappets.
15 Remove the power steering pump as described in Chapter 10 Section 21.
16 Remove the alternator as described in Chapter 5A Section 7.
17 Undo the retaining bolts and remove the power steering pump/alternator mounting bracket.
18 Undo the coolant outlet housing (left-hand end of the cylinder head) retaining bolts, slacken the two bolts securing the housing support bracket to the top of the transmission bellhousing, and move the outlet housing away from the cylinder head a little **(see illustration)**. There is no need to disconnect the hoses.
19 Disconnect the glow plug wiring plugs, then undo the 2 retaining bolts and move the wiring harness guide to one side.
20 Disconnect the coolant hose from the EGR valve (refer to Chapter 4B Section 2 if necessary).
21 Disconnect the high-pressure fuel pipe from the common rail to the pump, and disconnect the fuel supply and return hoses.

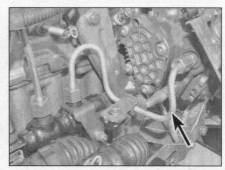

10.21 Remove the high-pressure pipe

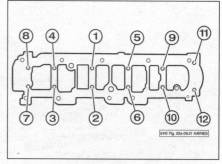

9.21 Tighten the bolts to the specified torque in the order shown

Where fitted, remove the bracket at the rear of the pump, then undo the bolt/nut and remove the pump and mounting bracket as an assembly **(see illustration)**. Immediately seal all the openings in the fuel system. Note that a new high-pressure pipe must be fitted – see Chapter 4A Section 2.
22 Slacken the unions and remove the high-pressure fuel pipes from the common rail to the injectors. Note that new pipes must be fitted.
23 Check that no components or electrical connectors are still fitted to the cylinder head.
24 Working in the reverse of the sequence shown **(see illustration 10.44)** undo the cylinder head bolts. Discard the bolts – new ones must be fitted.
25 Release the cylinder head from the cylinder block and location dowels by rocking it. The special manufacturers tool for doing this consists simply of two metal rods with 90-degree angled ends **(see illustration)**. Do not prise between the mating faces of the cylinder head and block, as this may damage the gasket faces.
26 Lift the cylinder head from the block, and recover the gasket.

Preparation for refitting

27 The mating faces of the cylinder head and cylinder block must be perfectly clean before refitting the head. The manufacturer

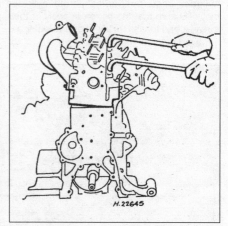

10.25 Free the cylinder head using angled rods

10.34 Measure the piston protrusion using a DTI gauge

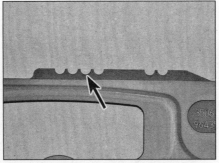

10.36 Cylinder head gasket thickness identification notches

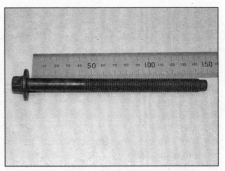

10.37 Measure the length from under the bolt head to its end

recommends that a scouring agent is used for this purpose, but acceptable results can be achieved by using a hard plastic or wood scraper to remove all traces of gasket and carbon. The same method can be used to clean the piston crowns. Take particular care to avoid scoring or gouging the cylinder head/cylinder block mating surfaces during the cleaning operations, as aluminium alloy is easily damaged. Make sure that the carbon is not allowed to enter the oil and water passages – this is particularly important for the lubrication system, as carbon could block the oil supply to the engine's components. Using adhesive tape and paper, seal the water, oil and bolt holes in the cylinder block. To prevent carbon entering the gap between the pistons and bores, smear a little grease in the gap. After cleaning each piston, use a small brush to remove all traces of grease and carbon from the gap, then wipe away the remainder with a clean rag.

28 Check the mating surfaces of the cylinder block and the cylinder head for nicks, deep scratches and other damage. If slight, they may be removed carefully with a file, but if excessive, machining may be the only alternative to renewal. If warpage of the cylinder head gasket surface is suspected, use a straight-edge to check it for distortion. Refer to Part D of this Chapter if necessary.

29 Thoroughly clean the threads of the cylinder head bolt holes in the cylinder block. Ensure that the bolts run freely in their threads, and that all traces of oil and water are removed from each bolt hole.

Gasket selection

30 The gasket thickness is indicated by notches/holes on the front edge of the gasket. If the crankshaft or pistons/connecting rods have not been disturbed, fit a new gasket with the same number of notches/holes as the previous one. If the crankshaft/piston or connecting rods have been disturbed, it's necessary to work out the piston protrusion as follows:

31 Remove the crankshaft timing pin, then turn the crankshaft until pistons 1 and 4 are at TDC (Top Dead Centre). Position a dial test indicator (dial gauge) on the cylinder block adjacent to the rear of No 1 piston, and zero it on the block face. Transfer the probe to the crown of No 1 piston (10.0 mm in from the rear edge), then slowly turn the crankshaft back-and-forth past TDC, noting the highest reading on the indicator. Record this reading as protrusion A.

32 Repeat the check described in paragraph 18, this time 10.0 mm in from the front edge of the No 1 piston crown. Record this reading as protrusion B.

33 Add protrusion A to protrusion B, then divide the result by 2 to obtain an average reading for piston No 1.

34 Repeat the procedure described in paragraphs 31 to 33 on piston 4, then turn the crankshaft through 180° and carry out the procedure on the piston Nos 2 and 3 **(see illustration)**. Check that there is a maximum difference of 0.07 mm protrusion between any two pistons.

35 If a dial test indicator is not available, piston protrusion may be measured using a straight-edge and feeler blades or Vernier calipers. However, this is much less accurate, and cannot therefore be recommended.

36 Note the greatest piston protrusion measurement, and use this to determine the correct cylinder head gasket from the table given in the Specifications. The series of notches/holes on the side of the gasket are used for thickness identification **(see illustration)**.

Head bolt examination

37 Carefully examine the cylinder head bolts for signs of damage to the threads or head, and for any sign of corrosion. If the bolts are in a satisfactory condition, measure the length of each bolt from the underside of the head to the end of the shank. The bolts may be re-used providing that the measured length does not exceed 149.0 mm **(see illustration)**. **Note:** *Considering the stress to which the cylinder head bolts are subjected, it is highly recommended that they be all renewed, regardless of their apparent condition.*

Refitting

38 Turn the crankshaft and position Nos 1 and 4 pistons at TDC, then turn the crankshaft a quarter turn (90°) anti-clockwise.

39 Thoroughly clean the surfaces of the cylinder head and block.

40 Make sure that the locating dowels are in place, then fit the correct gasket the right way round on the cylinder block **(see illustration)**.

41 Carefully lower the cylinder head onto the gasket and block, making sure that it locates correctly onto the dowels.

42 Apply a smear of grease to the threads, and to the underside of the heads of the new cylinder head bolts.

43 Carefully insert the cylinder head bolts into their holes (do not drop them in) and initially finger-tighten them.

44 Working progressively and in sequence, tighten the cylinder head bolts to their Stage 1 torque setting, using a torque wrench and suitable socket **(see illustration)**.

45 Once all the bolts have been tightened to their Stage 1 torque setting, working again in the specified sequence, tighten each

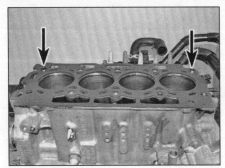

10.40 Ensure the gasket locates over the dowels

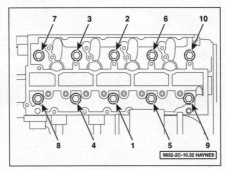

10.44 Cylinder head bolt tightening sequence

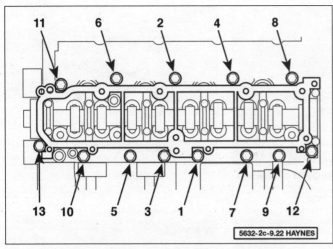

10.47 Camshaft housing bolts tightening sequence

11.3 Sump lower section retaining nuts/bolts

bolt to the specified Stage 2 setting. Finally, angle-tighten the bolts through the specified Stage 3 angle. It is recommended that an angle-measuring gauge is used during this stage of tightening, to ensure accuracy. **Note:** *Retightening of the cylinder head bolts after running the engine is not required.*

46 Refit the hydraulic tappets and rocker arms to their original locations as described in Section 9.

47 Ensure the mating faces are clean, then apply a thin smear of silicone sealant, and refit the camshaft housing (complete with camshaft) to the cylinder head. Tighten the bolts in the sequence shown to the specified torque **(see illustration)**.

48 Refit the timing belt as described in Section 7.

49 The remainder of refitting is a reversal of removal, noting the following points.

a) Use a new seal when refitting the coolant outlet housing.

b) When refitting a cylinder head, it is good practice to renew the thermostat.

c) Tighten all fasteners to the specified torque where given.

d) Refill the cooling system as described in Chapter 1 Section 23.

e) The engine may run erratically for the first few miles, until the engine management ECM relearns its stored values.

11 Sump – removal and refitting

Removal

1 Drain the engine oil, then clean and refit the engine oil drain plug, tightening it securely. If the engine is nearing its service interval when the oil and filter are due for renewal, it is recommended that the filter is also removed,

and a new one fitted. After reassembly, the engine can then be refilled with fresh oil. Refer to Chapter 1 Section 6 for further information.

2 Apply the handbrake, then jack up the front of the vehicle and support it on axle stands (see *Jacking and vehicle support*). Undo the bolts and remove the engine undershield (where fitted).

3 Undo the nuts/bolts securing the lower section of the sump to the upper section **(see illustration)**.

4 The lower section of the sump is held by sealant. Using the lugs provided, carefully prise the lower section of the sump from place. Take great care as the thin steel is easily deformed.

5 Progressively slacken and remove all the upper section of the sump inner and outer retaining bolts. Since the sump bolts vary in length, remove each bolt in turn, and store it in its correct fitted order by pushing it through a clearly-marked cardboard template. This will avoid the possibility of installing the bolts in the wrong locations on refitting.

6 Try to break the joint by striking the sump with the palm of your hand, then lower and withdraw the sump from under the car. If the sump is stuck (which is quite likely) use a putty knife or similar, carefully inserted between the sump and block. Ease the knife along the joint until the sump is released. While the sump is removed, take the opportunity to check the oil pump pick-up/strainer for signs of clogging or splitting. If necessary, remove the pump as described in Section 12, and clean or renew the strainer.

Refitting

7 Clean all traces of sealant from the mating surfaces of the cylinder block/crankcase and sump, then use a clean rag to wipe out the sump and the engine's interior.

8 Ensure that the sump upper section mating surfaces are clean and dry, then apply a 3mm diameter bead of silicone sealant to the sump

mating surface. The sealant must be applied to the inside of the bolt holes. Note that the sump must be installed within 10 minutes of applying the sealant, and the bolts tightened within a further 5 minutes.

9 Offer up the sump to the cylinder block/crankcase. Refit its retaining bolts, ensuring that each bolt is screwed into its original location. Tighten the bolts evenly and progressively to the specified torque setting.

10 Ensure the mating surfaces are clean, then apply a thin bead of silicone sealant to the lower section mating face. The sealant must be applied to the inside of the bolt holes. Note that the sump must be installed within 10 minutes of applying the sealant, and the bolts/nuts tightened within a further 5 minutes.

11 Refit the lower section of the sump and tighten the bolts/nuts to the specified torque.

12 Lower the vehicle to the ground, wait at least 30 minutes and then refill the engine with oil as described in Chapter 1 Section 6.

12 Oil pump – removal and refitting

Removal

1 Remove the sump as described in Section 11.

2 Remove the crankshaft sprocket as described in Section 8. Recover the locating key from the crankshaft.

3 Disconnect the wiring plug, undo the bolts and remove the crankshaft position sensor, located on the right-hand end of the cylinder block.

4 Undo the 3 bolts and remove the oil pump pick-up tube from the pump/block. Where fitted, discard the oil seal, a new one must be fitted.

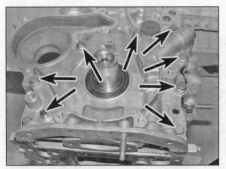

12.5 Oil pump retaining bolts

12.7 Apply a 4 mm wide bead of sealant

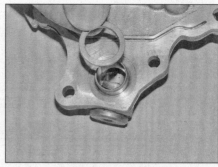

12.8a Fit a new seal...

5 Undo the 8 bolts, and remove the oil pump **(see illustration)**.

Refitting

6 Remove all traces of sealant, and thoroughly clean the mating surfaces of the oil pump and cylinder block.

7 Apply a 4 mm diameter bead of silicone sealant to the mating face of the cylinder block **(see illustration)**. Ensure that no sealant enters any of the holes in the block.

8 With a new oil seal fitted, refit the oil pump over the end of the crankshaft, aligning the flats in the pump drive gear with the flats machined in the crankshaft **(see illustrations)**. Note that new oil pumps are supplied with the oil seal already fitted, and a seal protector sleeve. The sleeve fits over the end of the crankshaft to protect the seal as the pump is fitted.

9 Install the oil pump bolts and tighten them to the specified torque.

10 Refit the oil pick-up tube to the pump/cylinder block using a new O-ring seal. Ensure the oil dipstick guide tube is correctly refitted.

11 Refit the sump as described in Section 11.

12 Refit the woodruff key to the crankshaft, and slide the crankshaft sprocket into place.

13 The remainder of refitting is a reversal of removal.

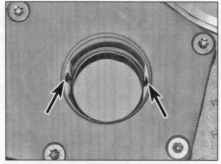

12.8b ...align the pump gear flats...

13 Oil cooler – removal and refitting

Removal

1 Apply the handbrake, then jack up the front of the vehicle and support it on axle stands (see *Jacking and vehicle support*). Undo the fasteners and remove the engine undershield (where fitted).

2 The oil cooler is fitted to the front of the oil filter housing. Drain the coolant as described in Chapter 1 Section 23.

3 Drain the engine oil as described in Chapter 1 Section 6, or be prepared for fluid spillage.

12.8c ...with those of the crankshaft

4 Undo the bolts/stud and remove the oil cooler **(see illustration)**. Recover the gasket.

Refitting

5 Fit a new gasket into the recesses in the oil filter housing, and refit the cooler. Tighten the bolts securely.

6 Refill or top-up the cooling system and engine oil level as described in Chapter 1 or *Weekly checks* (as applicable). Start the engine, and check the oil cooler for signs of leakage.

14 Oil seals – renewal

Crankshaft

Right-hand oil seal

1 Remove the crankshaft sprocket and Woodruff key as described in Section 8.

2 Measure and note the fitted depth of the oil seal.

3 Pull the oil seal from the housing using a screwdriver **(see illustration)**. Alternatively, drill a small hole in the oil seal, and use a self-tapping screw and a pair of pliers to remove it.

4 Clean the oil seal housing and the crankshaft sealing surface.

5 The new seal should be supplied with a protective sleeve, which fits over the end of the crankshaft to prevent any damage to

13.4 Undo the oil cooler bolts/stud

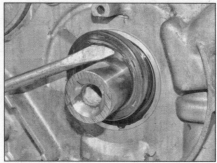

14.3 Take great care not to mark the crankshaft whilst levering out the oil seal

14.5a Slide the seal and protective sleeve over the end of the crankshaft...

14.5b ...and press the seal into place

14.12 Slide the seal and protective sleeve over the left-hand end of the crankshaft

14.16 Drill a hole, insert a self-tapping screw, and pull the seal from place using pliers

14.18a Use the correct tool to fit the seal...

14.18b ...or a suitable socket

the seal lip. With the sleeve in place, press the seal (open end first) into the pump to the previously-noted depth, using a suitable tube or socket (see illustrations).

6 Where applicable, remove the plastic sleeve from the end of the crankshaft.

7 Refit the crankshaft sprocket as described in Section 8.

Left-hand oil seal

8 Remove the flywheel, as described in Section 16.

9 Measure and note the fitted depth of the oil seal.

10 Pull the oil seal from the housing using a screwdriver. Alternatively, drill a small hole in the oil seal, and use a self-tapping screw and a pair of pliers to remove it (see illustration 14.3).

11 Clean the oil seal housing and the crankshaft sealing surface.

12 The new seal should be supplied with a protective sleeve, which fits over the end of the crankshaft to prevent any damage to the seal lip (see illustration). With the sleeve in place, press the seal (open end first) into the housing to the previously-noted depth, using a suitable tube or socket.

13 Where applicable, remove the plastic sleeve from the end of the crankshaft.

14 Refit the flywheel, as described in Section 16.

Camshaft

15 Remove the camshaft sprocket as

described in Section 8. In principle there is no need to remove the timing belt completely, but remember that if the belt has been contaminated with oil, it must be renewed.

16 Pull the oil seal from the housing using a hooked instrument. Alternatively, drill a small hole in the oil seal and use a self-tapping screw and a pair of pliers to remove it (see illustration).

17 Clean the oil seal housing and the camshaft sealing surface.

18 Press the seal (open end first) into the housing to the previously-noted depth, using either the correct tool (Fiat No. 2.000.023.500 or equivalent), a suitable tube or a socket which bears only of the outer edge of the seal (see illustrations). If the seal was supplied with a protective sleeve, remove it.

19 Refit the camshaft sprocket as described in Section 8.

20 Where necessary, fit a new timing belt with reference to Section 7.

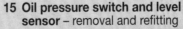

15 Oil pressure switch and level sensor – removal and refitting

Removal

Oil pressure switch

1 The oil pressure switch is located at the front of the cylinder block, adjacent to the oil dipstick guide tube. Remove the particulate

filter/catalytic converter as described in Chapter 4A Section 18.

2 Undo the retaining bolts and remove the heatshield and catalytic converter/particulate filter mounting bracket.

3 Remove the protective sleeve from the wiring plug (where applicable), then disconnect the wiring from the switch.

4 Unscrew the switch from the cylinder block, and recover the sealing washer (see illustration). Be prepared for oil spillage, and if the switch is to be left removed from the engine for any length of time, plug the hole in the cylinder block.

Oil level sensor

5 The oil level sensor is located at the rear of the cylinder block. Jack up the front of the

15.4 The oil pressure switch is located on the front face of the cylinder block

vehicle and support it securely on axle stands (see *Jacking and vehicle support*). Undo the bolts and remove the engine undershield.

6 Reach up between the driveshaft and the cylinder block, and disconnect the sensor wiring plug **(see illustration)**.

7 Using an open-ended spanner, unscrew the sensor and withdraw it from position.

Refitting

Oil pressure switch

8 Examine the sealing washer for any signs of damage or deterioration, and if necessary renew.

9 Refit the switch, complete with washer, and tighten it to the specified torque where given.

10 Refit the engine undershield, and lower the vehicle to the ground.

Oil level sensor

11 Smear a little silicone sealant on the threads and refit the sensor to the cylinder block, tightening it securely.

12 Reconnect the sensor wiring plug.

13 Refit the engine undershield, and lower the vehicle to the ground.

16 Flywheel – removal, inspection and refitting

Removal

1 Remove the transmission as described in, then remove the clutch assembly as described in Chapter 6 Section 6.

2 Prevent the flywheel from turning. Do not attempt to lock the flywheel in position using the crankshaft pulley locking tool described in Section 3. Insert a 12 mm diameter rod or drill bit through the hole in the sump, and into a slot in the flywheel **(see illustration)**.

3 Make alignment marks between the flywheel and crankshaft to aid refitment. Slacken and remove the flywheel retaining bolts, and remove the flywheel from the end of the crankshaft. Be careful not to drop it; it is heavy. If the flywheel locating dowel (where fitted) is a loose fit in the crankshaft end, remove it and store it with the flywheel for

safe-keeping. Discard the flywheel bolts; new ones must be used on refitting.

Inspection

4 Examine the flywheel for scoring of the clutch face, and for wear or chipping of the ring gear teeth. If the clutch face is scored, the flywheel may be surface-ground, but renewal is preferable. Seek the advice of an engine reconditioning specialist to see if machining is possible. If the ring gear is worn or damaged, the flywheel must be renewed, as it is not possible to renew the ring gear separately.

5 All engines are fitted with a dual-mass flywheel. The maximum travel of the primary mass in relation to the secondary must not exceed 15 teeth (or 20 degrees). If in doubt remove the flywheel and have a suitably equipped specialist check the flywheel. Inspect the flywheel for any grease or debris from the interface between the fixed part and the movable part of the flywheel. If any doubt to the condition of the flywheel exists, despite the expense we recommend replacing it.

Refitting

6 Clean the mating surfaces of the flywheel and crankshaft. Remove any remaining locking compound from the threads of the crankshaft holes, using the correct size of tap, if available.

7 If the new flywheel retaining bolts are not supplied with their threads already pre-coated, apply a suitable thread-locking compound to the threads of each bolt.

8 Ensure that the locating dowel is in position. Offer up the flywheel, locating it on the dowel (where fitted), and fit the new retaining bolts. Where no locating dowel is fitted, align the previously-made marks to ensure the flywheel is refitted in its original position.

9 Lock the flywheel using the method employed on dismantling, and tighten the retaining bolts to the specified torque **(see illustration)**.

10 Refit the clutch as described in Chapter 6 Section 6. Remove the flywheel locking tool, and refit the transmission as described in.

17 Engine/transmission mountings – inspection and renewal

General

1 The engine/transmission mountings seldom require attention, but broken or deteriorated mountings should be renewed immediately, or the added strain placed on the driveline components may cause damage or wear.

2 While separate mountings may be removed and refitted individually, if more than one is disturbed at a time – such as if the engine/transmission unit is removed from its mountings – they must be reassembled and their fasteners tightened in the position marked on removal.

3 On reassembly, the complete weight of the engine/transmission unit must not be taken by the mountings until all are correctly aligned with the marks made on removal. Tighten the engine/transmission mounting fasteners to their specified torque wrench settings.

Inspection

4 During the check, the engine/transmission unit must be raised slightly, to remove its weight from the mountings.

5 Raise the front of the vehicle, and support it securely on axle stands. Remove the engine undershield. Position a jack under the sump, with a large block of wood between the jack head and the sump, then carefully raise the engine/transmission just enough to take the weight off the mountings.

Warning: DO NOT place any part of your body under the engine when it is supported only by a jack.

6 Check the mountings to see if the rubber is cracked, hardened or separated from the metal components. Sometimes the rubber will split right down the centre.

7 Check for relative movement between each mounting's brackets and the engine/transmission or body (use a large screwdriver or lever to attempt to move the mountings). If movement is noted, lower the engine and check-tighten the mounting fasteners.

15.6 The oil level sensor is located on the rear face of the cylinder block

16.2 Insert a 12 mm bolt through the hole in the sump into the corresponding hole in the flywheel

16.9 Flywheel retaining Torx bolts

17.9 Coolant expansion tank retaining nut

17.10 Reaction rod-to-vehicle body bolt

17.11 Undo the bolt/nut and move the brackets to one side

Renewal

Note: *The following paragraphs assume the engine is supported beneath the sump as described earlier.*

Right-hand engine mounting

8 Raise the front of the vehicle, and support it securely on axle stands, then remove the engine undershield. Position a jack under the sump, with a large block of wood between the jack head and the sump, then carefully raise the jack just enough to support the weight of the engine.
9 Undo the nut and move the coolant expansion tank to one side **(see illustration)**.
10 Undo the bolt securing the reaction rod to the bracket on the vehicle body **(see illustration)**.
11 Undo the bolt/nut and move the pipe and wiring harness support brackets to one side **(see illustration)**.
12 Undo the 3 bolts/1 nut securing the reaction rod mounting bracket to the engine mounting bracket, and manoeuvre it from place.
13 If required, undo the bolt and separate the reaction rod from the mounting bracket.
14 Undo the 3 retaining bolts and remove the flexible mounting assembly from the vehicle body.
15 Refitting is a reversal of removal. Tighten the mounting bolts/nut to the specified torque.

Left-hand transmission mounting

16 Remove the air intake hose from the air cleaner assembly **(see illustration)**.

17 If not already done, undo the retaining bolts/nuts and remove the engine undershield (where fitted). Place a jack beneath the transmission, with a block of wood on the jack head. Raise the jack until it is supporting the weight of the transmission.
18 With the transmission supported, note the position of the mounting then first unscrew the centre retaining nut. Remove the retaining nuts, then lift the transmission mounting from its position on the inner wing mounting bracket **(see illustration)**.
19 If required, undo the bolts and detach the body-side mounting bracket **(see illustration)**.
20 If required, undo the 3 retaining bolts and remove the mounting bracket from the top of the transmission.
21 Refitting is a reversal of removal. Re-align the mounting in the position noted on removal (where applicable), then tighten all fasteners to the specified torque wrench settings.

Lower engine rear torque link

22 Firmly apply the handbrake, and then jack up the front of the vehicle and support it securely on axle stands (see *Jacking and vehicle support*). If not already done, undo the retaining bolts/nuts and remove the engine undershield (where fitted).
23 Unscrew and remove the bolt securing the rear mounting link to the subframe **(see illustration)**.
24 Remove the bolt securing the rear mounting link to the driveshaft inner bearing

17.16 Remove the air intake hose

bracket at the rear of the cylinder block, and then remove the mounting torque reaction link.
25 Check carefully for signs of wear or damage on all components, and renew them where necessary. The rubber bush fitted to the driveshaft bearing housing is available as a separate item on some models, check with your local dealer for availability of parts. If available, the rubber bush can be pressed out of the bearing housing, noting its fitted position, and then a new one pressed back into place.
26 Refit the rear mounting torque reaction link, and tighten both its bolts to their specified torque settings.
27 Refit the engine undershield (where applicable), and then lower the vehicle to the ground.

17.18 Undo the centre nut, and outer nuts

17.19 Undo the bolts and remove the mounting bracket

17.23 Rear mounting link retaining bolts

Chapter 2 Part B
1.6 litre DOHC engine in-car repair procedures

Contents

Degrees of difficulty

| **Easy,** suitable for novice with little experience | | **Fairly easy,** suitable for beginner with some experience | | **Fairly difficult,** suitable for competent DIY mechanic | | **Difficult,** suitable for experienced DIY mechanic | | **Very difficult,** suitable for expert DIY or professional | |

Specifications

General

Designation	DV6TED4
Engine code: *	
DV6TED4	9HU
Capacity	1560 cc
Bore	75.0 mm
Stroke	88.3 mm
Direction of crankshaft rotation	Clockwise (viewed from the right-hand side of vehicle)
No 1 cylinder location.	At the transmission end of block
Maximum power output	66 kW (90 hp) @ 4000 rpm
Maximum torque output.	180 Nm @ 1750 rpm
Compression ratio	18.0 : 1
Emissions level	Euro 4

*The engine code is stamped on a plate attached to the front of the cylinder block.

Compression pressures (engine hot, at cranking speed)

Normal (new engine).	20 ± 5 bar
Minimum	15 bar
Maximum difference between any two cylinders.	5 bar

Cylinder head gasket

Gasket thickness:

1 notch	1.35 mm
2 notch	1.25 mm
3 notch	1.30 mm
4 notch	1.40 mm
5 notch	1.45 mm

Piston protrusion (gasket required):

0.685 to 0.734 mm	1 notch
0.533 to 0.634 mm	2 notch
0.635 to 0.684 mm	3 notch
0.735 to 0.784 mm	4 notch
0.785 to 0.886 mm	5 notch

Cylinder head bolts

Maximum length (measured under head). . . . .   149 mm

Camshaft

Drive:
  Intake camshaft . . . .   Toothed belt from crankshaft
  Exhaust camshaft. . . . .   Chain-drive from intake camshaft
Number of teeth   19
Length:
  Intake camshaft . . . .   401.0 ± 0.15 mm
  Exhaust camshaft. . . . .   389.0 ± 0.5 mm
Endfloat . . . .   0.195 to 0.300 mm

Lubrication system

Oil pump type. . . . .   Gear-type, driven directly by the right-hand end of the crankshaft, by two flats machined along the crankshaft journal

Oil pressure at 110°C:
  1000 rpm . . . .   1.3 bar
  4000 rpm . . . .   3.5 bar

Torque wrench settings

	Nm	lbf ft
Ancillary drivebelt tensioner roller	20	15
Big-end bolts: *		
Stage 1	10	7
Stage 2	Slacken 180°	
Stage 3	30	22
Stage 4	Angle-tighten a further 140°	
Camshaft bearing caps	10	7
Camshaft cover/bearing ladder:		
Studs	10	7
Bolts	10	7
Camshaft position sensor bolt	5	4
Camshaft sprocket:		
Stage 1	20	15
Stage 2	Angle-tighten a further 50°	
Coolant outlet housing bolts	7	5
Crankshaft position/speed sensor bolt	5	4
Crankshaft pulley/sprocket bolt: *		
Stage 1	35	26
Stage 2	Angle-tighten a further 190 °	
Cylinder head bolts:		
Stage 1	20	15
Stage 2	40	30
Stage 3	Angle-tighten a further 260°	
Cylinder head cover/manifold	10	7
EGR valve.	10	7
Engine mountings:		
Left-hand engine/transmission mounting:		
Flexible mounting centre nut	65	48
Flexible mounting-to-bracket bolts	30	22
Mounting bracket-to-transmission bolts	60	44
Mounting bracket-to-vehicle body bolts	27	20
Rear engine/transmission mounting:		
Link rod-to-cylinder block bracket bolt	60	44
Link rod-to-subframe bolt.	87	64
Right-hand engine mounting:		
Flexible mounting-to-vehicle body bolts	30	22
Mounting bracket-to-engine bolts	60	44
Reaction rod mounting bracket-to-engine mounting bracket:		
Bolts	60	44
Nut	45	33
Reaction rod-to-vehicle body.	47	34
Reaction rod-to-mounting bracket bolt	47	34
Engine-to-transmission fixing bolts	54	40

Torque wrench settings (continued)

	Nm	lbf ft
Flywheel bolts: *		
Dual mass flywheel:		
Stage 1	25	18
Stage 2	Fully slacken	
Stage 3	8	6
Stage 4	30	22
Stage 5	Angle-tighten a further 90°	
Normal flywheel:		
Stage 1	25	18
Stage 2	Fully slacken	
Stage 3	8	6
Stage 4	17	13
Stage 5	Angle-tighten a further 75°	
Fuel pump sprocket	50	37
Main bearing ladder outer seam bolts:		
Stage 1	5	4
Stage 2	10	7
Main bearing ladder to cylinder block:		
Stage 1	10	7
Stage 2	Slacken 180°	
Stage 3	30	22
Stage 4	Angle-tighten a further 140°	
Piston oil jet spray tube bolt..........................	20	15
Oil filter cover..	25	18
Oil pick-up pipe	10	7
Oil pressure switch......................................	32	24
Oil pump to cylinder block.............................	10	7
Sump drain plug..	25	18
Sump bolts/nuts..	12	9
Timing belt idler pulley	35	26
Timing belt tensioner pulley	25	18
Timing chain tensioner	10	7
Vacuum pump:		
Stage 1	18	13
Stage 2	Angle-tighten a further 5°	

*Do not re-use

1 General Information

How to use this Chapter

1 This Chapter describes the repair procedures that can reasonably be carried out on the engine whilst it remains in the vehicle. If the engine has been removed from the vehicle and is being dismantled as described in Chapter 2D, any preliminary dismantling procedures can be ignored.

2 Note that, while it may be possible physically to overhaul items such as the piston/connecting rod assemblies while the engine is in the car, such tasks are not usually carried out as separate operations. Usually, several additional procedures are required (not to mention the cleaning of components and oil ways); for this reason, all such tasks are classed as major overhaul procedures, and are described in Chapter 2D.

3 Chapter 2D describes the removal of the engine/transmission from the car, and the full overhaul procedures that can then be carried out.

DV series engines

4 The 1.6 litre DV series engine is the result of development collaboration between Peugeot/Citroën and Ford. The engine in this Chapter is of double overhead camshaft (DOHC) 16-valve design. The direct injection, turbocharged, four-cylinder engine is mounted transversely, with the transmission mounted on the left-hand side.

5 A toothed timing belt drives the intake camshaft, high-pressure fuel pump and coolant pump. The intake camshaft drives the exhaust camshaft via a chain. The camshafts operate the intake and exhaust valves via rocker arms, which are supported at their pivot ends by hydraulic self-adjusting tappets. The camshafts are supported by bearings machined directly in the cylinder head and camshaft bearing housing.

6 The high-pressure fuel pump supplies fuel to the fuel rail, and subsequently to the electronically controlled injectors, which inject the fuel direct into the combustion chambers.

This design differs from the previous type where an injection pump supplies the fuel at high pressure to each injector. The earlier, conventional type injection pump required fine calibration and timing, and these functions are now completed by the high-pressure pump, electronic injectors and engine management ECM (Engine Control Module).

7 The crankshaft runs in five main bearings of the usual shell type. Endfloat is controlled by thrustwashers either side of No 2 main bearing.

8 The pistons are selected to be of matching weight, and incorporate fully floating gudgeon pins retained by circlips.

Repair operations precaution

9 The engine is a complex unit with numerous accessories and ancillary components. The design of the engine compartment is such that every conceivable space has been utilised, and access to virtually all of the engine components is extremely limited. In many cases, ancillary components will have to be removed, or moved to one side, and wiring, pipes and hoses will have to be

disconnected or removed from various cable clips and support brackets.

10 When working on this engine, read through the entire procedure first, look at the car and engine at the same time, and establish whether you have the necessary tools, equipment, skill and patience to proceed. Allow considerable time for any operation, and be prepared for the unexpected.

11 Because of the limited access, many of the engine photographs appearing in this Chapter were, by necessity, taken with the engine removed from the vehicle.

⚠️ **Warning: It is essential to observe strict precautions when working on the fuel system components of the engine, particularly the high-pressure side of the system. Before carrying out any engine operations that entail working on, or near, any part of the fuel system, refer to the special information given in Chapter 4A Section 1.**

Operations with engine in vehicle

a) *Compression pressure – testing.*
b) *Cylinder head cover – removal and refitting.*
c) *Crankshaft pulley – removal and refitting.*
d) *Timing belt covers – removal and refitting.*
e) *Timing belt – removal, refitting and adjustment.*
f) *Timing belt tensioner and sprockets – removal and refitting.*
g) *Camshaft oil seal – renewal.*
h) *Camshaft, rocker arms and hydraulic tappets – removal, inspection and refitting*
i) *Sump – removal and refitting.*
j) *Oil pump – removal and refitting.*
k) *Crankshaft oil seals – renewal.*
l) *Engine/transmission mountings – inspection and renewal.*

2 Compression and leakdown tests – description and interpretation

Compression test

Note: *A compression tester specifically designed for diesel engines must be used for this test.*

1 When engine performance is down, or if misfiring occurs which cannot be attributed to the fuel system, a compression test can provide diagnostic clues as to the engine's condition. If the test is performed regularly, it can give warning of trouble before any other symptoms become apparent.

2 A compression tester specifically intended for diesel engines must be used, because of the higher pressures involved. The tester is connected to an adapter, which screws into the glow plug or injector hole. On this engine, an adapter suitable for use in the glow plug holes will be required, so as not to disturb the fuel system components. It is unlikely to be worthwhile buying such a tester for occasional use, but it may be possible to borrow or hire one – if not, have the test performed by a garage.

3 Unless specific instructions to the contrary are supplied with the tester, observe the following points:
a) *The battery must be in a good state of charge, the air filter must be clean, and the engine should be at normal operating temperature.*
b) *All the glow plugs should be removed as described in Chapter 5B Section 2 before starting the test.*
c) *Disconnect the fuel injector wiring plugs (see Chapter 4A Section 11).*

4 The compression pressures measured are not so important as the balance between cylinders. Values are given in the Specifications.

5 The cause of poor compression is less easy to establish on a diesel engine than on a petrol one. The effect of introducing oil into the cylinders ('wet' testing) is not conclusive, because there is a risk that the oil will sit in the swirl chamber or in the recess on the piston crown instead of passing to the rings. However, the following can be used as a rough guide to diagnosis.

6 All cylinders should produce very similar pressures; any difference greater than that specified indicates the existence of a fault. Note that the compression should build-up quickly in a healthy engine; low compression on the first stroke, followed by gradually increasing pressure on successive strokes, indicates worn piston rings. A low compression reading on the first stroke, which does not build-up during successive strokes, indicates leaking valves or a blown head gasket (a cracked head could also be the cause). Deposits on the undersides of the valve heads can also cause low compression.

7 A low reading from two adjacent cylinders is almost certainly due to the head gasket having blown between them; the presence of coolant in the engine oil will confirm this.

8 If the compression reading is unusually high, the cylinder head surfaces, valves and pistons are probably coated with carbon deposits. If this is the case, the cylinder head should be removed and decarbonised (see Chapter 2D Section 7).

Leakdown test

9 A leakdown test measures the rate at which compressed air fed into the cylinder is lost. It is an alternative to a compression test, and in many ways it is better, since the escaping air provides easy identification of where pressure loss is occurring (piston rings, valves or head gasket).

10 The equipment needed for leakdown testing is unlikely to be available to the home mechanic. If poor compression is suspected, have the test performed by a suitably-equipped garage.

3 Engine assembly/valve timing holes – general information and usage

Note: *Do not attempt to rotate the engine whilst the crankshaft and camshaft are locked in position. If the engine is to be left in this state for a long period of time, it is a good idea to place suitable warning notices inside the vehicle, and in the engine compartment. This will reduce the possibility of the engine being accidentally cranked on the starter motor, which is likely to cause damage with the locking pins in place.*

1 Timing holes or slots are located only in the crankshaft pulley flange and camshaft sprocket hub. The holes/slots are used to position the pistons halfway up the cylinder bores. This will ensure that the valve timing is maintained during operations that require removal and refitting of the timing belt. When the holes/slots are aligned with their corresponding holes in the cylinder block and cylinder head, suitable diameter bolts/pins can be inserted to lock the crankshaft and camshaft in position, preventing rotation.

2 Note that the HDi/MultiJet type fuel system used on these engines does not have a conventional diesel injection pump, but instead uses a high-pressure fuel pump. Although it may be argued that timing of the fuel pump is irrelevant because it merely pressurises the fuel in the fuel rail, Peugeot/Citroën/Fiat include this procedure, using the same timing rod/pin used for crankshaft sprocket timing. **Note:** *The drive sprocket is keyed to the shaft. In addition, note that the hole in the fuel pump sprocket only aligns correctly with the hole in the mounting bracket every 12 revolutions of the crankshaft (or every 6 revolutions of the camshaft sprocket).*

3 To align the engine assembly/valve timing holes, proceed as follows.

4 Chock the rear wheels then jack up the front of the vehicle and support it on axle stands (see *Jacking and vehicle support*). Remove the right-hand front roadwheel.

5 To gain access to the crankshaft pulley, to enable the engine to be turned, the wheel arch plastic liner must be removed. The liner is secured by several plastic expanding rivets/nut/screws. To remove the rivets, push in the centre pins a little, and then prise the clips from place. Remove the liner from under the front wing. The crankshaft can then be turned using a suitable socket and extension bar fitted to the pulley bolt.

6 Remove the upper and lower timing belt covers as described in Section.

7 Temporarily refit the crankshaft pulley bolt, remove the crankshaft locking tool, then turn the crankshaft until the timing hole in the camshaft sprocket hub is aligned with the corresponding hole in the cylinder head. Note that the crankshaft must always be turned in a clockwise direction (viewed from the right-hand side of vehicle). Use a small mirror

3.9 Insert a 5.0 mm drill bit/bolt through the round hole in the sprocket flange, into the hole in the oil pump housing (lower timing belt cover removed for clarity)

3.10 Insert an 8.0 mm drill bit/bolt through the hole in the camshaft sprocket and into the corresponding hole in the cylinder head

3.11 Insert a 5.0 mm drill bit/bolt through the round hole in the fuel pump sprocket flange, into the hole in the cylinder head

so that the position of the sprocket hub timing slot can be observed. When the slot is aligned with the corresponding hole in the cylinder head, the camshaft is positioned correctly.

8 Remove the crankshaft drivebelt pulley as described in Section 5.

9 Insert a 5 mm diameter bolt, rod or drill through the hole in crankshaft sprocket flange and into the corresponding hole in the oil pump housing **(see illustration)**, if necessary, carefully turn the crankshaft either way until the rod enters the timing hole in the block.

10 Insert an 8 mm bolt, rod or drill through the hole in the camshaft sprocket hub and into engagement with the cylinder head **(see illustration)**.

11 If using this procedure during refitting of the timing belt, insert a 5 mm diameter bolt, rod or drill through the hole in the fuel pump sprocket and into the corresponding hole in the cylinder head **(see illustration)**. Note the comment in paragraph 2 – if the fuel pump sprocket holes are not aligned during removal of the timing belt, it is of no consequence, however it is important to align the holes during the refitting procedure. If timing alignment alone is being checked there is no need to check alignment of the pump sprocket.

12 The crankshaft and camshaft are now locked in position, preventing unnecessary rotation.

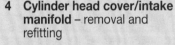

4 Cylinder head cover/intake manifold – removal and refitting

Removal

1 Disconnect the battery negative lead as described in Chapter 5A Section 4.

2 Drill out the rivet/undo the bolt securing the drain tube to the bonnet slam panel, then undo the retaining nuts and remove the cabin air intake cowling **(see illustrations)**.

3 Remove the air intake hoses, and air cleaner assembly as described in Chapter 4A Section 5.

4 Disconnect the wiring plugs from the top of

each injector, undo the guide bolts, then make sure all wiring harnesses are freed from any retaining brackets on the cylinder head cover/ intake manifold **(see illustration)**. Disconnect any vacuum pipes as necessary, having first noted their fitted positions.

5 Remove the EGR heat exchanger as described in Chapter 4B Section 2.

6 Depress the release buttons and disconnect the fuel feed and return hoses at the right-hand end of the cylinder head, then disconnect the fuel temperature sensor wiring plug, and move the pipe/priming bulb assembly to the rear **(see illustration)**.

7 Release the clamps, undo the bolts and remove the intake ducting between the

4.2a Undo the bolt/drill out the rivet securing the drain tube

4.2b Undo the nuts at the top of the intake cowling…

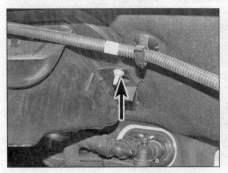

4.2c …and slacken the nut each side

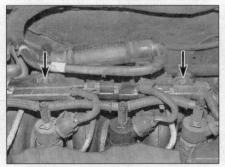

4.4 Undo the Allen screws and position the wiring harness/guide to one side

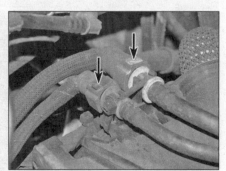

4.6 Depress the release buttons and disconnect the fuel feed and return hoses

4.7a Slacken the left-hand turbocharger outlet hose bolt, undo the right-hand bolt ...

4.7b ... then slacken the hose clamps ...

4.7c ... disconnect the wiring plugs ...

4.7d ... and undo the securing bolts

4.8 Undo the bolts and remove the oil separator

turbocharger and the intake manifold. Make a note of their fitted positions, and then disconnect the various wiring plugs, as the assembly is withdrawn **(see illustrations)**.

8 Undo the retaining bolts and remove the oil separator from the top of the cylinder head **(see illustration)**. Recover the rubber seal.

9 Prise out the retaining clips and disconnect the fuel return pipes from the injectors, then undo the unions and remove the high-pressure fuel pipes from the injectors and the common fuel rail at the rear of the cylinder head – counterhold the unions with a second spanner **(see illustrations)**. Plug the openings to prevent dirt ingress.

10 Undo the 2 bolts securing the cylinder head cover/intake manifold. Lift the assembly away **(see illustration)**. Recover the manifold rubber seals.

Refitting

11 Refitting is a reversal of removal, bearing in mind the following points:

a) *Examine the seals for signs of damage and deterioration, and renew if necessary. Smear a little clean engine oil on the manifold seals.*

b) *Renew the fuel injector high-pressure pipes – see Chapter 4A Section 11.*

c) *Refit the air intake hoses and filter element – see Chapter 1 Section 24.*

5 Crankshaft pulley – removal and refitting

Removal

1 Remove the auxiliary drivebelt as described in Chapter 1 Section 20.

2 To lock the crankshaft, working underneath the engine, insert Peugeot/Citroën tool No. 0194-C/Fiat tool No. 2.000.022.500 into the hole in the right-hand face of the engine block casting over the lower section of the flywheel.

4.9a Prise out the clip and pull the return hose from the top of each injector

4.9b Use a second spanner to hold the injector port whilst slackening the fuel pipe unions

4.10 Undo the 2 remaining bolts and pull the cover/manifold upwards

5.2 The locking pin/bolt must locate in the hole in the flywheel to prevent rotation

5.3a Undo the retaining bolt …

5.3b … and remove the crankshaft pulley

Rotate the crankshaft until the tool engages in the corresponding hole in the flywheel. In the absence of the special tool, insert a 12 mm rod or drill into the hole **(see illustration)**. Note: The hole in the casting and the hole in the flywheel are provided purely to lock the crankshaft whilst the pulley bolt is undone, it doesnotposition the crankshaft at TDC.

3 Using a suitable socket and extension bar, unscrew the retaining bolt, remove the washer, then slide the pulley off the end of the crankshaft **(see illustrations)**. If the pulley is tight fit, it can be drawn off the crankshaft using a suitable puller. If a puller is being used, refit the pulley retaining bolt without the washer to avoid damaging the crankshaft as the puller is tightened.
Caution: Do not touch the outer magnetic sensor ring of the sprocket with your fingers, or allow metallic particles to come into contact with it.

Refitting

4 Refit the pulley to the end of the crankshaft, making sure the locating lug on the end of the crankshaft aligns with the slot in the rear of the pulley **(see illustration)**.
5 Thoroughly clean the threads of the pulley retaining bolt, then apply a coat of locking compound to the bolt threads. Peugeot/Citroën/Fiat recommend the use of Loctite (available from your franchised dealer); in the absence of this, any good-quality locking compound may be used.
6 Refit the crankshaft pulley retaining bolt and washer. Tighten the bolt to the specified

torque, and then through the specified angle, preventing the crankshaft from turning using the method employed on removal.
7 Refit and tension the auxiliary drivebelt as described in Chapter 1 Section 20.

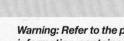
6 Timing belt covers – removal and refitting

⚠ *Warning: Refer to the precautionary information contained in 2A Section 1 before proceeding.*

Removal

Upper cover

1 Remove the air cleaner assembly as described in Chapter 4A Section 5.
2 Where fitted, release the fasteners and remove the acoustic cover from the top of the engine.
3 Remove the throttle body as described in Chapter 4A Section 12.
4 Disconnect the fuel feed pipe from the connector, then undo the screw, prise out the plastic rivet, and move the pipe assembly to one side. Plug the openings to prevent contamination.
5 Release the fuel lines from the support bracket next to the cover and then unclip the wiring loom from the upper cover **(see illustration)**.

5.4 Crankshaft sprocket alignment lug

6 Undo the 3 bolts and remove the timing belt upper cover **(see illustration)**.

Lower cover

7 Remove the crankshaft pulley as described in 2ASection 5.
8 Remove the timing belt upper cover as described previously in this Section.
9 Undo the 6 bolts and remove the lower cover **(see illustration)**.

6.5 Unclip the fuel pipes and release the wiring loom

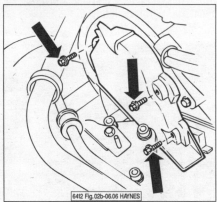

6.6 Timing belt upper cover bolts

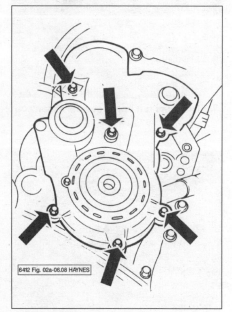

6.9 Lower timing cover retaining bolts

Refitting

10 Refitting of all the covers is a reversal of the relevant removal procedure, ensuring that each cover section is correctly located, and that the cover retaining bolts are securely tightened. Ensure that all disturbed hoses are reconnected and retained by their relevant clips.

7 Timing belt – removal, inspection, refitting and tensioning

General

1 The timing belt drives the intake camshaft, high-pressure fuel pump, and coolant pump from a toothed sprocket on the end of the crankshaft. If the belt breaks or slips in service, the pistons are likely to hit the valve heads, resulting in expensive damage.

2 The timing belt should be renewed at the specified intervals, or earlier if it is contaminated with oil, or at all noisy in operation (a 'scraping' noise due to uneven wear).

3 If the timing belt is being removed, it is a wise precaution to check the condition of the coolant pump at the same time (check for signs of coolant leakage). This may avoid the need to remove the timing belt again at a later stage should the coolant pump fail.

Removal

4 Chock the rear wheels then jack up the front of the vehicle and support it on axle stands (see *Jacking and vehicle support*). Remove the front right-hand roadwheel, wheel arch liner (to expose the crankshaft pulley), and the engine undershield. The wheel arch liner is secured by several plastic expanding rivets/plastic clips. Pull the centre pins out a little then prise the rivets from place. The engine undershield is retained by several bolts/nuts.

5 Remove the upper and lower timing belt covers, as described in Section 6.

6 Undo the mounting nut, and move the coolant expansion tank to one side **(see illustration)**. There's no need to disconnect the pipes/hoses.

7 Position a trolley jack under the engine, and using a block of wood on the jack head, take the weight of the engine.

8 Undo the bolts/nut and remove the right-hand engine mounting and support bracket as described in Section 17.

9 Lock the crankshaft and camshaft in the correct position as described in Section 3. If necessary, temporarily refit the crankshaft pulley bolt to enable the crankshaft to be rotated. At this stage, it is of no consequence whether the fuel pump sprocket aligns correctly with the hole in the pump mounting bracket.

10 Insert a hexagon key into the belt tensioner pulley centre, slacken the pulley bolt, and allow the tensioner to rotate, relieving the belt tension **(see illustration)**. With the belt slack, temporarily tighten the pulley bolt.

11 Note its routing, then remove the timing belt from the sprockets.

Inspection

12 Renew the belt as a matter of course, regardless of its apparent condition. The cost of a new belt is nothing compared with the cost of repairs should the belt break in service. If signs of oil contamination are found, trace the source of the oil leak and rectify it. Wash down the engine timing belt area and all related components, to remove all traces of oil. Check that the tensioner and idler pulleys rotate freely without any sign of roughness, and also check that the coolant pump pulley rotates freely. Due to the complexity of this procedure, it is recommended that the tensioner and idler pulleys be renewed when fitting a new timing belt **(see illustration)**.

Refitting and tensioning

13 Commence refitting by ensuring that the crankshaft and camshaft timing pins are still in position correctly. Also, where a Bosch high-pressure fuel pump is fitted, locate and lock the fuel pump sprocket in its correct position as described in Section 3.

14 Locate the timing belt on the crankshaft sprocket then, keeping it taut, locate it around the idler pulley, camshaft sprocket, high-pressure pump sprocket, coolant pump sprocket, and the tensioner pulley **(see illustrations)**. If the timing belt has directional arrows on it, make sure that they point in the direction of normal engine rotation.

7.6 Undo the nut and move the expansion tank to one side

7.10 Slacken the bolt and allow the tensioner to rotate, relieving the tension on the belt

7.12 Tensioner and idler pulleys

7.14a Feed the timing belt around the crankshaft sprocket first ...

7.14b ... and then finally around the tensioner pulley

7.14c Timing belt routing

7.16 The index arm must align with the lug

15 Refit the timing belt protection bracket and tighten the retaining bolt securely.
16 Slacken the tensioner pulley bolt and, using a hexagonal key, rotate the tensioner anti-clockwise, which moves the index arm clockwise, until the index arm is aligned as shown **(see illustration)**.
17 Remove the camshaft and crankshaft and fuel pump timing pins and, using a socket on the crankshaft pulley bolt, crankshaft clockwise 6 complete revolutions. Align the camshaft and crankshaft timing holes and check that the timing pins can be inserted, then remove them. There is no requirement to check the fuel pump sprocket alignment, as it will only be aligned after 12 complete revolutions.
18 Check that the tensioner index arm is still aligned between the edges of the area shown **(see illustration 7.16)**. If it is not, remove and belt and begin the refitting process again.
19 The remainder of refitting is a reversal of removal. Tighten all fasteners to the specified torque where given.

8 Timing belt sprockets and tensioner – removal and refitting

Camshaft sprocket
Removal
1 Remove the timing belt as described in Section 7.
2 Remove the locking tool from the camshaft sprocket/hub. Slacken the sprocket hub retaining bolt. To prevent the camshaft rotating

8.11a Slide the sprocket from the crankshaft …

A sprocket holding tool can be made from two lengths of steel strip bolted together to form a forked end. Drill holes and insert bolts in the ends of the fork to engage with the sprocket spokes.

as the bolt is slackened, a sprocket holding tool will be required. In the absence of the special Peugeot/Citroën/Fiat tool, an acceptable substitute can be fabricated at home (see **Tool Tip**). Do not attempt to use the engine assembly/valve timing locking tool to prevent the sprocket from rotating whilst the bolt is slackened.
3 Remove the sprocket hub retaining bolt, and slide the sprocket and hub off the end of the camshaft.
4 Clean the camshaft sprocket thoroughly, and renew it if there are any signs of wear, damage or cracks.
Refitting
5 Refit the camshaft sprocket to the camshaft **(see illustration)**.
6 Refit the sprocket hub retaining bolt. Tighten the bolt to the specified torque, preventing the camshaft from turning as during removal.
7 Align the engine assembly/valve timing slot in the camshaft sprocket hub with the hole in the cylinder head and refit the timing pin to lock the camshaft in position.
8 Fit the timing belt around the pump sprocket and camshaft sprocket, and tension the timing belt as described in Section 7.

Crankshaft sprocket
Removal
9 Remove the timing belt as described in Section 7.

8.11b … and recover the Woodruff key

8.5 Ensure the lug on the sprocket hub engages with the slot on the end of the camshaft

10 Check that the engine assembly/valve timing holes are still aligned as described in Section 3, and the camshaft sprocket and flywheel are locked in position.
11 Slide the sprocket off the end of the crankshaft and collect the Woodruff key **(see illustrations)**.
12 Examine the crankshaft oil seal for signs of oil leakage and, if necessary, renew it as described in Section 14.
13 Clean the crankshaft sprocket thoroughly, and renew it if there are any signs of wear, damage or cracks. Recover the crankshaft locating key.
Refitting
14 Refit the key to the end of the crankshaft, then refit the crankshaft sprocket (with the flange facing the crankshaft pulley).
15 Fit the timing belt around the crankshaft sprocket, and tension the timing belt as described in Section 7.

Fuel pump sprocket
Removal
16 Remove the timing belt as described in Section 7.
17 Using a socket, undo the pump sprocket retaining nut. The sprocket can be held stationary by inserting a locking pin, drill or rod through the hole in the sprocket, and into the corresponding hole in the backplate **(see illustration)**, or by using a forked tool engaged with the holes in the sprocket (see **Tool Tip** in paragraph 2). Note: On some

8.17 Insert a suitable drill bit through the sprocket into the hole in the backplate

Make a sprocket releasing tool from a short strip of steel. Drill two holes in the strip to correspond with the two holes in the sprocket. Drill a third hole just large enough to accept the flats of the sprocket retaining nut.

8.25 Remove the tensioner retaining bolt

8.28 Make sure the tensioner is fitted to the lug on the engine casing

engines, a hole is provided at the 5 o'clock position for locking purposes only, however, the timing position hole is at the 12 o'clock position.

18 The pump sprocket is a taper fit on the pump shaft and it will be necessary to make up another tool to release it from the taper (see **Tool Tip**).

19 On late models where the sprocket is keyed to the shaft, unscrew the retaining nut and remove the sprocket, then recover the Woodruff key. On early models where the sprocket is not keyed to the shaft, partially unscrew the sprocket retaining nut, then fit the home-made tool, and secure it to the sprocket with two suitable bolts. Prevent the sprocket from rotating as before, and unscrew the sprocket retaining nut. The nut will bear against the tool, as it is undone, forcing the sprocket off the shaft taper. Once the taper is released, remove the tool, unscrew the nut fully, and remove the sprocket from the pump shaft.

20 Clean the sprocket thoroughly, and renew it if there are any signs of wear, damage or cracks.

Refitting

21 Refit the Woodruff key (later models only) then refit the pump sprocket and retaining nut,

and tighten the nut to the specified torque. Prevent the sprocket rotating as the nut is tightened using the sprocket holding tool.

22 Fit the timing belt around the pump sprocket, and tension the timing belt as described in Section 7.

Coolant pump sprocket

23 The coolant pump sprocket is integral with the pump, and cannot be removed. Coolant pump removal is described in Chapter 3 Section 8.

Tensioner pulley

Removal

24 Remove the timing belt as described in Section 7.

25 Remove the tensioner pulley retaining bolt, and remove the pulley from the cylinder block **(see illustration)**.

26 Clean the tensioner pulley, but do not use any strong solvent, which may enter the pulley bearings. Check that the pulley rotates freely, with no sign of stiffness or free play. Renew the pulley if there is any doubt about its condition, or if there are any obvious signs of wear or damage.

27 Examine the pulley locating stud for signs of damage.

Refitting

28 Refit the tensioner pulley to the cylinder block making sure it is positioned over the

locating stud **(see illustration)**, and then fit the retaining bolt.

29 Refit the timing belt as described in Section 7.

Idler pulley

Removal

30 Remove the timing belt as described in Section 7.

31 Undo the retaining nut and withdraw the idler pulley from the engine **(see illustration)**.

32 Clean the idler pulley, but do not use any strong solvent which may enter the bearings. Check that the pulley rotates freely, with no sign of stiffness or free play. Renew the idler pulley if there is any doubt about its condition, or if there are any obvious signs of wear or damage.

Refitting

33 Locate the idler pulley on the engine, and fit the retaining nut. Tighten the nut to the specified torque.

34 Refit the timing belt (see Section 7).

9 Camshafts, rocker arms and hydraulic tappets – removal, inspection and refitting

Removal

1 Remove the cylinder head cover/manifold as described in Section 4.

2 Remove the injectors as described in Chapter 4A Section 11.

3 Remove the camshaft sprocket as described in Section 8.

4 Refit the right-hand engine mounting, but only tighten the bolts moderately; this will keep the engine supported during the camshaft removal.

5 Undo the bolts and remove the vacuum pump. Recover the pump O-ring seals **(see illustration)**.

6 Remove the fuel filter (see Chapter 1 Section 11), then undo the bolts and remove the fuel filter mounting bracket.

7 Release the wiring harness clips, then undo

8.31 Undo the timing belt idler pulley retaining nut

9.5 Vacuum pump retaining bolts

the bolts and remove the timing belt inner, upper cover **(see illustration)**.

8 Disconnect the wiring plug, unscrew the retaining bolt, and remove the camshaft position sensor from the camshaft cover/bearing ladder.

9 Undo the 5 bolts and remove the upper rear section of the turbocharger heat shield, then working gradually and evenly, slacken and remove the bolts securing the camshaft cover/bearing ladder to the cylinder head in sequence **(see illustrations)**. Lift the cover/ladder from position complete with the camshafts.

10 Undo the retaining bolts and remove the bearing caps. Note their fitted positions, as they must be refitted into their original positions **(see illustration)**. Note that the bearing caps are marked A for intake, and E for exhaust, and 1 to 4 from the flywheel end of the cylinder head.

11 Undo the bolts securing the chain tensioner assembly to the camshaft cover/bearing ladder, and then lift the camshafts, chain and tensioner from place **(see illustrations)**. Discard the camshaft oil seal.

12 Obtain 16 small, clean plastic containers, and number them 1 to 8 intake and 1 to 8 exhaust; alternatively, divide a larger container into 16 compartments.

13 Lift out each rocker arm. Place the rocker arms in their respective positions in the box or containers.

14 A compartmentalised container filled with engine oil is now required to retain the hydraulic tappets while they are removed from the cylinder head. Withdraw each hydraulic follower and place it in the container, keeping them each identified for correct refitting. The tappets must be totally submerged in the oil to prevent air entering them.

Inspection

15 Inspect the cam lobes and the camshaft bearing journals for scoring or other visible evidence of wear. Once the surface hardening of the cam lobes has been eroded, wear will occur at an accelerated rate. **Note:** *If these symptoms are visible on the tips of the camshaft lobes, check the corresponding rocker arm, as it will probably be worn as well.*

9.7 Timing belt inner, upper cover bolts

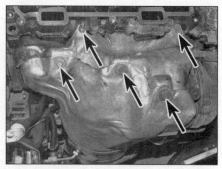

9.9a Undo the bolts and remove the rear section of the heat shield

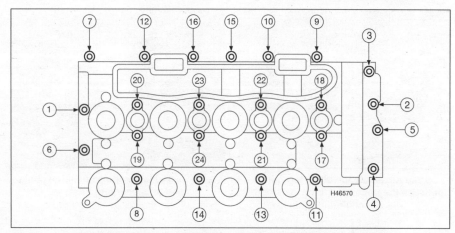

9.9b Camshaft cover/bearing ladder bolt slackening sequence

16 Examine the condition of the bearing surfaces in the cylinder head and camshaft bearing housing. If wear is evident, the cylinder head and bearing housing will both have to be renewed, as they are a matched assembly.

17 Inspect the rocker arms and tappets for scuffing, cracking or other damage and renew any components as necessary. Also check the condition of the tappet bores in the cylinder head. As with the camshafts, any wear in this area will necessitate cylinder head renewal.

Refitting

18 Thoroughly clean the sealant from the mating surfaces of the cylinder head and camshaft bearing housing. Use a suitable liquid gasket dissolving agent together with a soft putty knife; do not use a metal scraper or the faces will be damaged. As there is no conventional gasket used, the cleanliness of the mating faces is of the utmost importance. Prise out the oil injector oil seals from the camshaft bearing housing.

19 Clean off any oil, dirt or grease from both components and dry with a clean lint-free cloth. Ensure that all the oilways are completely clean.

20 Liberally lubricate the hydraulic tappet bores in the cylinder head with clean engine oil.

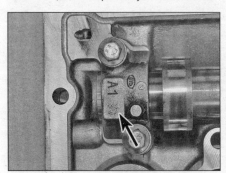

9.10 Bearing caps are numbered 1 to 4 from the flywheel end – A for intake, and E for exhaust

9.11a Undo the tensioner bolts ...

9.11b ... then lift the camshafts, chain and tensioner from place

9.21 Refit the hydraulic tappets …

9.22 … and rocker arms to their original locations

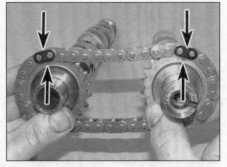

9.23 Align the marks on the sprockets with the centre of the black-coloured chain links. There must be 12 link pins between the sprocket marks

9.24a Assemble the chain tensioner between the upper and lower runs of the chain …

9.24b … and lower the camshafts, chain and tensioner into position

26 Check that the black-coloured links on the chain are still aligned with the marks on the camshaft sprockets, then refit the camshaft cover/bearing ladder, and gradually and evenly tighten the retaining bolts until the cover/ladder is in contact with the cylinder head, then tighten the bolts to the specified torque in sequence (see illustration). Note: Ensure the cover/ladder is correctly located by checking the bores of the vacuum pump and camshaft oil seal at each end of the cover/ladder.

27 Fit a new camshaft oil seal as described in Section 14.

28 Refit the camshaft sprocket, and tighten the retaining bolt finger-tight.

29 Using a spanner on the camshaft sprocket bolt, rotate the camshafts approximately 40 complete revolutions clockwise. Check the black-coloured links on the chain still align with the marks on the camshaft sprockets.

30 If the marks still align, refit the camshaft sprocket as described in Section 8.

31 Refit the camshaft position sensor as described in Chapter 4A Section 12.

32 Press the new seals into the bearing housing, using a tube/socket of approximately 20 mm outside diameter, ensuring the inner lip of the seal fits around the injector guide

21 Insert the hydraulic tappets into their original bores in the cylinder head unless they have been renewed (see illustration).

22 Lubricate the rocker arms and place them over their respective tappets and valve stems (see illustration).

23 Engage the timing chain around the camshaft sprockets, aligning the black-coloured links with the marked teeth on the camshaft sprockets (see illustration). If the black colouring has been lost, there must be 12 chain link pins between the marks on the sprockets.

24 Fit the chain tensioner between the upper and lower runs of the chain, then lubricate the bearing surfaces with clean engine oil, and fit the camshafts into position on the underside of the camshaft cover/bearing ladder. Refit the bearing caps to their original positions and tighten the retaining bolts to the specified torque (see illustrations). Tighten the tensioner retaining bolts to the specified torque.

25 Apply a thin bead of sealant to the mating surface of the camshaft cover/bearing ladder as shown. Peugeot/Citroën/Fiat recommend the use of Autojoint Noir (see illustration). Do not allow the sealant to obstruct the oil channels for the hydraulic chain tensioner.

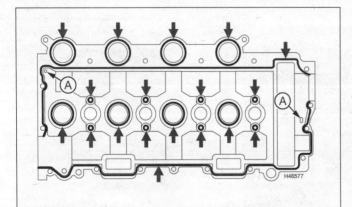

9.25 Apply sealant to the camshaft cover/bearing ladder as indicated by the heavy black lines. Ensure sealant does not enter the tensioner oil holes – marked A

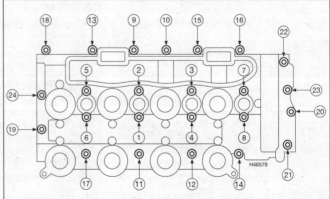

9.26 Camshaft cover/bearing ladder bolt tightening sequence

tube **(see illustrations)**. Refit the injectors as described in, Section.

33 Refit the cylinder head cover/manifold as described in Section 4.

10 Cylinder head – removal and refitting

Removal

1 Chock the rear wheels then jack up the front of the vehicle and support it on axle stands (see *Jacking and vehicle support*). Remove the front right-hand roadwheel, the engine undershield, and the front wheel arch liner. The undershield is secured by several screws, and the wheel arch liner is secured by several plastic expanding rivets/nuts/plastic clips. Push the centre pins in a little, then prise the rivet from place.

2 Disconnect the battery negative lead as described in Chapter 5A Section 4.

3 Drain the cooling system as described in Chapter 1 Section 23.

4 Remove the camshafts, rocker arms and hydraulic tappets as described in Section 9.

5 Remove the turbocharger as described in Chapter 4A Section 16.

6 Remove the glow plugs as described in Chapter 5B Section 2.

7 Undo the upper mounting bolts, and pivot the alternator away from the engine, undo the oil dipstick guide tube bolt, then undo the bolts securing the alternator/power steering

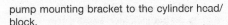

9.32a Fit the new seal around a 20 mm outside diameter socket ...

pump mounting bracket to the cylinder head/block.

8 Undo the coolant outlet housing (left-hand end of the cylinder head) retaining bolts, slacken the two bolts securing the housing support bracket to the top of the transmission bellhousing, and move the outlet housing away from the cylinder head a little **(see illustration)**. There is no need to disconnect the hoses.

9 Disconnect the high-pressure fuel pipe from the common rail to the pump, and disconnect the fuel supply and return hoses. Remove the bracket at the rear of the pump, then undo the bolt/nut and remove the pump and mounting bracket as an assembly **(see illustrations)**. Note that a new high-pressure pipe must be fitted.

10 Working in the reverse of the sequence shown **(see illustration 10.32)** undo the cylinder head bolts.

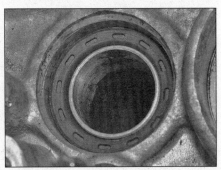

9.32b ... and push it into place

11 Release the cylinder head from the cylinder block and location dowels by rocking it. The Peugeot/Citroën/Fiat tool for doing this consists simply of two metal rods with 90-degree angled ends **(see illustration)**. Do not prise between the mating faces of the cylinder head and block, as this may damage the gasket faces.

12 Lift the cylinder head from the block, and recover the gasket.

13 If necessary, remove the exhaust manifold with reference to Chapter 4A Section 14.

Preparation for refitting

14 The mating faces of the cylinder head and cylinder block must be perfectly clean before refitting the head. Peugeot/Citroën/Fiat recommend the use of a scouring agent for this purpose, but acceptable results can be achieved by using a hard plastic or wood scraper to remove all traces of gasket and carbon.

15 The same method can be used to clean the piston crowns. Take particular care to avoid scoring or gouging the cylinder head/cylinder block mating surfaces during the cleaning operations, as aluminium alloy is easily damaged. Make sure that the carbon is not allowed to enter the oil and water passages – this is particularly important for the lubrication system, as carbon could block the oil supply to the engine's components.

10.8 Coolant outlet housing retaining bolts

10.9a Remove the high-pressure pipe ...

10.9b ... and the bracket

10.9c Pump mounting bracket upper nut and lower mounting bolt

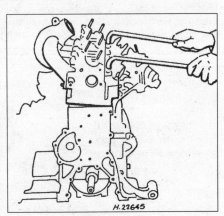

10.11 Free the cylinder head using angled rods

10.17a Pull the non-return valve from the cylinder head ...

10.17b ... and push a new one into place

10.21 Measure the piston protrusion using a DTI gauge

Using adhesive tape and paper, seal the water, oil and bolt holes in the cylinder block. To prevent carbon entering the gap between the pistons and bores, smear a little grease in the gap. After cleaning each piston, use a small brush to remove all traces of grease and carbon from the gap, and then wipe away the remainder with a clean rag.

16 Check the mating surfaces of the cylinder block and the cylinder head for nicks, deep scratches and other damage. If slight, they may be removed carefully with a file, but if excessive, machining may be the only alternative to renewal. If warpage of the cylinder head gasket surface is suspected, use a straight-edge to check it for distortion. Refer to Chapter 2D Section 7 if necessary.

17 Thoroughly clean the threads of the cylinder head bolt holes in the cylinder block. Ensure that the bolts run freely in their threads, and that all traces of oil and water are removed from each bolt hole. If required, pull the oil feed non-return valve from the cylinder head, and check the ball moves freely. Push a new valve into place if necessary **(see illustrations)**.

Gasket selection

18 Remove the crankshaft timing pin, then turn the crankshaft until pistons 1 and 4 are at TDC (Top Dead Centre). Position a dial test indicator (dial gauge) on the cylinder block adjacent to the rear of No 1 piston, and zero it on the block face. Transfer the probe to the crown of No 1 piston (10.0 mm in from the rear edge), and then slowly turn the crankshaft

back-and-forth past TDC, noting the highest reading on the indicator. Record this reading as protrusion A.

19 Repeat the check described in paragraph 18, this time 10.0 mm in from the front edge of the No 1 piston crown. Record this reading as protrusion B.

20 Add protrusion A to protrusion B, then divide the result by 2 to obtain an average reading for piston No 1.

21 Repeat the procedure described in paragraphs 18 to 20 on piston 4, then turn the crankshaft through 180° and carry out the procedure on the piston Nos 2 and 3 **(see illustration)**. Check that there is a maximum difference of 0.07 mm protrusion between any two pistons.

22 If a dial test indicator is not available, piston protrusion may be measured using a straight-edge and feeler blades or Vernier calipers. However, this is much less accurate, and cannot therefore be recommended.

23 Note the greatest piston protrusion measurement, and use this to determine the correct cylinder head gasket from the following table. The series of notches/holes on the side of the gasket are used for thickness identification **(see illustration)**.

Piston protrusion	Gasket identification
0.685 to 0.734 mm	1 notch
0.533 to 0.634 mm	2 notch
0.635 to 0.684 mm	3 notch
0.735 to 0.784 mm	4 notch
0.785 to 0.886 mm	5 notch

Head bolt examination

24 Carefully examine the cylinder head bolts for signs of damage to the threads or head, and for any sign of corrosion. If the bolts are in a satisfactory condition, measure the length of each bolt from the underside of the head to the end of the shank. The bolts may be re-used providing that the measured length does not exceed 149.0 mm **(see illustration)**. Note: Considering the stress to which the cylinder head bolts are subjected, it is highly recommended that they be all renewed, regardless of their apparent condition.

Refitting

25 Turn the crankshaft and position Nos 1 and 4 pistons at TDC, then turn the crankshaft a quarter turn (90°) anti-clockwise.

26 Thoroughly clean the surfaces of the cylinder head and block.

27 Make sure that the locating dowels are in place, then fit the correct gasket the right way round on the cylinder block **(see illustration)**.

28 If necessary, refit the exhaust manifold to the cylinder head as described in Chapter 4A Section 14.

29 Carefully lower the cylinder head onto the gasket and block, making sure that it locates correctly onto the dowels.

30 Apply a smear of grease to the threads, and to the underside of the heads, of the cylinder head bolts. Peugeot/Citroën/Fiat recommend the use of Molykote G Rapid Plus; in the absence of the specified grease, any good-quality high melting-point grease may be used.

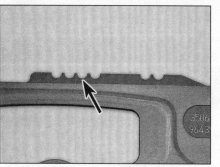

10.23 Cylinder head gasket thickness identification notches

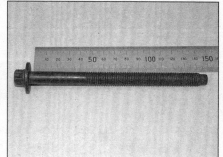

10.24 Measure the length from under the bolt head to its end

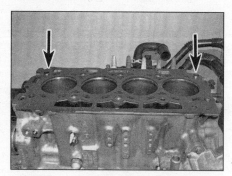

10.27 Ensure the gasket locates over the dowels

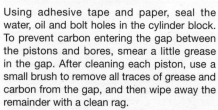

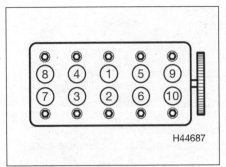

10.32 Cylinder head bolt tightening sequence

H44687

31 Carefully insert the cylinder head bolts into their holes (do not drop them in) and initially finger-tighten them.

32 Working progressively and in sequence, tighten the cylinder head bolts to their Stage 1 torque setting, using a torque wrench and suitable socket **(see illustration)**.

33 Once all the bolts have been tightened to their Stage 1 torque setting, working again in the specified sequence, tighten each bolt to the specified Stage 2 setting. Finally, angle-tighten the bolts through the specified Stage 3 angle. It is recommended that an angle-measuring gauge be used during this stage of tightening, to ensure accuracy. **Note:** *Retightening of the cylinder head bolts after running the engine is not required.*

34 Refit the hydraulic tappets, rocker arms, and camshaft housing (complete with camshafts) as described in Section 9.

35 Refit the timing belt as described in Section 7.

36 The remainder of refitting is a reversal of removal, noting the following points.
a) Use a new seal when refitting the coolant outlet housing.
b) When refitting a cylinder head, it is good practice to renew the thermostat.

c) Refit the camshaft position sensor with reference to Chapter 4A Section 12.
d) Tighten all fasteners to the specified torque where given.
e) Refill the cooling system as described in Chapter 1 Section 23.
f) The engine may run erratically for the first few miles, until the engine management ECM relearns its stored values.

11 Sump – removal and refitting

Removal

1 Drain the engine oil, then clean and refit the engine oil drain plug, tightening it securely. If the engine is nearing the service interval when the oil and filter are due for renewal, it is recommended that the filter is also removed, and a new one fitted. After reassembly, the engine can then be refilled with fresh oil. Refer to Chapter 1 Section 6 for further information.

2 Chock the rear wheels then jack up the front of the vehicle and support it on axle stands (see *Jacking and vehicle support*). Undo the screws and remove the engine undershield.

3 Remove the exhaust front pipe as described in Chapter 4A Section 18.

4 Where necessary, disconnect the wiring connector from the oil temperature sender unit, which is screwed into the sump.

5 Progressively slacken and remove all the sump retaining bolts/nuts. Since the sump bolts vary in length, remove each bolt in turn, and store it in its correct fitted order by pushing it through a clearly marked cardboard template. This will avoid the possibility of installing the bolts in the wrong locations on refitting.

6 Try to break the joint by striking the sump with the palm of your hand, then lower and withdraw the sump from under the car. If the

sump is stuck (which is quite likely) use a putty knife or similar, carefully inserted between the sump and block. Ease the knife along the joint until the sump is released. While the sump is removed, take the opportunity to check the oil pump pick-up/strainer for signs of clogging or splitting. If necessary, remove the pump as described in Section 12, and clean or renew the strainer.

Refitting

7 Clean all traces of sealant from the mating surfaces of the cylinder block/crankcase and sump, and then use a clean rag to wipe out the sump and the engine's interior.

8 On engines where the sump was fitted without a gasket, ensure that the sump mating surfaces are clean and dry, then apply a thin coating of suitable sealant to the sump or crankcase mating surface **(see illustration)**.

9 Offer up the sump to the cylinder block/crankcase. Refit its retaining bolts/nuts, ensuring that each bolt is screwed into its original location. Tighten the bolts evenly and progressively to the specified torque setting **(see illustration)**.

10 Reconnect the wiring connector to the oil temperature sensor (where fitted).

11 Lower the vehicle to the ground, then refill the engine with oil as described in Chapter 1 Section 6.

12 Oil pump – removal, inspection and refitting

Removal

1 Remove the sump as described in Section 11.

2 Remove the crankshaft sprocket as described in Section 8. Recover the locating key from the crankshaft.

3 Disconnect the wiring plug, undo the bolts and

11.8 Apply a bead of sealant to the sump or crankcase mating surface. Ensure the sealant is applied on the inside of the retaining bolt holes

11.9 Refit the sump and tighten the bolts

12.4 Oil pick-up tube retaining screws

12.5 Oil pump retaining bolts

12.6 Undo the Torx bolts and remove the pump cover

remove the crankshaft position sensor, located on the right-hand end of the cylinder block.

4 Undo the screws and remove the oil pump pick-up tube from the pump/block **(see illustration)**. Discard the oil seal; a new one must be fitted.

5 Undo the 8 bolts, and remove the oil pump **(see illustration)**.

Inspection

6 Undo and remove the Torx bolts securing the cover to the oil pump **(see illustration)**. Examine the pump rotors and body for signs of wear and damage. If worn, the complete pump must be renewed.

7 Remove the circlip, and extract the cap, valve piston and spring, noting which way around they are fitted **(see illustrations)**. The condition of the relief valve spring can only be measured by comparing it with a new one; if there is any doubt about its condition, it should also be renewed.

8 Refit the relief valve piston and spring, and then secure them in place with the circlip.

9 Refit the cover to the oil pump, and tighten the Torx bolts securely.

Refitting

10 Remove all traces of sealant, and thoroughly clean the mating surfaces of the oil pump and cylinder block.

11 Apply a 4 mm wide bead of silicone sealant to the mating face of the cylinder block **(see illustration)**. Ensure that no sealant enters any of the holes in the block.

12 With a new oil seal fitted, refit the oil pump over the end of the crankshaft, aligning the flats in the pump drivegear with the flats machined in the crankshaft **(see illustrations)**.

12.7a Remove the circlip …

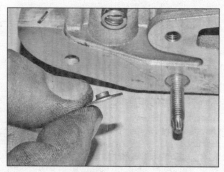

12.7b … cap …

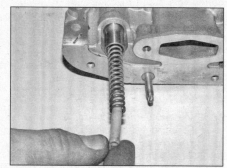

12.7c … spring …

12.7d … and piston

12.11 Apply a bead of sealant to the cylinder block mating surface

12.12a Fit a new seal …

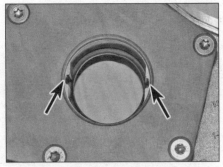

12.12b … align the pump gear flats …

12.12c … with those of the crankshaft

Note that new oil pumps are supplied with the oil seal already fitted, and a seal protector sleeve. The sleeve fits over the end of the crankshaft to protect the seal as the pump is fitted.

13 Install the oil pump bolts and tighten them to the specified torque.

14 Refit the oil pick-up tube to the pump/cylinder block using a new O-ring seal. Ensure the oil dipstick guide tube is correctly refitted.

15 Refit the Woodruff key to the crankshaft, and slide the crankshaft sprocket into place.

16 The remainder of refitting is a reversal of removal.

13.4a Undo the oil cooler bolts/stud

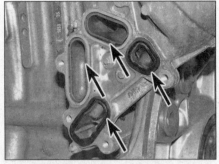

13.4b Renew the O-ring seals

13 Oil cooler –
removal and refitting

Removal

1 Chock the rear wheels then jack up the front of the vehicle and support it on axle stands (see *Jacking and vehicle support*). Undo the retaining bolts/nuts and remove the engine undershield (where fitted).

2 The oil cooler is fitted to the front of the oil filter housing. Drain the coolant as described in Chapter 1 Section 23.

3 Drain the engine oil as described in Chapter 1 Section 6, or be prepared for fluid spillage.

4 Undo the 5 bolts/stud and remove the oil cooler. Recover the O-ring seals **(see illustrations)**.

Refitting

5 Fit new O-ring seals into the recesses in the oil filter housing, and refit the cooler. Tighten the bolts securely.

6 Refill or top-up the cooling system and engine oil level as described in Chapter 1 Section 23 and Chapter 1 Section 6, or *Weekly checks* (as applicable). Start the engine, and check the oil cooler for signs of leakage.

14 Oil seals – renewal

Crankshaft
Right-hand oil seal

1 Remove the crankshaft sprocket and Woodruff key as described in Section 8.

2 Measure and note the fitted depth of the oil seal.

3 Pull the oil seal from the housing using a screwdriver. Alternatively, drill a small hole in the oil seal, and use a self-tapping screw and a pair of pliers to remove it **(see illustration)**.

4 Clean the oil seal housing and the crankshaft sealing surface.

5 The seal has a Teflon lip and must not be oiled or marked. The new seal should be supplied with a protector sleeve, which fits over the end of the crankshaft to prevent any damage to the seal lip. With the sleeve in place, press the seal (open end first) into the pump to the previously-noted depth, using a suitable tube or socket **(see illustrations)**.

6 Where applicable, remove the plastic sleeve from the end of the crankshaft.

7 Refit the timing belt crankshaft sprocket as described in Section 8.

14.3 Take great care not to mark the crankshaft whilst levering out the oil seal

14.5a Slide the seal and protective sleeve over the end of the crankshaft …

14.5b … and press the seal into place

2B•18 1.6 litre DOHC engine in-car repair procedures

14.12 Slide the seal and protective sleeve over the left-hand end of the crankshaft

14.16 Drill a hole, insert a self-tapping screw, and pull the seal from place using pliers

14.18 Fit the protective sleeve and seal over the end of the camshaft

Left-hand oil seal

8 Remove the flywheel, as described in Section 16.

9 Measure and note the fitted depth of the oil seal.

10 Pull the oil seal from the housing using a screwdriver **(see illustration 14.3)**. Alternatively, drill a small hole in the oil seal, and use a self-tapping scread a pair of pliers to remove it.

11 Clean the oil seal housing and the crankshaft sealing surface.

12 The seal has a Teflon lip and must not be oiled or marked. The new seal should be supplied with a protector sleeve, which fits over the end of the crankshaft to prevent any damage to the seal lip **(see illustration)**. With the sleeve in place, press the seal (open end first) into the housing to the previously-noted depth, using a suitable tube or socket.

13 Where applicable, remove the plastic sleeve from the end of the crankshaft.

14 Refit the flywheel, as described in Section 16.

Camshaft

15 Remove the camshaft sprocket as described in Section 8. In principle there is no need to remove the timing belt completely, but remember that if the belt has been contaminated with oil, it must be renewed.

16 Pull the oil seal from the housing using a hooked instrument. Alternatively, drill a small hole in the oil seal and use a self-tapping screw and a pair of pliers to remove it **(see illustration)**.

17 Clean the oil seal housing and the camshaft sealing surface.

18 The seal has a Teflon lip and must not be oiled or marked. The new seal should be supplied with a protector sleeve, which fits over the end of the camshaft to prevent any damage to the seal lip **(see illustration)**. With the sleeve in place, press the seal (open end first) into the housing, using a suitable tube or socket, which bears only of the outer edge of the seal.

19 Refit the camshaft sprocket as described in Section 8.

20 Where necessary, fit a new timing belt with reference to Section 7.

15 Oil pressure switch and level sensor – removal and refitting

Removal

Oil pressure switch

1 The oil pressure switch is located at the front of the cylinder block, adjacent to the oil dipstick guide tube. Remove the particulate filter/catalytic converter as described in Chapter 4A Section 18.

2 Undo the retaining bolts and remove the heatshield and catalytic converter/particulate filter mounting bracket.

3 Remove the protective sleeve from the wiring plug (where applicable), then disconnect the wiring from the switch.

4 Unscrew the switch from the cylinder block, and recover the sealing washer **(see illustration)**. Be prepared for oil spillage, and if the switch is to be left removed from the engine for any length of time, plug the hole in the cylinder block.

Oil level sensor

5 The oil level sensor is located at the rear of the cylinder block. Jack up the front of the vehicle and support it securely on axle stands (see *Jacking and vehicle support*). Undo the bolts and remove the engine undershield (where fitted).

6 Reach up between the driveshaft and the cylinder block, and disconnect the sensor wiring plug **(see illustration)**.

7 Using an open-ended spanner, unscrew the sensor and withdraw it from position.

15.4 The oil pressure switch is located on the front face of the cylinder block

15.6 The oil level sensor is located on the rear face of the cylinder block

Refitting

Oil pressure switch

8 Examine the sealing washer for any signs of damage or deterioration, and if necessary renew.
9 Refit the switch, complete with washer, and tighten it to the specified torque where given.
10 Refit the engine undershield, and lower the vehicle to the ground.

Oil level sensor

11 Smear a little silicone sealant on the threads and refit the sensor to the cylinder block, tightening it securely.
12 Reconnect the sensor wiring plug.
13 Refit the engine undershield, and lower the vehicle to the ground.

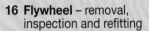

16 Flywheel – removal, inspection and refitting

Removal

1 Remove the transmission as described in, then remove the clutch assembly as described in Chapter 6 Section 6.
2 Prevent the flywheel from turning by locking the ring gear teeth **(see illustration)**. Alternatively, bolt a strap between the flywheel and the cylinder block/crankcase. Do not attempt to lock the flywheel in position using the crankshaft pulley locking tool described in Section 3. Insert a 12 mm diameter rod or drill bit through the hole in the flywheel cover casting, and into a slot in the flywheel.
3 Make alignment marks between the flywheel and crankshaft to aid refitting. Slacken and remove the flywheel retaining bolts, and remove the flywheel from the end of the crankshaft. Be careful not to drop it; it is heavy. If the flywheel locating dowel (where fitted) is a loose fit in the crankshaft end, remove it and store it with the flywheel for safekeeping. Discard the flywheel bolts; new ones must be used on refitting.

Inspection

4 Examine the flywheel for scoring of the clutch face, and for wear or chipping of the ring gear teeth. If the clutch face is scored, the flywheel may be surface-ground, but renewal is preferable. Seek the advice of an engine reconditioning specialist to see if machining is possible. If the ring gear is worn or damaged, the flywheel must be renewed, as it is not possible to renew the ring gear separately.

Refitting

5 Clean the mating surfaces of the flywheel and crankshaft. Remove any remaining locking compound from the threads of the crankshaft holes, using the correct size of tap, if available.
6 If the new flywheel retaining bolts are not supplied with their threads already

16.2 Using a tool to lock the flywheel ring gear and prevent rotation

pre-coated, apply a suitable thread-locking compound to the threads of each bolt.

Engines with normal flywheel

7 Ensure that the locating dowel is in position. Offer up the flywheel, locating it on the dowel (where fitted), and fit the new retaining bolts. Where no locating dowel is fitted, align the previously-made marks to ensure the flywheel is refitted in its original position.
8 Lock the flywheel using the method employed on dismantling, and tighten the retaining bolts to the specified torque **(see illustration)**.

Engines with dual mass flywheel

9 The dual mass flywheel is designed to reduce harshness and vibration in the action of the engine, clutch and transmission. With this type of flywheel, two flywheel centralising tools are needed (available from franchised dealers). These are screwed into two opposite flywheel bolt holes in the crankshaft. As the tools are screwed down, their conical shape centralises the flywheel with regard to the crankshaft.
10 With the flywheel centralised, fit the new bolts into the remaining flywheel holes, then lock the flywheel using the same method employed on dismantling, and tighten the bolts to the specified torque.
11 Remove the two centralising tools, fit the new bolts and tighten them to the specified torque.

All models

12 Refit the clutch as described in. Remove the flywheel locking tool, and refit the transmission as described in Chapter 6 Section 6.

17 Engine/transmission mountings – inspection and renewal

General

1 The engine/transmission mountings seldom require attention, but broken or deteriorated mountings should be renewed immediately, or the added strain placed on the driveline components may cause damage or wear.

16.8 Flywheel retaining Torx bolts

2 While separate mountings may be removed and refitted individually, if more than one is disturbed at a time – such as if the engine/transmission unit is removed from its mountings – they must be reassembled and their fasteners tightened in the position marked on removal.
3 On reassembly, the complete weight of the engine/transmission unit must not be taken by the mountings until all are correctly aligned with the marks made on removal. Tighten the engine/transmission mounting fasteners to their specified torque wrench settings.

Inspection

4 During the check, the engine/transmission unit must be raised slightly, to remove its weight from the mountings.
5 Raise the front of the vehicle, and support it securely on axle stands. Remove the engine undershield. Position a jack under the sump, with a large block of wood between the jack head and the sump, then carefully raise the engine/transmission just enough to take the weight off the mountings.

 Warning: DO NOT place any part of your body under the engine when it is supported only by a jack.

6 Check the mountings to see if the rubber is cracked, hardened or separated from the metal components. Sometimes the rubber will split right down the centre.
7 Check for relative movement between each mounting's brackets and the engine/transmission or body (use a large screwdriver or lever to attempt to move the mountings). If movement is noted, lower the engine and check-tighten the mounting fasteners.

Renewal

Note: *The following paragraphs assume the engine is supported beneath the sump as described earlier.*

Right-hand engine mounting

8 Raise the front of the vehicle, and support it securely on axle stands, then remove the engine undershield. Position a jack under the sump, with a large block of wood between the jack head and the sump, then carefully raise the jack just enough to support the weight of the engine.

17.9 Coolant expansion tank retaining nut

17.10 Reaction rod-to-vehicle body bolt

17.11 Undo the nut/bolt and move the support brackets to one side

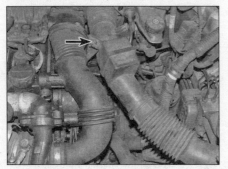

17.15 Undo the retaining bolt and remove the air intake hose

9 Undo the nut and move the coolant expansion tank to one side **(see illustration)**.
10 Undo the bolt securing the reaction rod to the bracket on the vehicle body **(see illustration)**.
11 Undo the nut/bolt release the support brackets, then undo the 3 bolts/1 nut securing the reaction rod mounting bracket to the engine mounting bracket, and manoeuvre it from place **(see illustration)**.
12 If required, undo the bolt and separate the reaction rod from the mounting bracket.
13 Undo the 3 retaining bolts and remove the

flexible mounting assembly from the vehicle body.
14 Refitting is a reversal of removal. Tighten the mounting bolts/nut to the specified torque.

Left-hand transmission mounting

15 Undo the bolt and remove the air intake hose from the air cleaner assembly **(see illustration)**.
16 If not already done, undo the retaining bolts/nuts and remove the engine undershield (where fitted). Place a jack beneath the transmission, with a block of wood on the jack head. Raise the jack until it is supporting the weight of the transmission.
17 With the transmission supported, note the position of the mounting then first unscrew the centre retaining nut. Remove the retaining nuts, then lift the transmission mounting from its position on the inner wing mounting bracket **(see illustration)**.
18 If required, undo the bolts and detach the body-side mounting bracket **(see illustration)**.
19 If required, undo the 3 retaining bolts and remove the mounting bracket from the top of the transmission.
20 Refitting is a reversal of removal. Re-align the mounting in the position noted on removal

(where applicable), then tighten all fasteners to the specified torque wrench settings.

Lower engine rear torque link

21 Firmly apply the handbrake, and then jack up the front of the vehicle and support it securely on axle stands (see *Jacking and vehicle support*). If not already done, undo the retaining bolts/nuts and remove the engine undershield (where fitted).
22 Unscrew and remove the bolts securing the rear mounting link to the subframe and the driveshaft bracket at the rear of the cylinder head **(see illustration)**. Manoeuvre the link from place.
23 Check carefully for signs of wear or damage on all components, and renew them where necessary. The rubber bush fitted to the driveshaft bearing housing is available as a separate item on some models, check with your local dealer for availability of parts. If available, the rubber bush can be pressed out of the bearing housing, noting its fitted position, and then a new one pressed back into place.
24 Refit the rear mounting torque reaction link, and tighten both its bolts to their specified torque settings.
25 Refit the engine undershield (where applicable), and then lower the vehicle to the ground.

17.17 Transmission mounting centre nut and outer retaining nuts

17.18 Body-side mounting bracket retaining bolts

17.22 Undo the rear link-to-subframe mounting bolt...

Chapter 2 Part C
2.0 litre diesel engine in-car repair procedures

Contents

Degrees of difficulty

Easy, suitable for novice with little experience	**Fairly easy,** suitable for beginner with some experience	**Fairly difficult,** suitable for competent DIY mechanic	**Difficult,** suitable for experienced DIY mechanic	**Very difficult,** suitable for expert DIY or professional

Specifications

General

Designation:		*Code
2006 to 2016.	DW10UTED / 120 Multijet	RHK
2006 to 2012.	DW10BTED4 / 140 Multijet	RHR
2008 to 2016.	DW10UTED4	RHG
2010 to 2016.	DW10CD / 130 Multijet	AHZ, RH02
2010 to 2016.	DW10CTED4 / 165 Multijet	RHH
2011 to 2016.	DW10CE	AHY

Capacity . . . . 1997 cc
Bore . . . . 85.00 mm
Stroke . . . . 88.00 mm
Direction of crankshaft rotation . . . . Clockwise (viewed from the right-hand side of vehicle)
No 1 cylinder location. . . . . At the transmission end of block
Maximum power output:
   RHK, RHG . . . . 88 kW (120 hp) @ 4000 rpm
   RHR . . . . 100 kW (136 hp) @ 4000 rpm
   AHZ, RH02 . . . . 94 kW (128 hp) @ 4000 rpm
   RHH . . . . 120 kW (163 hp) @ 3750 rpm
   AHY . . . . 72 kW (98 hp) @ 4000 rpm
Maximum torque output. . . . . 300 to 340 Nm @ 1750 rpm
Compression ratio . . . . 18.0 : 1
Emissions standard:
   Euro 4 . . . . RHK, RHG, RHR,
   Euro 5 . . . . AHZ, RH02, RHH, AHY

The engine code is stamped on a plate attached to the front of the cylinder block

Compression pressures (engine hot, at cranking speed)
Normal (new engine) . . . . 20 ± 5 bar
Maximum difference between any two cylinders . . . . 5 bar

Cylinder head bolts
Maximum length (measured under head):
   All engines . . . . 128 mm
Note: *The bolts may only be re-used once.*

Camshaft
Drive . . . . Toothed belt

Lubrication system
Oil pump type . . . . Gear-type, chain-driven off the crankshaft right-hand end
Minimum oil pressure @ 110°C:
   2000 rpm . . . . 2.0 bar
   4000 rpm . . . . 4.0 bar
Oil pressure warning switch operating pressure . . . . 0.8 bar

Torque wrench settings

	Nm	lbf ft
Big-end bearing cap nuts: *		
Stage 1	20	15
Stage 2	Angle-tighten a further 70°	
Camshaft bearing housing bolts	10	7
Camshaft position sensor bolt	6	4
Camshaft sprocket bolt:		
Stage 1	20	15
Stage 2	Angle-tighten a further 60°	
Clutch bellhousing closure plate	18	13
Coolant outlet housing	18	13
Crankshaft pulley bolt:		
Stage 1	70	52
Stage 2	Angle-tighten a further 60°	
Crankshaft right-hand oil seal housing bolts	14	10
Crankshaft sensor bolt	7	5
Cylinder head bolts:		
Stage 1	20	15
Stage 2	60	44
Stage 3	Slacken 360° (in sequence)	
Stage 4	20	15
Stage 5	60	44
Stage 6	Angle-tighten a further 220° ± 5°	
Cylinder head cover bolts	10	7
Engine mountings:		
Left-hand engine/transmission mounting:		
Bracket-to-transmission bolts	60	44
Bracket-to-transmission nut	65	48
Mounting to body/bracket	27	20
Rear engine mounting/torque rod bolts:		
Torque rod-to-driveshaft support bracket	58	43
Torque rod-to-subframe	87	64
Right-hand engine mounting:		
Reaction rod-to-vehicle body	50	37
Reaction rod-to-mounting bracket	45	33
Mounting bracket nut/bolts-to-engine bracket	60	44
Flexible mounting-to-vehicle body	30	22
Engine bracket-to-engine	55	41
Engine-to-transmission bolts	55	41
Exhaust manifold nuts	25	18
Flywheel bolts: *		
Stage 1	30	22
Stage 2	Angle-tighten a further 90°	
High-pressure fuel pump bolts	20	15
Main bearing cap bolts:		
Stage 1	25	18
Stage 2	Angle-tighten a further 60°	
Oil filter cap	25	18
Oil pressure switch	27	20

Torque wrench settings

	Nm	lbf ft
Oil level sensor	27	20
Oil pump mounting bolts	16	12
Piston oil jet spray tube bolt	10	7
Sump bolts:		
Euro 4 engines	16	12
Euro 5 engines:		
Lower section	10	7
Upper section	16	12
Sump drain plug	34	25
Timing belt idler pulley bolt	56	41
Timing belt tensioner	21	15
Timing chain tensioner bolts	6	4
Vacuum pump	9	7

Do not re-use

---

1 General Information

How to use this Chapter

1 This Chapter describes the repair procedures that can reasonably be carried out on the engine while it remains in the vehicle. If the engine has been removed from the vehicle and is being dismantled as described in Chapter 2D, any preliminary dismantling procedures can be ignored.

2 Note that, while it may be possible physically to overhaul items such as the piston/connecting rod assemblies while the engine is in the car, such tasks are not usually carried out as separate operations. Usually, several additional procedures are required (not to mention the cleaning of components and oilways); for this reason, all such tasks are classed as major overhaul procedures, and are described in Chapter 2D.

3 Chapter 2D describes the removal of the engine/transmission from the car, and the full overhaul procedures that can then be carried out.

DW engines

4 This engine is based on the well-proven DW10 SOHC direct injection engine, which has appeared in many Peugeot and Citroën vehicles. In particular, the cylinder block components are very similar but the remainder of the engine has been completely redesigned. The engine is of double overhead camshaft (DOHC) 16-valve design. The turbocharged, four-cylinder engine is mounted transversely, with the transmission mounted on the left-hand side.

5 A toothed timing belt drives the exhaust camshaft, and coolant pump. The exhaust camshaft drives the intake camshaft via a chain at the timing belt end. The camshafts operate the intake and exhaust valves via rocker arms, which are supported at their pivot ends by hydraulic self-adjusting tappets. The camshafts are supported by bearings machined directly in the cylinder head and camshaft bearing housing.

6 The high-pressure fuel pump is driven from the left-hand end of the exhaust camshaft. The high-pressure fuel pump supplies fuel to the fuel rail, and subsequently to the electronically-controlled injectors that inject the fuel directly into the combustion chambers. This design differs from the previous type where an injection pump supplies the fuel at high pressure to each injector. The earlier conventional type injection pump required fine calibration and timing, and these functions are now completed by the high-pressure pump, electronic injectors and engine management ECU.

7 The crankshaft runs in five main bearings of the usual shell type. Endfloat is controlled by thrustwashers either side of No 2 main bearing.

8 The pistons are selected to be of matching weight, and incorporate fully-floating gudgeon pins retained by circlips.

9 The oil pump is chain-driven from the right-hand end of the crankshaft.

10 Throughout the manual it is often necessary to identify the engines not only by their cubic capacity, but also by their engine code. The engine code consists of three letters (eg, RHR). The code is stamped on a plate attached to the front of the cylinder block.

Repair operations precaution

11 The engine is a complex unit with numerous accessories and ancillary components. The design of the engine compartment is such that every conceivable space has been utilised, and access to virtually all of the engine components is extremely limited. In many cases, ancillary components will have to be removed, or moved to one side, and wiring, pipes and hoses will have to be disconnected or removed from various cable clips and support brackets.

12 When working on this engine, read through the entire procedure first, look at the car and engine at the same time, and establish whether you have the necessary tools, equipment, skill and patience to proceed. Allow considerable time for any operation, and be prepared for the unexpected.

13 Because of the limited access, many of the engine photographs appearing in this Chapter were, by necessity, taken with the engine removed from the vehicle.

14 Warning: It is essential to observe strict precautions when working on the fuel system components of the engine, particularly the high-pressure side of the system. Before carrying out any engine operations that entail working on, or near, any part of the fuel system, refer to the special information given in Chapter 4A Section 2.

Operations with engine in vehicle

a) Compression pressure – testing.
b) Cylinder head cover(s) – removal and refitting.
c) Crankshaft pulley – removal and refitting.
d) Timing belt covers – removal and refitting.
e) Timing belt – removal, refitting and adjustment.
f) Timing belt tensioner and sprockets – removal and refitting.
g) Camshaft oil seal – renewal.
h) Camshafts, rocker arms and hydraulic tappets – removal, inspection and refitting.
i) Sump – removal and refitting.
j) Oil pump – removal and refitting.
k) Crankshaft oil seals – renewal.
l) Engine/transmission mountings – inspection and renewal.

2 Compression and leakdown tests – description and interpretation

Compression test

Note: *A compression tester specifically designed for diesel engines must be used for this test.*

1 When engine performance is down, or if misfiring occurs which cannot be attributed to the fuel system, a compression test can provide diagnostic clues as to the engine's condition. If the test is performed regularly, it can give warning of trouble before any other symptoms become apparent.

2 A compression tester specifically intended for diesel engines must be used, because of the higher pressures involved. The tester is connected to an adapter that screws into the glow plug or injector hole. On these engines, an adapter suitable for use in the glow plug holes will be required, so as not to disturb the fuel system components. It is unlikely to be worthwhile buying such a tester for occasional use, but it may be possible to borrow or hire one – if not, have the test performed by a garage.

3 Unless specific instructions to the contrary are supplied with the tester, observe the following points:

a) *The battery must be in a good state of charge, the air filter must be clean, and the engine should be at normal operating temperature.*

b) *All the glow plugs should be removed as described in Chapter 5B Section 2 before starting the test.*

c) *The wiring connector on the engine management system ECU must be disconnected*

4 The compression pressures measured are not so important as the balance between cylinders. Values are given in the Specifications.

5 The cause of poor compression is less easy to establish on a diesel engine than on a petrol one. The effect of introducing oil into the cylinders ('wet' testing) is not conclusive, because there is a risk that the oil will sit in the swirl chamber or in the recess on the piston crown instead of passing to the rings. However, the following can be used as a rough guide to diagnosis.

6 All cylinders should produce very similar pressures; any difference greater than that specified indicates the existence of a fault. Note that the compression should build-up quickly in a healthy engine; low compression on the first stroke, followed by gradually increasing pressure on successive strokes, indicates worn piston rings. A low compression reading on the first stroke, which does not build-up during successive strokes, indicates leaking valves or a blown head gasket (a cracked head could also be the cause). Deposits on the undersides of the valve heads can also cause low compression.

7 A low reading from two adjacent cylinders is almost certainly due to the head gasket having blown between them; the presence of coolant in the engine oil will confirm this.

8 If the compression reading is unusually high, the cylinder head surfaces, valves and pistons are probably coated with carbon deposits. If this is the case, the cylinder head should be removed and decarbonised (see Chapter 2D Section 7).

Leakdown test

9 A leakdown test measures the rate at which compressed air fed into the cylinder is lost. It is an alternative to a compression test, and in many ways it is better, since the escaping air provides easy identification of where pressure loss is occurring (piston rings, valves or head gasket).

10 The equipment needed for leakdown testing is unlikely to be available to the home mechanic. If poor compression is suspected, have the test performed by a suitably-equipped garage.

3 Engine assembly/valve timing holes – general information and usage

Note: *Do not attempt to rotate the engine whilst the crankshaft and camshaft are locked in position. If the engine is to be left in this state for a long period of time, it is a good idea to place suitable warning notices inside the vehicle, and in the engine compartment. This will reduce the possibility of the engine being accidentally cranked on the starter motor, which is likely to cause damage with the locking pins in place.*

1 Timing holes or slots are located only in the flywheel/driveplate and camshaft sprocket hub. The holes/slots are used to align the crankshaft and camshaft at the TDC position for Nos 1 and 4. This will ensure that the valve timing is maintained during operations that require removal and refitting of the timing belt. When the holes/slots are aligned with their corresponding holes in the cylinder block and cylinder head, suitable diameter bolts/pins can be inserted to lock the crankshaft and camshaft in position, preventing rotation. Note

that with the timing holes aligned, No 4 piston is at TDC on its compression stroke.

2 To align the engine assembly/valve timing holes, proceed as follows.

3 Slacken the right-hand front roadwheel bolts, chock the rear wheels then jack up the front of the vehicle and support it on axle stands (see *Jacking and vehicle support*). Remove the right-hand front roadwheel.

4 To gain access to the crankshaft pulley, to enable the engine to be turned, the wheel arch plastic liner must be removed. The liner is secured by several plastic expanding rivets. To remove the rivets, push in the centre pins a little, and then prise the clips from place. Remove the liner from under the front wing. Where necessary, unclip the coolant hoses from under the wing to improve access further. The crankshaft can then be turned using a suitable socket and extension bar fitted to the pulley bolt.

5 Remove the upper timing belt cover as described in Section 6.

6 Turn the crankshaft until the timing hole in the camshaft sprocket is aligned with the corresponding hole in the cylinder head. Note that the crankshaft must always be turned in a clockwise direction (viewed from the right-hand side of vehicle). Use a small mirror so that the position of the sprocket timing slot can be observed. When the slot is aligned with the corresponding hole in the cylinder head, the camshaft is positioned correctly.

7 Insert Citroën/Peugeot tool No (-).0188.X/ Fiat tool No. 1860.863.000 or an 8 mm diameter bolt, rod or drill through the hole in the left-hand flange of the cylinder block by the starter motor; if necessary, carefully turn the crankshaft either way until the rod enters the timing hole in the flywheel/driveplate **(see illustrations)**. Note that if a bolt/rod/drill bit is used, it must be flat (not tapered at all) at the end. If improved access is required, remove the starter motor as described in Chapter 5A Section 10.

8 Insert the 8 mm bolt, rod or drill through the hole in the camshaft sprocket hub and into engagement with the cylinder head **(see illustration)**.

9 The crankshaft and camshaft are now locked in position, preventing unnecessary rotation.

3.7a The tool fits through the hole in the cylinder block flange …

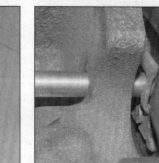

3.7b … and into a hole in the rear of the flywheel

3.8 Fit the tool through the hole in the exhaust camshaft sprocket, into the timing hole in the cylinder head

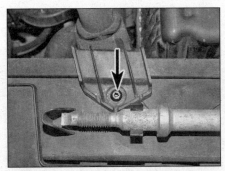

4.2a Drill out the rivet or undo the bolt securing the drain hose to the bonnet slam panel

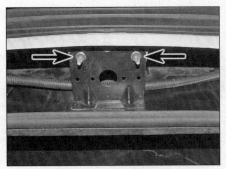

4.2b Undo the 2 nuts at the top…

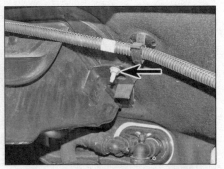

4.2c …slacken the nut each side and remove the cabin air intake cowling

---

4 Cylinder head cover/intake manifold – removal and refitting

Removal

1 Disconnect the battery negative lead as described in Chapter 5A Section 4.

2 Drill out the rivet/undo the bolt, release the water drain hose, then undo the 4 retaining nuts and remove the cabin air intake cowling **(see illustrations)**.

3 Remove the air filter assembly as described in Chapter 4A Section 5, then if improved access is required, undo the retaining nut and move the coolant expansion tank to one side **(see illustration)**.

Euro 4 engines

4 To improve access, release the clamps and remove the turbocharger intake hose.

5 Release the clamp, undo the bolts and remove the metal EGR pipe from the EGR cooler to the intake manifold **(see illustration)**.

6 The cylinder head cover is integral with the intake manifold. Disconnect the wiring plugs from the fuel injectors, glow plugs and turbocharger boost pressure/temperature sensor.

7 Disconnect the wiring plug, and then unscrew the camshaft position sensor from the cover **(see illustration)**.

8 Release the clamps and disconnect the breather hoses from the cover/manifold **(see illustration)**.

9 Undo the bolts securing the upper timing belt cover to the cylinder head cover/intake manifold **(see illustration)**.

10 Disconnect the wiring connectors and disconnect the air intake hose(s) from the front of the intake manifold **(see illustration)**.

11 Undo the manifold/cover retaining bolts in the reverse of the sequence shown in illustration 4.30a. Check around the manifold/cover for any wiring or hoses, and then remove the manifold/cover and discard the gaskets. New gaskets must be used on refitting.

4.3 Undo the nut and move the expansion tank to one side

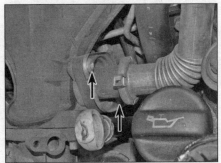

4.5 Undo the bolts securing the EGR pipe to the manifold

4.7 Undo the bolt and remove the camshaft position sensor

4.8 Release the breather hose clamp

4.9 Undo the upper cover bolt

4.10 Disconnect the wiring plug and release the hose clamp

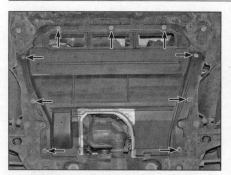

4.12 Engine undershield fasteners

4.13 Pull the insulation material upwards to release the mountings

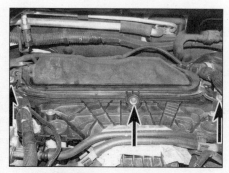

4.14 Rubber cover retaining bolts

Euro 5 engines

12 Raise the front of the vehicle and support it securely on axle stands (see *Jacking and vehicle support*). Undo the fasteners and remove the engine undershield **(see illustration)**.

13 Pull up the sound insulation material from the top of the engine **(see illustration)**.

14 Undo the 3 bolts and remove the rubber cover from the top of the engine **(see illustration)**.

15 Remove the throttle body as described in Chapter 4A Section 12.

16 Undo the unions and remove the high-pressure fuel pipes from the common rail to each injector – refer to Chapter 4A Section 11.

17 Undo the unions and remove the high-pressure fuel pipe from the pump to the common rail – refer to Chapter 4A Section 10.

18 Remove the camshaft position sensor as described in Chapter 4A Section 12.

19 Note their fitted positions, then disconnect the wiring plugs from the injectors, fuel pressure sensor, and fuel heater, then release the wiring loom from the manifold.

20 Slide out the green locking clips and pull the return pipes from each injector **(see illustration)**. Disconnect the

return pipe from the pump in the same manner. Examine the pipe O-ring seals and renew if necessary.

21 Undo the bolts and remove the fuel (common) rail from the cylinder head cover **(see illustration)**.

22 Undo the screws and disconnect the EGR pipe from the EGR valve **(see illustrations)**. Access to the upper bolt is extremely limited, and a long-reach Allen key/bit will be required.

23 Disconnect the fuel supply and return pipes at the quick release connectors, then unclip them from the manifold **(see illustrations)**.

4.20 Slide out the locking clip and disconnect the return pipes

4.21 Common rail retaining bolts

4.22a Use a long reach Allen key/bit to unscrew the upper bolt

4.22b Unscrew the EGR pipe lower bolt

4.23a Prise up the center section, press down the outer sections, pull the pipe from the connector…

4.23b …then unclip the pipes from the manifold

4.24a The heatshield is secured by 1 bolt at the right-hand end...

4.24b ...1 at the left-hand end...

4.24c ...and 1 bolt in the centre

4.25 Disconnect the drain hose

4.26a Remove the vacuum solenoids...

4.26b ...and disconnect the vacuum pipes

24 Undo the 3 bolts and remove the heatshield at the rear of the cylinder head **(see illustrations)**. Access is extremely limited.
25 Disconnect the drain hose from the left-hand rear corner of the cylinder head cover **(see illustration)**.
26 Undo the retaining nuts/bolts and move the vacuum solenoids on the rear of the cover/manifold to one side **(see illustrations)**. Note their fitted positions, then disconnect the vacuum pipes from the manifold.
27 Undo the manifold/cover retaining bolts in the reverse of the sequence shown in illustration 4.30b. Check around the manifold/cover for any wiring or hoses, and then remove the manifold/cover and discard the gaskets. New gaskets must be used on refitting **(see illustration)**.

Refitting

28 Clean the sealing surfaces of the manifold/cover and the cylinder head.
29 Fit the new seals/gasket to the intake manifold/cover, and then fit it to the cylinder head **(see illustration)**. Use a little petroleum jelly on the manifold O-rings to ease reassembly (where applicable).

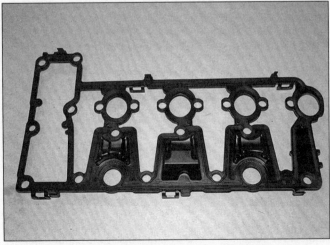

4.27 Intake manifold/cover gasket – Euro 5 engines shown

4.29 Renew the manifold seals

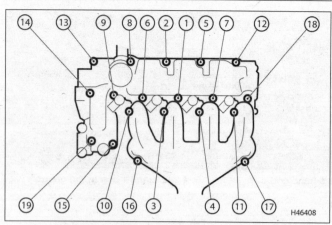

4.30a Intake manifold/cylinder head cover bolt tightening sequence – Euro 4 engines

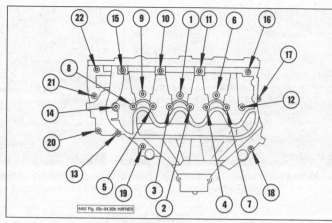

4.30b Intake manifold/cylinder head cover bolt tightening sequence – Euro 5 engines

30 Tighten the bolts to the specified torque in sequence **(see illustrations)**.

31 The remainder of refitting is a reversal of removal, noting the following points:

a) *Tighten all fasteners to their specified torque.*

b) *Before refitting the timing belt upper cover, adjust the camshaft position sensor air gap as described in Chapter 4A Section 12.*

5 Crankshaft pulley – removal and refitting

Removal

1 Remove the auxiliary drivebelt as described in Chapter 1 Section 20.

2 Position the camshaft and crankshaft as described in Section 3. **Note:** *It is essential that the crankshaft and camshaft timing pins are in place as described in Section 3. This is because on these engines, the crankshaft sprocket has a wider keyway to allow it to rotate a little independently of the crankshaft during the belt tensioning procedure. Failure to lock the crankshaft and camshaft could result in the timing being lost.*

3 To prevent crankshaft turning whilst the pulley retaining bolt is being slackened, the flywheel/driveplate ring gear can be locked using (Citroën tool No (-).0188.F/Fiat tool

No. 1.870.890.000) or a suitable tool made from steel angle. Remove the starter motor as described in Chapter 5A Section 10, and bolt the tool to the bellhousing flange so it engages with the ring gear teeth **(see illustration)**. Do not attempt to lock the pulley by only inserting a bolt/drill through the timing hole.

4 Where applicable, prise out the cover from the centre of the crankshaft pulley **(see illustration)**.

5 Using a suitable socket and extension bar, unscrew the retaining bolt, remove the washer, then slide the pulley off the end of the crankshaft **(see illustration)**. If the pulley is a tight fit, it can be drawn off the crankshaft using a suitable puller. If a puller is being used, refit the pulley retaining bolt without the washer, to avoid damaging the crankshaft as the puller is tightened.

Refitting

6 Ensure the camshaft and crankshaft are positioned at TDC as described previously, and the flywheel/driveplate ring gear is locked in position, as described in paragraph 3.

7 Thoroughly clean the threads of the pulley retaining bolt, then apply a coat of locking compound to the bolt threads. Citroën/Peugeot/Fiat/Toyota recommend the use of Loctite; in the absence of this, any good-quality locking compound may be used.

8 Refit the crankshaft pulley retaining bolt and washer. Tighten the bolt to the specified torque, then through the specified angle.

9 Where applicable, press the cover back into the centre of the crankshaft pulley.

10 Remove the crankshaft, camshaft and flywheel/driveplate locking tools.

11 Refit and tension the auxiliary drivebelt as described in Chapter 1 Section 20.

6 Timing belt covers – removal and refitting

⚠ *Warning: Refer to the precautionary information contained in Section 1 before proceeding.*

Removal

Upper cover

1 Drill out the rivet/undo the bolt, release the water drain hose, then undo the 4 retaining nuts and remove the cabin air intake ducting **(see illustrations 4.2a, 4.2b and 4.2c)**.

2 Release the two fuel hoses from the retaining clips at the right-hand end of the cylinder head.

3 Move the electrical harness to one side,

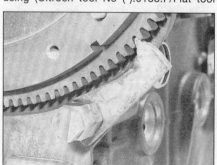

5.3 Use a fabricated tool similar to this to lock the flywheel ring gear and prevent crankshaft rotation

5.4 Prise the pulley centre cover from place

5.5 Undo the bolt and remove the crankshaft pulley

then undo the screws/nut and remove the upper timing belt cover **(see illustration)**.

Lower cover

4 Remove the upper cover as described previously.

5 Remove the crankshaft pulley as described in Section 5.

6 Carefully pull the crankshaft sensor signal disc from the crankshaft **(see illustration)**. If the disc is reluctant to move, screw in two 6.0 mm bolts into the threaded holes in the disc and force it from place.

7 Undo the bolts and remove the lower timing belt cover.

Refitting

8 Refitting of all the covers is a reversal of the relevant removal procedure, ensuring that each cover section is correctly located, and that the cover retaining bolts are securely tightened. Ensure that all disturbed hoses are reconnected and retained by their relevant clips.

---

7 Timing belt – removal, inspection, refitting and tensioning

General

1 The timing belt drives the exhaust camshaft and coolant pump from a toothed sprocket on the end of the crankshaft. If the belt breaks or slips in service, the pistons are likely to hit the valve heads, resulting in expensive damage.

2 The timing belt should be renewed at the specified intervals, or earlier if it is contaminated with oil or at all noisy in operation (a 'scraping' noise due to uneven wear).

3 If the timing belt is being removed, it is a wise precaution to check the condition of the coolant pump at the same time (check for signs of coolant leakage). This may avoid the need to remove the timing belt again at a later stage should the coolant pump fail.

Removal

4 Chock the rear wheels then jack up the front

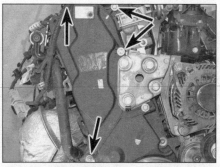
6.3 Upper timing belt cover fasteners

of the vehicle and support it on axle stands (see *Jacking and vehicle support*). Remove the front right-hand roadwheel, wheel arch liner (to expose the crankshaft pulley), and the engine undershield. The wheel arch liner is secured by several plastic expanding rivets, or push-in clips. Push the centre pins in a little then prise the rivet from place. Undo the retaining screws and remove the engine undershield.

5 Remove the crankshaft pulley as described in Section 5, then use 6.0 mm bolts to draw the sensor disc from the end of the crankshaft **(see illustration 6.6)**.

6 Remove the upper and lower timing belt covers as described in Section 6.

7 Ensure the engine is positioned at TDC as described in Section 3, with the camshaft and crankshaft locking tools described in place.

8 Loosen the bolt on the tensioner pulley, and turn the tensioner clockwise to release the tension on the timing belt. Use an Allen key in the hole provided, to turn the tensioner bracket against the spring tension. Retighten the bolt sufficiently to hold the tensioner in its released position; do not fully-tighten the bolt in this position.

9 Mark the timing belt with an arrow to indicate its running direction as a reference for refitting. Remove the belt from the sprockets.

Inspection

10 Renew the belt as a matter of course, regardless of its apparent condition. The

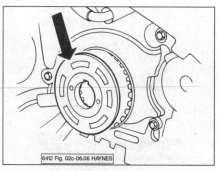
6.6 Sensor signal disc

cost of a new belt is nothing compared with the cost of repairs should the belt break in service. If signs of oil contamination are found, trace the source of the oil leak and rectify it. Wash down the engine timing belt area and all related components, to remove all traces of oil. Check that the tensioner and idler pulleys rotate freely without any sign of roughness, and also check that the coolant pump rotates freely. If necessary, renew these items.

Refitting and tensioning

11 Commence refitting by ensuring that the TDC timing pins are still in position correctly.

12 Centre the crankshaft sprocket by inserting Citroën/Peugeot tool (-).0188.AH/ Fiat tool 2.000.020.300 either side of the crankshaft key, and into the keyway in the sprocket. In the absence of the tool, position the sprocket centrally, ensuring a gap exists each side of the key **(see illustration)**.

13 Fit the timing belt to the camshaft sprocket. Citroën technicians use a clip to retain the belt on the sprocket; if necessary, use a plastic cable-tie to hold it.

14 Continue to fit the belt in the following order, keeping the belt taut as it's fitted around the idler pulley and the crankshaft sprocket **(see illustration)** :

a) Idler pulley.
b) Crankshaft sprocket.
c) Coolant pump sprocket.
d) Tensioner pulley.

7.12 Position the crankshaft sprocket so that equal gaps exists each side of the key

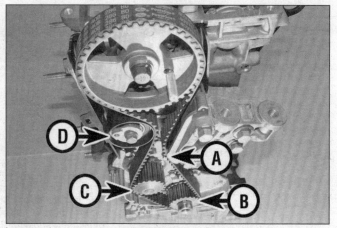
7.14 Timing belt routing

7.16a Use an Allen key in the tensioner

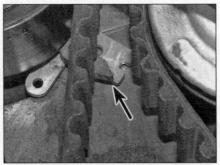

7.16b Rotate the tensioner anti-clockwise until the index pointer is aligned with the lower edge of the reference plate.

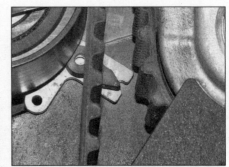

7.21 Align the index pointer with the notch in the reference plate

15 Remove the tool/cable-tie securing the belt to the camshaft sprocket, and the crankshaft sprocket centring tool.

16 Slacken the tensioner pulley retaining bolt, then using an Allen key, rotate the tensioner anti-clockwise until the index pointer is aligned with the lower, outside edge of the reference plate **(see illustrations)**. Tighten the tensioner pulley retaining bolt to the specified torque.

17 Ensure the crankshaft/flywheel ring gear locking tool is still in place, then refit the lower timing belt cover, sensor disc and crankshaft pulley, and tighten the retaining bolt to 70 Nm (52 lbf ft).

18 Remove the camshaft sprocket and crankshaft locking/timing tools.

19 Rotate the crankshaft 10 times in the normal direction of rotation, and refit the camshaft sprocket and crankshaft locking/timing tools.

TOOL TiP

To make a sprocket holding tool, obtain two lengths of steel strip about 6.0 mm thick by about 30 mm wide or similar, one 600 mm long, the other 200 mm long (all dimensions approximate). Bolt the two strips together to form a forked end, leaving the bolt slack so that the shorter strip can pivot freely. At the other end of each 'prong' of the fork, drill a suitable hole and fit a nut and bolt to engage with the spokes or holes in the sprocket. It may be necessary to cut-off or grind the side slightly to allow them to fit in the sprocket holes.

20 With the flywheel ring gear locked, slacken the crankshaft pulley bolt.

21 Slacken the timing belt tensioner retaining bolt, then use an Allen key to rotate the tensioner clockwise until the index pointer aligns with the notch in the reference plate **(see illustration)**. Tighten the tensioner pulley bolt to the specified torque.

22 Tighten the crankshaft pulley bolt to 70 Nm (52 lbf ft), at this stage.

23 Remove the camshaft sprocket and crankshaft/flywheel ring gear locking/aligning tools, and rotate the crankshaft 2 complete revolutions in the normal direction of rotation (clockwise).

24 Check that the camshaft sprocket and crankshaft/flywheel aligning tools can still be inserted, and that the tensioner index pointer is still aligned with the notch in the reference plate. If necessary, repeat the tensioning procedure until the pointer and notch align.

25 Lock the flywheel ring gear using the previously described tool and undo the crankshaft pulley bolt.

26 Apply a little thread-locking compound to the threads, then tighten the crankshaft pulley retaining bolt to the specified torque.

27 Remove the camshaft sprocket and crankshaft/flywheel ring gear locking/aligning tools.

28 The remainder of refitting is a reversal of removal.

8 Timing belt sprockets and tensioner – removal and refitting

Camshaft sprocket

Removal

1 Remove the timing belt as described in Section 7.

2 Remove the locking tool from the camshaft sprocket, then slacken the sprocket retaining bolt. To prevent the camshaft rotating as the bolt is slackened, Citroën technicians use tool No 6016-T. In the absence of this tool, fabricate a substitute as described (see **Tool Tip**). Do not attempt to use the camshaft sprocket locking tool to prevent the sprocket

from rotating whilst the bolt is slackened. **Note:** *Take care not to damage the sensor signal disc integral with the sprocket.*

3 Remove the bolt, and slide the sprocket from the camshaft. If the Woodruff key is a loose fit in the camshaft, remove it for safekeeping. Examine the camshaft oil seal for signs of oil leakage and, if necessary, renew it as described in Section 14.

4 Clean the camshaft sprocket thoroughly, and renew it if there are any signs of wear, damage or cracks.

Refitting

5 Where applicable, refit the Woodruff key to the end of the camshaft, and then refit the camshaft sprocket and hub.

6 Refit the sprocket retaining bolt and washer. Tighten the bolt to the specified torque, preventing the camshaft from turning as during removal.

7 Align the timing slot in the camshaft sprocket with the hole in the cylinder head and refit the tool locking the camshaft in position.

8 Refit the timing belt as described in Section 7.

Crankshaft sprocket

Removal

9 Remove the timing belt as described in Section 7.

10 Slide the sprocket off the end of the crankshaft and collect the Woodruff key **(see illustrations)**.

8.10a Slide off the crankshaft pulley ...

2.0 litre diesel engine in-car repair procedures

8.10b ... and recover the Woodruff key

9.7 Lift up the upper chain guide rail and insert a 2.0 mm diameter rod/drill bit into the hole in the tensioner body

9.8 Undo the tensioner retaining bolts

11 Examine the crankshaft oil seal for signs of oil leakage and, if necessary, renew it as described in Section 14.

12 Clean the crankshaft sprocket thoroughly, and renew it if there are any signs of wear, damage or cracks.

Refitting

13 Refit the Woodruff key to the end of the crankshaft, and then refit the crankshaft sprocket (with the flange nearest the cylinder block).

14 Refit the timing belt as described in Section 7.

Coolant pump sprocket

15 The coolant pump sprocket is integral with the pump, and cannot be removed.

Tensioner pulley

Removal

16 Remove the timing belt as described in Section 7.

17 Remove the tensioner pulley retaining bolt, and slide the pulley off its mounting stud.

18 Clean the tensioner pulley, but do not use any strong solvent that may enter the pulley bearings. Check that the pulley rotates freely, with no sign of stiffness or free play. Renew the pulley if there is any doubt about its condition, or if there are any obvious signs of wear or damage.

Refitting

19 Refit the tensioner pulley, and insert the retaining bolt.

20 Refit the timing belt as described in Section 7.

Idler pulley

Removal

21 Remove the timing belt as described in Section 7.

22 Undo the retaining bolt and withdraw the idler pulley from the engine.

23 Clean the idler pulley, but do not use any strong solvent, which may enter the bearings. Check that the pulley rotates freely, with no sign of stiffness or free play. Renew the idler pulley if there is any doubt about its condition, or if there are any obvious signs of wear or damage.

Refitting

24 Locate the idler pulley on the engine, and fit the retaining bolt. Tighten the bolt to the specified torque.

25 Fit the timing belt around the idler pulley, and tension the timing belt as described in Section 7.

---

9 Camshafts, rocker arms and hydraulic tappets – removal, inspection and refitting

Removal

1 Remove the cylinder head cover as described in Section 4.

2 Remove the camshaft sprocket as described in Section 8.

3 Slacken the retaining clamps and disconnect the air intake hose from the left-hand end of the cylinder head. Remove the intercooler air duct from the left-hand end of the cylinder head.

4 Remove the high-pressure fuel pump (Chapter 4A Section 9), and fuel injectors (Chapter 4A Section 11).

5 Disconnect the vacuum pipe from the brake vacuum pump on the left-hand end of the cylinder head.

6 Remove the vacuum pump from the cylinder head with reference to Chapter 9 Section 22.

7 Compress the timing chain tensioner and insert a 2.0 mm drill bit into the tensioner body to lock the piston in the compressed state **(see illustration)**.

8 Undo the bolts and remove the timing chain tensioner **(see illustration)**.

9 Working in a spiral pattern from the outside to the inside, progressively loosen the camshaft bearing cap housing bolts until they can be removed.

10 Withdraw the bearing cap housing from the cylinder head. The housing is likely to be initially tight to release, as it is located by two dowels on the forward facing side of the cylinder head. If necessary, very carefully prise up the housing using a screwdriver inserted in the slotted lug adjacent to each dowel location. Once the bearing housing is free, lift it squarely from the cylinder head. The camshaft will rise up slightly under the pressure of the valve springs – be careful it doesn't tilt and jam in the cylinder head or bearing housing section.

11 Check that the camshafts and chain are marked in relation to each other – the chain should have two black or copper links that align with marks on the teeth. If necessary, mark the chain and teeth with dabs of paint. The marks on the teeth are the most important as they determine the valve timing, however the chain links can be marked as they are 7 links (inclusive) apart **(see illustrations)**.

12 Simultaneously, lift the camshafts and

9.11a The coloured links on the chain align with the marks on the camshaft sprockets ...

9.11b ... the mark on the sprockets is a dot and a line

9.14 Lift out the rocker arms with the hydraulic tappets

9.23 Insert the tappets and rocker arms into their original locations

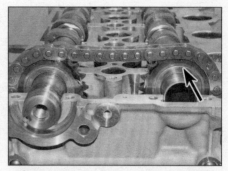

9.26 Position the camshafts so the mark on the intake camshaft is in the 12 o'clock position

chain from the cylinder head. Release the camshafts from the chain.

13 Either get sixteen small, clean plastic containers, and number them 1 to 16, or divide a larger container into sixteen compartments.

14 Lift out each rocker arm and release it from the spring clip on the tappet (see illustration). Place the rocker arms in their respective positions in the box or containers.

15 A compartmentalised container filled with engine oil is now required to retain the hydraulic tappets while they are removed from the cylinder head. Using a rubber sucker, withdraw each hydraulic tappet and place it in the container, keeping them each identified for correct refitting. The tappets must be totally submerged in the oil to prevent air entering them.

Inspection

16 Inspect the cam lobes and the camshaft bearing journals for scoring or other visible evidence of wear. Once the surface hardening of the cam lobes has been eroded, wear will occur at an accelerated rate. **Note:** *If these symptoms are visible on the tips of the camshaft lobes, check the corresponding rocker arm, as it will probably be worn as well.*

17 Examine the condition of the bearing surfaces in the cylinder head and camshaft bearing housing. If wear is evident, the cylinder head and bearing housing will both have to be renewed, as they are a matched assembly.

18 Inspect the rocker arms and tappets for scuffing, cracking or other damage and renew any components as necessary. Also check the condition of the tappet bores in the cylinder head. As with the camshafts, any wear in this area will necessitate cylinder head renewal.

Refitting

19 Thoroughly clean the sealant from the mating surfaces of the cylinder head and camshaft bearing housing. Use a suitable liquid gasket dissolving agent together with a soft putty knife; do not use a metal scraper or the faces will be damaged. As there is no conventional gasket used, the cleanliness of the mating faces is of the utmost importance.

20 Clean off any oil, dirt or grease from both components and dry with a clean lint-free cloth. Ensure that all the oilways are completely clean.

21 To prevent any possibility of the valves contacting the pistons as the camshaft is refitted, remove the locking pin/drill from the flywheel/driveplate and turn the crankshaft a quarter turn in the opposite direction to normal rotation (ie, anti-clockwise), to position all the pistons at mid-stroke.

22 Liberally lubricate the hydraulic tappet bores in the cylinder head with clean engine oil.

23 Insert the hydraulic tappets into their original bores in the cylinder head unless they have been renewed (see illustration).

24 Lubricate the rocker arms and place them over their respective tappets and valve stems. Ensure that the ends of the rocker arms engage with the spring clips on the tappets.

25 Lubricate the camshaft bearing journals in the cylinder head sparingly with oil, taking care not to allow the oil to spill over onto the camshaft bearing housing contact areas.

26 Engage the camshafts with the chain, making sure that the coloured links are aligned with the marked teeth, fit the tensioner between the chain runs, and then lower them into position. The longer exhaust camshaft must go at the rear of the cylinder head. Rotate the camshaft so the mark on the intake camshaft is in the 12 o'clock position (see illustration).

27 Fit a new camshaft oil seal as described in Section 14.

28 Refit the camshaft sprocket, lightly tighten the retaining bolt, and then fit the camshaft sprocket locking tool.

29 Check the marks on the camshaft sprockets still align with the coloured links on the chain.

30 Ensure that the mating faces of the cylinder head and camshaft bearing housing are clean and free of any oil or grease.

31 Sparingly apply a bead of sealant (Loctite 518) to the mating face of the camshaft bearing housing, taking care not to allow the product to contaminate the camshaft bearing journal areas (see illustrations).

32 Lower the housing into place, then insert

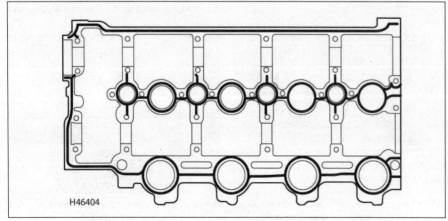

H46404

9.31a Apply a thin bead of sealant as indicated by the heavy black line

9.31b We inserted a tapered rod into the tensioner oil supply hole to prevent any sealant from entering

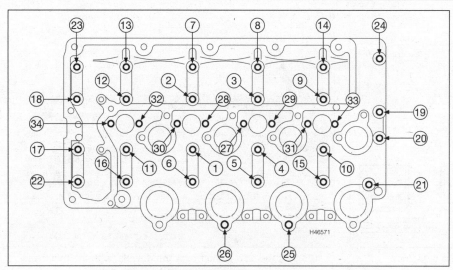

9.32 Camshaft bearing cap housing bolts tightening sequence

and tighten the camshaft bearing housing bolts to the specified torque, in sequence **(see illustration)**.

33 Refit the chain tensioner, tighten the retaining bolts to the specified torque, then pull out the locking pin and allow the tensioner to act upon the chain.

34 The remainder of refitting is a reversal of removal.

10 Cylinder head – removal and refitting

Note: *This is an involved procedure, and it is suggested that the Section is read thoroughly before starting work. To aid refitting, make notes on the locations of all relevant brackets and the routing of hoses and cables before removal.*

Removal

1 Disconnect the battery negative lead as described in Chapter 5A Section 4.
2 Remove the right-hand driveshaft as described in Chapter 8 Section 2.
3 Remove the wiper motor assembly as described in Chapter 12 Section 14.
4 Drain the cooling system as described in Chapter 1 Section 23.
5 Remove the camshafts, rocker arms and hydraulic tappets as described in Section 9.
6 Remove the fuel filter and bracket.
7 Remove the common (fuel) rail as described in Chapter 4A Section 10.
8 Support the engine from underneath, then remove the right-hand engine mounting assembly as described in Section 17.
9 Note their fitted positions and routing, then disconnect all coolant and vacuum hoses from the cylinder head.
10 Undo the bolts/studs securing the coolant outlet housing to the left-hand end of the

cylinder head. Pull the housing away from the cylinder head **(see illustration)**.
11 Remove the turbocharger and exhaust manifold as described in Section and Chapter 4A Section 14.
12 Progressively slacken the cylinder head bolts, in the reverse order to that shown for tightening **(see illustration 10.32)**.
13 When all the bolts are loose, unscrew them fully and remove them from the cylinder head.
14 Release the cylinder head from the cylinder block and location dowels by rocking it. The Citroën/Peugeot/Fiat tool for doing this consists simply of two metal rods with 90-degree angled ends. Do not prise between the mating faces of the cylinder head and block, as this may damage the gasket faces.
15 Lift the cylinder head from the block, and recover the gasket.

Preparation for refitting

16 The mating faces of the cylinder head and cylinder block must be perfectly clean before refitting the head. The manufacturers recommend the use of a scouring agent for this purpose, but acceptable results can be achieved by using a hard plastic or wood scraper to remove all traces of gasket and

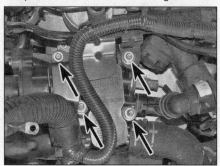

10.10 Undo the nuts and remove the coolant outlet housing

carbon. The same method can be used to clean the piston crowns. Take particular care to avoid scoring or gouging the cylinder head/cylinder block mating surfaces during the cleaning operations, as aluminium alloy is easily damaged. Make sure that the carbon is not allowed to enter the oil and water passages – this is particularly important for the lubrication system, as carbon could block the oil supply to the engine's components. Using adhesive tape and paper, seal the water, oil and bolt holes in the cylinder block. To prevent carbon entering the gap between the pistons and bores, smear a little grease in the gap. After cleaning each piston, use a small brush to remove all traces of grease and carbon from the gap, and then wipe away the remainder with a clean rag.

17 Check the mating surfaces of the cylinder block and the cylinder head for nicks, deep scratches and other damage. If slight, they may be removed carefully with a file, but if excessive, machining may be the only alternative to renewal. If warpage of the cylinder head gasket surface is suspected, use a straight-edge to check it for distortion. Refer to Chapter 2D Section 7 if necessary.
18 Thoroughly clean the threads of the cylinder head bolt holes in the cylinder block. Ensure that the bolts run freely in their threads, and that all traces of oil and water are removed from each bolt hole. If possible, use a M12 x 150 tap to clean out the threads.
19 Measure the length of the cylinder head bolts from the underside of the bolt head to the tip of the threads. The bolts must be renewed if their length exceeds 128 mm. The manufacturers insist that the bolts may only be re-used once.
Note: *Given the stresses applied to the cylinder head bolts, we consider it prudent to renew the bolts regardless of the apparent condition.*

Gasket selection

20 Turn the crankshaft until pistons 1 and 4 are at TDC (Top Dead Centre). Position a dial test indicator (dial gauge) on the cylinder block adjacent to the rear of No 1 piston, and zero it on the block face **(see illustration)**. Transfer the probe to the crown of No 1 piston (10.0 mm in from the rear edge), and then

10.20 Zero the DTI on the gasket face

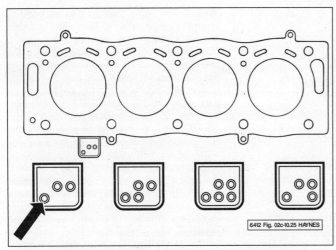

10.25 Gasket identification holes – Euro 5 engines

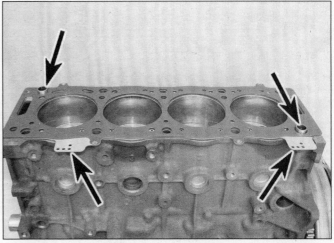

10.28 Fit the new gasket over the dowels, with the thickness identification holes at the front

slowly turn the crankshaft back-and-forth past TDC, noting the highest reading on the indicator. Record this reading as protrusion A.
21 Repeat the check described in paragraph 20, this time 10.0 mm in from the front edge of the No 1 piston crown. Record this reading as protrusion B.
22 Add protrusion A to protrusion B, then divide the result by 2 to obtain an average reading for piston No 1.
23 Repeat the procedure described in paragraphs 20 to 22 on piston 4, then turn the crankshaft through 180° and carry out the procedure on the piston Nos 2 and 3. Check that there is a maximum difference of 0.07 mm protrusion between any two pistons.
24 If a dial test indicator is not available, piston protrusion may be measured using a straight-edge and feeler blades or Vernier calipers. However, this is much less accurate, and cannot therefore be recommended.
25 Note the greatest piston protrusion measurement, and use this to determine the correct cylinder head gasket from the following table. The series of holes on the front side of the gasket are used for thickness identification **(see illustration)**.

Euro 4 engines

Piston protrusion	Gasket identification
0.55 to 0.60 mm	1 hole
0.61 to 0.65 mm	2 holes
0.66 to 0.70 mm	3 holes
0.71 to 0.75 mm	4 holes

Euro 5 engines

Piston protrusion	Gasket identification (arrangement of holes at front edge)
0.55 to 0.60 mm	1 – 0 – 0
0.601 to 0.650 mm	1 – 1 – 0
0.651 to 0.700 mm	1 – 1 – 1
0.701 to 0.750 mm	1 – 0 – 1

Refitting

26 Turn the crankshaft and position Nos 1 and 4 pistons at TDC, then turn the crankshaft a quarter turn (90°) anti-clockwise.
27 Thoroughly clean the surfaces of the cylinder head and block.
28 Make sure that the locating dowels are in place, then fit the correct gasket the right way round on the cylinder block **(see illustration)**.
29 Carefully lower the cylinder head onto the gasket and block, making sure that it locates correctly onto the dowels.
30 Apply a light smear of grease to the threads, and to the underside of the heads, of the cylinder head bolts.
31 Carefully insert the cylinder head bolts into their holes (do not drop them in) and initially finger-tighten them.
32 Working progressively and in sequence, tighten the cylinder head bolts to their Stage 1 torque setting, using a torque wrench and suitable socket **(see illustration)**.
33 Once all the bolts have been tightened to their Stage 1 torque setting, working again in the specified sequence, tighten each bolt following the Stages given in the Specifications. Finally, angle-tighten the bolts through the specified Stage 6 angle. It is recommended that an angle-measuring gauge be used during this stage of tightening,

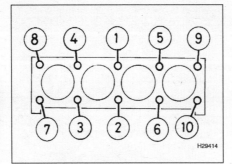

10.32 Cylinder head bolt tightening sequence

to ensure accuracy. **Note:** *Retightening of the cylinder head bolts after running the engine is not required.*
34 The remainder of refitting is a reversal of removal, noting the following points.
a) *Use a new seal when refitting the coolant outlet housing.*
b) *Refit the camshaft position sensor and set the air gap with reference to Chapter 4A Section 12.*
c) *Tighten all fasteners to the specified torque where given.*
d) *Refill the cooling system as described in Chapter 1 Section 23.*
e) *The engine may run erratically for the first few miles, until the engine management ECU relearns its stored values.*

11 Sump – removal and refitting

Removal

1 Drain the engine oil, then clean and refit the engine oil drain plug, tightening it securely. If the engine is nearing its service interval when the oil and filter are due for renewal, it is recommended that the filter is also removed, and a new one fitted. After reassembly, the engine can then be refilled with fresh oil. Refer to Chapter 1 Section 6 for further information.
2 Chock the rear wheels then jack up the front of the vehicle and support it on axle stands (see *Jacking and vehicle support*). Undo the retaining bolts/nuts and remove the engine undershield (where applicable).
3 On models with air conditioning, where the compressor is mounted onto the side of the sump, remove the drivebelt as described in Chapter 1 Section 20. Unbolt the compressor, and position it clear of the sump. Support the weight of the compressor by tying it to the vehicle, to prevent any excess strain being placed on the compressor lines. Do

11.4 Remove the charge air pipe securing bolts

11.7a Undo the screws securing the sump lower section

11.7b Carefully insert a putty knife between the lower and upper sump sections

not disconnect the refrigerant lines from the compressor (refer to the warnings given in Chapter 3 Section 11).

Euro 4 engines

4 Slacken the clamps, undo the bolts and remove the charge air pipe from under the sump **(see illustration)**.

5 Where necessary, disconnect the wiring connector from the oil temperature sender unit, which is screwed into the sump.

Euro 5 engines

Note: *A long 6 mm Allen (hexagonal) key/bit will be required to remove the upper sump retaining bolts.*

6 Release the clamps and disconnect the rubber hoses from the supply pipe between the turbocharger and the intercooler, then undo the retaining bolts and remove the supply pipe.

7 Undo the retaining screws and remove the lower section of the sump **(see illustrations)**. Note that the lower section will be reluctant to release due to the use of silicone sealant. Use a putty knife or similar carefully inserted between the lower and upper sections of the sump. Ease the knife along the joint until the lower section of the sump is released.

Caution: Be prepared for oil spillage!

8 Disconnect the oil level sensor wiring plug, then unscrew the sensor from the sump.

9 Release the clamp and disconnect the oil filler hose from the upper section of the sump **(see illustration)**.

10 Undo the lower bolt securing the catalytic

11.9 Release the clamp and disconnect the oil filler hose

converter/particulate filter bracket to the sump.

11 Undo the 2 retaining bolts and pull the engine oil level dipstick guide tube from the sump.

12 Undo the bolt and remove the oil decanter pipe **(see illustration)**.

All engines

13 Where applicable, remove the bolt securing the air conditioning compressor mounting bracket to the sump **(see illustration)**.

14 Progressively slacken and remove all the sump retaining bolts **(see illustrations)**. Since the sump bolts vary in length, remove each bolt in turn, and store it in its correct fitted order by pushing it through a clearly marked cardboard template. This will avoid the possibility of installing the bolts in the wrong locations on refitting.

11.12 Oil decanter retaining bolt

15 Try to break the joint by striking the sump with the palm of your hand, then lower and withdraw the sump from under the car. If the sump is stuck (which is quite likely) use a putty knife or similar carefully inserted between sump and block. Ease the knife along the joint until the sump is released. While the sump is removed, take the opportunity to check the oil pump pick-up/strainer for signs of clogging or splitting. If necessary, remove the pump as described in Section 12, and clean or renew the strainer.

16 If required, remove the oil baffle plate.

Refitting

17 Clean all traces of sealant/gasket from the mating surfaces of the cylinder block/crankcase and sump, and then use a clean rag to wipe out the sump and the engine's interior.

11.13 Compressor bracket-to-sump bolt

11.14a Undo the bolts securing the sump to the transmission …

11.14b … access to the sump end bolts is through the holes

11.18 Refit the oil baffle plate

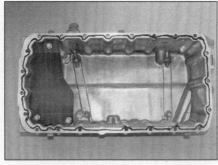

11.19a Apply a bead of sealant around the inside of the bolt holes – Euro 4 engines…

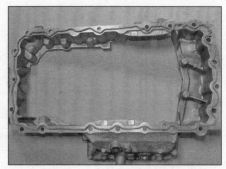

11.19b …and Euro 5 engines

18 Where applicable, refit the oil baffle plate (**see illustration**).

19 Ensure that the sump mating surfaces are clean and dry, then apply a thin coating of suitable sealant (E10 – available from Citroën/Peugeot dealers or Autojoint OR from Fiat dealers or equivalent) to the sump or crankcase mating surface (**see illustrations**).

20 Offer up the sump to the cylinder block/crankcase. Refit its retaining bolts, ensuring that each bolt is screwed into its original location. Tighten the bolts evenly and progressively to the specified torque setting.

21 Where applicable, refit the oil decanter tube. Tighten the retaining bolt securely.

22 Where applicable, apply sealant to the lower sump mating face, position it against the upper sump, then insert and tighten the bolts to the specified torque.

23 The remainder of refitting is a reversal of removal, remembering to refill the engine with oil as described in Chapter 1 Section 6.

12 Oil pump – removal, inspection and refitting

Removal

Euro 4 engines

1 Remove the timing belt as described in Section 7, then slide off the crankshaft sprocket. Recover the Woodruff key from the end of the crankshaft.

2 Remove the sump as described in Section 11.

3 Undo the retaining bolts and remove the front cover and crankshaft seal. Note the original locations of the cover screws – they are different lengths.

4 Undo the bolt securing the oil level pipe (**see illustration**).

5 Pull out the key from the end of the crankshaft sprocket, then undo the pump mounting bolts, slide the pump, chain and crankshaft sprocket from the end of the engine (**see illustrations**). Recover the O-ring between the sprocket and crankshaft.

Euro 5 engines

6 Remove the upper section of the sump as described in Section 11.

7 Undo the oil pump mounting bolts, and manoeuvre the pump, along with the oil pick up duct, from place, disengaging the drive sprocket from the chain as it's withdrawn (**see illustration**).

Inspection

8 Examine the oil pump sprocket for signs of damage and wear, such as chipped or missing teeth. If the sprocket is worn, the pump assembly must be renewed, since the sprocket is not available separately. It is also recommended that the chain and drive sprocket, fitted to the crankshaft, be renewed at the same time.

9 If a faulty pump is suspected, renewal is the only option. No separate parts are available, therefore the complete pump assembly must be renewed.

10 Prime the pump by filling it with clean engine oil before refitting.

12.4 Oil level pipe bracket bolt

12.5a Remove the sprocket key …

12.5b … undo the pump mounting bolts, slide the assembly from the crankshaft …

12.5c … and recover the O-ring between the sprocket and the crankshaft

12.7 Oil pump mounting bolts

12.12 Fit the O-ring to the end of the crankshaft

13.2 Oil cooler retaining bolts

13.10 Oil cooler location

Refitting

11 Before refitting the oil pump, ensure the mating faces of the pump and engine block are completely clean.

Euro 4 engines

12 Fit the O-ring to the end of the crankshaft **(see illustration)**.

13 Engage the drive chain with the oil pump and crankshaft sprockets, then slide the crankshaft sprocket into place (aligning the slot in the sprocket with the keyway in the crankshaft) as the pump is refitted. Refit the crankshaft key.

14 Refit the mounting bolts and tighten them to the specified torque. Note that the front, left-hand bolt is slightly longer than the others.

15 Apply a 3 mm bead of sealant to the oil seal housing flange. Refit the housing and tighten the bolts to the specified torque.

16 Fit a new oil seal to the carrier as described in Section 14.

17 Refit the bolt securing the oil level pipe.

18 The remainder of refitting is a reversal of removal.

Euro 5 engines

19 Engage the pump sprocket with the drive chain, then manoeuvre the pump into position, and tighten the retaining bolts to the specified torque.

20 The remainder of refitting is a reversal of removal.

13 Oil cooler – removal and refitting

Note: *New sealing rings will be required on refitting – check for availability prior to commencing work.*

Removal

Euro 4 engines

1 The cooler is fitted to the oil filter housing on the front of the cylinder block. Access is from under the vehicle. Undo the retaining bolts/nuts and remove the engine undershield. To further improve access, undo the mounting bolts and move the air conditioning compressor to one side. Suspend the

compressor using wire or straps. There is no need to disconnect the refrigerant pipes.

2 Undo the 4 retaining bolts and detach the cooler from the housing **(see illustration)**. Recover the sealing rings and be prepared for coolant/oil spillage.

Euro 5 engines

3 Raise the front of the vehicle and support it securely on axle stands (see *Jacking and vehicle support*). Undo the fasteners and remove the engine undershield **(see illustration 4.12)**.

4 Remove the throttle body as described in Chapter 4A Section 12.

5 Undo the 2 retaining bolts and remove the engine oil level dipstick guide tube.

6 Clamp the hose then disconnect the coolant hose from the oil cooler. Be prepared for coolant spillage.

7 Disconnect the engine oil level and temperature sensor wiring plugs.

8 Release the clamp and disconnect the engine oil filler hose.

9 Release the clamp and disconnect the air outlet hose from the intercooler.

10 Undo the retaining bolts and remove the oil cooler located under the oil filter location **(see illustration)**. Recover the sealing rings and be prepared for coolant/oil spillage.

Refitting

11 Refitting is a reversal of removal, bearing in mind the following points:

a) Use new sealing rings.
b) Tighten the cooler mounting bolts securely.

c) Refit the engine undershield.
d) On completion lower the car to the ground. Check and if necessary top-up the oil and coolant levels, then start the engine and check for signs of oil or coolant leakage.

14 Oil seals – renewal

Crankshaft

Right-hand oil seal

1 Remove the crankshaft sprocket as described in Section 8.

2 Measure and note the fitted depth of the oil seal.

3 Pull the oil seal from the housing using a hooked instrument. Alternatively, drill a small hole in the oil seal, and use a self-tapping screw and a pair of pliers to remove it **(see illustrations)**.

4 Clean the oil seal housing and the crankshaft sealing surface.

5 Lubricate the inner lip of the oil seal with clean engine oil, then press the new seal into the housing (open end first) to the previously-noted depth, using a suitable tube or socket. A piece of thin plastic or tape wound around the front of the crankshaft is useful to prevent damage to the oil seal as it is fitted. Note that special tools to guide the seal onto the crankshaft and drive it into place may be

14.3a Drill a small hole in the seal …

14.3b … insert a self-tapping screw and pull out the seal

14.5a Locate the new seal and guide over the end of the crankshaft ...

14.5b ... then drive the seal home until it's flush with housing

14.10a Drill a hole in the seal ...

14.10b ... then insert a self-tapping screw and pull out the seal

14.19a Use a socket or similar to drive the seal into place ...

14.19b ... until it's flush with the casing surface

available from Citroën/Peugeot/Fiat (see illustrations).

6 Where applicable, remove the plastic or tape from the end of the crankshaft.

7 Refit the crankshaft sprocket as described in Section 8.

Left-hand oil seal

8 Remove the flywheel/driveplate, as described in Section 16.

9 Measure and note the fitted depth of the oil seal.

10 Pull the oil seal from the housing using a hooked instrument. Alternatively, drill a small hole in the oil seal, and use a self-tapping screw and a pair of pliers to remove it (see illustrations).

11 Clean the oil seal housing and the crankshaft sealing surface.

12 Lubricate the inner lip of the seal with clean engine oil, then press the new seal into the housing (open end first) to the previously-noted depth, using a suitable tube or socket. A piece of thin plastic or tape wound around the end of the crankshaft is useful to prevent damage to the oil seal as it is fitted.

13 Where applicable, remove the plastic or tape from the end of the crankshaft.

14 Refit the flywheel/driveplate, as described in Section 16.

Camshaft

15 Remove the camshaft sprocket as

described in Section 8. In principle there is no need to remove the timing belt completely, but remember that if the belt has been contaminated with oil, it must be renewed.

16 Pull the oil seal from the housing using a hooked instrument. Alternatively, drill a small hole in the oil seal and use a self-tapping screw and a pair of pliers to remove it (see illustration 14.3b).

17 Clean the oil seal housing and the camshaft sealing surface.

18 Fit it over the end of the camshaft, open end first. Note that the seal must not be oiled prior to fitting. A piece of thin plastic or tape wound around the end of the camshaft is

15.1 Oil pressure warning light switch

useful to prevent damage to the oil seal as it is fitted.

19 Press the seal into the housing until it is flush with the end face of the cylinder head. Use an M10 bolt (screwed into the end of the camshaft), washers and a suitable tube or socket that bears only on the outer edge of the seal to press it into position (see illustrations).

20 Refit the camshaft sprocket as described in Section 8.

21 Where necessary, fit a new timing belt with reference to Section 7.

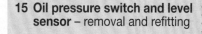

15 Oil pressure switch and level sensor – removal and refitting

Removal

Oil pressure switch

1 The oil pressure switch is located at the front of the cylinder block, in the lower part of the oil filter housing (see illustration). Note that on some models, access to the switch may be improved if the vehicle is jacked up and supported on axle stands, then undo the bolts/nuts and remove the engine undershield so that the switch can be reached from underneath (see *Jacking and vehicle support*).

15.2 Disconnect the wiring plug from the switch

15.5a Oil level sensor – Euro 4 engines…

15.5b …and Euro 5 engines

2 Remove the protective sleeve from the wiring plug (where applicable), and then disconnect the wiring from the switch **(see illustration)**.

3 Unscrew the switch from the filter housing, and recover the sealing washer. Be prepared for oil spillage, and if the switch is to be left removed from the engine for any length of time, plug the hole in the cylinder block.

Oil level sensor

4 The oil level sensor is located at the front of the engine, at the transmission end of the sump. Jack up the front of the vehicle and support it securely on axle stands (see *Jacking and vehicle support*). Undo the retaining bolts/nuts and remove the engine undershield.

5 Reach up and disconnect the sensor wiring plug **(see illustrations)**.

6 Using an open-ended spanner, unscrew the sensor and withdraw it from position.

Refitting

Oil pressure switch

7 Examine the sealing washer for any signs of damage or deterioration, and if necessary renew.

8 Refit the switch, complete with washer, and tighten it to the specified torque.

9 Refit the engine undershield, and lower the vehicle to the ground.

10 Check the engine oil level, and top-up as required (see *Weekly checks*).

11 Check for correct operation of the warning light, and for signs of oil leaks once the engine has been started and warmed-up to normal operating temperature.

Oil level sensor

12 Smear a little silicone sealant on the threads and refit the sensor to the sump, tightening it securely.

13 Reconnect the sensor wiring plug.

14 Refit the engine undershield, and lower the vehicle to the ground.

15 Check the engine oil level, and top-up as required (see *Weekly checks*).

16 Check for correct operation of the warning light, and for signs of oil leaks once the engine has been started and warmed-up to normal operating temperature.

16 Flywheel – removal, inspection and refitting

Removal

1 Remove the clutch assembly as described in Chapter 6 Section 6.

2 Prevent the flywheel from turning by locking the ring gear teeth **(see illustration 5.3)**. Alternatively, bolt a strap between the flywheel and the cylinder block/crankcase. Do not attempt to lock the flywheel in position using the crankshaft pulley locking tool described in Section 3.

3 Slacken and remove the flywheel retaining bolts, and remove the flywheel from the end of the crankshaft **(see illustration)**. Be careful not to drop it; it is heavy. If the flywheel locating dowel is a loose fit in the crankshaft end, remove it and store it with the flywheel for safe-keeping. Discard the flywheel bolts; new ones must be used on refitting.

Inspection

4 Examine the flywheel for scoring of the clutch face, and for wear or chipping of the ring gear teeth. If the clutch face is scored, the flywheel may be surface-ground, but renewal is preferable. Seek the advice of a Citroën/Peugeot/Fiat dealer or engine reconditioning specialist to see if machining is possible. If the ring gear is worn or damaged, the flywheel must be renewed, as it is not possible to renew the ring gear separately.

16.3 Flywheel retaining bolts

Refitting

5 Clean the mating surfaces of the flywheel and crankshaft. Remove any remaining locking compound from the threads of the crankshaft holes, using the correct size of tap, if available.

6 If the new flywheel retaining bolts are not supplied with their threads already pre-coated, apply a suitable thread-locking compound to the threads of each bolt.

7 Ensure that the locating dowel is in position. Offer up the flywheel, locating it on the dowel, and fit the new retaining bolts **(see illustration)**.

8 Lock the flywheel using the method employed on dismantling, and tighten the retaining bolts to the specified torque.

9 Refit the clutch as described in Chapter 6 Section 6.

17 Engine/transmission mountings – inspection and renewal

Inspection

1 If improved access is required, chock the rear wheels then jack up the front of the car and support it on axle stands (see *Jacking and vehicle support*). Undo the retaining bolts/nuts and remove the engine undershield.

2 Check the mounting rubbers to see if they are cracked, hardened or separated from the metal at any point; renew the mounting if any such damage or deterioration is evident.

16.7 Note the locating dowel and the corresponding hole

17.7 Reaction rod-to-vehicle body bracket bolt

17.8 Engine mounting bracket bolts/nut (one bolt hidden)

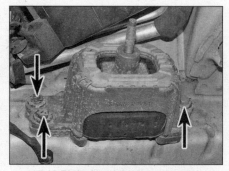

17.10 Right-hand engine mounting retaining bolts

3 Check that all the mountings fasteners are securely tightened; use a torque wrench to check if possible.

4 Using a large screwdriver or a crowbar, check for wear in each mounting by carefully levering against it to check for free play. Where this is not possible, enlist the aid of an assistant to move the engine/transmission back-and-forth, or from side-to-side, while you watch the mounting. While some free play is to be expected even from new components, excessive wear should be obvious. If excessive free play is found, check first that the fasteners are correctly secured, and then renew any worn components as described below.

Renewal

Right-hand engine mounting

5 Raise the front of the vehicle, and support it securely on axle stands, then remove the engine undershield. Position a jack under the sump, with a large block of wood between the jack head and the sump, then carefully raise the jack just enough to support the weight of the engine.

6 Undo the nut securing the coolant expansion tank and move it to one side (see illustration 4.3).

7 Undo the bolt securing the reaction rod to the bracket on the vehicle body (see illustration).

8 Undo the 4 bolts/1 nut securing the reaction rod mounting bracket to the engine mounting bracket, and manoeuvre it from place (see illustration).

9 If required, undo the bolt and separate the reaction rod from the mounting bracket.

10 Undo the 3 retaining bolts and remove the flexible mounting assembly from the vehicle body (see illustration).

11 Refitting is a reversal of removal. Tighten the fasteners to the specified torque.

Left-hand transmission mounting

12 Remove the air cleaner assembly as described in Chapter 4A Section 5.

13 If not already done, undo the retaining bolts/nuts and remove the engine undershield (where fitted). Place a jack beneath the transmission, with a block of wood on the jack head. Raise the jack until it is supporting the weight of the transmission.

14 With the transmission supported, note the position of the mounting then first unscrew the centre retaining nut. Remove the retaining bolts, then lift the transmission mounting from its position on the inner wing mounting bracket (see illustration).

15 If required, undo the bolts and detach the body-side mounting bracket (see illustration).

16 If required, undo the 3 retaining bolts and remove the mounting bracket from the top of the transmission.

17 Refitting is a reversal of removal. Re-align the mounting in the position noted on removal (where applicable), then tighten all fasteners to the specified torque wrench settings.

Lower engine rear torque link

18 Firmly apply the handbrake, and then jack up the front of the vehicle and support it securely on axle stands (see *Jacking and vehicle support*). If not already done, undo the retaining bolts/nuts and remove the engine undershield (where fitted).

19 Unscrew and remove the bolts securing the rear mounting link to the subframe and driveshaft bearing bracket (see illustration).

20 Check carefully for signs of wear or damage on all components, and renew them where necessary. The rubber bush fitted to the driveshaft bearing housing is available as a separate item on some models, check with your local dealer for availability of parts. If available, the rubber bush can be pressed out of the bearing housing, noting its fitted position, and then a new one pressed back into place.

21 Refit the rear mounting torque reaction link, and tighten both its bolts to their specified torque settings.

22 Refit the engine undershield (where applicable), and then lower the vehicle to the ground.

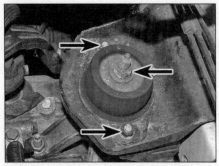

17.14 Transmission mounting centre nut and retaining bolts

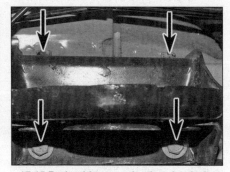

17.15 Body-side mounting bracket bolts

17.19 Undo the rear link bolts

Chapter 2 Part D
Engine removal and overhaul procedures

Contents

Degrees of difficulty

Easy, suitable for novice with little experience	Fairly easy, suitable for beginner with some experience	Fairly difficult, suitable for competent DIY mechanic	Difficult, suitable for experienced DIY mechanic	Very difficult, suitable for expert DIY or professional

Specifications

Cylinder block

Cylinder bore diameter . . . . 75.00 mm (nominal)

Cylinder head

1.6 litre engines:
  Maximum gasket face distortion . . . . 0.03 mm
  Maximum permitted re-grind . . . . No re-grind permitted
2.0 litre engines:
  New cylinder head height . . . . 132.6 ± 0.05 mm
  Maximum gasket face distortion . . . . 0.05 mm
  Maximum permitted re-grind . . . . 0.4 mm

Valves

	Intake	Exhaust
Valve stem diameter:		
1.6 litre engines	Not available	Not available
2.0 litre engines	5.978 ± 0.009 mm	5.968 ± 0.009 mm

Pistons

Piston diameter:
1.6 litre engines:
  Nominal dimension . . . . 74.945 mm ± 0.075 mm
  Repair dimension . . . . 75.345 mm ± 0.075 mm
2.0 litre engines . . . . Not available

Piston ring end gaps

1.6 litre engines:
  Top compression ring . . . . 0.15 to 0.25 mm
  Second compression (sealing) ring . . . . 0.30 to 0.50 mm
  Oil control (scraper) ring . . . . 0.35 to 0.55 mm
2.0 litre engines:
  Top compression ring . . . . 0.20 to 0.35 mm
  Second compression ring . . . . 0.80 to 1.0 mm
  Oil control ring . . . . 0.25 to 0.50 mm

Crankshaft

Endfloat:
    1.6 litre engines . . . . 0.10 to 0.30 mm (thrustwasher thickness 2.40 ± 0.05 mm)
    2.0 litre engines . . . . 0.07 to 0.32 mm (thrustwasher thickness 2.30 mm)

Torque wrench settings

1.6 litre SOHC engines

Refer to Chapter 2A, Specifications

1.6 litre DOHC engines

Refer to Chapter 2B, Specifications

2.0 litre engines

Refer to Chapter 2C Specifications

1 General Information

1 Included in this Chapter are details of removing the engine/transmission from the car and general overhaul procedures for the cylinder head, cylinder block/crankcase and all other engine internal components.
2 The information given ranges from advice concerning preparation for an overhaul and the purchase of parts, to detailed step-by-step procedures covering removal, inspection, renovation and refitting of engine internal components.
3 After Section 5, all instructions are based on the assumption that the engine has been removed from the car. For information concerning in-car engine repair, as well as the removal and refitting of those external components necessary for full overhaul, refer to Chapter 2A or Chapter 2B, as applicable and to Section 5. Ignore any preliminary dismantling operations that are no longer relevant once the engine has been removed from the car.
4 Apart from torque wrench settings, which are given at the beginning of Chapter 2A, Chapter 2B or Chapter 2C, all specifications relating to engine overhaul are at the beginning of this Chapter.

2 Engine overhaul – general information

1 It is not always easy to determine when, or if, an engine should be completely overhauled, as a number of factors must be considered.
2 High mileage is not necessarily an indication that an overhaul is needed, while low mileage does not preclude the need for an overhaul. Frequency of servicing is probably the most important consideration. An engine, which has had regular and frequent oil and filter changes, as well as other required maintenance, should give many thousands of miles of reliable service. Conversely, a neglected engine may require an overhaul very early in its life.
3 Excessive oil consumption is an indication

that piston rings, valve seals and/or valve guides are in need of attention. Make sure that oil leaks are not responsible before deciding that the rings and/or guides are worn. Perform a compression test, as described in Chapter 2A, Chapter 2B or Chapter 2C (as applicable), to determine the likely cause of the problem.
4 Check the oil pressure with a gauge fitted in place of the oil pressure switch, and compare it with that specified. If it is extremely low, the main and big-end bearings, and/or the oil pump, are probably worn out.
5 Loss of power, rough running, knocking or metallic engine noises, excessive valve gear noise, and high fuel consumption may also point to the need for an overhaul, especially if they are all present at the same time. If a complete service does not remedy the situation, major mechanical work is the only solution.
6 A full engine overhaul involves restoring all internal parts to the specification of a new engine. During a complete overhaul, the pistons and the piston rings are renewed. New main and big-end bearings are generally fitted; if necessary, the crankshaft may be reground, to compensate for wear in the journals. The valves are also serviced as well, since they are usually in less-than-perfect condition at this point. While the engine is being overhauled, other components, such as the starter and alternator, can be overhauled as well. Always pay careful attention to the condition of the oil pump when overhauling the engine, and renew it if there is any doubt as to its serviceability. The end result should be an as-new engine that will give many trouble-free miles.
7 Critical cooling system components such as the hoses, thermostat and water pump should be renewed when an engine is overhauled. The radiator should be checked carefully, to ensure that it is not clogged or leaking. Also, it is a good idea to renew the oil pump whenever the engine is overhauled.
8 Before beginning the engine overhaul, read through the entire procedure, to familiarise yourself with the scope and requirements of the job. Overhauling an engine is not difficult if you follow carefully all of the instructions, have the necessary tools and equipment, and pay close attention to all specifications. It can, however, be time-consuming. Plan on the

car being off the road for a minimum of two weeks, especially if parts must be taken to an engineering works for repair or reconditioning. Check on the availability of parts and make sure that any necessary special tools and equipment are obtained in advance. Most work can be done with typical hand tools, although a number of precision measuring tools are required for inspecting parts to determine if they must be renewed. Often the engineering works will handle the inspection of parts and offer advice concerning reconditioning and renewal.
9 Always wait until the engine has been completely dismantled, and until all components (especially the cylinder block/crankcase and the crankshaft) have been inspected, before deciding what service and repair operations must be performed by an engineering works. The condition of these components will be the major factor to consider when determining whether to overhaul the original engine, or to buy a reconditioned unit. Do not, therefore, purchase parts or have overhaul work done on other components until they have been thoroughly inspected. As a general rule, time is the primary cost of an overhaul, so it does not pay to fit worn or sub-standard parts.
10 As a final note, to ensure maximum life and minimum trouble from a reconditioned engine, everything must be assembled with care, in a spotlessly clean environment.

3 Engine removal – methods and precautions

1 If you have decided that the engine must be removed for overhaul or major repair work, several preliminary steps should be taken.
2 Locating a suitable place to work is extremely important. Adequate workspace, along with storage space for the car, will be needed. Engine/transmission removal is extremely complicated and involved on these vehicles. It must be stated, that unless the vehicle can be positioned on a ramp, or raised and supported on axle stands over an inspection pit, it will be more difficult to carry out the work involved.

3 Cleaning the engine compartment and engine/transmission before beginning the removal procedure will help keep tools clean and organised.

4 An engine hoist or A-frame will also be necessary. Make sure the equipment is rated in excess of the weight of the engine. Safety is of primary importance, considering the potential hazards involved in lifting the engine/transmission out of the car.

5 The help of an assistant is essential. Apart from the safety aspects involved, there are many instances when one person cannot simultaneously perform all of the operations required during engine/transmission removal.

6 Plan the operation ahead of time. Before starting work, arrange for the hire of or obtain all of the tools and equipment you will need. Some of the equipment necessary to perform engine/transmission removal and installation safely and with relative ease (in addition to an engine hoist) is as follows: a heavy duty trolley jack, complete sets of spanners and sockets (see Tools and working facilities), wooden blocks, and plenty of rags and cleaning solvent for mopping-up spilled oil, coolant and fuel. If the hoist must be hired, make sure that you arrange for it in advance, and perform all of the operations possible without it beforehand. This will save you money and time.

7 Plan for the car to be out of use for quite a while. An engineering machine shop or engine reconditioning specialist will be required to perform some of the work, which cannot be accomplished without special equipment. These places often have a busy schedule, so it would be a good idea to consult them before removing the engine, in order to accurately estimate the amount of time required to rebuild or repair components that may need work.

8 During the engine/transmission removal procedure, it is advisable to make notes of the locations of all brackets, cable-ties, earthing points, etc, as well as how the wiring harnesses, hoses and electrical connections are attached and routed around the engine and engine compartment. An effective way of doing this is to take a series of photographs

of the various components before they are disconnected or removed; the resulting photographs will prove invaluable when the engine/transmission is refitted.

9 The engine can be removed complete with the transmission as an assembly. Remove the front bumper, crossmember and radiator panel, and then the assembly is removed from the front of the vehicle.

10 Always be extremely careful when removing and refitting the engine/transmission. Serious injury can result from careless actions. Plan ahead and take your time, and a job of this nature, although major, can be accomplished successfully.

4 Engine – removal and refitting

Note: *Such is the complexity of the power unit arrangement on these vehicles, and the variations that may be encountered according to model and optional equipment fitted, the following should be regarded as a guide to the work involved, rather than a step-by-step procedure. Where differences are encountered, or additional component disconnection or removal is necessary, make notes of the work involved as an aid to refitting.*

Removal

1 On vehicles equipped with air conditioning, have the system evacuated by a suitably equipped repairer.

2 Apply the handbrake, then jack up the front of the vehicle and support it on axle stands (see *Jacking and vehicle support*). Remove both front roadwheels. Undo the retaining bolts/nuts and remove the engine undershield, also release the securing clips and remove the front wheel arch liners.

3 Remove the radiator grille as described in Chapter 11 Section 23.

4 Remove the front bumper as described in Chapter 11 Section 6.

5 Remove both front headlights as described in Chapter 12 Section 8.

6 Undo the retaining nuts and remove the front crossmember (see illustration).

7 Undo the nuts, remove the lock protection, then disconnect the release cable from the bonnet lock.

8 Undo the retaining bolts and remove the bonnet lock. Disconnect the wiring plug as the lock is withdrawn.

9 Drain the cooling system with reference to Chapter 1 Section 23.

10 Drain the transmission oil/fluid as described in. Refit the drain and filler plugs, and tighten them to their specified torque settings.

11 If the engine is to be dismantled, drain the engine oil and remove the oil filter as described in Chapter 1 Section 6. Clean and refit the drain plug, tightening it securely.

12 Disconnect the electric cooling fans(s) wiring plug(s), unclip the wiring loom and move it one side.

13 Undo the bolts and move the relay box attached to the bonnet slam panel to one side.

14 Remove the air cleaner assembly as described in Chapter 4A Section 5.

15 Disconnect the remaining hoses from the radiator, and where applicable, disconnect the refrigerant pipes from the condenser. Plug the openings to prevent contamination.

16 Release the clamps, undo the retaining bolts and remove the air ducting/pipes between the turbocharger, intercooler and intake manifold.

17 Undo the 4 retaining bolts at the upper edge, then lift the cooling fan(s), radiator and condenser (where applicable) upwards and manoeuvre the assembly from place (see illustration). Be prepared for coolant spillage.

18 Release the fasteners, and remove the sound insulation material from the top of the engine (where fitted).

19 Undo the retaining bolts and remove the radiator supporting crossmember (see illustration). Where applicable, undo the bolt securing the power steering pipe to the crossmember.

20 Disconnect the hoses, then undo

4.6 Undo the nuts each side and remove the crossmember

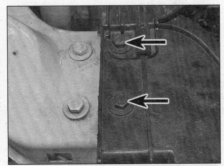

4.17 Undo the bolts securing the panel to the inner wings each side (right-hand bolts arrowed)

4.19 Left-hand crossmember bolt, and power steering pipe bracket bolt

4.20 Coolant expansion tank retaining nut

4.21 Air cleaner mounting bracket nuts (2.0 litre models)

4.23 Disconnect the earth strap from the left-hand chassis member

the retaining nut and remove the coolant expansion tank (see illustration).

21 On 2.0 litre models, undo the nuts, unclip the earth lead, and remove the air cleaner mounting bracket (see illustration).

22 Disconnect the reversing light switch wiring plug.

23 Undo the retaining bolt and disconnect the main earth strap from the left-hand front chassis member (see illustration).

24 Remove the engine management ECM as described in Chapter 4A Section 12.

25 Disconnect the wiring plug from the pre-heater control unit, then release any retaining clips/wiring plugs and lay the wiring loom on top of the engine.

26 Note their fitted positions, then disconnect

the various wiring plugs/leads from the engine compartment junction box (see illustration).

27 Where applicable, undo the nuts and disconnect the refrigerant pipes from the air conditioning compressor. Plug the openings to prevent contamination.

28 Disconnect the fuel supply and return pipes at the quick-release connectors at the fuel filter (see illustrations). Plug the end of the hoses to prevent dirt ingress.

29 On 1.6 litre models, clamp the hose and disconnect the fluid supply pipe from the clutch slave cylinder as described in Chapter 6 Section 4. On 2.0 litre models, undo the retaining bolts, withdraw the clutch slave cylinder from the transmission casing, release

the pipe from the bracket and move it to one side.

30 Disconnect the heater hoses from the matrix connections at the engine compartment bulkhead (see illustration).

31 Disconnect the gear change/selector cables from the transmission as described in.

32 Disconnect the servo hose from the vacuum pump.

33 Refer to Chapter 8 Section 2 and remove both front driveshafts.

34 On 1.6 litre models, remove the upstream catalytic converter as described in Chapter 4A Section 18 On 2.0 litre models, slacken the clamp and disconnect the main catalytic converter/particulate filter flexible pipe from the upstream catalytic converter.

35 Where applicable, release the fasteners and remove the sump sound insulation material.

36 From underneath the vehicle, slacken and remove the nuts and bolts securing the rear engine mounting connecting link to the mounting assembly and subframe, and remove the connecting link.

37 Undo the bolts and remove the heatshield above the rear engine mounting.

38 Where applicable, undo the retaining bolt and remove the reverse gear inhibitor switch from the transmission casing (see illustration).

39 Disconnect the wiring plugs from the power steering electric pump (2.0 litre

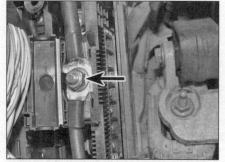

4.26 Open the cover, undo the nut and disconnect the battery positive lead from the engine compartment junction box

4.28a Prise out the centre section of the clip a little, then press-in the outer section to release the pipe

4.28b Prise out the centre section a little, then squeeze together the side of the clip

4.28c Fuel supply and return pipes (2.0 litre engine shown)

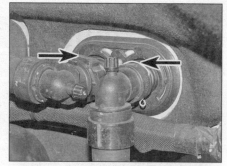

4.30 Prise up the wire clip to disconnect the hose on the passengers side, then rotate the collar to disconnect the remaining hose

4.38 Reverse gear inhibitor switch retaining bolt – viewed through the wheelarch aperture

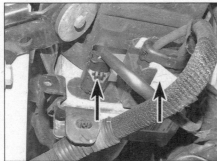

4.39 Electric power steering pump wiring plugs

engines), and the engine oil pressure sensor **(see illustration)**.

40 On 1.6 litre engines, remove as much fluid as possible from the power steering fluid reservoir using a syringe (or similar), then disconnect the fluid supply hose from the base of the reservoir.

41 On 1.6 litre models, undo the support bracket bolts, then undo the union and disconnect the fluid pressure pipe from the power steering pump. Be prepared for fluid spillage.

42 Using a hoist attached to the lifting eyes on the cylinder head and transmission, take the weight of the engine and transmission **(see illustration)**.

43 Remove the right-hand and left-hand engine mountings and support brackets as described in Chapter 2A Section 17, Chapter 2B Section 17 or Chapter 2C Section 17.

44 Make a final check to ensure all wiring; hoses and brackets that would prevent the removal of the assembly have been disconnected.

45 Move the engine/transmission forwards and out from the front of the vehicle. Enlist the help of an assistant during this procedure, as it may be necessary to tilt and twist the assembly slightly to clear the body panels and

adjacent components. Move the unit clear of the car and lower it to the ground.

Separation

46 With the engine/transmission assembly removed, support the assembly on suitable blocks of wood on a workbench (or failing that, on a clean area of the workshop floor).

47 Undo the retaining bolts, and remove the flywheel lower cover plate (where fitted) from the transmission.

48 Slacken and remove the retaining bolts, and remove the starter motor from the transmission.

49 Disconnect any remaining wiring connectors at the transmission, then move the main engine wiring harness to one side.

50 Ensure that both engine and transmission are adequately supported, then slacken and remove the remaining bolts securing the transmission housing to the engine. Note the correct fitted positions of each bolt (and the relevant brackets) as they are removed, to use as a reference on refitting.

51 Carefully withdraw the transmission from the engine, ensuring that the weight of the transmission is not allowed to hang on the input shaft while it is engaged with the clutch friction disc.

52 If they are loose, remove the locating

dowels from the engine or transmission, and keep them in a safe place.

Refitting

53 If the engine and transmission have not been separated, perform the operations described below from paragraph 40 onwards.

54 The manufacturers recommend that no lubricant/grease is applied to the transmission input shaft splines.

55 Ensure that the locating dowels are correctly positioned in the engine or transmission, and then carefully offer the transmission to the engine until the locating dowels are engaged. On manual transmission models, ensure that the weight of the transmission is not allowed to hang on the input shaft as it is engaged with the clutch friction disc.

56 Refit the transmission housing-to-engine bolts, ensuring that all the necessary brackets are correctly positioned, and tighten them securely.

57 Refit the starter motor, and securely tighten its retaining bolts.

58 Refit the lower flywheel cover plate (where fitted) to the transmission, and securely tighten the bolts.

59 Reconnect the hoist and lifting tackle to the engine lifting brackets. With the aid of an assistant, lift the assembly into the engine compartment, taking care not to damage surrounding components.

60 Refit the right-hand engine mounting and support bracket, but leave the bolts finger-tight at this stage.

61 Working on the left-hand mounting, refit the mounting to the transmission and finger-tighten.

62 Remove the hoist.

63 From underneath the vehicle, refit the rear mounting connecting link and finger-tighten the bolts.

64 Rock the engine to settle it on its mountings, then go around and tighten all the mounting nuts and bolts to their specified torque settings.

65 The remainder of the refitting procedure is a direct reversal of the removal sequence, with reference to the relevant chapters and noting the following points:

a) Ensure that the wiring loom is correctly routed and retained by all the relevant retaining clips; all connectors should be correctly and securely reconnected.

b) Prior to refitting the driveshafts to the transmission, renew the driveshaft oil seals as described in

c) Ensure that all coolant hoses are correctly reconnected, and securely retained by their retaining clips.

d) Refill the engine and transmission with the correct quantity and type of lubricant.

e) Refill the cooling system as described in Chapter 1 Section 23.

f) Initialise the engine management ECM as follows. Start the engine and run to normal temperature. Carry out a road test during which the following procedure should be made. Engage third gear and stabilise the engine at 1000 rpm. Now accelerate fully to 3500 rpm.

4.42 Attach a hoist to the cylinder head and transmission

5 Engine overhaul – dismantling sequence

1 It is much easier to dismantle and work on the engine if it is mounted on a portable engine stand. These stands can often be hired from a tool hire shop. Before the engine is mounted on a stand, the flywheel/driveplate should be removed, so that the stand bolts can be tightened into the end of the cylinder block/crankcase.

2 If a stand is not available, it is possible to dismantle the engine with it blocked up on a sturdy workbench, or on the floor. Be extra careful not to tip or drop the engine when working without a stand.

3 If you are going to obtain a reconditioned engine, all the external components must be removed first, to be transferred to the new engine (just as they will if you are doing a complete engine overhaul yourself). These components include the following:

6.5a Compress the valve spring using a spring compressor …

6.5c Remove the spring retainer …

6.5e … and the spring seat (not all models)

a) *Ancillary unit mounting brackets (oil filter, starter, alternator, power steering pump, etc)*
b) *Thermostat and housing (Chapter 3 Section 5).*
c) *Dipstick tube/sensor.*
d) *All electrical switches and sensors.*
e) *Intake and exhaust manifolds – where applicable.*
f) *Flywheel (Chapter 2A Section 16 or Chapter 2B Section 16 or Chapter 2C Section 16).*

Note: *When removing the external components from the engine, pay close attention to details that may be helpful or important during refitting. Note the fitted position of gaskets, seals, spacers, pins, washers, bolts, and other small items.*

4 If you are obtaining a 'short' engine (which consists of the engine cylinder block/crankcase, crankshaft, pistons and connecting rods all assembled), then the cylinder head, sump, oil pump, and timing belt will have to be removed also.

5 If you are planning a complete overhaul, the

6.5b … then extract the collets and release the spring compressor

6.5d … followed by the valve spring …

6.5f Use a pair of pliers to remove the valve stem oil seal. On some models the spring seat is integral with the seal

engine can be dismantled, and the internal components removed, in the order given below, referring to Chapter 2A or Chapter 2B or Chapter 2C unless otherwise stated.

a) *Intake and exhaust manifolds – where applicable (Chapter 4A).*
b) *Timing belts, sprockets and tensioner(s).*
c) *Cylinder head.*
d) *Flywheel/driveplate.*
e) *Sump.*
f) *Oil pump.*
g) *Piston/connecting rod assemblies (Section 9).*
h) *Crankshaft (Section 10).*

6 Before beginning the dismantling and overhaul procedures, make sure that you have all of the correct tools necessary. Refer to Tools and working facilities 13 Section 6 for further information.

6 Cylinder head – dismantling

Note: *New and reconditioned cylinder heads are available from the manufacturer, and from engine overhaul specialists. Be aware that some specialist tools are required for the dismantling and inspection procedures, and new components may not be readily available. It may therefore be more practical and economical for the home mechanic to purchase a reconditioned head, rather than dismantle, inspect and recondition the original head.*

1 Remove the cylinder head as described in Chapter 2A Section 10 or Chapter 2B Section 10 or Chapter 2C Section 10 (as applicable).

2 If not already done, remove the intake and the exhaust manifolds with reference to Chapter 4A. Remove any remaining brackets or housings as required.

3 Remove the camshafts, hydraulic followers and rockers (as applicable) as described in Chapter 2A or Chapter 2B or Chapter 2C.

4 If not already done, remove the glow plugs as described in Chapter 5B Section 2.

5 On all models, using a valve spring compressor, compress each valve spring in turn until the split collets can be removed. Release the compressor, and lift off the spring retainer, spring and, where fitted, the spring seat. Using a pair of pliers, carefully extract the valve stem oil seal from the top of the guide. On 16-valve engines, the valve stem oil seal also forms the spring seat and is deeply recessed in the cylinder head. It is also a tight fit on the valve guide making it difficult to remove with pliers or a conventional valve stem oil seal removal tool. It can be easily removed, however, using a self-locking nut of suitable diameter screwed onto the end of a bolt and locked with a second nut. Push the nut down onto the top of the seal; the locking portion of the nut will grip the seal allowing it to be withdrawn from the top of the valve guide. Access to the valves is limited, and it may be necessary to make up an adapter out of metal tube – cut out a 'window' so that the valve collets can be removed **(see illustrations).**

6 If, when the valve spring compressor is screwed down, the spring retainer refuses to free and expose the split collets, gently tap the top of the tool, directly over the retainer, with a light hammer. This will free the retainer.

7 Withdraw the valve from the combustion chamber. Remove the valve stem oil seal from the top of the guide, then lift out the spring seat where fitted.

8 It is essential that each valve is stored together with its collets, retainer, spring, and spring seat. The valves should also be kept in their correct sequence, unless they are so badly worn that they are to be renewed. If they are going to be kept and used again, place each valve assembly in a labelled polythene bag or similar small container **(see illustration)**. Note that No 1 valve is nearest to the transmission (flywheel/driveplate) end of the engine.

6.8 Place each valve and its associated components in a labelled bag

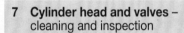

7 Cylinder head and valves – cleaning and inspection

1 Thorough cleaning of the cylinder head and valve components, followed by a detailed inspection, will enable you to decide how much valve service work must be carried out during the engine overhaul. **Note:** *If the engine has been severely overheated, it is best to assume that the cylinder head is warped – check carefully for signs of this.*

Cleaning

2 Scrape away all traces of old gasket material from the cylinder head.

3 Scrape away the carbon from the combustion chambers and ports, then wash the cylinder head thoroughly with paraffin or a suitable solvent.

4 Scrape off any heavy carbon deposits that may have formed on the valves, then use a power-operated wire brush to remove deposits from the valve heads and stems.

Inspection

Note: *Be sure to perform all the following*

inspection procedures before concluding that the services of a machine shop or engine overhaul specialist are required. Make a list of all items that require attention.

Cylinder head

5 Inspect the head very carefully for cracks, evidence of coolant leakage, and other damage. If cracks are found, a new cylinder head should be obtained. Use a straight-edge and feeler blade to check that the cylinder head gasket surface is not distorted **(see illustration)**. If it is, it may be possible to have it machined, provided that the cylinder head height is not significantly reduced.

6 Examine the valve seats in each of the combustion chambers. If they are severely pitted, cracked, or burned, they will need to be renewed or recut by an engine overhaul specialist. If they are only slightly pitted, this can be removed by grinding-in the valve heads and seats with fine valve grinding compound, as described below. If in any doubt, have the cylinder head inspected by an engine overhaul specialist.

7 Check the valve guides for wear by inserting the relevant valve, and checking for side-to-side motion of the valve. A very small amount of movement is acceptable. If the movement seems excessive, remove the valve. Measure the valve stem diameter (see below), and renew the valve if it is worn. If the valve stem is not worn, the wear must

be in the valve guide, and the guide must be renewed. The renewal of valve guides is best carried out by a Citroën/Peugeot dealer or engine overhaul specialist, who will have the necessary tools available. Where no valve stem diameter is specified, seek the advice of a Citroën/Peugeot dealer on the best course of action.

8 If renewing the valve guides, the valve seats should be recut or reground only after the guides have been fitted.

9 Where applicable, examine the camshaft oil supply non-return valve in the oil feed bore at the timing belt/chain end of the cylinder head. Check that the valve is not loose in the cylinder head and that the ball is free to move within the valve body. If the valve is a loose fit in its bore, or if there is any doubt about its condition, it should be renewed. The non-return valve can be removed (assuming it is not loose), using compressed air, such as that generated by a tyre foot pump. Place the pump nozzle over the oil feed bore of the camshaft bearing journal and seal the corresponding oil feed bore with a rag. Apply the compressed air and the valve will be forced out of its location in the underside of the cylinder head **(see illustrations)**. Fit the new non-return valve to its bore on the underside of the head ensuring it is fitted the correct way. Oil should be able to pass upwards through the valve to the camshafts, but the ball in the valve should prevent the oil from returning back to the cylinder block. Use a thin socket or similar to push the valve fully into position.

Valves

10 Examine the head of each valve for pitting, burning, cracks, and general wear. Check the valve stem for scoring and wear ridges. Rotate the valve, and check for any obvious indication that it is bent. Look for pits or excessive wear on the tip of each valve stem. Renew any valve that shows any such signs of wear or damage.

11 If the valve appears satisfactory at this stage, measure the valve stem diameter at several points using a micrometer **(see**

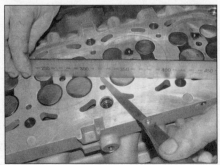
7.5 Check the cylinder head gasket surface for distortion

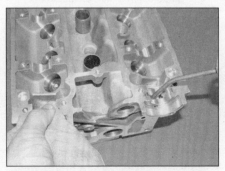
7.9a Apply compressed air to the oil feed bore of the intake camshaft, seal the bore in the exhaust camshaft bore with a rag ...

7.9b ... and the camshaft oil supply non-return valve will be ejected from the underside of the cylinder head

7.11 Measure the valve stem diameter with a micrometer

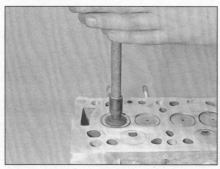

7.14 Grinding-in a valve

Valve components

17 Examine the valve springs for signs of damage and discoloration. No minimum free length is specified by Peugeot/Citroën/Fiat, so the only way of judging valve spring wear is by comparison with a new component.

18 Stand each spring on a flat surface, and check it for squareness. If any of the springs are damaged, distorted or have lost their tension, obtain a complete new set of springs. It is normal to renew the valve springs as a matter of course if a major overhaul is being carried out.

19 Renew the valve stem oil seals regardless of their apparent condition.

---

illustration). Any significant difference in the readings obtained indicates wear of the valve stem. Should any of these conditions be apparent, the valve must be renewed.

12 If the valves are in satisfactory condition, they should be ground (lapped) into their respective seats, to ensure a smooth, gas-tight seal. If the seat is only lightly pitted, or if it has been recut, fine grinding compound only should be used to produce the required finish. Coarse valve-grinding compound should not be used, unless a seat is badly burned or deeply pitted. If this is the case, the cylinder head and valves should be inspected by an expert, to decide whether seat recutting, or even the renewal of the valve or seat insert (where possible) is required.

13 Valve grinding is carried out as follows. Place the cylinder head upside-down on a bench.

14 Smear a trace of (the appropriate grade of) valve-grinding compound on the seat face,

and press a suction grinding tool onto the valve head **(see illustration)**. With a semi-rotary action, grind the valve head to its seat, lifting the valve occasionally to redistribute the grinding compound. A light spring placed under the valve head will greatly ease this operation.

15 If coarse grinding compound is being used, work only until a dull, matt even surface is produced on both the valve seat and the valve, then wipe off the used compound, and repeat the process with fine compound. When a smooth unbroken ring of light grey matt finish is produced on both the valve and seat, the grinding operation is complete. Do not grind-in the valves any further than absolutely necessary, or the seat will be prematurely sunk into the cylinder head.

16 When all the valves have been ground-in, carefully wash off all traces of grinding compound using paraffin or a suitable solvent, before reassembling the cylinder head.

8 Cylinder head – reassembly

1 Working on the first valve assembly, refit the spring seat then dip the new valve stem oil seal in fresh engine oil. Locate the seal on the valve guide and press the seal firmly onto the guide using a suitable socket **(see illustrations)**. Note that the seal is integral with the lower spring seat.

2 Lubricate the stem of the first valve, and insert it in the guide **(see illustration)**.

3 Locate the valve spring on top of its seat, and then refit the spring retainer.

4 Compress the valve spring, and locate the split collets in the recess in the valve stem. Release the compressor, then repeat the procedure on the remaining valves. Ensure that each valve is inserted into its original location. If new valves are being fitted, insert them into the locations to which they have been ground.

5 With all the valves installed, support the cylinder head and, using a hammer and interposed block of wood, tap the end of each valve stem to settle the components.

6 Refit the camshafts, hydraulic followers and rocker arms (as applicable) as described in Chapter 2A or Chapter 2B or Chapter 2C.

7 Refit any remaining components using the reverse of the removal sequence and with new seals or gaskets as necessary.

8 The cylinder head can then be refitted as described in Chapter 2A Section 10 or Chapter 2B Section 10 or Chapter 2C Section 10.

8.1a Locate the valve stem oil seal on the valve guide …

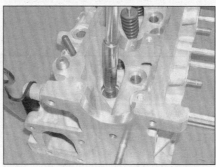

8.1b … and press the seal firmly onto the guide using a suitable socket

8.1c On some models, the valve stem oil seal is integral with the spring seat

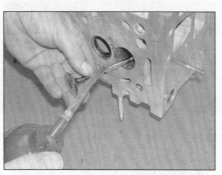

8.2 Lubricate the stem of the valve and insert it into the guide

9 Piston/connecting rod assembly – removal

Note: *The main bearing ladder must be removed before the piston/connecting rods, can be withdrawn.*

1 Remove the cylinder head, sump and oil pump as described in Chapter 2A or Chapter 2B or Chapter 2C.

2 If there is a pronounced wear ridge at the top of any bore, it may be necessary to remove it with a scraper or ridge reamer, to avoid piston damage during removal. Such a ridge indicates excessive wear of the cylinder bore.

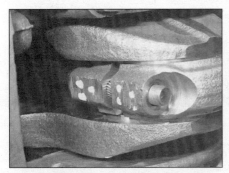

9.3 Connecting rod and big-end bearing cap identification marks (No 3 shown)

9.5 Remove the big-end bearing shell and cap

9.6 To protect the crankshaft journals, tape over the connecting rod stud threads

3 Using quick-drying paint, mark each connecting rod and big-end bearing cap with its respective cylinder number on the flat machined surface provided; if the engine has been dismantled before, note carefully any identifying marks made previously **(see illustration)**. Note that No 1 cylinder is at the transmission (flywheel) end of the engine.
4 Turn the crankshaft to bring pistons 1 and 4 to BDC (Bottom Dead Centre). On 1.6 litre engines, remove the main bearing ladder, as described in Section 10.
5 Unscrew the nuts or bolts, as applicable, from No 1 piston big-end bearing cap. Take off the cap, and recover the bottom half bearing shell **(see illustration)**. If the bearing shells are to be re-used, tape the cap and the shell together.
6 Where applicable, to prevent the possibility of damage to the crankshaft bearing journals, tape over the connecting rod stud threads **(see illustration)**.
7 Using a hammer handle, push the piston up through the bore, and remove it from the top of the cylinder block. Recover the bearing shell, and tape it to the connecting rod for safekeeping.
8 Loosely refit the big-end cap to the connecting rod, and secure with the nuts/bolts – this will help to keep the components in their correct order.
9 Remove number 4 piston assembly in the same way.

10 Turn the crankshaft through 180° to bring pistons 2 and 3 to BDC (Bottom Dead Centre), and remove them in the same way.

10 Crankshaft – removal

1 Remove the crankshaft sprocket and the oil pump as described in Chapter 2A or Chapter 2B or Chapter 2C (as applicable).
2 Remove the pistons and connecting rods, as described in Section 9. If no work is to be done on the pistons and connecting rods, there is no need to remove the cylinder head, or to push the pistons out of the cylinder bores. The pistons should just be pushed far enough up the bores so that they are positioned clear of the crankshaft journals. **Note:** *On 1.6 litre engines, the main bearing ladder must be removed before the piston/connecting rods, can be withdrawn.*
3 Check the crankshaft endfloat as described in Section 13, then proceed as follows.

1.6 litre engines

4 Work around the outside of the cylinder block, and unscrew all the small bolts securing the main bearing ladder to the base of the cylinder block. Note the correct fitted depth of the left-hand crankshaft oil seal in the cylinder block/main bearing ladder.
5 Working in a diagonal sequence, evenly and progressively slacken the large main bearing ladder retaining bolts by a turn at a time. Once all the bolts are loose, remove them from the ladder. **Note:** *Prise up the two caps at the flywheel end of the ladder to expose the two end main bearing bolts* **(see illustration)**.
6 With all the retaining bolts removed, carefully lift the main bearing ladder casting away from the base of the cylinder block. Recover the lower main bearing shells, and tape them to their respective locations in the casting. If the two locating dowels are a loose fit, remove them and store them with the casting for safekeeping.
7 Undo the big-end bolts and remove the pistons/connecting rods as described in Section 9. Lift out the crankshaft, and discard both the oil seals.
8 Recover the upper main bearing shells, and store them along with the relevant lower bearing shell. Also recover the two thrustwashers (one fitted either side of No 2 main bearing) from the cylinder block.

2.0 litre engines

9 Slacken and remove the retaining bolts, and remove the oil seal housing from the right-hand (timing belt) end of the cylinder block **(see illustration)**.

10.5 Prise up the two caps to expose the main bearing bolts at the flywheel end

10.9 Remove the oil seal housing from the right-hand end of the cylinder block

10.10a Remove the oil pump drive chain ...

10.10b ... then slide off the drive sprocket ...

10.10c ... and remove the Woodruff key from the crankshaft

10.11 Main bearing cap identification markings

10.12 Note the thrustwasher fitted to the No 2 main bearing cap

Section 9. Lift out the crankshaft, and discard the left-hand (flywheel end) oil seal **(see illustration)**.

14 Recover the upper bearing shells from the cylinder block, and tape them to their respective caps for safekeeping **(see illustration)**. Remove the upper thrustwasher halves from the side of No 2 main bearing, and store them with the lower halves.

11 Cylinder block/crankcase – cleaning and inspection

Cleaning

1 Remove all external components and electrical switches/sensors from the block. For complete cleaning, the core plugs should ideally be removed **(see illustration)**. Drill a small hole in the plugs, and then insert a self-tapping screw into the hole. Pull out the plugs by pulling on the screw with a pair of grips, or by using a slide hammer.

2 Where applicable, undo the retaining bolts and remove the piston oil jet spray tubes (there is one for each piston) from inside the cylinder block **(see illustration)**.

3 Scrape all traces of gasket from the cylinder block/crankcase, and from the main bearing ladder/caps (as applicable), taking care not to damage the gasket/sealing surfaces.

4 Remove all oil gallery plugs (where fitted). The plugs are usually very tight – they may have to be drilled out, and the holes retapped. Use new plugs when the engine is reassembled.

10.13 Lift out the crankshaft

10.14 Remove the upper main bearing shells

10 Remove the oil pump drive chain, and slide the drive sprocket and spacer (where fitted) off from the crankshaft. Remove the Woodruff key, and store it with the sprocket for safekeeping **(see illustrations)**.

11 The main bearing caps should be numbered 1 to 5, starting from the transmission (flywheel) end of the engine **(see illustration)**. If not, mark them accordingly using a centre-punch. Also note the correct fitted depth of the crankshaft oil seal in the bearing cap.

12 Slacken and remove the main bearing cap retaining bolts, and lift off each bearing cap. Recover the lower bearing shells, and tape them to their respective caps for safekeeping. Also recover the lower thrustwasher halves from the side of No 2 main bearing cap **(see illustration)**. Remove the sealing strips from

the sides of No 1 main bearing cap, and discard them.

13 Undo the big-end bolts and remove the pistons/connecting rods as described in

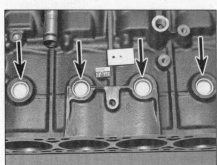

11.1 Cylinder block core plugs

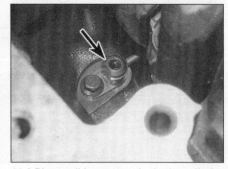

11.2 Piston oil jet spray tube in the cylinder block

5 If any of the castings are extremely dirty, all should be steam-cleaned.

6 After the castings are returned, clean all oil holes and oil galleries one more time. Flush all internal passages with warm water until the water runs clear. Dry thoroughly, and apply a light film of oil to all mating surfaces, to prevent rusting. If you have access to compressed air, use it to speed up the drying process, and to blow out all the oil holes and galleries.

 Warning: Wear eye protection when using compressed air.

7 If the castings are not very dirty, you can do an adequate cleaning job with hot (as hot as you can stand), soapy water and a stiff brush. Take plenty of time, and do a thorough job. Regardless of the cleaning method used, be sure to clean all oil holes and galleries very thoroughly, and to dry all components well. On cast-iron block engines, protect the cylinder bores as described above, to prevent rusting.

8 All threaded holes must be clean, to ensure accurate torque readings during reassembly. To clean the threads, run the correct-size tap into each of the holes to remove rust, corrosion, thread sealant or sludge, and to restore damaged threads **(see illustration)**. If possible, use compressed air to clear the holes of debris produced by this operation.

9 Apply suitable sealant to the new oil gallery plugs, and insert them into the holes in the block. Tighten them securely. Also apply suitable sealant to new core plugs, and drive them into the block using a tube or socket.

10 Where applicable, clean the threads of the piston oil jet retaining bolts, and apply a drop of thread-locking compound (Peugeot/Citroën/Fiat recommend Loctite) to each bolt threads. Refit the piston oil jet spray tubes to the cylinder block, and tighten the retaining bolts to the specified torque setting.

11 If the engine is not going to be reassembled right away, cover it with a large plastic bag to keep it clean; protect all mating surfaces and the cylinder bores as described above, to prevent rusting.

Inspection

12 Visually check the castings for cracks and corrosion. Look for stripped threads in the threaded holes. If there has been any history of internal water leakage, it may be worthwhile having an engine overhaul specialist check the cylinder block/crankcase with special equipment. If defects are found, have them repaired if possible, or renew the assembly.

13 Check each cylinder bore for scuffing and scoring. Check for signs of a wear ridge at the top of the cylinder, indicating that the bore is excessively worn.

14 If the necessary measuring equipment is available, measure the bore diameter of each cylinder at the top (just under the wear ridge), centre, and bottom of the cylinder bore, parallel to the crankshaft axis.

15 Next, measure the bore diameter at the

11.8 Use a suitable tap to clean the cylinder block threaded holes

same three locations, at right angles to the crankshaft axis. Compare the results with the figures given in the Specifications. If there is any doubt about the condition of the cylinder bores, seek the advice of a Citroën/Peugeot/Fiat dealer or suitable engine reconditioning specialist.

16 At the time of writing, it was not clear whether oversize pistons were available for all models. Consult your Peugeot/Citroën/Fiat dealer or engine specialist for the latest information on piston availability. If oversize pistons are available, then it may be possible to have the cylinder bores rebored and fit the oversize pistons. If oversize pistons are not available, and the bores are worn, renewal of the block seems to be the only option.

12 Piston/connecting rod assembly – inspection

1 Before the inspection process can begin, the piston/connecting rod assemblies must be cleaned, and the original piston rings removed from the pistons.

2 Carefully expand the old rings over the top of the pistons. The use of two or three old feeler blades will be helpful in preventing the rings dropping into empty grooves **(see illustration)**. Be careful not to scratch the piston with the ends of the ring. The rings are brittle, and will snap if they are spread too far. They are also very sharp – protect your hands and fingers. Note that the third ring incorporates an expander. Always remove the rings from the top of the piston. Keep each set of rings with its piston if the old rings are to be re-used.

3 Scrape away all traces of carbon from the top of the piston. A hand-held wire brush (or a piece of fine emery cloth) can be used, once the majority of the deposits have been scraped away.

4 Remove the carbon from the ring grooves in the piston, using an old ring. Break the ring in half to do this (be careful not to cut your fingers – piston rings are sharp). Be careful to remove only the carbon deposits – do not remove any metal, and do not nick or scratch the sides of the ring grooves.

5 Once the deposits have been removed,

12.2 Remove the piston rings with the aid of a feeler gauge

clean the piston/connecting rod assembly with paraffin or a suitable solvent, and dry thoroughly. Make sure that the oil return holes in the ring grooves are clear.

6 If the pistons and cylinder bores are not damaged or worn excessively, and if the cylinder block does not need to be re-bored (where possible), the original pistons can be refitted. Normal piston wear shows up as even vertical wear on the piston thrust surfaces, and slight looseness of the top ring in its groove. New piston rings should always be used when the engine is reassembled.

7 Carefully inspect each piston for cracks around the skirt, around the gudgeon pin holes, and at the piston ring 'lands' (between the ring grooves).

8 Look for scoring and scuffing on the piston skirt, holes in the piston crown, and burned areas at the edge of the crown. If the skirt is scored or scuffed, the engine may have been suffering from overheating, and/or abnormal combustion, which caused excessively high operating temperatures. The cooling and lubrication systems should be checked thoroughly. Scorch marks on the sides of the pistons show that blow-by has occurred. A hole in the piston crown, or burned areas at the edge of the piston crown, indicates that abnormal combustion (pre-ignition, knocking, or detonation) has been occurring. If any of the above problems exist, the causes must be investigated and corrected, or the damage will occur again. The causes may include incorrect ignition/injection pump timing, or a faulty injector (as applicable).

9 Corrosion of the piston, in the form of pitting, indicates that coolant has been leaking into the combustion chamber and/or the crankcase. Again, the cause must be corrected, or the problem may persist in the rebuilt engine.

10 Examine each connecting rod carefully for signs of damage, such as cracks around the big-end and small-end bearings. Check that the rod is not bent or distorted. Damage is highly unlikely, unless the engine has been seized or badly overheated. Detailed checking of the connecting rod assembly can only be carried out by a Citroën/Peugeot/Fiat dealer or engine specialist with the necessary equipment.

12.13a Prise out the circlip ...

12.13b ... and withdraw the gudgeon pin

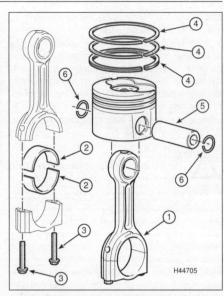

12.17 Piston and connecting rod assembly

1 Connecting rod   *4 Piston rings*
2 Big-end shells   *5 Gudgeon pin*
3 Big-end bolt   *6 Circlips*

11 The connecting rod big-end cap bolts/ nuts must be renewed whenever they are disturbed. Although Citroën/Peugeot/Fiat do not specify that the bolts must also renewed, it is recommended that the nuts and bolts are renewed as a complete set.

12 The gudgeon pins are of the floating type, secured in position by two circlips. On these engines, the pistons and connecting rods can be separated as described in the following paragraphs.

13 Using a small flat-bladed screwdriver, prise out the circlips, and push out the gudgeon pin **(see illustrations)**. Hand pressure should be sufficient to remove the pin. Identify the piston and rod to ensure correct reassembly. Discard the circlips – new ones must be used on refitting.

14 Examine the gudgeon pin and connecting rod small-end bearing for signs of wear or damage. Wear can be cured by renewing both the pin and bush (where possible) or connecting rod. Bush renewal, however, is a specialist job – press facilities are required, and the new bush must be reamed accurately.

15 The connecting rods themselves should not be in need of renewal, unless seizure or some other major mechanical failure has occurred. Check the alignment of the connecting rods visually, and if the rods are not straight, take them to an engine overhaul specialist for a more detailed check.

16 Examine all components, and obtain any new parts from your Peugeot/Citroën/Fiat dealer. If new pistons are purchased, they will be supplied complete with gudgeon pins and

circlips. These circlips can also be purchased individually.

17 Position the piston as shown **(see illustration)**.

18 Ensure the piston and connecting rod are correctly positioned then apply a smear of clean engine oil to the gudgeon pin. Slide it into the piston and through the connecting rod small-end. Check that the piston pivots freely on the rod, then secure the gudgeon pin in position with two new circlips. Ensure that each circlip is correctly located in its groove in the piston.

13 Crankshaft – inspection

Checking endfloat

1 If the crankshaft endfloat is to be checked, this must be done when the crankshaft is still installed in the cylinder block/crankcase, but is free to move (see Section 10).

2 Check the endfloat using a dial gauge in contact with the end of the crankshaft. Push the crankshaft fully one way, and then zero the gauge. Push the crankshaft fully the other way, and check the endfloat. The result can be compared with the specified amount, and will give an indication as to whether new thrustwashers are required **(see illustration)**.

3 If a dial gauge is not available, feeler blades can be used. First push the crankshaft fully towards the flywheel end of the engine, and

then use feeler blades to measure the gap between the web of No 2 crankpin and the thrustwasher **(see illustration)**.

Inspection

4 Clean the crankshaft using paraffin or a suitable solvent, and dry it, preferably with compressed air if available. Be sure to clean the oil holes with a pipe cleaner or similar probe, to ensure that they are not obstructed.

⚠ *Warning: Wear eye protection when using compressed air.*

5 Check the main and big-end bearing journals for uneven wear, scoring, pitting and cracking.

6 Big-end bearing wear is accompanied by distinct metallic knocking when the engine is running (particularly noticeable when the engine is pulling from low speed) and some loss of oil pressure.

7 Main bearing wear is accompanied by severe engine vibration and rumble – getting progressively worse as engine speed increases – and again by loss of oil pressure.

8 Check the bearing journal for roughness by running a finger lightly over the bearing surface. Any roughness (which will be accompanied by obvious bearing wear) indicates that the crankshaft requires regrinding (where possible) or renewal.

9 Check the oil seal contact surfaces at each end of the crankshaft for wear and damage. If the seal has worn a deep groove in the surface of the crankshaft, consult an engine overhaul specialist; repair may be possible, but otherwise a new crankshaft will be required.

10 Take the crankshaft to a Peugeot/Citroën/ Fiat dealer or engine reconditioning specialist

13.2 The crankshaft endfloat can be checked with a dial gauge ...

13.3 ... or with feeler gauges

to have it measured for journal wear. If excessive wear is evident, they will be able to advise you with regard to regrinding the crankshaft and supplying new bearing shells.

11 If the crankshaft has been reground, check for burrs around the crankshaft oil holes (the holes are usually chamfered, so burrs should not be a problem unless regrinding has been carried out carelessly). Remove any burrs with a fine file or scraper, and thoroughly clean the oil holes as described previously.

12 At the time of writing, it was not clear whether Peugeot/Citroën/Fiat produce undersize bearing shells for all of these engines. On some engines, if the crankshaft journals have not already been reground, it may be possible to have the crankshaft reconditioned, and to fit undersize shells. If no undersize shells are available and the crankshaft has worn beyond the specified limits, it will have to be renewed. Consult your Peugeot/Citroën/Fiat dealer or engine specialist for further information on parts availability.

14 Main and big-end bearings – inspection

1 Even though the main and big-end bearings should be renewed during the engine overhaul, the old bearings should be retained for close examination, as they may reveal valuable information about the condition of the engine. The bearing shells are graded by thickness, the grade of each shell being indicated by the colour code marked on it.

2 Bearing failure can occur due to lack of lubrication, the presence of dirt or other foreign particles, overloading the engine, or corrosion **(see illustration)**. Regardless of the cause of bearing failure, the cause must

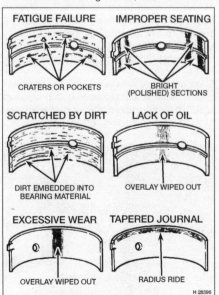

14.2 Typical bearing failures

be corrected (where applicable) before the engine is reassembled, to prevent it from happening again.

3 When examining the bearing shells, remove them from the cylinder block/crankcase, the main bearing ladder/caps (as appropriate), the connecting rods and the connecting rod big-end bearing caps. Lay them out on a clean surface in the same general position as their location in the engine. This will enable you to match any bearing problems with the corresponding crankshaft journal. Do not touch any shell's bearing surface with your fingers while checking it, or the delicate surface may be scratched.

4 Dirt and other foreign matter gets into the engine in a variety of ways. It may be left in the engine during assembly, or it may pass through filters or the crankcase ventilation system. It may get into the oil, and from there into the bearings. Metal chips from machining operations and normal engine wear are often present. Abrasives are sometimes left in engine components after reconditioning, especially when parts are not thoroughly cleaned using the proper cleaning methods. Whatever the source, these foreign objects often end up embedded in the soft bearing material, and are easily recognised. Large particles will not embed in the bearing, and will score or gouge the bearing and journal. The best prevention for this cause of bearing failure is to clean all parts thoroughly, and keep everything spotlessly clean during engine assembly. Frequent and regular engine oil and filter changes are also recommended.

5 Lack of lubrication (or lubrication breakdown) has a number of interrelated causes. Excessive heat (which thins the oil), overloading (which squeezes the oil from the bearing face) and oil leakage (from excessive bearing clearances, worn oil pump or high engine speeds) all contribute to lubrication breakdown. Blocked oil passages, which usually are the result of misaligned oil holes in a bearing shell, will also oil-starve a bearing, and destroy it. When lack of lubrication is the cause of bearing failure, the bearing material is wiped or extruded from the steel backing of the bearing. Temperatures may increase to the point where the steel backing turns blue from overheating.

6 Driving habits can have a definite effect on bearing life. Full-throttle, low-speed operation (labouring the engine) puts very high loads on bearings, tending to squeeze out the oil film. These loads cause the bearings to flex, which produces fine cracks in the bearing face (fatigue failure). Eventually, the bearing material will loosen in pieces, and tear away from the steel backing.

7 Short-distance driving leads to corrosion of bearings, because insufficient engine heat is produced to drive off the condensed water and corrosive gases. These products collect in the engine oil, forming acid and sludge. As the oil is carried to the engine bearings, the acid attacks and corrodes the bearing material.

8 Incorrect bearing installation during engine assembly will lead to bearing failure as well. Tight-fitting bearings leave insufficient bearing running clearance, and will result in oil starvation. Dirt or foreign particles trapped behind a bearing shell result in high spots on the bearing, which lead to failure.

9 Do not touch any shell's bearing surface with your fingers during reassembly; there is a risk of scratching the delicate surface, or of depositing particles of dirt on it.

10 As mentioned at the beginning of this Section, the bearing shells should be renewed as a matter of course during engine overhaul; to do otherwise is false economy.

15 Engine overhaul – reassembly sequence

1 Before reassembly begins, ensure that all new parts have been obtained, and that all necessary tools are available. Read through the entire procedure to familiarise yourself with the work involved, and to ensure that all items necessary for reassembly of the engine are at hand. In addition to all normal tools and materials, thread-locking compound will be needed. A tube of suitable liquid sealant will also be required for the joint faces that are fitted without gaskets. It is recommended that the manufacturers own product(s) be used, which are specially formulated for this purpose; the relevant product names are quoted in the text of each Section where they are required.

2 In order to save time and avoid problems, engine reassembly can be carried out in the following order, referring to Chapter 2A or Chapter 2B or Chapter 2C unless otherwise stated:

a) *Crankshaft (see Section 17).*
b) *Piston/connecting rod assemblies (See Section 18).*
c) *Oil pump.*
d) *Sump.*
e) *Flywheel/driveplate.*
f) *Cylinder head.*
g) *Injection pump and mounting bracket.*
h) *Timing belt tensioner pulley(s) and sprockets, and timing belt.*
i) *Engine external components.*

3 At this stage, all engine components should be absolutely clean and dry, with all faults repaired. The components should be laid out (or in individual containers) on a completely clean work surface.

16 Piston rings – refitting

1 Before fitting new piston rings, the ring end gaps must be checked as follows.

2 Lay out the piston/connecting rod assemblies and the new piston ring sets, so that the ring sets will be matched with the

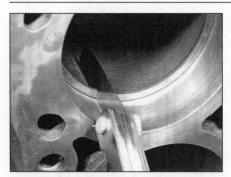

16.5 Measure the piston rings end gaps with a feeler gauge

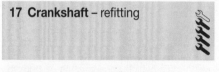

J44877

16.9a Piston ring fitting diagram (typical)

1 Oil control ring
2 Second compression ring
3 Top compression ring

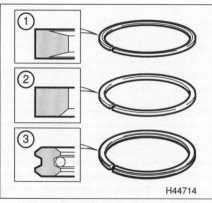

H44714

16.9b Piston rings

1 Top compression ring
2 Second compression ring
3 Oil control ring

same piston and cylinder during the end gap measurement and subsequent engine reassembly.

3 Insert the top ring into the first cylinder, and push it down the bore using the top of the piston. This will ensure that the ring remains square with the cylinder walls. Position the ring near the bottom of the cylinder bore, at the lower limit of ring travel. Note that the top and second compression rings are different. The second ring can be identified by its taper and the top ring has a chamfer on its upper/outer edge.

4 Measure the end gap using feeler blades.

5 Repeat the procedure with the ring at the top of the cylinder bore, at the upper limit of its travel **(see illustration)**, and compare the measurements with the figures given in the Specifications. If the end gaps are incorrect, check that you have the correct rings for your engine and for the cylinder bore size.

6 Repeat the checking procedure for each ring in the first cylinder, and then for the rings in the remaining cylinders. Remember to keep rings, pistons and cylinders matched up.

7 Once the ring end gaps have been checked and if necessary corrected, the rings can be fitted to the pistons.

8 Fit the oil control ring expander (where fitted) then install the ring. The ring gap should be positioned 180° from the expander gap.

9 The second and top rings are different and can be identified from their cross-

sections; the top ring is symmetrical whilst the second ring is tapered. Fit the second ring, ensuring its identification (TOP) marking is facing upwards, and then install the top ring **(see illustrations)**. Arrange the second and top ring end gap so they are equally spaced 120° apart. **Note:** *Always follow any instructions supplied with the new piston ring sets – different manufacturers may specify different procedures. Do not mix up the top and second compression rings, as they have different cross-sections.*

17 Crankshaft – refitting

Selection of bearing shells

1 Have the crankshaft inspected and measured by an engine reconditioning specialist. They will be able to carry out any regrinding/repairs, and supply suitable main and big-end bearing shells.

Crankshaft refitting

1.6 litre diesel engine

2 Place the bearing shells in their locations. If new shells are being fitted, ensure that all

traces of protective grease are cleaned off using paraffin. Wipe dry the shells with a lint-free cloth. The upper bearing shells all have a grooved surface, whereas the lower shells have a plain surface. On these engines, it's essential that the lower bearing shells are centrally located in the bearing cap housing/ladder. To ensure this use Citroën/Peugeot/Fiat tool No 0194-QZ positioned over the housing/ladder, and insert the bearing shells through the slots in the tool **(see illustration)**.

3 Liberally lubricate each bearing shell in the cylinder block with clean engine oil then lower the crankshaft into position.

4 Insert the thrustwashers to either side of No 2 main bearing upper location and push them around the bearing journal until their edges are horizontal **(see illustration)**. Ensure that the oilway grooves on each thrustwasher face outwards (away from the bearing journal).

5 Thoroughly degrease the mating surfaces of the cylinder block and the crankshaft bearing cap housing. Apply a thin bead of RTV sealant to the bearing cap housing mating surface **(see illustration)**. The manufacturers recommend the use of Loctite Autojoint Noir for this purpose.

6 Lubricate the lower bearing shells with clean engine oil, then refit the bearing cap housing, ensuring that the shells are not displaced, and that the locating dowels engage correctly.

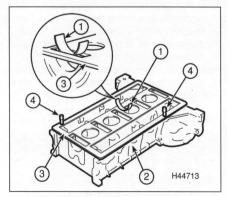

17.2 Main bearing shell refitment

1 Bearing shell
2 Main bearing ladder
3 Citroën tool
4 Aligning pins

17.4 Place the thrustwashers each side of the No 2 bearing upper location

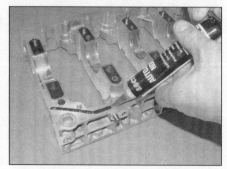

17.5 Apply a thin bead of RTV sealant to the bearing cap housing mating surface

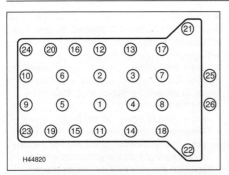

17.8 Main bearing ladder bolts tightening sequence

17.12a Ensure the grooved main bearing shells are fitted to the cylinder block …

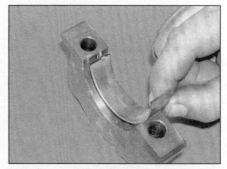

17.12b … and the plain bearing shells are fitted to the bearing caps

7 Install the ten large diameter and sixteen smaller diameter crankshaft bearing cap housing retaining bolts, and screw them in until they are just making contact with the housing.

8 Working in sequence, tighten the bolts to the torque settings given in Chapter 2A Specifications 0 or Chapter 2B Specifications 0 **(see illustration)**.

9 With the bearing cap housing in place, check that the crankshaft rotates freely.

10 Refit the piston/connecting rod assemblies to the crankshaft as described in Section 18.

2.0 litre diesel engine

11 Using a little grease, stick the thrustwashers to each side of No 2 main bearing upper location and bearing cap **(see illustration 17.4)**. Ensure that the oilway grooves on each thrustwasher face outwards (away from the cylinder block).

12 Place the bearing shells in their locations **(see illustrations)**. If new shells are being fitted, ensure that all traces of protective grease are cleaned off using paraffin. Wipe dry the shells and connecting rods with a lint-free cloth. Liberally lubricate each bearing shell in the cylinder block/crankcase and cap with clean engine oil.

13 Lower the crankshaft into position so that Nos 2 and 3 cylinder crankpins are at TDC; Nos 1 and 4 cylinder crankpins will be at BDC, ready for fitting No 1 piston. Check the crankshaft endfloat, referring to Section 13.

14 Lubricate the lower bearing shells in the

17.15 Fit the No 2 to 5 bearing caps and install the bolts

main bearing caps with clean engine oil. Make sure that the locating lugs on the shells engage with the corresponding recesses in the caps.

15 Fit main bearing caps Nos 2 to 5 to their correct locations, ensuring that they are fitted the correct way round (the bearing shell tab recesses in the block and caps must be on the same side) **(see illustration)**. Ensure the thrustwashers remain correctly fitted to No 2 bearing cap then refit the bearing cap bolts, tightening them only lightly at this stage.

16 Apply a small amount of sealant to the No 1 main bearing cap mating face on the cylinder block, around the sealing strip holes and in the corners **(see illustration)**.

17 Locate the tab of each sealing strip over

17.16 Apply sealant to the No 1 main bearing cap mating face on the cylinder block, around the sealing strip holes and in the corners

the pins on the base of No 1 bearing cap, and press the strips into the bearing cap grooves. It is now necessary to obtain two thin metal strips, of 0.25 mm thickness or less, in order to prevent the strips moving when the cap is being fitted. Citroën/Peugeot/Fiat garages use the tool shown, which acts as a clamp. Metal strips (such as old feeler blades) can be used, provided all burrs that may damage the sealing strips are first removed **(see illustrations)**.

18 Where applicable, oil both sides of the metal strips, and hold them on the sealing strips. Fit the No 1 main bearing cap, insert the bolts loosely, and then carefully pull out the metal strips in a horizontal direction, using a pair of pliers **(see illustration)**.

17.17a Fit the sealing strips to each side of No 1 main bearing cap, ensuring they are correctly engaged

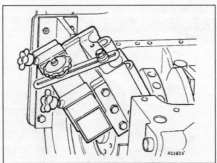

17.17b Using the manufacturers tool to fit the No 1 main bearing cap

17.18 Using 2 metal strips to hold the sealing strips in place as the bearing cap is fitted

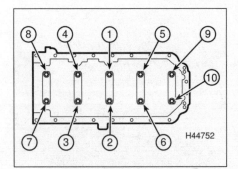

17.19 Main bearing cap bolt tightening sequence

19 Working in sequence **(see illustration)**, tighten the main bearing cap bolts evenly and progressively to the specified Stage 1 torque wrench setting. Once all the bolts have been tightened to the Stage 1 setting, working in the specified sequence, angle-tighten the bolts through the specified Stage 2 angle, using a socket and extension bar. It is recommended that an angle-measuring gauge be used during this stage of the tightening, to ensure accuracy. If a gauge is not available, use a dab of white paint to make alignment marks between the bolt head and casting prior to tightening; the marks can then be used to check that the bolt has been rotated sufficiently during tightening.
20 Check that the sealing strips protrude slightly from above the cylinder block/crankcase mating surface by approximately 1 mm. If not, remove the bearing cap again and refit; the seals are supplied the correct length and should not be cut. Also check that the crankshaft rotates freely.
21 Fit a new crankshaft left-hand (flywheel end) oil seal as described in Chapter 2C Section 14.
22 Refit the piston/connecting rod assemblies to the crankshaft as described in Section 18.
23 Fit a new sealing ring (where fitted) the crankshaft then refit the Woodruff key and slide on the oil pump drive sprocket

and spacer. Locate the drive chain on the sprocket.
24 Ensure that the mating surfaces of the right-hand (timing belt end) oil seal housing and cylinder block are clean and dry. Note the correct fitted depth of the oil seal then, using a large flat-bladed screwdriver, lever the old seal out of the housing.
25 Apply a smear of suitable sealant to the oil seal housing mating surface. Ensure that the locating dowels are in position, and then slide the housing over the end of the crankshaft and into position on the cylinder block. Tighten the housing retaining bolts to the specified torque.
26 Fit a new crankshaft right-hand (timing belt end) oil seal as described in Chapter 2C Section 14.
27 Ensuring that the drive chain is correctly located on the sprocket, refit the oil pump and sump as described in Chapter 2C.
28 Refit the flywheel as described in Chapter 2C Section 16.
29 Refit the cylinder head (where removed) and also refit the crankshaft sprocket and timing belt.

18 Piston/connecting rod assembly – refitting

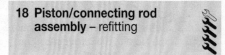

Note: *New big-end cap nuts/bolts must be used on refitting.*
1 Clean the backs of the bearing shells, and the bearing locations in both the connecting rod and bearing cap.

2.0 litre engines

2 Press the bearing shells into their locations, ensuring that the tab on each shell engages in the notch in the connecting rod and cap. Take care not to touch any shell's bearing surface with your fingers **(see illustration)**.

All engines

3 Lubricate the cylinder bores, the pistons and piston rings, then lay out each piston/connecting rod assembly in its respective position.

4 Start with assembly No 1. Make sure that the piston rings are still spaced as described in Section 16, and then clamp them in position with a piston ring compressor.
5 Insert the piston/connecting rod assembly into the top of cylinder number 1; ensuring the piston is correctly positioned as follows.
a) *On 1.6 litre diesel engines, ensure that the DIST mark or arrow on the piston crown is towards the timing belt end of the engine.*
b) *On 2.0 litre diesel engines, ensure that the valve recesses on the piston crown are towards the rear of the cylinder block.*
6 Once the piston is correctly positioned, using a block of wood or hammer handle against the piston crown, tap the assembly into the cylinder until the piston crown is flush with the top of the cylinder **(see illustration)**.

2.0 litre engines

7 Ensure that the bearing shell is still correctly installed. Liberally lubricate the crankpin and both bearing shells. Taking care not to mark the cylinder bores, pull the piston/connecting rod assembly down the bore and onto the crankpin. Refit the big-end bearing cap and fit the new nuts, tightening them finger-tight at first **(see illustration)**. Note that the faces with the identification marks must match (which means that the bearing shell locating tabs abut each other).
8 Tighten the bearing cap retaining nuts evenly and progressively to the specified torque setting.

1.6 litre engines

9 On these engines, the connecting rod is made in one piece, and the big-end bearing cap is 'cracked' off. This ensures that the cap fits onto the connecting rod only in one position, and with maximum rigidity. Consequently, there are no locating notches for the bearing shells to fit into.
10 To ensure that the big-end bearing shells are centrally located in the connecting rod and cap, two special tools are available from the engine manufacturers. These half-moon shaped tools are pressed in from either side of the rod/cap and locate the shell exactly in

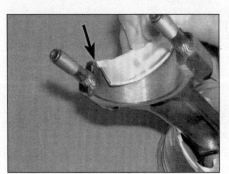

18.2 Ensure the bearing shell tab locates correctly in the cut-out

18.6 Tap the piston into the bore using a hammer handle

18.7 Fit the big-end bearing cap, ensuring it is fitted the right way around, and screw on the new nuts

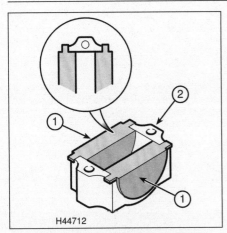

18.10 Big-end bearing shell positioning
1 Tool No 0194-P   2 Bearing shell

the centre **(see illustration)**. Fit the shells into the connecting rods and big-end caps and lubricate them with plenty of clean engine oil.
11 Pull the connecting rods and pistons down the bores and onto the crankshaft journals. Fit the big-end caps – they will only

fit properly one way round (see paragraph 9), and insert the new bolts.
12 Tighten the bolts to the Stage 1 torque setting, then slacken them 180° (Stage 2). Tighten the bolts to the Stage 3 setting, followed by the Stage 4 angle-tightening setting.

All engines

13 Once the bearing cap retaining nuts have been correctly tightened, rotate the crankshaft. Check that it turns freely; some stiffness is to be expected if new components have been fitted, but there should be no signs of binding or tight spots.

19 Engine –
initial start-up after overhaul

1 With the engine refitted in the vehicle, double-check the engine oil and coolant levels. Make a final check that everything has been reconnected, and that there are no tools or rags left in the engine compartment.
2 Prime the fuel system (refer to Chapter 4A Section 4).

3 Fully depress the accelerator pedal, turn the ignition key to position M, and wait for the preheating warning light to go out.
4 Start the engine, noting that this may take a little longer than usual, due to the fuel system components having been disturbed.
5 While the engine is idling, check for fuel, water and oil leaks. Don't be alarmed if there are some odd smells and smoke from parts getting hot and burning off oil deposits.
6 Assuming all is well; keep the engine idling until hot water is felt circulating through the top hose, then switch off the engine.
7 After a few minutes, recheck the oil and coolant levels as described in *Weekly checks*, and top-up as necessary.
8 Note that there is no need to retighten the cylinder head bolts once the engine has first run after reassembly.
9 If new pistons, rings or crankshaft bearings have been fitted, the engine must be treated as new, and run-in for the first 500 miles. Do not operate the engine at full-throttle, or allow it to labour at low engine speeds in any gear. It is recommended that the oil and filter be changed at the end of this period.

Notes

Chapter 3
Cooling, heating and ventilation systems

Contents

Degrees of difficulty

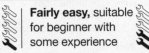

Easy, suitable for novice with little experience	**Fairly easy,** suitable for beginner with some experience	**Fairly difficult,** suitable for competent DIY mechanic	**Difficult,** suitable for experienced DIY mechanic	**Very difficult,** suitable for expert DIY or professional

Specifications

General

Maximum system pressure	1.4 bars
Engine coolant temperature sensor resistance (approx):	
60°C	1266 ohms
80°C	642 ohms
Cooling fan operating temperatures:	
1st speed	97°C (or climate control operating)
2nd speed	101°C
3rd speed	105°C
Post-cooling period	6 minutes

Thermostat

Start of opening temperature	83°C

Air conditioning compressor oil

Quantity	135 cc
Type	Sanden SP10

Note: *DENSO ND8 oil is compatible with SANDEN SP10 oil*

Refrigerant

Quantity	540 ± 25 g
Type	R134a

Torque wrench settings

	Nm	lbf ft
Air conditioning compressor mounting bolts	25	18
Coolant outlet housing:		
Stage 1	3	2
Stage 2	8	6
Coolant pump:		
Stage1	5	4
Stage 2	9	7
Thermostat housing bolts:		
1.6 litre models	8	6
2.0 litre models	Not available	

1 General information and precautions

1 The cooling system is of pressurised type, comprising a coolant pump driven by the timing belt, an aluminium radiator, an expansion tank, an electric cooling fan, a thermostat, a heater matrix, and all associated hoses and switches.

2 The system functions as follows. Cold coolant in the bottom of the radiator passes through the bottom hose to the coolant pump, where it is pumped around the cylinder block and head passages. After cooling the cylinder bores, combustion surfaces and valve seats, the coolant reaches the underside of the thermostat, which is initially closed. The coolant passes through the heater, and is returned via the cylinder block to the coolant pump.

3 When the engine is cold, the coolant circulates only through the cylinder block, cylinder head, and heater. When the coolant reaches a predetermined temperature, the thermostat opens, and the coolant passes through the top hose to the radiator. As the coolant passes down through the radiator, it is cooled by the inrush of air when the car is in forward motion. The airflow is supplemented by the action of the electric cooling fan when necessary. Upon reaching the bottom of the radiator, the coolant has now cooled, and the cycle is repeated.

4 On models fitted with an engine oil cooler, the coolant is also passed through the oil cooler.

5 The operation of the electric cooling fan(s) is controlled by the engine management control unit.

⚠️ **Warning: Do not attempt to remove the expansion tank filler cap, or to disturb any part of the cooling system, while the engine is hot, as there is a high risk of scalding. If the expansion tank filler cap must be removed before the engine and radiator have fully cooled (even though this is not recommended), the pressure in the cooling system must first be relieved. Cover the cap with a thick layer of cloth to avoid scalding, and slowly unscrew the filler cap** until a hissing sound is heard. When the hissing has stopped, indicating that the pressure has reduced, slowly unscrew the filler cap until it can be removed; if more hissing sounds are heard, wait until they have stopped before unscrewing the cap. At all times keep well away from the filler cap opening, and protect your hands.

⚠️ **Warning: Do not allow antifreeze to come into contact with your skin, or with the painted surfaces of the vehicle. Rinse off spills immediately, with plenty of water. Never leave antifreeze lying around in an open container, or in a puddle in the driveway or on the garage floor. Children and pets are attracted by its sweet smell, but antifreeze can be fatal if ingested.**

⚠️ **Warning: If the engine is hot, the electric cooling fan(s) may start rotating even if the engine is not running. Be careful to keep your hands, hair, and any loose clothing well clear when working in the engine compartment.**

⚠️ **Warning: Refer to Section 11 for precautions to be observed when working on models equipped with air conditioning.**

2 Cooling system hoses – disconnection and renewal

Note: *Refer to the warnings given in Section 1 of this Chapter before proceeding. Hoses should only be disconnected once the engine has cooled sufficiently to avoid scalding.*

1 If the checks described in the hose and fluid leak check in Chapter 1 Section 7 reveal a faulty hose, it must be renewed as follows.

2 First drain the cooling system (see Chapter 1 Section 23). If the coolant is not due for renewal, it may be re-used, providing it is collected in a clean container.

3 To disconnect a hose, proceed as follows, according to the type of hose connection.

Conventional connections

4 On conventional connections, the clips used to secure the hoses in position may be either standard worm-drive clips, spring clips or disposable crimped types **(see illustration)**. The crimped type of clip is not designed to be re-used and should be updated with a worm-drive type on reassembly,

5 To disconnect a hose, release the retaining clips and move them along the hose, clear of the relevant inlet/outlet. Carefully work the hose free. The hoses can be removed with relative ease when new – on an older car they may have stuck **(see illustration)**.

6 If a hose proves to be difficult to remove, try to release it by rotating its ends before attempting to free it. Gently prise the end of the hose with a blunt instrument (such as a flat-bladed screwdriver), but do not apply too much force, and take care not to damage the pipe stubs or hoses. Note in particular that the radiator inlet stub is fragile; do not use excessive force when attempting to remove the hose. If all else fails, cut the hose with a sharp knife, then slit it so that it can be peeled off in two pieces. Although this may prove expensive if the hose is otherwise undamaged, it is preferable to buying a new radiator. Check first, however, that a new hose is readily available.

7 When fitting a hose, first slide the clips onto the hose, and then work the hose into position. If crimped-type clips were originally fitted, use standard worm-drive clips when refitting the hose.

8 Work the hose into position, checking that it is correctly routed, and the alignment markings **(see illustration)** on the hoses, are in line with the markings on the coolant pipe stubs. Once in position, slide each clip back along the hose until it passes over the flared end of the relevant inlet/outlet, before tightening the clip securely.

9 Refill the cooling system (see Chapter 1 Section 23).

10 Check thoroughly for leaks as soon as possible after disturbing any part of the cooling system.

Click-fit connections

Note: *New sealing ring should be used when reconnecting the hose.*

11 On certain models, some cooling system hoses are secured in position with click-fit connectors where the hose is retained by a large circlip.

12 To disconnect this type of hose fitting, carefully prise the wire clip out of position

2.4 Spring clip type upper hose retaining clip

2.5 Release the retaining clip and move it along the hose

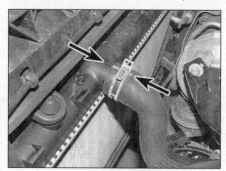

2.8 Hose alignment markings

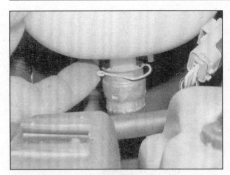

2.12 Where click-fit connectors are used, prise out the circlip then disconnect the hose

2.13 Ensure the sealing ring and circlip are correctly fitted to the hose union before reconnecting a connector

3.2 Squeeze the clips to disconnect the coolant pipes

then disconnect the hose connection **(see illustration)**. Once the hose has been disconnected, refit the wire clip to the hose union. Inspect the hose unit sealing ring for signs of damage or deterioration and renew if necessary.

13 On refitting, ensure that the sealing ring is in position and the wire clip is correctly located in the groove in the union **(see illustration)**. Lubricate the sealing ring with a smear of soapy water, to ease installation, and then push the hose into its union until it is heard to click into position.

14 Ensure the hose is securely retained by the wire clip then refill the cooling system as described in Chapter 1 Section 23.

15 Check thoroughly for leaks as soon as possible after disturbing any part of the cooling system.

3 Coolant expansion tank – removal and refitting

Removal

1 Referring to Chapter 1 Section 23, drain the cooling system sufficiently to empty the contents of the expansion tank. Do not drain any more coolant than is necessary.

2 Squeeze together the collars, and then pull

the plastic hose(s) from the expansion tank **(see illustration)**.

3 Disconnect the level sensor wiring plug – where fitted.

4 Unscrew the mounting nut and free the tank from its mount **(see illustration)**. Withdraw the expansion tank forwards from the mounting rubbers in the mounting bracket. Lift the expansion tank upwards to access the lower coolant hose.

5 Release the securing clip and disconnect the remaining hose from the bottom of the expansion tank, as it is removed.

Refitting

6 Refitting is the reverse of removal, ensuring the hoses are securely reconnected. On completion, top-up the coolant level as described in *Weekly checks*.

4 Radiator – removal, inspection and refitting

Note: *If leakage is the reason for removing the radiator, bear in mind that minor leaks can often be cured using a radiator sealant with the radiator still in position.*

Removal

1 Drain the cooling system (see Chapter 1 Section 23).

3.4 Coolant reservoir mounting nut

2.0 litre models

2 Remove the air cleaner assembly as described in Chapter 4A Section 5.

3 Release the clamps and remove the air hose from the intercooler to the intake manifold **(see illustration)**.

All models

4 Release the clamps, then disconnect the radiator upper and lower hoses (if not already done so) **(see illustration)**.

5 Squeeze together the collar and disconnect the plastic pipe from the top of the radiator **(see illustration)**. Unclip the pipe from any retaining clips along the top of the radiator.

6 Using a flat-bladed screwdriver, release

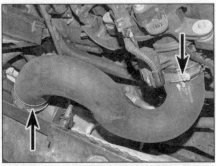

4.3 Intake manifold-to-intercooler hose clamps

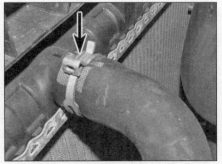

4.4 Radiator upper hose clamp

4.5 Squeeze together the collar and disconnect the plastic pipe

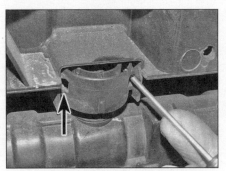

4.6 Press-in the clip each side, and pull the radiator rearwards

4.10 Radiator lower rubber mountings

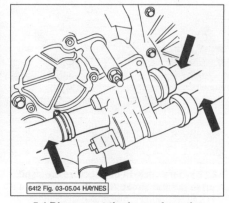

5.4 Disconnect the hoses from the thermostat housing

the two retaining clips, pull the top of the radiator rearwards, and lift it from place **(see illustration)**.

Inspection

7 If the radiator has been removed due to suspected blockage, reverse-flush it as described in Chapter 1 Section 23. Clean dirt and debris from the radiator fins, using an airline (in which case, wear eye protection) or a soft brush. Be careful, as the fins are sharp, and easily damaged.
8 If necessary, a radiator specialist can perform a 'flow test' on the radiator, to establish whether an internal blockage exists.
9 A leaking radiator must be referred to a specialist for permanent repair. Do not attempt to weld or solder a leaking radiator, as damage to the plastic components may result.
10 Inspect the condition of the radiator mounting rubbers, and renew them if necessary. Check that the two radiator lower mounting rubbers are in position **(see illustration)**, before refitting.

Refitting

11 Refitting is a reversal of removal, bearing in mind the following points:
a) *Ensure that the lower lugs on the radiator are correctly engaged with the mounting rubbers in the body panel*
b) *Reconnect the hoses with reference to Section 2, using new sealing rings where applicable.*
c) *On completion, refill the cooling system as described in Chapter 1 Section 23.*

5 Thermostat – removal, testing and refitting

Removal

1 Drain the cooling system (see Chapter 1 Section 23).

1.6 litre models

2 Remove the air filter assembly as described in Chapter 4A Section 5.
3 The thermostat housing is located at the left-hand end of the cylinder head. Disconnect

the coolant temperature sensor wiring plug **(see illustration 7.4a)**.
4 Note their fitted positions, then disconnect the various coolant hoses from the housing **(see illustration)**.
5 Unscrew the four retaining bolts, and then remove the housing from the left-hand end of the cylinder head. Recover the gasket/seal a new one will be required for refitting.

2.0 litre models

6 The thermostat is located in a housing at the left-hand end of the cylinder head. The thermostat is integral with the housing.
7 Remove the air cleaner assembly as described in Chapter 4A Section 5.
8 Release the clamps, undo the retaining bolt, and remove the hose from the air filter to the turbocharger air inlet pipe.
9 Unclip the wiring loom from the mounting bracket(s), and then remove the mounting

5.9a Unclip the loom, then remove the outer mounting bracket...

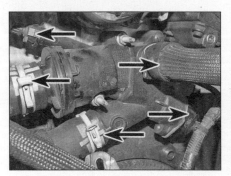

5.11 Disconnect the hoses from the coolant housing

bracket(s) to access the coolant housing **(see illustrations)**.
10 Disconnect the wiring connector from the temperature sensor in the coolant housing.
11 Note the fitted position of the hoses, and then disconnect them from the coolant housing **(see illustration)**.
12 Unscrew the retaining bolts, and then remove the housing from the left-hand end of the cylinder head **(see illustration)**. Recover the gasket/seal a new one will be required for refitting.

Testing

13 A rough test of the thermostat may be made by suspending it with a piece of string in a container full of water. Heat the water to bring it to the boil – the thermostat must open by the time the water boils. If not, renew it.

5.9b ...then remove the inner bracket

5.12 Thermostat housing retaining nuts

14 If a thermometer is available, the precise opening temperature of the thermostat may be determined; compare with the figures given in the Specifications. The opening temperature may also be marked on the thermostat.
15 A thermostat which fails to close as the water cools must also be renewed.

Refitting

16 Refitting is a reversal of removal, bearing in mind the following points.
a) Renew the coolant housing gasket/seal.
b) Make sure all wiring connectors are fitted securely.
c) On completion, refill the cooling system as described in Chapter 1 Section 23.

6 Electric cooling fan – removal and refitting

Removal

1 Disconnect the battery negative lead as described in Chapter 5A Section 4.
2 Remove the front bumper as described in Chapter 11 Section 6.
3 Release the locking clips, then disconnect the fan wiring plugs and release them from the securing clips on the radiator front panel (see illustration).
4 Undo the retaining bolts and lift the fan from place (see illustration).

Refitting

5 Refitting is a reversal of removal.

7 Coolant temperature sensor – general information, removal and refitting

General information

1 The coolant temperature sensor is fitted to the coolant housing on the left-hand end of

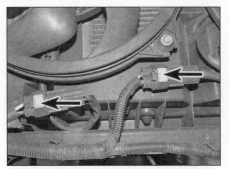
6.3 Slide out the locking clips and disconnect the fan wiring plugs

the cylinder head (see Section 5). The coolant temperature gauge and the cooling fan are all operated by the engine management ECM (Electronic Control Module), using the signal supplied by this sensor.
2 To make access easier remove the air cleaner and ducting as described in Chapter 4A Section 5.

Removal

Note: Ensure the engine is cold before removing a temperature sensor.
3 Partially drain the cooling system to just below the level of the sensor (as described in Chapter 1 Section 23). Alternatively, have ready a suitable bung to plug the sensor aperture whilst the sensor is removed. If this method is used, take great care not to damage the switch aperture or use anything that will allow foreign matter to enter the cooling system.
4 Disconnect the wiring connector from the sensor (see illustrations). Note: Depending on model, the sensor may be on the front or rear of the coolant housing.
5 The sensor is clipped in place; prise out the sensor retaining circlip, and then remove the sensor and sealing ring from the housing. If the system has not been drained, plug the

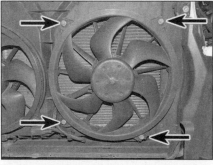
6.4 Left-hand cooling fan retaining bolts

sensor aperture to prevent further coolant loss.

Refitting

6 Fit a new sealing ring to the sensor, and then apply some lubricant (coolant) to the seal to aid refitting. Push the sensor firmly into the housing and secure it in position with the circlip, ensuring it is correctly located in the housing groove.
7 Reconnect the wiring connector then refit any components removed from access. Refit the air cleaner and if removed, refit the battery.
8 Top-up the cooling system as described in Weekly checks.

8 Coolant pump – removal and refitting

1 Drain the cooling system (see Chapter 1 Section 23).
2 Remove the timing belt as described in Chapter 2A Section 7 or Chapter 2B Section 7 or Chapter 2C Section 7.
3 Slacken and remove the retaining bolts from the coolant pump, and then withdraw it from the cylinder block. Recover the pump sealing ring/gasket (as applicable) and discard it; a

7.4a Temperature sensor – 1.6 litre models

7.4b Temperature sensor – 2.0 litre models

**8.5a Coolant pump retaining bolts –
1.6 litre engine**

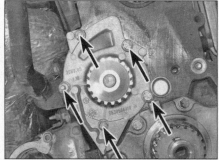

**8.5b Coolant pump retaining bolts –
2.0 litre engine**

8.5c Renew the pump gasket

new one must be used on refitting. **Note:** *The sealing ring may not be available separately from the pump – check with your Citroën/Peugeot/Fiat dealer.*

4 Ensure that the pump and cylinder block/housing mating surfaces are clean and dry.

5 Fit the new sealing ring/gasket (as applicable) to the pump, and then refit the pump assembly, tightening its retaining bolts to the specified torque **(see illustrations)**.

6 Refit the timing belt as described in Chapter 2A Section 7 or Chapter 2B Section 7 or Chapter 2C Section 7.

7 Refill the cooling system as described in Chapter 1 Section 23 (as applicable).

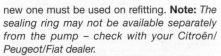

**9   Heating and ventilation
system** – general information

Note: *Refer to Section 11 for information on the air conditioning side of the system.*

Manually-controlled system

1 The heating/ventilation system consists of a four-speed blower motor (housed behind the left-hand side of the facia), face level vents in the centre and at each end of the facia, and air ducts to the front footwells.

2 The control unit is located in the facia, and the controls operate flap valves to deflect and mix the air flowing through the various parts of the heating/ventilation system. The flap valves are contained in the air distribution housing, which acts as a central distribution unit, passing air to the various ducts and vents.

3 Cold air enters the system through the grille in the scuttle. If required, the airflow is boosted by the blower, and then flows through the various ducts, according to the settings of the controls. Stale air is expelled through ducts at the rear of the vehicle. If warm air is required, the cold air is passed over the heater matrix, which is heated by the engine coolant.

4 A recirculation button enables the outside air supply to be closed off, while the air inside the vehicle is recirculated. This can be useful to prevent unpleasant odours entering from outside the vehicle, but should only be used briefly, as the recirculated air inside the vehicle will soon become stale.

Automatic climate control

5 A fully automatic electronic climate control system was offered as an option on some models. The main components of the system are exactly the same as those described for the manual system, the only major difference being that the temperature and distribution flaps in the heating/ventilation housing are operated by electric motors rather than cables.

6 The operation of the system is controlled by the electronic control module (which is incorporated in the blower motor assembly) along with the following sensors.

a) *The passenger compartment sensor – informs the control module of the temperature of the air inside the passenger compartment.*

b) *Evaporator temperature sensor – informs the control module of the evaporator temperature.*

c) *Heater matrix temperature sensor – informs the control module of the heater matrix temperature.*

7 Using the information from the above sensors, the control module determines the appropriate settings for the heating/ventilation system housing flaps to maintain the passenger compartment at the desired setting on the control panel.

8 If the system develops a fault, the vehicle should be taken to a Peugeot/Citroën/Fiat dealer. A complete test of the system can then be carried out, using a special electronic diagnostic test unit, which is simply plugged into the system's diagnostic connector. This is located inside the storage compartment on the drivers side of the facia **(see illustration)**.

**10 Heater/ventilation
components** –
removal and refitting

Control panel

1 Remove the facia centre switch panel as described in Chapter 11 Section 27.

2 Pull the control panel from the facia complete with wiring and control cables (on manually-operated system).

3 Disconnect the wiring connectors from the rear of the control panel **(see illustration)**.

4 On manually-operated systems, note the position of the control cables, then release the securing clips from the outer cables and unhook the inner cable from the operating levers on the control panel **(see illustration)**.

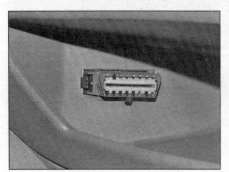

9.8 Vehicle diagnostic plug connector

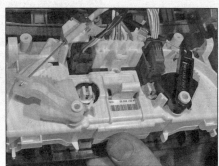

10.3 Disconnect the wiring connectors

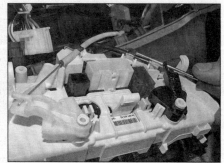

10.4 Prise out the securing clips

10.11a Release the outer cable retaining clip – left-hand side cable...

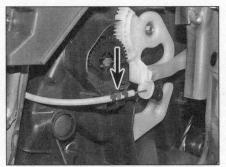

10.11b ...and right-hand side cable

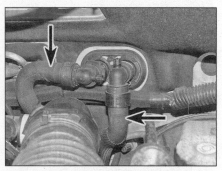

10.14 Heater matrix hoses at the engine compartment bulkhead

5 Refitting is the reverse of removal. On manually-operated systems, ensure the control cables are correctly reconnected and securely held by the retaining clips; check the operation of the control knobs before refitting the trim panels and switch panel (where removed).

Control cables – manually operated system

6 Remove the control panel as described previously in this Section.

7 Before disconnecting the cables from the rear of the control panel note their fitted position. The cable with the black outer cable connects to the black operating lever (temperature control), and the cable with the white outer cable connects to the white operating lever (air flow direction control).

8 Release the retaining clip and then detach the relevant cable from the lever on the rear of the control panel (see illustration 10.4).

9 To access the lower end of the cable on the passenger side, remove the glovebox as described in Section 11 Section 26. To access the lower end of the cable on the drivers side, remove the lower facia panel as described in Chapter 11 Section 27.

10 Unclip the heater ducting from the side of the heater housing (see illustration 10.16).

11 Unclip the outer cable from the retaining clip and then detach the inner cable from the lever on the heater housing (see illustrations).

The cable can then be withdrawn out from the facia panel.

12 Refitting is the reverse of removal, ensuring the cable is routed correctly and secured in place by its retaining clips. Check the operation of the control panel and cables.

Heater matrix

13 To improve access to the matrix unions on the bulkhead, remove the air cleaner assembly and intake duct (see Chapter 4A Section 5).

14 Drain the cooling system (see Chapter 1 Section 23). Alternatively, clamp the heater matrix coolant hoses at the engine compartment bulkhead to minimise coolant loss (see illustration).

15 Remove the gear lever console as described in Chapter 11 Section 27.

10.16 Remove the passengers air duct

16 Unclip the passengers footwell air duct (see illustration).

17 Undo the screw and remove the plastic cover from the matrix pipes (see illustration).

18 Release the clips and detach the coolant pipes from the matrix connections (see illustrations). Be prepared for coolant spillage, and renew the pipe seals.

19 Slide the matrix out from the heater housing (see illustration). Keep the matrix unions uppermost as the matrix is removed to prevent any coolant spillage.

20 On refitting, ease the matrix into the housing, until it is fitted securely in the heater housing.

21 Reconnect the pipes, with new O-ring seals, and secure them to the matrix with

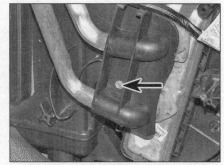

10.17 Undo the screw and remove the plastic cover

10.18a Release the pipe clips

10.18b Renew the pipe O-ring seals

10.19 Slide the matrix from the housing

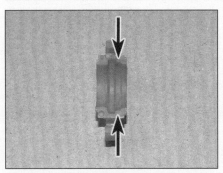

10.21 The 'stepped' side of the clip is on the matrix side

10.25 Undo the 2 screws and lower the blower motor

10.28 Release the resistor wiring plug clip

the retaining clips. Note that the clips are not symmetrical – the 'stepped' side of the clip must be placed on the matrix side **(see illustration)**.

22 Where fitted, remove the clamps from the heater hoses and refill the cooling system (see Chapter 1 Section 23).

23 The remainder of refitting is a reversal of removal.

Heater blower motor

24 Remove the passengers glovebox as described in Chapter 11 Section 27.

25 Disconnect the wiring connector from the blower motor, undo the 2 retaining screws and lower the heater blower motor out from under the facia **(see illustration)**.

26 Refitting is the reverse of removal.

Heater blower motor resistor

27 The resistor is located at the side of the heater blower motor, in the heater housing. Remove the passengers glovebox as described in Chapter 11 Section 27.

28 Reach under the facia and disconnect the wiring connector from the resistor **(see illustration)**.

29 Undo the retaining bolt and withdraw the resistor from the heater housing.

30 To refit manoeuvre the resistor into position in the heater housing and tighten the securing screw. Connect the wiring connector and refit any components removed for access.

Housing assembly

31 On models with air conditioning, have the refrigerant system evacuated by a suitably equipped repairer.

32 Disconnect the battery negative lead as described in Chapter 5A Section 4.

33 To improve access to the matrix unions on the bulkhead, remove the air cleaner housing and intake duct (see Chapter 4A Section 5).

34 Drain the cooling system (see

Chapter 1 Section 23). Alternatively, working in the engine compartment, clamp the heater matrix coolant hoses to minimise coolant loss.

35 Release the retaining clips and disconnect the coolant hoses from the heater matrix pipe unions on the engine compartment bulkhead **(see illustration)**.

36 Undo the screw securing the plate at the heater pipe connection at the bulkhead **(see illustration)**.

37 On models with air conditioning, undo the 2 retaining nuts and pull the refrigerant pipes from the expansion valve at the engine compartment bulkhead **(see illustration)**. Plug the openings to prevent contamination. Renew the pipe O-ring seals.

38 Remove the facia assembly as described in Chapter 11 Section 27.

39 Undo the nut securing the heater housing to the bulkhead in the passenger cabin **(see illustration)**.

40 Undo the bolts and remove the support bracket between the facia crossmember and the vehicle body in the centre **(see illustration)**.

10.35 Prise out the right-hand wire clip a little, and rotate the left-hand collar to release the hoses

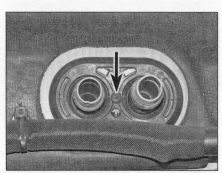

10.36 Undo the Torx screw securing the plate

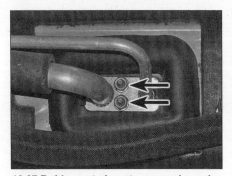

10.37 Refrigerant pipes-to-expansion valve nuts

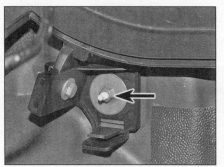

10.39 Undo the nut under the blower motor housing

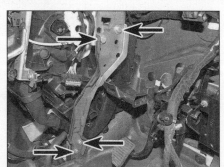

10.40 Support bracket retaining bolts

10.41 Undo the crossmember bolt at the engine compartment bulkhead

10.43a Disconnect the earth lead at the drivers end of the crossmember...

10.43b ...and the one in the centre

41 Working in the engine compartment, undo the bolt securing the crossmember to the bulkhead **(see illustration)**.
42 Note the routing, then release the wiring loom from any retaining clips along the crossmember.
43 Note their fitted positions, then disconnect the earth leads from the crossmember **(see illustrations)**.
44 Undo the nuts securing the gearchange lever assembly to the crossmember **(see illustration)**.
45 Undo the 3 bolts securing the heater housing to the crossmember **(see illustrations)**.
46 The facia crossmember is now secured by 2 bolts at each end. Use paint (or a marker pen) to make alignment marks between the crossmember and the vehicle body, then undo the bolts, and with the help of an assistant,

carefully manoeuvre the crossmember from the vehicle cabin. Take great care as the un-finished edges of the crossmember may be extremely sharp **(see illustration)**.
47 On models with air conditioning, disconnect the water drain hose from the base of the housing **(see illustration)**.
48 Unclip the air duct, then undo the bolt securing the heater housing to the floor bracket at the right-hand lower edge of the housing **(see illustration)**.
49 Manoeuvre the heating/ventilation housing from the vehicle. Keep the heater matrix pipe unions uppermost as the assembly is removed to prevent coolant spillage.
50 Recover the seal and retaining plate from the heater matrix pipes, and the seal from the housing mounting. Renew the seals if they show signs of damage or deterioration.

51 Refitting is the reverse of removal ensuring the seals are in position on the pipes and housing mounting. On completion, refill the cooling system (see Chapter 1 Section 23).

Air control motors

52 On models with an automatic (climate control) heater control system, there may be a number of control motors fitted to the heater housing assembly. On manually-operated heater systems, control cables operate the heater flaps.
53 Remove the facia as described in Chapter 11 Section 27.
54 Disconnect the wiring plug from the control motor, then undo the retaining bolts, and remove it from the side of the heater housing.

10.44 Gearchange lever assembly retaining nuts

10.45a The heater housing is secured to the crossmember by 2 bolts in the centre...

10.45b ...and 1 bolt at the left-hand end

10.46 Undo the 2 bolts at each end of the crossmember

10.47 Pull the drain hose from the housing

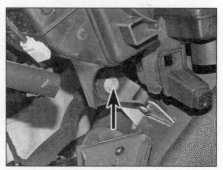

10.48 Undo the housing-to-floor bracket bolt

10.55 Air flap control motor

11.5 The air conditioning high- and low-pressure circuits service ports are located on the right-hand side of the engine compartment

55 All models have an air flap control motor fitted to the heater housing above the air blower motor **(see illustration)**.
56 Refitting is a reversal of removal.

Sunlight sensor

57 Disconnect the battery negative lead as described in Chapter 5A Section 4.
58 Using a blunt, flat-bladed tool, carefully prise the sensor from the centre of the facia. Take care not to mark the facia surface.
59 Disconnect the wiring plug from the base of the sensor as it's withdrawn.
60 Attach a length of string or self-adhesive tape to the sensor wiring to prevent it falling through the aperture into the facia.
61 Refitting is a reversal of removal.

11 Air conditioning system – general information and precautions

1 An air conditioning system is available on all models. It enables the temperature of incoming air to be lowered, and also dehumidifies the air, which makes for rapid demisting and increased comfort.
2 The cooling side of the system works in the same way as a domestic refrigerator. Refrigerant gas is drawn into a belt-driven compressor, and passes into a condenser mounted on the front of the radiator, where it loses heat and becomes liquid. The liquid passes through an expansion valve to an evaporator, where it changes from liquid under

high pressure to gas under low pressure. This change is accompanied by a drop in temperature, which cools the evaporator. The refrigerant returns to the compressor, and the cycle begins again.
3 Air blown through the evaporator passes to the heating/ventilation housing, where it is mixed with hot air blown through the heater matrix to achieve the desired temperature in the passenger compartment.
4 The heating side of the system works in the same way as on models without air conditioning (see Section 9).
5 The operation of the system is controlled electronically by the ECM integral with the control panel. Any problems with the system should be referred to a Peugeot/Citroën/Fiat dealer, or suitably-equipped specialist **(see illustration)**.

Precautions

6 When an air conditioning system is fitted, it is necessary to observe special precautions whenever dealing with any part of the system, or its associated components. The refrigerant is potentially dangerous, and should only be handled by qualified persons. Uncontrolled discharging of the refrigerant is dangerous and damaging to the environment for the following reasons.
● If it is splashed onto the skin, it can cause frostbite.
● The refrigerant is heavier then air and so displaces oxygen. In a confined space, which is not adequately ventilated, this

could lead to a risk of suffocation. The gas is odourless and colourless so there is no warning of its presence in the atmosphere.
● Although not poisonous, in the presence of a naked flame (including a cigarette) it forms a noxious gas that causes headaches, nausea, etc.

⚠ *Warning: Never attempt to open any air conditioning system refrigerant pipe/hose union without first having the system fully discharged by an air conditioning specialist. On completion of work, have the system recharged with the correct type and amount of fresh refrigerant.*

⚠ *Warning: Always seal disconnected refrigerant pipe/hose unions as soon as they are disconnected. Failure to form an airtight seal on any union will result in the dehydrator reservoir become saturated, necessitating its renewal. Also renew all sealing rings disturbed.*
Caution: Do not operate the air conditioning system if it is known to be short of refrigerant as this could damage the compressor.

12 Air conditioning system components – removal and refitting

⚠ *Warning: Refer to the precautions given in Section 11 and have the system discharged by an air conditioning specialist before carrying out any work on the air conditioning system.*

Compressor

1 Have the air conditioning system fully discharged and evacuated by an air conditioning specialist.
2 Remove the auxiliary drivebelt as described in Chapter 1, Section 20.
3 Disconnect the compressor wiring connector(s), and unclip the wiring harness from the retaining clips **(see illustrations)**.
4 Unscrew the nuts securing the refrigerant pipes retaining plates to the compressor **(see illustration)**. Separate the pipes from the

12.3a Disconnect the wiring connector

12.3b On some models there are two connectors

12.4 Undo the nuts securing the refrigerant pipes to the compressor

compressor and quickly seal the pipe and compressor unions to prevent the entry of moisture into the refrigerant circuit. Discard the sealing rings, new ones must be used on refitting.

⚠️ *Warning: Failure to seal the refrigerant pipe unions will result in the dehydrator reservoir become saturated, necessitating its renewal.*

5 Unscrew the compressor mounting bolts and nuts then free the compressor from its mounting bracket and remove it from the engine **(see illustration)**. Take care not to lose the spacers from the compressor rear mountings (where fitted).

6 If the compressor is to be renewed, drain and measure the refrigerant oil from the old compressor. The specialist who recharges the refrigerant system will need to add this amount of oil to the system. Check for the amount of oil to be added, depending on specific model.

7 Ensure the spacers are correctly fitted to the rear mountings then manoeuvre the compressor into position and fit the mounting bolts and nuts.

8 Tighten the compressor front (drivebelt pulley) end mounting bolts to the specified torque first then tighten the rear bolts.

9 Lubricate the new refrigerant pipe sealing rings with compressor oil. Remove the plugs and install the sealing rings then quickly fit the refrigerant pipes to the compressor. Ensure the refrigerant pipes are correctly joined then refit the retaining bolt, tighten it securely.

10 Reconnect the wiring connector then refit the auxiliary drivebelt (see Chapter 1 Section 20).

11 Have the air conditioning system recharged with the correct type and amount of refrigerant by a specialist before using the system. Remember to inform the specialist which components have been renewed, so they can add the correct amount of oil.

Condenser

12 Have the air conditioning system fully discharged by an air conditioning specialist.
13 Remove the radiator as described in, Section 4.
14 Undo the retaining nuts and disconnect

12.5 Remove the compressor mounting bolts

the refrigerant pipes from the right-hand side of the condenser. Recover the O-ring seals **(see illustration)**. Plug the openings to prevent contamination.

⚠️ *Warning: Failure to seal the refrigerant pipe unions will result in the dehydrator reservoir become saturated, necessitating its renewal.*

15 Move the top of the condenser to the rear and withdraw it upwards and out from the engine compartment **(see illustration)**.
16 Refitting is a reversal of removal. Noting the following points:

d) Ensure the upper and lower mounting rubbers are correctly fitted then seat the condenser in position in the front panel **(see illustration)**

e) Lubricate the sealing rings with compressor oil. Remove the plugs and install the sealing rings then quickly fit the refrigerant pipes to the condenser. Securely tighten the dehydrator pipe union nut and ensure the compressor pipe is correctly joined.

f) Have the air conditioning system recharged with the correct type and amount of refrigerant by a specialist before using the system.

Receiver/drier

17 The receiver/drier is located on the side of the condenser. Condenser removal and refitting is described earlier in this Section. The receiver/drier is not available separately; see your local dealer for further information.

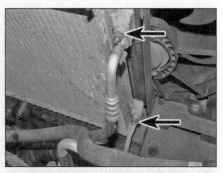

12.14 Undo the nuts securing the refrigerant pipes to the condenser

Pressure switch

18 The switch is located in the high-pressure pipe on the right-hand side of the engine compartment at the bulkhead **(see illustration)**.
19 Have the air conditioning system fully discharged by an air conditioning specialist.
20 Disconnect the wiring connector, and then unscrew the switch from the high-pressure pipe. Quickly seal the condenser union to prevent the entry of moisture into the refrigerant circuit.

⚠️ *Warning: Failure to seal the refrigerant pipe unions will result in the dehydrator reservoir become saturated, necessitating its renewal.*

21 Refitting is a reversal of removal noting the following points:

g) Lubricate the switch seal with compressor oil.

h) Have the air conditioning system recharged with the correct type and amount of refrigerant by a specialist prior to using the system.

Evaporator

22 Have the air conditioning system fully discharged and evacuated by an air conditioning specialist.
23 Remove the heating/ventilation housing as described in Section 10.
24 Note their fitted positions, and then disconnect the wiring plugs and harness from the housing.
25 Remove the rubber pad around the

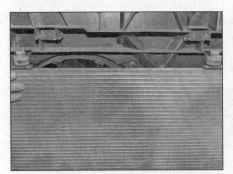

12.15 Move the top of the condenser rearwards to release the mountings

12.16 Make sure the rubber mountings are fitted securely

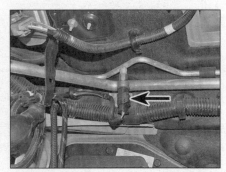

12.18 Air conditioning pressure switch

12.25 Remove the pad around the pipes

12.26 Undo the screws and remove the cover

12.27 Unclip the air duct

12.28 Undo the bolt and remove the bracket

refrigerant pipes/expansion valve **(see illustration)**.
26 Undo the screws and remove the cover from the base of the housing **(see illustration)**.

27 Unclip the footwell air vent **(see illustration)**.
28 Undo the bolt and remove the bracket from the top of the housing **(see illustration)**.

29 Use a sharp craft knife to cut through the foam seals **(see illustration)**.
30 Undo the screws around the housing, and lift one half from the other half **(see illustrations)**.

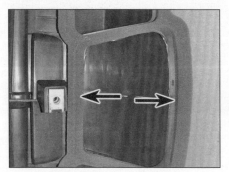

12.29 Cut through the foam

12.30a Undo the screws around the circumference…

12.30b …and separate the halves of the housing

12.31 Lift the evaporator from place

12.34 Drill out the rivet securing the water drain pipe

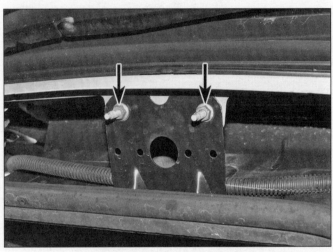

12.35a Undo the 2 nuts at the top...

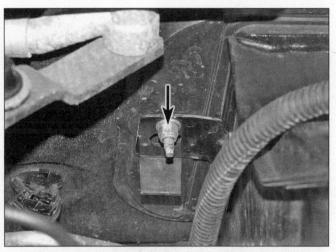

12.35b ...and slacken the nut each side of the intake cowl

31 Slide the evaporator from the housing **(see illustration)**.
32 Refitting is a reversal of removal but have the air conditioning system recharged with the correct type and amount of refrigerant by a specialist prior to using the system.

Expansion valve

33 Have the air conditioning system fully discharged and evacuated by an air conditioning specialist.
34 Remove the rivet and detach the cabin air intake assembly water drain pipe from the front panel **(see illustration)**.
35 Undo the retaining nuts and remove the cabin air intake cowl **(see illustrations)**.
36 Undo the nuts securing the refrigerant pipes to the connection at the engine compartment bulkhead **(see illustration 10.37)**. Plug/cover the openings to prevent

contamination/saturation. Recover and discard the O-ring seals – new ones must be fitted.

 Warning: Failure to seal the refrigerant pipe unions will result in the receiver/drier becoming saturated, necessitating its renewal.

37 Undo the 2 studs using a Torx socket, and remove the expansion valve. Recover and discard the O-ring seals – new ones must be fitted. If the expansion valve is reluctant to release, insert an M6 bolt into the threaded hole in the centre of the valve. As the bolt is tightened, the valve should release **(see illustration)**.
38 Refitting is a reversal of removal but have the air conditioning system recharged with the correct type and amount of refrigerant by a specialist prior to using the system.

12.37 Unscrew the 2 studs

Chapter 4 Part A
Fuel and exhaust systems

Contents

Degrees of difficulty

| **Easy,** suitable for novice with little experience | | **Fairly easy,** suitable for beginner with some experience | **Fairly difficult,** suitable for competent DIY mechanic | **Difficult,** suitable for experienced DIY mechanic | **Very difficult,** suitable for expert DIY or professional | |

Specifications

General

System type	HDi/Multijet (high-pressure diesel injection) with full electronic control, direct injection and turbocharger
Designation	Bosch EDC 16C 34, Siemens SID 803 or Delphi 3.5
Firing order	1-3-4-2 (No 1 at flywheel end)
Fuel system operating pressure	200 to 1800 bars (according to engine and engine speed)

Injectors

Type . . . . Piezo

Turbocharger

Type:
    1.6 litre engines . . . . MHI – TD025S2 or Garrett GT1544V
    2.0 litre engines:
        Euro 4 emissions level . . . . Garrett GT1749V
        Euro 5 emissions level . . . . Not available
Boost pressure (approximate):
    1.6 litre engines . . . . 0.9 bar @ 3500 rpm
    2.0 litre engines . . . . 1.0 bar @ 4000 rpm

Torque wrench settings

	Nm	lbf ft
Camshaft position sensor bolt	6	4
Common rail mounting bolts	23	17
Engine knock sensor	20	15
Exhaust manifold nuts:		
1.6 litre engines	20	15
2.0 litre engines	25	18
Exhaust system fasteners:		
Catalytic converter-to-manifold nuts	40	30
Clamping ring nuts	20	15
Fuel filter water sensor	25	18
Fuel injector clamp bolts/nuts:		
1.6 litre engines:		
DOHC engines:		
Stage 1	4	3
Stage 2	Angle-tighten a further 65°	
SOHC engines:		
Stage 1	7	5
Stage 2	Angle-tighten a further 85°	
2.0 litre engines:		
Siemens:		
Stage 1	4	3
Stage 2	Angle-tighten a further 45°	
Delphi:		
Stage 1	4	3
Stage 2	Angle-tighten a further 77°	
Euro 5 engines:		
Stage 1	7	5
Stage 2	Angle-tighten a further 45°	
Fuel pipe unions:		
1.6 litre engines	25	18
2.0 litre engines:		
Stage 1	23	17
Stage 2	30	22
Fuel temperature sensor (Delphi systems)	15	11
High-pressure fuel pump mounting bolts:		
1.6 litre engines	25	18
2.0 litre engines:		
Siemens	20	15
Delphi:		
2 lower bolts	20	15
1 upper bolt (from engine side)	8	6
High-pressure fuel pump rear mounting bolts/nut (8 mm)	17	13
High-pressure fuel pump sprocket nut	50	37
Intake manifold bolts	10	7
Turbocharger mounting bolts/nuts	25	18
Turbocharger oil supply pipe banjo bolts:		
1.6 litre engines	30	20
2.0 litre engines:		
Engine pipe to cylinder block	40	30
All other connections	25	18
Turbocharger oil return pipe bolts:		
1.6 litre engines	30	20
2.0 litre engines	10	7

1 General information and system operation

1 The fuel system consists of a rear-mounted fuel tank with an immersed level sensor, a fuel pump, a fuel filter with integral water separator, a fuel cooler mounted under the car (depending on model), and an electronically-controlled high-pressure diesel injection (HDi) system, together with a single turbocharger.

2 The exhaust system is conventional, but to meet the latest emission levels an unregulated catalytic converter and an exhaust gas recirculation system are fitted to all models. On some models, an exhaust emission particulate filter may be fitted – refer to Section 18, for further details.

3 The HDi system (generally known as a 'common rail' system) derives its name from the fact that a common rail, or fuel reservoir, is used to supply fuel to all the fuel injectors. Instead of an in-line or distributor type injection pump, which distributes the fuel directly to each injector, a high-pressure pump is used, which generates a very high fuel pressure (up to 1800 bar at high engine speed) in the common rail. The common rail stores fuel, and maintains a constant fuel pressure with the aid of a pressure control valve. Each injector is supplied with high-pressure fuel from the common rail, and the injectors are individually controlled via signals from the system Electronic Control Module (ECM). The injectors are electronically operated.

4 In addition to the various sensors used on models with a conventional fuel injection pump; common rail systems also have a fuel pressure sensor. The fuel pressure sensor allows the ECM to maintain the required fuel pressure, via the pressure control valve.

System operation

5 For the purposes of describing the operation of a common rail injection system, the components can be divided into three sub-systems; the low-pressure fuel system, the high-pressure fuel system and the electronic control system.

Low-pressure fuel system

6 The low-pressure fuel system consists of the following components:
a) Fuel tank.
b) Fuel pump.
c) Fuel cooler.
d) Fuel heater (not all models).
e) Fuel filter/water trap.
f) Low-pressure fuel lines.

7 The low-pressure system (fuel supply system) is responsible for supplying clean fuel to the high-pressure fuel system.

High-pressure fuel system

8 The high-pressure fuel system consists of the following components:
a) High-pressure fuel pump with pressure control valve.
b) High-pressure fuel common rail.
c) Fuel injectors.
d) High-pressure fuel lines.

9 After passing through the fuel filter, the fuel reaches the high-pressure pump, which forces it into the common rail. As diesel fuel has certain elasticity, the pressure in the common rail remains constant, even though fuel leaves the rail each time one of the injectors operates. Additionally, a pressure control valve mounted on the high-pressure pump ensures that the fuel pressure is maintained within preset limits.

10 The pressure control valve is operated by the ECM. When the valve is opened, fuel is returned from the high-pressure pump to the tank, via the fuel return lines, and the pressure in the common rail falls. To enable the ECM to trigger the pressure control valve correctly, the pressure in the common rail is measured by a fuel pressure sensor.

11 The electronically controlled fuel injectors are operated individually, via signals from the ECM, and each injector injects fuel directly into the relevant combustion chamber. The fact that high fuel pressure is always available allows very precise and highly flexible injection in comparison to a conventional injection pump: for example combustion during the main injection process can be improved considerably by the pre-injection of a very small quantity of fuel.

Electronic control system

12 The electronic control system consists of the following components:
a) Electronic control module (ECM).
b) Crankshaft speed/position sensor.
c) Camshaft position sensor.
d) Accelerator pedal position sensor.
e) Coolant temperature sensor.
f) Fuel temperature sensor.
g) Airflow meter.
h) Fuel pressure sensor.
i) Fuel injectors.
j) Fuel pressure control valve.
k) Preheating control module.
l) EGR solenoid valve.
m) Air temperature sensor.
n) Atmospheric pressure sensor – integral with the ECM.
o) Intake manifold pressure sensor.

13 The information from the various sensors is passed to the ECM, which evaluates the signals. The ECM contains electronic 'maps' which enable it to calculate the optimum quantity of fuel to inject, the appropriate start of injection, and even pre- and post-injection fuel quantities, for each individual engine cylinder under any given condition of engine operation.

14 Additionally, the ECM carries out monitoring and self-diagnostic functions. Any faults in the system are stored in the ECM memory, which enables quick and accurate fault diagnosis using appropriate diagnostic equipment (such as a suitable fault code reader).

2 High-pressure diesel injection system – special information

Warnings and precautions

1 It is essential to observe strict precautions when working on the fuel system components, particularly the high-pressure side of the system. Before carrying out any operations on the fuel system, refer to the precautions given in *Safety first!* at the beginning of this manual, and to the following additional information.
● Do not carry out any repair work on the high-pressure fuel system unless you are competent to do so, have all the necessary tools and equipment required, and are aware of the safety implications involved.
● Before starting any repair work on the fuel system, wait at least 30 seconds after switching off the engine to allow the fuel circuit pressure to reduce.
● Never work on the high-pressure fuel system with the engine running.
● Keep well clear of any possible source of fuel leakage, particularly when starting the engine after carrying out repair work. A leak in the system could cause an extremely high-pressure jet of fuel to escape, which could result in severe personal injury.
● Never place your hands or any part of your body near to a leak in the high-pressure fuel system.
● Do not use steam cleaning equipment or compressed air to clean the engine or any of the fuel system components.

Procedures and information

2 Strict cleanliness must be observed at all times when working on any part of the fuel system. This applies to the working area in general, the person doing the work, and the components being worked on.

3 Before working on the fuel system components, they must be thoroughly cleaned with a suitable degreasing fluid. Specific cleaning products may be obtained from Citroën/Peugeot/Fiat dealers. Alternatively, a suitable brake cleaning fluid may be used. Cleanliness is particularly important when working on the fuel system connections at the following components:
a) Fuel filter.
b) High-pressure fuel pump.
c) Common rail.
d) Fuel injectors.
e) High-pressure fuel pipes.

4 After disconnecting any fuel pipes or components, the open union or orifice must be immediately sealed to prevent the entry of dirt or foreign material. Plastic plugs and caps in various sizes are available in packs from motor factors and accessory outlets, and are particularly suitable for this application **(see**

2.4 Typical plastic plug and cap set for sealing disconnected fuel pipes and components

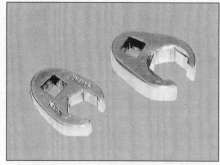

2.7 Two crow-foot adapters will be necessary for tightening the fuel pipe unions

illustration). Fingers cut from disposable rubber gloves should be used to protect components such as fuel pipes, fuel injectors and wiring connectors, and can be secured in place using elastic bands. Suitable gloves of this type are available at no cost from most petrol station forecourts.

5 Whenever any of the high-pressure fuel pipes are disconnected or removed, new pipes must be obtained for refitting.

6 On the completion of any repair on the high-pressure fuel system, Peugeot/Citroën/Fiat recommend the use of a leak-detecting compound. This is a powder which is applied to the fuel pipe unions and connections, and turns white when dry. Any leak in the system will cause the product to darken indicating the source of the leak.

7 The torque wrench settings given in the Specifications must be strictly observed when tightening component mountings and connections. This is particularly important when tightening the high-pressure fuel pipe unions. To enable a torque wrench to be used

on the fuel pipe unions, two Peugeot/Citroën/Fiat crow-foot adapters are required. Suitable alternatives are available from motor factors and accessory outlets **(see illustration)**.

3 Fuel pipes and fittings – general information and disconnection

1 Disconnect the cable from the negative battery terminal (Chapter 5A Section 4) before proceeding.

2 The fuel supply pipe connects the fuel pump in the fuel tank to the fuel rail on the engine.

3 Whenever you're working under the vehicle, be sure to inspect all fuel and evaporative emission pipes for leaks, kinks, dents and other damage. Always replace a damaged fuel pipe immediately.

4 If you find signs of dirt in the pipes during disassembly, disconnect all pipes and blow them out with compressed air. Inspect the

fuel strainer on the fuel pump pick-up unit for damage and deterioration.

Steel tubing

5 It is critical that the fuel pipes be replaced with pipes of equivalent type and specification.

6 Some steel fuel pipes have threaded fittings. When loosening these fittings, hold the stationary fitting with a spanner while turning the union nut.

Plastic tubing

⚠️ *Warning: When removing or installing plastic fuel tubing, be careful not to bend or twist it too much, which can damage it. Also, plastic fuel tubing is NOT heat resistant, so keep it away from excessive heat.*

7 When replacing fuel system plastic tubing, use only original equipment replacement plastic tubing.

Flexible hoses

8 When replacing fuel system flexible hoses, use original equipment replacements, or hose to the same specification.

9 Don't route fuel hoses (or metal pipes) within 100 mm of the exhaust system or within 280 mm of the catalytic converter. Make sure that no rubber hoses are installed directly against the vehicle, particularly in places where there is any vibration. If allowed to touch some vibrating part of the vehicle, a hose can easily become chafed and it might start leaking. A good rule of thumb is to maintain a minimum of 8.0 mm clearance around a hose (or metal pipe) to prevent contact with the vehicle underbody.

Disconnecting Fuel pipe Fittings

10 Typical fuel pipe fittings:

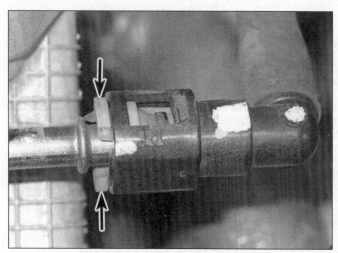

3.10a Two-tab type fitting; depress both tabs with your fingers, then pull the fuel pipe and the fitting apart

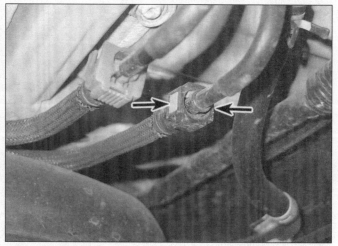

3.10b On this type of fitting, depress the two buttons on opposite sides of the fitting, then pull it off the fuel pipe

3.10c Threaded fuel pipe fitting; hold the stationary portion of the pipe or component (A) while loosening the union nut (B) with a flare-nut spanner

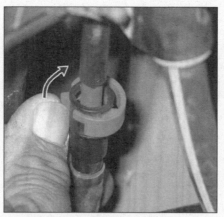

3.10d Plastic collar-type fitting; rotate the outer part of the fitting

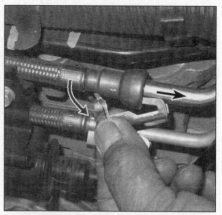

3.10e Metal collar quick-connect fitting; pull the end of the retainer off the fuel pipe and disengage the other end from the female side of the fitting ...

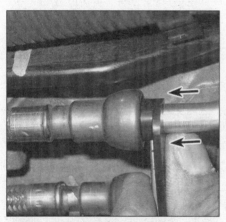

3.10f ... insert a fuel pipe separator tool into the female side of the fitting, push it into the fitting and pull the fuel pipe off the pipe

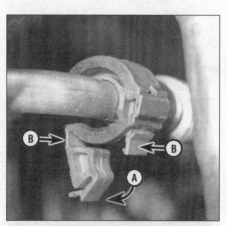

3.10g Some fittings are secured by lock tabs. Release the lock tab (A) and rotate it to the fully-opened position, squeeze the two smaller lock tabs (B) ...

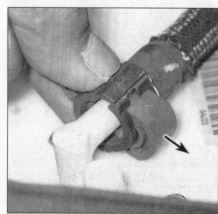

3.10h ... then push the retainer out and pull the fuel pipe off the pipe

3.10i Spring-lock coupling; remove the safety cover, install a coupling release tool and close the tool around the coupling ...

3.10j ... push the tool into the fitting, then pull the two pipes apart

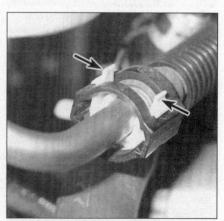

3.10k Hairpin clip type fitting: push the legs of the retainer clip together, then push the clip down all the way until it stops and pull the fuel pipe off the pipe

4.1a Hand-priming pump – early engines

4.1b Hand-priming pump – later engines

4.1c Hand-priming pump – 2.0 litre Euro 5 engines

4.2a Bleed screw location

4.2b Operate the pump until fuel emerges

4 Fuel system – priming and bleeding

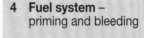

1 Should the fuel supply system be disconnected between the fuel tank and high-pressure pump, it is necessary to prime the fuel system. This is achieved by operating the hand-priming pump until resistance is felt **(see illustrations)**.

2 Where fitted, unscrew the bleed screw on the top of the fuel filter housing, place rags around the screw location, then operate the hand priming pump until fuel emerges from the bleed screw hole **(see illustrations)**. Refit the bleed screw and tighten it securely.

3 If vehicle will still not run, it may be necessary to connect a hose (special Peugeot/Citroën hose No 444-T may be available) from the fuel filter outlet pipe to the fuel return pipe and forcing fuel through the filter into the return system. If the special manufacturer hose is not available, it will suffice to connect a length of hose to the filter outlet, with the other end of the hose into a container.

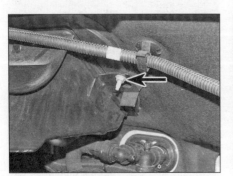

5.1 Drill out the rivet or undo the bolt securing the hose to the bonnet slam panel

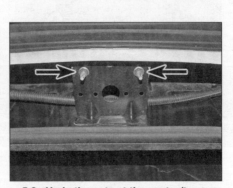

5.2a Undo the nuts at the centre/top...

5 Air cleaner assembly – removal and refitting

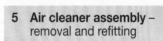

Removal

1 Drill out the rivet/undo the bolt securing the cabin air intake drain hose to the front panel **(see illustration)**.

2 Undo the 2 central retaining nuts, slacken the rear nuts and remove the cabin air intake cowl **(see illustrations)**.

1.6 litre engines

3 Release the clips, and remove the air filter intake hose **(see illustration)**.

4 Unclip and remove the air outlet hose from the air cleaner to the turbocharger **(see illustration)**.

5.2b ...then slacken the nut each side and remove the cabin air intake cowl

5.3 Unclip and remove the air intake pipe

5.4 Unclip the air outlet hose

5.5a Undo the bolts at the front edge of the air filter housing

5.5b Note how the filter housing locates on the lugs at the rear

5.8 Slacken the hose clamp

5.10a Depress the clip…

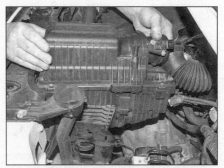

5.10b …and lift out the air cleaner

SOHC engines

5 Unclip any pipes/wiring, undo the 2 retaining bolts at the front edge, then pull the air filter housing upwards from the mountings **(see illustrations)**. Where applicable, disconnect the air flow meter wiring plug. Note how the housing locates on the lugs at the rear.

DOHC engines

6 Remove the air filter element as described in Chapter 1 Section 24.
7 Lift the air cleaner assembly from place.

2.0 litre engines

8 Release the clamp and disconnect the air outlet hose from the air cleaner housing **(see illustration)**.

9 Disconnect the air flow meter wiring plug.
10 Release the clip and lift out the air cleaner assembly **(see illustrations)**.

Refitting

11 Refitting is a reverse of the removal procedure. Examine the condition of the seals and retaining clips, and renew if necessary.

6 Accelerator pedal – removal and refitting

Removal

1 Disconnect the battery negative lead as described in Chapter 5A Section 4.

2 Remove the drivers side lower facia panel as described in Chapter 11 Section 27.
3 Unscrew the plastic fasteners and fold back the carpet to expose the pedal bracket nuts **(see illustration)**.
4 Undo the nuts and lower the assembly from place **(see illustration)**.
5 Prise up the locking clip and disconnect the accelerator pedal position sensor wiring plug **(see illustration)**.
6 If required, undo the nuts and detach the pedal assembly from the bracket.

Refitting

7 Refitting is a reversal of the removal procedure.

6.3 Unscrew the carpet retainers

6.4 Pedal assembly retaining nuts

6.5 Slide up the locking clip and disconnect the wiring plug

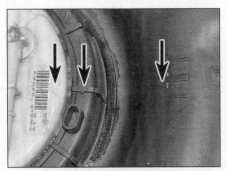

7.2a Alignment marks are provided on the tank, cover, and locking ring

7.2b Using a special tool to slacken the locking ring

7.3 Take care not to damage the float arm as the assembly is withdrawn

7 Fuel lift pump and level sensor – removal and refitting

Note: *The fuel pump/gauge sender unit is only available as a complete assembly – no components are available separately.*
Note: *On some models, only a fuel level sender unit is fitted – no lift pump.*

Removal

1 The fuel pump/gauge sender unit is located in the top of the fuel tank. Therefore the fuel tank will need to be removed as described in Section 8.
2 Note the alignment marks on the tank **(see illustrations)**, pump/sensor cover and the locking ring, then unscrew the ring and remove it from the tank. This is best accomplished by using a special tool, which fits over the locking ring and allows it to be released using a spanner or a ratchet and socket. Alternatively, it may be possible to undo the locking ring using a screwdriver on the raised ribs of the locking ring. Carefully tap the screwdriver to turn the ring anti-clockwise until it can be unscrewed by hand.
3 Carefully lift the fuel pump/sender assembly out of the fuel tank, taking great care not to damage the fuel gauge sender unit float arm **(see illustration)**. The pump/gauge sender will hold fuel, so be aware of spillage. Recover the rubber sealing ring and discard it – a new one must be used on refitting.

4 If the fuel pump is going to be left out of the fuel tank for a while, screw the ring back to the top of the fuel tank to prevent it from going out of shape. Cover the access hole in the tank to prevent dirt ingress.
5 The function of the level sender can be checked using a digital multimeter. Connect the multimeter across the sender terminals, and measure the resistance with the float in the empty position (zero deflection) and full position (maximum deflection) **(see illustration)**. If the resistances vary significantly from those specified, the sender may be defective.

Full tank (maximum float deflection)	70 ohms
Empty tank (zero deflection)	352 ohms

Refitting

6 Fit the new sealing ring to the top of the fuel tank **(see illustration)**.
7 Carefully manoeuvre the pump assembly into the fuel tank, taking care not to damage the float arm.
8 Align the notch in the top of the fuel tank with the lug on the fuel pump/sensor cover to locate the pump assembly into position **(see illustration)**.
9 Press down on the pump/sensor and refit the locking ring, tighten it securely until its alignment mark aligns with the alignment marks on the fuel tank, as noted on removal **(see illustration 7.2a)**.

10 Securely reconnect the fuel pipe(s) to the pump/gauge sender unit, then reconnect the pump wiring connector.
11 Refit the fuel tank as described in Section 8.
12 Prime the fuel system (see Section 4). Start the engine and check the fuel pump feed and return hoses unions for signs of leakage.

8 Fuel tank and cooler – removal and refitting

Fuel tank

Note: *Refer to the warnings and precautions in Section 2 before proceeding.*
1 Before removing the fuel tank, all fuel must be drained from the tank. Since a fuel tank drain plug is not provided, it is therefore preferable to carry out the removal operation when the tank is nearly empty. Before proceeding, disconnect the battery (Chapter 5A Section 4), and then siphon or hand-pump the remaining fuel from the tank. Do not refit the fuel filler cap.
2 Chock the front wheels then jack up the rear of the vehicle and support it on axle stands (see *Jacking and vehicle support*). **Note:** *As the filler neck of the fuel tank is part of the fuel tank assembly and cannot be removed separately, there will need to be sufficient height to remove the complete assembly.*
3 Remove the fuel filler cap.

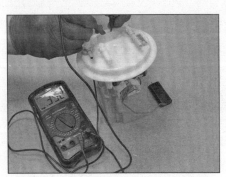

7.5 Measure the senders resistance with a multimeter

7.6 Fit a new sealing ring to the top of the tank

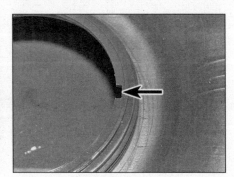

7.8 Align the pump/sensor with the cut-out in the fuel tank

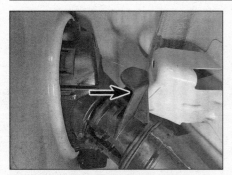

8.5a Undo the bolt at the top…

8.5b …and the bolt halfway along the filler neck

8.7 Disconnect the wiring plug

4 Remove the left hand rear roadwheel and inner wheelarch liner.

5 Inside the wheelarch, undo the 2 retaining bolts from the filler neck **(see illustrations)**.

6 Place a trolley jack with a flat/long piece of wood beneath the tank, to spread the weight. Then raise the jack until it is supporting the weight of the tank.

7 To improve clearance, disconnect the wiring plug at the front of the tank **(see illustration)**.

8 Slacken and remove the bolts securing the fuel tank to the body **(see illustration)**. Release the filler neck from the body at the filler cap aperture.

9 Start to lower the fuel tank, unclip the various pipes from the top of the tank. Once it is lowered enough, reach up and disconnect the fuel pipes and wiring connector(s) from the top of the fuel pump/gauge sender unit. Depress the retaining clips and detach the fuel pipe(s), bearing in mind the information given in, Section 2 on warnings and precautions to be taken with the fuel system before disconnecting. Plug the pipe end(s) to minimise fuel loss and prevent the entry of dirt **(see illustration)**. Depending on model, the amount of pipes to the top of the pump will vary note their fitted position, before removal.

10 With the wiring and fuel pipes disconnected slowly lower the fuel tank; ensuring the filler neck assembly is guided out of position without placing any stress on it. Check all pipes and wiring are disconnected from the fuel tank as it is lowered.

11 If the tank is contaminated with sediment or water, remove the fuel pump/sensor (Section 7), and swill the tank out with clean

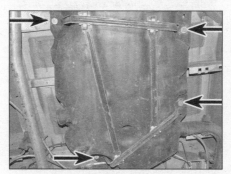

8.8 Fuel tank retaining bolts

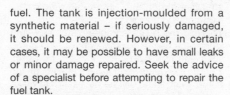

fuel. The tank is injection-moulded from a synthetic material – if seriously damaged, it should be renewed. However, in certain cases, it may be possible to have small leaks or minor damage repaired. Seek the advice of a specialist before attempting to repair the fuel tank.

12 It is not possible to separate the filler neck from the tank. If damaged, the complete assembly must be renewed.

13 Refitting is the reverse of the removal procedure, noting the following points:

a) *Ensure the wiring connectors and fuel pipes are securely reconnected and retained by all the relevant clips. When lifting the tank back into position, take care to ensure that the pipes/wiring do not become trapped between the tank and vehicle body.*

b) *Make sure the spacer(s) are fitted correctly between the fuel tank and the floor panel.*

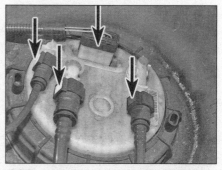

8.9 Depress the release button each side, disconnect the pipes and the wiring plug

c) *Refit the particulate filter additive tank as described in Chapter 4B, Section 2.*

d) *Refit the exhaust as described in Section 18.*

e) *On completion, refill the tank with a small amount of fuel and prime the fuel system as described in Section 4. Check for signs of leakage prior to taking the vehicle out on the road.*

Fuel cooler

Note: *The fuel cooler is not fitted to all models.*

14 The fuel cooler is located under the left-hand side of the vehicle **(see illustration)**. Jack up the front of the vehicle, and support it on axle stands (see *Jacking and vehicle support*).

15 Depress the release buttons, and disconnect the fuel feed and return hoses from the cooler. Be prepared for fuel spillage, and plug the hose and cooler openings to prevent dirt ingress **(see illustrations)**.

8.14 Fuel cooler assembly

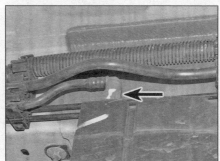

8.15a Disconnect the fuel pipe on the right-hand…

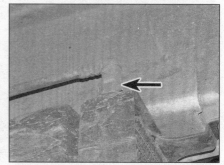

8.15b …and left-hand side of the cooler

8.16 Fuel cooler retaining nuts

A sprocket holding tool can be made from two lengths of steel strip bolted together to form a forked end. Bend the ends of the strip through 90° to form the fork 'prongs'.

Make a sprocket releasing tool from a short strip of steel. Drill two holes in the strip to correspond with the two holes in the sprocket. Drill a third hole just large enough to accept the flats of the sprocket retaining nut.

16 Undo the 2 retaining nuts and remove the fuel cooler assembly **(see illustration)**.
17 Refitting is a reversal of removal.

9 High-pressure fuel pump – removal and refitting

 Warning: Refer to the information contained in Section 2 before proceeding.

Note: *A new fuel pump-to-common rail high-pressure fuel pipe will be required for refitting.*

Removal

1.6 litre engines

1 Disconnect the battery negative lead as described in Chapter 5A Section 4.
2 Remove the timing belt as described in Chapter 2A Section 7 or Chapter 2B Section 7. After removal of the timing belt, temporarily refit the right-hand engine mounting but do not fully-tighten the bolts.
3 Remove the air cleaner assembly as described in Section 5.
4 Remove the EGR heat exchanger/cooler as described in Chapter 4B Section 2.
5 Remove the intake manifold as described in Section 13.
6 Remove the rear engine mounting/torque road as described in Chapter 2A Section 17 or Chapter 2B Section 17.
7 Note it's fitted position and routing, then unclip and remove the fuel return manifold

9.20a Unscrew the high-pressure fuel pipe – Euro 4 engines...

assembly from the rear/top of the engine. Plug the openings to prevent contamination.
8 Undo the bolts/nuts and remove the 3 support brackets above the fuel common rail and the high-pressure pump.
9 Undo the union nuts and remove the high-pressure fuel pipe between the fuel common rail and the high-pressure pump. Plug the openings to prevent contamination.
10 Disconnect the wiring plug from the high-pressure fuel pump.
11 Hold the pump sprocket stationary, and loosen the centre nut securing it to the pump shaft (see **Tool Tip 1**).
12 The fuel pump sprocket is a taper fit on the pump shaft and it will be necessary to make up a tool to release it from the taper (see **Tool Tip 2**). Partially unscrew the sprocket retaining nut, fit the home-made tool, and secure it to the sprocket with two 7.0 mm bolts and nuts. Prevent the sprocket from rotating as before, and screw down the nuts, forcing the sprocket off the shaft taper. Once the taper is released, remove the tool, unscrew the nut fully, and remove the sprocket from the pump shaft.
13 Undo the three bolts, and remove the pump from the mounting bracket.
Caution: The high-pressure fuel pump is manufactured to extremely close tolerances and must not be dismantled in

9.20b ...and Euro 5 emissions level engines

any way. Do not unscrew the fuel pipe male union on the rear of the pump, or attempt to remove the sensor, piston de-activator switch, or the seal on the pump shaft. No parts for the pump are available separately and if the unit is in any way suspect, it must be renewed.
14 Undo the bolts securing the bracket to the rear of the pump (where fitted), then undo the 3 bolts and pull the pump from the inner timing cover.

2.0 litre engines

15 Disconnect the battery negative lead as described in Chapter 5A Section 4.
16 Remove the air cleaner assembly as described in Section 5.
17 Release the clamps, undo the bolts and remove the EGR pipe from the EGR valve to the intake manifold.
18 Raise the front of the vehicle, and support it securely on axle stands (see Vehicle jacking and support 13 Section 5). Undo the fasteners and remove the engine undershield (where fitted).
19 Disconnect the breather hose, undo the retaining bolts and securing clip and remove the turbocharger intake duct from the engine compartment **(see illustrations 16.37a and 16.37b)**.
20 Thoroughly clean the high-pressure fuel pipe unions on the fuel pump and common rail. Using an open-ended spanner, unscrew the union nuts securing the high-pressure fuel pipe to the fuel pump and common rail. Counterhold the unions on the pump and common rail with a second spanner, while unscrewing the union nuts. Withdraw the high-pressure fuel pipe and plug or cover the open unions to prevent dirt entry **(see illustrations)**. Note that a new high-pressure fuel pipe will be required for refitting.
Note: *The fuel lines must be renewed every time they are removed, as it is possible for minute metal particles to enter them as a result of tightening the union nuts. If these*

9.21 Depress the outer edges of the release buttons and disconnect the hoses

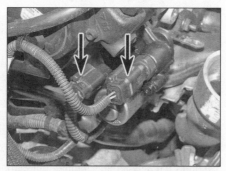

9.22 Disconnect the wiring plugs from the pump

d) *Take the car for a short road test and check for leaks once again on return. If any leaks are detected, obtain and fit another new high-pressure fuel pipe. Do not attempt to cure even the slightest leak by further tightening of the pipe unions.*

10 Common rail –
   removal and refitting

 Warning: Refer to the information contained in Section 2 before proceeding.

Note: *A complete new set of high-pressure fuel pipes will be required for refitting.*

Removal

1 Disconnect the battery negative lead as described in Chapter 5A Section 4.

1.6 litre engines

2 Raise the front of the vehicle and support is securely on axle stands (see *Jacking and vehicle support*). Where applicable, undo the fasteners and remove the engine undershield.

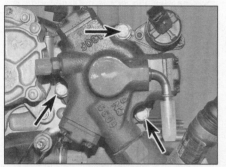

9.24a Unscrew the three bolts and remove the pump

9.24b Delphi fuel pumps have a mounting bolt on the cylinder head side of the pump

particles enter the fuel injectors, fuel at high pressure can enter the combustion chambers unrestricted.

21 Disconnect the fuel supply and return hoses from the high-pressure pump **(see illustration)**. Plug the openings to prevent contamination.

22 Note their fitted positions, and disconnect the wiring plugs from the pump **(see illustration)**. Move the wiring harness to one side.

23 Where applicable, undo the retaining nuts and remove the wiring support bracket from the pump.

24 Undo the 3 bolts and withdraw the fuel pump from the cylinder head **(see illustrations)**. Note on Delphi fuel pumps the upper bolt is accessed from the cylinder head side of the fuel pump.

Caution: The high-pressure fuel pump is manufactured to extremely close tolerances and must not be dismantled in

any way. Do not unscrew the fuel pipe male union on the rear of the pump, or attempt to remove the pressure control valve, piston de-activator switch, or the seal on the pump shaft. No parts for the pump are available separately and if the unit is in any way suspect, it must be renewed.

Refitting

25 Refitting is a reversal of removal, noting the following points:
a) *Always renew the pump-to-common rail high-pressure pipe.*
b) *Renew the fuel pump drive seal.*
c) *With everything reassembled and reconnected, start the engine and allow it to idle. Check for leaks at the high-pressure fuel pipe unions with the engine idling. If satisfactory, increase the engine speed to 3000 rpm and check again for leaks.*

DOHC engines

3 Drain the cooling system as described in Chapter 1 Section 23.
4 Remove the air cleaner assembly as described in Section 5.
5 Remove the fuel filter (Chapter 1 Section 11) and filter mounting.
6 Remove the EGR heat exchanger/cooler as described in Chapter 4B Section 2.
7 Remove the engine oil level sensor.
8 Undo the 2 mounting bolts, slacken the clamps, and move the coolant pump outlet assembly aside **(see illustration)**.
9 Remove the starter motor as described in Chapter 5A Section 10.
10 Clean around the pipes, then undo the unions and remove the high-pressure pipe from the common rail to the high-pressure pump, and the pipes from the common rail to each injector. Plug the openings to prevent contamination.
11 Disconnect the wiring plug(s) from the common rail **(see illustration)**.
12 Unscrew the two rail mounting bolts and manoeuvre it from place **(see illustration)**.

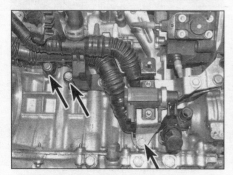

10.8 Undo the bolts and move the coolant pump outlet assembly aside

10.11 Disconnect the common rail wiring plug(s)

10.12 Accumulator rail mounting bolt/stud

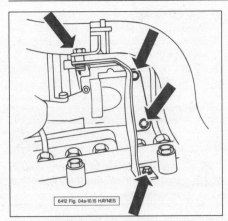

10.15 EGR valve mounting bracket retaining bolts

Caution: The manufacturers insist that the fuel pressure sensor on the common rail must not be removed.

Caution: Do not attempt to remove the four high-pressure fuel pipe male unions from the common rail. These parts are not available separately and if disturbed are likely to result in fuel leakage on reassembly.

SOHC engines

13 Remove the starter motor as described in Chapter 5A Section 10.
14 Undo the nuts and remove the starter motor cover bracket.

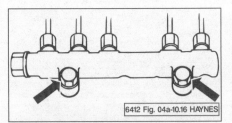

10.16 High-pressure fuel pipe unions and common rail mounting bolts

15 Undo the 4 bolts and remove the EGR valve mounting bracket (see illustration).
16 Clean around the pipes, then undo the unions and remove the high-pressure pipe from the common rail to the high-pressure pump, and the pipes from the common rail to each injector (see illustration). Plug the openings to prevent contamination.
17 Disconnect any wiring plugs from the common rail.
18 Undo the 2 retaining bolts and manoeuvre the common rail from place.
19 No further dismantling of the common rail is recommended.

2.0 litre engines – Euro 4 emissions engines

20 Remove the air filter assembly, as described in Section 5.
21 Remove the wiper motor and linkage as described in Chapter 12 Section 14.
22 Remove the intake manifold as described in Section 13.

23 Release the clamps, undo the retaining bolts and remove the EGR pipe from the EGR valve to the intake manifold.
24 Thoroughly clean all the high-pressure fuel pipe unions on the common rail, fuel pump and injectors. Using an open-ended spanner, unscrew the union nuts securing the high-pressure fuel pipe to the fuel pump and common rail. Counterhold the unions on the pump and common rail (where applicable) with a second spanner, while unscrewing the union nuts. Withdraw the high-pressure fuel pipe and plug or cover the open unions to prevent dirt entry (see illustrations).
25 Again using two spanners, hold the unions and unscrew the union nuts securing the high-pressure fuel pipes to the fuel injectors and common rail (see illustration). Withdraw the high-pressure fuel pipes and plug or cover the open unions to prevent dirt entry.
26 Undo the 2 mounting nuts and manoeuvre the common rail from position. Recover the mounting spacers. Disconnect the sensor wiring plug(s) as the common rail is withdrawn.
Caution: The manufacturers insist that the fuel pressure sensor on the common rail must not be removed.

2.0 litre engines – Euro 5 emissions level engines

27 Remove the air cleaner assembly as described in Section 5.
28 Pull the acoustic cover upwards from the top of the engine, then undo the 3 bolts and remove the rubber cover from the intake manifold/cylinder head cover.
29 Clean around the pipes, then undo the unions and remove the high-pressure pipe from the common rail to the high-pressure pump, and the pipes from the common rail to each injector (see illustration). Plug the openings to prevent contamination.
30 Disconnect the wiring plug from the fuel pressure sensor on the common rail.
31 Undo the 3 retaining bolts and manoeuvre the common rail from place (see illustration).
32 No further dismantling of the common rail is recommended.

Refitting

33 Locate the common rail in position, refit and finger-tighten the mounting bolts/nuts.

10.24a Unscrew the unions from the rail ...

10.24b ... and plug the ends to prevent contamination

10.25 Counterhold the injector with a second spanner whilst slackening the pipe union

10.29 Pump-to-common rail pipe unions

10.31 Common rail retaining bolts

11.10 Wiring harness support bracket bolts

11.12 Prise out the clip and pull the return pipe from each injector

11.13 Use a second spanner to counterhold the high-pressure pipe union nuts

34 Reconnect the common rail wiring plug(s).
35 Fit the new pump-to-rail high-pressure pipe, and only finger-tighten the unions at first, then tighten the unions to the specified torque setting. Use a second spanner to counterhold the union screwed into the pump body.
36 Fit the new set of rail-to-injector high pressure pipes, and finger-tighten the unions. If it's not possible to fit the new pipes to the injector unions, remove and refit the injectors as described in Section 11, and then try again.
37 Tighten the common rail mounting bolts/nuts to the specified torque.
38 Tighten the rail-to-injector pipe unions to the specified torque setting. Use a second spanner to counterhold the injector unions.
39 The remainder of refitting is a reversal of removal, noting the following points:
a) Ensure all wiring connectors and harnesses are correctly refitting and secured.
b) Reconnect the battery as described in Chapter. 5A Section 4
c) Start the engine and allow it to idle. Check for leaks at the high-pressure fuel pipe unions with the engine idling. If satisfactory, increase the engine speed to 3000 rpm and check again for leaks. Take the car for a short road test and check for leaks once again on return.
d) If any leaks are detected, obtain and fit additional new high-pressure fuel pipes as required. Do not attempt to cure even the slightest leak by further tightening of the pipe unions.

11 Fuel injectors – removal and refitting

 Warning: Refer to the information contained in Section 2 before proceeding.

Removal

1 Disconnect the battery negative lead as described in Chapter 5A Section 4.

1.6 litre engines

DOHC engines

Note: The following procedure describes the removal and refitting of the injectors as a

complete set, however each injector may be removed individually if required. New copper washers, upper seals, and a high-pressure fuel pipe will be required for each disturbed injector when refitting.
2 Raise the front of the vehicle and support is securely on axle stands (see Jacking and vehicle support). Where applicable, undo the fasteners and remove the engine undershield.
3 Drain the cooling system as described in Chapter 1 Section 23.
4 Remove the fuel filter assembly (Chapter 1 Section 11), and the filter mounting bracket.
5 Remove the EGR heat exchanger/cooler as described in Chapter 4B Section 2.
6 Remove the engine oil level sensor.
7 Undo the 2 mounting bolts, slacken the clamps, and move the coolant pump outlet assembly aside **(see illustration 10.8)**.
8 Remove the starter motor as described in Chapter 5A Section 10.
9 Disconnect the injector wiring plugs.
10 Undo the bolts and move aside the wiring harness support bracket **(see illustration)**.
11 Release the manual fuel priming pump and its support.
12 Extract the retaining circlip and disconnect the leak-off pipe from each fuel injector **(see illustration)**.
13 Clean the area around the high-pressure fuel pipes between the injectors and the common rail, then unscrew the pipe unions. Use a second spanner to counterhold the union screwed into the injector body **(see illustration)**. The injectors' screwed-in unions must not be allowed to move. Remove the

bracket above the common rail unions, and then remove the pipes. Plug the openings in the common rail and injectors to prevent dirt ingress.
14 Unscrew the injector retaining nuts, and carefully pull or lever the injector from place. If necessary, use an open-ended spanner and twist the injector to free it from position **(see illustrations)**. Do not lever against or pull on the solenoid housing at the top of the injector. Note down the injectors position – if the injectors are to be re-used, they must be refitted to their original locations. If improved access is required, undo the bolts and remove the oil separator housing from the front of the cylinder head cover.
15 Remove the copper washer and the upper seal from each injector, or from the cylinder head if they remained in place during injector removal. New copper washers and upper seals will be required for refitting. Cover the injector hole in the cylinder head to prevent dirt ingress.
16 Examine each injector visually for any signs of obvious damage or deterioration. If any defects are apparent, renew the injector(s). Note down the 8-digit injector classification number – this may be needed during the refitting procedure if the ECU has been renewed **(see illustrations 11.31a and 11.31b)**.
Caution: The injectors are manufactured to extremely close tolerances and must not be dismantled in any way. Do not unscrew the fuel pipe union on the side of the injector, or separate any parts of the injector body. Do not attempt to clean

11.14a Injector retaining nuts

11.14b Use a spanner to twist the injector and free it from position

11.18 Depress the clip and disconnect the wiring plug

11.19 Pull up the catches and disconnect the return hoses

11.20 Unscrew the high-pressure pipe unions

11.21a Undo the retaining bolt…

11.21b …and withdraw the injector

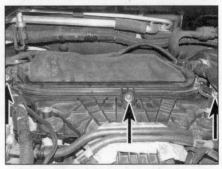

11.25 Undo the 3 bolts and remove the rubber cover

carbon deposits from the injector nozzle or carry out any form of ultrasonic or pressure testing.

SOHC engines

17 Remove the air cleaner assembly as described in Section 5.

18 Disconnect the wiring plug from each injector **(see illustration)**.

19 Pull up the catches and disconnect the fuel return hoses from the top of the injectors **(see illustration)**. Plug the openings to prevent contamination.

20 Clean the area around the high-pressure fuel pipes at the injectors, then unscrew the pipe unions. Use a second spanner to counterhold the union screwed into the injector body **(see illustration)**. The injectors' screwed-in unions must not be allowed to move.

21 Undo the retaining bolt and remove the injector along with its mounting clamps **(see illustrations)**.

2.0 litre engines

Note: *New copper washers, upper seals, studs and a high-pressure fuel pipe will be required for each disturbed injector when refitting.*

22 Remove the air cleaner assembly as described in Section 5.

23 Pull the acoustic cover upwards from the top of the engine (where fitted).

24 On Euro 4 emissions level engines, remove the intake manifold as described in Section 13.

25 On Euro 5 emissions level engines, undo the 3 bolts and remove the rubber cover from the top of the engine **(see illustration)**.

26 Thoroughly clean all the high-pressure fuel pipe unions on the fuel injectors and common rail. Using two open-ended spanners, unscrew the union nuts securing the high-pressure fuel pipes to the fuel injectors and common rail **(see illustration)**. Withdraw the high-pressure fuel pipes and plug or cover the open unions on the injectors and common rail to prevent dirt entry. Note that a new high-pressure fuel pipe will be required for each removed injector when refitting.

27 If not already done so, disconnect the wiring plugs from the injectors **(see illustration)**.

11.26 Remove the high pressure pipes – Euro 5 emissions level shown

11.27 Squeeze together the wire clips and disconnect the wiring plugs – Euro 5 engines shown

11.28a On Siemens injectors, prise down the lower edge of the retaining clip (shown with the hose disconnected for clarity) …

11.28b … then pull the hose from the injector

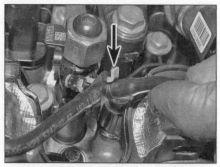

11.28c Slide out the green clip and disconnect the pipes – Euro 5 engines

11.29a Cover the intake ports to prevent anything being dropped inside

11.29b Undo the injector retaining nuts

11.29c Injector retaining bolt – Euro 5 engines

11.30a Use a spanner to slightly twist the injector …

11.30b … and then free it from its position in the cylinder head

11.30c Euro 5 emissions level injector

28 Release the retaining clip and disconnect the leak-off pipe from each fuel injector **(see illustrations)**.

29 Undo the fasteners securing the injectors **(see illustrations)**.

30 Carefully pull the injectors upwards from the cylinder head **(see illustrations)**. Note down the injectors' position – if the injectors are to be re-used, they must be refitting to their original locations.

31 Remove the injector seals, then examine each injector visually for any signs of obvious damage or deterioration. If any defects are apparent, renew the injector(s). Note down the injector classification number – this may be needed during the refitting procedure if the ECU has been renewed **(see illustrations)**.
Caution: The injectors are manufactured to extremely close tolerances and must not be

dismantled in any way. Do not unscrew the fuel pipe union on the side of the injector, or separate any parts of the injector body.

11.31a Note the Bosch injector classification number …

Do not attempt to clean carbon deposits from the injector nozzle or carry out any form of ultrasonic or pressure testing.

11.31b … and the Delphi injector classification number

11.33 The injectors should be stored upright, in order

11.34a Unscrew the old injector retaining studs ...

11.34b ... and fit new studs

11.35 Make sure the injector recess is clean

11.36a Fit a new upper seal ...

32 If the injectors are in a satisfactory condition, plug the fuel pipe union (if not already done) and suitably cover the electrical element and the injector nozzle.

33 Ideally, the injectors should be stored upright in order **(see illustration)**.

Refitting

34 Where applicable, unscrew the injector retaining studs from the cylinder head and renew **(see illustrations)**.

35 Clean out the injector recess in the cylinder head and make sure it is free from any dirt **(see illustration)**.

36 Where applicable, locate a new upper seal in the cylinder head or injector (as applicable), and place a new sealing washer down the injector recess in the cylinder head or onto the injector **(see illustrations)**.

37 Where fitted, refit the injector clamp locating dowels to the cylinder head.

38 Ensure the injector clamps are in place over their respective circlips on the injector bodies (where applicable), and then fit the injectors into place in the cylinder head. If the original injectors are being refitted, ensure they are fitted into their original positions **(see illustrations)**.

39 Fit the injector retaining bolts/nuts, but only finger-tighten them at this stage **(see**

11.36b ... and use a length of wire to guide the new sealing washer into place

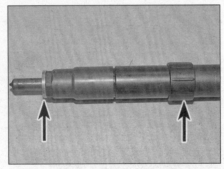

11.36c On Euro 5 engines, replace the sealing washer and upper seal

11.38a Ensure the circlip is in place (where applicable) ...

11.38b ... then fit the injectors into their original positions

**11.39a Fit new injector securing nuts –
Euro 4 engines**

**11.39b Injector clamp position – Euro 5
engines**

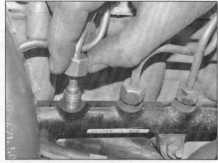

**11.40 Screw the high-pressure fuel pipes
to the fuel rail**

illustrations). When tightening the nuts/bolts, ensure the clamps stay horizontal.

40 Working on one fuel injector at a time, remove the blanking plugs from the fuel pipe unions on the common rail and the relevant injector. Locate the high-pressure fuel pipe over the unions and screw on the union nuts **(see illustration)**. Take care not to cross-thread the nuts or strain the fuel pipes as they are fitted. Once the union nut threads have started, finger-tighten the nuts to the ends of the threads.

41 When all the fuel pipes are in place, tighten the injector clamp retaining nuts/bolts to the specified torque and angle **(see illustration)**.

42 Using an open-ended spanner, hold each fuel pipe union in turn and tighten the union nut to the specified torque using a torque wrench and crow-foot adapter **(see illustration)**. Tighten all the disturbed union nuts in the same way.

43 If new injectors have been fitted, their classification numbers must be programmed into the engine management ECU using dedicated diagnostic equipment/scanner. If this equipment is not available, entrust this task to a Citroën/Peugeot/Fiat dealer or suitably-equipped repairer. Note that it should be possible to drive the vehicle, albeit with reduced performance/increased emissions, to a repairer for the numbers to be programmed.

44 The remainder of refitting is a reversal of removal, noting the following points:

a) *Ensure all wiring connectors and harnesses are correctly refitting and secured.*
b) *Reconnect the battery as described in Chapter 5A Section 4.*
c) *Observing the precautions listed in Section 2, start the engine and allow it to idle. Check for leaks at the high-pressure fuel pipe unions with the engine idling. If satisfactory, increase the engine speed to 3000 rpm and check again for leaks. Take the car for a short road test and check for leaks once again on return. If any leaks are detected, obtain and fit additional new high-pressure fuel pipes as required. Do not attempt to cure even the slightest leak by further tightening of the pipe unions.*

12 Electronic control system components – testing, removal and refitting

Testing

1 If a fault is suspected in the electronic control side of the system, first ensure that all the wiring connectors are securely connected and free of corrosion. Ensure that the suspected problem is not of a mechanical nature, or due to poor maintenance; ie, check that the air filter element is clean, the engine breather hoses are clear and undamaged, and

that the cylinder compression pressures are correct.

2 If these checks fail to reveal the cause of the problem, the vehicle should be taken to a Peugeot/Citroën/Fiat dealer or suitably-equipped garage for testing. A diagnostic socket is located beneath the drivers side of the facia **(see illustration)** to which a fault code reader or other suitable test equipment can be connected. By using the code reader or test equipment, the engine management ECM – Engine Control Module (and the various other vehicle system ECMs) can be interrogated, and any stored fault codes can be retrieved. This will allow the fault to be quickly and simply traced, alleviating the need to test all the system components individually, which is a time-consuming operation that carries a risk of damaging the ECM.

Removal and refitting

3 Before carrying out any of the following procedures, disconnect the battery as described in Chapter 5A Section 4. Reconnect the battery on completion of refitting.

Electronic control Module (ECM)

Note: *If a new ECM is being fitted, the vehicle will not start until the immobiliser ECM has been matched to the engine management ECM. This can only be performed using dedicated test equipment. Consequently, entrust the procedure to a Peugeot/Citroën/Fiat dealer or suitably-equipped specialist.*

11.41 Using an angle gauge to tighten the injector securing nuts/bolts

11.42 Using a crow-foot adapter to tighten the injector pipes

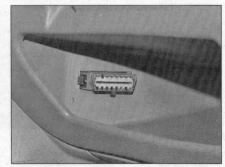

12.2 Vehicle diagnostic socket

12.4 The ECM is located on the left-hand side of the engine compartment

12.6a Undo the nut, drill out the rivets at the top…

12.6b …and undo the nut at the base of the bracket

4 The ECM is located on the left-hand side of the engine compartment **(see illustration).**

5 On models with self-levelling suspension, undo the nuts, disconnect the wiring plug and remove the suspension ECU.

6 Undo the nuts, drill out the rivets and remove the bracket above the ECM **(see illustrations).** Unclip the wiring loom as the bracket is withdrawn.

7 Undo the retaining nuts and pull the engine management ECM from place **(see illustration).**

8 Pivot over the locking catches, and disconnect the wiring plugs from the base of the ECM **(see illustration).**

9 Refitting is a reverse of the removal procedure ensuring the wiring connectors are securely reconnected.

Crankshaft speed/position sensor

10 The crankshaft position sensor is located adjacent to the crankshaft pulley on the right-hand end of the engine. Slacken the right-hand front roadwheel bolts, and then jack the front of the vehicle up and support it on axle stands (see *Jacking and vehicle support*). Remove the right-hand front roadwheel.

11 Push in the centre pins a little, then prise out the rivets and remove the wheel arch liner.

12 Disconnect the sensor wiring plug **(see illustration).**

13 Undo the bolt and remove the sensor. If necessary, slacken the lower timing belt cover bolts a few turns and move the cover away from the engine slightly.

14 Refitting is a reversal of removal, tightening the sensor retaining bolt securely.

Camshaft position sensor

1.6 litre engines

15 The camshaft position sensor is mounted on the right-hand end of the cylinder head cover, directly behind the camshaft sprocket.

16 On DOHC engines, remove the timing belt upper cover as described in Chapter 2A Section 6.

17 Unplug the sensor wiring connector.

18 To access the sensor, undo the retaining bolts and hose clips and remove the air intake pipes from the top of the engine **(see illustration).**

19 Undo the bolt and pull the sensor from position **(see illustrations).**

20 On DOHC engines, upon refitting, position the sensor so that the air gap between the

12.7 ECM retaining nuts

12.8 ECM wiring plugs

12.12 Disconnect the crankshaft position sensor wiring plug

12.18 Remove the air intake pipes assembly (SOHC shown)

12.19a Camshaft sensor retaining bolt – DOHC engine

12.19b Camshaft sensor retaining bolt – SOHC engine

12.20a The gap between the end of the used sensor and signal wheel …

12.20b … must be 1.2 mm measured with a feeler gauge

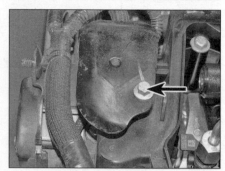

12.23 Vent retaining bolt

sensor end and the webs of the signal wheel is 1.2 mm, measured with feeler gauges **(see illustrations)**. If a new sensor is being fitted, position it so the nipple of the sensor is just in contact with the camshaft signal wheel. Tighten the sensor retaining bolt to the specified torque.

21 The remainder of refitting is a reversal of removal.

2.0 litre engines

22 The camshaft position sensor is mounted on the right-hand end of the cylinder head cover, directly behind the camshaft sprocket.

23 Where applicable, pull the acoustic cover upwards from the top of the engine, then undo the bolt and remove the plastic vent assembly from the right-hand end of the cylinder head cover (where fitted) **(see illustration)**. Move the vent to one side – there's no need to disconnect the pipe.

24 Disconnect the sensor wiring plug **(see illustration)**.

25 Undo the retaining bolt and remove the sensor **(see illustration)**.

26 To refit and adjust the sensor position, locate the sensor on the cylinder head cover and loosely refit the retaining bolt.

27 When refitting a used sensor, insert a 7.5 mm drill bit in between the sensor and the timing belt cover to get the sensor in position **(see illustration)**. Tighten the retaining bolt securely.

28 When fitting a new sensor, slide the sensor into position until the plastic nipple on the tip of the sensor just comes into contact with the spoke on the camshaft sprocket. Tighten the retaining bolt securely. Note that, depending on the position of the camshaft sprocket, it may need to be rotated slightly to get one of the spokes on sprocket to align with the hole for the sensor.

Accelerator pedal position sensor

29 The pedal sensor is integral with the accelerator pedal assembly. Refer to Section 6 of this Chapter for the pedal removal procedure.

Coolant temperature sensor

30 Refer to Chapter 3 Section 7.

Fuel temperature sensor

⚠️ *Warning: Refer to the information contained in Section 2 before proceeding.*

1.6 litre engines

31 The sensor (where fitted) is clipped in to the plastic fuel manifold at the right-hand rear end of the cylinder head. To remove the sensor, disconnect the wiring plug, and then unclip the sensor from the manifold. Be prepared for fuel spillage **(see illustration)**.

32 Refitting is a reversal of removal. Observing the precautions listed in Section 2, start the engine and allow it to idle. Check for leaks at the fuel temperature sensor with the engine idling. If satisfactory, increase the engine speed to 4000 rpm and check again for leaks. Take the car for a short road test and check for leaks once again on return. If any leaks are detected, obtain and fit a new sensor.

2.0 litre engines – Siemens

33 Remove the air cleaner assembly as described in Section 5.

34 The fuel temperature sensor (where fitted) is located in the fuel supply pipe between the fuel filter and the high-pressure pump, in the vicinity of the common rail.

35 Disconnect the fuel temperature sensor wiring connector.

36 Thoroughly clean the area around the sensor and its location.

37 Suitably protect the components below the sensor and have plenty of clean rags handy. Be prepared for considerable fuel spillage.

38 Release the retaining clips and detach the sensor from the fuel pipes.

39 Refitting is a reversal of removal.

40 Observing the precautions listed in Section 2, start the engine and allow it to idle. Check for leaks at the fuel temperature sensor with the engine idling. If satisfactory, increase

12.24 Disconnect the wiring connector

12.25 Withdraw the sensor from the cover

12.27 Using an 7.5 mm drill bit to measure the position of the sensor

12.31 Fuel temperature sensor

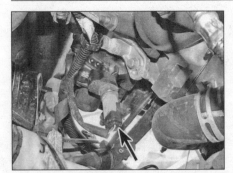

12.41 Fuel temperature sensor

12.51a Disconnect airflow meter wiring plug – 1.6 litre DOHC engine

12.51b Airflow meter wiring plug – 1.6 litre SOHC engine

the engine speed to 4000 rpm and check again for leaks. Take the car for a short road test and check for leaks once again on return. If any leaks are detected, obtain and fit a new sensor.

2.0 litre engines – Delphi

41 The fuel temperature sensor is located in the high-pressure fuel pump (see illustration).
42 Disconnect the fuel temperature sensor wiring connector.
43 Thoroughly clean the area around the sensor and its location.
44 Suitably protect the components below the sensor and have plenty of clean rags handy. Be prepared for considerable fuel spillage.
45 Undo the sensor and remove it from the fuel pump.
46 Refitting is a reversal of removal, tightening the sensor to the specified torque.
47 Observing the precautions listed in Section 2, start the engine and allow it to idle. Check for leaks at the fuel temperature sensor with the engine idling. If satisfactory, increase the engine speed to 4000 rpm and check again for leaks. Take the car for a short road test and check for leaks once again on return. If any leaks are detected, obtain and fit a new sensor.

Airflow meter

48 The airflow meter is located in the intake ducting from the air cleaner housing.

1.6 litre DOHC engines

49 Drill out the rivet and detach the cabin air intake cowl drain tube from the front panel (see illustration 5.1).
50 Undo the 4 retaining nuts and remove the

cabin air intake cowl (see illustration 5.2a and 5.2b).

All engines

51 Disconnect the meter wiring plug (see illustrations).
52 Slacken the retaining clips (where fitted) and disconnect the air intake ducting from the airflow meter. Suitably plug or cover the turbocharger intake duct, using clean rag to prevent any dirt or foreign material from entering.
53 Undo the retaining screws and disconnect the airflow meter from the air cleaner housing.
54 Refitting is reverse of the removal procedure.

Fuel pressure sensor

55 The fuel pressure sensor is integral with the common rail, and is not available separately. The manufacturers insist that the sensor is not removed from the rail.

Fuel pressure regulator

56 The fuel pressure regulator is located in the high-pressure fuel pump. Depending on fuel system, the regulator may be screwed into the fuel pump or it may have two retaining screws securing it to the fuel pump (see illustration).
57 Disconnect the wiring connector from the fuel pressure regulator.
58 Thoroughly clean the area around the sensor and its location.
59 Suitably protect the components below the sensor and have plenty of clean rags handy. Be prepared for considerable fuel spillage.

60 Depending on type fitted, either unscrew the regulator and remove it from the fuel pump or undo the two retaining screws and remove the regulator from the pump.
61 Refitting is a reversal of removal, tightening the sensor to the specified torque.
62 Observing the precautions listed in Section 2, start the engine and allow it to idle. Check for leaks at the fuel temperature sensor with the engine idling. If satisfactory, increase the engine speed to 4000 rpm and check again for leaks. Take the car for a short road test and check for leaks once again on return. If any leaks are detected, obtain and fit a new sensor.

EGR solenoid valve

63 Refer to Chapter 4B Section 2.

Throttle body

1.6 litre DOHC

64 Undo the 2 retaining screws, and move the relay box attached to the front panel, to one side.
65 Slacken the clamps and remove the air intake pipe between the intercooler and the throttle body.
66 Undo the retaining nut and move the engine coolant expansion tank to one side.
67 Note their fitted positions, then disconnect the various wiring plugs from the throttle body (see illustration).

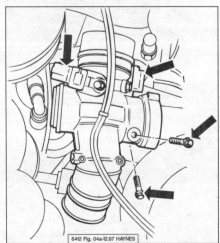

12.67 Throttle body wiring plugs and retaining bolts

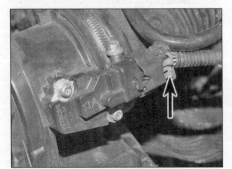

12.51c Slide out the clip and disconnect the airflow meter wiring plug – 2.0 litre engines

12.56 Delphi fuel pressure regulator – 2.0 litre engine shown

12.72 Release the clamps and remove the air hose

12.74 Throttle body retaining bolts

12.75 Release the clamps and remove the hose

68 Release the clamp, undo the 2 retaining bolts and remove the throttle body.

1.6 litre SOHC

69 Undo the bolt securing the cabin air intake cowl drain tube to the front panel.
70 Undo the 2 retaining nuts and remove the cabin air intake cowl.
71 Where applicable, release the fasteners and remove the acoustic cover from the top of the engine.
72 Release the clamps and remove the air hose from the throttle body **(see illustration)**.
73 Disconnect the throttle body wiring plug.
74 Undo the 4 retaining bolts and remove the throttle body **(see illustration)**. Note that one of the bolts is accessed from the rear of the manifold. Check the condition of the O-ring seal and renew if necessary.

2.0 litre engines

Euro 4 emissions level engines

75 Release the clamps and remove the air hose between the intercooler and the throttle body **(see illustration)**.
76 Disconnect the vacuum hose, and the wiring plug(s) from the throttle body.
77 Undo the 2 retaining bolts and remove the throttle body. Renew the gasket.

Euro 5 emissions level engines

78 Remove the air cleaner assembly as described in Section 5.
79 Pull up and remove the acoustic cover from the top of the engine.

12.81 Disconnect the wiring plugs from the throttle body

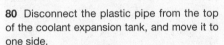

80 Disconnect the plastic pipe from the top of the coolant expansion tank, and move it to one side.
81 Note their fitted positions, then disconnect the wiring plugs and vacuum hoses from the throttle body **(see illustration)**. Release the hose(s) and wiring loom from any retaining clips on the throttle body.
82 Release the clamp then disconnect the air inlet hose from the throttle body **(see illustration)**.
83 Undo the 6 retaining bolts, and manoeuvre the throttle body from place **(see illustrations)**. Renew the rubber seal.

All engines

84 Refitting is a reversal of removal, renewing any gasket or seal as necessary.

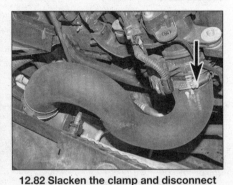

12.82 Slacken the clamp and disconnect the hose

13 Intake manifold – removal and refitting

1.6 litre DOHC engines and 2.0 litre engines

1 The intake manifold is integral with the cylinder head cover. For the removal and refitting procedure, refer to Chapter 2B Section 4 or Chapter 2C Section 4.

1.6 litre SOHC engines

Removal

2 Drain the engine coolant as described in Chapter 1 Section 23.
3 Disconnect the battery negative lead as described in Chapter 5A Section 4.
4 Remove the air cleaner assembly as described in Section 5.
5 Remove the fuel filter assembly as described in Chapter 1 Section 11.
6 Remove the throttle body as described in Section 12.
7 Remove the starter motor as described in Chapter 5A Section 10.
8 Remove the EGR cooler as described in Chapter 4B Section 2.
9 Undo the retaining bolts and remove the wiring harness guide above the manifold.
10 The intake manifold is removed along with the fuel filter mounting bracket. Undo the 3 bolts securing the manifold to the cylinder head.

12.83a Throttle body retaining bolts

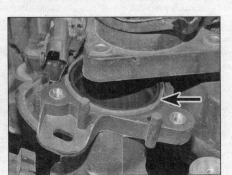

12.83b Renew the seal

11 Undo the 3 bolts securing the fuel filter mounting bracket, release the fuel pipe from the retaining clip, then manoeuvre the manifold and bracket from place.

Refitting

12 Refitting is a reversal of removal. Renew any seals/gaskets as necessary.

14 Exhaust manifold – removal and refitting

Removal

1 Remove the turbocharger as described in Section 16.
2 Where applicable, undo the bolts and remove the heatshield(s) from the exhaust manifold **(see illustration)**.
3 Undo the retaining nuts, recover the spacers (where fitted), and remove the manifold. Recover the gasket **(see illustrations)**.

Refitting

4 Refitting is a reverse of the removal procedure, bearing in mind the following points:
a) *Ensure that the manifold and cylinder head mating faces are clean, with all traces of old gasket removed.*
b) *Use new gaskets when refitting the manifold to the cylinder head.*
c) *Tighten the exhaust manifold retaining nuts to the specified torque, starting with the ones at the centre and then working your way to the outer ones.*

15 Turbocharger – description and precautions

1 A turbocharger is fitted to increase engine efficiency by raising the pressure in the intake manifold above atmospheric pressure. Instead of the air simply being sucked into the cylinders, it is forced in.
2 Energy for the operation of the turbocharger comes from the exhaust gas. The gas flows through a specially shaped housing (the turbine housing) and, in so doing, spins the turbine wheel. The turbine wheel is attached to a shaft, at the end of which is another vaned wheel known as the compressor wheel. The compressor wheel spins in its own housing, and compresses the intake air on the way to the intake manifold.
3 Boost pressure (the pressure in the intake manifold) is limited by a wastegate, which diverts the exhaust gas away from the turbine wheel in response to a pressure-sensitive actuator. The turbocharger incorporates a variable intake nozzle to improve boost pressure at low engine speeds.
4 The turbo shaft is pressure-lubricated by an oil feed pipe from the main oil gallery. The shaft 'floats' on a cushion of oil. A drain pipe returns the oil to the sump.

Precautions

5 The turbocharger operates at extremely high speeds and temperatures. Certain precautions must be observed, to avoid premature failure of the turbo, or injury to the operator.
● Do not operate the turbo with any of its parts exposed, or with any of its hoses removed. Foreign objects falling onto the rotating vanes could cause excessive damage, and (if ejected) personal injury.
● Do not race the engine immediately after start-up, especially if it is cold. Give the oil a few seconds to circulate.
● Always allow the engine to return to idle speed before switching it off – do not blip the throttle and switch off, as this will leave the turbo spinning without lubrication.
● Allow the engine to idle for several minutes before switching off after a high-speed run.
● Observe the recommended intervals for oil and filter changing, and use a reputable oil of the specified quality. Neglect of oil changing, or use of inferior oil, can cause carbon formation on the turbo shaft, leading to subsequent failure.

16 Turbocharger – removal, inspection and refitting

Removal

1 Chock the rear wheels then jack up the front of the vehicle and support it on axle stands (see *Jacking and vehicle support*). Undo the screws and remove the engine undershield (where fitted).

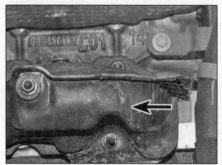

14.2 Remove the manifold heatshield

14.3a Undo the exhaust manifold nuts, recover the spacers, and remove the manifold

14.3b Recover the manifold gasket – 1.6 litre engines

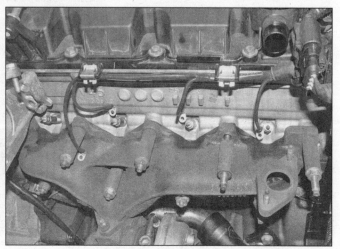

14.3c Exhaust manifold – 2.0 litre engines

16.6 Disconnect the vacuum pipe from the wastegate control assembly

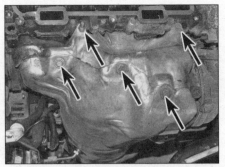

16.7 Undo the bolts and remove the turbocharger heat shield

16.9 Turbocharger oil supply and return pipes

2 Disconnect the battery negative lead as described in Chapter 5A Section 4.

1.6 litre engines

3 Remove the air cleaner assembly as described in Section 5.
4 Place a sheet of thick cardboard over the rear of the radiator to protect it from accidental damage.

DOHC engines

5 Slacken the clamps, undo the bolts, and remove the air ducts to and from the turbocharger and intake manifold. Note their fitted positions and disconnect the various wiring plugs, as the assembly is withdrawn.
6 Disconnect the vacuum hose from the turbocharger wastegate control assembly **(see illustration)**.
7 Undo the mounting bolts **(see illustration)**, and remove the heat shield from above turbocharger.
8 Remove the catalytic converter/particulate filter (where applicable) as described in Section 18.
9 Undo the oil supply pipe banjo bolts and recover the sealing washers **(see illustration)**.
10 Slacken the retaining clip and disconnect the oil return pipe from the turbocharger and cylinder block.
11 Unscrew the nuts, and the nut securing the support bracket, then remove the turbocharger from the exhaust manifold **(see illustration)**.

SOHC engines

12 Remove the catalytic converter/particulate filter as described in Section 18.

16.11 Undo the 3 nuts (arrowed – one hidden) and remove the support bracket bolt

13 Release the clamps and remove the air hose from the air cleaner to the turbocharger.
14 Undo the retaining screws, disconnect the breather hose and remove the turbocharger intake assembly **(see illustration)**.
15 Disconnect the wiring plug from the turbocharger vane position sensor.
16 Undo the banjo bolt and detach the oil supply pipe from the top of the turbocharger **(see illustration)**. Renew the sealing washers.
17 Slacken the clamp and disconnect the lower end of the turbocharger oil return hose.
18 Undo the 4 nuts securing the turbocharger to the exhaust manifold, and manoeuvre it from place **(see illustration)**. Renew the turbocharger-to-exhaust manifold gasket.

2.0 litre engines

Note: *Access to the turbocharger is extremely*

16.14 Disconnect the breather hose and disconnect the air intake assembly

limited. Most photographs in this Section were taken with the engine removed for clarity.
19 Remove the air cleaner assembly as described in Section 5.
20 Remove the right-hand driveshaft as described in Chapter 8 Section 2.
21 Remove the catalytic converter/particulate filter as described in Section 18.

Euro 4 emissions level engines

22 Undo the retaining bolts and disconnect the turbocharger air intake and outlet ducts **(see illustration)**.
23 Remove the windscreen wiper motor and linkage as described in Chapter 12 Section 14.
24 Remove the EGR cooler as described in Chapter 4B Section 2.
25 Unclip the metal cover from over the steering rack.

16.16 Oil supply pipe banjo bolt

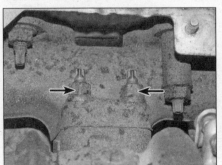

16.18 Turbocharger upper retaining bolts

16.22 Remove the air intake and outlet ducts

16.26 Disconnect the wiring connector and the vacuum pipe

16.27a Disconnect the turbocharger oil supply pipe…

16.27b … and the return pipe

26 Disconnect the vacuum pipe and wiring plug from the turbocharger control valve **(see illustration)**.

27 Disconnect the oil supply and return pipes from the engine cylinder block **(see illustrations)**. Tape over the openings.

28 Remove the support bracket beneath the turbocharger **(see illustration)**.

29 Undo the nuts/bolt securing the turbocharger to the exhaust manifold, lift the assembly slightly, then lower the turbocharger downwards from position **(see illustration)**.

Euro 5 emissions level engines

Note: *In theory, it is possible to remove the turbocharger with the engine and transmission in place. Access is extremely limited. Consequently, we recommend that the front subframe is removed as described in Chapter 10 Section 9.*

30 Remove the pre-catalytic converter as described in Section 18.

31 On engines fitted with a water-cooled turbocharger, drain the coolant system as described in Chapter 1 Section 23, or be prepared for coolant spillage when the turbocharger coolant hoses are disconnected.

32 Undo the bolts and remove the rigid air pipe between the turbocharger and intercooler **(see illustration)**.

33 Release the clamp, disconnect the breather hose, undo the retaining bolts and remove the turbocharger air inlet pipe/hose assembly **(see illustrations)**.

34 Undo the retaining bolts and remove the exhaust manifold heatshield **(see illustration)**. Note the it may be necessary to remove the left-hand rear engine lifting eye bracket from the rear corner of the cylinder head, then disconnect the vacuum pipe and wiring plug from the wastegate actuator.

35 Release the clamp securing the lower end of the turbocharger oil return hose **(see illustration)**.

16.28 Turbocharger lower mounting bracket bolt

16.29 Turbocharger upper mounting nuts and bolt

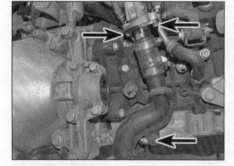

16.32 Undo the bolts and remove air outlet pipe assembly

16.33a Rotate the collar and disconnect the breather hose

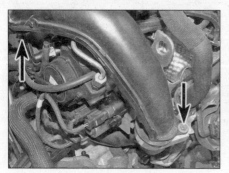

16.33b Air inlet pipe retaining bolts

16.34 Undo the bolts and remove the heatshield

16.35 Release the clamp and disconnect the oil return hose

16.36 Undo the oil supply banjo bolt

16.38 Disconnect the vacuum hose and wiring plug

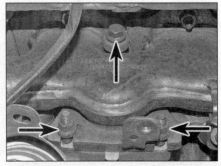

16.39 Turbocharger retaining nuts/bolt

36 Undo the banjo bolt and disconnect the turbocharger oil supply pipe from the cylinder block **(see illustration)**. Renew the sealing washers.
37 Where applicable, release the clamps and disconnect the coolant supply and return hoses from the turbocharger.
38 If not already done so, disconnect the wiring plug and vacuum hose from the turbocharger vane control valve and actuator **(see illustration)**.
39 Undo the nuts/bolt securing the turbocharger to the exhaust manifold **(see illustration)**.
40 Remove the support bracket bolt and manoeuvre the turbocharger from place **(see illustration)**.

Inspection

41 With the turbocharger removed, inspect the housing for cracks or other visible damage.
42 Spin the turbine or the compressor wheel to verify that the shaft is intact and to feel for excessive shake or roughness. Some play is normal, since in use the shaft is 'floating' on a film of oil. Check that the wheel vanes are undamaged.
43 If oil contamination of the exhaust or induction passages is apparent, it is likely that turbo shaft oil seals have failed.
44 No DIY repair of the turbo is possible and none of the internal or external parts are available separately. If the turbocharger is suspect in any way a complete new unit must

16.40 Undo the bracket-to-turbocharger bolt

be obtained. Do not attempt to dismantle the turbocharger control assemblies.
45 Where applicable, clean the fine filter inserted into the turbocharger oil supply pipe banjo bolt **(see illustration)**.

Refitting

46 Refitting is a reverse of the removal procedure, bearing in mind the following points:
a) Renew the turbocharger retaining nuts and gaskets.
b) When fitting the new clamp to the pre-catalyst, align the clamp on the flange **(see illustrations)**.
c) If a new turbocharger is being fitted, change the engine oil and filter. Also renew the filter in the oil feed pipe.
d) Prime the turbocharger by injecting clean

16.45 Clean the filter in the oil supply banjo bolt

engine oil through the oil feed pipe union before reconnecting the union.
e) Top up the engine coolant where necessary (see Weekly checks).

17 Intercooler – removal and refitting

Removal

1.6 litre models

1 The intercooler is located at the front of the engine compartment, on the right-hand side of the radiator.
2 Undo the retaining bolts and move the relay box on the front panel to one side **(see illustration)**. Unclip the wiring loom from the panel.

16.46a Unclip the old inner sealing washer from the old clamp

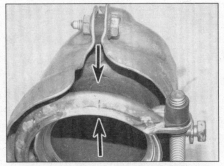

16.46b Fit the alignment mark on the new clamp with the upper flange of the pre-cat

17.2 Undo the bolts and move the relay box to one side

17.3 Remove the upper hose clamps from the intercooler

17.4 Use a pair of screwdrivers to depress the catch each side, and pull the upper mounting rearwards

17.6 Relay box retaining bolts

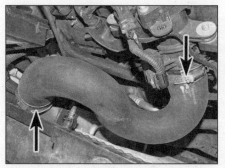

17.7 Intake manifold-to-intercooler hose clamps

17.9 Turbocharger-to-intercooler hose clamps

3 Slacken the retaining clips and disconnect the air intake and outlet hoses from the top of the intercooler **(see illustration)**.
4 Release the upper mounting, and then lift the intercooler, releasing it from its lower mountings in the radiator front panel **(see illustration)**.

2.0 litre models

5 The intercooler is located at the front of the engine compartment, on the right-hand side of the radiator.
6 Undo the 2 retaining bolts and move the relay box on the front panel to one side **(see illustration)**.
7 Release the clamps and remove the air intake hose from the intake manifold to the intercooler **(see illustration)**.
8 Raise the front of the vehicle and support it securely on axle stands (see *Jacking and*

vehicle support). Undo the fasteners and remove the engine undershield.
9 Slacken the clamps, and disconnect the air hose from the turbocharger to the intercooler **(see illustration)**.
10 Release the upper mounting clips, then lift the intercooler, releasing it from its lower mountings in the radiator front panel **(see illustrations)**.

Refitting

11 Refitting is a reversal of removal.

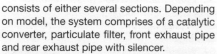

18 Exhaust system – general information and component renewal

General information

1 According to model, the exhaust system

consists of either several sections. Depending on model, the system comprises of a catalytic converter, particulate filter, front exhaust pipe and rear exhaust pipe with silencer.
2 The exhaust joints are of either the spring-loaded ball type (to allow for movement in the exhaust system) or clamp-ring type.
3 The system is suspended throughout its entire length by rubber mountings.

Removal

4 Each exhaust section can be removed individually, or alternatively, the complete system can be removed as a unit.
5 To remove the system or part of the system, first jack up the front or rear of the car, and support it on axle stands (see *Jacking and vehicle support*). Alternatively, position the car over an inspection pit, or on car ramps.

Catalytic converter/particulate filter

6 Undo the retaining bolts/nuts and remove the engine undershield.

1.6 litre engines

7 Drill out the rivet securing the drain hose to the front panel **(see illustration 5.1)**.
8 Undo the retaining nuts and remove the cabin air intake cowl **(see illustrations 5.2a and 5.2b)**.
9 Release the clamps, undo the bolts and remove the turbocharger inlet hose assembly **(see illustration)**.
10 Undo the nuts/bolt and remove the

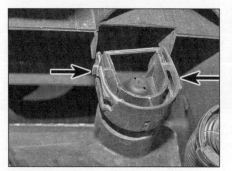

17.10a Press-in the clip each side and pull the upper mounting rearwards

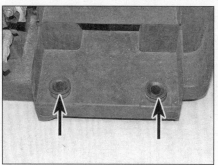

17.10b Intercooler lower mountings

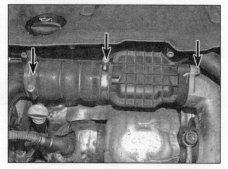

18.9 Release the clamps, undo the bolts and remove the inlet assembly

18.10 Heatshield retaining nuts/bolt

18.11 Unscrew the pressure take-off unions from the side/base of the catalyst/filter

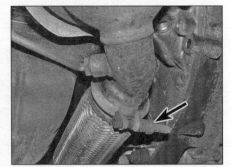

18.13 Exhaust flexible pipe-to-catalyst/ filter clamp

heatshield from the turbocharger **(see illustration)**.

11 Unscrew the pressure take-off unions from the side and base of the assembly **(see illustration)**.

12 Disconnect the sensor wiring plug(s) on the side of the catalytic converter.

13 Slacken the retaining clamps joining the catalytic converter to the turbocharger and exhaust pipe. Take care not to damage the flexible section of the front exhaust pipe **(see illustration)**.

14 Slacken the clamp securing the catalytic converter to the turbocharger **(see illustration)**.

15 Undo the 2 nuts securing the catalytic converter/particulate filter to the cylinder block and manoeuvre it down and out of the engine compartment **(see illustration)**.

16 If required, note its fitted position, then slacken the clamp and detach the particulate filter from the base of the catalytic converter **(see illustration)**.

2.0 litre engines

17 Slacken and gently spread the clamp securing the pre-catalytic converter to the catalytic converter/particulate filter flexible hose **(see illustration)**.

18 Undo the catalyst/filter mounting bolts.

19 Label the hoses to aid refitting, then release the clamps and disconnect the rubber hoses from the particulate filter **(see illustration)**.

20 Unscrew the exhaust temperature sensor from the side of the particulate filter.

18.14 Slacken the turbo-to-catalytic converter clamp

18.15 Catalytic converter/particulate filter retaining nuts

18.16 Undo the clamp and slide the particulate filter from the catalytic converter

18.17 Release the clamp securing the particulate filter/catalytic converter to the pre-catalytic converter

21 Slacken and gently spread the clamp securing the particulate filter to the intermediate/rear exhaust pipe.

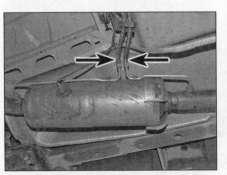

18.19 Disconnect the hoses from the particulate filter

18.25 Slacken the bolt and spread the clamp

22 Manoeuvre the catalytic converter/ particulate filter from place.

Pre-catalytic converter – 2.0 litre engines

23 In theory, it is possible to remove the pre-catalytic converter (upstream) with the subframe in place, however, access is extremely limited. Consequently, we recommend the front subframe is removed as described in Chapter 10 Section 9.

24 Slacken and gently spread the clamp securing the pre-catalytic converter to the main catalytic converter/particulate filter **(see illustration 18.17)**.

25 Slacken and gently spread the clamp securing the pre-catalytic converter to the turbocharger **(see illustration)**.

26 Disconnect the oxygen sensor wiring plug.

27 Undo the retaining bolts/nut and manoeuvre the pre-catalytic converter from place **(see illustration)**.

Intermediate pipe/silencer

28 Raise the rear of the vehicle and support it securely on axle stands (see *Jacking and vehicle support*).
29 Remove the spare wheel, then unhook the spare wheel carrier.
30 Slacken the clamp securing the pipe to the catalytic converter/particulate filter.
31 Release the pipe from its mountings and remove it from underneath the vehicle **(see illustration)**. Alternatively, undo the nuts securing the mounting bracket to the vehicle body.
32 The rear silencer may be available as a separate component. Consult a Citroen/Peugeot/Fiat dealer or parts specialist.

Heat shield(s)

33 The heat shields are secured to the underside of the body by various fasteners. Each shield can be removed once the relevant exhaust section has been removed. If a shield is being removed to gain access to a component located behind it, it may prove sufficient in some cases to remove the

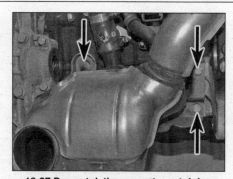

18.27 Pre-catalytic converter retaining bolts/nut

18.31 Release the pipe from the rubber mountings

fasteners and simply lower the shield, without disturbing the exhaust system.

Refitting

34 Each section is refitted by reversing the removal sequence, noting the following points:
a) Ensure that all traces of corrosion have been removed from the flanges, and renew all necessary gaskets.
b) Inspect the rubber mountings for signs of damage or deterioration, and renew as necessary.
c) On joints secured together by a clamping ring, apply a smear of exhaust system jointing paste to the flange joint, to ensure a gas-tight seal. Tighten the clamping ring nuts evenly and progressively, so that the clearance between the clamp halves remains equal on either side.
d) Prior to tightening the exhaust system fasteners, ensure that all rubber mountings are correctly located, and that there is adequate clearance between the exhaust system and vehicle underbody.

Chapter 4 Part B
Emission control systems

Contents

Degrees of difficulty

Easy, suitable for novice with little experience	**Fairly easy,** suitable for beginner with some experience	**Fairly difficult,** suitable for competent DIY mechanic

Difficult, suitable for experienced DIY mechanic	**Very difficult,** suitable for expert DIY or professional

1 General Information

1 All diesel engines are designed to meet strict emission requirements and are equipped with a crankcase emission control system and a catalytic converter. To further reduce exhaust emissions, all diesel engines are also fitted with an exhaust gas recirculation (EGR) system. Additionally, some models may be equipped with a particulate emission filter, which uses porous silicon carbide substrate to trap particulates of carbon as the exhaust gases pass through. The models with particulate filters may also be equipped with an additive system, where a cerium oxide based additive (EOLYS 176 or EOLYS Powerflex) is injected into the fuel tank each time is is refilled. The additive lowers the temperature at which the particles in the exhaust gases are burnt, reducing exhaust emissions further, and assisting in the 'regenerative' function, cleaning the particulate filter.

Crankcase emission control

2 To reduce the emission of unburned hydrocarbons from the crankcase into the atmosphere, the engine is sealed and the blow-by gases and oil vapour are drawn from inside the crankcase, through a wire mesh oil separator, into the intake tract to be burned by the engine during normal combustion.
3 Under all conditions the gases are forced out of the crankcase by the (relatively) higher crankcase pressure; if the engine is worn, the raised crankcase pressure (due to increased blow-by) will cause some of the flow to return under all manifold conditions.

Exhaust emission control

4 To minimise the level of exhaust pollutants released into the atmosphere, a catalytic converter is fitted in the exhaust system of all models.
5 The catalytic converter consists of a canister containing a fine mesh impregnated with a catalyst material, over which the hot exhaust gases pass. The catalyst speeds up the oxidation of harmful carbon monoxide, un-burnt hydrocarbons and soot, effectively reducing the quantity of harmful products released into the atmosphere via the exhaust gases.

Exhaust gas recirculation system

6 This system is designed to recirculate small quantities of exhaust gas into the intake tract, and therefore into the combustion process.

This process reduces the level of oxides of nitrogen present in the final exhaust gas, which is released into the atmosphere.

7 The volume of exhaust gas recirculated is controlled by the system electronic control unit.

8 A vacuum-operated valve is fitted to the exhaust manifold, to regulate the quantity of exhaust gas recirculated. The valve is operated by the vacuum supplied by the solenoid valve.

Particulate filter system

9 The particulate filter is combined with the catalytic converter in the exhaust system on some models, and its purpose it to trap particles of carbon (soot) as the exhaust gases pass through, in order to comply with latest emission regulations.

10 The filter can be automatically regenerated (cleaned) by the system's ECM on-board the vehicle. The engine's high-pressure injection system is utilised to inject fuel into the exhaust gases during the post-injection period; this causes the filter temperature to increase sufficiently to oxidise the particulates, leaving an ash residue. The regeneration period is automatically controlled by the on-board ECM. Subsequently, at the correct service interval the filter must be removed from the exhaust system, and renewed.

11 To assist the combustion of the trapped carbon (soot) during the regeneration process, a fuel additive (cerium-based Eolys) is automatically mixed with the diesel fuel in the fuel tank. The additive is stored in a container attached to the underside of the vehicle adjacent to the fuel tank, and the ECM regulates the amount of additive to send to the fuel tank by means of an additive injector located on the top of the fuel tank.

2 Emission control systems – testing and component renewal

Crankcase emission control

1 The components of this system require no attention other than to check that the hose(s) are clear and undamaged at regular intervals.

Exhaust emission control

2 The performance of the catalytic converter can be checked only by measuring the exhaust gases, using a good quality, carefully calibrated exhaust gas analyser.

3 If the catalytic converter is thought to be faulty, before assuming the catalytic converter is faulty, it is worth checking the problem is not due to a faulty injector. Refer to your Citroën/Peugeot/Fiat dealer for further information.

Catalytic converter renewal

4 Refer to Chapter 4A Section 18.

Exhaust gas recirculation system

5 Testing of the system should ideally be entrusted to a Peugeot/Citroën dealer since a vacuum pump and vacuum gauge are required.

EGR valve renewal

6 Disconnect the battery negative lead as described in Chapter 5A Section 4.

7 Drill out the rivet securing the cabin air intake cowling drain tube to the front panel, then undo the 4 retaining nuts and remove the cowling (see illustrations).

8 On 1.6 litre models, to improve access, remove the windscreen wiper linkage assembly as described in Chapter 12 Section 14.

9 On 1.6 litre models, the EGR valve is located at the rear of the cylinder head, bolted to the left-hand end of the heat exchanger, whilst on 2.0 litre models the EGR valve and cooler are located on the front, left-hand side of the engine. On 1.6 litre models, the EGR valve can be removed separately from the heat exchanger. On 2.0 litre models, the EGR valve and heat exchanger have to be removed as one complete unit.

1.6 litre engine

Note: The EGR valve is located at the rear of the engine. Access is extremely limited.

10 Remove the air cleaner housing and air ducting, as described in Chapter 4A Section 5, and then remove the heat shield from over the EGR valve (where fitted).

11 Remove the fuel filter and mounting as described in Chapter 1 Section 11.

12 Disconnect the EGR valve wiring plug.

13 Undo the 2 retaining bolts and pull the EGR valve from place. Discard the metal gasket from the valve, and the O-ring seal from the pipe – new ones must be fitted.

14 Refitting is a reversal of removal.

2.0 litre engine – Euro 4 emissions level engines

Note: The EGR valve is located at the rear of the engine. Access is extremely limited.

15 Remove the catalytic converter assembly as described in Chapter 4A Section 18.

16 Drain the cooling system as described in Chapter 1 Section 23.

17 Remove the air cleaner assembly and air ducts as described in Chapter 4A Section 5.

18 Release the clamp, undo the bolts and remove the EGR pipe between the EGR cooler and the intake manifold.

19 Disconnect the EGR valve wiring plug.

20 Release the clamps and disconnect the coolant hoses from the EGR cooler.

21 Release the metal collar securing the EGR pipe to the cooler from the exhaust manifold.

22 Undo the 3 retaining bolts, then lift out the EGR valve complete with heat exchanger from the rear of the engine.

23 To remove the EGR solenoid valve and housing from the heat exchanger, undo the two retaining bolts (see illustration).

24 Refitting is a reversal of removal.

2.0 litre engine – Euro 5 emissions level engines

25 Drain the cooling system as described in Chapter 1 Section 23.

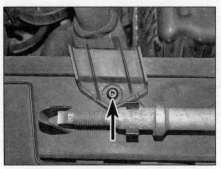

2.7a Drill out the rivet securing the drain tube

2.7b Undo the nuts at the top of the cowling…

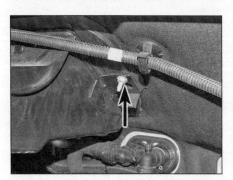

2.7c …and slacken the nut each side

2.23 Cooler-to-EGR valve housing securing bolts

2.28 Slide out the locking clip and disconnect the EGR valve wiring plug

2.29 Undo the nuts/bolt and remove the plastic support bracket

2.30 Coolant hose clamp

26 Undo the retaining bolt and remove the engine oil level dipstick guide tube.

27 Remove the cylinder head cover/ intake manifold as described in Chapter 2C Section 4.

28 Disconnect the EGR valve wiring plug, release the retaining clips and slide the wiring loom plastic guide upwards from the plastic support bracket **(see illustration)**.

29 Undo the 2 nuts, and 1 bolt, then manoeuvre the plastic support bracket from place **(see illustration)**.

30 Release the clamp and disconnect the coolant pipe from the underside of the EGR cooler **(see illustration)**.

31 Disconnect the vacuum hose from the EGR valve.

32 Undo the nut and move the engine oil level dipstick guide tube to one side.

33 Undo the retaining bolts/nuts, and manoeuvre the EGR valve/cooler from place **(see illustration)**.

34 Refitting is a reversal of removal. Renew any gaskets/seal as necessary.

EGR heat exchanger renewal

Note: *The following procedure is for 1.6 litre diesel engines, for 2.0 litre diesel models, see EGR valve renewal described previously in this Section.*

35 Drain the cooling system as described in Chapter. 1 Section 23

36 Disconnect the battery negative lead as described in Chapter 5A Section 4.

37 Remove the starter motor as described in Chapter 5A Section 10.

38 Remove the air cleaner housing and air ducting, as described in Chapter 4A Section 5, and then remove the heat shield from over the EGR valve.

39 Loosen the clips and disconnect the coolant hoses from the EGR heat exchanger **(see illustration)**.

40 Undo the bolts securing the EGR pipe to the cooler.

41 If not already done, undo the heat exchanger mounting bracket nuts and remove the heat exchanger from the rear of the engine.

42 Refitting is a reversal of removal.

Particulate filter

Fuel additive system

43 It is possible to check the fuel additive pump delivery pressure, but this should be made by a Peugeot/Citroën/Fiat dealer or specialist.

Fuel additive reservoir renewal

Note: *Ideally, the additive reservoir should be empty before removing it, otherwise take precautions against spillage.*

⚠️ **Warning: Wear protective gloves and eye protection when handling the reservoir.**

44 To remove the fuel additive reservoir, chock the front wheels then jack up the rear of the vehicle and support on axle stands (see *Jacking and vehicle support*). The reservoir is adjacent to the fuel tank.

2.33 EGR valve/cooler retaining nuts/bolts

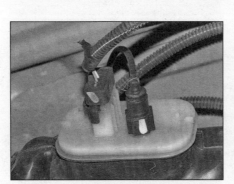

2.46 Disconnect the wiring plug and the fluid supply pipe

45 Disconnect the battery negative lead as described in Chapter 5A Section 4.

46 Disconnect the wiring plug, then depress the release buttons and disconnect the supply pipe from the additive reservoir **(see illustration)**.

47 Undo the 3 retaining bolts and lower the reservoir from place **(see illustration)**.

48 Refitting is a reversal of removal.

49 As the engine management ECU will need to be reset using dedicated diagnostic equipment, have the reservoir refilled by a Peugeot/Citroën/Fiat dealer or specialist.

Particulate filter

50 Renewal of the particulate filter is described in Chapter 4A Section 18.

Exhaust gas pressure sensor

51 This sensor measures the pressure at the entrance and exit of the particulate filter,

2.39 Release the coolant hose retaining clamps

2.47 Fuel additive reservoir retaining bolts

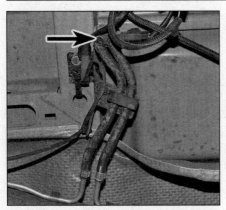

2.51 The exhaust gas pressure sensor is located under the vehicle floor

and is located under the vehicle adjacent to the particulate filter **(see illustration)**. **Note:** *Depending on model and year of the vehicle this location may change.*

52 Note the fitted position of the hoses, and then disconnect the hoses and wiring connectors from the pressure sensor.

53 Undo the mounting nuts and remove the sensor from the mounting bracket.

54 Refitting is a reversal of removal.

---

3 Catalytic converter – general information and precautions

1 The catalytic converter is a reliable and simple device which needs no maintenance in itself, but there are some facts of which an owner should be aware if the converter is to function properly for its full service life.

a) *DO NOT use fuel or engine oil additives – these may contain substances harmful to the catalytic converter.*

b) *DO NOT continue to use the car if the engine burns oil to the extent of leaving a visible trail of blue smoke.*

c) *Remember that the catalytic converter operates at very high temperatures. DO NOT, therefore, park the car in dry undergrowth, over long grass or piles of dead leaves after a long run.*

d) *Remember that the catalytic converter is FRAGILE – do not strike it with tools.*

e) *If the converter is no longer effective it must be renewed.*

Chapter 5 Part A
Starting and charging systems

Contents

Degrees of difficulty

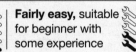

Easy, suitable for novice with little experience	**Fairly easy,** suitable for beginner with some experience	**Fairly difficult,** suitable for competent DIY mechanic	**Difficult,** suitable for experienced DIY mechanic	**Very difficult,** suitable for expert DIY or professional

Specifications

System type . . . . 12 volt, negative earth

Battery
Type . . . . Lead/Calcium, 'maintenance-free' sealed for life
Capacity . . . . 50, 60 or 70 Ah (depending on model)

Alternator
Type . . . . Valeo, Denso, Bosch, Magneti Marelli or Mitsubishi (depending on model)
Rating . . . . 120 or 150 amp

Starter motor
Type . . . . Valeo, Bosch, Ducellier, Mitsubishi or Iskra (depending on model)

Torque wrench settings	**Nm**	**lbf ft**
Alternator mounting bolts:		
Front upper bolt	40	30
Rear bolts	49	36
Auxiliary belt idler pulley bolt	45	33
Auxiliary belt tensioner-to-cylinder block bolt	20	15
Oil level sensor	27	20
Oil pressure switch	20	15
Starter motor bolts:		
1.6 litre engines	20	15
2.0 litre engines	35	26

1 General information and precautions

General information

1 The engine electrical system consists mainly of the charging and starting systems. Because of their engine-related functions, these components are covered separately from the body electrical devices such as the lights, instruments, etc (which are covered in Chapter 12). Refer to Section for information on the preheating system.

2 The electrical system is of the 12 volt negative earth type.

3 The battery is of the 'maintenance-free' (sealed for life) type and is charged by the alternator, which is belt-driven from the crankshaft pulley.

4 The starter motor is of the pre-engaged type incorporating an integral solenoid. On starting, the solenoid moves the drive pinion into engagement with the flywheel ring gear before the starter motor is energised. Once the engine has started, a one-way clutch prevents the motor armature being driven by the engine until the pinion disengages from the flywheel.

Precautions

5 Further details of the various systems are given in the relevant Sections of this Chapter. While some repair procedures are given, the usual course of action is to renew the component concerned.

6 It is necessary to take extra care when working on the electrical system to avoid damage to semi-conductor devices (diodes and transistors), and to avoid the risk of personal injury. In addition to the precautions given in *Safety first!* at the beginning of this manual, observe the following when working on the system:

● Always remove rings, watches, etc, before working on the electrical system. Even with the battery disconnected, capacitive discharge could occur if a component's live terminal is earthed through a metal object. This could cause a shock or nasty burn.

● Do not reverse the battery connections. Components such as the alternator, electronic control units, or any other components having semi-conductor circuitry could be irreparably damaged.

● If the engine is being started using jump leads and a slave battery, connect the batteries positive-to-positive and negative-to-negative (see Jump starting). This also applies when connecting a battery charger.

● Never disconnect the battery terminals, the alternator, any electrical wiring or any test instruments when the engine is running.

● Do not allow the engine to turn the alternator when the alternator is not connected.

● Never 'test' for alternator output by 'flashing' the output lead to earth.

● Never use an ohmmeter of the type incorporating a hand-cranked generator for circuit or continuity testing.

● Always ensure that the battery negative lead is disconnected when working on the electrical system.

● Before using electric-arc welding equipment on the car, disconnect the battery, alternator and components such as the fuel injection/ignition electronic control unit to protect them from the risk of damage.

2 Electrical fault finding – general information

1 Refer to Chapter 12 Section 2.

3 Battery – testing and charging

Testing

1 A 'sealed for life' maintenance-free battery is fitted to these models, topping-up and testing of the electrolyte in each cell is not possible. The condition of the battery can therefore only be tested using a battery condition indicator or a voltmeter.

2 Certain models may be fitted with a built-in charge condition indicator. The indicator is located in the top of the battery casing, and indicates the condition of the battery from its colour **(see illustration)**. If the indicator shows green, then the battery is in a good state of charge. If the indicator shows black, then the battery requires charging, as described later in this Section. If the indicator shows white, then the electrolyte level in the battery is too low to allow further use, and the battery should be renewed. **Caution: Do not attempt to charge, load or jump start a battery when the indicator shows clear/yellow.**

3 If testing the battery using a voltmeter, connect the voltmeter across the battery and check for a reading of approx. 12.7 volts. The test is only accurate if the battery has not been subjected to any kind of charge for the previous six hours. If this is not the case, switch on the headlights for 30 seconds, then wait four to five minutes

before testing the battery after switching off the headlights. All other electrical circuits must be switched off, so check that the doors and tailgate are fully shut when making the test.

4 If the voltage reading is less than 12.2 volts, then the battery is discharged, whilst a reading of 12.2 to 12.4 volts indicates a partially discharged condition.

5 If the battery is to be charged, remove it from the vehicle (Section 4) and charge it as described later in this Section.

Charging

Note: *The following is intended as a guide only. Always refer to the manufacturer's recommendations (often printed on a label attached to the battery) before charging a battery.*

6 A maintenance-free battery takes considerably longer to fully recharge than the standard type, the time taken being dependent on the extent of discharge, but it can take anything up to three days.

7 A constant voltage type charger is required to be set, when connected, to 13.9 to 14.9 volts with a charger current below 25 amps. Using this method, the battery should be usable within three hours, giving a voltage reading of 12.5 volts, but this is for a partially discharged battery and, as mentioned, full charging can take considerably longer.

8 If the battery is to be charged from a fully discharged state (condition reading less than 12.2 volts), have it recharged by your Peugeot/Citroën dealer or local automotive electrician, as the charge rate is higher and constant supervision during charging is necessary.

4 Battery – disconnection, reconnection, removal and refitting

Note: *Prior to disconnecting the battery, wait 5 minutes after switching off the ignition to allow the vehicle's ECMs to store all learned values in their memories, and also the power consuming equipment can switch to standby.*

Disconnection

1 Open the passengers door, then lift the outer edge and remove the battery cover **(see illustration)**. Where applicable, lift out the foam padding.

3.2 Battery charge condition indicator

4.1 Lift the outer edge and remove the battery cover

4.2 Slacken the nut and pull the negative lead clamp from the terminal

4.3 Lift the positive lead release lever

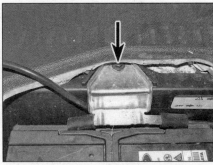

4.13 Battery retaining clamp bolt

2 Slacken the nut, then with a twisting motion, pull the negative lead clamp from the battery terminal **(see illustration)**. Position the lead clamp away from the battery terminal to prevent accidental reconnection.

3 Lift the release lever and pull the positive lead from the battery terminal **(see illustration)**.

Reconnection

4 Position the positive lead clamp over the positive battery terminal, then press it down fully into place. Tighten the clamp retaining nut securely.

5 Press the negative lead clamp over the battery negative terminal, and push down the locking lever. Check the clamp is secure.

6 Smear petroleum jelly on the terminals after reconnecting the leads.

7 Refit the battery cover.

8 Wait at least 1 minute before starting the engine.

9 To initialise the electric windows, lower the window completely, then fully close the window, keeping the switch operated for 2 seconds after the window has closed. Repeat this procedure on the remaining windows.

10 Close the tailgate using the key, then open it to reactivate the electric opening function.

11 After reconnection, the following may need to be carried out using the information contained in the Owners Handbook supplied with the vehicle:

● Update the time, date, measurement unit for outside temperature, and reconfigure the multifunction display.

● Reprogram the radio stations.

● Reprogram the navigation equipment

Note: *Bear in mind that any speed limiter settings will have been deleted.*

Removal

12 Disconnect the battery negative and positive leads as described previously in this Section.

13 Unscrew the securing bolt and remove the battery retaining clamp **(see illustration)**.

14 The battery can now be lifted out of the engine compartment.

Refitting

15 Refitting is a reversal of removal.

---

5 Charging system – testing

Note: *Refer to the warnings given in 'Safety first!' and in Section 1 of this Chapter before starting work.*

1 If the ignition warning light fails to illuminate when the ignition is switched on, first check the alternator wiring connections for security. If satisfactory, check that the warning light bulb has not blown, and that the bulbholder is secure in its location in the instrument panel. If the light still fails to illuminate, check the continuity of the warning light feed wire from the alternator to the bulbholder. If all is satisfactory, the alternator is at fault and should be renewed or taken to an auto-electrician for testing and repair.

2 If the ignition warning light illuminates when the engine is running, stop the engine and check that the drivebelt is correctly fitted and tensioned (see Chapter 1 Section 20) and that the alternator connections are secure. If all is so far satisfactory, have the alternator checked by an auto-electrician for testing and repair.

3 If the alternator output is suspect even though the warning light functions correctly, the regulated voltage may be checked as follows.

4 Connect a voltmeter across the battery terminals and start the engine.

5 Increase the engine speed until the voltmeter reading remains steady; the reading should be approximately 12 to 13 volts, and no more than 14 volts.

6 Switch on as many electrical accessories as possible (eg, the headlights, heated rear window and heater blower), and check that the alternator maintains the regulated voltage of around 13 to 14 volts.

7 If the regulated voltage is not as stated,

the fault may be due to worn brushes, weak brush springs, a faulty voltage regulator, a faulty diode, a severed phase winding or worn or damaged slip-rings. The alternator should be renewed or taken to an auto-electrician for testing and repair.

---

6 Alternator drivebelt – removal, refitting and tensioning

1 Refer to the procedure given for the auxiliary drivebelt in Chapter 1, Section 20.

---

7 Alternator – removal and refitting

Removal

1 Remove the auxiliary drivebelt as described in Chapter 1 Section 20.

2 Disconnect the battery negative lead as described in Section 4.

1.6 litre engines

3 Undo the central bolt and remove the auxiliary drivebelt idler pulley **(see illustration)**.

4 Remove the rubber cover from the

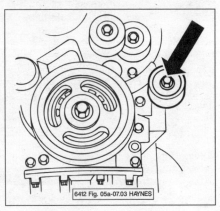

7.3 Idler pulley central bolt

7.4a Remove the rubber cover and undo the securing nut …

7.4b … then disconnect the alternator wiring and plug …

7.4c … release the wiring loom from the rear of the alternator

7.5a Alternator outer mounting bolts …

7.5b … and inner mounting bolts

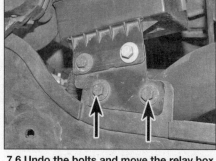

7.6 Undo the bolts and move the relay box

7.8 Release the clip and slide the oil filler neck upwards

alternator terminal, then unscrew the retaining nut and disconnect the wiring from the rear of the alternator **(see illustrations)**. Prise out the retaining clip to release the wiring harness routed around the end of the alternator.

5 Unscrew the alternator mounting bolts **(see illustrations)**. Manoeuvre the alternator away from its mounting brackets and out from the engine compartment.

2.0 litre engines

6 Undo the retaining bolts and move the relay box at the front panel to one side **(see illustration)**.

7 Undo the retaining nut and move the engine coolant expansion tank to one side. There's no need to disconnect the hoses.

8 On Euro 5 emissions level engines, unclip the oil filler neck and move it to one side **(see illustration)**.

9 Where fitted, pull up the acoustic cover from the top of the engine.

10 Undo the nuts and remove the insulation guard (where fitted) over the alternator to one side **(see illustration)**.

11 Remove the rubber cover from the alternator terminal, then undo the nut and disconnect the wiring from the alternator. Disconnect the wiring plug at the same time **(see illustration)**.

7.10 Undo the nuts and remove the plastic guard

7.11 Prise up the rubber cover, undo the nut, then release the clip and disconnect the wiring plug

12 Undo the mounting bolts and manoeuvre the alternator from place **(see illustrations)**.

Refitting

13 Refitting is a reversal of removal, tensioning the auxiliary drivebelt as described in Chapter 1, Section 20, and ensuring that the alternator mountings are securely tightened. Note that on some models, one of the bolts acts as a centraliser and should be tightened first **(see illustration)**.

8 Alternator brushes, regulator and drive pulley – inspection and renewal

Note: *If the alternator is thought to be suspect, check on the cost of repairs before proceeding, as it may prove more economical to obtain a new or exchange alternator. The alternator fitted may vary slightly, depending on model and age; the model shown in the following sequence is for a Valeo type alternator.*

Brushes and regulator

1 Remove the alternator as described in Section 7.
2 Unscrew the nuts/screws securing the cover to the rear of the alternator **(see illustration)**.
3 Using a screwdriver, lever off the cover, and remove it from the rear of the alternator.
4 Unscrew and remove the three retaining screws, and remove the regulator/brush holder from the rear of the alternator **(see illustration)**.
5 Check the brushes for excessive wear and damage. No specifications for brush length are given by the manufacturer. If the brushes are suspect, renew them along with the regulator as a complete assembly.
6 If the brushes are in good condition, clean them and check that they move freely in their holders.
7 Wipe clean the alternator slip-rings, and check them for signs of scoring or burning **(see illustration)**. It may be possible to have the slip-rings renovated by an electrical specialist.
8 Use a paper clip to restrain the brushes, then refit the regulator/brush holder assembly and securely tighten the retaining screws **(see illustration)**.
9 Refit the cover, then insert and tighten the retaining screws/nuts.
10 Refit the alternator with reference to Section 7.

Drive pulley

11 The alternator drive pulley on some models is fitted with a one-way clutch to reduced wear and stress on the auxiliary drivebelt. In order to remove the pulley, a special tool will be required to hold the alternator shaft whilst unscrewing the pulley. This tool should be available from

7.12a Alternator outer retaining bolts

7.12b On Euro 5 engines, the lower alternator mounting is a clamp secured by an Allen bolt

7.12c Access to the inner, upper bolt is extremely limited

7.13 On some models, the upper bolt acts as a centraliser

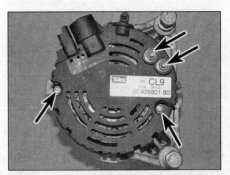

8.2 Undo the screw/nuts and remove the cover from the alternator

8.4 Undo the bolts and remove the regulator/brush pack

8.7 Check the condition of the slip-rings

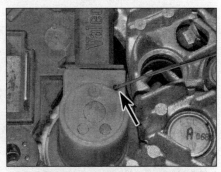

8.8 Use a screwdriver to push back the brushes against the springs, then insert a thin rod to hold them in place

8.13a A special tool is required to remove the alternator pulley

8.13b Insert the central Torx bit into the end of the alternator shaft, unscrew the pulley …

8.13c … and remove the pulley from the shaft

auto electrical specialists/automotive tool specialists.

12 Prise the plastic cap from the pulley.

13 Insert the special tool into the splines of the pulley, engaging the central Torx bit with the alternator shaft **(see illustrations)**. Unscrew the pulley anti-clockwise whilst holding the shaft with the Torx bit, and remove the pulley.

14 Fit the pulley to the alternator shaft, and tighten it securely using the special tool.

9 Starting system – testing

Note: *Refer to the precautions given in 'Safety first!' and in Section 1 of this Chapter before starting work.*

1 If the starter motor fails to operate when the ignition key is turned to the appropriate position, the following possible causes may be to blame.

a) *The engine immobiliser is faulty.*

b) *The battery is faulty.*

c) *The electrical connections between the switch, solenoid, battery and starter motor are somewhere failing to pass the necessary current from the battery through the starter to earth.*

d) *The solenoid is faulty.*

e) *The starter motor is mechanically or electrically defective.*

2 To check the battery, switch on the

headlights. If they dim after a few seconds, this indicates that the battery is discharged – recharge (see Section 3) or renew the battery. If the headlights glow brightly, operate the ignition switch and observe the lights. If they dim, then this indicates that current is reaching the starter motor, therefore the fault must lie in the starter motor. If the lights continue to glow brightly (and no clicking sound can be heard from the starter motor solenoid), this indicates that there is a fault in the circuit or solenoid – see following paragraphs. If the starter motor turns slowly when operated, but the battery is in good condition, then this indicates that either the starter motor is faulty, or there is considerable resistance somewhere in the circuit.

3 If a fault in the circuit is suspected, disconnect the battery leads (including the earth connection to the body), the starter/solenoid wiring and the engine/transmission earth strap – located on the top of the transmission housing **(see illustration)**. Thoroughly clean the connections and reconnect the leads and wiring, then use a voltmeter or test lamp to check that full battery voltage is available at the battery positive lead connection to the solenoid, and that the earth is sound. Smear petroleum jelly around the battery terminals to prevent corrosion – corroded connections are among the most frequent causes of electrical system faults.

4 If the battery and all connections are in good

condition, check the circuit by disconnecting the wire from the solenoid blade terminal. Connect a voltmeter or test lamp between the wire end and a good earth (such as the battery negative terminal), and check that the wire is live when the ignition switch is turned to the 'start' position. If it is, then the circuit is sound – if not the circuit wiring can be checked as described in Chapter 12 Section 2.

5 The solenoid contacts can be checked by connecting a voltmeter or test lamp between the battery positive feed connection on the starter side of the solenoid, and earth. When the ignition switch is turned to the 'start' position, there should be a reading or lighted bulb, as applicable. If there is no reading or lighted bulb, the solenoid is faulty and should be renewed.

6 If the circuit and solenoid are proved sound, the fault must lie in the starter motor. In this event, it may be possible to have the starter motor overhauled by a specialist, but check on the cost of spares before proceeding, as it may prove more economical to obtain a new or exchange motor.

10 Starter motor – removal and refitting

Removal

1 Disconnect the battery negative lead as described in Section 4.

2 So that access to the motor can be gained both from above and below, apply the handbrake then jack up the front of the vehicle and support it on axle stands (see *Jacking and vehicle support*). Undo the retaining bolts/nuts and remove the engine undershield (where fitted)

1.6 litre engines

3 Where applicable, release the fasteners and remove the heatshield above the starter motor.

4 Disconnect the wiring connectors from the starter motor solenoid, and where fitted, recover the washers under the nuts **(see illustration)**.

5 Undo the three mounting bolts (two at

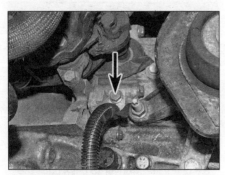

9.3 The earth strap is attached to the top of the transmission housing

10.4 Undo the nuts and disconnect the starter wiring

10.5 Starter motor mounting bolts

10.6 Remove the starter motor

the rear of the motor, and one which comes through from the top of the transmission housing), supporting the starter motor as the bolts are withdrawn. Recover the washers from under the bolt heads and note the locations of any wiring or hose brackets secured by the bolts (see illustration).

6 Manoeuvre the starter motor out from underneath the engine; recover the locating dowel(s) from the motor/transmission so that they do not get lost (see illustration).

2.0 litre engines

7 Disconnect the wiring connectors from the starter motor solenoid, and where fitted, recover the washers under the nuts (see illustration).

8 Disconnect the wiring plug from the engine oil level and temperature sensor, then undo the mounting bolts and move the clutch slave cylinder to one side. There's no need to disconnect the fluid pipe from the cylinder.

9 Undo the retaining bolts and manoeuvre the starter motor from place (see illustration).

Refitting

10 Refitting is a reversal of removal, ensuring that the locating dowel(s) are correctly positioned. Also make sure that any wiring

10.7 Undo the nuts and disconnect the wiring

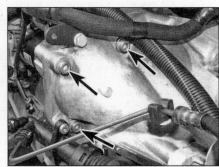

10.9 Starter motor retaining bolts

or hose brackets are in place under the bolt heads as noted prior to removal.

11 Starter motor –
testing and overhaul

1 If the starter motor is thought to be suspect, it should be removed from the vehicle and taken to an auto-electrician for testing. Most auto-electricians will be able to supply and fit brushes at a reasonable cost. However, check

on the cost of repairs before proceeding, as it may prove more economical to obtain a new or exchange motor.

12 Ignition switch –
removal and refitting

1 The ignition switch is integral with the steering column lock, and can be removed as described in Chapter 10, Section 17.

Notes

Chapter 5 Part B
Pre/post-heating system

Contents

Degrees of difficulty

Easy, suitable for novice with little experience	**Fairly easy,** suitable for beginner with some experience	**Fairly difficult,** suitable for competent DIY mechanic	**Difficult,** suitable for experienced DIY mechanic	**Very difficult,** suitable for expert DIY or professional

Specifications

Preheating system

Preheating period at ambient temperatures of (approximate values): .

-30°C	15 seconds
-25°C	10 seconds
-10°C	5 seconds
0°C	0.5 seconds
20°C	0 seconds

Post-heating system

Post-heating period at ambient temperatures of (approximate values):

-30°C	3 minutes
-20°C	3 minutes
-10°C	3 minutes
0°C	3 minutes
20°C	0.5 seconds
80°C	0 seconds

Torque wrench settings

	Nm	lbf ft
Glow plugs:		
All engines	9	7

1 Pre/post-heating system – description and testing

Description

1 To assist cold starting, diesel engines are fitted with a preheating system, which consists of four glow plugs (one per cylinder), a glow plug relay unit, a facia-mounted warning lamp, the engine management ECU, and the associated electrical wiring.

2 The glow plugs are miniature electric heating elements, encapsulated in a metal case with a probe at one end and electrical connection at the other. Each combustion chamber has one glow plug threaded into it, with the tip of the glow plug probe positioned directly in line with incoming spray of fuel from the injectors. When the glow plug is energised, it heats up rapidly, causing the fuel passing over the glow plug probe to be heated to its optimum temperature, ready for combustion. In addition, some of the fuel passing over the glow plugs is ignited and this helps to trigger the combustion process.

3 The preheating system begins to operate as soon as the ignition key is switched to the second position, but only if the engine coolant temperature is below 20° C and the engine is turned at more than 70 rpm for 0.2 seconds. A facia-mounted warning lamp informs the driver that preheating is taking place. The lamp extinguishes when sufficient preheating has taken place to allow the engine to be started, but power will still be supplied to the glow plugs for a further period until the engine is started. If no attempt is made to start the engine, the power supply to the glow plugs is switched off after 10 seconds, to prevent battery drain and glow plug burn-out.

4 With the electronically controlled diesel injection systems fitted to models in this manual, the glow plug relay unit is controlled by the engine management system ECU, which determines the necessary preheating time based on inputs from the various system sensors. The system monitors the temperature of the intake air, and then alters the preheating time (the length for which the glow plugs are supplied with current) to suit the conditions.

5 Post-heating takes place after the ignition key has been released from the 'start' position, but only if the engine coolant temperature is below 20ºC, the injected fuel flow is less than a certain rate, and the engine speed is less than 2000 rpm. The glow plugs continue to operate for a maximum of 60 seconds, helping to improve fuel combustion whilst the engine is warming-up, resulting in quieter, smoother running and reduced exhaust emissions.

Testing

6 If the system malfunctions, testing is ultimately by substitution of known good units, but some preliminary checks may be made as follows.

7 Connect a voltmeter or 12 volt test lamp between the glow plug supply cable and earth (engine or vehicle metal). Make sure that the live connection is kept clear of the engine and bodywork.

8 Have an assistant switch on the ignition, and check that voltage is applied to the glow plugs. Note the time for which the warning light is lit, and the total time for which voltage is applied before the system cuts out. Switch off the ignition.

9 Compare the results with the information given in the Specifications. Warning light time will increase with lower temperatures and decrease with higher temperatures.

10 If there is no supply at all, the control module or associated wiring is at fault.

11 To gain access to the glow plugs for further testing, remove the following components, according to model:

a) *1.6 litre DOHC engine: Remove the cylinder head cover/manifold assembly as described in Chapter 2B Section 4.*

b) *1.6 litre SOHC engine: Remove the air cleaner assembly (Chapter 4A Section 5) and fuel filter assembly (Chapter 1 Section 11).*

c) *2.0 litre engine: Working as described in Chapter 4B Section 2, undo the bolts and move the EGR heat exchanger and valve assembly to one side.*

12 Disconnect the main supply cable and the interconnecting wire or strap from the top of the glow plugs. Be careful not to drop the nuts and washers.

13 Use a continuity tester or a 12 volt test lamp connected to the battery positive terminal to check for continuity between each glow plug terminal and earth. The resistance of a glow plug in good condition is very low (less than 1 ohm), so if the test lamp does not light or the continuity tester shows a high resistance, the glow plug is certainly defective.

14 If an ammeter is available, the current draw of each glow plug can be checked. After an initial surge of 15 to 20 amps, each plug should draw 12 amps. Any plug that draws much more or less than this is probably defective.

15 As a final check, the glow plugs can be removed and inspected as described in the following Section. On completion, refit any components removed for access.

2 Glow plugs – removal, inspection and refitting

Caution: If the preheating system has just been energised, or if the engine has been running, the glow plugs will be very hot.

Removal

1 Ensure the ignition is turned off. To gain access to the glow plugs, remove the components described in Section 1, according to engine.

2 Either pull the connector upwards to disconnect the wiring connector from the top of the glow plug or unscrew the nuts from the glow plug terminals, and recover the washers **(see illustrations)**.

3 Where applicable, carefully move any

2.2a Using a pair of long-nose pliers to disconnect connector

2.2b Undo the nuts securing the glow plug connections

2.2c Access to the glow plugs can be extremely limited

2.4a Unscrew the glow plugs – SOHC 1.6 litre engine …

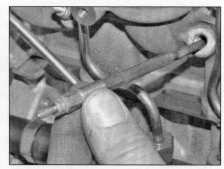

2.4b … and remove them from the cylinder head – DOHC 1.6 and 2.0 litre engines

obstructing pipes or wires to one side to enable access to the relevant glow plug(s).

4 Unscrew the glow plug(s) and remove from the cylinder head **(see illustrations)**.

Inspection

5 Inspect each glow plug for physical damage. Burnt or eroded glow plug tips can be caused by a bad injector spray pattern. Have the injectors checked if this sort of damage is found.

6 If the glow plugs are in good physical condition, check them electrically using a 12 volt test lamp or continuity tester as described in the previous Section.

7 The glow plugs can be energised by applying 12 volts to them to verify that they heat up evenly and in the required time. Observe the following precautions.

a) *Support the glow plug by clamping it carefully in a vice or self-locking pliers. Remember it will become red-hot.*

b) *Make sure that the power supply or test lead incorporates a fuse or overload trip to protect against damage from a short circuit.*

c) *After testing, allow the glow plug to cool for several minutes before attempting to handle it.*

8 A glow plug in good condition will start to glow red at the tip after drawing current for 5 seconds or so. Any plug that takes much longer to start glowing, or which starts glowing in the middle instead of at the tip is defective.

Refitting

9 Refit by reversing the removal operations. Apply a smear of copper-based anti-seize compound to the plug threads and tighten the glow plugs to the specified torque. Do not overtighten, as this can damage the glow plug element.

10 Refit any components removed for access.

---

3 Pre/post-heating system relay unit – removal and refitting

Removal

1 The unit is located on the left-hand front side of the engine compartment **(see illustration)**.

3.1 The pre/post-heating relay is mounting on the left-hand inner wing

2 Disconnect the battery negative lead as described in Chapter 5A Section 4.

3 Slide out the wiring connector locking clip and disconnect the wiring connector from the relay unit, then undo the securing nut and remove the relay unit from the front of the engine compartment fusebox.

Refitting

4 Refitting is a reversal of removal, ensuring that the wiring connector is correctly connected.

Chapter 6
Clutch

Contents

Degrees of difficulty

Easy, suitable for novice with little experience	**Fairly easy,** suitable for beginner with some experience	**Fairly difficult,** suitable for competent DIY mechanic	**Difficult,** suitable for experienced DIY mechanic	**Very difficult,** suitable for expert DIY or professional

Specifications

Type
All models. . . . . Single dry disc with diaphragm spring, hydraulic operation

Torque wrench setting

	Nm	lbf ft
Pressure plate retaining bolts.	20	15

1 General Information

1 The clutch consists of a friction disc, a pressure plate assembly, and a release bearing; all of these components are contained in the large cast-aluminium alloy bellhousing, sandwiched between the engine and the transmission. The release mechanism is hydraulic, operated by a master cylinder and a slave cylinder. The hydraulic master cylinder is located in the bulkhead, directly behind the brake pedal, and the clutch fluid reservoir is shared with the brake fluid reservoir on top of the brake master cylinder.

2 The friction disc is fitted between the engine flywheel and the clutch pressure plate, and is allowed to slide on the transmission input shaft splines.

3 The pressure plate assembly is bolted to the engine flywheel. When the engine is running, drive is transmitted from the crankshaft, via the flywheel, to the friction disc (these components being clamped securely together by the pressure plate assembly) and from the friction disc to the transmission input shaft.

4 To interrupt the drive, the spring pressure must be relaxed by the hydraulically operated release mechanism. Depressing the clutch pedal operates the master cylinder, which in turn, through the hydraulic system, presses the release bearing against the pressure plate spring fingers. This causes the springs to deform and releases the clamping force on the pressure plate. When the pedal is released the diaphragm spring forces the pressure plate into contact with the friction linings on the friction plate. The friction disc is now firmly sandwiched between the pressure plate and the flywheel, thus transmitting engine power to the transmission.

5 The clutch pedal is connected to the clutch master cylinder by a short pushrod. The master cylinder is mounted on the passengers side of the bulkhead in front of the driver and receives its hydraulic fluid supply from the brake master cylinder reservoir. Depressing the clutch pedal moves the piston in the master cylinder forwards, so forcing hydraulic fluid through the clutch hydraulic pipe to the slave cylinder.

6 The piston in the slave cylinder moves forward on the entry of the fluid and actuates the clutch release fork by means of a short pushrod. The release fork pivots on its mounting stud, and the other end of the fork then presses the release bearing against the pressure plate spring fingers. This causes the springs to deform and releases the clamping force on the pressure plate.

7 On all models the clutch operating mechanism is self-adjusting, and no manual adjustment is required.

2 Clutch hydraulic system – bleeding

 Warning: Hydraulic fluid is poisonous; wash off immediately and thoroughly in the case of skin contact, and seek immediate medical advice if any fluid is swallowed or gets into the eyes. Certain types of hydraulic fluid are inflammable, and may ignite when allowed into contact with hot components; when servicing any hydraulic system, it is safest to assume that the fluid IS inflammable, and to take precautions against the risk of fire as though it is petrol that is being handled. Hydraulic fluid is also an effective paint stripper, and will attack plastics. If any is spilt, it should be washed off immediately, using copious quantities of clean water. When topping-up or renewing the fluid, always use the recommended type, and ensure that it comes from a freshly opened sealed container.

2.4 Slave cylinder bleed screw

1 Obtain a clean container, a suitable length of rubber or clear plastic tubing that is a tight fit over the bleed screw on the clutch slave cylinder, and a tin of the specified hydraulic fluid. The help of an assistant will also be required. If a one-man do-it-yourself bleeding kit for bleeding the brake hydraulic system is available, this can be used quite satisfactorily for the clutch also. Full information on the use of these kits may be found in Chapter 9 Section 2.

2 On 2.0 litre engines, remove the air cleaner assembly as described in Chapter 4A Section 5, to access the clutch bleed screw.

3 Remove the filler cap from the brake master cylinder reservoir, and if necessary top-up the fluid. Keep the reservoir topped-up during subsequent operations.

4 Remove the dust cap from the slave cylinder bleed screw, located on the lower front facing side of the transmission **(see illustration)**.

5 Connect one end of the bleed tube to the bleed screw, and insert the other end of the tube in the jar containing sufficient clean hydraulic fluid to keep the end of the tube submerged.

6 Open the bleed screw half a turn and have your assistant depress the clutch pedal and then slowly release it. Continue this procedure until clean hydraulic fluid, free from air bubbles, emerges from the tube. Now tighten the bleed screw at the end of a downstroke. Make sure that the brake master cylinder reservoir is checked frequently to ensure that the level does not drop too far, allowing air into the system.

7 Check the operation of the clutch pedal. After a few strokes it should feel normal. Any sponginess would indicate air still present in the system.

8 On completion remove the bleed tube and refit the dust cover. Top-up the master cylinder reservoir if necessary and refit the cap. Fluid expelled from the hydraulic system should now be discarded, as it will be contaminated with moisture, air and dirt, making it unsuitable for further use.

3 Clutch master cylinder – removal and refitting

Note: *Before starting work, refer to the note at the beginning of Section 2 concerning the dangers of hydraulic fluid.*

Removal

1 To improve access, remove the drivers side lower facia panel as described in Chapter 11 Section 27.

2 Using a syringe, remove fluid from the brake/clutch fluid reservoir to bring the level below the clutch fluid supply hose at the side of the reservoir.

3 Prise out the clip and detach the lower end of the pedal over-centre spring from the pedal **(see illustration)**.

⚠️ *Warning: The over-centre spring will release suddenly.*

4 Remove the circlip from the left-hand end of the pedal shaft **(see illustration)**.

5 Prise the end of the master cylinder pushrod from the pin on the pedal, then slide the pedal from the shaft **(see illustration)**.

6 Undo the 2 retaining bolts, and pull the master cylinder into the cabin slightly **(see illustration)**.

7 Prise out the clip and disconnect the fluid supply hose from the master cylinder **(see illustration)**. Be prepared for fluid spillage.

8 Push down the rubber grommet, slide out the clip and disconnect the pressure pipe from the base of the cylinder **(see illustration)**.

Refitting

9 Refitting the master cylinder is the reverse sequence to removal, bearing in mind the following points.

a) Ensure all retaining clips are correctly refitted.

b) Bleed the clutch hydraulic system as described in Section 2.

3.3 Prise out the clip

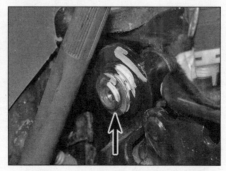

3.4 Remove the circlip at the end of the shaft

3.5 Prise the end of the pushrod from the pin, and slide the pedal from the shaft

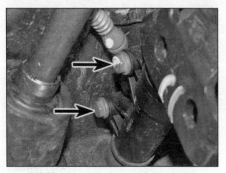

3.6 Master cylinder retaining bolts

3.7 Fluid supply pipe retaining clip

3.8 Prise out the pressure pipe retaining clip

4 Clutch slave cylinder – removal and refitting

Note: *Before starting work, refer to the note at the beginning of Section 2 concerning the dangers of hydraulic fluid.*

Removal

1 Raise the front of the vehicle and support is securely on axle stand (see *Jacking and vehicle support*). Release the fasteners and remove the engine undershield (where fitted).
2 To minimise hydraulic fluid loss, remove the brake master cylinder reservoir filler cap then tighten it down onto a piece of polythene to obtain an airtight seal.
3 On 2.0 litre models, remove the air cleaner assembly as described in Chapter 4A Section 5. On 1.6 litre models, remove the air cleaner intake ducting from the front left-hand side of the engine compartment (see Chapter 4A Section 5), to access the clutch slave cylinder.
4 Place absorbent rags under the clutch slave cylinder located on the lower front facing side of the transmission. Be prepared for hydraulic fluid loss.
5 Where necessary for access, release the wiring harness from the retaining clips and move the harness clear of the slave cylinder.
6 Lever out the retaining clip a little, and then disconnect the hydraulic pipe from the side of the slave cylinder **(see illustration)**. Suitably plug or cap the pipe end to prevent further fluid loss and dirt entry.
7 Undo the two retaining bolts and remove the cylinder from the transmission housing **(see illustration)**.

Refitting

8 Refitting the slave cylinder is the reverse sequence to removal, bearing in mind the following points.
a) Apply a little Molykote BR2 Plus grease to the end of the slave cylinder pushrod.
b) Remove the piece of polythene from the top of the reservoir.
c) Bleed the clutch hydraulic system as described in Section 2.

6.2 Mark the position of the pressure plate on the flywheel

4.6 Lever out the hydraulic pipe retaining clip

5 Clutch pedal – removal and refitting

1 Removal of the pedal is described within the master cylinder removal procedure, described in Section 3.
2 Check the condition of the pedal, pivot bush and return spring assembly and renew any components as necessary.

6 Clutch assembly – removal, inspection and refitting

⚠ *Warning: Dust created by clutch wear and deposited on the clutch components may be a health hazard. DO NOT blow it out with compressed air, nor inhale any of it. DO NOT use petrol or petroleum-based solvents to clean off the dust. Brake system cleaner or methylated spirit should be used to flush the dust into a suitable receptacle. After the clutch components are wiped clean with rags, dispose of the contaminated rags and cleaner in a sealed, marked container.*
Note: *Although most friction materials no longer contain asbestos, it is safest to assume that some still do, and to take precautions accordingly.*

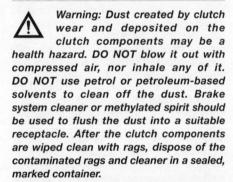

6.3 Undo the pressure plate bolts

4.7 Undo the two bolts and remove the clutch slave cylinder

Removal

1 Unless the complete engine/transmission unit is to be removed from the car and separated for major overhaul (see Chapter 2D Section 3), the clutch can be reached by removing the transmission as described in.
2 Before disturbing the clutch, use chalk or a marker pen to mark the relationship of the pressure plate assembly to the flywheel **(see illustration)**.
3 Working in a diagonal sequence, slacken the pressure plate bolts by half a turn at a time, until spring pressure is released and the bolts can be unscrewed by hand **(see illustration)**.
4 Prise the pressure plate assembly off its locating dowels, and collect the friction disc, noting which way round the disc is fitted.

Inspection

Note: *Due to the amount of work necessary to remove and refit clutch components, it is considered good practice to renew the clutch friction disc, pressure plate assembly and release bearing as a matched set, even if only one of these is worn enough to require renewal. It is worth considering the renewal of the clutch components on a preventative basis if the engine and/or transmission have been removed for some other reason.*
5 When cleaning clutch components, read the warning at the beginning of this Section first; remove dust using a clean, dry cloth, and working in a well-ventilated atmosphere.
6 Check the friction disc facings for signs of wear, damage or oil contamination. If the friction material is cracked, burnt, scored or damaged, or if it is contaminated with oil or grease (shown by shiny black patches), the friction disc must be renewed.
7 If the friction material is still serviceable, check that the centre boss splines are unworn, that the torsion springs are in good condition and securely fastened, and that all the rivets are tight. If any wear or damage is found, the friction disc must be renewed.
8 If the friction material is fouled with oil, this must be due to an oil leak from the crankshaft left-hand oil seal, from the sump-to-cylinder block joint, or from the transmission input shaft. Renew the seal or repair the joint, as appropriate, as described in Chapter 2A,

6.13a Fit the disc so the spring hub assembly faces away from the flywheel

6.13b ... or the protruding hub away from the flywheel

6.16 Using some threaded rod, washers and nuts, compress the spring and the pressure plate together ...

Chapter 2B or Chapter 2C, or, before installing the new friction disc.

9 Check the pressure plate assembly for obvious signs of wear or damage; shake it to check for loose rivets or worn or damaged fulcrum rings, and check that the drive straps securing the pressure plate to the cover do not show signs (such as a deep yellow or blue discoloration) of overheating. If the diaphragm spring is worn or damaged, or if its pressure is in any way suspect, the pressure plate assembly should be renewed.

10 Examine the machined bearing surfaces of the pressure plate and of the flywheel; they should be clean, completely flat, and free from scratches or scoring. If either is discoloured from excessive heat, or shows signs of cracks, it should be renewed – although minor damage of this nature can sometimes be polished away using emery paper.

11 Check that the release bearing contact surface rotates smoothly and easily, with no sign of noise or roughness. Also check that the surface itself is smooth and unworn, with no signs of cracks, pitting or scoring. If there is any doubt about its condition, the bearing must be renewed.

Refitting

12 On reassembly, ensure that the bearing surfaces of the flywheel and pressure plate are completely clean, smooth, and free from oil or grease. Use solvent to remove any protective grease from new components.

13 Fit the friction disc so that its spring hub assembly faces away from the flywheel; there may be a marking showing which way round the disc is to be refitted **(see illustrations)**.

Models with self-adjusting clutch

Type 1

14 On these models, the clutch pressure plate has a pre-adjustment mechanism to compensate for wear in the friction disc (this is termed by Peugeot/Citroën/Fiat as a self-adjusting clutch (SAC), which is slightly ambiguous as all clutches fitted to these models are essentially self-adjusting). However, this mechanism must be reset before refitting the pressure plate. A new plate may be supplied preset, in which case this procedure can be ignored.

15 A large diameter bolt (M14 at least) long enough to pass through the pressure plate, a matching nut, and several large diameter washers, will be needed for this procedure. Mount the bolt head in the jaws of a sturdy bench vice, with one large washer fitted.

16 Offer the plate over the bolt, friction disc surface facing down, and locate it centrally over the bolt and washer – the washer should bear on the centre hub **(see illustration)**.

17 Fit several further large washers over the bolt, so that they bear on the ends of the spring fingers, then add the nut and tighten by hand to locate the washers.

18 The purpose of the procedure is to turn the plate's internal adjuster disc so that the three small coil springs visible on the plate's outer surface are fully compressed. Tighten the nut just fitted until the adjuster disc is free to turn. Using a pair of thin-nosed, or circlip, pliers in one of the two windows in the top surface, open the jaws of the pliers to turn the adjuster disc anti-clockwise, so that the springs are fully compressed **(see illustration)**.

19 Hold the pliers in this position, and then unscrew the centre nut. Once the nut is released, the adjuster disc will be gripped in position, and the pliers can be removed. Take the pressure plate from the vice, and it is ready to fit.

Type 2

20 On this type of clutch, the self adjusting mechanism is fully automatic **(see illustration)**. New clutch assemblies are supplied with the mechanism set, and ready for fitting. If refitting the original clutch pressure plate, the mechanism should be left as originally set during removal.

6.18 ... then move the adjusting ring anti-clockwise to the stop

6.20 This type of self adjusting mechanism is fully automatic

6.23 Centralise the friction plate on the flywheel using a clutch aligning tool

7.2 Squeeze the tabs of the retaining clip together and remove the release fork ...

All models

21 Refit the pressure plate assembly, aligning the marks made on dismantling (if the original pressure plate is re-used), and locating the pressure plate on its three locating dowels. Fit the pressure plate bolts, but tighten them only finger-tight, so that the friction disc can still be moved.

22 The friction disc must now be centralised, so that when the transmission is refitted, its input shaft will pass through the splines at the centre of the friction disc.

23 Centralisation can be achieved by passing a screwdriver or other long bar through the friction disc and into the hole in the crankshaft; the friction disc can then be moved around until it is centred on the crankshaft hole. Alternatively, a clutch-aligning tool can be used to eliminate the guesswork; these can be obtained from most accessory shops **(see illustration)**.

24 When the friction disc is centralised, tighten the pressure plate bolts evenly and in a diagonal sequence to the specified torque setting.

25 Apply a very thin smear of molybdenum disulphide grease (Peugeot/Citroën/Fiat recommend the use of Molykote BR2 Plus) to the splines of the friction disc and the transmission input shaft, and also to the release bearing bore and release fork shaft.

26 Refit the transmission as described in Chapter 7.

7 Clutch release mechanism – removal, inspection and refitting

Note: *Refer to the warning concerning the dangers of asbestos dust at the beginning of Section 2.*

Removal

1 Unless the complete engine/transmission unit is to be removed from the car and separated for major overhaul (see Chapter 2D Section 4), the clutch release mechanism can be reached by removing the transmission only, as described in.

2 With the transmission removed, squeeze

7.3 ... disengage the release bearing as the fork is removed

together the tabs of the retaining clip and pull the release fork off the pivot ball-stud **(see illustration)**.

3 Slide the release bearing off the guide tube and disengage the arms off the release fork **(see illustration)**.

4 If required, recover the shim where fitted and unscrew the mounting stud from the transmission housing **(see illustrations)**.

7.4a Recover the shim ...

7.4b ... then unscrew the pivot ball-stud

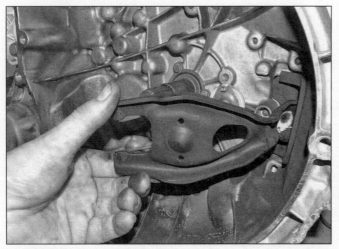

7.8a Refit the release fork into the rubber gaiter and release bearing

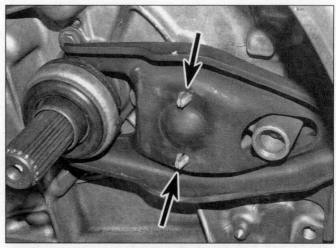

7.8b Ensure the retaining tabs (arrowed) engage correctly with the release fork

Inspection

5 Check that the release bearing contact surface rotates smoothly and easily, with no sign of noise or roughness, and that the surface itself is smooth and unworn, with no signs of cracks, pitting or scoring. If there is any doubt about its condition, the bearing must be renewed.
6 Check the bearing surfaces and points of contact on the release fork and pivot ball-stud, renewing any component, which is worn or damaged.

Refitting

7 Apply a smear of molybdenum disulphide grease to the pivot ball-stud.
8 Insert the outer end of the release fork through the rubber boot in the side of the transmission bellhousing. Engage the arms of the release fork with the release bearing collar, then slide the release bearing onto the guide tube. Position the shim over the tabs of the pivot ball-stud clip, then push the fork over

the stud, ensuring the tabs of the retaining clip engage correctly with the fork **(see illustrations)**.
9 Refit the transmission as described in.

8 Clutch pedal switch – removal and refitting

Removal

1 Disconnect the battery negative lead as described in Chapter 5A Section 4.
2 Remove the drivers side lower facia panel as described in Chapter 11 Section 27.
3 Reach up under the drivers side of the facia, and disconnect the wiring plug from the switch **(see illustration)**.
4 Pull the switch from the mounting bracket plastic fitting.

Refitting

5 Depress the clutch pedal slightly.

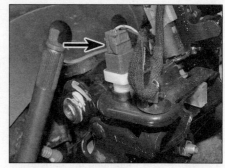

8.3 Disconnect the pedal switch wiring plug

6 Push the switch down into the mounting bracket plastic fitting, then slowly release the clutch pedal to the stop. The switch will settle in the correct position.
7 The remainder of refitting is a reversal of removal.

Chapter 7
Manual transmission

Contents

Degrees of difficulty

Easy, suitable for novice with little experience	**Fairly easy,** suitable for beginner with some experience	**Fairly difficult,** suitable for competent DIY mechanic	**Difficult,** suitable for experienced DIY mechanic	**Very difficult,** suitable for expert DIY or professional

Specifications

General
Type .... Manual, five or six forward speeds and reverse. Synchromesh on all forward speeds

Designation:
1.6 litre BE4/5
2.0 litre ML6C

Lubrication
Capacity .... Refer to Chapter 1 Section 1
Recommended oil type .... See Lubricants and fluids 0 Section 6

Torque wrench settings

	Nm	lbf ft
BE4/5 transmission		
Clutch release bearing guide sleeve bolts	15	11
Engine-to-transmission fixing bolts	Refer to Chapter 2A or Chapter 2B specifications	
Gearchange lever mounting nuts	8	6
Left-hand engine/transmission mounting	Refer to Chapter 2A or Chapter 2B specifications	
Neutral sensor bolt	10	7
Oil drain plug	35	26
Oil filler/level plug	22	16
Reversing light switch	25	18
Roadwheel bolts	100	74
Speedometer drive housing bolts	15	11
ML6C transmission		
Clutch release bearing guide sleeve bolts	10	7
Driveshaft seal thrust plate bolts (left-hand side)	20	15
Engine movement limiter to subframe	65	48
Engine-to-transmission fixing bolts	Refer to Chapter 2C specifications	
Gearchange lever housing bolts	10	7
Left-hand engine/transmission mounting	Refer to Chapter 2C specifications	
Oil drain plug	33	24
Reversing light switch	25	18
Roadwheel bolts	100	74

1 General Information

1 The transmission is contained in a cast-aluminium alloy casing bolted to the engine's left-hand end, and consists of the gearbox and final drive differential – often called a transaxle.

2 Drive is transmitted from the crankshaft via the clutch to the input shaft that has a splined extension to accept the clutch friction disc, and rotates in sealed ball-bearings. From the input shaft, drive is transmitted to the output shaft, which rotates in a roller bearing at its right-hand end, and a sealed ball-bearing at its left-hand end. From the output shaft, the drive is transmitted to the differential crownwheel, which rotates with the differential case and planetary gears, thus driving the sun gears and driveshafts. The rotation of the planetary gears on their shaft allows the inner roadwheel to rotate at a slower speed than the outer roadwheel when the car is cornering.

3 The input and output shafts are arranged side-by-side, parallel to the crankshaft and driveshafts, so that their gear pinion teeth are in constant mesh. In the neutral position, the output shaft gear pinions rotate freely, so that drive cannot be transmitted to the crownwheel.

4 Two different manual transmissions are used on the models covered in this manual; 1.6 litre diesel engines use the BE4/5 and 2.0 litre diesel engines use the ML6C transmission.

5 All transmissions do not require regular maintenance and are filled for life. If the transmission develops a leak or is removed for other work, the oil needs to be completely drained and refilled with the correct amount of oil. The transmission will then be refilled through the vent on the top of the transmission.

6 Gear selection is via a console-mounted lever and cables, which pass through the floor panel to the top of the transmission housing. The selector/gearchange cables cause the appropriate selector fork to move its respective synchro-sleeve along the shaft, to lock the gear pinion to the synchro-hub. Since the synchro-hubs are splined to the output shaft, this locks the pinion to the shaft, so that drive can be transmitted. To ensure that gearchanging can be made quickly and quietly, a synchromesh system is fitted to all forward gears, consisting of baulk rings and spring-loaded fingers, as well as the gear pinions and synchro-hubs. The synchromesh cones are formed on the mating faces of the baulk rings and gear pinions.

2 Manual transmission – draining and refilling

Note: *A suitable square section wrench may be required to undo the transmission filler/level and drain plugs on some models. These wrenches can be obtained from most motor factors or your dealer.*

1 This operation is much quicker and more efficient if the car is first taken on a journey of sufficient length to warm the engine/transmission up to normal operating temperature.

2 Park the car on level ground, switch off the ignition and apply the handbrake firmly. For improved access, jack up the front of the car and support it securely on axle stands (see *Jacking and vehicle support*). Note that the vehicle must be level to ensure accuracy when refilling and checking the oil level. Undo the screws and remove the engine undershield (where fitted).

3 Position a suitable container under the drain plug (situated on the final drive casing at the rear of the transmission) and unscrew the plug **(see illustrations)**.

4 Allow the oil to drain completely into the container. If the oil is hot, take precautions against scalding. Clean the drain plug, being especially careful to wipe any metallic particles off the magnetic inserts. Discard the original sealing washer, as it should be renewed whenever it is disturbed.

5 To improve access to the filler/level plug, remove the left-hand front wheel and wheelarch liner.

6 Wipe clean the area around the filler/level plug (BE4/5 transmission) or the breather cap (ML6C transmission); The filler/level plug is situated on the left-hand end of the transmission, next to the end cover, and the breather cap is located on the top of the transmission. Remove the filler/level plug from the transmission and recover the sealing washer, on BE4/5 transmissions, or prise off the breather cap on ML6C transmissions **(see illustrations)**.

7 When the oil has finished draining, clean the drain plug threads and those of the transmission casing, fit a new sealing washer and refit the drain plug, tightening it to the specified torque wrench setting (where given). Refit the undercover (where fitted), and then check that the vehicle is level before refilling.

BE4/5 transmission

8 Refilling the transmission is an extremely awkward operation. Above all, allow plenty of time for the oil level to settle properly before checking it. Note that the car must be parked on flat level ground when checking the oil level.

9 Refill the transmission with the exact amount of the specified type of oil. The level is correct when the oil comes up to the lower edge of the filler opening. if the correct amount was poured into the transmission and a large amount flows out on checking the level, refit the filler/level plug and take the car on a short journey so that the new oil is distributed fully around the transmission components, then check the level again on your return.

10 Once the oil level is correct securely refit the inner cover/wheel arch liner and roadwheel; tighten to the specified torque.

2.3a Oil drain plug – BE4/5 transmission

2.3b Oil drain plug – ML6C transmission

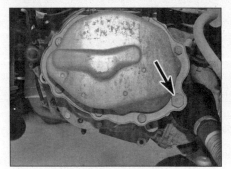
2.6a Oil filler/level plug – BE4/5 transmission

2.6b Breather cap – ML6C transmission

3.3 Prise the cable balljoints from the levers on the transmission

3.4 Pull back the collar and pull the outer cable from the bracket

3.6 Gear lever assembly retaining nuts

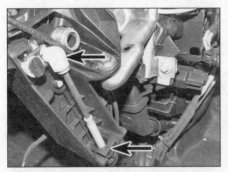

3.7a Prise the end of the cable from the balljoint, and slide the outer cable from the bracket – right-hand cable shown

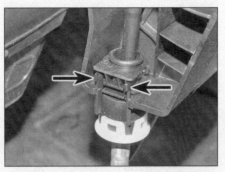

3.7b Squeeze together the clips to release the outer cables

3.7c Disconnect the reverse inhibitor cable from the lever/knob

ML6C transmission

11 Add the exact amount of fluid through the breather opening at the top of the transmission. Refit the breather cap.

3 Gearchange lever and cables – removal and refitting

Removal

1 Slacken the left-hand front roadwheel bolts, then raise the front of the vehicle and support it securely on axle stands (see *Jacking and vehicle support*). Remove the roadwheel.
2 Disconnect the battery negative lead as described in Chapter 5A Section 4.

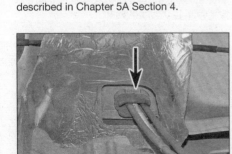

3.8 Release the grommet from the vehicle body

3 Note their fitted locations, then carefully prise the two gearchange cable balljoints from the selector levers on the transmission **(see illustration)**. Note that the rear cable is accessible from the aperture in the left-hand wheelarch.
4 Pull back the collars, then disengage the outer cables from the support brackets **(see illustration)**.
5 Remove the gear lever console as described in Chapter 11 Section 27.
6 Undo the lever assembly retaining nuts **(see illustration)**.
7 Note their fitted positions, then prise the end of the gearchange cables from the lever balljoints, release the outer cable stops, and detach them from the lever assembly **(see illustrations)**. Where

applicable, disconnect the reverse inhibitor cable.
8 Release the rubber grommet from the vehicle body at the rear of the engine compartment, and pull the cable assembly into the cabin **(see illustration)**.

Refitting

9 Refitting is a reversal of the removal procedure.

4 Oil seals – renewal

Driveshaft oil seals

1 Remove the appropriate driveshaft as described in Chapter 8 Section 2.

All except left-hand side seal on ML6C transmissions

2 Carefully prise the oil seal out of the transmission, using a large flat-bladed screwdriver **(see illustration)**.
3 Remove all traces of dirt from the area around the oil seal aperture, then apply a smear of grease to the outer lip of the new oil seal. Fit the new seal into its aperture, and drive it squarely into position using a suitable tubular drift (such as a socket) which bears only on the hard outer edge of the seal until it abuts its locating shoulder. If the seal was supplied with a plastic protector sleeve, leave

4.2 Use a large flat-bladed screwdriver to prise out the driveshaft oil seals

4.3a Fit the new seal to the transmission, noting the plastic seal protector ...

4.3b ... and tap it into position using a tubular drift/socket

4.4 Thrust plate on left-hand side of transmission

4.5a Remove the thrust plate from the transmission ...

4.5b ... and drift out the oil seal

4.6a Fit the new seal to the thrust plate ...

this in position until the driveshaft has been refitted **(see illustrations)**.

Left-hand side seal on ML6C transmissions

4 On the ML6C transmission, the passenger side oil seal is fitted to a thrust plate bolted to the differential casing **(see illustration)**.

5 Undo the four retaining bolts and remove the thrust plate, noting the fitted position of the oil seal. Remove the seal from the thrust plate **(see illustrations)**.

6 Remove all traces of dirt from around the thrust plate, and then apply a smear of grease to the outer lip of the new oil seal. Fit the new seal into its aperture, and drive it squarely into position using a suitable tubular drift, which bears only on the hard outer edge of the seal, until it's located in the thrust plate to the position noted on removal **(see illustrations)**.

7 Apply a bead of sealant around the outer

edge of the thrust plate, and then refit to the transmission casing **(see illustration)**. Tighten the oil seal thrust plate bolts to the specified torque setting.

All oil seals

8 Apply a thin film of grease to the oil seal lip.

9 Refit the driveshaft as described in Chapter 8 Section 2.

Input shaft oil seal

Note: *On some transmission, the oil seal appears to be integral with the guide sleeve. Check with your Citroën/Peugeot/Fiat parts specialist before removal.*

10 Remove the transmission as described in Section 6, and the clutch release mechanism as described in Chapter 6 Section 7.

11 Undo the 3 bolts (2 bolts on some models) securing the clutch release bearing guide sleeve in position, and slide the guide off

4.6b ... using a drift; make sure it is fitted squarely

the input shaft, along with its sealing ring or gasket (as applicable) **(see illustrations)**. Recover any shims or thrustwashers, which have stuck to the rear of the guide sleeve, and refit them to the input shaft.

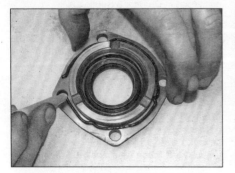

4.7 Apply a bead of sealant around the thrust plate

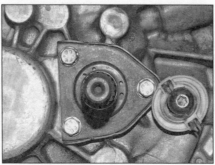

4.11a Undo the 3 bolts and remove the guide sleeve ...

4.11b ... and any shims, where fitted – BE4/5 transmission

12 Where applicable, carefully lever the oil seal out of the guide using a suitable flat-bladed screwdriver **(see illustration)**.

13 Before fitting a new seal, check the input shaft's seal rubbing surface for signs of burrs, scratches or other damage, which may have caused the seal to fail in the first place. It may be possible to polish away minor faults of this sort using fine abrasive paper; however, more serious defects will require the renewal of the input shaft. Ensure that the input shaft is clean and greased, to protect the seal lips on refitting.

14 Where applicable, dip the new seal in clean oil, and fit it to the guide sleeve.

15 On transmissions where the seals are integral with the guide sleeve, lubricate the lips of the seal before refitting.

16 Fit a new sealing ring or gasket (as applicable) to the rear of the guide sleeve, then carefully slide the sleeve into position over the input shaft. Refit the retaining bolts and tighten them to the specified torque setting **(see illustration)**.

17 Take the opportunity to inspect the clutch components if not already done (). Finally, refit the transmission as described in Section 6.

Selector shaft oil seal

BE4/5 transmissions

18 Park the car on level ground, apply the handbrake, slacken the left-hand front roadwheel bolts, then jack up the front of the vehicle and support it on axle stands (see *Jacking and vehicle support*). Remove the left-hand front roadwheel.

19 Using a large flat-bladed screwdriver, lever the link rod balljoint off the transmission selector shaft, and disconnect the link rod.

20 Using a large flat-bladed screwdriver, carefully prise the selector shaft seal out of the housing, and slide it off the end of the shaft.

21 Before fitting a new seal, check the selector shaft's seal rubbing surface for signs

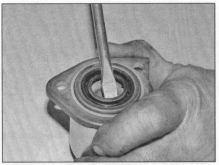

4.12 Remove the input shaft seal from the guide sleeve – BE4/5 transmission

of burrs, scratches or other damage, which may have caused the seal to fail in the first place. It may be possible to polish away minor faults of this sort using fine abrasive paper; however, more serious defects will require the renewal of the selector shaft.

22 Apply a smear of grease to the new seal's outer edge and sealing lip, then carefully slide the seal along the selector rod. Press the seal fully into position in the transmission housing.

23 Refit the link rod to the selector shaft, ensuring that its balljoint is pressed firmly onto the shaft. Lower the car to the ground.

ML6C transmissions

24 To renew the selector shaft oil seal on these models, the transmission must be dismantled. This task should therefore be entrusted to a Citroën/Peugeot/Fiat dealer or transmission specialist.

5 Reversing light switch – testing, removal and refitting

Testing

1 The reversing light circuit is controlled by a plunger-type switch, which is screwed into

4.16 Fit a new O-ring/gasket (as applicable) to the guide sleeve – BE4/5 transmission

the front of the transmission housing **(see illustrations)**. If a fault develops, first ensure that the circuit fuse has not blown.

2 To test the switch, disconnect the wiring connector, and use a multimeter (set to the resistance function) or a battery-and-bulb test circuit to check that there is continuity between the switch terminals only when reverse gear is selected. If this is not the case, and there are no obvious breaks or other damage to the wires, the switch is faulty, and must be renewed.

Removal

3 Where necessary, to improve access to the switch, remove the air cleaner housing intake duct from the front left-hand side of the engine compartment (see Chapter 4A Section 5).

4 Disconnect the wiring connector, and then unscrew the switch from the transmission casing along with its sealing washer.

Refitting

5 Fit a new sealing washer to the switch, then screw it back into position in the top of the transmission housing and tighten it to the specified torque setting where given. Refit the wiring plug, and test the operation of the circuit. Refit any components removed for access.

5.1a Location of reversing light switch – BE4/5 transmission

5.1b Location of reversing light switch – ML6C transmission

6 Manual transmission – removal and refitting

1 The transmission can only be removed along with the engine, as described in Chapter 2D Section 4.

7 Manual transmission overhaul – general information

1 Overhauling a manual transmission is a difficult and involved job for the DIY home mechanic. In addition to dismantling and reassembling many small parts, clearances must be precisely measured and, if necessary, changed by selecting shims and spacers. Internal transmission components are also often difficult to obtain, and in many instances, extremely expensive. Because of this, if the transmission develops a fault or becomes noisy, the best course of action is to have the unit overhauled by a specialist repairer, or to obtain an exchange reconditioned unit.

2 Nevertheless, it is not impossible for the more experienced mechanic to overhaul the transmission, provided the special tools are available, and the job is done in a deliberate step-by-step manner, so that nothing is overlooked.

3 The tools necessary for an overhaul include internal and external circlip pliers, bearing pullers, slide hammer, set of pin punches, dial test indicator, and possibly a hydraulic press. In addition, a large, sturdy workbench and a vice will be required.

4 During dismantling of the transmission, make careful notes of how each component is fitted, to make reassembly easier and more accurate.

5 Before dismantling the transmission, it will help if you have some idea what area is malfunctioning. Certain problems can be closely related to specific areas in the transmission, which can make component examination and renewal easier. Refer to Fault finding for more information.

Chapter 8
Driveshafts

Contents

Driveshaft overhaul – general information 4
Driveshaft rubber gaiters – renewal 3
Driveshafts – removal and refitting. 2

General Information 1
Right-hand driveshaft intermediate bearing – renewal. 5

Section number

Section number

Degrees of difficulty

| Easy, suitable for novice with little experience | | Fairly easy, suitable for beginner with some experience | | Fairly difficult, suitable for competent DIY mechanic | | Difficult, suitable for experienced DIY mechanic | | Very difficult, suitable for expert DIY or professional | |

Specifications

Lubrication (overhaul only – see text)

Lubricant type/specification.	Use only special grease supplied in sachets with gaiter kits – joints are otherwise pre-packed with grease and sealed

Torque wrench settings

	Nm	lbf ft
Anti-roll bar link nut	90	66
Driveshaft retaining nut	345	254
Right-hand driveshaft intermediate bearing retaining bolt.	10	7
Roadwheel bolts.	100	74
Suspension strut-to-hub carrier bolts	90	66
Track rod end nut	25	18

1 General Information

1 Drive is transmitted from the differential to the front wheels by means of two solid-steel driveshafts of unequal length.

2 Both driveshafts are splined at their outer ends, to accept the wheel hubs, and are threaded so that each hub can be fastened by a large nut. The inner end of each driveshaft is splined, to accept the differential sun gear.

3 Constant velocity (CV) joints are fitted to each end of the driveshafts, to ensure that the smooth and efficient transmission of power at all suspension and steering angles. The outer constant velocity joints are of the ball-and-cage type, and the inner constant velocity joints are of the tripod type.

4 On the right-hand side, due to the length of the driveshaft, the inner constant velocity joint is situated approximately halfway along the shaft's length, and an intermediate support bearing is mounted in the engine/transmission rear mounting bracket. The inner end of the driveshaft passes through the bearing (which prevents any lateral movement of the driveshaft inner end) and the inner constant velocity joint outer member. On automatic transmission models, the inboard end of the right-hand driveshaft fits over a splined shaft from the transmission differential.

2 Driveshafts –
removal and refitting

Removal

1 Chock the rear wheels of the car, firmly apply the handbrake, and then jack up the front of the car and support it on axle stands (see *Jacking and vehicle support*). Remove the appropriate front roadwheel.

2 Pull out the R-clip securing the driveshaft nut, then refit the roadwheel, lower the vehicle again and slacken the driveshaft nut. Jack the vehicle up again and remove the roadwheel.

3 Drain the transmission oil as described in Chapter 7 Section 2.

4 Unclip the wiring for the ABS wheel speed sensor, to make sure that it does not get damaged as the hub assembly is moved.

5 Slacken and remove the driveshaft retaining nut. If the nut was not slackened with the wheels on the ground (see paragraph 2), withdraw the R-clip and remove the locking cap **(see illustration)**. Refit at least two roadwheel bolts to the front hub, tightening them securely, then have an assistant firmly depress the brake pedal to prevent the front hub from rotating, whilst you slacken and remove the driveshaft retaining nut. Alternatively, a tool can be fabricated from

2.5a Use a screwdriver to prise out the R-clip

2.5b Using a fabricated tool to hold the front hub stationary whilst the driveshaft nut is slackened

2.8 Disconnect the track rod end using a balljoint separator

two lengths of steel strip (one long, one short) and a nut and bolt; the nut and bolt forming the pivot of a forked tool **(see illustration)**.

6 Undo the brake caliper guide pin or guide pin bolts and slide the caliper from the disc (refer to Chapter 9, Section 9, if required). Suspend the caliper from the suspension coil spring using a cable-tie to prevent straining the brake hose. Discard the guide pin bolts, new ones must be fitted.

7 Undo the nut and disconnect the upper end of the anti-roll bar link rod from the suspension strut as described in Chapter 10 Section 8.

8 Undo the retaining nut and using a balljoint

separator tool, disconnect the track rod end from the hub carrier **(see illustration)**.

Left-hand driveshaft

9 Slacken and remove the two bolts securing the hub carrier to the base of the suspension strut **(see illustration)**.

10 Pull the hub carrier outwards to free it from the strut. **Note:** *After releasing the hub carrier, rotate the base of the strut 90° towards the rear of the vehicle to minimise the chances of damaging the rubber driveshaft gaiter.*

11 Turn the steering to full left-hand lock, carefully pull the swivel hub assembly outwards, and withdraw the driveshaft outer

constant velocity joint from the hub assembly. If necessary, the shaft can be tapped out of the hub using a soft-faced mallet.

12 Support the driveshaft, and then lever the inner constant velocity joint from the transmission, taking care not to damage the driveshaft oil seal **(see illustration)**. Remove the driveshaft from the vehicle. **Note:** *Do not allow the vehicle to rest on its wheels with one or both driveshafts removed, as damage to the wheel bearing(s) may result. If moving the vehicle is unavoidable, temporarily insert the outer end of the driveshaft(s) in the hub(s) and tighten the driveshaft nut(s). Support the inner end(s) of the driveshaft(s) to avoid damage.*

Right-hand driveshaft

13 Slacken and remove the two bolts securing the steering hub carrier to the base of the suspension strut. Pull the hub carrier outwards to free it from the strut. **Note:** *After releasing the hub carrier, rotate the base of the strut 90° towards the rear of the vehicle to minimise the chances of damaging the rubber driveshaft gaiter* **(see illustration 2.9)**.

14 Slacken the upper and remove the lower intermediate bearing retaining bolts, then remove the retaining plate **(see illustrations)**.

15 Carefully pull the swivel hub assembly outwards, and withdraw the driveshaft outer constant velocity joint from the hub assembly.

2.9 The strut-to-hub carrier bolts are inserted from the rear

2.12 Lever the constant velocity joint from the transmission

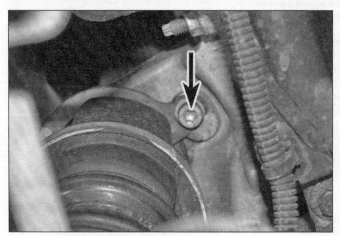

2.14a Slacken the upper bolt...

2.14b ...then remove the lower bolt and retaining plate

2.25a Tighten the driveshaft nut to the specified torque, then refit the locking cap ...

2.25b ... and secure it in position with the R-clip

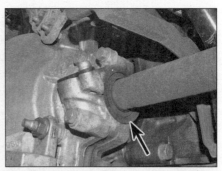

2.30 Locate the dust seal (where fitted) on the inner end of the right-hand driveshaft

If necessary, the shaft can be tapped out of the hub using a soft-faced mallet.

16 Support the outer end of the driveshaft, then pull on the inner end of the shaft to free the intermediate bearing from its mounting bracket.

17 Once the driveshaft end is free from the transmission, slide the dust seal (where fitted) off the inner end of the shaft, noting which way around it is fitted, and remove the driveshaft from the vehicle. Check the condition of the splined shaft O-ring. **Note:** *Do not allow the vehicle to rest on its wheels with one or both driveshafts removed, as damage to the wheel bearing(s) may result. If moving the vehicle is unavoidable, temporarily insert the outer end of the driveshaft(s) in the hub(s) and tighten the driveshaft nut(s). Support the inner end(s) of the driveshaft(s) to avoid damage.*

Refitting

18 Before installing the driveshaft, examine the driveshaft oil seal in the transmission for signs of damage or deterioration and, if necessary, renew it as described in Chapter 7 Section 4. It is highly recommended that the seal be renewed, regardless of its apparent condition.

19 Thoroughly clean the driveshaft splines, and the apertures in the transmission and hub assembly. Apply a thin film of grease to the oil seal lips, and to the driveshaft splines and shoulders. Check that all gaiter clips are securely fastened.

Left-hand driveshaft

20 Offer up the driveshaft, and locate the joint splines with those of the differential sun gear, taking great care not to damage the oil seal. Push the joint fully into position.

21 Locate the outer constant velocity joint splines with those of the swivel hub, and slide the joint back into position in the hub.

22 Rotate the base of the strut 90° and align the hub carrier with the brackets on the strut. Insert the bolts and tighten them to the specified torque.

23 Refit the track rod end to the stub axle and tighten the retaining nut.

24 Refit the ABS wheel speed sensor wiring back into its retaining clips and refit the brake caliper as described in Chapter 9, Section 9.

25 Lubricate the inner face and threads of the

driveshaft nut with clean engine oil, and refit it to the end of the driveshaft. Use the method employed on removal to prevent the hub from rotating (see paragraph 5), and tighten the driveshaft retaining nut to the specified torque. Check that the hub rotates freely then engage the locking cap with the driveshaft nut, so that one of its cut-outs is aligned with the driveshaft hole, and secure the cap in position with the R-clip **(see illustrations)**. Alternatively, depending on type of wheel fitted, lightly tighten the nut at this stage, and tighten it to the specified torque once the car is resting on its wheels again.

26 Refit the roadwheel, then lower the vehicle to the ground and tighten the roadwheel bolts to the specified torque. If not already done, tighten the driveshaft retaining nut to the specified torque then refit the locking cap, aligning its cut-outs with the driveshaft hole, and secure it in position with the R-clip.

27 Refill the transmission with the specified type and amount of oil, and check the level using the information given in Chapter 7 Section 2.

Right-hand driveshaft

28 Check that the intermediate bearing rotates smoothly, without any sign of roughness or undue free play between its inner and outer races. If necessary, renew the bearing as described in Section 5. Examine the dust seal for signs of damage or deterioration, and renew if necessary. Check the condition of the differential splined shaft O-ring seal and renew if necessary.

29 Apply a smear of grease to the outer race of the intermediate bearing, and to the inner lip of the dust seal (where fitted).

30 Pass the inner end of the shaft through the bearing mounting bracket then, where necessary, carefully slide the dust seal into position on the driveshaft, ensuring that its flat surface is facing the transmission **(see illustration)**.

31 Carefully locate the inner driveshaft splines with those of the differential sun gear, taking care not to damage the oil seal.

32 Align the intermediate bearing with its mounting bracket, and push the driveshaft fully into position. If necessary, use a soft-faced mallet to tap the outer race of

the bearing into position in the mounting bracket.

33 Locate the outer constant velocity joint splines with those of the swivel hub, and slide the joint back into position in the hub.

34 Ensure that the intermediate bearing is correctly seated, and then rotate its retaining plate back into position against the bearing outer race. Tighten the retaining bolts to the specified torque. Where necessary, ensure that the dust seal is tight against the driveshaft oil seal.

35 Carry out the operations described above in paragraphs 19 to 26.

3 Driveshaft rubber gaiters – renewal

Note: *There are three makes of driveshaft fitted to these models: GKN, PSA and NTN (see illustration).*
Note: *The outer joint on GKN type driveshaft cannot be removed from the driveshaft; to renew the outer gaiter on this type, the inner joint will need to be removed and the gaiter fitted from that end.*
Note: *The inner tripod joint on PSA type driveshaft cannot be removed from the driveshaft; to renew the inner gaiter on this type, the outer joint will need to be removed and the gaiter fitted from that end.*

Outer joint (PSA and NTN type)

1 Remove the driveshaft from the vehicle as described in Section 2.

3.0a Make of driveshaft (PSA) written on label

3.3a Pull back the gaiter ...

3.3b ... and clean out the old grease

3.4 Using a soft metal drift to release the outer joint

3.6 Where applicable, remove the plastic bush

2 Secure the driveshaft in a vice equipped with soft jaws, and release the two outer gaiter retaining clips. If necessary, the gaiter retaining clips can be cut to release them.
3 Slide the rubber gaiter down the shaft, to expose the outer constant velocity joint. Scoop out the excess grease **(see illustrations)**.
4 Using a hammer and suitable soft metal drift, sharply strike the inner member of the outer joint to drive it off the end of the shaft **(see illustration)**. The joint is retained on the driveshaft by a circlip, and striking the joint in this manner forces the circlip into its groove, so allowing the joint to slide off.
5 Once the joint assembly has been removed, remove the circlip from the groove in the driveshaft splines, and discard it. A new circlip must be fitted on reassembly.
6 Withdraw the rubber gaiter from the driveshaft. Where applicable, slide the gaiter inner end plastic bush off the driveshaft **(see illustration)**.

7 With the constant velocity joint removed from the driveshaft, thoroughly clean the joint using paraffin, or a suitable solvent, and dry it thoroughly. Carry out a visual inspection of the joint.
8 Move the inner splined driving member from side-to-side, to expose each ball in turn at the top of its track. Examine the balls for cracks, flat spots, or signs of surface pitting.
9 Inspect the ball tracks on the inner and outer members. If the tracks have widened, the balls will no longer be a tight fit. At the same time, check the ball cage windows for wear or cracking between the windows.
10 If, on inspection, any of the constant velocity joint components are found to be worn or damaged, it will be necessary to renew the complete joint assembly (where available), or even the complete driveshaft (where no joint components are available separately). Refer to your Peugeot/Citroën/Fiat dealer for further information on parts

availability. If the joint is in satisfactory condition, obtain a repair kit consisting of a new gaiter, circlip, retaining clips, and the correct type and quantity of grease.
11 To install the new gaiter, perform the operations shown **(see illustrations)**. Be sure to stay in order, and follow the captions carefully. Note that the hard plastic rings and plastic bushes are not fitted to all gaiters, and the gaiter retaining clips supplied with the repair kit may be different to those shown in the sequence.
12 To secure the other type of clip in position, lock the ends of the clip together, and then remove any slack in the clip by carefully compressing the raised section of the clip using a pair of special pliers or side-cutters **(see illustration)**.
13 Check that the constant velocity joint moves freely in all directions, and then refit the driveshaft to the vehicle as described in Section 2.

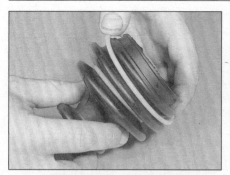

3.11a Where applicable, fit the hard plastic rings to the outer gaiter …

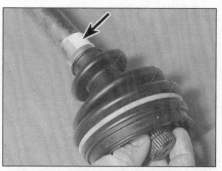

3.11b … then slide on the new plastic bush (where fitted), and seat it in its recess in the shaft. Slide the gaiter onto the shaft …

3.11c … and seat the gaiter inner end on top of the plastic bush (as applicable)

3.11d Fit the new circlip to its groove in the driveshaft splines …

3.11e … then locate the joint outer member on the splines, and slide it into position over the circlip. Ensure that the joint is securely retained by the circlip

3.11f Pack the joint with grease, working it into the ball tracks while twisting the joint, then locate the gaiter outer lip in its groove on the outer member

3.11g Fit the outer gaiter retaining clip and, using a hook fabricated out of welding rod and a pair of pliers, pull the clip tight to remove all the slack

3.11h Bend the clip end back over the buckle, then cut off the excess

3.11i Fold the clip end underneath the buckle …

3.11j … then fold the buckle firmly down onto the clip to secure the clip in position

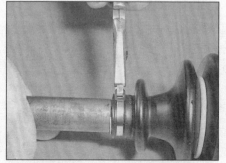

3.11k Carefully lift the gaiter inner end to equalise the air pressure in the gaiter, then secure the inner gaiter retaining clip in position using the same method

3.12 Using a pair of special pliers to secure the retaining clip

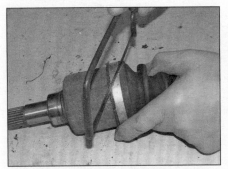

3.15a Cut the retaining clip ...

3.15b ... and remove the clip and gaiter

3.18a Slide the joint apart ...

3.18b ... and retrieve the spring (where applicable)

3.19a Release the circlip ...

3.19b ... and mark the position of the joint on the shaft

Inner joint (GKN and NTN type)

14 Remove the driveshaft from the vehicle as described in Section 2.

15 Secure the driveshaft in a vice equipped with soft jaws, and release the two outer gaiter retaining clips. If necessary, the gaiter retaining clips can be cut to release them **(see illustrations)**. Take care not to damage the driveshaft when cutting the retaining clip.

16 Slide the rubber gaiter down the shaft to expose the outer constant velocity joint. Scoop out the excess grease.

17 If the gaiter is to be renewed, it can be cut off and removed from the driveshaft.

18 Slide the outer member off the tripod joint and remove the spring and/or cup from inside the outer member of the joint **(see illustrations)**.

19 Using circlip pliers, extract the circlip securing the tripod joint to the driveshaft **(see illustrations)**. Mark the position of the tripod in relation to the driveshaft, using a dab of paint or a punch.

20 The tripod joint can now be removed **(see illustration)**. If it is tight, draw the joint off the driveshaft end using a puller. Ensure that the legs of the puller are located behind the joint inner member and do not contact the joint rollers. Alternatively, support the inner member of the tripod joint, and press the shaft out using a hydraulic press, again ensuring that no load is applied to the joint rollers.

21 With the tripod joint removed, if not removed already, slide the gaiter off the end of the driveshaft.

22 Wipe clean the joint components, taking care not to remove the alignment marks made on dismantling. Do not use paraffin or other solvents to clean this type of joint.

23 Examine the tripod joint, rollers and outer member for any signs of scoring or wear. Check that the rollers move smoothly on the tripod stems. If wear is evident, check with your local dealer to see if the tripod joint and roller assembly can be renewed. Obtain a new gaiter, retaining clips and a quantity of the special lubricating grease.

24 Tape over the splines on the end of the driveshaft, then carefully slide the inner retaining clip and gaiter onto the shaft **(see illustration)**.

25 Remove the tape, then, aligning the marks made on dismantling, engage the tripod joint with the driveshaft splines **(see illustration)**. Use a hammer and soft metal drift to tap the joint onto the shaft, taking great care not to damage the driveshaft splines or joint rollers. Alternatively, support the driveshaft, and press the joint into position using a hydraulic press

3.20 Slide the joint from the end of the shaft

3.24 Make sure the inner retaining clip is put on the shaft

3.25 Align the marks up for refitting

3.26 Refit the circlip to secure the tripod joint

3.27a Pack the outer joint with grease …

3.27b … and insert the spring (where fitted)

and suitable tubular spacer, which bears only on the joint inner member.

26 Secure the tripod joint in position with the circlip, ensuring that it is correctly located in the driveshaft groove **(see illustration)**.

27 Evenly distribute the grease contained in the repair kit inside the outer member, and then refit the spring and cup (where fitted) in the outer member **(see illustrations)**.

28 Pack the gaiter with the remainder of the grease and slide the two halves of the joint together **(see illustration)**.

29 Slide the gaiter up the driveshaft. Locate the gaiter in the grooves on the driveshaft and outer member.

30 Fit the inner retaining clip into place over the inner end of the gaiter.

31 Using a blunt rod, carefully lift the outer lip of the gaiter to equalise the air pressure.

32 Slip the new retaining clip into place to secure the outer lip of the gaiter to the outer member. Remove any slack in the gaiter retaining clip by carefully compressing the raised section of the clip (depending on type of clip supplied). In the absence of the special tool, a pair of pincers may be used **(see illustration)**. Secure the small retaining clip using the same procedure.

33 Check that the constant velocity joint moves freely in all directions, then refit the driveshaft as described in Section 2.

Inner gaiter (PSA type)

34 Remove the outer constant velocity joint as described above in paragraphs 1 to 5.

35 Tape over the splines on the driveshaft, and

3.28 Refit the tripod joint into the outer joint

carefully remove the outer constant velocity joint rubber gaiter, and (where fitted) the gaiter inner end plastic bush. It is recommended that the outer joint gaiter be also renewed, regardless of its apparent condition.

36 Release the retaining clips, then slide the inner gaiter off the shaft and (where fitted) remove its plastic bush **(see illustration 3.6)**.

37 As the gaiter is released, the joint outer member will also be freed from the end of the shaft **(see illustrations)**.

38 Thoroughly clean the joint using paraffin, or a suitable solvent, and dry it thoroughly. Check the tripod joint bearings and joint outer member for signs of wear, pitting or scuffing on their bearing surfaces. Check that the bearing rollers rotate smoothly and easily around the tripod joint, with no traces of roughness.

39 If, on inspection, the tripod joint or outer

3.32 Secure the gaiter in position with the securing clips

member reveal signs of wear or damage, it will be necessary to renew the complete driveshaft assembly, since the joint is not available separately. If the joint is in a satisfactory condition, obtain a repair kit consisting of a new gaiter, retaining clips, and the correct type and quantity of grease.

40 On reassembly, pack the inner joint with the grease supplied in the gaiter kit. Work the grease well into the bearing tracks and rollers, while twisting the joint.

41 Clean the shaft, using emery cloth to remove any rust or sharp edges which may damage the gaiter, then slide the plastic bush (where fitted) and inner joint gaiter along the driveshaft. Locate the plastic bush in its recess on the shaft, and seat the inner end of the gaiter on top of the bush; where no bush is fitted, seat the inner end of the driveshaft in the recess on the shaft **(see illustration)**.

3.37a Release the inner gaiter retaining clips and remove the joint outer member

3.37b Slide the gaiter off the end of the driveshaft

3.41 Locate the new gaiter in the groove on the driveshaft

3.42 Fit the new clips and crimp them into place

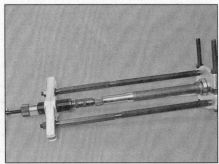

5.3 Using a long-reach bearing puller to remove the intermediate bearing from the right-hand driveshaft

42 Fit the outer member over the end of the shaft, and locate the gaiter in the groove on the joint outer member. Push the outer member onto the joint, so that it's spring-loaded plunger is compressed, then lift the outer edge of the gaiter to equalise air pressure in the gaiter. Fit both the inner and outer retaining clips, securing them in position using the information given in paragraph 11. Ensure that the gaiter retaining clips are securely tightened, and then check that the joint moves freely in all directions **(see illustration)**.

43 Refit the outer constant velocity joint components using the information given in paragraphs 11 to 13.

4 Driveshaft overhaul – general information

1 If any of the checks described in Chapter 1, Section 9, reveal wear in any driveshaft joint, first remove the roadwheel trim or centre cap (as appropriate).

2 If the R-clip is still in position, the driveshaft nut should be correctly tightened; if in doubt, remove the R-clip and locking cap, and use a torque wrench to check that the nut is securely fastened. Once tightened, refit the locking cap and R-clip, and then refit the centre cap or trim. Repeat this check on the remaining driveshaft nut.

3 Road test the vehicle, and listen for a metallic clicking from the front as the vehicle is driven slowly in a circle on full-lock. If a clicking noise is heard, this indicates wear in the outer constant velocity joint. This means that the joint must be renewed; reconditioning is not possible.

4 If vibration, consistent with roadspeed, is felt through the car when accelerating, there is a possibility of wear in the inner joints.

5 To check the joints for wear, remove the driveshafts, and then dismantle them as described in Section 3 ; if any wear or free play is found, the affected joint must be renewed. In the case of the inner joints (and on some models, the outer joints), this means that the complete driveshaft assembly must be renewed, as the joints are not available separately. Refer to your Peugeot/Citroën/Fiat dealer for latest information on the availability of driveshaft components.

5 Right-hand driveshaft intermediate bearing – renewal

Note: *A suitable bearing puller will be required, to draw the bearing and collar off the driveshaft end.*

1 Remove the right-hand driveshaft as described in Section 2 of this Chapter.

2 Check that the bearing outer race rotates smoothly and easily, without any signs of roughness or undue free play between the inner and outer races. If necessary, renew the bearing as follows.

3 Using a long-reach universal bearing puller, carefully draw the collar and intermediate bearing off the driveshaft inner end **(see illustration)**. Apply a smear of grease to the inner race of the new bearing, and then fit the bearing over the end of the driveshaft. Using a hammer and suitable piece of tubing which presses only against the bearing inner race, tap the new bearing into position on the driveshaft, until it abuts the constant velocity joint outer member. Once the bearing is correctly positioned, tap the bearing collar onto the shaft until it contacts the bearing inner race.

4 Check that the bearing rotates freely, then refit the driveshaft as described in Section 2.

Chapter 9
Braking system

Contents

Degrees of difficulty

Easy, suitable for novice with little experience | **Fairly easy,** suitable for beginner with some experience | **Fairly difficult,** suitable for competent DIY mechanic | **Difficult,** suitable for experienced DIY mechanic | **Very difficult,** suitable for expert DIY or professional

Specifications

Front brakes

Type	Vented disc, with twin-piston sliding caliper
Caliper make	TRW
Piston diameters	45 and 60 mm
Disc diameter:	
1.6 litre 1000kg models	280 mm
All other models	304 mm
Disc thickness:	
All discs:	
New	28 mm
Minimum	26 mm
Maximum disc run-out	0.05 mm
Brake pad friction material thickness:	
New	12.0 mm
Minimum	2.0 mm

Rear disc brakes

Type	Solid disc (non-vented), with single-piston sliding caliper
Caliper make	TRW
Piston diameter	41 mm
Disc diameter	290 mm
Disc thickness:	
New	14 mm
Minimum thickness	12 mm
Maximum disc run-out	0.05 mm
Brake pad friction material thickness:	
New	11.0 mm
Minimum	2.0 mm

Rear drum brakes

Drum internal diameter:

New	254 mm
Maximum	256 mm
Shoe friction material minimum thickness	1.5 mm

Vacuum pump pressure (engine at idle)

Engine temperature at 80°C:

4.5 seconds	500 mbars
18 seconds	800 mbars

ABS hydraulic valve block

Make	Bosch
Type	ABS 8.0

Torque wrench settings

	Nm	lbf ft
ABS system components:		
Hydraulic hose/pipe union nuts:		
Without ESP	15	11
With ESP	18	13
Hydraulic/modulator unit mounting nuts	8	6
Hydraulic/modulator unit mounting bracket bolts	15	11
Wheel sensor retaining bolts	8	6
Gyrometer/accelerometer sensor nuts	8	6
Caliper bleed screws	10	7
Disc retaining screws	10	7
Front brake caliper:		
Hydraulic hose to caliper	15	11
Guide pin bolts*	27	26
Mounting bracket bolts*	190	140
Master cylinder:		
Retaining nuts	25	18
Hydraulic hose/pipe union nuts:		
Without ESP	15	11
With ESP	18	13
Rear brake caliper:		
Hydraulic hose to caliper	18	13
Guide pin bolts*	35	26
Mounting bracket bolts*	108	80
Rear wheel cylinder bolts	15	11
Roadwheel bolts	100	74
Vacuum pump:		
Stage 1	5	4
Stage 2	18	13
Vacuum servo unit mounting nuts	22	16

Do not re-use

1 General Information

1 The braking system is of the servo-assisted, dual-circuit hydraulic type. The arrangement of the hydraulic system is such that each circuit operates one front and one rear brake from a tandem master cylinder. Under normal circumstances, both circuits operate in unison. However, in the event of hydraulic failure in one circuit, full braking force will still be available at two wheels.

2 All models are equipped with disc brakes on all wheels, except the 1000kg 1.6 litre models, which are equipped with rear drum brakes. ABS is fitted as standard (refer to Section 20 for further information on ABS operation).

3 The front disc brakes are actuated by twin-piston sliding calipers, whereas the rear disc brakes are actuated by single-piston sliding type calipers, which ensure that equal pressure is applied to each disc pad.

4 On all models, the handbrake provides an independent mechanical means of rear brake application. All models except the 1000kg 1.6 litre, are fitted with rear brake calipers with an integral handbrake function. The handbrake cable operates a lever on the caliper that forces the piston to press the pad against the disc surface. A self-adjust mechanism is incorporated to automatically compensate for brake pad wear. On 1000kg 1.6 litre models, the handbrake cable acts upon the rear shoes, forcing them out against the drum inner surface.

5 There is a vacuum pump fitted to provide sufficient vacuum to operate the servo unit, this is mounted on the left-hand end of the cylinder head, and is driven directly off the end of the camshaft.

Note: *When servicing any of the system, work carefully and methodically; also observe scrupulous cleanliness when overhauling any of the hydraulic system. Always renew components (in axle sets, where applicable) if in doubt about their condition, and use only genuine Peugeot/Citroën/Fiat parts, or at least those of known good quality. Note the warnings given in ' Safety first 0 Section 2 !' and at relevant points in this Chapter concerning the dangers of asbestos dust and hydraulic fluid.*

2 Hydraulic system – bleeding

⚠ **Warning: Hydraulic fluid is poisonous; wash off immediately and thoroughly in the case of skin contact, and seek immediate medical advice if any fluid is swallowed or gets into the eyes. Certain types of hydraulic fluid are inflammable, and may ignite when allowed into contact with hot components; when servicing any hydraulic system, it is safest to assume that the fluid is inflammable, and to take precautions against the risk of fire as though it is petrol that is being handled. Hydraulic fluid is also an effective paint stripper, and will attack plastics; if any is spilt, it should be washed off immediately, using copious quantities of fresh water. Finally, it is hygroscopic (it absorbs moisture from the air) – old fluid may be contaminated and unfit for further use. When topping-up or renewing the fluid, always use the recommended type, and ensure that it comes from a freshly opened sealed container.**

Caution: Ensure the ignition is switched off before starting the bleeding procedure, to avoid any possibility of voltage being applied to the hydraulic modulator before the bleeding procedure is complete. Ideally, the battery should be disconnected. If voltage is applied to the modulator before the bleeding procedure is complete, this will effectively drain the hydraulic fluid in the modulator, rendering the unit unserviceable. Do not, therefore, attempt to 'run' the modulator in order to bleed the brakes.

Note: If difficulty is experienced in bleeding the braking circuit, this maybe due to air being trapped in the ABS modulator unit. If this is the case then the vehicle should be taken to a Peugeot/Citroën/Fiat dealer or suitably-equipped specialist so that the system can be bled using special electronic test equipment.

Note: A hydraulic clutch shares its fluid reservoir with the braking system, and may also need to be bled (see Chapter 6 Section 2).

General

1 The correct operation of any hydraulic system is only possible after removing all air from the components and circuit; this is achieved by bleeding the system.

2 During the bleeding procedure, add only clean, unused hydraulic fluid of the recommended type; never re-use fluid that has already been bled from the system. Ensure that sufficient fluid is available before starting work.

3 If there is any possibility of incorrect fluid being already in the system, the brake components and circuit must be flushed completely with uncontaminated, correct fluid, and new seals should be fitted to the various components.

4 If hydraulic fluid has been lost from the system, or air has entered because of a leak, ensure that the fault is cured before proceeding further.

5 Park the vehicle on level ground, switch off the engine and select first or reverse gear, then chock the wheels and release the handbrake.

6 Check that all pipes and hoses are secure, unions tight and bleed screws closed. Clean any dirt from around the bleed screws.

7 Unscrew the master cylinder reservoir cap, and top the master cylinder reservoir up to the MAX level line **(see illustration)**; refit the cap loosely, and remember to maintain the fluid level at least above the MIN/DANGER level line throughout the procedure, or there is a risk of further air entering the system.

8 There is a number of one-man, do-it-yourself brake bleeding kits currently available from motor accessory shops. It is recommended that one of these kits is used whenever possible, as they greatly simplify the bleeding operation, and also reduce the risk of expelled air and fluid being drawn back into the system. If such a kit is not available, the basic (two-man) method must be used, which is described in detail below.

9 If a kit is to be used, prepare the vehicle as described previously, and follow the kit manufacturer's instructions, as the procedure may vary slightly according to the type being used; generally, they are as outlined below in the relevant sub-section.

10 Whichever method is used, the same sequence must be followed (paragraphs 11 and 12) to ensure that the removal of all air from the system.

Bleeding

Sequence

11 If the system has been only partially disconnected, and suitable precautions were taken to minimise fluid loss, it should be necessary only to bleed that of the system (ie, the primary or secondary circuit).

12 If the complete system is to be bled, then it should be done working in the following sequence:
a) Left-hand front brake.
b) Right-hand front brake.
c) Left-hand rear brake.
d) Right-hand rear brake.

Basic (two-man) method

13 Collect a clean glass jar, a suitable length of plastic or rubber tubing which is a tight fit over the bleed screw, and a ring spanner to fit the screw. The help of an assistant will also be required.

14 Remove the dust cap from the first screw in the sequence. Fit the spanner and tube to the screw, place the other end of the tube in the jar, and pour in sufficient fluid to cover the end of the tube.

15 Ensure that the master cylinder reservoir fluid level is maintained at least above the MIN/DANGER level line throughout the procedure.

16 Have the assistant fully depress the brake pedal several times to build up pressure, and then maintain it on the final downstroke.

17 While pedal pressure is maintained, unscrew the bleed screw (approximately one turn) and allow the compressed fluid and air to flow into the jar. The assistant should maintain pedal pressure, following it down to the floor if necessary, and should not release it until instructed to do so. When the flow stops, tighten the bleed screw again, have the assistant release the pedal slowly, and recheck the reservoir fluid level.

18 Repeat the steps given in paragraphs 16 and 17 until the fluid emerging from the bleed screw is free from air bubbles. If the master cylinder has been drained and refilled, and air is being bled from the first screw in the sequence, allow approximately five seconds between cycles for the master cylinder passages to refill.

19 When no more air bubbles appear, tighten the bleed screw securely, remove the tube and spanner, and refit the dust cap. Do not overtighten the bleed screw.

20 Repeat the procedure on the remaining screws in the sequence, until all air is removed from the system and the brake pedal feels firm again.

Using a one-way valve kit

21 As their name implies, these kits consist of a length of tubing with a one-way valve fitted, to prevent expelled air and fluid being drawn back into the system; some kits include a translucent container, which can be positioned so that the air bubbles can be more easily seen flowing from the end of the tube.

22 The kit is connected to the bleed screw, which is then opened **(see illustration)**. The user returns to the driver's seat, depresses the brake pedal with a smooth, steady stroke, and slowly releases it; this is repeated until the expelled fluid is clear of air bubbles.

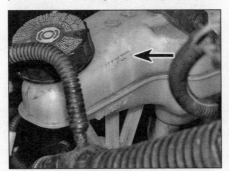

2.7 Fluid MAX level line

2.22 Connect the bleed kit to the bleed screw

23 Note that these kits simplify work so much that it is easy to forget the master cylinder reservoir fluid level; ensure that this is maintained at least above the MIN/DANGER level line at all times.

Using a pressure-bleeding kit

24 These kits are usually operated by the reservoir of pressurised air contained in the spare tyre. However, note that it will probably be necessary to reduce the pressure to a lower level than normal; refer to the instructions supplied with the kit.

25 By connecting a pressurised, fluid-filled container to the master cylinder reservoir, bleeding can be carried out simply by opening each screw in turn (in the specified sequence), and allowing the fluid to flow out until no more air bubbles can be seen in the expelled fluid.

26 This method has the advantage that the large reservoir of fluid provides an additional safeguard against air being drawn into the system during bleeding.

27 Pressure-bleeding is particularly effective when bleeding 'difficult' systems, or when bleeding the complete system at the time of routine fluid renewal.

All methods

28 When bleeding is complete, and firm pedal feel is restored, wash off any spilt fluid, tighten the bleed screws securely, and refit their dust caps.

29 Check the hydraulic fluid level in the master cylinder reservoir, and top-up if necessary (see *Weekly checks*).

30 Discard any hydraulic fluid that has been bled from the system; it will not be fit for re-use.

31 Check the feel of the brake pedal. If it feels at all spongy, air must still be present in the system, and further bleeding is required. Failure to bleed satisfactorily after a reasonable repetition of the bleeding procedure may be due to worn master cylinder seals.

3 Hydraulic pipes and hoses – renewal

Caution: Ensure the ignition is switched off before disconnecting any braking system hydraulic union and do not switch it on until after the hydraulic system has been bled. Failure to do this could lead to air entering the modulator unit requiring the unit to be bled using special test equipment (see Section 2).

Note: *Before starting work, refer to the note at the beginning of Section 2 concerning the dangers of hydraulic fluid.*

1 If any pipe or hose is to be renewed, minimise fluid loss by first removing the master cylinder reservoir cap, then tightening it down onto a piece of polythene to obtain an airtight seal. Alternatively, flexible hoses can be sealed, if required, using a proprietary

3.2 Slacken the union nut and then remove the spring clip

brake hose clamp; metal brake pipe unions can be plugged (if care is taken not to allow dirt into the system) or capped immediately they are disconnected. Place a wad of rag under any union that is to be disconnected, to catch any spilt fluid.

2 If a flexible hose is to be disconnected, unscrew the brake pipe union nut before removing the spring clip that secures the hose to its mounting bracket **(see illustration)**.

3 To unscrew the union nuts, it is preferable to obtain a brake pipe spanner of the correct size; these are available from most large motor accessory shops. Failing this, a close-fitting open-ended spanner will be required, though if the nuts are tight or corroded, their flats may be rounded-off if the spanner slips. In such a case, a self-locking wrench is often the only way to unscrew a stubborn union, but it follows that the pipe and the damaged nuts must be renewed on reassembly. Always clean a union and surrounding area before disconnecting it. If disconnecting a component with more than one union, make a careful note of the connections before disturbing any of them.

4 If a brake pipe is to be renewed, it can be obtained cut to length and with the union nuts and end flares in place, from Peugeot/Citroën/Fiat dealers. All that is then necessary is to bend it to shape, following the line of the original, before fitting it to the car. Alternatively, most motor accessory shops can make up

brake pipes from kits, but this requires very careful measurement of the original, to ensure that the new one is of the correct length. The safest answer is usually to take the original to the shop as a pattern.

5 On refitting, do not overtighten the union nuts. It is not necessary to exercise brute force to obtain a sound joint.

6 Ensure that the pipes and hoses are correctly routed, with no kinks, and that they are secured in the clips or brackets provided. After fitting, remove the polythene from the reservoir, and bleed the hydraulic system as described in Section 2. Wash off any spilt fluid, and then check the brake system carefully for fluid leaks.

4 Front brake pads – renewal

⚠️ *Warning: Disc brake pads must be renewed on both front wheels at the same time – never renew the pads on only one wheel, as uneven braking may result. Also, the dust created by wear of the pads may be a health hazard. Never blow it out with compressed air and don't inhale any of it. An approved filtering mask should be worn when working on the brakes. DO NOT use petroleum based solvents to clean brake parts. Use brake cleaner or methylated spirit only.*

1 Slacken the front roadwheel bolts, then jack up the front of the vehicle and support it on axle stands (see *Jacking and vehicle support*). Remove the front roadwheels.

Note: *A new guide pin bolt must be fitted upon reassembly.*

2 Follow the accompanying photos **(illustrations 4.2a to 4.2u)** for the actual pad renewal procedure. Be sure to stay in order and read the caption under each illustration.

3 Refit the roadwheel, then repeat the renewal procedure on the remaining front brake.

4 Depress the brake pedal repeatedly, until

4.2a If there's a wear lip at the edge of the disc, use a large screwdriver to lever the caliper outwards a little to retract the pistons

4.2b Disconnect the pad wear sensor wiring plug, and unclip the wiring – left hand brake only

4.2c Undo the bolt securing the flexible brake hose to the bracket

4.2d Holding the guide with an open-ended spanner, unscrew the upper guide pin bolt

4.2e Pivot the caliper downwards

4.2f Lift out the inner brake pad…

4.2g …and the outer brake pad

4.2h Remove the upper and lower shims

4.2i Measure the thickness of the pads friction material. If any pad is worn down to 1.5 mm or less, all 4 front pads must be renewed

4.2j Clean the caliper and mounting bracket with brake cleaner and a soft brush

4.2k If new pads are to be fitted, the pistons must be pushed back fully into the caliper body, using a piston retraction tool, or G-clamp. Keep an eye on the fluid level in the reservoir as the pistons are pushed back. Remove any surplus fluid using a syringe

4.2l Before refitting the pads, check that the guide pins are free to slide in the caliper and check that the rubber dust excluders around the guide pins are undamaged

4.2m Refit the upper…

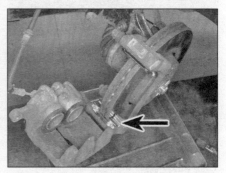

4.2n …and lower shims

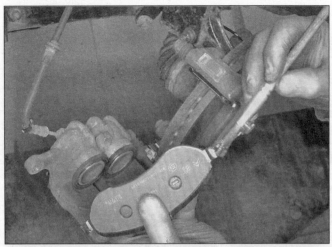

4.2o Apply a thin smear of high-temperature grease to the edges of pad backing plates, where they contact the caliper mounting bracket

4.2p Fit the outer brake pad...

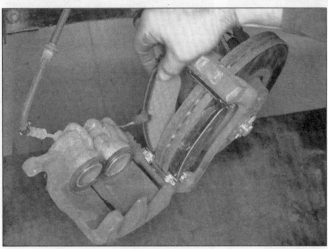

4.2q ...and the inner pad, feeding the wear sensor wiring through the aperture in the caliper body

4.2r Pivot the caliper back up into place

the pads are pressed into firm contact with the brake disc, and normal (non-assisted) pedal pressure is restored.

5 If not already done, refit the roadwheels, and then lower the vehicle to the ground and tighten the roadwheel bolts to the specified torque.

6 On completion, check the fluid level in the reservoir, check the hydraulic fluid level as described in *Weekly checks*.

Caution: New pads will not give full braking efficiency until they have bedded-in. Be prepared for this, and avoid hard braking as far as possible for the first hundred miles or so after pad renewal.

4.2s Fit the new upper guide pin bolt and tighten it to the specified torque

4.2t Refit the brake hose to the bracket and tighten the retaining bolt securely

4.2u Reconnect the pad wear sensor wiring plug, and clip the wiring back into place – left-hand brake only

5 Rear brake pads – renewal

⚠️ **Warning: Renew both sets of rear brake pads at the same time – never renew the pads on only one wheel, as uneven braking may result. Note that the dust created by wear of the pads may be a health hazard. Never blow it out with compressed air, and don't inhale any of it. An approved filtering mask should be worn when working on the brakes. DO NOT use petrol or petroleum-based solvents to clean brake parts; use brake cleaner or methylated spirit only.**

Note: *A new lower guide pin bolt must be fitted on reassembly.*

1 Chock the front wheels, slacken the rear roadwheel bolts, and then jack up the rear of the vehicle and support it on axle stands (see *Jacking and vehicle support*). Remove the rear roadwheels. Fully release the handbrake.

2 Follow the accompanying photos **(illustrations 5.2a to 5.2v)** for the actual pad renewal procedure. Be sure to stay in order and read the caption under each illustration.

3 Depress the brake pedal repeatedly until the pads are pressed into firm contact with the brake disc, and normal (non-assisted) pedal pressure is restored.

4 Repeat the above procedure on the remaining rear brake caliper.

5 Check the operation of the handbrake, and if necessary, carry out the adjustment procedure as described in Section 16.

6 Refit the roadwheels, then lower the vehicle to the ground and tighten the roadwheel bolts to the specified torque setting.

7 Check the hydraulic fluid level as described in *Weekly checks*.

Caution: New pads will not give full braking efficiency until they have bedded-in. Be prepared for this, and avoid hard braking as far as possible for the first hundred miles or so after pad renewal.

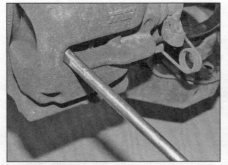
5.2a If there's a wear lip at the edge of the disc, use a large screwdriver to lever the caliper outwards a little to retract the piston

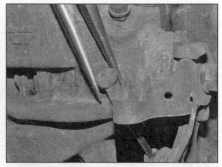
5.2b Using a pair of pliers, unhook the end of the handbrake cable from the caliper lever…

5.2c …then slide out the retaining clip and pull the cable from the bracket

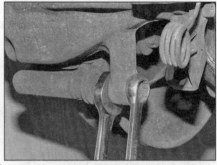
5.2d Hold the lower guide pin with an open-ended spanner, then unscrew the guide pin bolt

5.2e Pivot up the caliper, and secure it to the bodywork/suspension with wire/string etc.

5.2f Remove the outer brake pad…

5.2g …and the inner pad

5.2h Remove the lower shim…

5.2i …and the upper shim

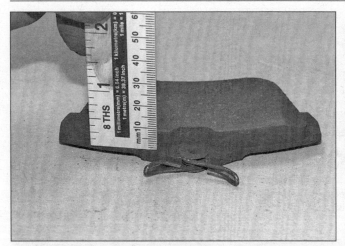

5.2j Measure the thickness of the pad friction material. If any pad is worn down to 1.5 mm or less, all 4 rear pads must be renewed

5.2k Clean the caliper mounting bracket using brake cleaner and a soft brush

5.2l Prior to fitting the pads, check that the guide sleeves are free to slide easily in the caliper body, and check that the rubber guide sleeve gaiters are undamaged

5.2m If new brake pads are to be fitted, the caliper piston must be pushed back into the cylinder to make room for them. In order to retract the piston, the piston must be turned clockwise as it is pushed into the caliper using a piston retraction tool. Keep an eye on the fluid level in the reservoir as the piston is retracted. Remove any surplus fluid with a syringe.

5.2n Press the lower…

5.2o …and upper shims into place

5.2p Apply a very thin smear of high-temperature grease to the pad backing plates where they contact the mounting bracket

5.2q Fit the outer brake pad…

5.2r …and the inner brake pad. Make sure the friction material is against the disc face!

5.2s Lower the caliper back down into place…

5.2t …then fit the new guide pin bolt and tighten it to the specified torque

5.2u Insert the handbrake cable into the caliper bracket, refit the retaining clip….

5.2v …and engage the end of the cable with the caliper lever

6 Rear brake shoes – renewal

Renewal

1 Remove the rear brake drums as described in Section 11.

2 Clean the components with brake cleaner, and allow to dry. Position a tray beneath the backplate to catch the fluid and residue.

3 Note its fitted position, then using pliers/ screwdriver, carefully remove the lower return spring (see illustration).

4 Remove the two shoe hold-down springs by using a pair of pliers to compress and twist the cups so that they can be withdrawn off the pins. Remove the hold-down pins from the backplate (see illustration).

5 Pull the lower ends of the brake shoes from behind the lower anchor, and manoeuvre them, along with the upper spring and adjustment rod, from the backplate (see illustrations). Take care not to damage the wheel cylinder rubber boots.

6.3 Remove the lower return spring

6.4 Compress the spring cup and twist it 90°

6.5 Pull out the lower ends and manoeuvre the shoes and springs assembly from place

6.6 Disengage the cable end fitting from the lever

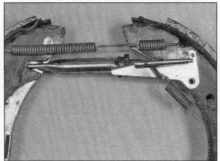

6.8 Note the positions of the springs and adjustment rod

6.10 Apply a thin smear of grease to the areas shown

6 Disengage the handbrake cable end fitting from the lever on the shoes **(see illustration)**.
7 To prevent the wheel cylinder pistons from being accidentally ejected, fit a suitable elastic band or wire lengthways over the cylinder/pistons. DO NOT press the brake pedal while the shoes are removed.
8 If required, note their fitted positions, then unhook the upper return spring and adjustment rod from the shoes **(see illustration)**.
9 Clean the backplate with brake cleaner and a soft brush.
10 Apply a very thin smear of high-temperature grease to the areas on the backplate where it contacts the edge of the brake shoes **(see illustration)**. Take great care to ensure no grease is able to contaminate the shoe friction material.
11 Fit the new brake shoes using a reversal of the removal procedure, but set the adjuster rod to its minimum length before assembling it to the trailing shoe **(see illustration)**.
12 Carry out the renewal procedures on the remaining rear brake.
13 Refit the brake drum as described in Section 11.
14 With the roadwheels refitting, depress the brake pedal several times, in order to operate the self-adjusting mechanism and set the shoes at their normal operating position.
15 Make several forward and reverse stops, and operate the handbrake fully two or three times (adjust the handbrake as required – see

Section 16). Give the car a road test, to make sure that the brakes are functioning correctly, and to bed-in the new shoes to the contours of the drum. Remember that the new shoes will not give full braking efficiency until they have bedded-in.

7 Front brake disc – inspection, removal and refitting

Note: *Before starting work, refer to the note at the beginning of Section 4 concerning the dangers of asbestos dust.*

Inspection

Note: *If either disc requires renewal, BOTH should be renewed at the same time, to ensure even and consistent braking. New brake pads should also be fitted.*
1 Apply the handbrake, slacken the front roadwheel bolts, then jack up the front of the car and support it on axle stands (see *Jacking and vehicle support*). Remove the appropriate front roadwheel.
2 Slowly rotate the brake disc so that the full area of both sides can be checked; remove the brake pads if better access is required to the inboard surface. Light scoring is normal in the area swept by the brake pads, but if heavy scoring or cracks are found, the disc must be renewed.
3 It is normal to find a lip of rust and brake

dust around the disc's perimeter; this can be scraped off if required. If, however, a lip has formed due to excessive wear of the brake pad swept area, then the disc's thickness must be measured using a micrometer. Take measurements at several places around the disc, at the inside and outside of the pad swept area; if the disc has worn at any point to the specified minimum thickness or less, the disc must be renewed **(see illustration)**.
4 If the disc is thought to be warped, it can be checked for run-out. Either use a dial gauge mounted on any convenient fixed point, while the disc is slowly rotated, or use feeler blades to measure (at several points all around the disc) the clearance between the disc and a fixed point, such as the caliper mounting bracket **(see illustration)**. If the measurements obtained are at the specified maximum or beyond, the disc is excessively warped, and must be renewed; however, it is worth checking first that the hub bearing is in good condition (Chapter 1, Section 8). Also try the effect of removing the disc and turning it through 180°, to reposition it on the hub; if the run-out is still excessive, the disc must be renewed.
5 Check the disc for cracks, especially around the wheel bolt holes, and any other wear or damage, and renew if necessary.

Removal

6 Slacken and remove the two bolts securing the brake caliper mounting bracket to the hub

6.11 Rotate the wheel to set the adjuster rod to the minimum length

7.3 Use a micrometer to measure the disc thickness

7.4 Check the disc run-out using a dial gauge

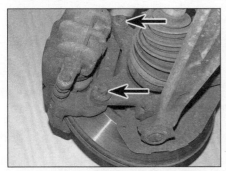

7.6 Undo the caliper mounting bracket bolts

7.7 Undo the two Torx screws, and remove the disc

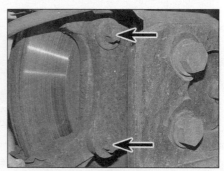

8.4 Slacken the two caliper mounting bracket Torx screws

carrier **(see illustration)**, discard the bolts, as new ones will be required for refitting. Slide the assembly off the disc and tie it to the coil spring, using a piece of wire or string, to avoid placing any strain on the hydraulic brake hose. Where necessary, unclip the pad wear sensor wiring. Note that new bolts will be required.

7 Use chalk or paint to mark the relationship of the disc to the hub, then remove the screws securing the brake disc to the hub, and remove the disc **(see illustration)**. If it is tight, lightly tap its rear face with a hide or plastic mallet.

Refitting

8 Refitting is the reverse of the removal procedure, noting the following points:
a) Ensure that the mating surfaces of the disc and hub are clean and flat.
b) Align (if applicable) the marks made on removal, and tighten the disc retaining screws to the specified torque setting.
c) If a new disc has been fitted, use a suitable solvent to wipe any preservative coating from the disc, before refitting the caliper.
d) Fit new bolts to the caliper mounting bracket and tighten to the specified torque setting.
e) Refit the roadwheels, and then lower the vehicle to the ground and tighten the wheel bolts to the specified torque.
f) Apply the footbrake several times to force the pads back into contact with the disc before driving the vehicle.

---

8 Rear brake disc – inspection, removal and refitting

Note: Before starting work, refer to the warning at the beginning of Section 5 concerning the dangers of harmful brake dust.

Inspection

Note: If either disc requires renewal, BOTH should be renewed at the same time, to ensure even and consistent braking. New brake pads should also be fitted.

1 Chock the front wheels, engage reverse gear and release the handbrake. Jack up the rear of the vehicle and support it securely on

axle stands (see *Jacking and vehicle support*). Remove the relevant roadwheel.
2 Inspect the rear brake discs, as described for the front brake discs in Section 7.

Removal

Note: *New hub/disc retaining nut must be fitted on reassembly.*
3 Remove the brake pads as described in Section 5. then undo the remaining guide pin bolt and suspend the caliper from the suspension/body using wire/string etc. Take care not to strain the flexible hose.
4 Unscrew the two screws securing the brake caliper mounting bracket to the hub carrier, and move it clear of the disc **(see illustration)**.
5 Undo the 2 screws and remove the disc from the hub **(see illustration)**.

Refitting

6 If a new disc is being fitted, use a suitable solvent to wipe any preservative coating from the disc before refitting.
7 Slide the disc into position on the hub, then tighten the retaining screws securely.
8 Refit the caliper mounting bracket and tighten the new retaining bolts to their specified torque.
9 Refit the brake pads as described in Section 5.
10 Refit the roadwheel, then lower the vehicle to the ground and tighten the roadwheel bolts to the specified torque.
11 On completion, depress the brake pedal several times to bring the brake pads into contact with the disc.

8.5 The disc is retained by 2 Torx screws

9 Front brake caliper – removal, overhaul and refitting

Caution: Ensure the ignition is switched off before disconnecting any braking system hydraulic union and do not switch it on until after the hydraulic system has been bled. Failure to do this could lead to air entering the modulator unit requiring the unit to be bled using special Peugeot/Citroën/Fiat test equipment (see Section 2).
Note: *Before starting work, refer to the note at the beginning of Section 2 concerning the dangers of hydraulic fluid, and to the warning at the beginning of Section 4 concerning the dangers of harmful dust.*

Removal

1 Apply the handbrake, slacken the relevant front roadwheel bolts, then jack up the front of the vehicle and support it on axle stands (see *Jacking and vehicle support*). Remove the appropriate roadwheel.
2 Minimise fluid loss by first removing the master cylinder reservoir cap, and then tightening it down onto a piece of polythene, to obtain an airtight seal. Alternatively, use a brake hose clamp, a G-clamp or a similar tool to clamp the flexible hose **(see illustration)**.
3 Clean the area around the caliper hose

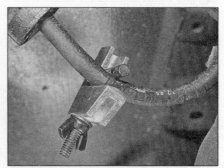

9.2 To minimise fluid loss, fit a brake hose clamp to the flexible hose

9.3 Slacken the brake hose nut

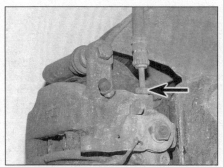

10.3 Unscrew the brake pipe union nut

11.2 Align the 'unlocked' symbol with the lug

union and place a wad of rag under the union, to catch any spilt fluid, then undo the brake hose union (see illustration).

4 If working on the left-hand caliper, disconnect the brake pad wear sensor wiring plug.

5 Slacken and remove the upper and lower caliper guide pin bolts, refer to Section 4. Lift the caliper away from the brake disc. Note that the brake pads need not be disturbed, and can be left in position in the caliper mounting bracket. Note that new guide pin bolts will be required.

6 If required, the caliper mounting bracket can be unbolted from the hub carrier. Discard the bolts, as new ones must be fitted.

Overhaul

7 At the time of writing, it would appear that no overhaul kits are available for the brake calipers. Check availability with your Citroen/Peugeot/Fiat dealer or parts specialist.

Refitting

8 If previously removed, refit the caliper mounting bracket to the hub carrier, and tighten the new bolts to the specified torque.

9 Ensure that the brake pads are correctly fitted in the caliper mounting bracket and refit the caliper (see Section 4).

10 Insert the new guide pin bolts and tighten them to the specified torque.

11 Where applicable, reconnect the brake pad wear sensor wiring plug.

12 Tighten the brake hose union nut to the specified torque, then remove the brake hose clamp or polythene (where fitted).

13 Bleed the hydraulic system as described in Section 2. Note that, providing the precautions described were taken to minimise brake fluid loss, it should only be necessary to bleed the relevant front brake.

14 Depress the brake pedal repeatedly, until the pads are pressed into firm contact with the brake disc, and normal (non-assisted) pedal pressure is restored.

15 Refit the roadwheel, then lower the vehicle to the ground and tighten the roadwheel bolts to the specified torque.

10 Rear brake caliper – removal, overhaul and refitting

Caution: Ensure the ignition is switched off before disconnecting any braking system hydraulic union and do not switch it back on until after the hydraulic system has been bled. Failure to do this could lead to air entering the modulator unit requiring the unit to be bled using special Peugeot/Citroën/Fiat test equipment (see Section 2).
Note: *Before starting work, refer to the note at the beginning of Section 2 concerning the dangers of hydraulic fluid, and to the warning at the beginning of Section 5 concerning the dangers of asbestos dust.*
Note: *New caliper mounting bracket bolts and guide pin bolts when be required on reassembly.*

Removal

1 Chock the front wheels, slacken the relevant rear roadwheel bolts, then jack up the rear of the vehicle and support on axle stands (see *Jacking and vehicle support*). Remove the relevant rear wheel.

2 Minimise fluid loss by first removing the master cylinder reservoir cap, and then tightening it down onto a piece of polythene to obtain an airtight seal. Alternatively, use a brake hose clamp, a G-clamp or a similar tool to clamp the flexible hose at the nearest convenient point to the brake caliper (see illustration 9.2).

3 Wipe away all traces of dirt around the brake pipe union on the caliper (see illustration). Unscrew the union nut and disconnect the brake pipe from the caliper. Plug the pipe and caliper unions to minimise fluid loss and prevent dirt entry.

4 Remove the brake pads (see Section 5).

5 Slacken and remove the remaining guide pin bolt, to remove the caliper from the vehicle. If required, the caliper mounting bracket can be unbolted from the hub carrier. Discard the bolts, as new ones must be fitted.

Overhaul

6 At the time of writing, it would appear that

no parts were available to recondition the rear caliper assembly, with the exception of the guide pin bolts, guide pins and guide pin gaiters. Check with a Citroen/Peugeot/Fiat dealer or parts specialist. Check the condition of the guide pins and their gaiters; both pins should be undamaged and (when cleaned) a reasonably tight sliding fit in the caliper bracket. If there is any doubt about the condition of any component, renew it.

Refitting

7 If previously removed, refit the caliper mounting bracket to the hub carrier, and tighten the new bolts to the specified torque.

8 Refit the brake pads as described in Section 5.

9 Refit the caliper and insert the new guide pin bolt, tightening it to the specified torque settings.

10 Reconnect the brake pipe to the caliper, and tighten the brake hose union nut to the specified torque. Remove the brake hose clamp or polythene (where fitted).

11 Bleed the hydraulic system as described in Section 2. Note that, providing the precautions described were taken to minimise brake fluid loss, it should only be necessary to bleed the relevant rear brake.

12 Depress the brake pedal repeatedly, until the pads are pressed into firm contact with the brake disc, and normal (non-assisted) pedal pressure is restored.

13 Refit the roadwheel, then lower the vehicle to the ground and tighten the roadwheel bolts to the specified torque.

11 Rear brake drum – removal and refitting

Removal

1 Chock the front wheels, fully release the handbrake, slacken the rear wheel bolts, then raise the rear of the vehicle and support it securely on axle stands (see *Jacking and vehicle support*). Remove the rear roadwheels.

2 Working underneath the vehicle, rotate the handbrake cable collar anti-clockwise until the 'unlocked' symbol aligns with the arrow mark/lug on the cable fitting (see illustration).

11.3a Undo the retaining bolt…

11.3b …and remove the drum protection ring

11.4 Pull the drum from place

3 Undo the retaining bolt and remove the brake drum protection **(see illustrations)**.
4 Undo the retaining bolt, and pull the drum squarely from place **(see illustration)**.

Refitting

5 Refitting is a reversal of removal. Tighten the drum retaining screw to the specified torque, and adjust the handbrake as described in Section 16.

12 Rear wheel cylinder – removal, overhaul and refitting

1 Refer to the precautions in Section 1 before proceeding. Also bear in mind that if the brake shoes have been contaminated by fluid leaking from the wheel cylinder, they must be renewed. The shoes on BOTH sides of the car must be renewed, even if they are only contaminated on one side.

Removal

2 Remove the brake drum as described in Section 11. If the wheel cylinders have been leaking, there will probably be a significant build-up of brake dust on the failed seals (the dust sticks to the leaking fluid). A leak can be confirmed by carefully prising up the outer lip of the seal – any wetness means a new cylinder will be needed.
3 In recent years, the availability of wheel cylinder repair kits has greatly decreased, but it may still be worth asking. Wheel cylinders do not have to be fitted in pairs (providing they are the same size), but if one is leaking, it's reasonable to assume the other one soon will be too. If the leak has been going on for some time, it may be serious enough to have contaminated the brake shoes, in which case new shoes should be fitted on BOTH sides.
4 Minimise fluid loss either by removing the master cylinder reservoir cap, and then tightening it down onto a piece of polythene to obtain an airtight seal, or by using a brake hose clamp or similar tool, to clamp the flexible hose at the nearest convenient point to the wheel cylinder.
5 Pull the brake shoes apart at their top

ends, so that they are just clear of the wheel cylinder. The automatic adjuster will hold the shoes in this position so that the cylinder can be withdrawn.
6 Wipe away all traces of dirt around the hydraulic union at the rear of the wheel cylinder, then undo the union nut **(see illustration)**. This nut may well be very tight – it pays to apply penetrating oil in advance, and to use a proper brake spanner when loosening it.
7 Unscrew the bolts securing the wheel cylinder to the backplate.
8 Withdraw the wheel cylinder from the backplate so that it is clear of the brake shoes. Plug the open hydraulic unions to prevent entry of dirt, and to minimise further fluid loss whilst the cylinder is detached.

Overhaul

9 No overhaul procedures or parts were available at the time of writing – check availability of spares before dismantling. Renewing a wheel cylinder as a unit is recommended.

Refitting

10 Wipe clean the backplate and remove the plug from the end of the hydraulic pipe. Fit the cylinder onto the backplate and screw in the hydraulic union nut by hand, being careful not to cross-thread it.
11 Tighten the mounting bolt to the specified torque, and then fully- tighten the hydraulic union nut.

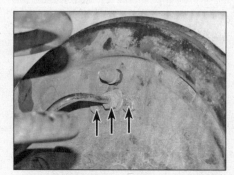

12.6 Brake pipe union nut and wheel cylinder retaining bolts

12 Retract the automatic brake adjuster mechanism, so that the brake shoes engage with the pistons of the wheel cylinder. To do this, prise the shoes apart slightly, turn the automatic adjuster to its minimum position, and release the shoes.
13 Remove the clamp from the flexible brake hose, or the polythene from the master cylinder (as applicable).
14 Refit the brake drum with reference to Section 11.
15 Bleed the hydraulic system as described in Section 2. Providing suitable precautions were taken to minimise loss of fluid, it should only be necessary to bleed the relevant rear brake.
16 Test the brakes carefully before returning the car to normal service.

13 Master cylinder – removal, overhaul and refitting

Caution: Ensure the ignition is switched off before disconnecting any braking system hydraulic union and do not switch it back on until after the hydraulic system has been bled. Failure to do this could lead to air entering the modulator unit requiring the unit to be bled using special Peugeot/Citroën/Fiat test equipment (see Section 2).
Note: *Before starting work, refer to the warning at the beginning of Section 2 concerning the dangers of hydraulic fluid.*

Removal

1 Disconnect the battery negative lead as described in Chapter 5A Section 4.
2 Remove the master cylinder reservoir cap and filter, and using a syringe, remove as much fluid as possible from the reservoir. Alternatively, open any convenient bleed screw in the system, and gently pump the brake pedal to expel the fluid through a plastic tube connected to the screw until the reservoir is emptied (see Section 2).
3 Disconnect the wiring connector from the

13.3 Fluid level sensor wiring plug

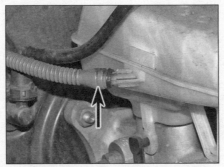

13.4 Disconnect the clutch fluid supply pipe

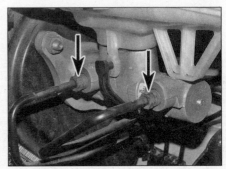

13.5 Unscrew the brake pipe unions

brake fluid level sender unit fitted to top of the reservoir **(see illustration)**.

4 Disconnect clutch fluid supply pipe from the reservoir **(see illustration)**. Plug the pipe opening to prevent dirt ingress.

5 Wipe clean the area around the brake pipe unions on the side of the master cylinder, and place absorbent rags beneath the pipe unions to catch any surplus fluid. Make a note of the correct fitted positions of the unions, then unscrew the union nuts and carefully withdraw the pipes **(see illustration)**. Plug or tape over the pipe ends and master cylinder orifices, to minimise the loss of brake fluid, and to prevent the entry of dirt into the system. Wash off any spilt fluid immediately with cold water.

6 Slacken and remove the two nuts securing the master cylinder to the vacuum servo unit. Withdraw the master cylinder from the engine compartment. If the sealing ring fitted to the rear of the master cylinder shows signs of damage or deterioration, it must be renewed.

7 If required, remove the retaining clip and separate the reservoir from the master cylinder.

Overhaul

8 It may be that the master cylinder can be overhauled after obtaining the relevant repair kit from a Peugeot/Citroën/Fiat dealer or parts specialist. Check availability prior to dismantling. Ensure that the correct repair kit is obtained for the master cylinder being worked on. Note the locations of all components to ensure correct refitting, and lubricate the new seals using clean brake fluid. Follow the assembly instructions supplied with the repair kit.

Refitting

9 Remove all traces of dirt from the master cylinder and servo unit mating surfaces and ensure that the sealing ring is correctly fitted to the rear of the master cylinder.

10 If removed, press the mounting seals fully into the master cylinder ports then carefully ease the fluid reservoir into position. Secure it in position, making sure the retaining clips are correctly located.

11 Fit the master cylinder to the servo unit. Refit the master cylinder mounting nuts, and tighten them to the specified torque.

12 Wipe clean the brake pipe unions and refit

them to the master cylinder ports, tightening them to the specified torque.

13 Reconnect the clutch master cylinder supply pipe (where applicable), and level sensor wiring plug.

14 Reconnect the battery as described in Chapter 5A Section 4.

15 Refit any other components removed to improve access then refill the master cylinder reservoir with new fluid. Bleed the complete hydraulic system as described in Section 2. **Note:** *A hydraulic clutch shares its fluid reservoir with the braking system, and may also need to be bled (see Chapter 6, Section 2).*

14 Vacuum servo unit –
testing, removal and refitting

Testing

1 To test the operation of the servo unit, depress the footbrake several times to exhaust the vacuum, then start the engine whilst keeping the pedal firmly depressed. As the engine starts, there should be a noticeable 'give' in the brake pedal as the vacuum builds-up. Allow the engine to run for at least two minutes, and then switch it off. If the brake pedal is now depressed it should feel normal, but further applications should result in the pedal feeling firmer, with the pedal stroke decreasing with each application.

2 If the servo does not operate as described, first inspect the servo unit check valve as described in Section 15, also check the

14.6 Disconnect the vacuum pipe from the servo

operation of the vacuum pump as described in Section 23.

3 If the servo unit still fails to operate satisfactorily, the fault lies within the unit itself. Repairs to the unit are not possible – if faulty, the servo unit must be renewed.

Removal

4 Remove the master cylinder as described in Section 13.

5 Release the wiring harness adjacent to the servo from its retaining clips, and move it to one side.

6 Depress the release button, then disconnect the vacuum pipe from the servo unit **(see illustration)**.

7 Working on the passengers side of the engine compartment bulkhead, slide out the retaining clip and pull the pushrod clevis pin from the cross-shaft.

8 Slacken and remove the four nuts securing the servo to the bulkhead.

9 Working back in the engine compartment, manoeuvre the servo unit out of position, along with its gasket which is fitted between the servo and housing. Renew the gasket if it shows signs of damage.

Refitting

10 Refitting is the reverse of removal, noting the following points.
a) Lubricate all linkage pivot points with multipurpose grease.
b) Tighten the servo unit nuts to their specified torque settings, where applicable.
c) Make sure the servo pushrod locates correctly with the pedal
d) Refit the master cylinder as described in Section 13 and bleed the complete hydraulic system as described in Section 2.
e) Test the brakes and servo operation as described at the beginning of this Section.

15 Vacuum servo unit check
valve – removal, testing and refitting

Removal

1 Release the retaining clip, and then

15.3 Servo pipe check valve

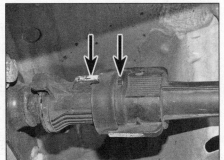

16.3 Rotate the collar anti-clockwise to align the arrow/protrusion with the 'unlocked' symbol

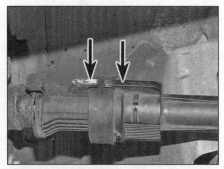

16.4 Rotate the collar clockwise to the locked position

disconnect the vacuum pipe from the servo unit **(see illustration 14.6)**.

2 Disconnect the other end of the vacuum pipe from the vacuum pump at the cylinder head. The check valve is integral with the vacuum pipe.

Testing

3 Examine the check valve for signs of damage, and renew if necessary **(see illustration)**. The valve may be tested by blowing through it in both directions. Air should flow through the valve in one direction only – when blown through from the servo unit end of the valve. Renew the valve and pipe if this is not the case.

4 Examine the rubber sealing grommet and flexible vacuum hose for signs of damage or deterioration, and renew as necessary.

Refitting

5 Refitting is a reversal of removal.
6 On completion, start the engine and check for air leaks.

---

16 Handbrake – adjustment

1 To check the handbrake adjustment, pull the handbrake lever to the fully applied position, applying normal moderate pressure, counting the number of clicks emitted from the handbrake ratchet mechanism. If adjustment is correct, there should be 1 click before the brakes begins to apply, and the rear wheels locked from the 4th click onwards. If this is not the case, adjust as follows.
2 Chock the front wheels, then jack up the rear of the vehicle and support it on axle stands (see *Jacking and vehicle support*). Check the handbrake cables are routed correctly and move freely. Also check the handbrake levers on the rear of the brake calipers operate correctly.
3 With the handbrake in the off position, rotate the collar of the cable fitting anti-clockwise to align the arrow/protrusion

with the 'unlocked' symbol **(see illustration)**.
4 Now rotate the collar in a clockwise direction 90° to the locked position **(see illustration)**.
5 Fully apply the handbrake at least 12 times.
6 Release the handbrake, then rotate the cable collar anti-clockwise to align the arrow with the 'unlocked' symbol.
7 Now rotate the collar clockwise 90° to the locked position.
8 Check that the wheels rotate freely with the handbrake lever released. There should be slight friction at the wheels when the lever is pulled to the first notch, and the wheels should be locked from the 4th notch onwards.
9 Lower the vehicle to the ground.

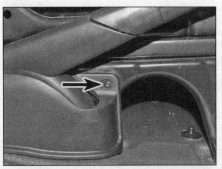

17.3a Undo the screw at the side of the cover...

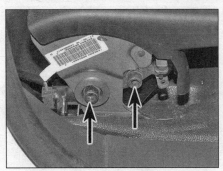

17.4 Handbrake lever retaining bolts

---

17 Handbrake lever and switch – removal and refitting

Removal

1 Disconnect the battery negative lead as described in Chapter 5A Section 4.
2 Chock the wheels and fully release the handbrake.
3 Undo the 2 screws and remove the handbrake lever cover **(see illustrations)**.
4 Undo the 2 Allen bolts securing the handbrake lever to the seat base **(see illustration)**.
5 Disconnect the wiring connector from the handbrake warning light switch.
6 Disengage the cable end fitting and manoeuvre the lever from place **(see illustration)**.

17.3b ...and the screw at the rear

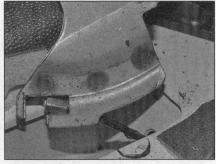

17.6 Disengage the cable from the lever

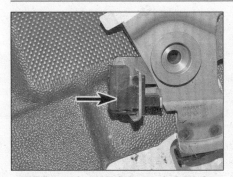

17.7 Press the switch forwards from the bracket

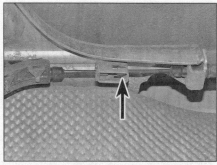

18.8 Disengage the cable from the coupling

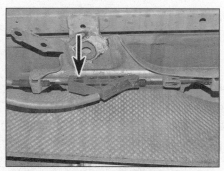

18.9 Disengage the distributor from the end of the cable

7 If required, press the handbrake warning light switch forwards from the bracket **(see illustration)**.

Refitting

8 Refitting is a reversal of removal. Tighten the lever retaining bolts, and adjust the handbrake (see Section 16).

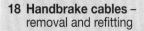

18 Handbrake cables – removal and refitting

Removal

1 Firmly chock the front wheels, slacken the relevant rear roadwheel bolts, and then jack up the rear of the vehicle and support it on axle stands (see *Jacking and vehicle support*).
2 Release the handbrake.
3 Rotate the cable collar anti-clockwise until the 'unlocked' symbol aligns with the arrow on the cable fitting **(see illustration 16.3)**.
4 Fully apply the handbrake.
5 Move the drivers seat fully forwards, and undo the 2 screws and remove the handbrake lever cover **(see illustration 17.3a and 17.3b)**.
6 Rotate the cable collar clockwise to the locked position **(see illustration 16.4)**.
7 Release the handbrake.

8 Disengage the end of the cable from the coupling **(see illustration)**.
9 Rotate the distributor, and release the end of the cable **(see illustration)**.
10 Disengage the end of the cable from the handbrake lever.
11 Working underneath the vehicle, release the main cable from any retaining clips along its length, and manoeuvre it from place.
12 Squeeze together the tabs and release the left-hand secondary cable outer fitting from the support bracket **(see illustration)**.
13 Squeeze together the tabs and release the right-hand secondary cable outer fitting from the support bracket.

Models with rear disc brakes

14 Release the cable end fitting from the lever on the brake caliper, and remove the cable from the support bracket **(see illustrations)**.

Models with rear drum brakes

15 Remove the rear brake shoes as described in Section 6.
16 Compress the clips and pull the cable from the backplate **(see illustration)**.

Refitting

17 Refitting is a reversal of the removal procedure, adjusting the handbrake as described in Section 16.

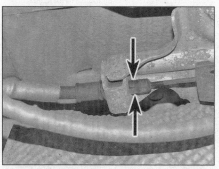

18.12 Squeeze together the tabs and pull the secondary cable from the bracket

18.14a Disengage the inner cable from the lever…

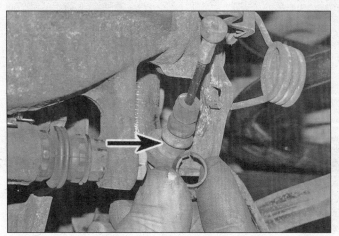

18.14b …then remove the clip from the groove and pull the outer cable from the bracket

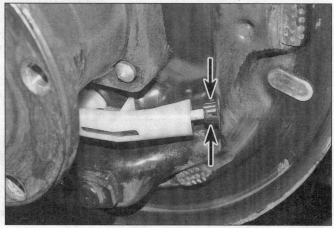

18.16 Compress the clips and pull the cable from the backplate

19.3a Disconnect the wiring plug…

19.3b …then rotate the switch 90° anti-clockwise

21.3 Depress the clip and fold up the wiring plug catch

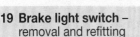

19 Brake light switch – removal and refitting

Removal

1 Disconnect the battery negative lead as described in Chapter 5A Section 4.
2 Remove the drivers side lower facia panel as described in Chapter 11 Section 27.
3 Disconnect the wiring, then rotate the switch 90° anti-clockwise and remove it from the bracket (see illustrations).

Refitting

4 Refit the switch back into position in the mounting bracket, and turn it 90° clockwise to lock it in position. No adjustment is necessary.
5 Reconnect the wiring connector, and check that the switch plunger is up against the brake pedal lever bracket.
6 Reconnect the battery as described in Chapter 5A Section 4, and check the operation of the brake lights.

20 Anti-lock braking system (ABS) – general information

1 ABS is fitted to all models as standard; the system comprises a hydraulic valve block/modulator unit and the four roadwheel sensors. The hydraulic/modulator unit contains the Electronic Control Module (ECM); the hydraulic solenoid valves and the electrically driven return pump. The purpose of the system is to prevent the wheel(s) locking during heavy braking. This is achieved by automatic release of the brake on the relevant wheel, followed by re-application of the brake.
2 The solenoid valves are controlled by the ECM, which itself receives signals from the four wheel speed sensors (front sensors are fitted to the swivel hubs, and the rear sensors are fitted to the rear hubs), which monitor the speed of rotation of each wheel. By comparing these signals, the ECM can determine the speed at which the vehicle is traveling. It can then use this speed to determine when a wheel is

decelerating at an abnormal rate, compared to the speed of the vehicle, and therefore predicts when a wheel is about to lock. During normal operation, the system functions in the same way as a non-ABS braking system.
3 If the ECM senses that a wheel is about to lock, it closes the relevant outlet solenoid valves in the hydraulic unit, which then isolates the relevant brake(s) on the wheel(s) which is/are about to lock from the master cylinder, effectively sealing-in the hydraulic pressure.
4 If the speed of rotation of the wheel continues to decrease at an abnormal rate, the ECM opens the inlet solenoid valves on the relevant brake(s), and operates the electrically-driven return pump which pumps the hydraulic fluid back into the master cylinder, releasing the brake. Once the speed of rotation of the wheel returns to an acceptable rate, the pump stops; the solenoid valves switch again, allowing the hydraulic master cylinder pressure to return to the caliper, which then re-applies the brake. This cycle can be carried out many times a second.
5 The action of the solenoid valves and return pump creates pulses in the hydraulic circuit. When the ABS system is functioning, these pulses can be felt through the brake pedal.
6 The operation of the ABS system is entirely dependent on electrical signals. To prevent the system responding to any inaccurate signals, a built-in safety circuit monitors all signals received by the ECM. If an inaccurate signal or low battery voltage is detected, the ABS system is automatically shut-down, and the warning light on the instrument panel is illuminated, to inform the driver that the ABS system is not operational. Normal braking should still be available, however.
7 Depending on model, it may also be equipped with additional safety features built around the ABS system. These systems are EBFD (electronic brake force distribution), which automatically apportions braking effort between the front and rear wheels, EBA (emergency brake assist) which guarantees full braking effort in the event of an emergency stop by monitoring the rate at which the brake pedal is depressed, and ESP (electronic stability program) which monitors the vehicle's cornering forces and steering

wheel angle, then applies the braking force to the appropriate roadwheel to enhance the stability of the vehicle.
8 If a fault does develop in the any of these systems, the vehicle must be taken to a Peugeot/Citroën/Fiat dealer or suitably-equipped specialist for fault diagnosis and repair.

21 Anti-lock braking system (ABS) components – removal and refitting

Hydraulic valve block/modulator and ECM

Caution: Disconnect the battery before disconnecting the modulator hydraulic unions, and do not reconnect the battery until after the hydraulic system has been bled. Also ensure that the unit is stored upright (in the same position as it is fitted to the vehicle) and is not tipped onto its side or upside down. Failure to do this could lead to air entering the modulator unit, requiring the unit to be bled using special Peugeot/Citroën/Fiat test equipment on refitting (see Section 2).
Note: Before starting work, refer to the warning at the beginning of Section 2 concerning the dangers of hydraulic fluid.
1 Disconnect the battery negative lead as described in Chapter 5A Section 4.
2 Use a brake pedal depressor tool, or length of wood jammed between the steering wheel and the brake pedal to firmly depress the brake pedal. This will prevent any flow of fluid when the brake pipes are disconnected.
3 Depress the clip, fold up the catch and disconnect the main wiring plug from the hydraulic valve block ECM (see illustration).
4 Mark the locations of the hydraulic fluid pipes to ensure correct refitting, then unscrew the union nuts, and disconnect the pipes from the modulator assembly. Be prepared for fluid spillage, and plug the open ends of the pipes and the modulator to prevent dirt ingress and further fluid loss.
5 Slacken and remove the modulator mounting nuts and remove the assembly from the engine compartment.

21.11 Front wheel speed sensor retaining bolt

21.19 Rear wheel speed sensor wiring plug

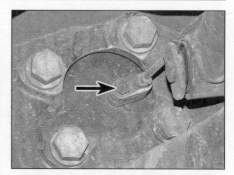

21.20 Undo the bolt and withdraw the sensor

6 Refitting is a reversal of removal, bearing in mind the following points:
a) New valve blocks/modulator are supplied pre-filled with fluid – remove the plugs prior to connecting the fluid pipes.
b) New ECMs must be initialised and programmed using dedicated diagnostic equipment. Entrust this task to a Peugeot/Citroën/Fiat dealer or suitably-equipped specialist.
c) Tighten the hydraulic pipes and mounting nuts securely
d) On completion, bleed the brake hydraulic system as described in Section 2.

Electronic Control Module (ECM)

7 The ECM is integral with the hydraulic valve block assembly, and is not available separately.

Front wheel speed sensor

8 Ensure the ignition is turned off.
9 Apply the handbrake, slacken the appropriate front roadwheel bolts, then jack up the front of the vehicle and support securely on axle stands (see Jacking and vehicle support). Remove the relevant front wheel.
10 Trace the wiring back from the sensor, releasing it from all the relevant clips and ties on the inner wing panel, whilst noting its correct routing, then disconnect the wiring connector.

11 Slacken and remove the retaining bolt and withdraw the sensor from the rear of the hub carrier (see illustration).
12 Ensure that the mating faces of the sensor and the swivel hub are clean, and apply a little anti-seize grease to the swivel hub bore before refitting.
13 Make sure the sensor tip is clean and ease it into position in the swivel hub.
14 Clean the threads of the sensor bolt and apply a few drops of thread-locking compound (Peugeot/Citroën/Fiat recommend Loctite). Refit the retaining bolt and tighten it to the specified torque.
15 Work along the sensor wiring, making sure it is correctly routed, and securing it in position with all the relevant clips and ties. Reconnect the wiring connector.
16 Refit the roadwheel, lower the vehicle to the ground and tighten the wheel bolts to the specified torque.

Rear wheel speed sensor

17 Ensure the ignition is turned off.
18 Chock the front wheels, slacken the relevant rear roadwheel bolts, and then jack up the rear of the vehicle and support it on axle stands (see Jacking and vehicle support). Remove the relevant roadwheel.
19 Trace the wiring back from the sensor, releasing it from all the relevant clips and ties whilst noting its correct routing, and disconnect the wiring connector (see illustration).

20 Working at the rear of the hub assembly, undo the retaining bolt and withdraw the sensor (see illustration).
21 Ensure that the mating faces of the sensor and the hub are clean, and apply a little anti-seize grease to the hub bore before refitting.
22 Make sure the sensor tip is clean and ease it into position in the rear of the hub.
23 Clean the threads of the sensor bolt and apply a few drops of thread-locking compound (Peugeot/CitroënFiat recommend Loctite). Refit the retaining bolt and tighten it to the specified torque.
24 Work along the sensor wiring, making sure it is correctly routed, and securing it in position with all the relevant clips and ties. Reconnect the wiring connector.
25 Refit the roadwheel, lower the vehicle to the ground and tighten the wheel bolts to the specified torque.

Gyrometer/accelerometer sensor

26 The sensor is located under the drivers side carpet. Remove front seats as described in Chapter 11 Section 24, to be able to pull the carpet back to expose the sensor.
27 Undo the nuts and remove the cover from the floor panel (see illustration).
28 Undo the 2 retaining nuts and lift the sensor from place (see illustration).
29 Release the retaining clip, and then disconnect the wiring plug.
30 Refitting is a reversal of removal, ensuring the arrow on the top of the sensor points to the front of the vehicle.

22 Vacuum pump – removal and refitting

Removal

1 The pump is located at the left-hand end of the cylinder head.
2 To access the vacuum pump, remove the air cleaner ducting and pipes from the left-hand side of the cylinder head. Refer to Chapter 4A, Section 5 for further information.

21.27 Undo the nuts and remove the cover

21.28 The arrow on the gyrometer/accelerometer sensor must point to the front of the vehicle

1.6 litre models

3 Depress the retaining clip/button and disconnect the vacuum hose(s) from the pump **(see illustration)**.

4 Slacken and remove the retaining bolts/nut (as applicable) securing the pump to the left-hand end of the cylinder head, then remove the pump. Discard the sealing rings – new ones must be used on refitting. One of the pump retaining bolts acts as a locating stud for the air intake ducting.

2.0 litre models

5 On Euro 5 emissions level models, disconnect the fuel supply and return hoses above the vacuum pump, and release them from the retaining clips.

6 Release the wiring loom from the bracket over the vacuum pump. then undo the retaining bolts and remove the bracket **(see illustration)**.

7 Disconnect the vacuum hoses from the pump, then undo the retaining bolts and manoeuvre the pump from place **(see illustration)**. Renew the gasket/seal.

Refitting

8 Fit new sealing ring(s) to the pump recess, then align the drive dog with the slot in the end of the camshaft, and refit the pump to the cylinder head, ensuring that the sealing ring(s) remain correctly seated **(see illustrations)**.

9 Refit the pump mounting bolts/nut (as applicable) and tighten them securely.

10 The remainder of refitting is a reversal of removal.

23 Vacuum pump – testing

1 The operation of the braking system vacuum pump can be checked using a vacuum gauge.

2 Start the engine and get it up to temperature, then allow it to idle.

3 Disconnect the vacuum pipe from the pump, and connect the gauge to the pump union using a suitable length of hose.

4 Measure the vacuum created by the pump; refer to specifications at the beginning of this Chapter. If the vacuum registered is

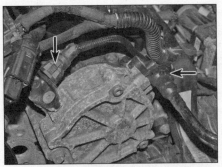
22.3 Depress the button and disconnect the vacuum hose(s)

22.6 Remove the bracket above the pump

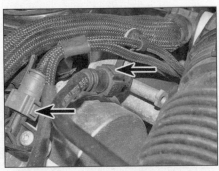
22.7 Depress the release buttons, and disconnect the hoses

22.8a Renew the vacuum pump O-ring seals

22.8b Some pumps may have two O-ring seals

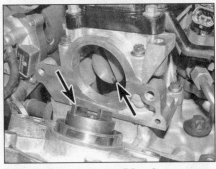
22.8c Ensure the pump drive dog engages with the slot in the end of the camshaft

significantly less than specified, it is likely that the pump is faulty. However, seek the advice of a Peugeot/Citroën/Fiat dealer before condemning the pump.

5 Overhaul of the vacuum pump is not possible, since no components are available separately for it. If faulty, the complete pump assembly must be renewed.

Notes

Chapter 10
Suspension and steering

Contents

Degrees of difficulty

Easy, suitable for novice with little experience	**Fairly easy,** suitable for beginner with some experience	**Fairly difficult,** suitable for competent DIY mechanic	**Difficult,** suitable for experienced DIY mechanic	**Very difficult,** suitable for expert DIY or professional

Specifications

Wheel alignment and steering angles (vehicle unladen with 5 litres of fuel)

Front wheels:

Toe setting:

Short wheelbase Combi van	-0°09' ± 0°09'
All other models	-0°17' ± 0°09'

Camber:

Combi models	0° ± 0°30'
Van models	0°05' ± 0°30'

Castor:

Combi models:

Short wheel base	+3°34' ± 0°30'
Long wheel base	+3°39' ± 30'

Van models:

Short wheel base	+4°15' ± 0°30'
Long wheel base	+4°18' ± 0°30'

Rear wheels:

Tracking (toe setting):

Combi models:

Short wheel base	0° 39' ± 0°09'
Long wheel base	0° 39' ± 0°09'

Van models:

Short wheel base	0°48' ± 0°09'
Long wheel base	0° 50' ± 0°09'

Roadwheels

Type	Pressed-steel or aluminium alloy (depending on model)
Tyre pressures	See *Lubricants, fluids and tyre pressures*

Torque wrench settings

	Nm	lbf ft
Front suspension		
Anti-roll bar:		
Connecting link nuts*	90	66
Mounting clamp bolts.	105	77
Driveshaft retaining nut	345	255
Hub carrier-to-strut*	92	68
Lower arm-to-subframe:		
Rear bolt	105	77
Front bolts	125	92
Lower balljoint clamp bolt	65	48
Subframe mounting bolts.	107	79
Suspension strut:		
Piston rod nut*	35	26
Strut mounting plate-to-body bolts	33	24
Trackrod end-to-hub carrier nut.	25	18
*Do not re-use		
Rear suspension		
Panhard bar:		
Nut	130	96
Bolt	85	63
Rear axle-to-mounting bracket bolts	196	145
Rear hub-to-axle bolts	127	94
Shock absorber bolts.	90	66
Steering		
High-pressure pipe-to-steering rack retaining bolt	20	15
High-pressure union on power steering pump.	20	15
High-pressure union on steering rack/ram.	10	7
Power steering pump mounting bolts:		
1.6 litre models	22	16
2.0 litre models	N/A	N/A
Steering column mounting bolts	22	16
Steering column universal joints pinch bolt	25	18
Steering rack mounting bolts.	160	118
Steering rack mounting stud	10	7
Steering wheel retaining bolt	20	15
Track rod:		
Balljoint-to-hub carrier nut*	57	42
*Do not re-use		
Roadwheels		
Wheel bolts.	100	74

1 General Information

1 The independent front suspension is of the MacPherson strut type, incorporating coil springs and integral telescopic shock absorbers. The MacPherson struts are located by transverse lower suspension arms, which utilise rubber inner mounting bushes. The front hub carriers, which carry the wheel bearings, the brake calipers and the hub/disc assemblies, are bolted to the MacPherson struts, and connected to the lower arms via balljoints. A front anti-roll bar is fitted to all models. The anti-roll bar is rubber-mounted onto the subframe, and is connected to the front suspension struts by link rods.
2 The rear suspension has separate telescopic shock absorbers and coil springs fitted between the beam axle and the vehicle body. The rear beam axle pivots around rubber bushes that are bolted to the front crossmember. To control body roll a Panhard rod is fitted between the vehicle body and the rear beam axle.
3 The steering column has a universal joint fitted to its lower end, which is connected to the steering rack pinion by means of a clamp bolt.
4 The steering rack is mounted onto the front subframe, and is connected by two track rods, with balljoints at their outer ends, to the steering arms projecting rearwards from the hub carriers. The track rod ends are threaded, to facilitate adjustment.
5 A variable power steering system is fitted. The hydraulic pump alters the hydraulic pressure supplied to the steering rack to suit all conditions, ie, supplies high pressure when the vehicle is being driven slowly/parked and lower pressure when the vehicle is being driven at speed. The hydraulic steering system is powered by an electrically operated pump, which is controlled by the engine management module (ECM) on 2.0 litre models, and by a traditional belt driven pump on 1.6 litre models.

2 Front hub carrier assembly
  – removal and refitting

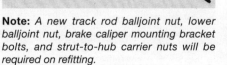

Note: *A new track rod balljoint nut, lower balljoint nut, brake caliper mounting bracket bolts, and strut-to-hub carrier nuts will be required on refitting.*

Removal

1 Remove the wheel trim/hub cap (as applicable) then withdraw the R-clip and remove the locking cap from the driveshaft

2.1 Prise out the R-clip, remove the locking collar and slacken the driveshaft nut

2.4 Using a fabricated tool to hold the front hub stationary whilst the driveshaft nut is slackened.

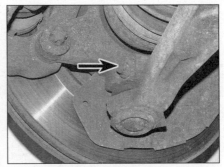

2.7 Remove the clamp bolt

retaining nut. Slacken the driveshaft nut with the vehicle resting on its wheels **(see illustration)**. Also slacken the wheel bolts.

2 Chock the rear wheels of the car, firmly apply the handbrake, and then jack up the front of the car and support it on axle stands (see *Jacking and vehicle support*). Remove the appropriate front roadwheel.

3 Unbolt the wheel sensor and position it clear of the hub assembly (see Chapter 9, Section 21). Note that there is no need to disconnect the wiring.

4 Slacken and remove the driveshaft retaining nut. If the nut was not slackened with the wheels on the ground (see paragraph 1), withdraw the R-clip and remove the locking cap. Refit at least two roadwheel bolts to the front hub, tightening them securely, then have an assistant firmly depress the brake pedal to prevent the front hub from rotating whilst you slacken and remove the driveshaft retaining nut. Alternatively, a tool can be fabricated to hold the hub stationary **(see illustration)**.

5 Slacken and remove the nut securing the steering rack track rod to the hub carrier then free the balljoint from the hub. If the balljoint is tight, use a universal balljoint separator to free it. Discard the nut; a new one should be used on refitting.

6 If the hub bearings are to be disturbed, remove the brake disc as described in Chapter 9, Section 7. If not, unscrew the two bolts securing the brake caliper mounting bracket assembly to the hub carrier, and slide the caliper assembly off the disc. Using a piece of wire or string, tie the caliper to the front suspension coil spring, to avoid placing any strain on the hydraulic brake hose.

7 Slacken and remove the clamp bolt, and free the balljoint shank from the hub carrier. If necessary, use a chisel to slightly spread the clamp, and plenty of releasing fluid **(see illustration)**.

8 Use a long bar to lever down the lower arm, and withdraw the balljoint from the hub carrier.

9 Undo the retaining nuts and withdraw the hub carrier-to-suspension strut bolts, noting that the bolts are inserted from the rear of the vehicle **(see illustration 4.6)**.

10 Free the hub carrier assembly from the

end of the strut, then release it from the outer constant velocity joint splines, and remove it from the vehicle. Suspend the driveshaft by string from the suspension strut to prevent any damage to the constant velocity joints.

Refitting

11 Ensure that the driveshaft outer constant velocity joint and hub splines are clean, and then slide the hub fully onto the driveshaft splines.

12 Slide the hub assembly fully into the suspension strut bracket and insert the bolts from the rear and fit the retaining nuts at the front.

13 Align the balljoint with the hub carrier, insert the bolt and tighten it to the specified torque.

14 Engage the track rod balljoint in the hub carrier, then fit the new retaining nut and tighten it to the specified torque.

15 Where necessary, refit the brake disc to the hub, referring to Chapter 9, Section 7 for further information. Slide the caliper into position, making sure the pads pass either side of the disc, and tighten the new caliper bracket bolts to the specified torque setting.

16 Refit the wheel sensor as described in Chapter 9, Section 21.

17 Lubricate the inner face and threads of the driveshaft retaining nut with clean engine oil, and refit it to the end of the driveshaft. Use the method employed on removal to

3.2 Press the hub flange from the bearing

prevent the hub from rotating (see paragraph 4), and tighten the driveshaft retaining nut to the specified torque. Check that the hub rotates freely then engage the locking cap with the driveshaft nut, so that one of its cut-outs is aligned with the driveshaft hole, and secure the cap in position with the R-clip. Alternatively, lightly tighten the nut at this stage and tighten it to the specified torque once the vehicle is resting on its wheels again.

18 Refit the roadwheel, then lower the vehicle to the ground and tighten the roadwheel bolts to the specified torque. If not already done, tighten the driveshaft retaining nut to the specified torque then refit the locking cap, aligning its cut-outs with the driveshaft hole, and secure it in position with the R-clip.

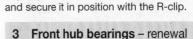

3 Front hub bearings – renewal

Note: *The bearing is a sealed, pre-adjusted and pre-lubricated, double-row roller type, and is intended to last the car's entire service life without maintenance or attention. Never overtighten the driveshaft nut beyond the specified torque wrench setting in an attempt to 'adjust' the bearing.*

Note: *A press will be required to dismantle and rebuild the assembly; if such a tool is not available, a large bench vice and spacers (such as large sockets) will serve as an adequate substitute. The bearing's inner races are an interference fit on the hub; if the inner race remains on the hub when it is pressed out of the hub carrier, a knife-edged bearing puller will be required to remove it. A new bearing retaining circlip must be used on refitting.*

1 Remove the hub carrier assembly as described in Section 2.

2 Support the hub carrier securely on blocks or in a vice. Using a tubular spacer, which bears only on the inner end of the hub flange, press the hub flange out of the bearing **(see illustration)**. If the bearing's outboard inner race remains on the hub, remove it using a bearing puller (see note above).

3 Extract the bearing retaining circlip from

3.3 Extract the circlip from the inner side of the hub carrier

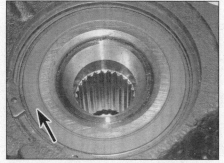

3.7 Take great care not to damage the seal in the bearing – it contains the encoder for the wheel speed sensor

3.8 Position the ends of the circlip either side of the ABS wheel speed sensor

the inner end of the hub carrier assembly **(see illustration)**.

4 Where necessary, refit the inner race back in position over the ball cage, and securely support the inner face of the hub carrier. Using a tubular spacer, which bears only on the inner race, press the complete bearing assembly out of the hub carrier.

5 Thoroughly clean the hub and hub carrier, removing all traces of dirt and grease, and polish away any burrs or raised edges that might hinder reassembly. Check both for cracks or any other signs of wear or damage, and renew them if necessary. Renew the circlip, regardless of its apparent condition.

6 On reassembly, apply a light film of oil (Peugeot/Citroën/Fiat recommend Molykote 321R) to the bearing outer race and hub flange shaft, to aid installation of the bearing.

7 Securely support the hub carrier, and locate

the bearing in the hub. Press the bearing fully into position, ensuring that it enters the hub squarely, using a tubular spacer which bears only on the bearing outer race. Note that the bearing is equipped with a magnetic encoder on its inboard face. When fitting the bearing, ensure this face is inboard adjacent to the ABS wheel speed sensor **(see illustration)**. Take care not to damage this encoder, or place it adjacent to a magnetic source. Ensure the encoder face is clean.

8 Once the bearing is correctly seated, secure the bearing in position with the new circlip, ensuring that it is correctly located in the groove in the hub carrier. Align the gap between the ends of the circlip with the gap for the ABS wheel speed sensor **(see illustration)**.

9 Securely support the outer face of the hub flange, and locate the hub carrier bearing

inner race over the end of the hub flange. Press the bearing onto the hub, using a tubular spacer that bears only on the inner race of the hub bearing, until it seats against the hub shoulder. Check that the hub flange rotates freely, and wipe off any excess oil or grease.

10 Refit the hub carrier assembly as described in Section 2.

4 Front strut – removal and refitting

Note: *Always renew any self-locking nuts when working on the suspension/steering components.*

Removal

1 Chock the rear wheels, apply the handbrake, slacken the appropriate front roadwheel bolts, then jack up the front of the car and support on axle stands (see *Jacking and vehicle support*). Remove the appropriate roadwheel.

2 Unscrew the nut securing the anti-roll bar connecting link to the strut **(see illustration)**. Position the link clear of the strut; if necessary, retain the balljoint shank with a Torx bit to prevent rotation whilst the nut is slackened. Refer to Section 8 for further information; discard the nut, a new one should be used on refitting.

3 Undo the bolt securing the flexible brake hose to the strut.

4 Unclip the wheel speed sensor wiring from the bracket on the suspension strut **(see illustration)**.

5 Unclip the front brake pad wear sensor wiring from the strut.

6 Undo the bolts and pull the hub carrier away from the lower end of the strut **(see illustration)**, prevent the hub carrier assembly dropping whilst the strut is removed by supporting the lower arm.

7 Working in the wheelarch, slacken and remove the strut upper mounting bolts. Support the strut, whilst removing the upper mounting bolts, then withdraw it from under the wheel arch **(see illustration)**.

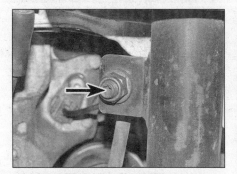

4.2 Use a Torx bit in the balljoint shaft to prevent rotation

4.4 Unclip the speed sensor and pad wear sensor wiring

4.6 Remove the strut-to-hub carrier bolts – noting their fitted position

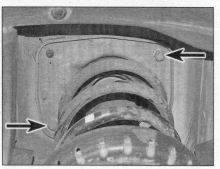

4.7 Remove the strut upper mounting bolts

Caution: As soon as the upper mounting bolts are removed, the strut will be unsupported.

Refitting

8 Manoeuvre the strut assembly into position, ensuring that the upper mounting plate correctly aligned with the corresponding hole in the inner wing. Fit the upper mounting bolts and tighten them to the specified torque.

9 Engage the lower end of the strut with the hub carrier, insert the bolts from the rear and fit the retaining nuts. Tighten the nuts/bolts to the specified torque.

10 The remainder of refitting is a reversal of removal.

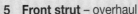 

5 Front strut – overhaul

Warning: Before attempting to dismantle the front suspension strut, a suitable tool to hold the coil spring in compression must be obtained. Adjustable coil spring compressors are readily available, and are recommended for this operation. Any attempt to dismantle the strut without such a tool is likely to result in damage or personal injury.

Note: *Always renew any self-locking nuts when working on the suspension/steering components.*

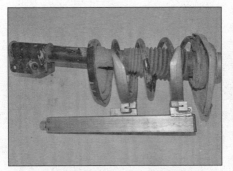

5.1 Compress the spring until all tension is relieved from the spring seats

5.2 Use an Allen key/bit to hold the piston rod whilst slackening the nut

1 With the strut removed from the car (as described in Section 4), clean away all external dirt. Fit the spring compressor and compress the coil spring until tension is relieved from the spring seats **(see illustration)**.

2 Slacken the piston rod nut whilst retaining the shock absorber piston with a suitable Allen key **(see illustration)**.

3 Remove the nut then lift off the spacer, followed by the upper mounting plate, thrust bearing and spring seat **(see illustrations)**.

4 Lift off the coil spring and remove the dust gaiter and rubber bump stop from the shock absorber piston **(see illustrations)**.

5 Examine the shock absorber for signs of fluid leakage. Check the piston for signs of pitting along its entire length, and check the shock body for signs of damage. While holding it in an upright position, test the

operation of the shock absorber by moving the piston through a full stroke, and then through short strokes of 50 to 100 mm. In both cases, the resistance felt should be smooth and continuous. If the resistance is jerky, or uneven, or if there is any visible sign of wear or damage to the shock absorber, renewal is necessary.

6 Inspect all other components for signs of damage or deterioration, and renew any that are suspect.

7 Slide the rubber bump stop onto the piston. Fit the dust gaiter and cap, making sure the lower end of gaiter is correctly positioned over the shock absorber end.

8 Refit the coil spring; making sure its lower end is correctly seated against the spring seat stop. Fit the upper spring seat, aligning its stop with the spring end, then the thrust

5.3a Remove the piston nut...

5.3b ...spacer...

5.3c ...upper mounting plate...

5.3d ...and thrust bearing/spring seat

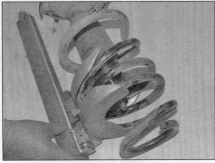

5.4a Remove the coil spring...

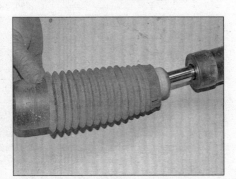

5.4b ...followed by the gaiter and bump stop

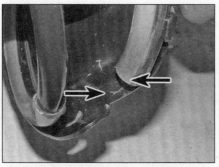

5.8a Align the ends of the coil spring with the 'stop' in the lower seat...

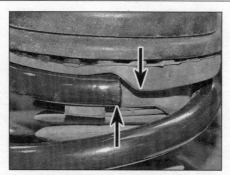

5.8b ...and the upper seat

bearing followed by the upper mounting plate **(see illustrations)**.

9 Refit the spacer and fit the new nut. Retain the shock absorber piston and tighten the piston rod nut to the specified torque.

10 With the nut securely tightened, refit the plastic cap, and gradually release the spring compressors.

6 Front lower arm – removal, overhaul and refitting

Note: *Always renew any self-locking nuts when working on the suspension/steering components.*

Removal

1 Slacken the appropriate front wheel bolts, raise the front of the vehicle and support it

securely on axle stands (see *Jacking and vehicle support*). Remove the roadwheel.

2 Release the fasteners and remove the relevant front wheelarch liner.

3 Slacken and remove the clamp bolt, then free the lower balljoint shank from the hub carrier **(see illustration 2.7)**. Liberally apply releasing fluid, and if necessary, slightly spread the clamp by inserting a wedge (chisel etc.) into the clamp slot.

4 Slacken and remove the lower arm front pivot bolts **(see illustration)**.

5 Slacken the bolts both sides securing the front anti-roll bar to the subframe (see Section 7). On the side having the lower arm removed, completely remove the anti-roll bar mounting bolts to provide sufficient clearance

6 Slacken and remove the rear pivot bolt **(see illustration)**.

7 Manoeuvre the lower arm assembly out from underneath the vehicle.

Overhaul

8 Thoroughly clean the lower arm and the area around the arm mountings, removing all traces of dirt and underseal if necessary, then check carefully for cracks, distortion or any other signs of wear or damage, paying particular attention to the pivot bushes, and renew components as necessary.

9 It would appear that replacement balljoint and bushes are not available. If the balljoint or the bushes are damaged/deteriorated, the complete lower arm assembly must be renewed. Check for parts availability at a Citroen/Peugeot/Toyota dealer or parts specialist.

Refitting

10 Manoeuvre the lower arm assembly into position, and refit the rear pivot bolt, tightening it to the specified torque.

11 Refit the front pivot bolts, and then tighten them to the specified torque.

12 Locate the balljoint shank in the hub carrier, then insert the clamp bolt and tighten it to the specified torque.

13 Refit the front anti-roll bar mounting bolts and tighten them to the specified torque.

14 Refit the wheelarch liner

15 Refit the roadwheel, then lower the vehicle and tighten the roadwheel bolts to the specified torque.

16 Check and, if necessary, adjust the front wheel alignment as described in Section 23.

7 Front anti-roll bar – removal and refitting

Note: *Always renew any self-locking nuts when working on the suspension/steering components.*

Removal

1 Slacken the front roadwheels bolts, raise the front of the vehicle and support it securely on axle stands (see *Jacking and vehicle support*). Remove the roadwheels, then undo the fasteners and remove the engine undershield (where fitted).

2 Unscrew the 4 bolts securing the anti-roll bar mountings to the subframe **(see illustration)**.

3 Lower the front subframe as described in Section 9. There's no need to detach the lower arms, steering rack or the rear engine mounting from the subframe. Lower it sufficiently to obtain the necessary clearance.

4 Slacken and remove the nuts securing the left- and right-hand connecting links to the anti-roll bar **(see illustration)**, and position the links clear of the bar. If necessary, retain the balljoint shank with a Torx bit to prevent rotation whilst the nut is slackened. Refer to Section 8 for further information; discard the nut, a new one should be used on refitting.

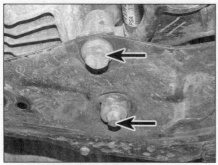

6.4 Remove the front pivot bolts

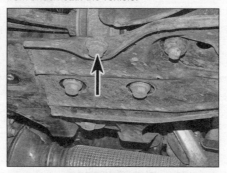

6.6 Rear pivot bolt

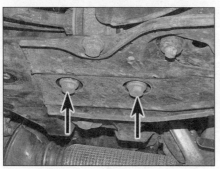

7.2 Remove the anti-roll bar mounting bolts each side

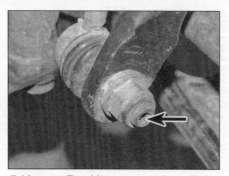

7.4 Insert a Torx bit to prevent the balljoint shank from rotating

5 Manoeuvre the anti-roll bar out from underneath the vehicle, and remove the mounting bushes from the bar.

6 Carefully examine the anti-roll bar components for signs of wear, damage or deterioration, paying particular attention to the mounting bushes. Renew worn components as necessary, noting the fitted position of the bushes if they are removed.

Refitting

7 Offer up the anti-roll bar, and manoeuvre it into position on the subframe. Refit the mounting bolts and tighten them to the specified torque.

8 The remainder of refitting is a reversal of removal.

8 Front anti-roll bar connecting link – removal and refitting

Note: New connecting link nuts will be required on refitting.

Removal

1 Chock the rear wheels, firmly apply the handbrake, slacken the relevant roadwheel bolts, then jack up the front of the vehicle and support on axle stands (see *Jacking and vehicle support*). Remove the relevant roadwheel.

2 Undo the upper balljoint where it secures to the suspension strut **(see illustration 4.2)**. If necessary, retain the balljoint shank with a Torx bit to prevent rotation whilst each nut is slackened.

3 Undo the lower balljoint where it secures to the end of the anti-roll bar. if necessary, retain the balljoint shank with a Torx bit to prevent rotation whilst each nut is slackened **(see illustration 7.4)**.

4 Inspect the link for signs of wear or damage and renew if necessary.

Refitting

5 Refitting is the reverse of removal, using new nuts and tightening them to the specified torque setting.

9 Front subframe – removal and refitting

Note: Always renew any self-locking nuts when working on the suspension/steering components.

Removal

1 Chock the rear wheels, firmly apply the handbrake, slacken the front roadwheel bolts, and then jack up the front of the vehicle and support it on axle stands (see *Jacking and vehicle support*). Remove both front roadwheels.

2 Release the fasteners and remove both wheelarch liners.

9.6 Undo the radiator crossmember bolts each side

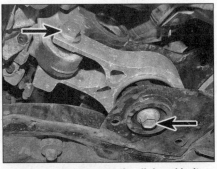
9.7 Rear engine mounting link rod bolts

3 Remove the front bumper as described in Chapter 11 Section 6.

4 Unclip the wiring harness from the radiator lower crossmember.

5 Undo the bolt securing the air conditioning refrigerant pipe (where applicable) to the lower crossmember.

6 Undo the 2 retaining bolts each side, and remove the radiator lower crossmember **(see illustration)**.

7 Slacken and remove the engine/transmission rear lower mounting bolt, then undo the bolt securing the link rod to the subframe and remove the link **(see illustration)**.

8 Undo the lower bolt securing the support rod between the subframe and vehicle body each side **(see illustration)**.

9 Where applicable, undo the bolt securing the power steering pipe support bracket to the subframe.

10 Slacken and remove the left-hand lower balljoint clamp bolt and free the balljoint shank from the hub carrier (refer to Section 6). Repeat the procedure on the right-hand side.

11 Slacken and remove the steering rack mounting bolts **(see illustration 18.5)**.

12 Undo the bolts securing the front anti-roll bar mountings to the subframe, and the lower ends of the link rods to the anti-roll bar (see Section 7).

13 Release the clamp and detach the front exhaust pipe from the catalytic converter/particulate filter beneath the engine.

14 Undo the bolts securing the exhaust pipe centre front mounting (where applicable).

15 Make a final check that all control cables/hoses that are attached to the subframe have been released and positioned clear so that they will not hinder the removal procedure.

16 Place a jack and a suitable block of wood under the subframe to support the subframe as it is lowered.

17 Slacken and remove the subframe mounting bolts then carefully lower the subframe assembly out of position and remove it from underneath the vehicle, taking great care to ensure that the subframe assembly does not catch the power steering pipes as it is lowered out of position **(see illustration)**.

Refitting

18 Refitting is a reversal of the removal procedure, noting the following points:

a) Tighten all nuts and bolts to the specified torque settings (where given).

b) On completion check and, if necessary, adjust the front wheel alignment as described in Section 23.

10 Rear hub and bearings – checking and renewal

Note: The bearing is a sealed, pre-adjusted and pre-lubricated, double-row ball type, and is intended to last the car's entire service life without maintenance or attention. The bearings are integral with the hub assembly, and should be renewed as a complete unit.

9.8 Support rod lower bolt

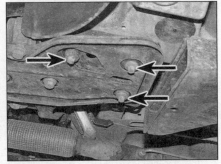
9.17 Subframe rear mounting bolts

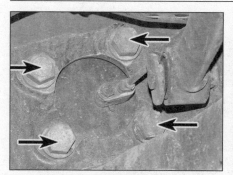

10.5 Rear hub retaining bolts

11.3 Raise the jack and slightly compress the spring

11.4 Rear shock absorber mounting bolts

Checking

1 Wear in the rear hub bearings can be checked for as described in Chapter 1 Section 8. However, the most common first symptom of bearing wear is a rumbling noise, noted at a particular roadspeed, or when the offending wheel is loaded-up during cornering. In this case, besides rocking the wheel, spin it and listen carefully to distinguish between the sound of the brake pads rubbing the disc, and the rumble of bearing wear. Compare the sound with the other rear wheel to confirm.

2 Wheel bearings do not have to be renewed in pairs. However, if the bearing on one side has worn, it may only be a short while before the other one needs renewal.

Removal

3 Remove the rear brake disc as described in Chapter 9, Section 8.

4 Undo the bolt and withdraw the wheel speed sensor from the inboard face of the hub (Chapter 9 Section 21).

5 Undo the 4 bolts securing the bearing/hub assembly, and detach it from the axle **(see illustration)**.

Refitting

6 Manoeuvre the bearing/hub assembly into position, and tighten the retaining nuts to the specified torque.

7 The remainder of refitting is a reversal of removal.

---

11 Rear shock absorber –
removal, testing and refitting

Note: *Always renew any self-locking nuts when working on the suspension/steering components.*

Removal

1 Chock the front wheels, slacken the relevant rear roadwheel bolts, and then jack up the rear of the vehicle and support it on axle stands (see *Jacking and vehicle support*). Remove the relevant rear roadwheel.

2 Undo the fasteners and remove the relevant rear wheelarch liner.

3 Using a trolley jack positioned under

the axle, raise the lower arm until the rear suspension coil spring is slightly compressed **(see illustration)**.

Caution: DO NOT lower the jack with the shock absorber removed, as the spring may come away from between the axle and vehicle body.

4 Undo the upper and lower mounting bolts, then manoeuvre the shock absorber from place **(see illustration)**.

Testing

5 Examine the shock absorber for signs of fluid leakage or damage. Test the operation of the shock absorber, while holding it in an upright position, by moving the piston through a full stroke and then through short strokes of 50 to 100 mm. In both cases, the resistance felt should be smooth and continuous. If the resistance is jerky, or uneven, or if there is any visible sign of wear or damage, renewal is necessary. Also check the rubber mountings for damage and deterioration. Renew worn components as necessary. Inspect the shank of the mounting bolt for signs of wear or damage, and renew as necessary. The self-locking nuts should be renewed as a matter of course.

Refitting

6 Prior to refitting the shock absorber, mount it upright in the vice, and operate it fully through several strokes in order to prime it.

7 Manoeuvre the shock absorber into position, then insert the upper and lower mounting bolts and tighten them to the specified torque.

8 The remainder of refitting is a reversal of removal.

---

12 Rear coil spring –
removal and refitting

Note: *Always renew any self-locking nuts when working on the suspension/steering components.*

Removal

1 Chock the front wheels, slacken the rear roadwheel bolts, and then jack up the rear of the vehicle and support it on axle stands (see

Jacking and vehicle support). Remove the rear roadwheels.

2 Position a trolley jack underneath one of the lower arms of the rear axle **(see illustration 11.3)**, and then raise the arm until the rear suspension coil spring one that side is slightly compressed.

3 Unscrew and remove the shock absorber lower mounting bolt **(see illustrations 11.4)**.

4 Slowly lower the jack as far as the lower arm will go, and remove the jack. At this point (unless the spring is broken) the spring should still stay in place between the axle and the vehicle body.

5 Now position the jack under the lower arm of the rear axle on the other side of the vehicle. Raise the arm until the coil spring on that side is slightly compressed. then slacken and remove the shock absorber lower mounting bolt.

Caution: Check that there is no stress applied to any of the brake cables or hoses, as the axle is fully lowered.

6 Slowly lower the jack until all tension in the both springs are released, then remove the springs. Note the fitted position of the upper spring seat before removal.

7 Inspect the coil spring and its upper and lower seats for signs of wear or damage, then renew if necessary.

Refitting

8 Fit the upper rubber seat on to the mounting **(see illustration)**.

9 Manoeuvre the springs into position and carefully raise one lower arm with the jack, ensuring that the lower end of the coil spring

12.8 Refit the upper spring seat

12.9 Align the end of the spring with the 'stop' on the seat

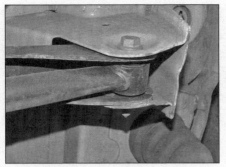

13.4a Remove the Panhard bar upper bolt…

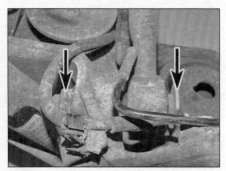

13.4b …and the bolt/nut securing it to the axle

locates correctly **(see illustration)**. Align the shock absorber with the lower arm and refit its mounting bolt. Tighten the bolt to the specified torque.

10 Remove the jack from underneath the lower arm, and position it under the rear axle lower arm on the remaining side. Raise the jack once again and align the lower mounting of the shock absorber with the arm. Insert the bolt, and tighten it to the specified torque.

11 Refit the rear roadwheel then lower the vehicle to the ground and tighten the wheel bolts to the specified torque.

13 Panhard bar – removal and refitting

Note: *Always renew any self-locking nuts when working on the suspension/steering components.*

Removal

1 Chock the front wheels, slacken the relevant rear roadwheel bolts, and then jack up the rear of the vehicle and support it on axle stands (see *Jacking and vehicle support*). Remove the relevant roadwheel.

2 Position a trolley jack under the centre of the rear axle, and raise the jack until the coil springs are slightly compressed.

3 Unscrew and remove the left-hand shock absorber lower mounting bolt **(see illustrations 12.5)**.

4 Undo the bolt at the upper end, and the nut at the lower end of the Panhard bar, then

withdraw the bar from under the vehicle **(see illustrations)**.

Refitting

5 Refitting is a reversal of removal. Tighten all fasteners to their specified torque where given.

14 Rear beam axle – removal, overhaul and refitting

Note: *Always renew any self-locking nuts when working on the suspension/steering components.*

Removal

1 Disconnect the battery negative lead as described in Chapter 5A Section 4.

2 Working as described in Section 11, remove the shock absorber lower mounting bolt each side.

3 Trace the ABS wheel speed sensors wiring back to the connectors, and unplug then. Free the sensor harness from any retaining clips on the axle **(see illustration)**.

4 Clamp the flexible brake hose, and undo the hose union where the flexible hose connects to the rigid hose. Plug the end of the hose/pipe to prevent dirt ingress. Repeat this procedure on the remaining side.

5 Release the handbrake cables from the retaining clips along the axle, then release the ends of the cables from the caliper levers and support brackets or brake shoes as applicable (see Chapter 9). Repeat the procedure on the remaining side.

6 Remove the upper bolt securing the Panhard rod to the vehicle body **(see illustration 13.4a)**.

7 Enlist the help of an assistant, then undo the bolt each side securing the axle to the vehicle body. With both bolts removed, lower the axle to the floor **(see illustration)**.

Overhaul

8 Thoroughly clean the axle and the area around the axle mountings, removing all traces of dirt and underseal if necessary, then check carefully for cracks, distortion or any other signs of wear or damage, paying particular attention to the pivot bushes.

9 Renewal of the pivot bushes will require the use of a hydraulic press and several spacers, and should therefore be entrusted to a specialist with access to the necessary equipment.

Refitting

10 Offer up the axle and mounting brackets, and insert the retaining bolts. Do not tighten them at this stage.

11 Insert the shock absorber lower mounting bolt each side. Do not tighten them at this stage.

12 With a trolley jack positioned under the centre of the rear axle, raise the axle until the distance between the shock asbsorber mounting bolts is as follows:

| Non-self leveling suspension | 334 mm |
| Self-levelling suspension | 346 mm |

13 Now tighten the axle mounting bolts to the specified torque.

14 Refit the Panhard bar and tighten the retaining nut/bolt to the specified torque.

15 Tighten the shock absorber lower mounting bolts to the specified torque.

16 The remainder of refitting is a reversal of removal, noting the following points:

a) *Bleed the brake hydraulic system as described in Chapter 9 Section 2.*

b) *Reconnect the battery negative lead as described in Chapter 5A Section 4.*

c) *Tighten all fasteners to their specified torque where given.*

14.3 Unclip the wiring harness from the axle

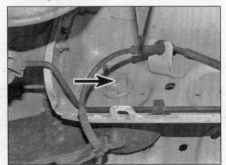

14.7 Undo the axle retaining bolt each side

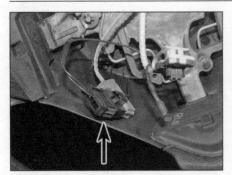

15.2 Disconnect the wiring plug, leaving the airbag wiring in place

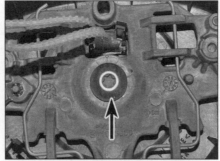

15.3a Undo the steering wheel retaining bolt …

15.3b … noting the master spline location

15 Steering wheel – removal and refitting

Warning: Refer to the precautions given in Chapter 12 Section 20 before proceeding.

Removal

1 Remove the airbag unit as described in Chapter 12 Section 21.

2 Disconnect the wiring plug from the steering wheel **(see illustration)**.

3 Slacken and remove the steering wheel retaining Torx bolt. Note the column shaft has a master spline. The wheel will only fit correctly in one position refitting **(see illustrations)**.

4 Withdraw the steering wheel assembly off the top of the steering column. As the steering wheel is removed, withdraw the wiring through the aperture in the top of the steering wheel.

16.3 Release the clips and slide the transponder from place

16.7a Undo the 2 bolts at the top of the column…

Refitting

5 Prior to refitting the steering wheel, ensure that the front wheels are still in the straight-ahead position.

6 Refitting is a reversal of removal, noting the following points:

a) *On refitting, align the master spline or the marks made on removal, taking great care not to damage the wiring loom, then tighten the retaining bolt to the specified torque.*

b) *On completion, refit the airbag unit as described in Chapter 12 Section 21.*

16 Steering column – removal, inspection and refitting

Note: As all models are equipped with a driver's airbag, refer to the precautions given in Chapter 12 Section 20 before proceeding.

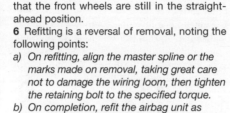

16.4 Unscrew the universal joint pinch bolt

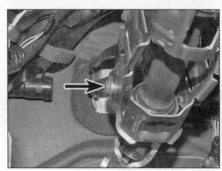

16.7b and the single lower bolt

Note: A new pinch-bolt nut will be needed on refitting.

Removal

1 Remove the steering wheel as described in Section 15.

2 Move the driver's seat as far back as possible.

3 Release the clips, disconnect the wiring plug and remove the transponder aerial from the ignition switch **(see illustration)**.

4 Working in the driver's footwell, undo and remove the pinch-bolt/nut from the universal joint at the base of the column **(see illustration)**. Note that the when refitting, the joint will only locate correctly in one position on the shaft.

5 Remove the combination switches from the top of the steering column as described in Chapter 12 Section 5.

6 Note their fitted positions, then disconnect any remaining wiring plugs from the column and, release the wiring loom from any retaining clips.

7 Slacken and remove the 2 mounting bolts from the top of the column, and the single lower bolt **(see illustrations)**. Slide the column assembly upwards and free from the lower shaft, and remove it from the vehicle.

Inspection

8 Before refitting the steering column, examine the column and mountings for signs of damage and deformation, and renew as necessary. Check the steering shaft for signs of free play in the column bushes, and check the universal joints for signs of damage or roughness in the joint bearings. If any damage or wear is found on the steering column universal joint or shaft bushes, the column must be renewed as an assembly.

Refitting

9 Align the marks made prior to removal and engage the column universal joint with the lower shaft.

10 Slide the column assembly into position making sure its mounting bracket is correctly engaged with the facia bracket. Refit the column mounting bolts and tighten them to the specified torque setting.

11 Refit the universal joint pinch-bolt, tighten it to the specified torque setting.

17.4 Disconnect the ignition switch wiring plug

17.5a Drill out the centre of the shear bolt ...

17.5b ... and use an extractor to remove the bolt

12 The remainder of refitting is a reversal of the removal procedure, noting the following.

a) Ensure that all wiring is correctly routed and retained by all the necessary clips and ties.

b) Refit the steering wheel as described in Section 15.

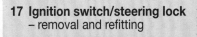

17 Ignition switch/steering lock – removal and refitting

Removal

1 Disconnect the battery negative lead as described in Chapter 5A Section 4.

2 Remove the steering column shrouds as described in Chapter 11 Section 27.

3 Carefully lift the two plastic retaining clips and withdraw the transponder immobiliser unit to release it from the ignition switch housing **(see illustration 16.3)**. Take care not to damage the transponder assembly.

4 Release the securing clip and disconnect the wiring plug from the rear of the ignition switch **(see illustration)**.

5 Use a centre punch to mark the centre of the lock housing retaining screw (shear bolt), then using a drill and an extractor, remove the screw **(see illustrations)**. Obviously, a new screw will be required for refitting. **Note:** It may be possible to use a hacksaw to cut a slot in the head of the bolt, and then use a large flat screwdriver to remove the old bolt.

6 Insert the key into the steering lock and turn it to the first position, and then using a small screwdriver, depress the locating peg and slide the ignition switch from the steering column housing **(see illustration)**.

Refitting

7 Refitting is a reversal of removal, noting the following points:

a) Ensure all wiring is correctly routed, and securely clipped back into its original positions.

b) Refit the steering lock housing with a new retaining/shear bolt **(see illustration)**

c) Tighten the bolt until the head shears off, leaving the threaded part securing the lock.

17.6 Depress the locating peg

17.7 Fit the new shear bolt – tighten until the head shears off

18 Steering rack assembly – removal, overhaul and refitting

Note: Always renew any self-locking nuts when working on the suspension/steering components.

Removal

1 Firmly apply the handbrake, slacken the front roadwheel bolts, and then jack up the front of the vehicle and support it on axle stands (see Jacking and vehicle support). Remove both front roadwheels.

2 Slacken and remove the nuts securing the steering rack track rod balljoints to the hub

carriers. Release the balljoint tapered shanks using a universal balljoint separator, see Section 22. Discard the nuts; new ones will be needed on refitting.

3 Unclip the metal cover, then clean the area around the rack pinion housing, then undo the bolts securing the fluid pipes to the rack pinion housing **(see illustrations)**, release the pipes from the retaining clamp, and drain the fluid into a container. To completely drain system, remove fluid reservoir cap and turn the steering wheel from lock-to-lock to assist the draining process; remember to recentre the steering wheel afterwards. Discard the pipes O-ring seals, new ones must be fitted. Plug the ends of the pipes to prevent dirt ingress.

4 Slacken and remove the universal joint

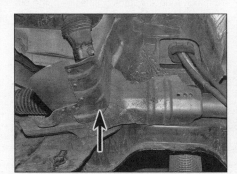

18.3a Pull the metal cover upwards to release the clips (engine removed for clarity)

18.3b Undo the bolt(s) securing the fluid pipes

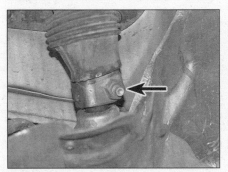

18.4 Remove the universal joint pinch bolt

18.5 Steering rack mounting bolts

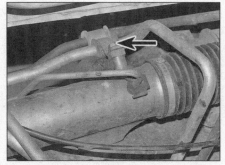

18.7 Undo the bolt securing the pipes bracket

pinch-bolt **(see illustration)**. The joint will only fit onto the rack pinion in one position.
5 Working underneath the vehicle, undo the remove the rack mounting bolts **(see illustration)**.
6 Remove the mounting half-washers.
7 Undo the bolt securing the steering rack pipes bracket to the subframe **(see illustration)**.
8 Free the steering rack pinion from the column universal joint and manoeuvre it out through the driver's side wheel arch aperture.

Overhaul

9 Examine the steering rack assembly for signs of wear or damage, and check that the rack moves freely throughout the full length of its travel, with no signs of roughness or excessive free play between the steering rack pinion and rack. Inspect all the steering rack fluid unions for signs of leakage, and check that all union nuts are securely tightened.
10 It is possible to overhaul the steering rack assembly housing components, but this task should be entrusted to a Peugeot/Citroën/Fiat dealer or specialist. The only components that can be renewed easily by the home mechanic are the steering rack gaiters, the track rod balljoints and the track rods, which are covered elsewhere in this Chapter.

Refitting

11 Manoeuvre the steering rack into position and engage it with the column universal joint, aligning the marks made prior to removal.
12 The remainder of refitting is a reversal of removal, noting the following points:
a) *Top-up the fluid reservoir and bleed the hydraulic system as described in Section 20.*
b) *On completion check and, if necessary, adjust the front wheel alignment as described in Section 23.*

19 Steering rack rubber gaiters – renewal

1 Remove the track rod balljoint as described in Section 22.
2 Mark the correct fitted position of the gaiter on the track rod, then release the retaining clips and slide the gaiter off the steering rack

housing and track rod end **(see illustration)**.
3 Thoroughly clean the track rod and the steering rack housing, using fine abrasive paper to polish off any corrosion, burrs or sharp edges which might damage the new gaiter's sealing lips on installation. Scrape off all the grease from the old gaiter, and apply it to the track rod inner balljoint. (This assumes that grease has not been lost or contaminated as a result of damage to the old gaiter. Use fresh grease if in doubt.)
4 Carefully slide the new gaiter onto the track rod end, and locate it on the steering rack housing. Align the outer edge of the gaiter with the mark made on the track rod prior to removal, and then secure it in position with new retaining clips (where fitted).
5 Refit the track rod balljoint as described in Section 22.

20 Power steering system – bleeding

1 This procedure will only be necessary when any of the hydraulic system has been disconnected.
2 Referring to *Weekly checks*, remove the fluid reservoir filler cap, and top-up with the specified fluid to the upper level mark.
3 Start the engine, then stop it after 5 seconds. Repeat this 3 times, pausing briefly between each start.
4 Check and if necessary, top up the fluid level.
5 Start the engine, slowly turn the steering from lock to lock approx 5 times to purge out

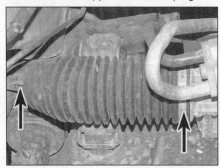

19.2 Steering rack gaiter retaining clips

any trapped air. Check the level and top up as necessary.
6 Start the engine and allow it to idle for 3 minutes without moving the steering wheel. Check the fluid level frequently during this period and top it up if necessary.
7 Turn the engine off and allow the system to cool. Once cool, check that fluid level is up to the upper mark on the power steering fluid reservoir, topping-up if necessary.

21 Power steering pump – removal and refitting

1.6 litre models

Removal

1 Remove the auxiliary drivebelt as described in Chapter 1 Section 20.
2 On Euro 4 emissions level engines, undo the 2 screws and move the relay box at the right-hand side of the bonnet slam panel to one side **(see illustration)**.
3 Slacken the clamps and remove the air hose between the intercooler and the throttle body pipe.
4 On Euro 4 emissions level engines, remove the throttle body as described in Chapter 4A Section 12, then undo the bolts and remove the heatshield from the catalytic converter.
5 On Euro 5 emissions level engines, remove the catalytic converter/particulate filter as described in Chapter 4A Section 18.

21.2 Undo the screws and move the relay box to one side

21.7 Power steering pump fluid return hose and supply pipe

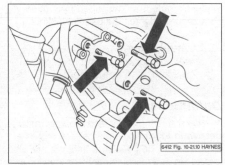

21.10 Power steering pump left-hand mounting bolts

22 Track rod balljoint –
removal and refitting

Note: *A new balljoint retaining nut will be required on refitting.*

Removal

1 Apply the handbrake, slacken the appropriate front roadwheel bolts, then jack up the front of the vehicle and support it on axle stands (see *Jacking and vehicle support*). Remove the appropriate front roadwheel.
2 If the balljoint is to be re-used, use a straight-edge and a scriber, or similar, to mark its relationship to the track rod.
3 Hold the track rod, and unscrew the balljoint locknut by a quarter of a turn **(see illustration)**. Do not move the locknut from this position, as it will serve as a handy reference mark on refitting.
4 Slacken and remove the nut securing the track rod balljoint to the hub carrier; discard the nut; a new one will be needed on refitting. Release the balljoint tapered shank using a universal balljoint separator **(see illustrations)**.
5 Counting the exact number of turns necessary to do so, unscrew the balljoint from the track rod end.
6 Count the number of exposed threads between the end of the balljoint and the locknut, and record this figure. If a new balljoint is to be fitted, unscrew the locknut from the old balljoint.
7 Carefully clean the balljoint and the threads. Renew the balljoint if its movement is sloppy

6 Undo the retaining bolts and remove the wiring bracket adjacent to the steering pump.
7 Release the clip and disconnect the fluid return hose from the pump **(see illustration)**. Be prepared for fluid spillage.
8 Undo the union and disconnect the fluid supply pipe from the pump.
9 Where necessary, undo the retaining bolt and pull the engine oil level dipstick guide tube from place.
10 Undo the mounting bolts at the left-hand side of the pump **(see illustration)**.
11 Working through the holes in the drive pulley, remove the pump right-hand mounting bolts **(see illustration)**. Manoeuvre the pump from place.
12 If the power steering pump is faulty it must be renewed. The pump is a sealed unit and cannot be overhauled.

2.0 litre models

13 Disconnect the battery negative lead as described in Chapter 5A Section 4.

14 Slacken the front roadwheel bolts, raise the front of the vehicle and support it securely on axle stands (see *Jacking and vehicle support*). Remove both roadwheels.
15 Release the fasteners and remove both front wheelarch liners.
16 Remove the front bumper as described in Chapter 11 Section 6.
17 Disconnect the wiring plugs from the electric power steering pump **(see illustration)**.
18 Apply hose clamps to the fluid hose attached to the pump, then release the clamps/undo the union bolt and disconnect the hoses **(see illustration)**. Be prepare for fluid spillage.
19 Undo the 3 retaining bolts and manoeuvre the power steering pump from place.

Refitting

20 Refitting is a reversal of removal. Tighten all fasteners to their specified torque where given.
21 On completion, bleed the hydraulic system as described in Section 20.

21.11 Access the mounting bolts through the pulley

21.17 Electric power steering pump wiring plugs

21.18 Power steering pump hoses

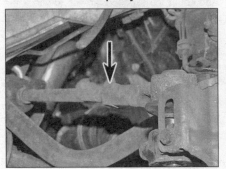

22.3 Slacken the track rod end locknut

22.4a Unscrew the track rod balljoint nut

22.4b Use a balljoint separator

or too stiff, if excessively worn, or if damaged in any way; carefully check the stud taper and threads. If the balljoint gaiter is damaged, the complete balljoint assembly must be renewed; it is not possible to obtain the gaiter separately.

Refitting

8 If a new balljoint is to be fitted, screw the locknut onto its threads, and position it so that the same number of exposed threads are visible, as was noted prior to removal.

9 Screw the balljoint into the track rod by the number of turns noted on removal. This should bring the balljoint locknut to within a quarter of a turn of the alignment marks that were made on removal (if applicable).

10 Ensure that the protector plate is in position then locate the balljoint shank in the hub carrier. Fit a new retaining nut and tighten it to the specified torque.

11 Refit the roadwheel, then lower the vehicle to the ground and tighten the roadwheel bolts to the specified torque.

12 Check and, if necessary, adjust the front

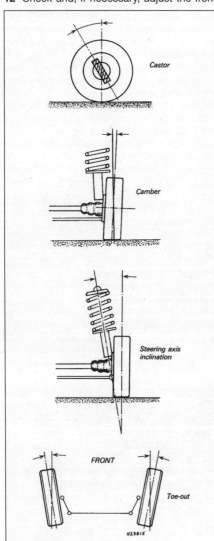

23.4 Front wheel geometry

wheel alignment as described in Section 23, then securely tighten the balljoint locknut.

23 Wheel alignment and steering angles – information, checking and adjustment

Definitions

1 A car's steering and suspension geometry is defined in four basic settings – all angles are expressed in degrees (toe settings are also expressed as a measurement); the steering axis is defined as an imaginary line drawn through the axis of the suspension strut, extended where necessary to contact the ground.

2 Camber is the angle between each roadwheel and a vertical line drawn through its centre and tyre contact patch, when viewed from the front or rear of the car. Positive camber is when the roadwheels are tilted outwards from the vertical at the top; negative camber is when they are tilted inwards. The camber angle is not adjustable.

3 Castor is the angle between the steering axis and a vertical line drawn through each roadwheel's centre and tyre contact patch, when viewed from the side of the car. Positive castor is when the steering axis is tilted so that it contacts the ground ahead of the vertical; negative castor is when it contacts the ground behind the vertical. The castor angle is not adjustable.

4 Toe is the difference, viewed from above, between lines drawn through the roadwheel centres and the car's centre-line. 'Toe-in' is when the roadwheels point inwards, towards each other at the front, while 'toe-out' is when they splay outwards from each other at the front **(see illustration)**.

5 The front wheel toe setting is adjusted by screwing the track rod in or out of its balljoints to alter the effective length of the track rod assembly.

6 Rear wheel toe setting is not adjustable.

Checking and adjustment

7 Due to the special measuring equipment necessary to check the wheel alignment and steering angles, and the skill required to use it properly, the checking and adjustment of these settings is best left to a Peugeot/Citroën/Fiat dealer or similar expert. Note that most tyre-fitting shops now possess sophisticated checking equipment. The following is provided as a guide, should the owner decide to carry out a DIY check.

Front wheel toe setting

8 The front wheel toe setting (tracking) is checked by measuring the angle of the wheels in relation to the longitudinal axis of the vehicle. Proprietary toe measurement gauges are available from motor accessory shops.

9 Adjustment is made by screwing the balljoints in or out of their track rods, to alter the effective length of the track rod assemblies.

10 Before starting work, check first that the tyre sizes and types are as specified, then check the tyre pressures and tread wear, the

roadwheel run-out, the condition of the hub bearings, the steering wheel free play, and the condition of the front suspension components (see *Weekly checks* and Chapter 1, Section 8. Correct any faults found.

11 Park the vehicle on level ground, check that the front roadwheels are in the straight-ahead position, then rock the rear and front ends to settle the suspension. Release the handbrake, and roll the vehicle backwards 1 metre, then forwards again, to relieve any stresses in the steering and suspension components.

12 Follow the tracking gauge manufacturer's instructions and measure the toe setting.

13 If adjustment is necessary, apply the handbrake, then jack up the front of the vehicle and support it securely on axle stands. Turn the steering wheel onto full-left lock, and record the number of exposed threads on the right-hand track rod end. Now turn the steering onto full-right lock, and record the number of threads on the left-hand side. If there are the same number of threads visible on both sides, then subsequent adjustment should be made equally on both sides. If there are more threads visible on one side than the other, it will be necessary to compensate for this during adjustment. **Note:** *It is most important that after adjustment, the same number of threads are visible on each track rod end.*

14 First clean the track rod threads; if they are corroded, apply penetrating fluid before starting adjustment. Release the rubber gaiter outboard clips (where necessary), and peel back the gaiters; apply a smear of grease to the inside of the gaiters, so that both are free, and will not be twisted or strained as their respective track rods are rotated.

15 Use a straight-edge and a scriber or similar to mark the relationship of each track rod to its balljoint then, holding each track rod in turn, unscrew its locknut fully.

16 Alter the length of the track rods, bearing in mind the note made in paragraph 13. Screw them into or out of the balljoints, rotating the track rod using an open-ended spanner fitted to the flats provided on the track rod. Shortening the track rods (screwing them into their balljoints) will reduce toe-in/increase toe-out.

17 When the setting is correct, hold the track rods and tighten the balljoint locknuts to the specified torque setting. Check that the balljoints are seated correctly in their sockets, and count the exposed threads to check the length of both track rods. If they are not the same, then the adjustment has not been made equally, and problems will be encountered with tyre scrubbing in turns; also, the steering wheel spokes will no longer be horizontal when the wheels are in the straight-ahead position.

18 If the track rod lengths are the same, lower the vehicle to the ground and recheck the toe setting; re-adjust if necessary. When the setting is correct, tighten the track rod balljoint locknuts to the specified torque. Ensure that the rubber gaiters are seated correctly, and are not twisted or strained, and secure them in position with new retaining clips (where necessary).

Chapter 11
Bodywork and fittings

Contents

Degrees of difficulty

Easy, suitable for novice with little experience	Fairly easy, suitable for beginner with some experience	Fairly difficult, suitable for competent DIY mechanic	Difficult, suitable for experienced DIY mechanic	Very difficult, suitable for expert DIY or professional

Specifications

Torque wrench setting	Nm	lbf ft
Seat belt mountings	30	22

1 General Information

1 The bodyshell is made of pressed-steel sections, and is available in Van or MPV format. Most components are welded together, but some use is made of structural adhesives.

2 The bonnet, doors and some other vulnerable panels are made of zinc-coated metal, and are further protected by being coated with an anti-chip primer prior to being sprayed.

3 Extensive use is made of plastic materials, mainly in the interior, but also in exterior components. The front and rear bumpers and the front grille are injection-moulded from a synthetic material which is very strong, yet light. Plastic components such as wheel arch liners are fitted to the underside of the vehicle, to improve the body's resistance to corrosion.

2 Maintenance – bodywork and underframe

1 The general condition of a vehicle's bodywork is the one thing that significantly affects its value. Maintenance is easy, but needs to be regular. Neglect, particularly after minor damage, can lead quickly to further deterioration and costly repair bills. It is important also to keep watch on those parts of the vehicle not immediately visible, for instance the underside, inside all the wheel arches, and the lower part of the engine compartment.

2 The basic maintenance routine for the bodywork is washing – preferably with a lot of water, from a hose. This will remove all the loose solids which may have stuck to the vehicle. It is important to flush these off in such a way as to prevent grit from scratching the finish. The wheel arches and underframe need washing in the same way, to remove any accumulated mud which will retain moisture and tend to encourage rust. Paradoxically enough, the best time to clean the underframe and wheel arches is in wet weather, when the mud is thoroughly wet and soft. In very wet weather, the underframe is usually cleaned of large accumulations automatically, and this is a good time for inspection.

3 Periodically, except on vehicles with a wax-based underbody protective coating, it is a good idea to have the whole of the underframe of the vehicle steam-cleaned, engine compartment included, so that a thorough inspection can be carried out to see what minor repairs and renovations are necessary. Steam-cleaning is available at many garages, and is necessary for the removal of the accumulation of oily grime, which sometimes is allowed to become thick in certain areas. If steam-cleaning facilities are not available, there are one or two excellent grease solvents available, which can be brush-applied; the dirt can then be simply hosed off. Note that these methods should not be used on vehicles with wax-based underbody protective coating, or the coating will be removed. Such vehicles should be inspected annually, preferably just prior to winter, when the underbody should be washed down, and any damage to the wax coating repaired using underseal. Ideally, a completely fresh coat should be applied. It would also be worth considering the use of wax-based protection for injection into door panels, sills, box sections, etc, as an additional safeguard against rust damage, where such protection is not provided by the vehicle manufacturer.

4 After washing paintwork, wipe off with a chamois leather to give an unspotted clear finish. A coat of clear protective wax polish will give added protection against chemical pollutants in the air. If the paintwork sheen has dulled or oxidised, use a cleaner/polisher combination to restore the brilliance of the shine. This requires a little effort, but such dulling is usually caused because regular washing has been neglected. Care needs to be taken with metallic paintwork, as a special non-abrasive cleaner/polisher is required to avoid damage to the finish. Always check that the door and ventilator opening drain holes and pipes are completely clear, so that water can be drained out. Brightwork should be treated in the same way as paintwork. Windscreens and windows can be kept clear of the smeary film which often appears, by the use of proprietary glass cleaner. Never use any form of wax or other body or chromium polish on glass.

3 Maintenance – upholstery and carpets

1 Mats and carpets should be brushed or vacuum-cleaned regularly, to keep them free of grit. If they are badly stained, remove them from the vehicle for scrubbing or sponging, and make quite sure they are dry before refitting. Seats and interior trim panels can be kept clean by wiping with a damp cloth and a proprietary upholstery cleaner. If they do become stained (which can be more apparent on light-coloured upholstery), use a little liquid detergent and a soft nail brush to scour the grime out of the grain of the material. Do not forget to keep the headlining clean in the same way as the upholstery. When using liquid cleaners inside the vehicle, do not over-wet the surfaces being cleaned. Excessive damp could get into the seams and padded interior, causing stains, offensive odours or even rot. If the inside of the vehicle gets wet accidentally, it is worthwhile taking some trouble to dry it out properly, particularly where carpets are involved. *Caution: Caution: Do not leave oil or electric heaters inside the vehicle for this purpose.*

4 Minor body damage – repair

Scratches

1 If the scratch is very superficial, and does not penetrate to the metal of the bodywork, repair is very simple. Lightly rub the area of the scratch with a paintwork renovator, or a very fine cutting paste, to remove loose paint from the scratch, and to clear the surrounding bodywork of wax polish. Rinse the area with clean water.

2 Apply touch-up paint to the scratch using a fine paint brush; continue to apply fine layers of paint until the surface of the paint in the scratch is level with the surrounding paintwork. Allow the new paint at least two weeks to harden, then blend it into the surrounding paintwork by rubbing the scratch area with a paintwork renovator or a very fine cutting paste. Finally apply wax polish.

3 Where the scratch has penetrated right through to the metal of the bodywork, causing the metal to rust, a different repair technique is required. Remove any loose rust from the bottom of the scratch with a penknife, then apply rust-inhibiting paint, to prevent the formation of rust in the future. Using a rubber or nylon applicator, fill the scratch with bodystopper paste. If required, this paste can be mixed with cellulose thinners, to provide a very thin paste which is ideal for filling narrow scratches. Before the stopper-paste in the scratch hardens, wrap a piece of smooth cotton rag around the top of a finger. Dip the finger in cellulose thinners, and quickly sweep it across the surface of the stopper-paste in the scratch; this will ensure that the surface of the stopper-paste is slightly hollowed. The scratch can now be painted over as described earlier in this Section.

Dents

4 When deep denting of the vehicle's bodywork has taken place, the first task is to pull the dent out, until the affected bodywork almost attains its original shape. There is little point in trying to restore the original shape completely, as the metal in the damaged area will have stretched on impact, and cannot be reshaped fully to its original contour. It is better to bring the level of the dent up to a point which is about 3 mm below the level of the surrounding bodywork. In cases where the dent is very shallow anyway, it is not worth trying to pull it out at all. If the underside of the dent is accessible, it can be hammered out gently from behind, using a mallet with a wooden or plastic head. Whilst doing this, hold a suitable block of wood firmly against the outside of the panel, to absorb the impact from the hammer blows and thus prevent a large area of the bodywork from being 'belled-out'.

5 Should the dent be in a section of the bodywork which has a double skin, or some other factor making it inaccessible from behind, a different technique is called for. Drill several small holes through the metal inside the area – particularly in the deeper section. Then screw long self-tapping screws into the holes, just sufficiently for them to gain a good purchase in the metal. Now the dent can be pulled out by pulling on the protruding heads of the screws with a pair of pliers.

6 The next stage of the repair is the removal of the paint from the damaged area, and from an inch or so of the surrounding 'sound' bodywork. This is accomplished most easily by using a wire brush or abrasive pad on a power drill, although it can be done just as effectively by hand, using sheets of abrasive paper. To complete the preparation for filling, score the surface of the bare metal with a screwdriver or the tang of a file, or alternatively, drill small holes in the affected area. This will provide a really good 'key' for the filler paste.

7 To complete the repair, see the Section on filling and respraying.

Rust holes or gashes

8 Remove all paint from the affected area, and from an inch or so of the surrounding 'sound' bodywork, using an abrasive pad or a wire brush on a power drill. If these are not available, a few sheets of abrasive paper will do the job most effectively. With the paint removed, you will be able to judge the severity of the corrosion, and therefore decide whether to renew the whole panel (if this is possible) or to repair the affected area. New body panels are not as expensive as most people think, and it is often quicker and more satisfactory to fit a new panel than to attempt to repair large areas of corrosion.

9 Remove all fittings from the affected area, except those which will act as a guide to the original shape of the damaged bodywork (eg headlight shells etc). Then, using tin snips or a hacksaw blade, remove all loose metal and any other metal badly affected by corrosion. Hammer the edges of the hole inwards, in order to create a slight depression for the filler paste.

10 Wire-brush the affected area to remove the powdery rust from the surface of the remaining metal. Paint the affected area with rust-inhibiting paint; if the back of the rusted area is accessible, treat this also.

11 Before filling can take place, it will be necessary to block the hole in some way. This can be achieved by the use of aluminium or plastic mesh, or aluminium tape.

12 Aluminium or plastic mesh, or glass-fibre matting, is probably the best material to use for a large hole. Cut a piece to the approximate size and shape of the hole to be filled, then position it in the hole so that its edges are below the level of the surrounding bodywork. It can be retained in position by several blobs of filler paste around its periphery.

13 Aluminium tape should be used for small or very narrow holes. Pull a piece off the roll, trim it to the approximate size and shape required, then pull off the backing paper (if used) and stick the tape over the hole; it can be overlapped if the thickness of one piece is insufficient. Burnish down the edges of the tape with the handle of a screwdriver or similar, to ensure that the tape is securely attached to the metal underneath.

Filling and respraying

14 Before using this Section, see the Sections on dent, minor scratch, rust holes and gash repairs.

15 Many types of bodyfiller are available, but generally speaking, those proprietary kits which contain a tin of filler paste and a tube of resin hardener are best for this type of repair; some can be used directly from the tube. A wide, flexible plastic or nylon applicator will be found invaluable for imparting a smooth and well-contoured finish to the surface of the filler.

16 Mix up a little filler on a clean piece of card or board – measure the hardener carefully (follow the maker's instructions on the pack), otherwise the filler will set too rapidly or too slowly. Using the applicator, apply the filler paste to the prepared area; draw the applicator across the surface of the filler to achieve the correct contour and to level the surface. As soon as a contour that approximates to the correct one is achieved, stop working the paste – if you carry on too long, the paste will become sticky and begin to 'pick-up' on the applicator. Continue to add thin layers of filler paste at 20-minute intervals, until the level of the filler is just proud of the surrounding bodywork.

17 Once the filler has hardened, the excess can be removed using a metal plane or file. From then on, progressively-finer grades of abrasive paper should be used, starting with a 40-grade production paper, and finishing with a 400-grade wet-and-dry paper. Always wrap the abrasive paper around a flat rubber, cork, or wooden block – otherwise the surface of the filler will not be completely flat. During the smoothing of the filler surface, the wet-and-dry paper should be periodically rinsed in water. This will ensure that a very smooth finish is imparted to the filler at the final stage.

18 At this stage, the 'dent' should be surrounded by a ring of bare metal, which in turn should be encircled by the finely 'feathered' edge of the good paintwork. Rinse the repair area with clean water, until all of the dust produced by the rubbing-down operation has gone.

19 Spray the whole area with a light coat of primer – this will show up any imperfections in the surface of the filler. Repair these imperfections with fresh filler paste or bodystopper, and once more smooth the surface with abrasive paper. If bodystopper is used, it can be mixed with cellulose thinners, to form a really thin paste which is ideal for filling small holes. Repeat this spray-and-repair procedure until you are satisfied that the surface of the filler, and the feathered edge of the paintwork, are perfect. Clean the repair area with clean water, and allow to dry fully.

20 The repair area is now ready for final spraying. Paint spraying must be carried out in a warm, dry, windless and dust-free atmosphere. This condition can be created artificially if you have access to a large indoor working area, but if you are forced to work in the open, you will have to pick your day very carefully. If you are working indoors, dousing the floor in the work area with water will help to settle the dust which would otherwise be in the atmosphere. If the repair area is confined to one body panel, mask off the surrounding panels; this will help to minimise the effects of a slight mismatch in paint colours. Bodywork fittings (eg chrome strips, door handles etc) will also need to be masked off. Use genuine masking tape, and several thicknesses of newspaper, for the masking operations.

21 Before commencing to spray, agitate the aerosol can thoroughly, then spray a test area (an old tin, or similar) until the technique is mastered. Cover the repair area with a thick coat of primer; the thickness should be built up using several thin layers of paint, rather than one thick one. Using 400 grade wet-and-dry paper, rub down the surface of the primer until it is really smooth. While doing this, the work area should be thoroughly doused with water, and the wet-and-dry paper periodically rinsed in water. Allow to dry before spraying on more paint.

22 Spray on the top coat, again building up the thickness by using several thin layers of paint. Start spraying at the top of the repair area, and then, using a side-to-side motion, work downwards until the whole repair area and about 2 inches of the surrounding original paintwork is covered. Remove all masking material 10 to 15 minutes after spraying on the final coat of paint.

23 Allow the new paint at least two weeks to harden, then, using a paintwork renovator or a very fine cutting paste, blend the edges of the paint into the existing paintwork. Finally, apply wax polish.

Plastic components

24 With the use of more and more plastic body components by the vehicle manufacturers (eg bumpers. spoilers, and in some cases major body panels), rectification of more serious damage to such items has become a matter of either entrusting repair work to a specialist in this field, or renewing complete components. Repair of such damage by the DIY owner is not really feasible, owing to the cost of the equipment and materials required for effecting such repairs. The basic technique involves making a groove along the line of the crack in the plastic, using a rotary burr in a power drill. The damaged part is then welded back together, using a hot air gun to heat up and fuse a plastic filler rod into the groove. Any excess plastic is then removed, and the area rubbed down to a smooth finish. It is important that a filler rod of the correct plastic is used, as body components can be made of a variety of different types (eg polycarbonate, ABS, polypropylene).

25 Damage of a less serious nature (abrasions, minor cracks etc) can be repaired by the DIY owner using a two-part epoxy filler repair material. Once mixed in equal proportions, this is used in similar fashion to the bodywork filler used on metal panels. The filler is usually cured in twenty to thirty minutes, ready for sanding and painting.

26 If the owner is renewing a complete component himself, or if he has repaired it with epoxy filler, he will be left with the problem of finding a suitable paint for finishing which is compatible with the type of plastic used. At one time, the use of a universal paint was not possible, owing to the complex range of plastics encountered in body component applications. Standard paints, generally speaking, will not bond to plastic or rubber satisfactorily. However, it is now possible to obtain a plastic body parts finishing kit which consists of a pre-primer treatment, a primer and coloured top coat. Full instructions are normally supplied with a kit, but basically, the method of use is to first apply the pre-primer to the component concerned, and allow it to dry for up to 30 minutes. Then the primer is applied, and left to dry for about an hour before finally applying the special-coloured top coat. The result is a correctly-coloured component, where the paint will flex with the plastic or rubber, a property that standard paint does not normally posses.

5 Major body damage – repair

1 Where serious damage has occurred, or large areas need renewal due to neglect, it means that complete new panels will need welding-in, and this is best left to professionals. If the damage is due to impact, it will also be necessary to check completely the alignment of the bodyshell, and this can only be carried out accurately by a Peugeot/Citroën/Fiat dealer, or accident repair specialist, using special jigs. If the body is left misaligned, it is primarily dangerous, as the car will not handle properly, and secondly, uneven stresses will be imposed on the steering, suspension and possibly transmission, causing abnormal wear, or complete failure, particularly to such items as the tyres.

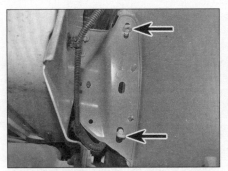

6.4 Rotate the fasteners 90° to release them

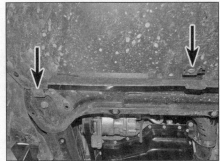

6.5 Undo the bolts along the lower edge of the bumper (right-hand and centre bolt arrowed)

rear corner of the bumper **(see illustration)**.

9 With the help of an assistant, carefully pull the bumper forwards from the vehicle.

Refitting

10 Refitting is a reversal of removal.

7 Rear bumper – removal and refitting

Note: *The help of an assistant is useful to support the bumper during the removal and refitting procedure.*

6 Front bumper – removal and refitting

Note: *The help of an assistant is useful to support the bumper during the removal and refitting procedure.*

Removal

1 Firmly apply the handbrake, prise off the wheel trims, slacken the front roadwheel bolts, jack up the front of the vehicle and support it securely on axle stands (see *Jacking and vehicle support*). Remove both front roadwheels.

2 Release the fasteners and remove both front wheelarch liners.

3 Remove the radiator grille as described in Section 23.

4 Working under the wheelarch, release the 2 fasteners each side securing the bumper to the front wings **(see illustration)**.

5 Undo the 3 bolts along the lower front edge of the bumper **(see illustration)**.

6 Depending on model, disconnect the wiring connector for the fog lights, parking sensors, etc.

7 Remove the 3 fasteners from along the upper edge of the front bumper assembly **(see illustration)**.

8 Undo the bolt each side at the upper,

Removal

1 Chock the front wheels, then jack up the rear of the vehicle and support securely on axle stands (see *Jacking and vehicle support*).

2 Prise out the centre pin, lever out the plastic expansion rivet each side at the lower edge of the wheelarchliners **(see illustration)**.

3 Undo the 3 screws/1 nut and remove the plastic panel from the underside of the bumper at each rear corner **(see illustrations)**.

4 With the rear section of the liners held forwards, remove the bumper upper retaining bolt each side **(see illustration)**.

5 Depending on model, working inside the left-hand corner of the rear bumper,

6.7 Remove the plastic rivets along the upper edge

6.8 Undo the bolt each side securing the bumper to the wing

7.2 Prise up the centre pin, and lever out the plastic rivet each side

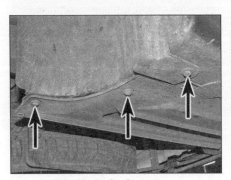

7.3a Undo the 3 screws...

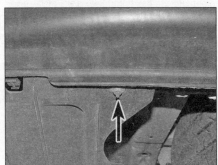

7.3b ...1 nut, and remove the panel

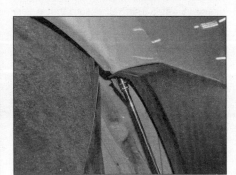

7.4 Undo the bolt each side at the front edge of the bumper

7.5 Disconnect the bumper wiring plug

7.6 Undo the upper bumper screws
(left-hand screws arrowed)

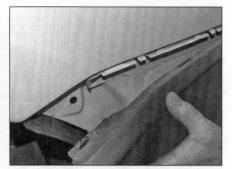

7.7 Gently pull the front edge of the
bumper from place

disconnect the wiring connector for the parking sensors **(see illustration)**.

6 Working your way along the upper edge of the bumper, remove the 6 Torx screws **(see illustration)**.

7 With the help of an assistant, unclip the bumper at each side from the wing panels **(see illustration)**, then carefully pull the bumper rearwards from the vehicle.

Refitting

8 Refitting is a reversal of removal, ensuring that the retaining clips each side correctly engage with the rear wings as it is located in position.

---

8 Bonnet – removal, refitting and adjustment

Removal

1 Open the bonnet and have an assistant support it then, using a pencil or felt tip pen, mark the outline of each bonnet hinge relative to the bonnet, to use as a guide on refitting.

2 Release the washer jet supply tubing from the right-hand bonnet hinge and disconnect the tubing from the connector **(see illustration)**.

3 With an assistant supporting the other side of the bonnet, unscrew the bonnet-to-hinge retaining nuts each side. Carefully lift the bonnet from the vehicle and store it out of the way in a safe place.

4 Inspect the bonnet hinges for signs of wear and free play at the pivots, and if necessary renew. Each hinge is secured to the body by two bolts. On refitting, apply a smear of multi-purpose grease to the hinges.

Refitting and adjustment

5 With the aid of an assistant, offer up the bonnet, and engage the retaining bolts. Align the hinges with the marks made on removal, then tighten the retaining bolts securely. Reconnect the washer jet tubing.

6 Close the bonnet, and check for alignment with the adjacent panels. If necessary, slacken the hinge bolts and re-align the bonnet to suit. When correctly aligned, tighten the hinge bolts securely.

7 Once the bonnet is correctly aligned, check that the bonnet fastens and releases in a satisfactory manner. If adjustment is necessary, slacken the bonnet lock retaining bolts, and adjust the position of the lock to suit. Once the lock is operating correctly, securely tighten its retaining bolts.

---

9 Bonnet lock and release cable – removal and refitting

Removal

1 Remove the radiator grille as described in Section 23.

8.2 Disconnect the washer tubing

2 Undo the 2 nuts and remove the security cover from the lock **(see illustration)**.

3 Undo the two bolts securing the bonnet lock to the radiator support frame **(see illustration)**. Unclip the cable from along the front of the crossmember, then withdraw the lock and disconnect the release cable.

4 Work along the length of the cable in the engine compartment along the left-hand inner wing panel, note their fitted locations, and release the cable retaining clips.

5 Remove the passenger side sill trim as described in Section 26.

6 Undo the retaining bolts and remove the release lever assembly from its location **(see illustration)**.

7 Tie a length of string to the end of the cable in the engine compartment, note its

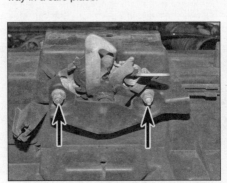

9.2 Undo the nuts and remove the cover

9.3 Bonnet lock retaining bolts

9.6 Release lever retaining bolts

9.7 Grommet for the bonnet release cable (facia removed for clarity)

routing, then carefully pull the cable through into the passenger compartment. Release the grommet from the bulkhead to withdraw the cable **(see illustration)**. Untie the string from the end of the cable, and leave it in position to aid refitting.

Refitting

8 Locate the cable in position in the passenger compartment.
9 Tie the end of the new cable to the string, and pull it through into the engine compartment.
10 Check that the bulkhead grommet is securely seated, then remove the string and connect the cable to the release lever.
11 Secure the release lever in place, tightening its retaining nut securely.
12 Reconnect the cable to the bonnet lock then refit the lock, tightening its retaining bolts securely.

13 Secure the cable in place with its retaining clips. Check the operation of the lock and, if necessary, adjust the position of the lock within the elongated bolt holes to achieve satisfactory operation prior to closing the bonnet.
14 The remainder of refitting is a reversal of removal.

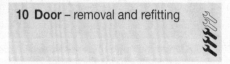

10 Door – removal and refitting

Front door

Removal

1 Disconnect the battery negative lead as described in Chapter 5A Section 4.
2 Open the door and pull back the rubber wiring harness boot **(see illustration)**.
3 Unscrew the securing bolt **(see illustration)**, and disconnect the door check strap from the door A-pillar.
4 Have an assistant support the door, then slide out the retaining clip, and extract the upper and lower hinge pins **(see illustration)**.
5 Move the door away a little, then pull the wiring harness from the A-pillar and disconnect the wiring plug.

Refitting

6 Refitting is a reversal of removal, but on completion check the fit of the door in relation to the surrounding body panels. If adjustment

is necessary, the door position can be altered by means of the elongated slots in the hinge plates attached to the door.

Sliding side door

Removal

7 Undo the Torx screw and remove the end cap from the rear of the centre door rail **(see illustration)**.
8 Undo the Torx screws and remove the end cap from the lower door rail **(see illustration)**.
9 With the help of an assistant, slide the door rearwards and manoeuvre it from place.

Refitting

10 Refitting is a reversal of removal.

Hinged rear door

Removal

11 Disconnect the battery negative lead as described in Chapter 5A Section 4.
12 When working on the left-hand rear door, first remove the trim panel (where fitted) from the rear pillar to access the wiring connector. Disconnect the wiring plug(s) and the washer jet tubing (where applicable).
13 With the help of an assistant to support the door, undo the 2 upper bolts and 2 lower bolts securing the hinges to the door **(see illustration)**. Carefully lift the door from the vehicle.

Refitting

14 Refitting is a reversal of removal, ensuring all wiring connectors are securely reconnected.

10.2 Pull back the wiring harness boot

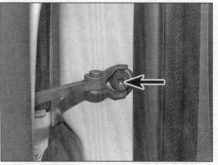

10.3 Check strap securing bolt

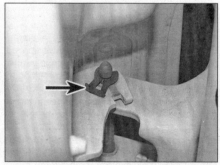

10.4 Slide out the retaining clip

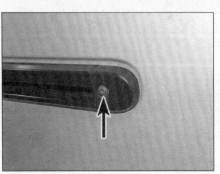

10.7 Undo the screw and remove the end cap

10.8 Undo the screws securing the lower rail end cap

10.13 Hinged rear door lower mounting bolts

11.1 Prise the switch panel assembly from the door trim panel

11.2 Prise the panel from the front of the door

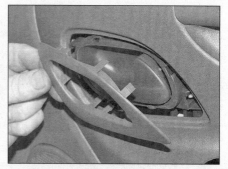

11.3 Prise away the interior release handle surround trim

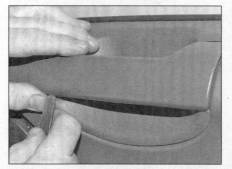

11.4a Prise out the lower edge of the pull handle cover

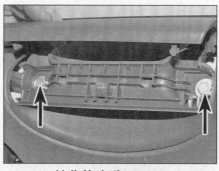

11.4b Undo the screws

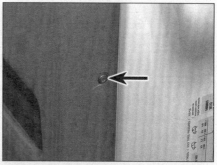

11.5a Undo the screw(s) at the rear edge…

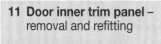

11 Door inner trim panel –
removal and refitting

Front door

Removal

1 Using a trim removal tool, prise the switch panel upwards from the door trim panel, and disconnect the wiring plug **(see illustration)**.
2 Using a trim removal tool, carefully prise off the trim panel from the front of the door **(see illustration)**.
3 Carefully prise the interior release handle surround trim from place **(see illustration)**.
4 Starting at the lower edge, prise up the door pull handle cover, then undo the 2 retaining screws **(see illustrations)**.
5 Undo the retaining screws from the door trim panel, one at the lower edge and one or two (depending on model) on the rear edge of the trim panel **(see illustrations)**.
6 Using a suitable forked tool, work around the edge of the trim panel, and release the securing clips **(see illustration)**.
7 Carefully pull the panel outwards, then lift it up and remove it from the door.

Refitting

8 Before refitting, check whether any of the trim panel retaining studs were broken on removal. Renew the panel retaining studs as necessary, then refit the panel using a reversal of removal.

11.5b …and the screw at the lower edge of the trim panel

Sliding side door

Note: *The securing clips that hold the trim panel in place are made of plastic, and can easily break on removal. It would be a good idea to purchase some new securing clips, before proceeding with this operation.*

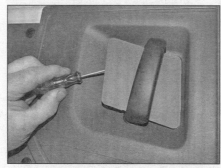

11.9a Prise out the trim panel…

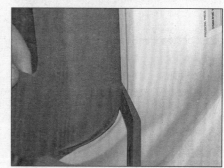

11.6 Prise the trim panel away to release the clips

Removal

9 Operate the interior door release handle, then using a trim removal tool, carefully prise out the trim panel from the handle recess. Undo the 2 Torx screws in the handle aperture and remove the handle surround **(see illustrations)**.

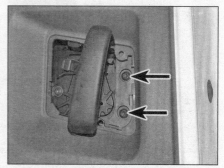

11.9b …and undo the Torx screws

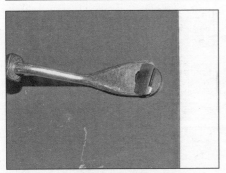

11.10 Prise out the centre pins a little, and release the securing clips and remove the trim panel

11.12 Prise the handle surround from place

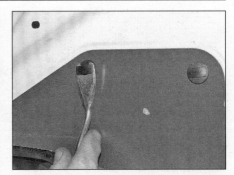

11.13 Prise up the centre pins, and lever out the fasteners

10 Using a suitable forked tool, work around the edge of the trim panel, and release the securing clips. Then remove the door trim panel from the door **(see illustration)**.

Refitting

11 Refitting is a reversal of removal.

Hinged rear door

Removal

12 Where applicable, prise the interior release handle surround from place **(see illustration)**.
13 Release the centre pin of the fasteners, then unclip them from around the outside edge of the panel. Remove the trim panel from the door **(see illustration)**.

Refitting

14 Refitting is a reversal of removal.

12 Front door handle and lock components – removal and refitting

Interior door release lever

1 Remove the door inner trim panel, as described in Section 11.
2 Remove the inner release lever by sliding the housing towards the rear edge of the door and then unclip it from the locating slots in the door **(see illustration)**.
3 Slide the outer cable from the housing and then disconnect the inner cable from the back of the release lever **(see illustration)**.
4 Refitting is a reversal of removal, but ensure that the operating cable is correctly fitted to the release lever. Refit the inner trim panel as described in Section 11.

Exterior door handle

5 Open the door and remove the rubber grommet/plastic blanking cover at the rear edge of the door to access the retaining screw **(see illustration)**.
6 Slacken the retaining screw until it cannot be turned no further and comes to a stop (DO NOT force the screw when it reaches the stop). The screw does not come completely out from the door panel. Carefully withdraw the push button/lock cylinder out from the door handle assembly **(see illustrations)**. Take care not to damage the paintwork as it is removed.
7 Detach the handle by sliding it to the rear of the door, and then pulling it out from the handle recess **(see illustration)**.
8 Refitting is a reversal of removal, but ensure that the handle locates securely inside the door lock housing.

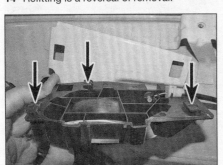

12.2 Slide the handle rearwards to release the clips from the slots

12.3 Slide the outer cable from the housing

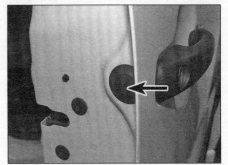

12.5 Remove the piece of tape covering the access hole

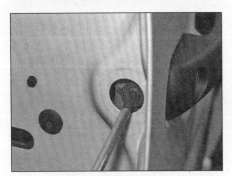

12.6a Slacken the Torx screw...

12.6b ...and withdraw the lock cylinder/ push button

12.7 Slide the handle to the rear and pull it out to disengage it from the door

12.10 Use a sharp knife to cut through the sealer

12.12 Remove the seal and slacken the screw

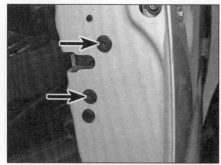

12.13 Undo the two screws securing the lock to the edge of the door

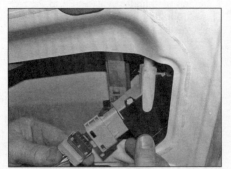

12.14 Disconnect the wiring from the lock assembly

12.17 Release the operating cable from the handle support

12.18 Release the outer cover and disconnect the cable

Door lock assembly

9 Make sure the window glass is in the fully closed position and remove the door trim panel, as described in Section 11.

10 Carefully cut around the edge of the inner sealing sheet, to release the sealer **(see illustration)**. Remove the sealing sheet and put it to one side for refitting.

11 Remove the interior door release lever as described previously in this Section.

12 Remove the exterior door handle as described previously in this Section, and then remove the seal and slacken the retaining screw (do not remove completely) for the door handle housing from the outside of the door **(see illustration)**.

13 Undo the two screws securing the lock assembly to the rear edge of the door **(see illustration)**.

14 Reach inside the door to the rear of the lock assembly and disconnect the wiring plug from the lock assembly **(see illustration)**.

15 Release the interior handle from the door panel **(see illustration 12.2)**.

16 Manoeuvre the lock, exterior handle frame, and interior handle from the door.

17 If required, unclip the lock operating outer cable from the lever on the exterior handle support bracket **(see illustration)**.

18 To remove the operating cable from the door lock assembly, release the securing clips and open the plastic cover **(see illustration)**. Release the outer cable from the housing and then unclip the inner cable from the operating lever inside the lock assembly.

19 Refitting is a reversal of removal. Fit a new inner sealing sheet to the door if the original was damaged in any way during removal. On completion, refit the door inner trim panel as described in Section 11.

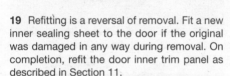

13 Sliding side door handle and lock components – removal and refitting

Note: *Although Peugeot/Citroen/Fiat recommend that the door to be removed for this operation, we found that if the door is secured in a partially open position, the door trim panel can be removed to access the lock components. Always make sure the door is secure before proceeding, so as to prevent it closing and trapping any body parts, whilst working on the door.*

13.2 Remove the handle Torx screw

Interior door release lever

1 Prise out the centre panel from the release lever, undo the 2 retaining screws, and remove the lever surround **(see illustration 11.9a and 11.9b)**.

2 Undo the retaining screw securing the lever assembly to the door **(see illustration)**.

3 Release the outer cable retaining clip from the housing and then disconnect the inner cable from the back of the release lever **(see illustration)**.

4 Refitting is a reversal of removal, but ensure that the operating cable is correctly fitted to the release lever. Refit the inner trim panel as described in Section 11.

Exterior door handle

5 Open the door and remove the rubber grommet/plastic blanking cover at the rear

13.3 Release the outer cable and inner cable from the lever assembly

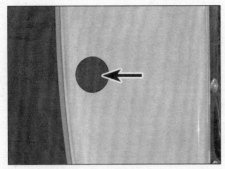

13.5 Remove the cover to expose the handle retaining screw

13.6a Slacken the retaining screw...

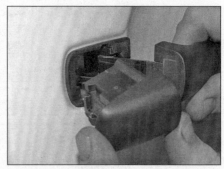

13.6b ...and withdraw the push button

edge of the door to access the retaining screw **(see illustration)**.

6 Slacken the retaining screw until it cannot be turned no further and comes to a stop (DO NOT force the screw when it reaches the stop). The screw does not come completely out from the door panel. Carefully withdraw the push button out from the door handle assembly **(see illustrations)**. Take care not to damage the paintwork as it is removed.

7 Detach the handle by sliding it to the rear of the door, and then pulling it out from the handle recess **(see illustration)**.

8 Refitting is a reversal of removal, but ensure that the handle locates securely inside the door lock housing. When fitting the rear of the door handle, make sure the leg on the rear of the handle is positioned behind the lever on the support bracket inside the door panel.

Door lock assembly

9 Make sure the window glass (where fitted) is in the fully closed position and remove the door trim panel, as described in Section 11.

10 Carefully cut around the edge of the inner sealing sheet, to release the sealer **(see illustration)**. Remove the sealing sheet and put it to one side for refitting.

11 Remove the interior door release lever as described previously in this Section.

12 Drill out the rivets and remove the interior door release lever support bracket **(see illustration)**. Unclip the cable from the bracket as it's withdrawn.

13 Remove the exterior door handle as described previously in this Section, and then remove the seal and slacken the retaining screw (do not remove completely) for the door handle housing from the outside of the door **(see illustration)**.

14 Undo the two screws securing the lock assembly to the rear edge of the door **(see illustration)**.

15 Reach inside the door to the rear of the lock assembly and disconnect the wiring plug from the lock assembly.

16 Release the interior handle operating cable from the clips on the door panel, then lower the lock assembly and manipulate it out through the door aperture.

17 If required, unclip the lock operating outer cable from the lever on the exterior handle support bracket **(see illustration)**.

18 To remove the operating cable from the door lock assembly, release the securing clips and open the plastic cover. Release the outer cable from the housing and then unclip the inner cable from the operating lever inside the lock assembly.

19 Refitting is a reversal of removal. Fit a new inner sealing sheet to the door if the original

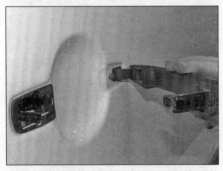

13.7 Slide the handle to the rear and pull it out to disengage it from the door

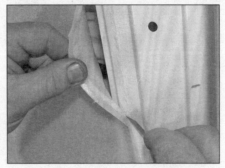

13.10 Remove the inner sealing sheet

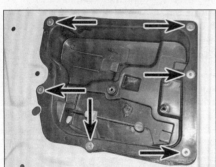

13.12 The lever support bracket is secured by 6 rivets

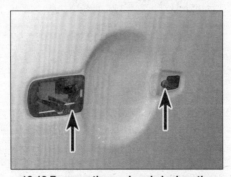

13.13 Remove the seal and slacken the Torx screw

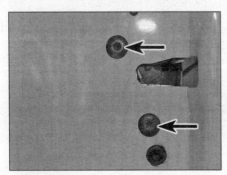

13.14 Undo the two screws securing the lock to the edge of the door

13.17 Slide the outer cable from the bracket, and disengage the inner cable

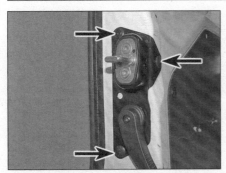

14.1 Undo the retaining screws

14.2 Slide the cables from the fittings

14.5 Make alignment marks, then unbolt the catch from the door panel

was damaged in any way during removal. On completion, refit the door inner trim panel as described in Section 11.

14 Hinged rear door handle and lock components – removal and refitting

Door release lever assembly

1 Undo the 3 retaining screws, to release the release lever assembly from the door panel **(see illustration)**.
2 Note their fitted position, then release the outer cables from the mounting bracket and the inner cables from the back of the release lever **(see illustration)**.
3 Refitting is a reversal of removal, but ensure that the operating cables are correctly fitted to the release lever, as noted on removal.

Door upper and lower catches

4 Remove the door release lever assembly as described previously in this Section.
5 Make alignment marks to aid refitting, then undo the retaining bolts and withdraw the catch from the door panel complete with cable **(see illustration)**.
6 To remove the operating cable from the door catch, release the outer cable from the mounting bracket and then unclip the inner cable from the operating lever **(see illustration)**.
7 Refitting is a reversal of removal. Refit

14.6 Slide the outer cable from the bracket and disengage the inner cable

the release lever, as described earlier in this section. Refit the inner trim panel as described in Section 11.

Exterior door handle

8 Open the door and remove the rubber grommet/plastic blanking cover (where fitted) at the rear edge of the door to access the retaining screw **(see illustration)**.
9 Slacken the retaining Torx screw until it cannot be turned no further and comes to a stop (DO NOT force the screw when it reaches the stop). The screw does not come completely out from the door panel. Carefully withdraw the push button/lock cylinder out from the door handle assembly **(see illustration)**. Take care not to damage the paintwork as it is removed.

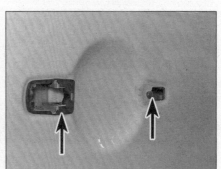

14.8 Remove the piece of tape covering the access hole

10 Detach the handle by sliding it to the side of the door, and then pulling it out from the handle recess **(see illustration)**.
11 Refitting is a reversal of removal, but ensure that the handle locates securely inside the door lock housing. When fitting the rear of the door handle, make sure the leg on the rear of the handle is positioned behind the lever on the support bracket inside the door panel.

Door lock assembly

12 Remove the door inner trim panel as described in Section 11.
13 Remove the exterior door handle as described previously in this Section, and then remove the seal and remove the retaining screw for the door handle housing from the outside of the door **(see illustration)**.

14.9 ...and withdraw the lock cylinder/push button

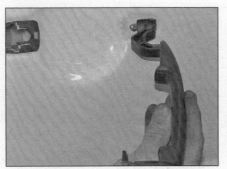

14.10 Slide the handle to the side and pull it out to disengage it from the door

14.13 Undo the Torx screws, and remove the seal

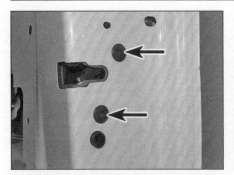

14.14 Door lock retaining screws

14.17 Withdraw the lock assembly out from inside the door

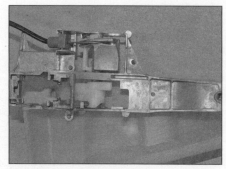

14.18 Release the operating cable from the handle support

14 Undo the 2 screws securing the lock assembly to the rear edge of the door **(see illustration)**.

15 Slide the interior release handle from the door frame.

16 Reach inside and manoeuvre the lock assembly from inside the door and disconnect the wiring plug.

17 Release the exterior handle support from the door panel, then lower the lock assembly and remove the lock assembly out through the door aperture **(see illustration)**.

18 If required, unclip the lock operating outer cable from the lever on the exterior handle support bracket **(see illustration)**.

19 To remove the operating cable from the door lock assembly, release the securing clips and open the plastic cover. Release the outer cable from the housing and then unclip the inner cable from the operating lever inside the lock assembly. **Note:** *On some models*

the cables are part of the lock assembly and cannot be renewed independently.

20 Refitting is a reversal of removal. On completion, refit the door inner trim panel as described in Section 11.

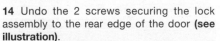

15 Front door window glass and regulator – removal and refitting

Door window glass

1 Position the window approximately three quarters of the way down.

2 Remove the door inner trim panel, as described in Section 11.

3 Unclip and partially remove the outer seal from the bottom of the window aperture **(see illustration)**.

4 Carefully cut around the edge of the inner

sealing sheet, to release the sealer **(see illustration 12.10)**, and fold it back to access the window regulator.

5 Slacken the window glass clamp screw, gently depress the retaining clip, and remove the window glass up through the aperture and out of the door **(see illustrations)**.

6 Refitting is a reversal of removal, clean and check the fixings on the window glass. Fit a new sealing sheet to the door if the original was damaged in any way during removal. On completion, refit the inner trim panel as described in Section 11.

Door window regulator

7 Remove the front door window glass, as described previously in this section.

8 Drill out the 5 rivets securing the regulator assembly to the door frame **(see illustration)**.

9 Disconnect the wiring plug connector from the window motor **(see illustration)**.

15.3 Pull up the lower, outer seal from the door

15.5a Slacken the window clamp screw…

15.5b …and gently push the clip outwards

15.5c Slide the glass upwards from the door

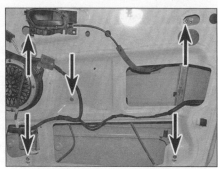

15.8 The window regulator is secured by 5 rivets

15.9 Disconnect the window motor wiring plug

10 Manoeuvre the window motor/regulator assembly out from inside the door aperture.

11 Refitting is a reversal of removal, but fit a new sealing sheet to the door if the original was damaged in any way during removal. On completion, refit the inner trim panel as described in Section 11.

16 Tailgate and support struts – removal and refitting

Tailgate

Removal

1 Undo the retaining bolts and remove the interior grab handle from the tailgate.

2 Undo the 7 screws around the edge securing the trim panel to the tailgate (see illustration). Remove the panel.

3 Disconnect the wiring connectors from the following components (where applicable):
a) Rear window wiper motor.
b) Tailgate lock motor.
c) Rear window demister elements.
d) High-level stop-light.
e) Number plate lights.

4 Release the wiring harness retaining clips from the tailgate.

5 Check that all wiring connectors have been disconnected, then release the wiring harness grommet and withdraw the harness from the top of the tailgate. **Note:** *Tie a length of string to the ends of the wiring loom connectors inside the tailgate, note its routing, then carefully pull the wiring loom out through the top of the grommet in the tailgate. Untie the string from the end of the wiring loom, and leave it in position to aid refitting.*

6 With the aid of an assistant to help support the tailgate, prise out the support strut spring clips, and pull the struts from the balljoints on the body as described later in this Section.

7 Unscrew the tailgate hinge retaining bolts (one at each side) and carefully lift the tailgate from the vehicle.

Refitting

8 If a new tailgate is to be fitted, transfer all serviceable components (lock mechanism, wiper motor, etc) to it.

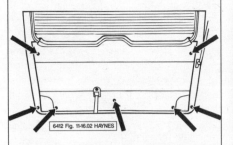

16.2 Tailgate trim panel retaining screws

9 Refitting is a reversal of removal, bearing in mind the following points:
a) If necessary, adjust the rubber buffers to obtain a good fit when the tailgate is shut.
b) If necessary, adjust the position of the tailgate lock striker to achieve satisfactory lock operation.
c) On completion, refit the tailgate trim panel.

Support struts

Removal

10 Support the tailgate in the open position, with the help of an assistant.

11 Using a suitable flat-bladed screwdriver, release the spring clip, and pull the support strut from its balljoint on the body.

12 Similarly, release the strut from the balljoint on the tailgate (see illustration), and withdraw the strut from the vehicle.

Refitting

13 Refitting is a reversal of removal, but ensure the spring clips are correctly engaged.

17 Tailgate lock components – removal and refitting

Tailgate lock

Removal

1 Remove the tailgate trim panel as described in Section 16.

2 Undo the 3 retaining bolts and lower

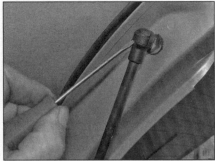

16.12 Prise out the spring clip slightly, and pull the strut from the tailgate

the lock support from the tailgate (see illustration). Disconnect the wiring plug.

3 If required, undo the 2 bolts and detach the lock from the support.

Refitting

4 Refitting is a reversal of removal. If necessary, adjust the position of the tailgate lock striker to achieve satisfactory lock operation. On completion, refit the tailgate trim panel as described in Section 16.

Tailgate lock striker

Removal

5 Undo the screws and remove the trim pane above the striker.

6 Mark the position of the striker on the body, for use when refitting. Unscrew the two securing bolts, and remove the striker from the body (see illustration).

Refitting

7 Refitting is a reversal of removal. Before tightening the securing bolts, the position of the striker should be altered (the securing bolt holes are elongated) until satisfactory lock operation is obtained. Use the marks made prior to removal, if appropriate.

Tailgate exterior release switch

8 Remove the tailgate lower trim panel as described in Section 16.

9 Disconnect the number plate lights wiring plugs.

10 Shear-off the heads of the rivets securing the release switch to the tailgate panel (see illustration).

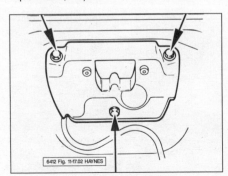

17.2 Lock support retaining bolts

17.6 Striker plate securing bolts

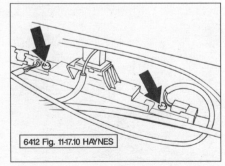

17.10 Shear-off the rivets securing the switch

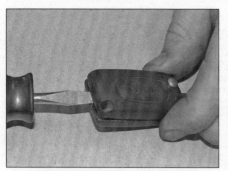

18.8 Twist the screwdriver in the slot provided and prise apart the two halves

18.9 Lift the circuit board and slide out the battery

11 Release the securing clips and remove the switch from the trim panel. Disconnect the wiring plug as the switch is withdrawn.
12 Refitting is a reversal of removal. On completion, refit the tailgate trim panel as described in Section 16.

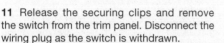

18 Central locking components – removal and refitting

Control unit

1 The central locking system is controlled by the Built-in Systems Interface (BSI) which is the vehicle central computer controlling the main body electrical system functions. The unit is located under the facia on the left-hand side. Refer to Chapter 12 Section 22 for further information.
2 Should any problems be experienced with the operation of the central locking system or any of the other functions controlled by the BSI, the vehicle should be taken to a Peugeot/Citroën/Fiat dealer for diagnostic investigation.

Front door lock motor

3 The motor is integral with the door lock assembly. Removal and refitting of the lock assembly is described in Section Section 12.

Sliding side door lock motor

4 The motor is integral with the door lock

assembly. Removal and refitting of the lock assembly is described in Section Section 13.

Hinged rear door lock motor

5 The motor is integral with the door lock assembly. Removal and refitting of the lock assembly is described in Section Section 14.

Tailgate lock motor

6 The motor is integral with the door lock assembly. Removal and refitting of the lock assembly is described in Section 17.

Remote control transmitter

Battery renewal

7 When the remote control transmitter battery is nearing the end of its life, an audible signal will be emitted from within the vehicle, accompanied by a message on the instrument panel multifunction screen. The battery should then be renewed with a type CR 1620 (3 volt) battery.
8 Using a small screwdriver in the slot at the upper end of the key, carefully prise the two halves of the transmitter apart **(see illustration)**.
9 Remove the printed circuit board and slide the battery out from its location in the circuit board, noting its fitted position – positive (+) side up **(see illustration)**.
10 Fit the new battery and reassemble the transmitter.

Initialisation

11 To initialise the unit after renewing the

battery, put the key in the ignition and leave it in the off position. Then switch on the ignition (without starting) and immediately press the locking button on the key for 10 seconds. Then switch off the ignition and remove the key from the ignition lock. The key remote should now be fully operational.

19 Exterior mirrors and glass – removal and refitting

Exterior mirror assembly

Removal

1 Ensure the ignition is turned off.
2 Remove the door inner trim panel as described in Section 11.
3 Disconnect the mirror wiring plug **(see illustration)**. Unclip the plug from the door panel.
4 Whilst supporting the weight of the mirror, peel away the covers, then undo the 3 retaining screws and remove the mirror from the door frame **(see illustration)**.

Refitting

5 Refitting is a reversal of removal.

Exterior mirror glass

Removal

6 Carefully press the mirror glass in at the inner edge, and then working through the gap at the outside edge of the mirror glass, use a lever to release the clips that secure the mirror glass to the mirror body **(see illustration)**.
Caution: Be prepared for mirror breakage. Wear gloves and eye protection.
7 Withdraw the glass, and where applicable, disconnect the wiring connectors for the heater element.

Refitting

8 Where applicable, reconnect the wiring connectors, then push the mirror glass into the mirror until it locks into position.

Exterior mirror shell

9 Remove the mirror glass as described previously in this Section.
10 Working from inside the mirror housing,

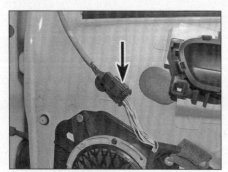

19.3 Disconnect and unclip the mirror wiring plug

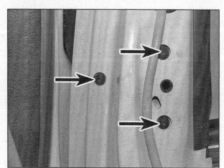

19.4 Mirror retaining screws

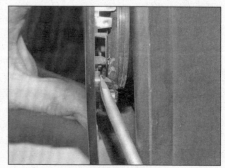

19.6 Carefully lever the outer edge of the mirror glass

release the retaining clips that secure the mirror shell to the mirror body **(see illustration)**.

11 Fold the mirror inwards, and unclip the outer shell from the mirror.

12 To refit, carefully push the mirror shell onto the mirror body until the securing clips lock into position. Refit mirror glass, as described previously in this section.

20 Windscreen, tailgate and rear door window glass – general information

1 These areas of glass are secured by the tight fit of the weatherstrip in the body aperture, and are bonded in position with a special adhesive. Renewal of such fixed glass is a difficult, messy and time-consuming task, which is considered beyond the scope of the home mechanic. It is difficult, unless one has plenty of practice, to obtain a secure, waterproof fit. Furthermore, the task carries a high risk of breakage; this applies especially to the laminated glass windscreen. In view of this, owners are strongly advised to have this sort of work carried out by one of the many specialist windscreen fitters.

21 Body exterior fittings – removal and refitting

Wheel arch liners

1 Firmly apply the handbrake, then jack up the front of the car and support it securely on axle stands (see *Jacking and vehicle support*). Remove the relevant front roadwheel.

2 The wheel arch liners are secured by a number of push-fit clips and screws **(see illustration)**. Release the centre pin, withdraw the plastic rivets/clips from the liner then undo the retaining screws.

3 Once all the clips have been removed, withdraw the liner from under the wheel arch.

Body trim strips and badges

4 The various body trim strips and badges are held in position with a special adhesive

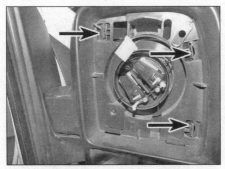

19.10 Release the retaining clips

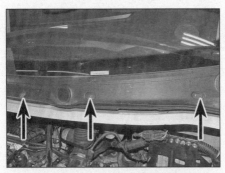

22.2a Scuttle panel retaining bolts (left-hand bolts arrowed)

membrane. Removal requires the trim/badge to be heated, to soften the adhesive, and then cut away from the surface. Due to the high risk of damage to the vehicle paintwork during this operation, it is recommended that this task should be entrusted to a Peugeot/ Citroën/Fiat dealer.

22 Windscreen scuttle panel – removal and refitting

Removal

1 Remove the windscreen wiper arms as described in Chapter 12 Section 13.

2 Undo the 5 retaining bolts and slide the scuttle panel downwards from the windscreen **(see illustrations)**.

21.2 Prise out the centre pin, and lever out the plastic rivet

22.2b Slide the panel downwards from the windscreen

Refitting

3 Refitting is a reversal of removal. Refit the wiper arms with reference to Chapter 12 Section 13.

23 Radiator grille – removal and refitting

Removal

1 Open the bonnet, then prise up the centre pins and remove the 4 plastic expansion rivets along the upper edge of the radiator grille **(see illustrations)**.

2 Release the lower retainers and lift the radiator grille from place **(see illustration)**.

Refitting

3 Refitting is a reversal of removal.

23.1a Prise up the centre pins, and lever out the plastic rivets…

23.1b …along the upper edge of the radiator grille (left-hand rivets arrowed)

23.2 Prise up the grille to release the lower retainers

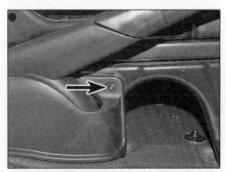

24.2a Undo the screw a the side of the cover...

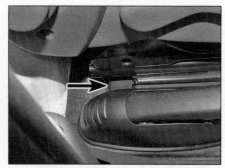

24.2b ...and the screw at the rear

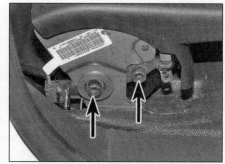

24.3 Handbrake lever retaining bolts

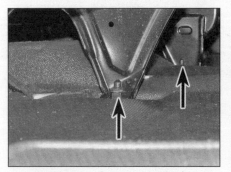

24.4 Undo the front mounting nuts

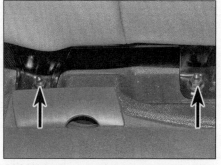

24.8 Undo the nuts at the outer edge of the seat base

8 Undo the nuts securing the seat base to the floor panel **(see illustration)**.
9 Disconnect the wiring plug on the underside, and manoeuvre the seat from the cabin.

Refitting

10 Refitting is a reversal of removal. Where applicable, reactivate the airbag system as described in Chapter 5A Section 4, before reconnecting the battery.

25 Seat belt components – removal and refitting

> **Warning: Depending on model, the front seats may be equipped with seat belt pretensioners, and side airbags are built into the outer sides of the seats. Refer to Chapter 12 Section 20 for the precautions which should be observed when dealing with an airbag system. Do not tamper with the seat belt pretensioner unit in any way, and do not attempt to test the unit. Note that the unit is triggered if the mechanism is supplied with an electrical current (including via an ohmmeter), or if the assembly is subjected to a temperature of greater than 100°C.**
> Note: *Record the positions of the washers and spacers on the seat belt anchors, and ensure they are refitted in their original positions.*

Outer front seat belts

Removal

1 Remove the B-pillar trim panels as described in Section 26.
2 Manoeuvre the inertia reel from the B-pillar, and disconnect the wiring plug **(see illustration)**.

Refitting

3 Refitting is a reversal of removal. Ensure that all washers and/or spacers are positioned as noted before removal, and tighten all mounting bolts to the specified torque.

Centre front seal belt

Removal

4 Remove the front fixed seat as described in Section 24.
5 Undo the lower anchorage bolt under the seat cushion **(see illustration)**.

24 Seats – removal and refitting

> **Warning: Depending on model, the front seats may be equipped with seat belt pretensioners, and side airbags may be built into the outer sides of the seats. Where side airbags are fitted, refer to Chapter 12 Section 20 for the precautions which should be observed when dealing with an airbag system. Do not tamper with the seat belt pretensioner unit in any way, and do not attempt to test the unit. Note that the unit is triggered if the mechanism is supplied with an electrical current (including via an ohmmeter), or if the assembly is subjected to a temperature of greater than 100°C.**

Removal

Sliding seat

1 Disconnect the battery negative lead as described in Chapter 5A Section 4.
2 Undo the screws and remove the handbrake lever cover **(see illustrations)**.
3 Undo the 2 Allen bolts securing the handbrake lever to the seat base **(see illustration)**.
4 Slide the seat fully rearwards, then undo the front mounting nuts **(see illustration)**.
5 Move the seat fully forwards, and remove the rear mounting nuts.
6 Disconnect the wiring plug(s) on the underside, and manoeuvre the seat from the cabin.

Fixed seat

7 Disconnect the battery negative lead as described in Chapter 5A Section 4.

25.2 Prise out the locking clip and disconnect the wiring plug

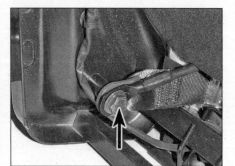

25.5 Undo the anchorage bolt under the cushion

6 Undo the screw each side of the cover at the top of the backrest **(see illustration)**.

7 Prise up the locking clip and disconnect the wiring plug from the inertia reel **(see illustration)**.

8 Undo the retaining bolt and manoeuvre the inertia reel from the backrest, along with the seat belt **(see illustration)**.

Refitting

9 Refitting is a reversal of removal.

Front seat belt stalk

Removal

10 To make access easier, remove the front seat as described in Section 24.

11 Disconnect the wiring connector from under the seat, and the undo the bolt securing the seat belt stalk to the seat frame **(see illustration)**.

Refitting

12 Refitting is a reversal of removal. Ensure that all washers and/or spacers are positioned as noted before removal, and tighten all mounting bolts to the specified torque.

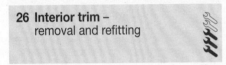

26 Interior trim – removal and refitting

Note: *There are numerous combinations of interior trim layout according to model year, vehicle type and whether or not sliding side doors are fitted. The following information is a guide to the most common arrangements.*

Door inner trim panels

1 Refer to Section 11.

Front A-pillar trim panel

2 Prise the weather seal from the front door aperture in the vicinity of the pillar trim. Take care not to damage the seal as it is being removed.

3 Pull the trim away from the pillar starting at the top, then work down the trim panel and release it from behind the facia panel **(see illustrations)**. Note that when removing the trim panel, the wiring loom or aerial lead may travel up the pillar (depending on which side is removed) and can make it awkward to disengage the bottom of the A-pillar trim panel from the facia, take care not to damage the wiring loom.

4 Refitting is a reversal of removal, but ensure that all retaining clips are fully engaged, and that the weatherstrip is fully seated.

Centre B-pillar trim panels

Lower section

5 Remove the relevant door sill trim panel as described later in this Section.

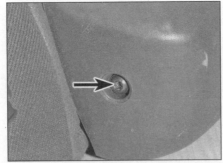

25.6 Undo the screw each side of the cover

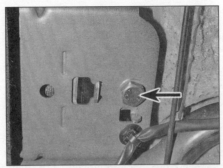

25.8 Centre seat belt inertia reel retaining bolt

6 Pull away the rubber weatherstrips each side of the B-pillar.

7 Slacken the centre screws, prise out the plastic expansion rivets, and pull the lower section of the B-pillar trim panel away **(see illustration)**.

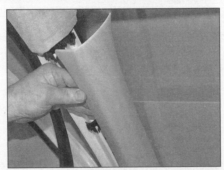

26.3a Pull the top of the A-pillar trim panel inwards...

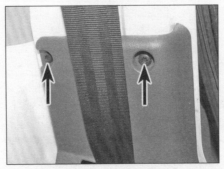

26.7 Slacken the screws and prise out the plastic rivets

25.7 Prise up the black locking clip and disconnect the plug

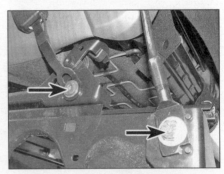

25.11 Seat belt stalk retaining bolts

8 Unscrew the seat belt lower anchorage bolt **(see illustration)**. Recover the spacer.

9 Feed the seat belt through the aperture, and remove the lower section of the B-pillar trim panel.

26.3b ...then upwards/rearwards to detach it from the facia

26.8 Seat belt lower anchorage bolt

26.10 Slide up the adjuster cover

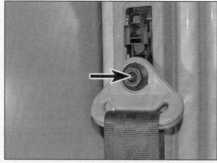

26.11 Seat belt upper anchorage bolt

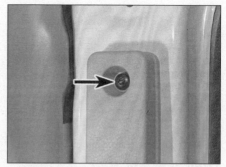

26.12 Undo the Torx screw at the top

Upper section

10 Carefully slide up and remove the seat belt height adjuster cover **(see illustration)**.
11 Undo the seat belt upper anchorage bolt **(see illustration)**.
12 Undo the screw at the top of the panel **(see illustration)**.
13 Fold down the cover, then release the 2 clips at the lower edge of the upper trim panel **(see illustration)**. Remove the panel.

Refitting

14 Refitting is a reversal of removal, but ensure that all retaining clips are fully engaged and that the weatherstrip is fully seated.

Luggage compartment side trim panel – van models

Removal

15 Release the fasteners and remove the wheelarch cover (where fitted).
16 Carefully work around the edge of the side trim panel, and release the retaining clips. Remove the panel.

Refitting

17 Refitting is a reversal of removal, but ensure that all retaining clips are fully engaged.

Headlining

Note: *Headlining removal requires considerable skill and experience if it is to be* carried out without damage, and is therefore best entrusted to a Peugeot/Citroën/Fiat dealer or bodywork specialist. A general overview of the procedure is given below for those with the expertise to attempt the operation on a DIY basis.

18 The headlining is clipped and glued to the roof, and can be withdrawn only once all fittings such as the grab handles, courtesy lights, sunvisors, sunroof (if fitted), pillar trim panels, and associated additional panels have been removed. The door, tailgate and sunroof aperture weatherstrips will also have to be prised clear and any additional screws and clips removed. Once the headlining attachments are released, the adhesive bonding in the centre panels must be broken using a hot air gun and spatula, starting at the front and working rearwards.
19 When refitting, a coat of neoprene adhesive (available from Peugeot/Citroën/Fiat dealers) must be applied to the centre panels in the locations noted during removal. Position the headlining carefully and refit all components disturbed during removal. Clean the headlining with soap and water or white spirit on completion.

Door sill trim panels

20 Undo the Torx screws securing the sill trim panel **(see illustrations)**.
21 Pull the trim panel upwards from place.
22 Refitting is a reversal of removal.

26.13 B-pillar trim lower clips

Sunvisors

23 Release the sunvisor from the inner mounting, then undo the 2 screws and remove the outer mounting **(see illustration)**.
24 Refitting is a reversal of removal.

27 Facia panel components – removal and refitting

1 Disconnect the battery negative lead as described in Chapter 5A Section 4.

Steering column shrouds

2 With the steering column in its highest position, undo the 2 upper Torx screws and

26.20a Undo the screws in the door aperture...

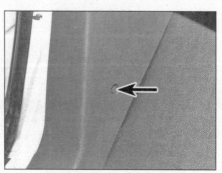

26.20b ...and the screw at the front

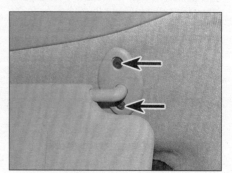

26.23 Undo the screws and remove the outer mounting

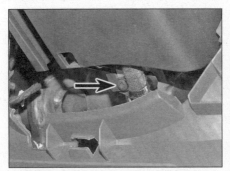

27.2a Undo the screw, and prise out the expansion rivet beneath the shroud...

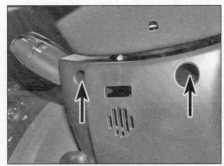

27.2b ...and remove the 2 Torx screws at the top

27.4 Remove the column upper shroud

lower plastic expansion rivet securing the column lower shroud **(see illustrations)**.

3 Unclip the upper shroud and remove the lower shroud.

4 If required, manoeuvre the upper shroud from place **(see illustration)**.

5 Refitting is a reversal of removal, making sure the lug on the lower shroud locates correctly in the slot on the steering column shroud.

Drivers side lower facia panels

6 Prise the panel from the drivers end of the facia **(see illustration 27.21)**.

7 Prise out and remove the facia drivers side lower cover **(see illustration)**.

8 Reach up behind the facia, and press the headlight range control switch from place. Disconnect the wiring plug.

9 Starting at the lower edge, pull rearwards the drivers side lower facia trim panel **(see illustration)**.

10 Open the cover (where fitted), release the clip, and push the diagnostic connector back into the facia recess **(see illustration)**.

11 Pull away the rubber weatherstrip from the pillar, then open the lower cover and undo the 2 screws at the right-hand edge of the lower facia panel/oddments tray **(see illustration)**.

12 Undo the 3 retaining screws, and manoeuvre the lower facia panel/oddments tray rearwards from place **(see illustration)**. Disconnect any wiring plugs as the assembly is withdrawn.

13 Refitting is a reversal of removal.

Centre switch panel

14 Depending on the equipment fitted, either remove the fault display unit or navigation screen from the top of the facia as described in Chapter 12 Section 11.

15 Remove the facia-mounted audio unit as described in Chapter 12 Section 17.

16 Prise the panel beneath the heater/air conditioning control panel rearwards **(see illustration)**.

17 On models with fully automatic climate control, carefully prise the audio unit console rearwards from the centre switch panel. On models with manual heating/air conditioning, pull the storage unit beneath the radio location

27.7 Remove the drivers side lower cover

27.9 Pull the lower edge of the panel rearwards

27.10 Push the diagnostic connector back into the facia recess

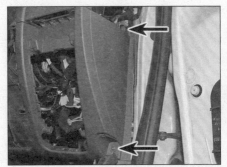

27.11 Undo the screws at the right-hand edge

27.12 Lower facia panel retaining screws

27.16 Carefully prise the panel rearwards

27.17 Pull the storage unit from the facia

27.18 Undo the Torx screws at the lower edge of the control panel

27.19a Undo the 2 screws...

27.19b ...release the clips...

27.19c ...and pull the switch panel rearwards

rearwards (see illustration). Disconnect any wiring plugs as the unit is withdrawn.

18 Undo the screws securing the heater/air conditioning control panel to the switch panel (see illustration).

19 Undo the 2 screws at the lower edge, release the clips at the top, then withdraw the switch panel from the facia and disconnect the wiring connectors from the switches (see illustrations).

20 Refitting is a reversal of removal, making sure all wiring connectors are fitted correctly.

Facia end panels

21 Carefully unclip the trim panels from each end of the facia, pulling them free from their retaining clips (see illustration). Disconnect any wiring as the panel is removed.

22 Refitting is a reversal of removal.

Passenger side glovebox

23 Prise the end panel from the passengers side of the facia (see illustration).

24 Prise away the lower cover from the facia (see illustration).

25 Pull away the rubber weatherstrip from the pillar adjacent to the glovebox.

26 Fold down the cover, then undo the 2 retaining screws at the outer edge of the glovebox (see illustration).

27 Working inside the glovebox, undo the 3 screws securing the glovebox to the facia (see illustration). Withdraw the glovebox

27.21 Starting at the rear edge, prise the panel from the end of the facia

27.23 Starting at the rear, prise the panel from the facia

27.24 Pull the lower cover rearwards to release it

27.26 Undo the screws at the outer edge

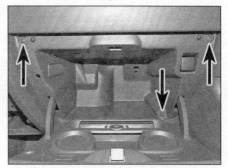

27.27 Undo the 3 screws and manoeuvre the glovebox rearwards

27.32 Prise up the gear lever gaiter

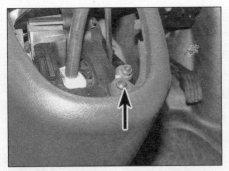

27.33a Undo the screw in the gear lever aperture...

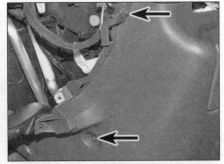

27.33b ...the 2 screws on the left-hand side...

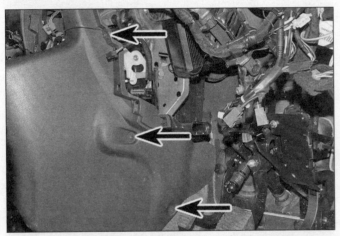

27.33c ...and 3 screws on the right-hand side of the console

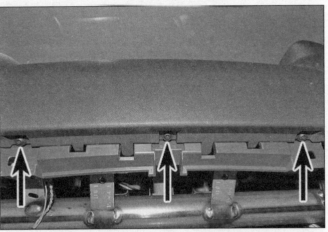

27.42a Undo the Torx screws at the lower edge...

from the facia. Disconnect any wiring plugs as the glovebox is withdrawn.
28 Refitting is a reversal of removal.

Gear lever console

29 Remove the centre switch panel as described previously in this Section.
30 Remove the passengers glovebox assembly as described in this Section.
31 Remove the drivers side lower facia panel as described in this Section
32 Carefully prise up the gear lever gaiter **(see illustration)**.
33 Undo the 6 screws securing the gear lever console, and release the clips securing the vent each side **(see illustrations)**. Manoeuvre the console over the lever, disconnecting any wiring plugs as they become accessible.
34 Refitting is a reversal of removal.

Instrument panel

35 Refer to Chapter 12 Section 10.

Multifunction display

36 Refer to Chapter 12 Section 11.

Complete facia assembly

Note: *This is an involved operation entailing the removal of numerous components and assemblies, and the disconnection of a multitude of wiring connectors. Make notes or take pictures of the location of all*

disconnected wiring, or attach labels to the connectors, to avoid confusion when refitting.
37 Disconnect the battery negative lead as described in Chapter 5A Section 4.
38 Move the front seats as far back as possible. Set the steering wheel in the straight-ahead position, and engage the steering lock.
39 Remove the following facia panels as described previously in this Section:
a) *Steering column shrouds.*
b) *Lower facia panels – driver's side.*
c) *Centre switch panel*
d) *Passenger side glovebox.*
e) *Facia end panels.*
f) *Gear lever console*
40 Remove the steering wheel and steering

column, as described in Chapter 10 Section 15 and Chapter 10 Section 16.
41 Remove the instrument panel as described in Chapter 12 Section 10.
42 Where fitted, remove the passenger airbag, as described in Chapter 12 Section 21. On models without a passengers airbag, undo the 3 screws at the lower edge, and carefully prise out the airbag panel **(see illustrations)**.
43 Remove the facia speaker as described in Chapter 12 Section 18.
44 Where applicable, prise up the solar sensor from the centre/top of the facia, and disconnect the wiring plug. Where no sensor is fitted, prise up the trim piece **(see illustration)**.

27.42b ...and pull the airbag panel rearwards

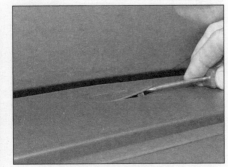

27.44 Prise up the trim piece from the centre of the facia

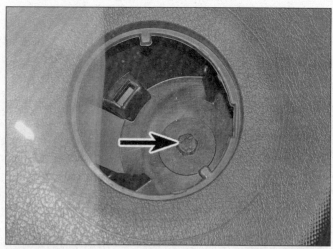

27.46a The facia is secured by 1 bolt in each tweeter speaker location...

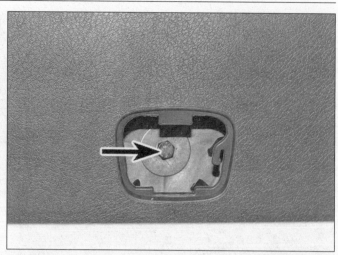

27.46b ...1 bolt in the centre (solar sensor location)...

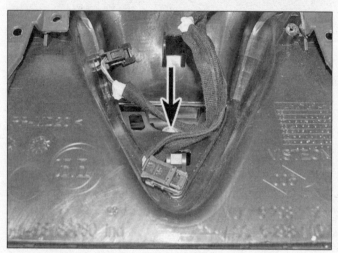

27.46c ...1 bolt in the centre between the vents...

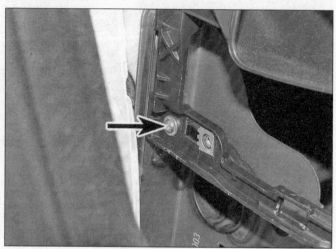

27.46d ...1 bolt at each end...

45 Remove both A-pillar trims as described in Section 26.
46 The facia is now secured by 10 retaining bolts **(see illustrations)**. Undo the bolts, and with the help of an assistant, manoeuvre the facia from the cabin.

47 Refitting is a reversal of removal ensuring that all wiring is correctly reconnected and all mountings securely tightened.

27.46e ...1 bolt in the passengers airbag aperture...

27.46f ...2 bolts in the centre, lower section...

27.46g ...and 1 bolt to the right-hand side of the steering column location

Chapter 12
Body electrical systems

Contents

Degrees of difficulty

| **Easy,** suitable for novice with little experience 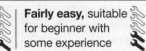 | **Fairly easy,** suitable for beginner with some experience | **Fairly difficult,** suitable for competent DIY mechanic | **Difficult,** suitable for experienced DIY mechanic | **Very difficult,** suitable for expert DIY or professional |

Specifications

General

System type.. 12 volt negative earth

Bulbs

	Type	Wattage
Brake/tail light	P21/5W Bayonet	21/5
Direction indicator light (amber)...................	PY21W Bayonet	21
Direction indicator side repeater (amber).....................	WY5W Push-fit	5
Foglight:		
Front	H1	55
Rear	P21W Bayonet	21
Front sidelights...................................	W5W Push-fit	5
Glovebox light	Push-fit	5
Headlights (Halogen)	H4	55
High-level brake light:		
Tailgate models.............................	P21W	21
Hinged-rear door models......................	5W5	5
Interior/courtesy lights	W5W Push-fit	5
Luggage compartment light.........................	Push-fit	5
Number plate light	W5W Push-fit	5
Reversing light	P21W Bayonet	21

Torque wrench setting

	Nm	lbf ft
Airbag control unit retaining nuts	8	6
Accelerometer sensor retaining bolts........................	8	6

1 General Information

⚠️ *Warning: Before carrying out any work on the electrical system, read through the precautions given in 'Safety first!' at the beginning of this manual, and in Chapter 5A Section 1.*

1 The electrical system is of 12 volt negative earth type. Power for the lights and all electrical accessories is supplied by a calcium-lead type battery, which is charged by the alternator.

2 Many of the body electrical systems are controlled by individual electronic control modules (ECMs), these are in turn controlled by a main ECM known as a built-in systems interface (BSI). The various ECMs and the BSI exchange data with each other via a multiplex network. The multiplex network is a two-wire system linking the BSI with the system ECMs and is termed by Peugeot/Citroën/Fiat as CAN (controlled area network) and VAN (vehicle area network). Essentially this means that the BSI and the ECMs controlling the 'comfort' systems, safety systems, security systems, and entertainment systems in the vehicle, are all interconnected via vehicle area networks.

3 An ECM connected to the multiplex network only receives some of the data needed for it to operate directly, with the remaining data being supplied by the other ECMs on the network. Because the ECMs share information via the network, several ECMs can control the operation of the same system. Also, one ECM can control several systems in an autonomous manner. The BSI is the manager of this information interchange as well as also being responsible for the control of certain vehicle systems itself. The BSI has a full diagnostic capability whereby any fault in any of the ECMs on the multiplex network can be traced using diagnostic equipment connected to the vehicle diagnostic connector, located inside storage compartment under the drivers side of the facia **(see illustration)**. Should any fault develop with a system on the network, have the self-diagnosis facility interrogated by a Peugeot/Citroën/Fiat dealer or suitably-equipped specialist.

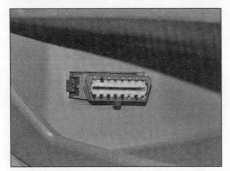

1.3 Vehicle diagnostic plug connector

4 This Chapter covers repair and service procedures for the various electrical components not associated with the engine. Information on the battery, alternator and starter motor can be found in Chapter 5A.

5 It should be noted that, prior to working on any component in the electrical system, the battery should first be disconnected; to prevent the possibility of electrical short-circuits (see Chapter 5A Section 1).

2 Electrical fault finding – general information

Note: *Refer to the precautions given in 'Safety first!' and in Chapter 5A Section 1 before starting work. The following tests relate to testing of the main electrical circuits, and should not be used to test delicate electronic circuits (such as anti-lock braking systems), particularly where an electronic control unit/module (ECU or ECM) or multiplexing is used (see Section 1).*

General

1 A typical electrical circuit consists of an electrical component; any switches, relays, motors, fuses, fusible links or circuit breakers related to that component, and the wiring and connectors which link the component to both the battery and the chassis. To help to pinpoint a problem in an electrical circuit, wiring diagrams are included at the end of this Chapter.

2 Before attempting to diagnose an electrical fault, first study the appropriate wiring diagram, to obtain a more complete understanding of the components included in the particular circuit concerned. The possible sources of a fault can be narrowed down, by noting whether other components related to the circuit are operating properly. If several components or circuits fail at one time, the problem is likely to be related to a shared fuse or earth connection.

3 Electrical problems usually stem from simple causes, such as loose or corroded connections, a faulty earth connection, a blown fuse, a melted fusible link, or a faulty relay (refer to Section 3 for details of testing relays). Visually inspect the condition of all fuses, wires and connections in a problem circuit before testing the components. Use the wiring diagrams to determine which terminal connections will need to be checked, in order to pinpoint the trouble spot.

4 The basic tools required for electrical fault finding include a circuit tester or voltmeter; an ohmmeter (to measure resistance); a battery and set of test leads; and a jumper wire, preferably with a circuit breaker or fuse incorporated, which can be used to bypass suspect wires or electrical components. Before attempting to locate a problem with test instruments, use the wiring diagram to determine where to make the connections.

5 To find the source of an intermittent wiring fault (usually due to a poor or dirty connection, or damaged wiring insulation), a 'wiggle' test can be performed on the wiring. This involves wiggling the wiring by hand, to see if the fault occurs as the wiring is moved. It should be possible to narrow down the source of the fault to a particular section of wiring. This method of testing can be used in conjunction with any of the tests described in the following sub-Sections.

6 Apart from problems due to poor connections, two basic types of fault can occur in an electrical circuit – open-circuit, or short-circuit.

7 Open-circuit faults are caused by a break somewhere in the circuit, which prevents current from flowing. An open-circuit fault will prevent a component from working, but will not cause the relevant circuit fuse to blow.

8 Short-circuit faults are caused by a 'short' somewhere in the circuit, which allows the current flowing in the circuit to 'escape' along an alternative route, usually to earth. Short-circuit faults are normally caused by a breakdown in wiring insulation, which allows a feed wire to touch either another wire, or an earthed component such as the bodyshell. A short-circuit fault will normally cause the relevant circuit fuse to blow. **Note:** *As an aid to economy and to prevent battery discharge, certain functions of the electrical system can only be used for 30 minutes after the engine has been stopped. Bear this in mind when tracing power supply faults on these systems.* After this period the BSI (built-in systems interface) cuts the power to these circuits. To restore power, start the engine. It is also possible for the BSI to turn off certain functions (heater blower, heated rear window) depending on the state of charge of the battery. When tracing a fault, ensure the battery is in a good state of charge.

Functions affected
- Windscreen wipers.
- Electric windows.
- Sunroof.
- Courtesy lights.
- Audio equipment.

Finding an open-circuit

9 To check for an open-circuit, connect one lead of a voltmeter to either the negative battery terminal or a known good earth.

10 Connect the other lead to a connector in the circuit being tested, preferably nearest to the battery or fuse.

11 Switch on the circuit, bearing in mind that some circuits are live only when the ignition switch is moved to a particular position.

12 If voltage is present (indicated either by the tester bulb lighting or a voltmeter reading, as applicable), this means that the section of the circuit between the relevant connector and the battery is problem-free.

13 Continue to check the remainder of the circuit in the same fashion.

14 When a point is reached at which no voltage is present, the problem must lie between that point and the previous test point with voltage. Most problems can be traced to a broken, corroded or loose connection.

Finding a short-circuit

15 To check for a short-circuit; first disconnect the load(s) from the circuit (loads are the components which draw current from a circuit, such as bulbs, motors, heating elements, etc).

16 Remove the relevant fuse from the circuit, and connect a circuit tester or voltmeter to the fuse connections.

17 Switch on the circuit, bearing in mind that some circuits are live only when the ignition switch is moved to a particular position.

18 If voltage is present (indicated either by the tester bulb lighting or a voltmeter reading, as applicable), this means that there is a short-circuit.

19 If no voltage is present, but the fuse still blows with the load(s) connected, this indicates an internal fault in the load(s).

Finding an earth fault

20 The battery negative terminal is connected to 'earth' – the metal of the engine/transmission and the car body – and most systems are wired so that they only receive a positive feed, the current returning via the metal of the car body. This means that the component mounting and the body form part of that circuit. Loose or corroded mountings can therefore cause a range of electrical faults, ranging from total failure of a circuit, to a puzzling partial fault. In particular, lights may shine dimly (especially when another circuit sharing the same earth point is in operation), motors (eg, wiper motors or the radiator cooling fan motor) may run slowly, and the operation of one circuit may have an apparently unrelated effect on another. Note that on many vehicles, earth straps are used between certain components, such as the engine/transmission and the body, usually where there is no metal-to-metal contact between components, due to flexible rubber mountings, etc **(see illustrations)**.

21 To check whether a component is properly earthed, disconnect the battery, and connect one lead of an ohmmeter to a known good earth point. Connect the other lead to the wire or earth connection being tested. The resistance reading should be zero; if not, check the connection as follows.

22 If an earth connection is thought to be faulty, dismantle the connection, and clean back to bare metal both the bodyshell and the wire terminal or the component earth connection mating surface. Be careful to remove all traces of dirt and corrosion, and then use a knife to trim away any paint, so that a clean metal-to-metal joint is made. On reassembly, tighten the joint fasteners securely; if a wire terminal is being refitted, use serrated washers between the terminal

2.20a The main earth lead is attached to the top of the transmission casing

2.20b Battery negative lead earth connection adjacent to the battery

2.20c Earth points may also be located at the front right-hand chassis member...

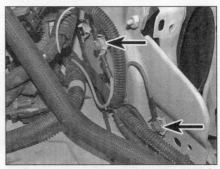

2.20d ...left-hand front chassis member...

2.20e ...facia crossmember (centre)...

2.20f ...and drivers side...

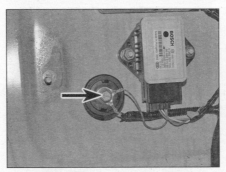

2.20g ...between the front seats...

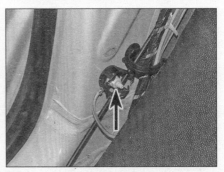

2.20h ...and lower A-pillar

and the bodyshell, to ensure a clean and secure connection. When the connection is remade, prevent the onset of corrosion in the future by applying a coat of petroleum jelly or silicone-based grease, or by spraying on (at regular intervals) a proprietary ignition sealer or water-dispersant lubricant.

3 Fuses and relays – general information

Fuses

1 Fuses are designed to break a circuit when a predetermined current is reached, in order to protect the components and wiring, which could be damaged by excessive current flow. Any excessive current flow will be due to a fault in the circuit, usually a short-circuit (see Section 2).

2 Three fuseboxes are fitted, with the majority of the fuses are located behind the storage compartment on the drivers side of the facia, with additional fuses located in the engine compartment, and in the battery compartment.

3 To gain access to the facia fuses, pull the storage compartment from the facia **(see illustrations)**.

4 To gain access to the fuses in the engine compartment, unclip and move the screenwash filler neck to one side, then unclip the cover from the fuse/relay box **(see illustrations)**.

5 To access the fuses in the battery compartment, remove the battery as described in Chapter 5A Section 4. The fuses are located at the front of the battery compartment **(see illustration)**.

6 To remove a fuse, first switch off the circuit concerned (or the ignition), and then pull the fuse out of its terminals **(see illustrations)**. The wire within the fuse should be visible; if the fuse has blown it will be broken or melted.

7 Always renew a fuse with one of the correct rating; never use a fuse with a different rating from that specified. The fuse rating is stamped on the top of the fuse; the fuses are also colour-coded as follows. Refer to the

3.3a Pull the storage compartment from the facia…

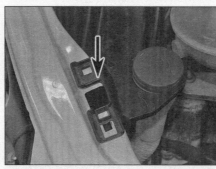

3.4a Slide the filler neck forwards to unclip it

wiring diagrams for details of the fuse ratings and the circuits protected.

COLOUR	RATING
Orange	5A
Red	10A
Blue	15A
Yellow	20A
White/Clear	25A
Green	30A

8 Never renew a fuse more than once without tracing the source of the trouble. If the new fuse blows immediately, find the cause before renewing it again; a short to earth as a result of faulty insulation is most likely. Where a fuse protects more than one circuit, try to isolate

3.3b …to access the fuses

3.4b Release the clips and open the cover

the fault by switching on each circuit in turn (where possible) until the fuse blows again. Always carry a supply of spare fuses of each relevant rating on the vehicle; a spare of each rating should be clipped into the fusebox.

Relays

Note: *The BSI unit is located on the drivers side of the facia*

9 The majority of relay functions are incorporated into the built-in system interface (BSI) unit (see Section 22). Other relays are located in the fuse/relay box in the engine compartment.

10 If a circuit or system controlled by a relay develops a fault and the relay is suspect, operate the system. If the relay is functioning, it should be possible to hear it 'click' as it is

3.5 Battery compartment fuses

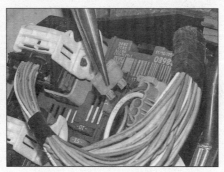

3.6a Pull the fuse from the terminals

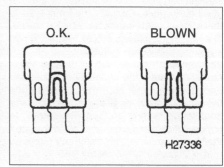

3.6b A blown fuse is recognised from its melted or broken wire

energised. If this is the case, the fault lies with the components or wiring of the system. If the relay is not being energised, then either the relay is not receiving a main supply or a switching voltage, or the relay itself is faulty. Testing is by the substitution of a known good unit, but be careful – while some relays are identical in appearance and in operation, others look similar but perform different functions.

11 To remove a relay, first ensure that the relevant circuit is switched off. The relay can then simply be pulled out from the socket, and pushed back into position.

4 Electrical connectors – general information

1 Most electrical connections on these vehicles are made with multiwire plastic connectors. The mating halves of many connectors are secured with locking clips molded into the plastic connector shells. The mating halves of some large connectors, such as some of those under the instrument panel, are held together by a bolt through the center of the connector.

2 To separate a connector with locking clips, use a small screwdriver to pry the clips apart carefully, then separate the connector halves. Pull only on the shell, never pull on the wiring harness, as you may damage the individual wires and terminals inside the connectors. Look at the connector closely before trying to separate the halves. Often the locking clips are engaged in a way that is not immediately clear. Additionally, many connectors have more than one set of clips.

3 Each pair of connector terminals has a male half and a female half. When you look at the end view of a connector in a diagram, be sure to understand whether the view shows the harness side or the component side of the connector. Connector halves are mirror images of each other, and a terminal shown on the right side end-view of one half will be on the left side end-view of the other half.

4 It is often necessary to take circuit voltage measurements with a connector connected. Whenever possible, carefully insert a small straight pin (not your meter probe) into the rear of the connector shell to contact the terminal inside, then clip your meter lead to the pin. This kind of connection is called "backprobing." When inserting a test probe into a terminal, be careful not to distort the terminal opening. Doing so can lead to a poor connection and corrosion at that terminal later. Using the small straight pin instead of a meter probe results in less chance of deforming the terminal connector. "T" pins are a good choice as temporary meter connections. They allow for a larger surface area to attach the meter leads too.

Electrical connectors

5 Typical electrical connectors:

4.5a Most electrical connectors have a single release tab that you depress to release the connector

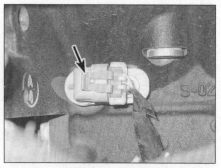
4.5b Some electrical connectors have a retaining tab which must be pried up to free the connector

4.5c Some connectors have two release tabs that you must squeeze to release the connector

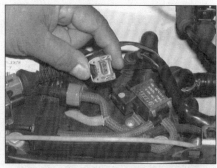
4.5d Some connectors use wire retainers that you squeeze to release the connector

4.5e Critical connectors often employ a sliding lock (1) that you must pull out before you can depress the release tab (2)

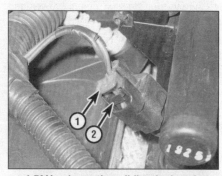
4.5f Here's another sliding-lock style connector, with the lock (1) and the release tab (2) on the side of the connector

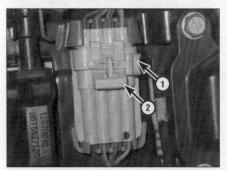
4.5g On some connectors the lock (1) must be pulled out to the side and removed before you can lift the release tab (2)

4.5h Some critical connectors, like the multi-pin connectors at the Electronic Control Module employ pivoting locks that must be flipped open

5.5 Disconnect the wiring plugs from the front face of the switch

5.6a Slacken the retaining clamp bolt

5.6b Lift the catches away from the lugs

5 Switches – removal and refitting

Note: *Disconnect the battery before removing any switch, and reconnect the lead after refitting the switch (see Chapter 5A Section 4).*

Ignition switch

1 Refer to Chapter 10 Section 17.

Steering column switches

2 Remove the driver's airbag as described in Section 21.

3 Remove the steering wheel as described in Chapter 10 Section 15.

4 Remove the steering column lower and upper shrouds as described in Chapter 11 Section 26.

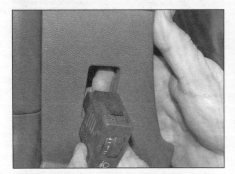

5.11 Push the adjustment switch from place

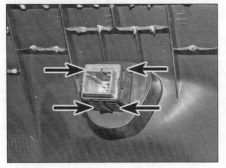

5.18 Depress the clips and detach the switch from the panel

5 Disconnect the wiring plugs from the switch assembly **(see illustration)**.

6 If the switch assembly is to be refitted, immobilise the airbag rotary contact disc with adhesive tape. Note that as long as the wheels are in the straight-ahead position, the contact disc should lock in position. Slacken the switch assembly retaining clamp, then using a small screwdriver, carefully prise the retaining catches away from the lug on the column and lift the switch assembly from place **(see illustrations)**.

Caution: Take great care not to damage the switch assembly retaining catches.

7 Although refitting is a reversal of removal, the airbag contact unit built into the switch assembly must be set in the correct position as follows:

8 Ensure the wheels are in the straight-ahead position.

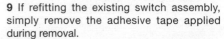

5.15 Switch retaining clips

5.20 Prise the switch assembly from the door trim panel

9 If refitting the existing switch assembly, simply remove the adhesive tape applied during removal.

10 New switch assemblies are supplied with the contact ring immobilised in the correct position by a self-adhesive label, which should be removed just prior to steering wheel refitment.

Headlight height adjustment switch

11 Reach inside the facia recess and push the adjustment switch rearwards from place **(see illustration)**.

12 Disconnect the switch wiring plug.

13 Refitting is the reversal of removal.

Centre panel switches (central locking, ESP, etc.)

14 Remove the facia centre switch panel as described in Chapter 11 Section 27.

15 Carefully release the clips and detach the relevant switch from the panel **(see illustration)**.

16 Refitting is a reversal of removal.

Hazard warning switch

17 Starting at the sides, carefully prise the switch panel from the top of the facia **(see illustration 11.2)**. Disconnect the wiring plugs as the panel is withdrawn.

18 Disconnect the wiring connector from the switch, and then release the securing clips and press the switch out from the switch panel **(see illustration)**.

19 Refitting is the reversal of removal.

Electric window/mirror switches

20 Using a blunt, flat-bladed tool, carefully prise the switch from the door trim panel **(see illustration)**. Disconnect the wiring plug as the switch is withdrawn.

21 Refitting is a reversal of removal.

Passenger airbag on/off switch

22 Remove the glovebox as described in Chapter 11 Section 27.

23 Reach through the aperture and push the switch rearwards from the facia. Disconnect the wiring plug as the switch is withdrawn.

24 Refitting is the reverse of removal.

5.28 Push the switch from the mounting bracket

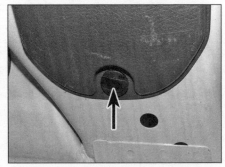

5.31 Prise out the centre pin a little, and lever out the plastic rivet

5.33 Push the courtesy light switch from the panel

Heating/ventilation control and heated rear window switch

25 The switches are an integral part of the heater/ventilation control panel, and cannot be renewed separately. If any switch is faulty, the complete control panel must be renewed – refer to Chapter 3 Section 10 for details.

Brake light switch

26 Refer to Chapter 9 Section 19.

Handbrake warning light switch

27 Remove the handbrake lever as described in Chapter 9 Section 17.
28 Press the switch forwards from the handbrake mounting bracket **(see illustration)**.
29 Refitting is the reverse of removal.

Courtesy light switch

30 The front door courtesy light switches are an integral part of the door lock assemblies. Refer to Chapter 11 Section 12 for door lock removal and refitting details.
31 To remove the sliding side door courtesy light switched, the plastic panel away adjacent to the door aperture must be removed. Prise out the centre pin, lever out the plastic rivet, and remove the panel **(see illustration)**.
32 Reach up behind the switch and disconnect the wiring plug.
33 Push the switch from the panel **(see illustration)**.
34 Refitting is a reversal of removal.

Luggage area light switch

35 The luggage compartment light switch function is integral with the tailgate lock assembly. For tailgate lock removal, refer to Chapter 11 Section 17.

6 Bulbs (exterior lights) – renewal

General

1 Whenever a bulb is renewed, note the following points:
a) Remember that, if the light has just been in use, the bulb may be extremely hot.

b) Always check the bulb contacts and holder, ensuring that there is clean metal-to-metal contact between the bulb and its live(s) and earth. Clean off any corrosion or dirt before fitting a new bulb.
c) Wherever bayonet-type bulbs are fitted (see Specifications), ensure that the live contact(s) bear firmly against the bulb contact.
d) Always ensure that the new bulb is of the correct rating, and that it is completely clean before fitting it; this applies particularly to headlight/foglight bulbs (see below)

Headlight

Note: *When handling the new bulb, use a tissue or clean cloth to avoid touching the glass with the fingers; moisture and grease from the skin can cause blackening and*

6.2 Unclip the headlight bulb protective cover

6.4a Move the clip to the side...

rapid failure of this type of bulb. If the glass is accidentally touched, wipe it clean using methylated spirit.
2 Reach behind the headlamp unit, pull the rubber tab at the edge of the protective cover and remove it **(see illustration)**.
3 Disconnect the wiring plug from the bulb **(see illustration)**.
4 Move the bulb retaining clip to the side, and withdraw the bulb **(see illustrations)**.
5 Install the new bulb, ensuring that its locating tabs are correctly seated in the light cut-outs, and secure it in position with the retaining clip.
6 Reconnect the wiring plug, and refit the protective cover.

Sidelight

7 Reach behind the headlamp and unclip the

6.3 Disconnect the headlight bulb wiring plug

6.4b ... and remove the bulb

6.7 Unclip the sidelight bulb protective cover

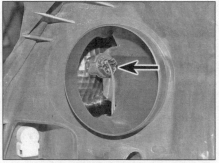

6.8 Pull the bulbholder to remove…

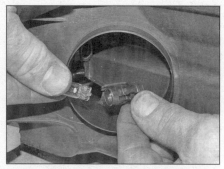

6.9 … then pull the bulb from its holder

6.17 Rotate the bulbholder 90° anti-clockwise

6.18 Press-in the bulb and twist it anti-clockwise

6.20 Push the light unit to the rear, then pull out the front edge

headlight bulb protective cover and remove it **(see illustration)**.

8 Pull the bulb holder from the rear of the light unit **(see illustration)**.

9 The bulb is a capless (push-fit) type, and can easily be removed by pulling it out of the bulbholder **(see illustration)**.

10 Refitting is the reverse of the removal procedure.

Front foglight

11 Remove the foglight as described in Section 8.

12 Pull the protective cover from the rear of the foglight.

13 Disconnect the wiring plug from the rear of the bulb.

14 Release the spring clip and withdraw then bulb.

15 When handling the new bulb, use a tissue

or clean cloth to avoid touching the glass with the fingers; moisture and grease from the skin can cause blackening and rapid failure of this type of bulb. If the glass is accidentally touched, wipe it clean using methylated spirit.

16 Fit the new bulb using a reversal of the removal procedure.

Front direction indicator

17 Reach behind the headlamp, rotate the bulbholder 90° anti-clockwise and remove it **(see illustration)**.

18 The bulb is a bayonet-fit in the holder, and can be removed by pressing it in and rotating it anti-clockwise **(see illustration)**.

19 Refitting is the reverse of the removal procedure.

Side repeater

20 Push the side repeater towards the

rearwards to free its retaining clip, then ease it out from the wing panel **(see illustration)**.

21 Release the clip and disconnect the wiring plug **(see illustration)**.

22 The side repeater is a sealed unit. If the bulb has failed the complete unit must be renewed.

23 Refitting is a reversal of the removal procedure.

Rear light cluster

24 Remove the relevant rear light unit as described in Section 8.

25 Release the retaining tabs and remove the bulbholder assembly, from the rear of the light unit **(see illustration)**.

26 All the bulbs have bayonet fittings. The relevant bulb can be removed by pressing it in and rotating it anti-clockwise **(see illustration)**.

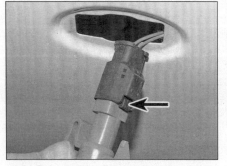

6.21 Release the clip and disconnect the plug

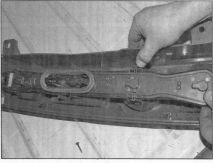

6.25 Release the bulbholder retaining tabs

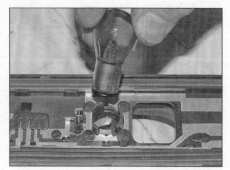

6.26 Press in the bulb and rotate it anti-clockwise to remove it

6.29 High-level brake light bulb – bayonet type

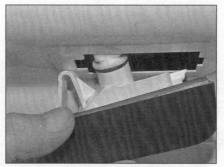

6.35 Push the light unit to the outside to compress the clip

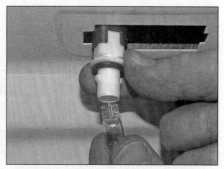

6.36 Pull the bulb from the bulbholder

27 Refitting is the reverse of removal, ensuring the light unit and bulbholder seals are in good condition.

High-level brake light

Hinged rear doors

28 Remove the high level light unit as described in Section 8.
29 Depending on model, the bulb may be a capless (push-fit) type, or bayonet (push-in, twist anti-clockwise and pull) type. Remove the bulb **(see illustration)**.
30 Refitting is a reversal of removal.

Tailgate

31 Undo the 2 Torx screws and remove the plastic cover from the inside of the high-level brake light.
32 Release the clips and remove the bulbholder.
33 Press-in the bulb slightly, rotate it anti-clockwise and pull it from the holder.
34 Refitting is the reverse of removal.

7.2 Carefully unclip the light lens

7.7 Rotate the bulbholders anti-clockwise

Number plate light

35 Push the light unit to the outside and unclip it **(see illustration)**.
36 Rotate the bulbholder anti-clockwise and pull it from the light unit. The bulb is of the capless (push-fit) type, and can easily be removed by pulling it out of the bulbholder **(see illustration)**.
37 Refitting is the reverse of the removal procedure.

7 Bulbs (interior lights) – renewal

General

1 Refer to Section 6, paragraph 1.

Passenger compartment lights

2 Using a flat bladed-screwdriver inserted into

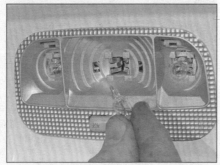

7.3 Pull the bulb from the light unit

7.12 Prise the front edge of the light unit from place

the slot each side, carefully unclip the plastic lens cover from the light unit **(see illustration)**.
3 The bulbs are of the capless (push-fit) type, and can be removed by simply pulling it out of the bulbholder **(see illustration)**.
4 Refitting is the reverse of the removal procedure

Instrument panel lights

5 The instrument panel and warning lights are illuminated by integral LEDs. It is not possible to renew them independently of the panel. Instrument panel renewal is described in Section 10.

Heating/ventilation control illumination

Note: *The following procedure is for models with manually operated heater controls. On models with automatic climate control, the heater control panel is illuminated by integral LEDs. It is not possible to renew them independently of the panel.*
6 Remove the heater control panel as described in Chapter 3 Section 10.
7 Twist the bulbholders anti-clockwise and remove them from the rear of the heater control panel **(see illustration)**.
8 The bulbs are of the capless (push-fit) type. Pull the bulb from the bulbholder.
9 Refitting is the reverse of the removal procedure

Multifunction display illumination

10 The multifunction display is illuminated by integral LEDs. It is not possible to renew them independently of the display. Remove the multifunction display as described in Section 11.

Switch illumination

11 All of the switches that are illuminated are done so by LEDs. These LEDs are an integral part of the switch and cannot be renewed separately. Renewal will therefore require renewal of the complete switch assembly (see Section 5).

Glovebox light

12 Open the glovebox, and carefully prise the light unit from place **(see illustration)**.
13 Pull the wedge-type bulb from the holder, and press the new one into place.
14 Refitting is a reversal of removal.

8.2a The headlight is secured by a bolt at the top…

8.2b …a bolt underneath…

8.2c …and a bolt at the inside edge

8 Exterior light units – removal and refitting

Headlight

1 Remove the front bumper (see Chapter 11 Section 6).

2 Undo the 3 retaining bolts (see illustrations).

3 Move the headlight forwards slightly, reach behind, slide out the locking clip and disconnect the wiring connector from the rear of the headlight unit (see illustration).

4 Reconnect the wiring plug and slide-in the locking clip.

5 Position the headlight in its aperture, and then refit and tighten the headlight mounting bolts.

6 Refit the front bumper.

7 Check the headlight beam alignment using the information given in Section 9.

Front indicator side repeater

8 Remove the indicator side repeater from the wing panel, as described in Section 6.

Rear light unit

9 Open the hinged rear doors/tailgate, then undo the two retaining nuts, and pull the light unit rearwards (see illustration).

10 Disconnect the wiring connector from the light unit as it is removed from the vehicle (see illustration).

11 Refitting is the reverse of removal, ensuring the light unit locating peg locates in the rear panel correctly (see illustration).

High-level brake light

Tailgate models

12 Undo the 2 Torx screws and remove the plastic cover from the inside of the high-level brake light.

13 Disconnect the wiring plug, unclip and remove the light unit.

14 Refitting is the reverse of removal.

Hinged-rear door models

15 Undo the 2 Torx screws and remove the light unit (see illustration). Disconnect the wiring plug as the light unit is withdrawn.

16 Refitting is the reverse of removal.

Number plate light

17 Removal of the number plate light unit is described as part of the bulb renewal procedure described in Section 6.

18 Refitting is the reverse of the removal procedure.

Front foglights

19 Slacken the appropriate front roadwheel bolts, raise the front of the vehicle and support is securely on axle stands (see *Jacking and vehicle support*). Remove the roadwheel.

20 Release the fasteners and remove the wheelarch liner.

21 Disconnect the wiring plug from the rear of the foglight.

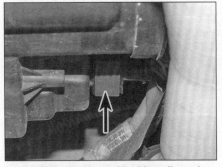

8.3 Slide out the red locking clip and disconnect the wiring plug

8.9 Undo the nuts and pull the light unit rearwards

8.10 Disconnect the wiring connector

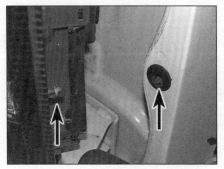

8.11 Ensure the peg locates into the corresponding hole

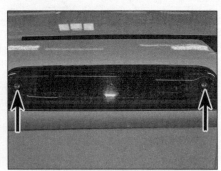

8.15 High-level brake light screws

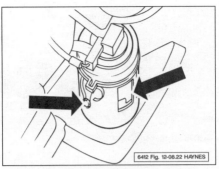

8.22 Undo the bolt and release the clip each side

9.2 The inner adjuster is for vertical alignment, the outer for horizontal adjustment

10.3 Pull the panel rearwards to release the clips

22 Undo the mounting bolt at the lower edge; release the clips and withdraw the foglight unit from the rear of the bumper **(see illustration)**.
23 Refitting is a reversal of removal.

9 Headlight beam alignment – general information

1 Accurate adjustment of the headlight beam is only possible using optical beam-setting equipment, and this work should therefore be carried out by a Peugeot/Citroën dealer or suitably-equipped workshop.
2 For reference, the vertical and horizontal alignment of the headlights can be adjusted by rotating the adjuster assemblies, which are accessible at the rear of the headlight casing **(see illustration)**. The inner adjuster is for vertical alignment, and the outer adjuster for horizontal alignment.
3 On models equipped with headlight leveling, ensure the adjuster switch on the facia panel inside the vehicle is set to position 0 before the headlights are adjusted.
4 The adjuster should be positioned as follows according to the load being carried in the vehicle:

0	No load
1	Partial load
2	Average load
3	Maximum load

10 Instrument panel – removal and refitting

Removal

1 Disconnect the battery negative lead as described in Chapter 5A Section 4.
2 Remove the headlight height adjustment switch as described in Section 5.
3 Starting at the lower edge, pull the panel beneath the steering column rearwards, and remove it **(see illustration)**.
4 Carefully prise the instrument panel

10.4 Prise the instrument panel surround trim rearwards

surround trim rearwards **(see illustration)**.
5 Undo the retaining screw at the upper centre part of the instrument panel, then pull it out at the top and lift it upwards from the lower locating pegs **(see illustration)**.
6 Fold over the locking clip and disconnect the wiring plug(s) as the unit is withdrawn **(see illustration)**.
7 Should the instrument panel develop a fault, have the vehicle's self-diagnosis facility interrogated by a Peugeot/Citroën/Fiat dealer or suitably-equipped specialist. No parts are available separately for the instrument panel, if faulty, the complete assembly must be renewed.

Refitting

8 Refitting is a reversal of removal, ensuring

10.5 Instrument panel retaining screw

that the wiring connectors are securely fitted and the retaining clips engage correctly when the instrument panel is pressed into position in the top of the facia.

11 Multifunction display/ On-board navigation unit – removal and refitting

Removal

1 Disconnect the battery negative lead as described in Chapter 5A Section 4.
2 Carefully unclip the display unit from the top of the facia panel, release the securing clip and disconnect the wiring plug as it is removed **(see illustration)**.

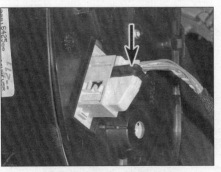

10.6 Fold over the locking clip

11.2 Starting at the sides, carefully prise the unit from the facia

12.1 The horn is located behind the right-hand end of the bumper

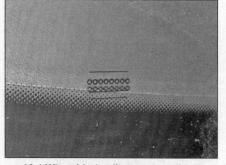

13.1 Wiper blade alignment mark on screen

13.2 Prise up the cover and slacken the nut beneath

Note: *Note that on our vehicle, the display unit was originally glued to the cover. Upon attempting to release the cover, the glue failed.*

Refitting

3 Refitting is a reversal of removal.

12 Horn – removal and refitting

Removal

1 The horn(s) are located behind the front bumper, on the right-hand side **(see illustration)**.
2 Unclip the inner wheel arch liner in front of the right-hand side front wheel, and then reach in to access the horns. If required, to make access easier, remove the front bumper as described in Chapter 11 Section 6.
3 Disconnect the wiring connector, then slacken the mounting bracket bolt and remove the horn from under the front crossmember.

Refitting

4 Refitting is a reversal of removal.

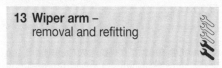
13 Wiper arm – removal and refitting

Note: *The wiper arms can be a very tight fit*

on their spindles, a puller may be needed to remove them safely and without damage.

Front wiper

1 There are alignment marks provided on the windscreen to aid refitting **(see illustration)**.
2 Prise up the plastic cover then slacken and remove the spindle nut **(see illustration)**.
3 Lift the blade off the glass, and move the wiper arms carefully side to side to release them from the spindle. If the arm is very tight, free it from the spindle using a suitable puller **(see illustration)**.
4 Ensure that the wiper arm and spindle splines are clean and dry, then refit the arm to the spindle, aligning the wiper blade with the alignment marks provided.
5 Refit the spindle nuts and tightening them securely.

Rear wiper

6 Operate the wiper motor, then switch it off so that the wiper arm returns to the at-rest position. Stick tape to the screen alongside the wiper blade to ensure the correct position for refitting.
7 Disconnect the washer fluid pipe.
8 Unclip the centre cap from the wiper arm spindle nut, then slacken and remove the spindle nut **(see illustration)**.
9 Remove the wiper arm spindle nut, lift the blade off the glass, and pull the wiper arm off its spindle. If the arm is very tight, free it from the spindle using a suitable puller.
10 Ensure that the wiper arm and spindle

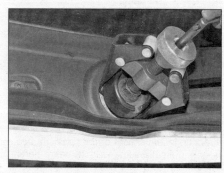

13.3 If the wiper arm is tight on the spindle, use a puller

splines are clean and dry, then refit the arm to the spindle, aligning the wiper blade with the tape fitted on removal. If the original position of the wiper has been lost, align the upper edge of the blade with the reference mark on the screen **(see illustration)**.
11 Refit the spindle nut, tightening it securely, and clip cover back into position.

14 Windscreen wiper motor and linkage – removal and refitting

Removal

1 Remove both wiper arms as described in Section 13.

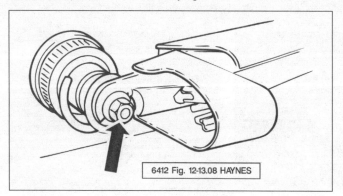

13.8 Lift the cap and undo the nut

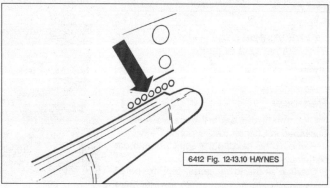

13.10 Align the blade with the reference mark on the screen

14.3a Undo the bolts at the top...

14.3b ...then slacken the nut behind the coolant expansion tank

14.5a Undo the nut around each wiper spindle...

2 Remove the windscreen scuttle panel as described in Chapter 11 Section 22.
3 Undo the 2 bolts at the top, slacken the rear nut, and slide the coolant expansion tank/bracket forwards **(see illustrations)**.
4 Release the retaining clip and disconnect the wiring plug from the wiper motor.
5 The wiper motor/linkage assembly is secured by a nut at each and and a lower nut **(see illustrations)**. Undo the nuts, recover the washers, then manoeuvre it from the engine compartment
6 If required, disconnect the linkage rods from the wiper motor spindle arm by levering them from their balljoints. Undo the retaining nut to remove the arm from the wiper spindle, noting its fitted position. To remove the wiper motor from the linkage bracket, undo the 4 retaining screws **(see illustration)**.

Refitting

7 Refitting is a reversal of removal, ensuring all fasteners are securely tightened.

15 Tailgate window wiper motor – removal and refitting

Removal

1 Ensure the ignition is turned off.
2 Remove the tailgate inner trim panel as described in Chapter 11 Section 17.
3 Remove the wiper arm as described in Section 13.
4 Unscrew the collar from the spindle.
5 Disconnect the wiring connector from the wiper motor.
6 Disconnect the screenwash fluid pipe from the motor assembly.
7 Undo the 3 retaining bolts securing the wiper motor to the tailgate, and manoeuvre it from position **(see illustration)**.

Refitting

8 Make sure that any rubber mountings and collars (where fitted) are correctly positioned in the wiper motor mounting bracket.
9 Manoeuvre the wiper motor into position and secure it in position with the retaining bolts.
10 Reconnect the wiring connector to the

14.5b ...and the nut underneath

motor then refit the trim panel to the tailgate. Turn on the ignition, then operate the wiper and allow it to stop in the park position.
11 Refit the wiper arm as described in Section 13.

16 Washer system components – removal and refitting

Note: *Before working on the reservoir or pump, it is advisable to drain as much fluid out of the reservoir as possible, to prevent any spillage.*
1 The washer reservoir is located behind the right-hand side of the front bumper and

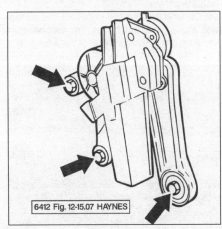

15.7 Tailgate wiper motor retaining bolts

14.6 Wiper motor retaining screws

supplies both the windscreen and tailgate washers via the same pump. On models equipped with headlight washers, the reservoir also supplies the headlight washer jets via an additional pump.

Washer fluid reservoir

2 Remove the front bumper as described in Chapter 11 Section 6.
3 Disconnect the wiring plug(s) from the washer pump(s) **(see illustration 16.10)**.
4 Note the correct fitted location of the washer hoses (if necessary, mark them for identification purposes) then disconnect the hoses from the washer pump(s). Position a container beneath the reservoir to catch any washer fluid from the pump and hoses.
5 Slacken and remove the retaining nut top of the reservoir, and the bolt at the side **(see illustration)**.

16.5 Undo the reservoir retaining nut and bolt

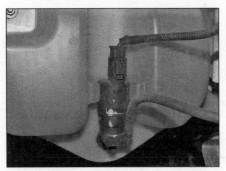

16.10 Disconnect the wiring plug and the hose

16.13 Pull the hose from the jet

17 Audio unit – removal and refitting

Note: *The following procedures show a basic and a higher range Audio unit, which are typical for the range of equipment fitted by Peugeot/Citroën/Fiat. There are many types of audio unit fitted depending on model; the type of removal clips (radio keys) will vary also.*

Removal

1 Disconnect the battery negative lead as described in Chapter 5A Section 4.
2 Insert the removal clips (radio keys) into the holes at the sides of the unit until they release the retaining clips. Push the clips outwards to release the unit from the facia **(see illustration)**. If the removal clips are not available, insert a small screwdriver/punch into the holes on each side of the unit to release the clips.
3 Once both retaining clips have been released, slide the audio unit out of position. Disconnect the wiring plugs and aerial lead, then remove the unit from the vehicle **(see illustration)**.

17.2 Insert two pins into each side of the audio unit

17.3 Disconnect the aerial lead and the wiring plugs

Refitting

4 Prior to refitting, remove the radio keys.
5 Securely reconnect the aerial lead and wiring plugs, then slide the unit back into position, taking care not to trap any wiring.

18 Loudspeakers – removal and refitting

Removal

Door speakers

1 Remove the door inner trim panel as described in Chapter 11 Section 11.
2 Undo the 4 screws and remove the speaker from the door **(see illustration)**, disconnecting the wiring plug as it becomes accessible.
3 If required, drill out the rivets and remove the speaker mounting from the door.

Front tweeter

4 Carefully prise the tweeter from place **(see illustration)**.
5 Disconnect the wiring plug connector from the tweeter is withdrawn. Secure the wiring connector to the top of the facia, to prevent losing the wiring inside the facia.

Refitting

6 Refitting is a reversal of removal. Making sure that all wiring connectors are secure and the trim panels are clipped securely in position.

6 Manoeuvre the reservoir out of position, releasing any wiring or hoses from locating clips in the side of the reservoir, disconnecting the filler neck as the reservoir is withdrawn.
7 Refitting is the reverse of removal, ensuring that the hoses are securely reconnected. Refill the reservoir and check for leaks.

Washer pump

8 Remove the front bumper as described in Chapter 11 Section 6.
9 Position a container beneath the reservoir to catch the washer fluid as the pump is removed.
10 Disconnect the washer fluid hose(s) and wiring plug from the washer pump **(see illustration)**.
11 Carefully ease the pump out from the

reservoir, and recover its sealing grommet. Wash off any spilt fluid with cold water.
12 Refitting is the reverse of removal, using a new sealing grommet if the original shows signs of damage or deterioration. Refill reservoir and check the pump grommet for leaks on completion.

Windscreen washer jet

13 Open the bonnet and disconnect the washer hoses from the jets **(see illustration)**. Release the clip under the bonnet and carefully prise the plastic grille from the outside of the bonnet. The jets are integral with the grille.
14 On refitting, clip the grille into the bonnet and make sure the hoses are reconnected securely; check the operation of the washer jets.

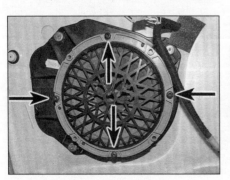

18.2 Door speaker retaining screws

18.4 Prise the tweeter and grille up from the facia

19 Radio aerial – removal and refitting

1 Removal of the radio aerial requires removal of the roof panel, which in turn requires removal of the headlining. Consequently, we recommend replacement of the aerial is entrusted to a Citroen/Peugeot/Fiat dealer, or suitable specialist.

20 Airbag system – general information and precautions

1 The airbag system is triggered in the event of a heavy frontal impact above a predetermined force, depending on the point of impact. The airbag is then inflated within milliseconds, and forms a safety cushion between the cabin occupants and the vehicle interior. This prevents contact between the upper body and vehicle interior, and therefore greatly reduces the risk of injury. The airbag then deflates almost immediately. The control unit also operates the front seat belt tensioner mechanisms at the same time.

2 There is a gyrometer/accelerometer sensor fitted to the floor panel between the two front seats.

3 The side airbags are fitted to the seat back of each front seat. The curtain airbags are fitted behind the windscreen pillars and headlining on each side of the passenger cabin.

4 Every time the ignition is switched on, the airbag control unit performs a self-test. The self-test takes approximately six seconds and during this time the warning light in the instrument panel will be illuminated. After the self-test is complete, the warning light will go out (unless the passenger airbag unit has been deactivated – see paragraph 5). If the warning light fails to come on, remains illuminated after the self-test period, or comes on at any time when the vehicle is being driven, there is a fault in the airbag system. The vehicle should be taken to a Peugeot/Citroën/Fiat dealer for examination at the earliest possible opportunity.

5 Most vehicles with a passenger airbag are equipped with a disabling switch fitted to the passengers end of the facia. The switch is operated using the ignition key and switches off the passenger airbag (it is not possible to disable the driver's or side/curtain airbags) to enable a rear-facing child seat to be installed in the passenger seat. Whilst the passenger airbag is disabled, the airbag warning light on the instrument panel will remain illuminated all the time.

Warning: Before carrying out any operations on the airbag system, disconnect the battery (see Chapter 5A Section 1) and wait at least five minutes. Remove the centre console (see Section), and then release the retaining clip and disconnect the wiring connector(s) from the airbag control unit. When the operations are complete, securely reconnect the control unit then refit the centre console. Make sure no one is inside the vehicle when the battery is reconnected then, with the driver's door open, switch the ignition on from outside vehicle and check the operation of the airbag warning light.

Warning: Do not subject the area of the body around the control unit to any form of shock, which could trigger the system.

Warning: Note that the airbags must not be subjected to temperatures in excess of 100ºC. When the airbag is removed, ensure that it is stored the correct way up (padded surface uppermost) to prevent possible inflation.

Warning: Do not allow any solvents or cleaning agents to contact the airbag assemblies. They must be cleaned using only a damp cloth.

Warning: The airbags and control unit are both sensitive to impact. If either is dropped or damaged they should be renewed.

Warning: Disconnect the airbag control unit wiring connector prior to using arc-welding equipment on the vehicle.

Warning: Never fit a rear-facing child seat to the front passenger seat unless the passenger airbag has been disabled (paragraph 5).

21 Airbag system components – removal and refitting

Warning: Refer to the precautions given in Section 20 before carrying out the following operations.

Driver's airbag

1 Disconnect the battery (see Chapter 5A Section 4) and wait at least five minutes.

2 Remove the steering column shrouds as described in Chapter 11 Section 27.

3 With the wheel in the straight-ahead position and the steering lock engaged, insert a screwdriver into the hole at the lower edge of the steering wheel boss, and press-in the spring clip (see illustration). Pull the airbag from the steering wheel.

4 Carefully lift the airbag unit away from the wheel, disconnecting the wiring plugs as they become accessible (see illustrations).

Warning: Do not knock or drop the airbag unit and store it with its padded surface uppermost.

5 Securely reconnect the wiring connectors then seat the airbag unit in the steering wheel, ensuring the wiring does not become trapped.

6 Fit the airbag unit; press it into place in the steering wheel until the retaining clips engage.

7 Refit the steering column shrouds as described in Chapter 11 Section 27.

8 Make sure no one is inside the vehicle then reconnect the battery. With the driver's door open, switch the ignition on from outside vehicle and check the operation of the warning light.

Passenger's airbag

9 Disconnect the battery as described in Chapter 5A Section 4, then wait at least five minutes.

10 Remove the passenger side glovebox assembly, as described in Chapter 11 Section 27.

21.3 Press-in the spring clip to release the airbag

21.4a Prise up the locking catch to release the main airbag plug

21.4b Disconnect the earth lead from the airbag

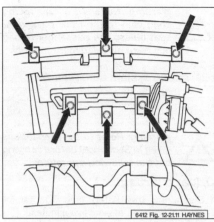

21.11 Passengers airbag retaining bolts

11 Working up inside the glovebox aperture, under the facia panel, undo the 6 retaining bolts securing the airbag unit to the vehicle crossmember **(see illustration)**.

12 Disconnect the airbag wiring plug and earth lead.

13 Carefully unclip the passenger side facia trim panel, complete with airbag from the main facia panel.

14 Refitting is the reversal of removal, ensuring the wiring is correctly connected and routed, and the retaining bolts are securely tightened.

15 On completion, make sure no one is inside the vehicle then reconnect the battery. With the door open, switch the ignition on from outside vehicle and check the operation of the warning light.

Airbag control unit

16 Disconnect the battery as described in Chapter 5A Section 4, then wait at least five minutes.

17 Remove the front seats as described in Chapter 11 Section 24.

18 Undo the fasteners and pull the drivers side door sill trim upwards.

19 Pull back the floor carpet to access the control.

20 Undo the retaining nuts and remove the ECU (Electronic Control Unit) cover **(see illustration)**.

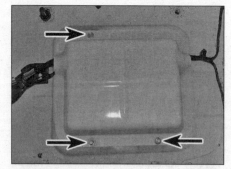

21.20 Undo the nuts and remove the cover

21 Pivot over the locking catches and disconnect the wiring plugs from the ECU.

22 Unscrew the control unit retaining nuts, and then remove the control unit from the floor of the vehicle.

23 Refit the control unit, making sure the arrow on the top of the unit is pointing towards the front of the vehicle **(see illustration)**. Refit the control unit retaining nuts and tighten them securely.

24 Securely reconnect the airbag control unit wiring connectors.

25 The remainder of refitting is a reversal of removal.

Gyrometer/accelerometer sensor

26 The sensor is located under the carpet, adjacent to the airbag control unit. Follow the airbag ECU removal procedure described previously in this Section.

27 Release the retaining clip, and then disconnect the wiring plug **(see illustration)**.

28 Undo the two nuts and remove the sensor.

29 Refitting is a reversal of removal, ensuring the arrow on the top of the sensor points to the front of the vehicle.

Side airbag sensor

30 Remove the B-pillar lower trim panel, as described in Chapter 11 Section 26.

31 Disconnect the wiring connector then undo the retaining bolt and remove the sensor from the inner sill panel.

32 Refitting is a reversal of removal, ensuring the bolt is tightened securely.

Side airbag

33 Removal and refitting of the side airbag units should be entrusted to a Peugeot/Citroën/Fiat dealer. The seat must be dismantled to enable the airbag unit to removed/refitted.

Curtain airbag

34 Removal and refitting of the curtain airbag units should be entrusted to a Peugeot/Citroën/Fiat dealer. The headlining must be partially removed to enable the airbag unit to removed/refitted.

Rotary contact unit

35 The rotary contact unit is integral with the steering column combination switch assembly. Removal is described in Section 5.

22 Built-in systems interface (BSI) unit/fusebox – general, removal and refitting

General information

1 The built-in systems interface (BSI) unit is an electronic control unit which controls a variety of functions normally controlled by individual control units and relays. The BSI unit is located behind the facia panel on the drivers side **(see illustration)**. The BSI unit controls the following functions (not all functions are fitted to all models).

a) *Direction indicator/hazard warning lights.*
b) *Windscreen/tailgate wiper motors.*
c) *Rear window heating element.*
d) *Immobiliser system.*
e) *Anti-theft alarm system.*
f) *Lights-on/ignition key warning buzzer.*
g) *Central locking/deadlocking, including the remote central locking receiver.*
h) *Door open indicator.*
i) *Courtesy light delay timer.*

2 Should any of the above functions become faulty, first check the condition of the fuses. If this fails to locate the problem, take the vehicle to a Peugeot/Citroën/Fiat dealer or

21.23 Airbag control unit

21.27 Gyrometer/accelerometer

22.1 Built in system interface (BSI) unit

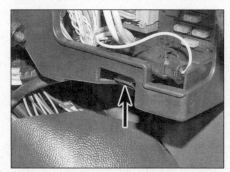

22.5a Release the clip at the base of the cover…

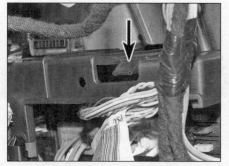

22.5b …and the clip at the base

22.6 Note the positions of the wiring plugs

suitably equipped repairer for testing. The only satisfactory way to test the BSI unit is by substitution with another unit that is known to be functioning correctly.

Removal

3 Disconnect the battery as described in Chapter 5A Section 4.
4 Remove the drivers side lower facia panel as described in Chapter 11 Section 27.

5 Release and remove the cover over the BSI unit **(see illustrations)**.
6 Release the securing clips and disconnect all of the wiring block connectors from the BSI unit. Most of the connectors are colour coded and can only be refitted in one position. Always make a note (or take a picture), as some of the connectors may be the same. Take your time to study the wiring connectors, and release them without using excessive

force as they are easily damaged **(see illustration)**.
7 Open the retaining clips and manoeuvre the BSI unit from place.

Refitting

8 Refitting is the reverse of removal, ensuring the wiring connectors are all securely reconnected and the BSI unit is secured.

BUILT-IN SYSTEM INTERFACE

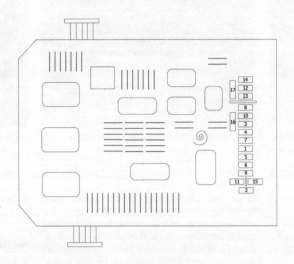

FUSE	VALUE	DESCRIPTION	OEM NAME
1	15 A	Rear wiper	F1
2	-	Not used	-
3	5 A	Airbag ECU	F3
4	10 A	Steering angle sensor, ESP dual sensor, Rear wiper relay, Diagnostic socket, Clutch switch, Manual air conditioning control panel, Manual headlamp height corrector, Particle filter pump	F4
5	30 A	Electric rear view mirrors, Passenger window motor	F5
6	30 A	Driver sequential window supply, Front passenger sequential window supply	F6
7	5 A	Stop lamps, Interior lamp, Glovebox lamp	F7
8	20 A	Multifunction display, Anti-theft alarm siren, Audio system, CD changer, Telephone system	F8
9	30 A	Cigar lighter, Diagnostic socket	F9
10	15 A	Rear height corrector, Steering wheel switch module, Instrument panel	F10
11	15 A	Diagnostic socket, Ignition switch	F11
12	15 A	Hands free kit, Airbag ECU, Parking assistance ECU	F12
13	5 A	Fuse box trailer relay unit	F13
14	15 A	Rain sensor, Rear additional air conditioning, Automatic air conditioning, Instrument panel	F14
15	-	Not used	-
16	-	Not used	-
17	10 A	Heated rear screen, Defroster rear view mirrors	F17

Fuses and relays

ENGINE COMPARTMENT CONNECTION BOARD-FUSE BOX

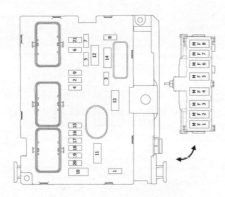

FUSE	VALUE	DESCRIPTION	OEM NAME
1	20 A	Engine ECU	F1
2	15 A	Horn	F2
3	10 A	Front and rear wash wiper pump	F3
4	20 A	Headlamp wash pump	F4
5	15 A	Engine ECU, Diesel fuel heater, Fuel additive pump, Fuel pump	F5
6	10 A	Mass air flow meter, Cooling fan high speed relay, Brake switch, Power steering pump, Sequential control switch, Gear lever locking control relay	F6
7	10 A	ESP ECU, ABS ECU	F7
8	20 A	Starter solenoid control	F8
9	10 A	Main brake switch	F9
10	30 A	Turbocharger pressure regulation solenoid, Engine ECU, Water presence sensor, Turbo air heating solenoid	F10
11	40 A	Air conditioning and heating unit, Left additional blower unit, Right additional blower unit	F11
12	30 A	Windscreen wiper	F12
13	40 A	Ignition BSI output	F13
14	-	Not used	-
15	10 A	Right hand headlamp	F15
16	10 A	Left hand headlamp	F16
17	15 A	Left hand headlamp	F17
18	15 A	Right hand headlamp	F18
19	15 A	Engine ECU, Throttle EGR solenoid, Oil vapour recirculation heating element, Air flowmeter, Diesel fuel heater	F19
20	10 A	Engine ECU, Turbocharger pressure regulation solenoid, Water presence sensor, Diesel injection pump	F20
21	5 A	Left cooling fan supply relay, Left and right in series cooling fan supply relay, Cooling fan fast speed supply relay	F21
MF1	-	Not used	-
MF2	40 A	ESP ECU, ABS ECU	MF2
MF3	30 A	ESP ECU, ABS ECU	MF3
MF4	60 A	Built-in system interface	MF4
MF5	70 A	Built-in system interface	MF5
MF6	20 A	Additional heating burner	MF6
MF7	20 A	Automatic gearbox ECU	MF7
MF8	30 A	Blower relay	MF8

Fuses and relays (continued)

FRONT FUSE MATRIX

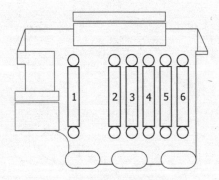

FUSE	VALUE	DESCRIPTION	OEM NAME
1	100 A	Power steering pump	F1
2	60 A	Fast speed fan supply relay	F2
3	60 A	Left hand fan supply relay	F3
4	40 A	Suspension control unit	F4
5	100 A	Pre post heating control unit	F5
6	-	Not used	-

FUSE BOX IN PASSENGER COMPARTMENT

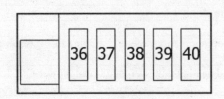

FUSE	VALUE	DESCRIPTION	OEM NAME
36	15 A	Tailgate/door lock relay	F36
37	10 A	Tailgate/door lock relay	F37
38	20 A	Rear wiper relay	F38
39	10 A	Additional heater control relay	F39
40	5 A	Folding rear view mirrors relays	F40

Fuses and relays (continued)

MAXI FUSE UNIT 1

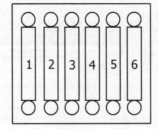

FUSE	VALUE	DESCRIPTION	OEM NAME
1	100 A	Electropump assembly	MF1
2	60 A	Electropump assembly	MF2
3	-	Not used	-
4	-	Not used	-
5	100 A	Preheating control unit	MF5
6	60 A	Electropump assembly	MF6

MAXI FUSE UNIT 2

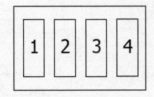

FUSE	VALUE	DESCRIPTION	OEM NAME
1	30 A	Heated seat relay	F1
2	20 A	12V socket	F2
3	50 A	Trailer fuse box, 40 A also used	F3
4	-	Not used	-

TRAILER FUSE BOX

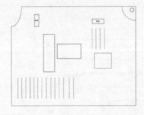

FUSE	VALUE	DESCRIPTION	OEM NAME
1	15 A	Trailer socket supply connector	F3
2	-	Not used	-

Fuses and relays (continued)

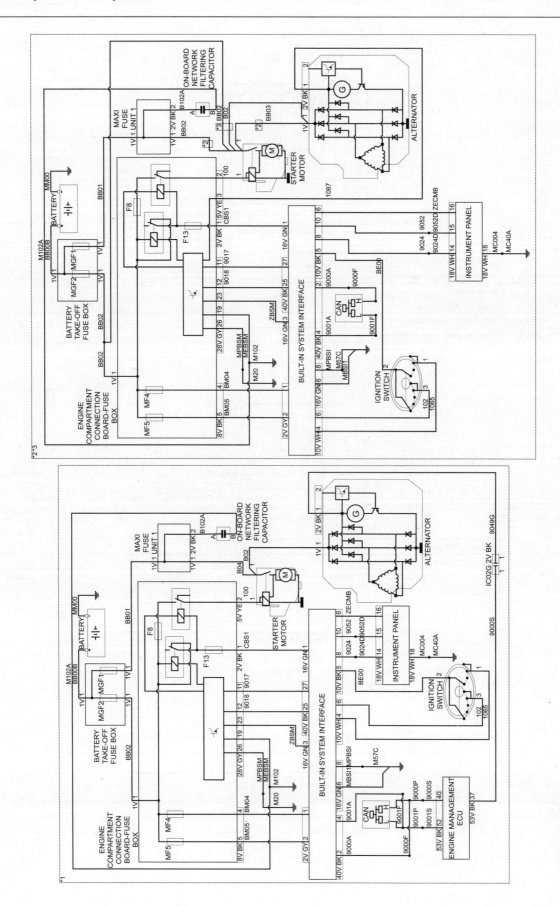

Starting and charging – Engines: DV6DU, DV6UC, DW10BTED4 and DV6UTED4

*1 Engine codes: DV6DU, DV6UC
*2 Engine codes: DW10BTED4
*3 Engine codes: DV6UTED4

Starting and charging – Engines: DW10CTED4, DW10CD, DW10CE and DW10UTED4

*1 Engine codes: DW10CTED4, DW10CD, DW10CE
*2 Engine codes: DW10UTED4

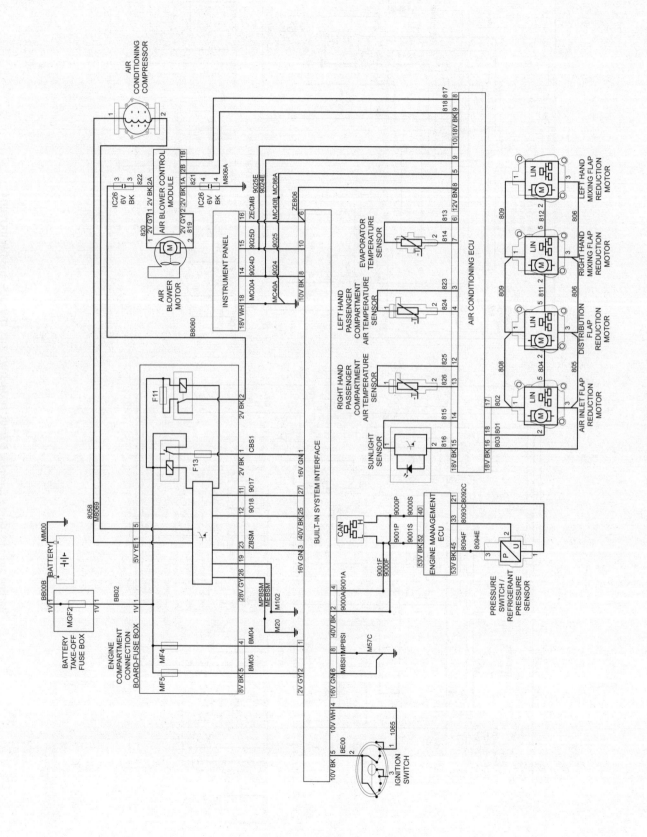

Automatic air conditioning

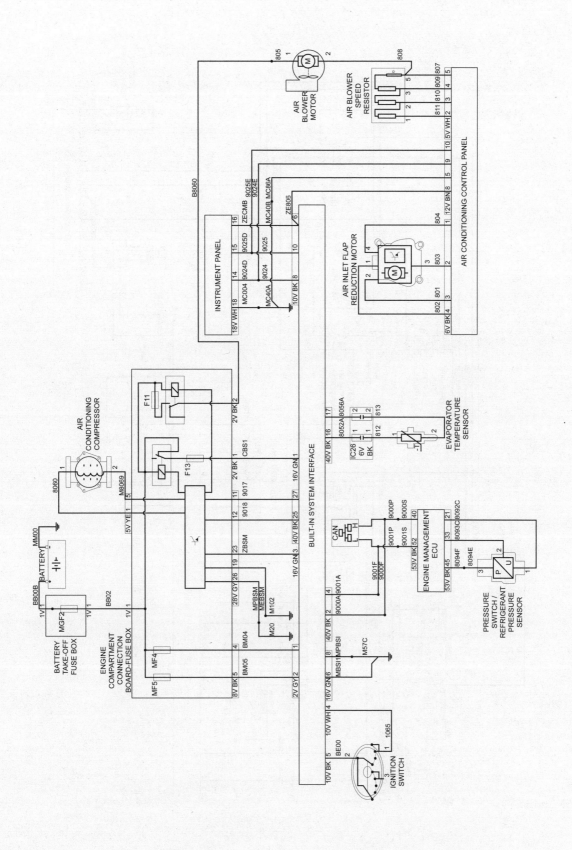

Manual air conditioning

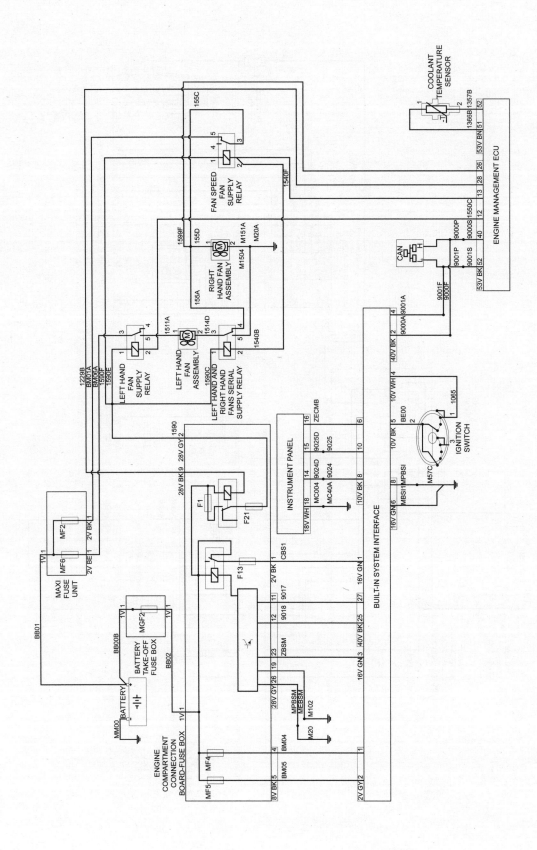

Engine cooling fan

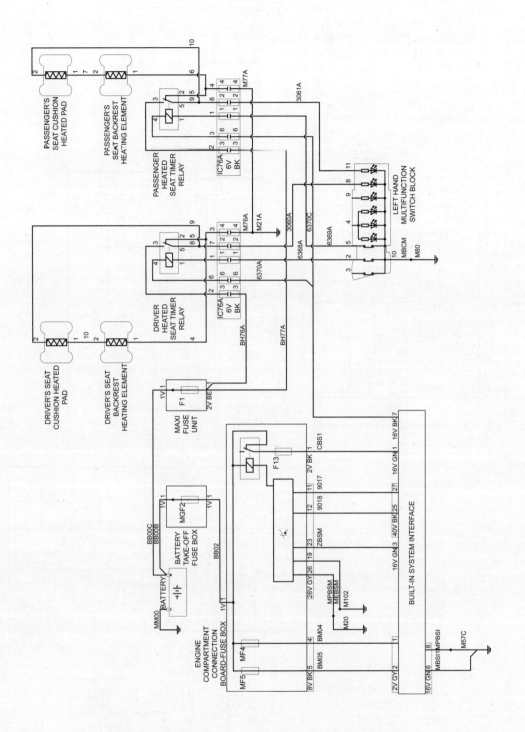

Seat heating

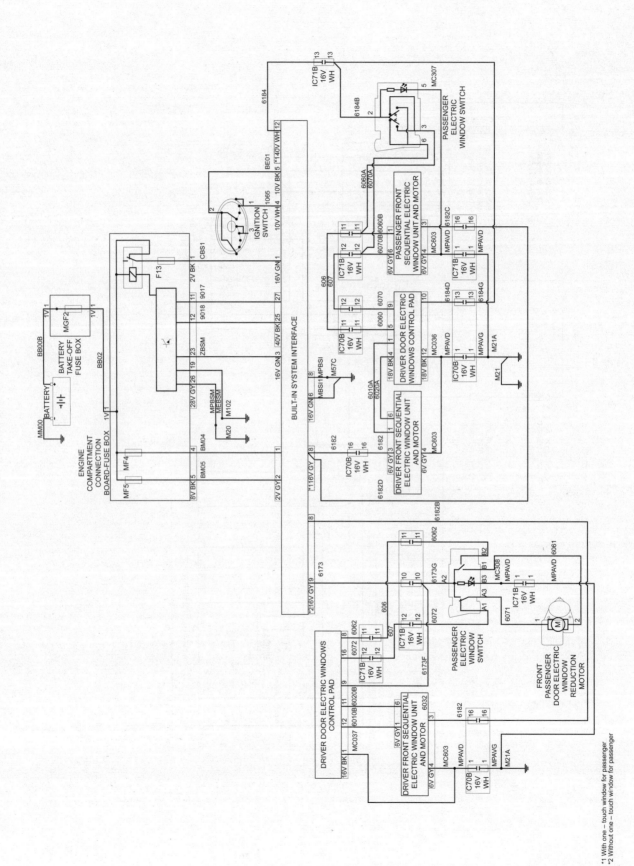

Power windows

*1 With one – touch window for passenger
*2 Without one – touch window for passenger

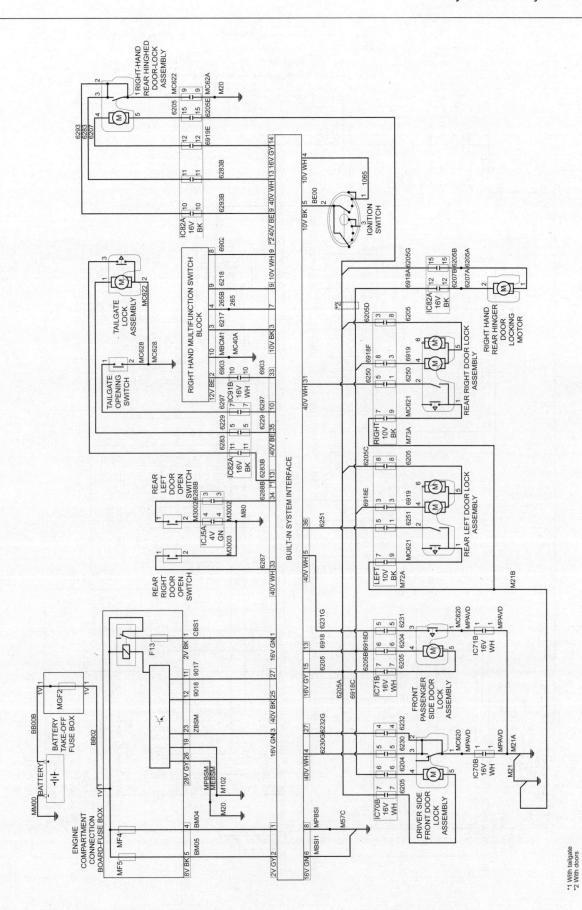

Central locking – without deadlocks

*1 With tailgate
*2 With doors

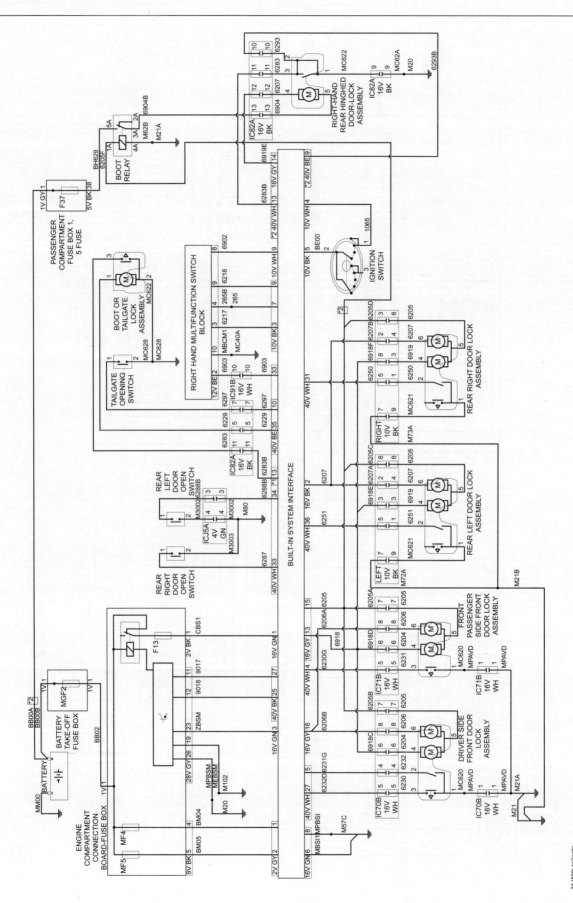

Central locking – with deadlocks

*1 With tailgate
*2 With doors

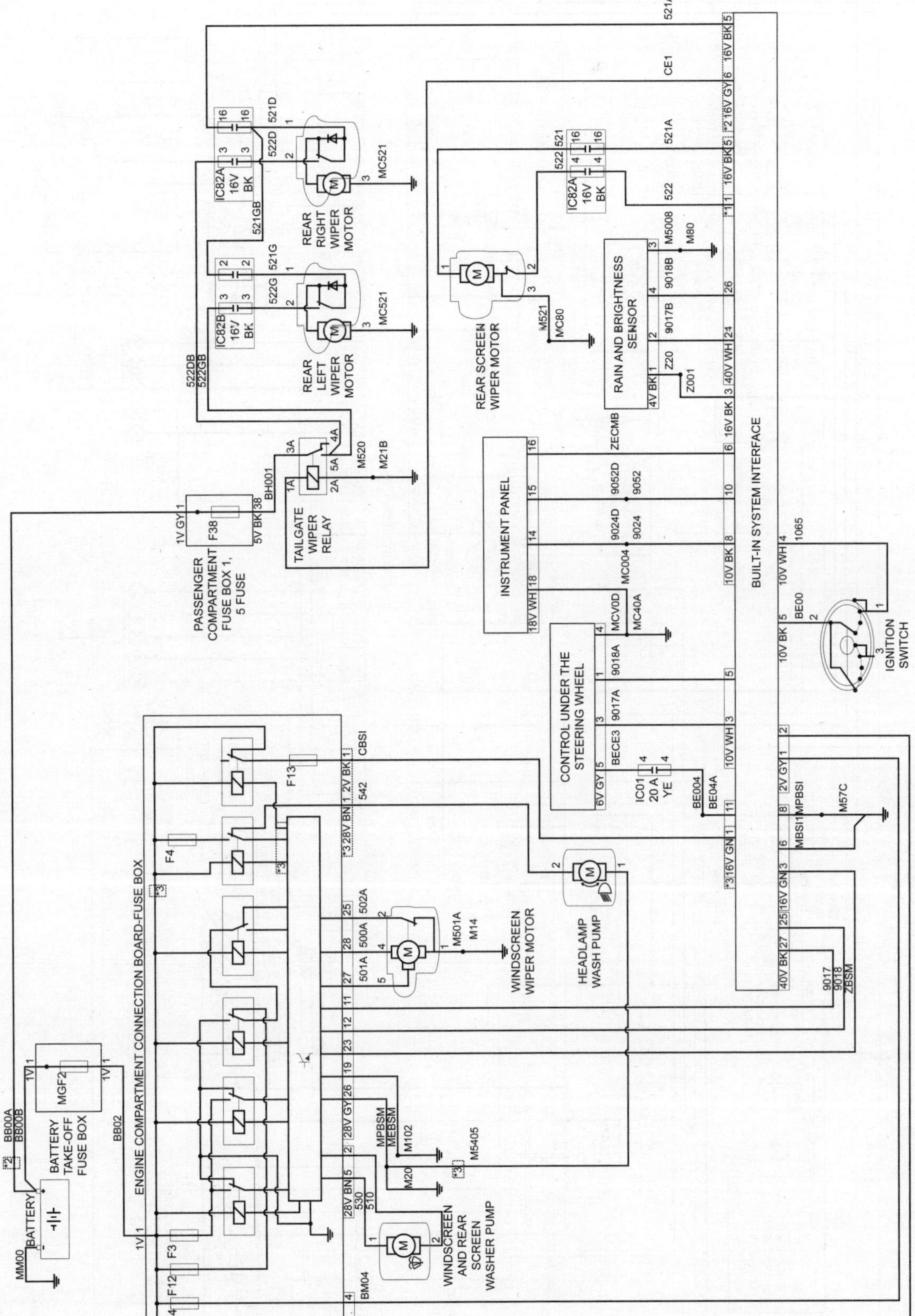

Wipers/washers

*1 With tailgate
*2 With doors
*3 Headlamp wash

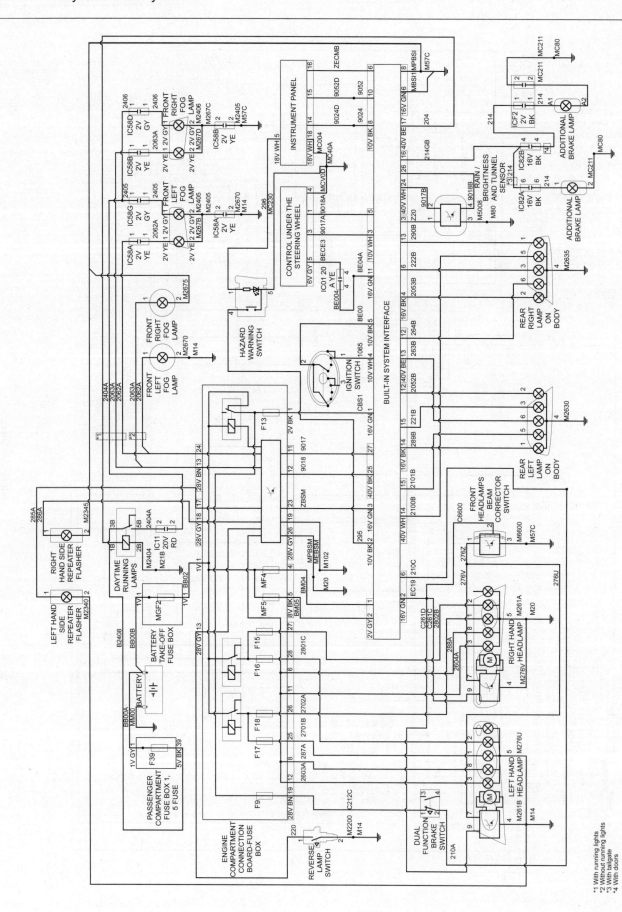

Exterior lighting

*1 With running lights
*2 Without running lights
*3 With tailgate
*4 With doors

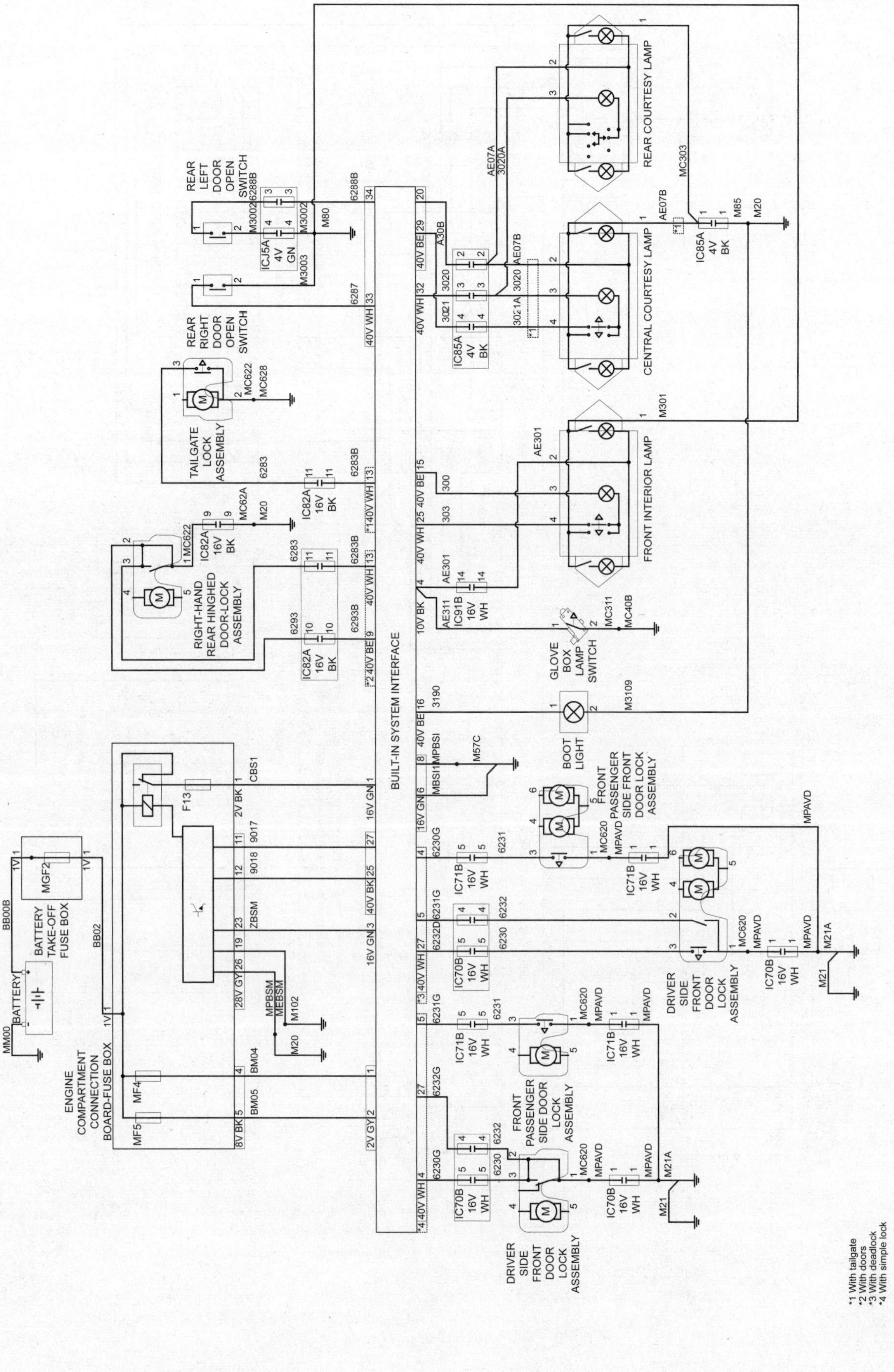

REAR LEFT DOOR OPEN SWITCH

REAR RIGHT DOOR OPEN SWITCH

TAILGATE LOCK ASSEMBLY

RIGHT-HAND REAR HINGHED DOOR-LOCK ASSEMBLY

REAR COURTESY LAMP

REAR COURTESY LAMP

CENTRAL COURTESY LAMP

FRONT INTERIOR LAMP

GLOVE BOX LAMP SWITCH

BUILT-IN SYSTEM INTERFACE

BOOT LIGHT

FRONT PASSENGER SIDE FRONT DOOR LOCK ASSEMBLY

DRIVER SIDE FRONT DOOR LOCK ASSEMBLY

FRONT PASSENGER SIDE DOOR LOCK ASSEMBLY

DRIVER SIDE FRONT DOOR LOCK ASSEMBLY

BATTERY

BATTERY TAKE-OFF FUSE BOX

ENGINE COMPARTMENT CONNECTION BOARD-FUSE BOX

Interior lighting

*1 With tailgate
*2 With doors
*3 With deadlock
*4 With simple lock

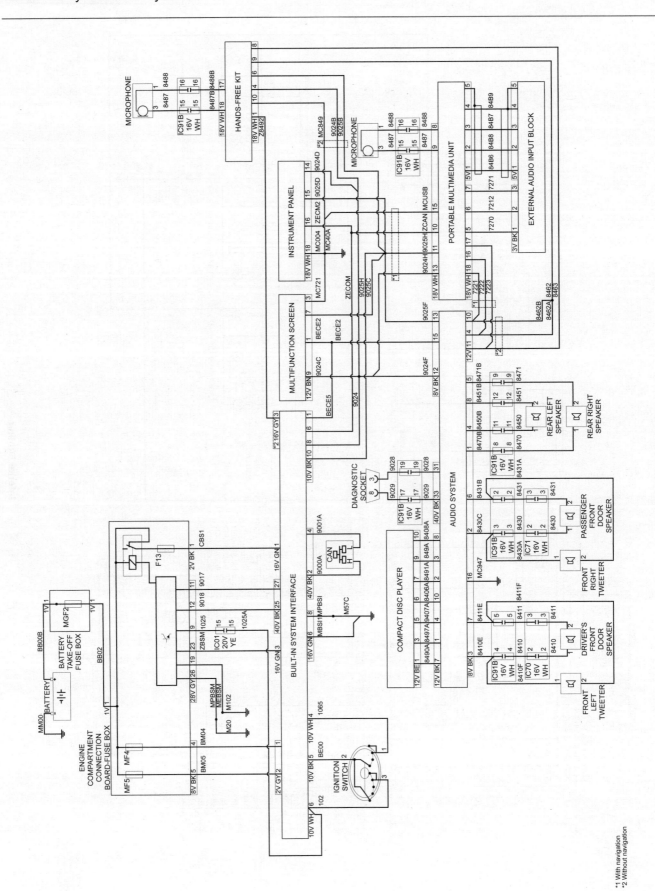

Sound system – Audio

*1 With navigation
*2 Without navigation

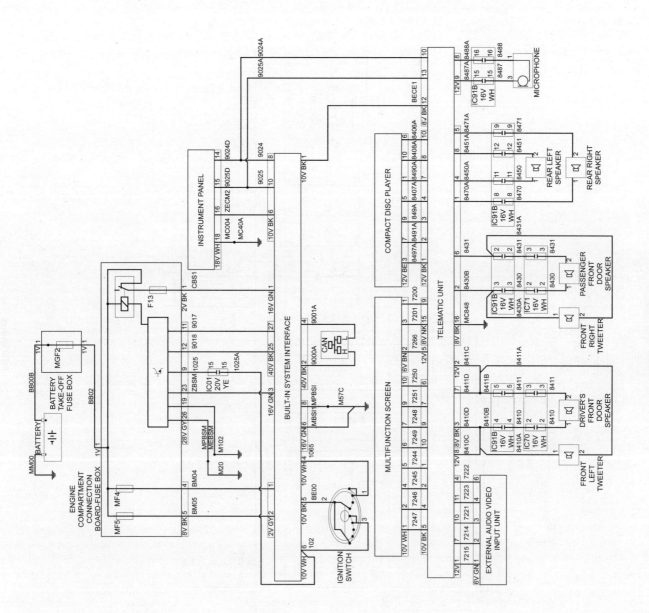

Sound system – Telematics

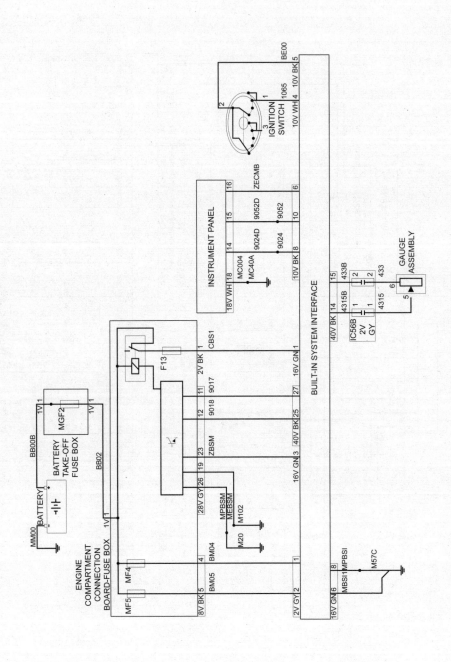

Fuel pump

Dimensions and weights

Note: *All figures are approximate, and may vary according to model. Refer to manufacturer's data for exact figures.*

Dimensions

Overall length	4813 mm (short) 5143 mm (long)
Overall height	1972 mm (Low) 2276 mm (high)
Mirrors folded	1986 mm
Mirrors unfolded	2193 mm
Wheelbase	3000 mm (short) 3122 (long)

Weights

Unladen weight :	
Van (short).	1661 – 1800 kg
Van (long)	1680 – 1839 kg
Maximum gross vehicle weight*:	
Van (short).	1960 – 2205 kg
Van (long)	2880 – 2992 kg

Note: * *Refer to the Vehicle Identification Plate for the exact figure for your vehicle – see 'Vehicle Identification Numbers'.*

Fuel economy

Although depreciation is still the biggest part of the cost of motoring for most car owners, the cost of fuel is more immediately noticeable. These pages give some tips on how to get the best fuel economy.

Working it out

Manufacturer's figures

Car manufacturers are required by law to provide fuel consumption information on all new vehicles sold. These 'official' figures are obtained by simulating various driving conditions on a rolling road or a test track. Real life conditions are different, so the fuel consumption actually achieved may not bear much resemblance to the quoted figures.

How to calculate it

Many cars now have trip computers which will

display fuel consumption, both instantaneous and average. Refer to the owner's handbook for details of how to use these.

To calculate consumption yourself (and maybe to check that the trip computer is accurate), proceed as follows.

1. Fill up with fuel and note the mileage, or zero the trip recorder.
2. Drive as usual until you need to fill up again.
3. Note the amount of fuel required to refill the tank, and the mileage covered since the previous fill-up.
4. Divide the mileage by the amount of fuel used to obtain the consumption figure.

For example:

Mileage at first fill-up (a) = 27,903
Mileage at second fill-up (b) = 28,346
Mileage covered (b - a) = 443
Fuel required at second fill-up = 48.6 litres

The half-completed changeover to metric units in the UK means that we buy our fuel

in litres, measure distances in miles and talk about fuel consumption in miles per gallon. There are two ways round this: the first is to convert the litres to gallons before doing the calculation (by dividing by 4.546, or see Table 1). So in the example:

48.6 litres ÷ 4.546 = 10.69 gallons
443 miles ÷ 10.69 gallons = 41.4 mpg

The second way is to calculate the consumption in miles per litre, then multiply that figure by 4.546 (or see Table 2).

So in the example, fuel consumption is:

443 miles ÷ 48.6 litres = 9.1 mpl
9.1 mpl x 4.546 = 41.4 mpg

The rest of Europe expresses fuel consumption in litres of fuel required to travel 100 km (l/100 km). For interest, the conversions are given in Table 3. In practice it doesn't matter what units you use, provided you know what your normal consumption is and can spot if it's getting better or worse.

Table 1: conversion of litres to Imperial gallons

litres	1	2	3	4	5	10	20	30	40	50	60	70
gallons	0.22	0.44	0.66	0.88	1.10	2.24	4.49	6.73	8.98	11.22	13.47	15.71

Table 2: conversion of miles per litre to miles per gallon

miles per litre	5	6	7	8	9	10	11	12	13	14
miles per gallon	23	27	32	36	41	46	50	55	59	64

Table 3: conversion of litres per 100 km to miles per gallon

litres per 100 km	4	4.5	5	5.5	6	6.5	7	8	9	10
miles per gallon	71	63	56	51	47	43	40	35	31	28

Maintenance

A well-maintained car uses less fuel and creates less pollution. In particular:

Filters

Change air and fuel filters at the specified intervals.

Oil

Use a good quality oil of the lowest viscosity specified by the vehicle manufacturer (see *Lubricants and fluids*). Check the level often and be careful not to overfill.

Spark plugs

When applicable, renew at the specified intervals.

Tyres

Check tyre pressures regularly. Under-inflated tyres have an increased rolling resistance. It is generally safe to use the higher pressures specified for full load conditions even when not fully laden, but keep an eye on the centre band of tread for signs of wear due to over-inflation.

When buying new tyres, consider the 'fuel saving' models which most manufacturers include in their ranges.

Driving style

Acceleration

Acceleration uses more fuel than driving at a steady speed. The best technique with modern cars is to accelerate reasonably briskly to the desired speed, changing up through the gears as soon as possible without making the engine labour.

Air conditioning

Air conditioning absorbs quite a bit of energy from the engine – typically 3 kW (4 hp) or so. The effect on fuel consumption is at its worst in slow traffic. Switch it off when not required.

Anticipation

Drive smoothly and try to read the traffic flow so as to avoid unnecessary acceleration and braking.

Automatic transmission

When accelerating in an automatic, avoid depressing the throttle so far as to make the transmission hold onto lower gears at higher speeds. Don't use the 'Sport' setting, if applicable.

When stationary with the engine running, select 'N' or 'P'. When moving, keep your left foot away from the brake.

Braking

Braking converts the car's energy of motion into heat – essentially, it is wasted. Obviously some braking is always going to be necessary, but with good anticipation it is surprising how much can be avoided, especially on routes that you know well.

Carshare

Consider sharing lifts to work or to the shops. Even once a week will make a difference.

Electrical loads

Electricity is 'fuel' too; the alternator which charges the battery does so by converting some of the engine's energy of motion into electrical energy. The more electrical accessories are in use, the greater the load on the alternator. Switch off big consumers like the heated rear window when not required.

Freewheeling

Freewheeling (coasting) in neutral with the engine switched off is dangerous. The effort required to operate power-assisted brakes and steering increases when the engine is not running, with a potential lack of control in emergency situations.

In any case, modern fuel injection systems automatically cut off the engine's fuel supply on the overrun (moving and in gear, but with the accelerator pedal released).

Gadgets

Bolt-on devices claiming to save fuel have been around for nearly as long as the motor car itself. Those which worked were rapidly adopted as standard equipment by the vehicle manufacturers. Others worked only in certain situations, or saved fuel only at the expense of unacceptable effects on performance, driveability or the life of engine components.

The most effective fuel saving gadget is the driver's right foot.

Journey planning

Combine (eg) a trip to the supermarket with a visit to the recycling centre and the DIY store, rather than making separate journeys.

When possible choose a travelling time outside rush hours.

Load

The more heavily a car is laden, the greater the energy required to accelerate it to a given speed. Remove heavy items which you don't need to carry.

One load which is often overlooked is the contents of the fuel tank. A tankful of fuel (55 litres / 12 gallons) weighs 45 kg (100 lb) or so. Just half filling it may be worthwhile.

Lost?

At the risk of stating the obvious, if you're going somewhere new, have details of the route to hand. There's not much point in

achieving record mpg if you also go miles out of your way.

Parking

If possible, carry out any reversing or turning manoeuvres when you arrive at a parking space so that you can drive straight out when you leave. Manoeuvering when the engine is cold uses a lot more fuel.

Driving around looking for free on-street parking may cost more in fuel than buying a car park ticket.

Premium fuel

Most major oil companies (and some supermarkets) have premium grades of fuel which are several pence a litre dearer than the standard grades. Reports vary, but the consensus seems to be that if these fuels improve economy at all, they do not do so by enough to justify their extra cost.

Roof rack

When loading a roof rack, try to produce a wedge shape with the narrow end at the front. Any cover should be securely fastened – if it flaps it's creating turbulence and absorbing energy.

Remove roof racks and boxes when not in use – they increase air resistance and can create a surprising amount of noise.

Short journeys

The engine is at its least efficient, and wear is highest, during the first few miles after a cold start. Consider walking, cycling or using public transport.

Speed

The engine is at its most efficient when running at a steady speed and load at the rpm where it develops maximum torque. (You can find this figure in the car's handbook.) For most cars this corresponds to between 55 and 65 mph in top gear.

Above the optimum cruising speed, fuel consumption starts to rise quite sharply. A car travelling at 80 mph will typically be using 30% more fuel than at 60 mph.

Supermarket fuel

It may be cheap but is it any good? In the UK all supermarket fuel must meet the relevant British Standard. The major oil companies will say that their branded fuels have better additive packages which may stop carbon and other deposits building up. A reasonable compromise might be to use one tank of branded fuel to three or four from the supermarket.

Switch off when stationary

Switch off the engine if you look like being stationary for more than 30 seconds or so. This is good for the environment as well as for your pocket. Be aware though that frequent restarts are hard on the battery and the starter motor.

Windows

Driving with the windows open increases air turbulence around the vehicle. Closing the windows promotes smooth airflow and

reduced resistance. The faster you go, the more significant this is.

And finally . . .

Driving techniques associated with good fuel economy tend to involve moderate acceleration and low top speeds. Be considerate to the needs of other road users who may need to make brisker progress; even if you do not agree with them this is not an excuse to be obstructive.

Safety must always take precedence over economy, whether it is a question of accelerating hard to complete an overtaking manoeuvre, killing your speed when confronted with a potential hazard or switching the lights on when it starts to get dark.

Conversion factors

Length (distance)

Inches (in)	x 25.4	= Millimetres (mm)	x 0.0394	= Inches (in)
Feet (ft)	x 0.305	= Metres (m)	x 3.281	= Feet (ft)
Miles	x 1.609	= Kilometres (km)	x 0.621	= Miles

Volume (capacity)

Cubic inches (cu in; in³)	x 16.387	= Cubic centimetres (cc; cm³)	x 0.061	= Cubic inches (cu in; in³)
Imperial pints (Imp pt)	x 0.568	= Litres (l)	x 1.76	= Imperial pints (Imp pt)
Imperial quarts (Imp qt)	x 1.137	= Litres (l)	x 0.88	= Imperial quarts (Imp qt)
Imperial quarts (Imp qt)	x 1.201	= US quarts (US qt)	x 0.833	= Imperial quarts (Imp qt)
US quarts (US qt)	x 0.946	= Litres (l)	x 1.057	= US quarts (US qt)
Imperial gallons (Imp gal)	x 4.546	= Litres (l)	x 0.22	= Imperial gallons (Imp gal)
Imperial gallons (Imp gal)	x 1.201	= US gallons (US gal)	x 0.833	= Imperial gallons (Imp gal)
US gallons (US gal)	x 3.785	= Litres (l)	x 0.264	= US gallons (US gal)

Mass (weight)

Ounces (oz)	x 28.35	= Grams (g)	x 0.035	= Ounces (oz)
Pounds (lb)	x 0.454	= Kilograms (kg)	x 2.205	= Pounds (lb)

Force

Ounces-force (ozf; oz)	x 0.278	= Newtons (N)	x 3.6	= Ounces-force (ozf; oz)
Pounds-force (lbf; lb)	x 4.448	= Newtons (N)	x 0.225	= Pounds-force (lbf; lb)
Newtons (N)	x 0.1	= Kilograms-force (kgf; kg)	x 9.81	= Newtons (N)

Pressure

Pounds-force per square inch (psi; lbf/in²; lb/in²)	x 0.070	= Kilograms-force per square centimetre (kgf/cm²; kg/cm²)	x 14.223	= Pounds-force per square inch (psi; lbf/in²; lb/in²)
Pounds-force per square inch (psi; lbf/in²; lb/in²)	x 0.068	= Atmospheres (atm)	x 14.696	= Pounds-force per square inch (psi; lbf/in²; lb/in²)
Pounds-force per square inch (psi; lbf/in²; lb/in²)	x 0.069	= Bars	x 14.5	= Pounds-force per square inch (psi; lbf/in²; lb/in²)
Pounds-force per square inch (psi; lbf/in²; lb/in²)	x 6.895	= Kilopascals (kPa)	x 0.145	= Pounds-force per square inch (psi; lbf/in²; lb/in²)
Kilopascals (kPa)	x 0.01	= Kilograms-force per square centimetre (kgf/cm²; kg/cm²)	x 98.1	= Kilopascals (kPa)
Millibar (mbar)	x 100	= Pascals (Pa)	x 0.01	= Millibar (mbar)
Millibar (mbar)	x 0.0145	= Pounds-force per square inch (psi; lbf/in²; lb/in²)	x 68.947	= Millibar (mbar)
Millibar (mbar)	x 0.75	= Millimetres of mercury (mmHg)	x 1.333	= Millibar (mbar)
Millibar (mbar)	x 0.401	= Inches of water (inH₂O)	x 2.491	= Millibar (mbar)
Millimetres of mercury (mmHg)	x 0.535	= Inches of water (inH₂O)	x 1.868	= Millimetres of mercury (mmHg)
Inches of water (inH₂O)	x 0.036	= Pounds-force per square inch (psi; lbf/in²; lb/in²)	x 27.68	= Inches of water (inH₂O)

Torque (moment of force)

Pounds-force inches (lbf in; lb in)	x 1.152	= Kilograms-force centimetre (kgf cm; kg cm)	x 0.868	= Pounds-force inches (lbf in; lb in)
Pounds-force inches (lbf in; lb in)	x 0.113	= Newton metres (Nm)	x 8.85	= Pounds-force inches (lbf in; lb in)
Pounds-force inches (lbf in; lb in)	x 0.083	= Pounds-force feet (lbf ft; lb ft)	x 12	= Pounds-force inches (lbf in; lb in)
Pounds-force feet (lbf ft; lb ft)	x 0.138	= Kilograms-force metres (kgf m; kg m)	x 7.233	= Pounds-force feet (lbf ft; lb ft)
Pounds-force feet (lbf ft; lb ft)	x 1.356	= Newton metres (Nm)	x 0.738	= Pounds-force feet (lbf ft; lb ft)
Newton metres (Nm)	x 0.102	= Kilograms-force metres (kgf m; kg m)	x 9.804	= Newton metres (Nm)

Power

Horsepower (hp)	x 745.7	= Watts (W)	x 0.0013	= Horsepower (hp)

Velocity (speed)

Miles per hour (miles/hr; mph)	x 1.609	= Kilometres per hour (km/hr; kph)	x 0.621	= Miles per hour (miles/hr; mph)

Fuel consumption*

Miles per gallon, Imperial (mpg)	x 0.354	= Kilometres per litre (km/l)	x 2.825	= Miles per gallon, Imperial (mpg)
Miles per gallon, US (mpg)	x 0.425	= Kilometres per litre (km/l)	x 2.352	= Miles per gallon, US (mpg)

Temperature

Degrees Fahrenheit = (°C x 1.8) + 32   Degrees Celsius (Degrees Centigrade; °C) = (°F - 32) x 0.56

It is common practice to convert from miles per gallon (mpg) to litres/100 kilometres (l/100km), where mpg x l/100 km = 282

Spare parts are available from many sources, including maker's appointed garages, accessory shops, and motor factors. To be sure of obtaining the correct parts, it will sometimes be necessary to quote the vehicle identification number. If possible, it can also be useful to take the old parts along for positive identification. Items such as starter motors and alternators may be available under a service exchange scheme – any parts returned should be clean.

Our advice regarding spare parts is as follows.

Officially appointed garages

This is the best source of parts which are peculiar to your car, and which are not otherwise generally available (eg, badges, interior trim, certain body panels, etc). It is also the only place at which you should buy parts if the car is still under warranty.

Accessory shops

These are very good places to buy materials and components needed for the maintenance of your car (oil, air and fuel filters, light bulbs, drivebelts, greases, brake pads, touch-up paint, etc). Components of this nature sold by a reputable shop are usually of the same standard as those used by the car manufacturer.

Besides components, these shops also sell tools and general accessories, usually have convenient opening hours, charge lower prices, and can often be found close to home. Some accessory shops have parts counters where components needed for almost any repair job can be purchased or ordered.

Motor factors

Good factors will stock all the more important components which wear out comparatively quickly, and can sometimes supply individual components needed for the overhaul of a larger assembly (eg, brake seals and hydraulic parts, bearing shells, pistons, valves). They may also handle work such as cylinder block reboring, crankshaft regrinding, etc.

Engine reconditioners

These specialise in engine overhaul and can also supply components. It is recommended that the establishment is a member of the Federation of Engine Re-Manufacturers, or a similar society.

Tyre and exhaust specialists

These outlets may be independent, or members of a local or national chain. They frequently offer competitive prices when compared with a main dealer or local garage, but it will pay to obtain several quotes before making a decision. When researching prices, also ask what extras may be added – for instance fitting a new valve, balancing the wheel and tyre disposal all both commonly charged on top of the price of a new tyre.

Other sources

Beware of parts or materials obtained from market stalls, car boot sales, on-line auctions or similar outlets. Such items are not invariably sub-standard, but there is little chance of compensation if they do prove unsatisfactory. In the case of safety-critical components such as brake pads, there is the risk not only of financial loss, but also of an accident causing injury or death.

Second-hand components or assemblies obtained from a car breaker can be a good buy in some circumstances, but this sort of purchase is best made by the experienced DIY mechanic.

Vehicle identification numbers

Modifications are a continuing and unpublicised process in vehicle manufacture, quite apart from major model changes. Spare parts manuals and lists are compiled upon a numerical basis, the individual vehicle identification numbers being essential for correct identification of the part concerned.

When ordering spare parts, always give as much information as possible. Quote the car model, year of manufacture, body and engine numbers, but most importantly, the after sales replacement parts number (referred to as RPO number: Replacement Parts Organisation number).

The vehicle identification number is on a label on the driver's door B-pillar **(see illustration)**.

The vehicle identification number (VIN) is stamped into the scuttle panel at the rear of the engine compartment, and repeated on a plate visible through the windscreen **(see illustration)**.

The engine number is stamped on the base of the cylinder block at the front, it is on the flat surface located on the right-hand side of the oil filter/cooler.

VIN plate on the drivers door pillar

VIN number stamped into the scuttle panel

VIN plate visible through the windscreen

Whenever servicing, repair or overhaul work is carried out on the car or its components, observe the following procedures and instructions. This will assist in carrying out the operation efficiently and to a professional standard of workmanship.

Joint mating faces and gaskets

When separating components at their mating faces, never insert screwdrivers or similar implements into the joint between the faces in order to prise them apart. This can cause severe damage which results in oil leaks, coolant leaks, etc upon reassembly. Separation is usually achieved by tapping along the joint with a soft-faced hammer in order to break the seal. However, note that this method may not be suitable where dowels are used for component location.

Where a gasket is used between the mating faces of two components, a new one must be fitted on reassembly; fit it dry unless otherwise stated in the repair procedure. Make sure that the mating faces are clean and dry, with all traces of old gasket removed. When cleaning a joint face, use a tool which is unlikely to score or damage the face, and remove any burrs or nicks with an oilstone or fine file.

Make sure that tapped holes are cleaned with a pipe cleaner, and keep them free of jointing compound, if this is being used, unless specifically instructed otherwise.

Ensure that all orifices, channels or pipes are clear, and blow through them, preferably using compressed air.

Oil seals

Oil seals can be removed by levering them out with a wide flat-bladed screwdriver or similar implement. Alternatively, a number of self-tapping screws may be screwed into the seal, and these used as a purchase for pliers or some similar device in order to pull the seal free.

Whenever an oil seal is removed from its working location, either individually or as part of an assembly, it should be renewed.

The very fine sealing lip of the seal is easily damaged, and will not seal if the surface it contacts is not completely clean and free from scratches, nicks or grooves. If the original sealing surface of the component cannot be restored, and the manufacturer has not made provision for slight relocation of the seal relative to the sealing surface, the component should be renewed.

Protect the lips of the seal from any surface which may damage them in the course of fitting. Use tape or a conical sleeve where possible. Where indicated, lubricate the seal lips with oil before fitting and, on dual-lipped seals, fill the space between the lips with grease.

Unless otherwise stated, oil seals must be fitted with their sealing lips toward the lubricant to be sealed.

Use a tubular drift or block of wood of the appropriate size to install the seal and, if the seal housing is shouldered, drive the seal down to the shoulder. If the seal housing is unshouldered, the seal should be fitted with its face flush with the housing top face (unless otherwise instructed).

Screw threads and fastenings

Seized nuts, bolts and screws are quite a common occurrence where corrosion has set in, and the use of penetrating oil or releasing fluid will often overcome this problem if the offending item is soaked for a while before attempting to release it. The use of an impact driver may also provide a means of releasing such stubborn fastening devices, when used in conjunction with the appropriate screwdriver bit or socket. If none of these methods works, it may be necessary to resort to the careful application of heat, or the use of a hacksaw or nut splitter device. Before resorting to extreme methods, check that you are not dealing with a left-hand thread!

Studs are usually removed by locking two nuts together on the threaded part, and then using a spanner on the lower nut to unscrew the stud. Studs or bolts which have broken off below the surface of the component in which they are mounted can sometimes be removed using a stud extractor.

Always ensure that a blind tapped hole is completely free from oil, grease, water or other fluid before installing the bolt or stud. Failure to do this could cause the housing to crack due to the hydraulic action of the bolt or stud as it is screwed in.

For some screw fastenings, notably cylinder head bolts or nuts, torque wrench settings are no longer specified for the latter stages of tightening, "angle-tightening" being called up instead. Typically, a fairly low torque wrench setting will be applied to the bolts/nuts in the correct sequence, followed by one or more stages of tightening through specified angles.

When checking or retightening a nut or bolt to a specified torque setting, slacken the nut or bolt by a quarter of a turn, and then retighten to the specified setting. However, this should not be attempted where angular tightening has been used.

Locknuts, locktabs and washers

Any fastening which will rotate against a component or housing during tightening should always have a washer between it and the relevant component or housing.

Spring or split washers should always be renewed when they are used to lock a critical component such as a big-end bearing retaining bolt or nut. Locktabs which are folded over to retain a nut or bolt should always be renewed.

Self-locking nuts can be re-used in non-critical areas, providing resistance can be felt when the locking portion passes over the bolt or stud thread. However, it should be noted that self-locking stiffnuts tend to lose their effectiveness after long periods of use, and should then be renewed as a matter of course.

Split pins must always be replaced with new ones of the correct size for the hole.

When thread-locking compound is found on the threads of a fastener which is to be re-used, it should be cleaned off with a wire brush and solvent, and fresh compound applied on reassembly.

Special tools

Some repair procedures in this manual entail the use of special tools such as a press, two or three-legged pullers, spring compressors, etc. Wherever possible, suitable readily-available alternatives to the manufacturer's special tools are described, and are shown in use. In some instances, where no alternative is possible, it has been necessary to resort to the use of a manufacturer's tool, and this has been done for reasons of safety as well as the efficient completion of the repair operation. Unless you are highly-skilled and have a thorough understanding of the procedures described, never attempt to bypass the use of any special tool when the procedure described specifies its use. Not only is there a very great risk of personal injury, but expensive damage could be caused to the components involved.

Environmental considerations

When disposing of used engine oil, brake fluid, antifreeze, etc, give due consideration to any detrimental environmental effects. Do not, for instance, pour any of the above liquids down drains into the general sewage system, or onto the ground to soak away, as this is likely to pollute your local environment. Many local council refuse tips provide a facility for waste oil disposal, as do some garages. You can find your nearest disposal point by calling the Environment Agency on 03708 506 506 or by visiting www.oilbankline.org.uk.

Note: It is illegal and anti-social to dump oil down the drain. To find the location of your local oil recycling bank, call 03708 506 506 or visit www.oilbankline.org.uk.

The jack supplied with the vehicle should only be used for changing the roadwheels – see Wheel changing at the front of this manual. When carrying out any other kind of work, raise the vehicle using a hydraulic (or 'trolley') jack, and always supplement the jack with axle stands at the vehicle jacking points.

When using a hydraulic jack or axle stands, always position the jack head or axle stand head under one of the relevant jacking points along the sills **(see illustration)**.

Do not attempt to jack the vehicle under the front crossmember, rear axle, engine, transmission or any of the suspension components.

The jack supplied with the vehicle locates at the jacking points on the underside of the sills – see Wheel changing. Ensure that the jack head is correctly engaged before attempting to raise the vehicle.

Never work under, around, or near a raised vehicle, unless it is adequately supported in at least two places.

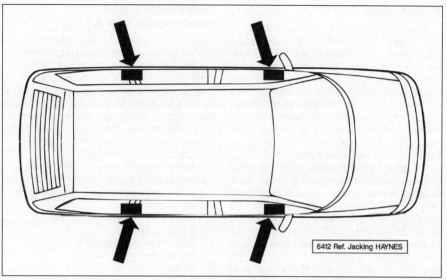

6412 Ref. Jacking HAYNES

Jacking points

Introduction

A selection of good tools is a fundamental requirement for anyone contemplating the maintenance and repair of a motor vehicle. For the owner who does not possess any, their purchase will prove a considerable expense, offsetting some of the savings made by doing-it-yourself. However, provided that the tools purchased meet the relevant national safety standards and are of good quality, they will last for many years and prove an extremely worthwhile investment.

To help the average owner to decide which tools are needed to carry out the various tasks detailed in this manual, we have compiled three lists of tools under the following headings: *Maintenance and minor repair, Repair and overhaul*, and *Special*. Newcomers to practical mechanics should start off with the *Maintenance and minor repair* tool kit, and confine themselves to the simpler jobs around the vehicle. Then, as confidence and experience grow, more difficult tasks can be undertaken, with extra tools being purchased as, and when, they are needed. In this way, a *Maintenance and minor repair* tool kit can be built up into a *Repair and overhaul* tool kit over a considerable period of time, without any major cash outlays. The experienced do-it-yourselfer will have a tool kit good enough for most repair and overhaul procedures, and will add tools from the *Special* category when it is felt that the expense is justified by the amount of use to which these tools will be put.

Maintenance and minor repair tool kit

The tools given in this list should be considered as a minimum requirement if routine maintenance, servicing and minor repair operations are to be undertaken. We recommend the purchase of combination spanners (ring one end, open-ended the other); although more expensive than open-ended ones, they do give the advantages of both types of spanner.

- [ ] *Combination spanners:*
  Metric - 8 to 19 mm inclusive
- [ ] *Adjustable spanner - 35 mm jaw (approx.)*
- [ ] *Spark plug spanner (with rubber insert) - petrol models*
- [ ] *Spark plug gap adjustment tool - petrol models*
- [ ] *Set of feeler gauges*
- [ ] *Brake bleed nipple spanner*
- [ ] *Screwdrivers:*
  Flat blade - 100 mm long x 6 mm dia
  Cross blade - 100 mm long x 6 mm dia
  Torx - various sizes (not all vehicles)
- [ ] *Combination pliers*
- [ ] *Hacksaw (junior)*
- [ ] *Tyre pump*
- [ ] *Tyre pressure gauge*
- [ ] *Oil can*
- [ ] *Oil filter removal tool (if applicable)*
- [ ] *Fine emery cloth*
- [ ] *Wire brush (small)*
- [ ] *Funnel (medium size)*
- [ ] *Sump drain plug key (not all vehicles)*

Repair and overhaul tool kit

These tools are virtually essential for anyone undertaking any major repairs to a motor vehicle, and are additional to those given in the *Maintenance and minor repair* list. Included in this list is a comprehensive set of sockets. Although these are expensive, they will be found invaluable as they are so versatile - particularly if various drives are included in the set. We recommend the half-inch square-drive type, as this can be used with most proprietary torque wrenches.

The tools in this list will sometimes need to be supplemented by tools from the *Special* list:

- [ ] *Sockets to cover range in previous list (including Torx sockets)*
- [ ] *Reversible ratchet drive (for use with sockets)*
- [ ] *Extension piece, 250 mm (for use with sockets)*
- [ ] *Universal joint (for use with sockets)*
- [ ] *Flexible handle or sliding T "breaker bar" (for use with sockets)*
- [ ] *Torque wrench (for use with sockets)*
- [ ] *Self-locking grips*
- [ ] *Ball pein hammer*
- [ ] *Soft-faced mallet (plastic or rubber)*
- [ ] *Screwdrivers:*
  Flat blade - long & sturdy, short (chubby), and narrow (electrician's) types
  Cross blade – long & sturdy, and short (chubby) types
- [ ] *Pliers:*
  Long-nosed
  Side cutters (electrician's)
  Circlip (internal and external)
- [ ] *Cold chisel - 25 mm*
- [ ] *Scriber*
- [ ] *Scraper*
- [ ] *Centre-punch*
- [ ] *Pin punch*
- [ ] *Hacksaw*
- [ ] *Brake hose clamp*
- [ ] *Brake/clutch bleeding kit*
- [ ] *Selection of twist drills*
- [ ] *Steel rule/straight-edge*
- [ ] *Allen keys (inc. splined/Torx type)*
- [ ] *Selection of files*
- [ ] *Wire brush*
- [ ] *Axle stands*
- [ ] *Jack (strong trolley or hydraulic type)*
- [ ] *Light with extension lead*
- [ ] *Universal electrical multi-meter*

Sockets and reversible ratchet drive

Brake bleeding kit

Torx key, socket and bit

Hose clamp

Angular-tightening gauge

Special tools

The tools in this list are those which are not used regularly, are expensive to buy, or which need to be used in accordance with their manufacturers' instructions. Unless relatively difficult mechanical jobs are undertaken frequently, it will not be economic to buy many of these tools. Where this is the case, you could consider clubbing together with friends (or joining a motorists' club) to make a joint purchase, or borrowing the tools against a deposit from a local garage or tool hire specialist.

The following list contains only those tools and instruments freely available to the public, and not those special tools produced by the vehicle manufacturer specifically for its dealer network. You will find occasional references to these manufacturers' special tools in the text of this manual. Generally, an alternative method of doing the job without the vehicle manufacturers' special tool is given. However, sometimes there is no alternative to using them. Where this is the case and the relevant tool cannot be bought or borrowed, you will have to entrust the work to a dealer.

☐ Angular-tightening gauge
☐ Valve spring compressor
☐ Valve grinding tool
☐ Piston ring compressor
☐ Piston ring removal/installation tool
☐ Cylinder bore hone
☐ Balljoint separator
☐ Coil spring compressors (where applicable)
☐ Two/three-legged hub and bearing puller
☐ Impact screwdriver
☐ Micrometer and/or vernier calipers
☐ Dial gauge
☐ Tachometer
☐ Fault code reader
☐ Cylinder compression gauge
☐ Hand-operated vacuum pump and gauge
☐ Clutch plate alignment set
☐ Brake shoe steady spring cup removal tool
☐ Bush and bearing removal/installation set
☐ Stud extractors
☐ Tap and die set
☐ Lifting tackle

Buying tools

Reputable motor accessory shops and superstores often offer excellent quality tools at discount prices, so it pays to shop around.

Remember, you don't have to buy the most expensive items on the shelf, but it is always advisable to steer clear of the very cheap tools. Beware of 'bargains' offered on market stalls, on-line or at car boot sales. There are plenty of good tools around at reasonable prices, but always aim to purchase items which meet the relevant national safety standards. If in doubt, ask the proprietor or manager of the shop for advice before making a purchase.

Care and maintenance of tools

Having purchased a reasonable tool kit, it is necessary to keep the tools in a clean and serviceable condition. After use, always wipe off any dirt, grease and metal particles using a clean, dry cloth, before putting the tools away. Never leave them lying around after they have been used. A simple tool rack on the garage or workshop wall for items such as screwdrivers and pliers is a good idea. Store all normal spanners and sockets in a metal box. Any measuring instruments, gauges, meters, etc, must be carefully stored where they cannot be damaged or become rusty.

Take a little care when tools are used. Hammer heads inevitably become marked, and screwdrivers lose the keen edge on their blades from time to time. A little timely attention with emery cloth or a file will soon restore items like this to a good finish.

Working facilities

Not to be forgotten when discussing tools is the workshop itself. If anything more than routine maintenance is to be carried out, a suitable working area becomes essential.

It is appreciated that many an owner-mechanic is forced by circumstances to remove an engine or similar item without the benefit of a garage or workshop. Having done this, any repairs should always be done under the cover of a roof.

Wherever possible, any dismantling should be done on a clean, flat workbench or table at a suitable working height.

Any workbench needs a vice; one with a jaw opening of 100 mm is suitable for most jobs. As mentioned previously, some clean dry storage space is also required for tools, as well as for any lubricants, cleaning fluids, touch-up paints etc, which become necessary.

Another item which may be required, and which has a much more general usage, is an electric drill with a chuck capacity of at least 8 mm. This, together with a good range of twist drills, is virtually essential for fitting accessories.

Last, but not least, always keep a supply of old newspapers and clean, lint-free rags available, and try to keep any working area as clean as possible.

Micrometers

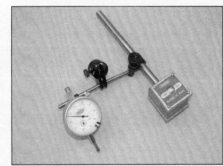

Dial test indicator ("dial gauge")

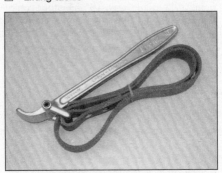

Oil filter removal tool (strap wrench type)

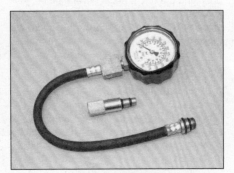

Compression tester

Bearing puller

This is a guide to getting your vehicle through the MOT test. Obviously it will not be possible to examine the vehicle to the same standard as the professional MOT tester. However, working through the following checks will enable you to identify any problem areas before submitting the vehicle for the test.

It has only been possible to summarise the test requirements here, based on the regulations in force at the time of printing. Test standards are becoming increasingly stringent, although there are some exemptions for older vehicles.

An assistant will be needed to help carry out some of these checks.

The checks have been sub-divided into four categories, as follows:

1 Checks carried out **FROM THE DRIVER'S SEAT**

2 Checks carried out **WITH THE VEHICLE ON THE GROUND**

3 Checks carried out **WITH THE VEHICLE RAISED AND THE WHEELS FREE TO TURN**

4 Checks carried out on **YOUR VEHICLE'S EXHAUST EMISSION SYSTEM**

---

1 Checks carried out **FROM THE DRIVER'S SEAT**

Handbrake (parking brake)

☐ Test the operation of the handbrake. Excessive travel (too many clicks) indicates incorrect brake or cable adjustment.
☐ Check that the handbrake cannot be released by tapping the lever sideways. Check the security of the lever mountings.

☐ If the parking brake is foot-operated, check that the pedal is secure and without excessive travel, and that the release mechanism operates correctly.
☐ Where applicable, test the operation of the electronic handbrake. The brake should engage and disengage without excessive delay. If the warning light does not extinguish when the brake is disengaged, this could indicate a fault which will need further investigation.

Footbrake

☐ Depress the brake pedal and check that it does not creep down to the floor, indicating a master cylinder fault. Release the pedal,

wait a few seconds, then depress it again. If the pedal travels nearly to the floor before firm resistance is felt, brake adjustment or repair is necessary. If the pedal feels spongy, there is air in the hydraulic system which must be removed by bleeding.

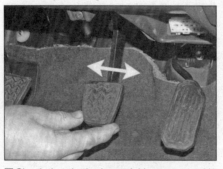

☐ Check that the brake pedal is secure and in good condition. Check also for signs of fluid leaks on the pedal, floor or carpets, which would indicate failed seals in the brake master cylinder.
☐ Check the servo unit (when applicable) by operating the brake pedal several times, then keeping the pedal depressed and starting the engine. As the engine starts, the pedal will move down slightly. If not, the vacuum hose or the servo itself may be faulty.

Steering wheel and column

☐ Examine the steering wheel for fractures or looseness of the hub, spokes or rim.
☐ Move the steering wheel from side to side and then up and down. Check that the steering wheel is not loose on the column, indicating wear or a loose retaining nut. Continue moving the steering wheel as before, but also turn it slightly from left to right.

☐ Check that the steering wheel is not loose on the column, and that there is no abnormal movement of the steering wheel, indicating wear in the column support bearings or couplings.
☐ Check that the ignition lock (where fitted) engages and disengages correctly.
☐ Steering column adjustment mechanisms (where fitted) must be able to lock the column securely in place with no play evident.

Windscreen, mirrors and sunvisor

☐ The windscreen must be free of cracks or other significant damage within the driver's field of view. (Small stone chips are acceptable.) Rear view mirrors must be secure, intact, and capable of being adjusted.

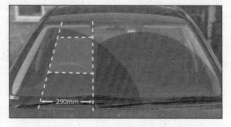

☐ The driver's sunvisor must be capable of being stored in the "up" position.

Seat belts and seats

Note: *The following checks are applicable to all seat belts, front and rear.*

☐ Examine the webbing of all the belts (including rear belts if fitted) for cuts, serious fraying or deterioration. Fasten and unfasten each belt to check the buckles. If applicable, check the retracting mechanism. Check the security of all seat belt mountings accessible from inside the vehicle, ensuring any height adjustable mountings lock securely in place.

☐ Seat belts with pre-tensioners, once activated, have a "flag" or similar showing on the seat belt stalk. This, in itself, is not a reason for test failure.

☐ The front seats themselves must be securely attached and the backrests must lock in the upright position.

Doors

☐ Both front doors must be able to be opened and closed from outside and inside, and must latch securely when closed.

Bonnet and boot/tailgate

☐ The bonnet and boot/tailgate must latch securely when closed.

2 Checks carried out WITH THE VEHICLE ON THE GROUND

Vehicle identification

☐ Number plates must be in good condition, secure and legible, with letters and numbers correctly spaced – spacing at (A) should be 33 mm and at (B) 11 mm. At the front, digits must be black on a white background and at the rear black on a yellow background. Other background designs (such as honeycomb) are not permitted.

☐ The VIN plate and/or homologation plate must be permanently displayed and legible.

Electrical equipment

☐ Switch on the ignition and check the operation of the horn.

☐ Check the windscreen washers and wipers, examining the wiper blades; renew damaged or perished blades. Also check the operation of the stop-lights.

☐ Check the operation of the sidelights and number plate lights. The lenses and reflectors must be secure, clean and undamaged.

☐ Check the operation and alignment of the headlights. The headlight reflectors must not be tarnished and the lenses must be undamaged.

☐ Switch on the ignition and check the operation of the direction indicators (including the instrument panel tell-tale) and the hazard warning lights. Operation of the sidelights and stop-lights must not affect the indicators - if it does, the cause is usually a bad earth at the rear light cluster. Indicators should flash at a rate of between 60 and 120 times per minute – faster or slower than this could indicate a fault with the flasher unit or a bad earth at one of the light units.

☐ Check the operation of the rear foglight(s), including the warning light on the instrument panel or in the switch.

☐ The warning lights must illuminate in accordance with the manufacturer's design. For most vehicles, the ABS and other warning lights should illuminate when the ignition is switched on, and (if the system is operating properly) extinguish after a few seconds. Refer to the owner's handbook.

Footbrake

☐ Examine the master cylinder, brake pipes and servo unit for leaks, loose mountings, corrosion or other damage. If ABS is fitted, this unit should also be examined for signs of leaks or corrosion.

☐ The fluid reservoir must be secure and the fluid level must be between the upper (**A**) and lower (**B**) markings.

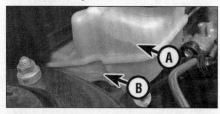

☐ Inspect both front brake flexible hoses for cracks or deterioration of the rubber. Turn the steering from lock to lock, and ensure that the hoses do not contact the wheel, tyre, or any part of the steering or suspension mechanism. With the brake pedal firmly depressed, check the hoses for bulges or leaks under pressure.

Steering and suspension

☐ Have your assistant turn the steering wheel from side to side slightly, up to the point where the steering gear just begins to transmit this movement to the roadwheels. Check for excessive free play between the steering wheel and the steering gear, indicating wear or insecurity of the steering column joints, the column-to-steering gear coupling, or the steering gear itself.

☐ Have your assistant turn the steering wheel more vigorously in each direction, so that the roadwheels just begin to turn. As this is done, examine all the steering joints, linkages, fittings and attachments. Renew any component that shows signs of wear or damage. On vehicles with power steering, check the security and condition of the steering pump, drivebelt and hoses.

☐ Check that the vehicle is standing level, and at approximately the correct ride height.

Shock absorbers

☐ Depress each corner of the vehicle in turn, then release it. The vehicle should rise and then settle in its normal position. If the vehicle continues to rise and fall, the shock absorber is defective. A shock absorber which has seized will also cause the vehicle to fail.

Exhaust system

☐ Start the engine. With your assistant holding a rag over the tailpipe, check the entire system for leaks. Repair or renew leaking sections.

3 Checks carried out **WITH THE VEHICLE RAISED AND THE WHEELS FREE TO TURN**

Jack up the front and rear of the vehicle, and securely support it on axle stands. Position the stands clear of the suspension assemblies. Ensure that the wheels are clear of the ground and that the steering can be turned from lock to lock.

Steering mechanism

☐ Have your assistant turn the steering from lock to lock. Check that the steering turns smoothly, and that no part of the steering mechanism, including a wheel or tyre, fouls any brake hose or pipe or any part of the body structure.
☐ Examine the steering rack rubber gaiters for damage or insecurity of the retaining clips. If power steering is fitted, check for signs of damage or leakage of the fluid hoses, pipes or connections. Also check for excessive stiffness or binding of the steering, a missing split pin or locking device, or severe corrosion of the body structure within 30 cm of any steering component attachment point.

Front and rear suspension and wheel bearings

☐ Starting at the front right-hand side, grasp the roadwheel at the 3 o'clock and 9 o'clock positions and rock gently but firmly. Check for free play or insecurity at the wheel bearings, suspension balljoints, or suspension mount-ings, pivots and attachments.
☐ Now grasp the wheel at the 12 o'clock and 6 o'clock positions and repeat the previous inspection. Spin the wheel, and check for roughness or tightness of the front wheel bearing.

☐ If excess free play is suspected at a component pivot point, this can be confirmed by using a large screwdriver or similar tool and levering between the mounting and the component attachment. This will confirm whether the wear is in the pivot bush, its retaining bolt, or in the mounting itself (the bolt holes can often become elongated).

☐ Carry out all the above checks at the other front wheel, and then at both rear wheels.

Springs and shock absorbers

☐ Examine the suspension struts (when applicable) for serious fluid leakage, corrosion, or damage to the casing. Also check the security of the mounting points.
☐ If coil springs are fitted, check that the spring ends locate in their seats, and that the spring is not corroded, cracked or broken.
☐ If leaf springs are fitted, check that all leaves are intact, that the axle is securely attached to each spring, and that there is no deterioration of the spring eye mountings, bushes, and shackles.

☐ The same general checks apply to vehicles fitted with other suspension types, such as torsion bars, hydraulic displacer units, etc. Ensure that all mountings and attachments are secure, that there are no signs of excessive wear, corrosion or damage, and (on hydraulic types) that there are no fluid leaks or damaged pipes.
☐ Inspect the shock absorbers for signs of serious fluid leakage. Check for wear of the mounting bushes or attachments, or damage to the body of the unit.

Driveshafts (fwd vehicles only)

☐ Rotate each front wheel in turn and inspect the constant velocity joint gaiters for splits or damage. Also check that each driveshaft is straight and undamaged.

Braking system

☐ If possible without dismantling, check brake pad wear and disc condition. Ensure that the friction lining material has not worn excessively, (A) and that the discs are not fractured, pitted, scored or badly worn (B).

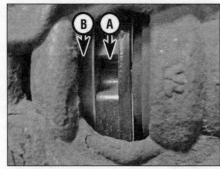

☐ Examine all the rigid brake pipes underneath the vehicle, and the flexible hose(s) at the rear. Look for corrosion, chafing or insecurity of the pipes, and for signs of bulging under pressure, chafing, splits or deterioration of the flexible hoses.
☐ Look for signs of fluid leaks at the brake calipers or on the brake backplates. Repair or renew leaking components.
☐ Slowly spin each wheel, while your assistant depresses and releases the footbrake. Ensure that each brake is operating and does not bind when the pedal is released.

black smoke means unburnt fuel (dirty air cleaner element, or other fuel system fault).

☐ An exhaust gas analyser for measuring carbon monoxide (CO) and hydrocarbons (HC) is now needed. If one cannot be hired or borrowed, have a local garage perform the check.

CO emissions (mixture)

☐ The MOT tester has access to the CO limits for all vehicles. The CO level is measured at idle speed, and at 'fast idle' (2500 to 3000 rpm). The following limits are given as a general guide:

At idle speed – Less than 0.5% CO
At 'fast idle' – Less than 0.3% CO
Lambda reading – 0.97 to 1.03

☐ If the CO level is too high, this may point to poor maintenance, a fuel injection system problem, faulty lambda (oxygen) sensor or catalytic converter. Try an injector cleaning treatment, and check the vehicle's ECU for fault codes.

HC emissions

☐ The MOT tester has access to HC limits for all vehicles. The HC level is measured at 'fast idle' (2500 to 3000 rpm). The following limits are given as a general guide:

At 'fast idle' – Less then 200 ppm

☐ Excessive HC emissions are typically caused by oil being burnt (worn engine), or by a blocked crankcase ventilation system ('breather'). If the engine oil is old and thin, an oil change may help. If the engine is running badly, check the vehicle's ECU for fault codes.

Diesel models

☐ The only emission test for diesel engines is measuring exhaust smoke density, using a calibrated smoke meter. The test involves accelerating the engine at least 3 times to its maximum unloaded speed.

Note: *On engines with a timing belt, it is VITAL that the belt is in good condition before the test is carried out.*

☐ With the engine warmed up, it is first purged by running at around 2500 rpm for 20 seconds. A governor check is then carried out, by slowly accelerating the engine to its maximum speed. After this, the smoke meter is connected, and the engine is accelerated quickly to maximum speed three times. If the smoke density is less than the limits given below, the vehicle will pass:

Non-turbo vehicles: 2.5m-1
Turbocharged vehicles: 3.0m-1

☐ If excess smoke is produced, try fitting a new air cleaner element, or using an injector cleaning treatment. If the engine is running badly, where applicable, check the vehicle's ECU for fault codes. Also check the vehicle's EGR system, where applicable. At high mileages, the injectors may require professional attention.

☐ Examine the handbrake mechanism, checking for frayed or broken cables, excessive corrosion, or wear or insecurity of the linkage. Check that the mechanism works on each relevant wheel, and releases fully, without binding.

☐ It is not possible to test brake efficiency without special equipment, but a road test can be carried out later to check that the vehicle pulls up in a straight line.

Fuel and exhaust systems

☐ Inspect the fuel tank (including the filler cap), fuel pipes, hoses and unions. All components must be secure and free from leaks. Locking fuel caps must lock securely and the key must be provided for the MOT test.

☐ Examine the exhaust system over its entire length, checking for any damaged, broken or missing mountings, security of the retaining clamps and rust or corrosion.

Wheels and tyres

☐ Examine the sidewalls and tread area of each tyre in turn. Check for cuts, tears, lumps, bulges, separation of the tread, and exposure of the ply or cord due to wear or damage. Check that the tyre bead is correctly seated on the wheel rim, that the valve is sound and properly seated, and that the wheel is not distorted or damaged.

☐ Check that the tyres are of the correct size for the vehicle, that they are of the same size and type on each axle, and that the pressures are correct.

☐ Check the tyre tread depth. The legal minimum at the time of writing is 1.6 mm over the central three-quarters of the tread width. Abnormal tread wear may indicate incorrect front wheel alignment or wear in steering or suspension components.

☐ If the spare wheel is fitted externally or in a separate carrier beneath the vehicle, check that mountings are secure and free of excessive corrosion.

Body corrosion

☐ Check the condition of the entire vehicle structure for signs of corrosion in load-bearing areas. (These include chassis box sections, side sills, cross-members, pillars, and all suspension, steering, braking system and seat belt mountings and anchorages.) Any corrosion which has seriously reduced the thickness of a load-bearing area (or is within 30 cm of safety-related components such as steering or suspension) is likely to cause the vehicle to fail. In this case professional repairs are likely to be needed.

☐ Damage or corrosion which causes sharp or otherwise dangerous edges to be exposed will also cause the vehicle to fail.

Towbars

☐ Check the condition of mounting points (both beneath the vehicle and within boot/hatchback areas) for signs of corrosion, ensuring that all fixings are secure and not worn or damaged. There must be no excessive play in detachable tow ball arms or quick-release mechanisms.

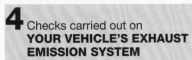

4 Checks carried out on **YOUR VEHICLE'S EXHAUST EMISSION SYSTEM**

Petrol models

☐ The engine should be warmed up, and running well (ignition system in good order, air filter element clean, etc).

☐ Before testing, run the engine at around 2500 rpm for 20 seconds. Let the engine drop to idle, and watch for smoke from the exhaust. If the idle speed is too high, or if dense blue or black smoke emerges for more than 5 seconds, the vehicle will fail. Typically, blue smoke signifies oil burning (engine wear);

Engine

☐ Engine fails to rotate when attempting to start
☐ Engine rotates, but will not start
☐ Engine difficult to start when cold
☐ Engine difficult to start when hot
☐ Starter motor noisy or excessively rough in engagement
☐ Engine starts, but stops immediately
☐ Engine idles erratically
☐ Engine misfires at idle speed
☐ Engine misfires throughout the driving speed range
☐ Engine hesitates on acceleration
☐ Engine stalls
☐ Engine lacks power
☐ Engine backfires
☐ Oil pressure warning light on with engine running
☐ Engine runs-on after switching off
☐ Engine noises

Cooling system

☐ Overheating
☐ Overcooling
☐ External coolant leakage
☐ Internal coolant leakage
☐ Corrosion

Fuel and exhaust systems

☐ Excessive fuel consumption
☐ Fuel leakage and/or fuel odour
☐ Excessive noise or fumes from exhaust system

Clutch

☐ Pedal travels to floor – no pressure or very little resistance
☐ Clutch fails to disengage (unable to select gears)
☐ Clutch slips (engine speed rises, with no increase in vehicle speed)
☐ Judder as clutch is engaged
☐ Noise when depressing or releasing clutch pedal

Manual transmission

☐ Noisy in neutral with engine running
☐ Noisy in one particular gear
☐ Difficulty engaging gears
☐ Jumps out of gear
☐ Vibration
☐ Lubricant leaks

Driveshafts

☐ Clicking or knocking noise on turns (at slow speed on full-lock)
☐ Vibration when accelerating or decelerating

Braking system

☐ Vehicle pulls to one side under braking
☐ Noise (grinding or high-pitched squeal) when brakes applied
☐ Excessive brake pedal travel
☐ Brake pedal feels spongy when depressed
☐ Excessive brake pedal effort required to stop vehicle
☐ Judder felt through brake pedal or steering wheel when braking
☐ Brakes binding
☐ Rear wheels locking under normal braking

Suspension and steering

☐ Vehicle pulls to one side
☐ Wheel wobble and vibration
☐ Excessive pitching and/or rolling around corners, or during braking
☐ Wandering or general instability
☐ Excessively-stiff steering
☐ Excessive play in steering
☐ Lack of power assistance
☐ Tyre wear excessive

Electrical system

☐ Battery won't hold a charge for more than a few days
☐ Ignition/no-charge warning light stays on with engine running
☐ Ignition/no-charge warning light fails to come on
☐ Lights inoperative
☐ Instrument readings inaccurate or erratic
☐ Horn inoperative, or unsatisfactory in operation
☐ Windscreen/tailgate wipers failed, or unsatisfactory in operation
☐ Windscreen/tailgate washers failed, or unsatisfactory in operation
☐ Electric windows inoperative, or unsatisfactory in operation
☐ Central locking system inoperative, or unsatisfactory in operation

Introduction

1 The vehicle owner who does his or her own maintenance according to the recommended service schedules should not have to use this section of the manual very often. Modern component reliability is such that, provided those items subject to wear or deterioration are inspected or renewed at the specified intervals, sudden failure is comparatively rare. Faults do not usually just happen as a result of sudden failure, but develop over a period of time. Major mechanical failures in particular are usually preceded by characteristic symptoms over hundreds or even thousands of miles. Those components that do occasionally fail without warning are often small and easily carried in the vehicle.

2 With any fault-finding, the first step is to decide where to begin investigations. Sometimes this is obvious, but on other occasions, a little detective work will be necessary. The owner who makes half a dozen haphazard adjustments or replacements may be successful in curing a fault (or its symptoms), but will be none the wiser if the fault recurs, and ultimately may have spent more time and money than was necessary. A calm and logical approach will be found

to be more satisfactory in the long run. Always take into account any warning signs or abnormalities that may have been noticed in the period preceding the fault – power loss, high or low gauge readings, unusual smells, etc – and remember that failure of components such as fuses or spark plugs may only be pointers to some underlying fault.

3 The pages that follow provide an easy-reference guide to the more common problems, which may occur during the operation of the vehicle. These problems and their possible causes are grouped under headings denoting various components or systems, such as Engine, Cooling system, etc. The general Chapter that deals with the problem is also shown in brackets; refer to the relevant part of that Chapter for system-specific information. Whatever the fault, certain basic principles apply. These are as follows:

4 Verify the fault. This is simply a matter of being sure that you know what the symptoms are before starting work. This is particularly important if you are investigating a fault for someone else, who may not have described it very accurately.

5 Don't overlook the obvious. For example, if the vehicle won't start, is there fuel in the tank? (Don't take anyone else's word on this particular point, and don't trust the fuel gauge either!) If an electrical fault is indicated, look for loose or broken wires before digging out the test gear.

6 Cure the disease, not the symptom. Substituting a flat battery with a fully charged one will get you off the hard shoulder, but if the underlying cause is not attended to, the new battery will go the same way. Similarly, changing oil-fouled spark plugs (petrol models) for a new set will get you moving again, but remember that the reason for the fouling (if it wasn't simply an incorrect grade of plug) will have to be found and corrected.

7 Don't take anything for granted. Particularly, don't forget that a 'new' component may itself be defective (especially if it's been rattling around in the boot for months), and don't leave components out of a fault diagnosis sequence just because they are new or recently fitted. When you do finally diagnose a difficult fault, you'll probably realise that all the evidence was there from the start.

Engine

Engine fails to rotate when attempting to start

☐ Battery terminal connections loose or corroded (*Weekly checks*).
☐ Battery discharged or faulty (Chapter 5A).
☐ Broken, loose or disconnected wiring in the starting circuit (Chapter 5A).
☐ Defective starter motor (Chapter 5A Section 9).
☐ Starter pinion or flywheel ring gear teeth loose or broken (Chapter 2A Section 16, Chapter 2B Section 16, Chapter 2C Section 16 or Chapter 5A Section 10).
☐ Engine earth strap broken or disconnected (Chapter 12 Section 2).

Engine rotates, but will not start

☐ Fuel tank empty.
☐ Battery discharged (engine rotates slowly) (Chapter 5A Section 3).
☐ Battery terminal connections loose or corroded (*Weekly checks*).
☐ Preheating system faulty (Chapter 5B).
☐ Air in fuel system (Chapter 4A Section 4).
☐ Fuel injector/injection pump fault (Chapter 4A).
☐ Low cylinder compressions (Chapter 2A Section 2, Chapter 2B Section 2 or Chapter 2C Section 2).
☐ Major mechanical failure (eg, camshaft drive) (Chapter 2A Section 7, Chapter 2B Section 7 or Chapter 2C Section 7).
☐ Faulty fuel pressure sensor (Chapter 4A Section 12).

Engine difficult to start when cold

☐ Battery discharged (Chapter 5A Section 3).
☐ Battery terminal connections loose or corroded (*Weekly checks*).
☐ Preheating system faulty (Chapter 5B).
☐ Fuel injector/injection pump fault (Chapter 4A).

Engine difficult to start when hot

☐ Fuel injector/injection pump fault (Chapter 4A).
☐ Low cylinder compressions (Chapter 2A Section 2, Chapter 2B Section 2 or Chapter 2C Section 2).

Starter motor noisy or excessively rough in engagement

☐ Starter pinion or flywheel/driveplate ring gear teeth loose or broken (Chapter 2A Section 16, Chapter 2B Section 16, Chapter 2C Section 16 or Chapter 5A Section 10).
☐ Starter motor mounting bolts loose or missing (Chapter 5A Section 10).
☐ Defective starter motor (Chapter 5A Section 11).

Engine starts, but stops immediately

☐ Air in fuel system (Chapter 4A Section 4).
☐ Fuel injector/injection pump fault (Chapter 4A).

Engine idles erratically

☐ Air in fuel system (Chapter 4A Section 4).
☐ Fuel injector/injection pump fault (Chapter 4A).
☐ Uneven or low cylinder compressions (Chapter 2A Section 2, Chapter 2B Section 2 or Chapter 2C Section 2).
☐ Timing belt incorrectly fitted (Chapter 2A Section 7, Chapter 2B Section 7 or Chapter 2C Section 7).
☐ Camshaft lobes worn (Chapter 2A Section 9, Chapter 2B Section 9 or Chapter 2C Section 9).

Engine (continued)

Engine misfires at idle speed

- [ ] Faulty injector(s) (Chapter 4A Section 11).
- [ ] Uneven or low cylinder compressions (Chapter 2A Section 2, Chapter 2B Section 2 or Chapter 2C Section 2).
- [ ] Timing belt incorrectly fitted (Chapter 2A Section 7, Chapter 2B Section 7 or Chapter 2C Section 7).
- [ ] Disconnected, leaking, or perished crankcase ventilation hoses (Chapter 4B).

Engine misfires throughout the driving speed range

- [ ] Fuel filter blocked (Chapter 1 Section 11).
- [ ] Fuel pump faulty (Chapter 4A Section 7).
- [ ] Fuel tank vent blocked, or fuel pipes restricted (Chapter 4A).
- [ ] Fuel injector/injection pump fault (Chapter 4A).
- [ ] Uneven or low cylinder compressions (Chapter 2A Section 2, Chapter 2B Section 2 or Chapter 2C Section 2).

Engine hesitates on acceleration

- [ ] Fuel injector/injection pump fault (Chapter 4A).

Engine stalls

- [ ] Fuel filter blocked (Chapter 1 Section 11).
- [ ] Fuel pump faulty (Chapter 4A Section 7).
- [ ] Fuel tank vent blocked, or fuel pipes restricted (Chapter 4A).
- [ ] Fuel injector/injection pump fault (Chapter 4A).

Engine lacks power

- [ ] Timing belt incorrectly fitted (Chapter 2A Section 7, Chapter 2B Section 7 or Chapter 2C Section 7).
- [ ] Fuel filter blocked (Chapter 1 Section 11).
- [ ] Fuel pump faulty (Chapter 4A Section 7).
- [ ] Uneven or low cylinder compressions (Chapter 2A Section 2, Chapter 2B Section 2 or Chapter 2C Section 2).
- [ ] Fuel injector/injection pump fault (Chapter 4A).
- [ ] Brakes binding (Chapter 1 or Chapter 9).
- [ ] Clutch slipping (Chapter 6).
- [ ] EGR valve faulty (Chapter 4B Section 2).
- [ ] Air intake/turbocharger duct leak (Chapter 4A).

Engine backfires

- [ ] Timing belt incorrectly fitted (Chapter 2A Section 7, Chapter 2B Section 7 or Chapter 2C Section 7).

Oil pressure warning light on with engine running

- [ ] Low oil level, or incorrect oil grade (*Weekly checks*).
- [ ] Faulty oil pressure warning light switch (Chapter 2A Section 15, Chapter 2B Section 15 or Chapter 2C Section 15).
- [ ] Worn engine bearings and/or oil pump (Chapter 2D).
- [ ] High engine operating temperature (Chapter 3).
- [ ] Oil pressure relief valve defective (Chapter 2A Section 12, Chapter 2B Section 12 or Chapter 2C Section 12).
- [ ] Oil pick-up strainer clogged (Chapter 2A Section 11, Chapter 2B Section 11 or Chapter 2C Section 11).

Engine runs-on after switching off

- [ ] Excessive carbon build-up in engine (Chapter 2D).
- [ ] High engine operating temperature (Chapter 3).

Engine noises

Pre-ignition (pinking) or knocking during acceleration or under load

- [ ] Excessive carbon build-up in engine (Chapter 2D).

Whistling or wheezing noises

- [ ] Leaking vacuum hose (Chapter 4A or Chapter 9).
- [ ] Blowing cylinder head gasket (Chapter 2A Section 10, Chapter 2B Section 10 or Chapter 2C Section 10).

Tapping or rattling noises

- [ ] Worn valve gear or camshaft (Chapter 2B Section 9, Chapter 2A Section 9 or Chapter 2C Section 9).
- [ ] Ancillary component fault (coolant pump, alternator, etc) (Chapter 3 or Chapter 5A etc).

Knocking or thumping noises

- [ ] Worn big-end bearings (regular heavy knocking, perhaps less under load) (Chapter 2D).
- [ ] Worn main bearings (rumbling and knocking, perhaps worsening under load) (Chapter 2D).
- [ ] Piston slap (most noticeable when cold) (Chapter 2D).
- [ ] Ancillary component fault (coolant pump, alternator, etc) (Chapter 3 or Chapter 5A etc).

Cooling system

Overheating

- ☐ Insufficient coolant in system (*Weekly checks*).
- ☐ Thermostat faulty (stuck closed) (Chapter 3 Section 5).
- ☐ Radiator core blocked, or grille restricted (Chapter 3 Section 4).
- ☐ Electric cooling fan or sensor faulty (Chapter 3).
- ☐ Pressure cap faulty (Chapter 3).
- ☐ Inaccurate temperature gauge/sensor (Chapter 3 Section 7).
- ☐ Airlock in cooling system (Chapter 1 Section 23).
- ☐ Engine management system fault (Chapter 4A).

Overcooling

- ☐ Thermostat faulty (stuck open) (Chapter 3 Section 5).
- ☐ Inaccurate temperature gauge/sensor (Chapter 3 Section 7).
- ☐ Damaged/Faulty relay (Chapter 12 Section 3).

External coolant leakage

- ☐ Deteriorated or damaged hoses or hose clips (Chapter 1 Section 7).
- ☐ Radiator core or heater matrix leaking (Chapter 3).
- ☐ Pressure cap faulty (Chapter 3).
- ☐ Coolant pump leaking (Chapter 3 Section 8).
- ☐ Boiling due to overheating (Chapter 3).
- ☐ Core plug leaking (Chapter 2D Section 11).

Internal coolant leakage

- ☐ Leaking cylinder head gasket (Chapter 2A Section 10, Chapter 2B Section 10 or Chapter 2C Section 10).
- ☐ Cracked cylinder head or cylinder bore (Chapter 2D).

Corrosion

- ☐ Infrequent draining and flushing (Chapter 1 Section 23).
- ☐ Incorrect coolant mixture or inappropriate coolant type (Chapter 1 Section 23).

Fuel and exhaust systems

Excessive fuel consumption

- ☐ Air filter element dirty or clogged (Chapter 1 Section 24).
- ☐ Engine management system fault (Chapter 4A).
- ☐ Faulty injector(s) (Chapter 4A Section 11).
- ☐ Tyres under-inflated (*Weekly checks*).
- ☐ Brakes binding (Chapter 1 and Chapter 9).

Fuel leakage and/or fuel odour

- ☐ Damaged or corroded fuel tank, pipes or connections (Chapter 4A).

Excessive noise or fumes from exhaust system

- ☐ Leaking exhaust system or manifold joints (Chapter 1 or Chapter 4A).
- ☐ Leaking, corroded or damaged silencers or pipe (Chapter 1 or Chapter 4A).
- ☐ Broken mountings causing body or suspension contact (Chapter 1 or Chapter 4A).

Clutch

Pedal travels to floor – no pressure or very little resistance

- [ ] Air in hydraulic system/faulty master or slave cylinder (Chapter 6 Section 2).
- [ ] Broken clutch release bearing or fork (Chapter 6 Section 7).
- [ ] Broken diaphragm spring in clutch pressure plate (Chapter 6 Section 6).

Clutch fails to disengage (unable to select gears)

- [ ] Air in hydraulic system/faulty master or slave cylinder (Chapter 6 Section 2).
- [ ] Clutch disc sticking on gearbox input shaft splines (Chapter 6 Section 6).
- [ ] Clutch disc sticking to flywheel or pressure plate (Chapter 6 Section 6).
- [ ] Faulty pressure plate assembly (Chapter 6 Section 6).
- [ ] Clutch release mechanism worn or incorrectly assembled (Chapter 6 Section 7).

Clutch slips (engine speed rises, with no increase in vehicle speed)

- [ ] Faulty hydraulic release system (Chapter 6 Section 7).
- [ ] Clutch disc linings excessively worn (Chapter 6 Section 6).
- [ ] Clutch disc linings contaminated with oil or grease (Chapter 6 Section 6).
- [ ] Faulty pressure plate or weak diaphragm spring (Chapter 6 Section 6).

Judder as clutch is engaged

- [ ] Clutch disc linings contaminated with oil or grease (Chapter 6 Section 6).
- [ ] Clutch disc linings excessively worn (Chapter 6 Section 6).
- [ ] Faulty or distorted pressure plate or diaphragm spring (Chapter 6 Section 6).
- [ ] Worn or loose engine or gearbox mountings (Chapter 2B Section 17, Chapter 2A Section 17 or Chapter 2C Section 17).
- [ ] Clutch disc hub or gearbox input shaft splines worn (Chapter 6 Section 6).

Noise when depressing or releasing clutch pedal

- [ ] Worn clutch release bearing (Chapter 6 Section 7).
- [ ] Worn or dry clutch pedal bushes (Chapter 6 Section 5).
- [ ] Faulty pressure plate assembly (Chapter 6 Section 6).
- [ ] Pressure plate diaphragm spring broken (Chapter 6 Section 6).
- [ ] Broken clutch disc cushioning springs (Chapter 6 Section 6).

Manual transmission

Noisy in neutral with engine running

- [ ] Input shaft bearings worn (noise apparent with clutch pedal released, but not when depressed) (Chapter 7 Section 7).*
- [ ] Clutch release bearing worn (noise apparent with clutch pedal depressed, possibly less when released) (Chapter 6 Section 7).

Noisy in one particular gear

- [ ] Worn, damaged or chipped gear teeth (Chapter 7 Section 7).*

Difficulty engaging gears

- [ ] Clutch fault (Chapter 6).
- [ ] Worn or damaged gear selection cables (Chapter 7 Section 3).*
- [ ] Worn synchroniser units (Chapter 7 Section 7).*

Jumps out of gear

- [ ] Worn or damaged gear selection cables (Chapter 7 Section 3).

- [ ] Worn synchroniser units (Chapter 7 Section 7).*
- [ ] Worn selector forks (Chapter 7 Section 7).*

Vibration

- [ ] Lack of oil (Chapter 1 Section 25 and Chapter 7 Section 2).
- [ ] Worn bearings (Chapter 7 Section 7).*

Lubricant leaks

- [ ] Leaking differential output oil seal (Chapter 7 Section 4).
- [ ] Leaking housing joint (Chapter 7 Section 7).*
- [ ] Leaking input shaft oil seal (Chapter 7 Section 4).

Note: *Although the corrective action necessary to remedy the symptoms described is beyond the scope of the home mechanic, the above information should be helpful in isolating the cause of the condition, so that the owner can communicate clearly with a professional mechanic.

Fault finding

Driveshafts

Clicking or knocking noise on turns (at slow speed on full-lock)

☐ Lack of constant velocity joint lubricant, possibly due to damaged gaiter (Chapter 8).
☐ Worn outer constant velocity joint (Chapter 8 Section 4).

Vibration when accelerating or decelerating

☐ Worn inner constant velocity joint (Chapter 8 Section 4).
☐ Bent or distorted driveshaft (Chapter 8 Section 4).
☐ Worn intermediate bearing (Chapter 8 Section 5).

Braking system

Vehicle pulls to one side under braking

Note: *Before assuming that a brake problem exists, make sure that the tyres are in good condition and correctly inflated, that the front wheel alignment is correct, and that the vehicle is not loaded with weight in an unequal manner. Apart from checking the condition of all pipe and hose connections, any faults occurring on the anti-lock braking system should be referred to a Citroën dealer for diagnosis.*

☐ Worn, defective, damaged or contaminated brake pads on one side (Chapter 9 Section 4).
☐ Seized or partially-seized front brake caliper (Chapter 9 Section 9).
☐ A mixture of brake pad materials fitted between sides (Chapter 9 Section 4).
☐ Brake caliper mounting bolts loose (Chapter 9 Section 9).
☐ Worn or damaged steering or suspension components (Chapter 1 or Chapter 10).

Noise (grinding or high-pitched squeal) when brakes applied

☐ Brake pad material worn down to metal backing (Chapter 1 or Chapter 9).
☐ Brake shoe material worn down to metal backing (Chapter 9 Section 6).
☐ Excessive corrosion of brake disc. May be apparent after the vehicle has been standing for some time (Chapter 9).
☐ Foreign object (stone chipping, etc) trapped between brake disc and shield (Chapter 9).

Excessive brake pedal travel

☐ Faulty master cylinder (Chapter 9).
☐ Air in hydraulic system (Chapter 9).
☐ Faulty vacuum servo unit (Chapter 9).

Brake pedal feels spongy when depressed

☐ Air in hydraulic system (Chapter 9).
☐ Deteriorated flexible rubber brake hoses (Chapter 1 or Chapter 9).
☐ Master cylinder mounting nuts loose (Chapter 9).
☐ Faulty master cylinder (Chapter 9).

Excessive brake pedal effort required to stop vehicle

☐ Faulty vacuum servo unit (Chapter 9).
☐ Disconnected, damaged or insecure brake servo vacuum hose (Chapter 9).
☐ Primary or secondary hydraulic circuit failure (Chapter 9).
☐ Seized brake caliper (Chapter 9).
☐ Brake pads incorrectly fitted (Chapter 9).
☐ Incorrect grade of brake pads fitted (Chapter 9).
☐ Brake pads contaminated (Chapter 9).
☐ Brake shoes contaminated (Chapter 9 Section 6).
☐ Brake shoe adjusting mechanism faulty (Chapter 9 Section 6).

Judder felt through brake pedal or steering wheel when braking

☐ Excessive run-out or distortion of discs (Chapter 9).
☐ Brake drums distorted/worn (Chapter 9 Section 11).
☐ Brake pads worn (Chapter 1 or Chapter 9).
☐ Brake shoes excessively worn (Chapter 9 Section 6).
☐ Brake caliper mounting bolts loose (Chapter 9).
☐ Wear in suspension or steering components or mountings (Chapter 1 or Chapter 10).

Brakes binding

☐ Seized brake caliper (Chapter 9).
☐ Wheel cylinder seized (Chapter 9 Section 12).
☐ Incorrectly-adjusted handbrake mechanism (Chapter 9).
☐ Faulty master cylinder (Chapter 9).

Rear wheels locking under normal braking

☐ Rear brake pads contaminated (Chapter 9 Section 5).
☐ Rear brake shoes contaminated (Chapter 9 Section 6).
☐ ABS system fault (Chapter 9).

Suspension and steering

Vehicle pulls to one side

Note: *Before diagnosing suspension or steering faults, be sure that the trouble is not due to incorrect tyre pressures, mixtures of tyre types, or binding brakes.*

☐ Defective tyre (*Weekly checks*).
☐ Excessive wear in suspension or steering components (Chapter 1 orChapter 10).
☐ Incorrect front wheel alignment (Chapter 10 Section 23).
☐ Damage to steering or suspension components (Chapter 1 Section 8 or Chapter 10).

Wheel wobble and vibration

☐ Front roadwheels out of balance (vibration felt mainly through the steering wheel) (Chapter 1 or Chapter 10).
☐ Rear roadwheels out of balance (vibration felt throughout the vehicle) (Chapter 1 or Chapter 10).
☐ Roadwheels damaged or distorted (Chapter 1 or Chapter 10).
☐ Faulty or damaged tyre (*Weekly checks*).
☐ Worn steering or suspension joints, bushes or components (Chapter 1 Section 8 or Chapter 10).
☐ Wheel bolts loose (Chapter 1 Section 8 or Chapter 10).

Excessive pitching and/or rolling around corners, or during braking

☐ Defective shock absorbers (Chapter 1 Section 8 or Chapter 10).
☐ Broken or weak spring and/or suspension part (Chapter 1 or Chapter 10).
☐ Worn or damaged anti-roll bar or mountings (Chapter 10 Section 7).

Wandering or general instability

☐ Incorrect front wheel alignment (Chapter 10 Section 23).
☐ Worn steering or suspension joints, bushes or components (Chapter 1 Section 8 or Chapter 10).
☐ Roadwheels out of balance (Chapter 1 Section 8 or Chapter 10).
☐ Faulty or damaged tyre (*Weekly checks*).
☐ Wheel bolts loose (Chapter 1 Section 8 or Chapter 10).
☐ Defective shock absorbers (Chapter 1 Section 8 or Chapter 10).

Excessively-stiff steering

☐ Lack of power steering fluid (*Weekly checks*).
☐ Seized track rod end balljoint or suspension balljoint (Chapter 1 Section 8 or Chapter 10).

☐ Incorrect front wheel alignment (Chapter 10 Section 23).
☐ Steering rack or column bent or damaged (Chapter 10).
☐ Power steering pump fault (Chapter 10 Section 21).

Excessive play in steering

☐ Worn steering column universal joint (Chapter 10 Section 16).
☐ Worn steering track rod end balljoints (Chapter 1 Section 8 or Chapter 10 Section 22).
☐ Worn steering rack (Chapter 10 Section 18).
☐ Worn steering or suspension joints, bushes or components (Chapter 1 Section 8 or Chapter 10).

Lack of power assistance

☐ Incorrect power steering fluid level (*Weekly checks*).
☐ Restriction in power steering fluid hoses (Chapter 1).
☐ Faulty power steering pump (Chapter 10 Section 21).
☐ Faulty steering rack (Chapter 10 Section 18).
☐ Relay or fuse fault (Chapter 12 Section 3).

Tyre wear excessive

Tyre treads exhibit feathered edges

☐ Incorrect toe setting (Chapter 10 Section 23).

Tyres worn in centre of tread

☐ Tyres over-inflated (*Weekly checks*).

Tyres worn on inside and outside edges

☐ Tyres under-inflated (*Weekly checks*).

Tyres worn on inside or outside edges

☐ Incorrect camber/castor angles (wear on one edge only) (Chapter 10 Section 23).
☐ Worn steering or suspension joints, bushes or components (Chapter 1 Section 8 or Chapter 10).
☐ Excessively-hard cornering.
☐ Accident damage.

Tyres worn unevenly

☐ Tyres/wheels out of balance (*Weekly checks*).
☐ Excessive wheel or tyre run-out (Chapter 10 Section 23).
☐ Worn shock absorbers (Chapter 1 Section 8 or Chapter 10).
☐ Faulty tyre (*Weekly checks*).

Electrical system

Battery won't hold a charge for more than a few days

Note: *For problems associated with the starting system, refer to the faults listed under 'Engine' earlier in this Section.*

☐ Battery defective internally (Chapter 5A Section 3).
☐ Battery terminal connections loose or corroded (*Weekly checks*).
☐ Auxiliary drivebelt broken, worn or incorrectly adjusted (Chapter 1 Section 20).
☐ Alternator not charging at correct output (Chapter 5A Section 5).
☐ Alternator or voltage regulator faulty (Chapter 5A Section 5).
☐ Short-circuit causing continual battery drain (Chapter 5A and Chapter 12 Section 2).

Ignition/no-charge warning light stays on with engine running

☐ Auxiliary drivebelt broken, worn, or incorrectly adjusted (Chapter 1 Section 20).
☐ Internal fault in alternator or voltage regulator (Chapter 5A Section 5).
☐ Broken, disconnected, or loose wiring in charging circuit (Chapter 5A Section 5).

Ignition/no-charge warning light fails to come on

☐ Broken, disconnected, or loose wiring in warning light circuit (Chapter 12).
☐ Alternator faulty (Chapter 5A Section 5).
☐ Instrument panel faulty (Chapter 12 Section 10).

Electrical system

Lights inoperative

- ☐ Bulb blown (Chapter 12).
- ☐ Corrosion of bulb or bulbholder contacts (Chapter 12 Section 6, 7).
- ☐ Blown fuse (Chapter 12 Section 3).
- ☐ Faulty relay (Chapter 12 Section 3).
- ☐ Broken, loose, or disconnected wiring (Chapter 12 Section 2).
- ☐ Faulty switch (Chapter 12 Section 2, 5).

Instrument readings inaccurate or erratic

Fuel or temperature gauges give no reading

- ☐ Faulty gauge sensor unit (Chapter 3 Section 7 or Chapter 4A Section 7).
- ☐ Wiring open-circuit (Chapter 12 Section 2).
- ☐ Faulty instrument panel (Chapter 12 Section 10).

Fuel or temperature gauges give continuous maximum reading

- ☐ Faulty gauge sensor unit (Chapter 3 Section 7 or Chapter 4A Section 7).
- ☐ Wiring short-circuit (Chapter 12 Section 2).
- ☐ Faulty instrument panel (Chapter 12 Section 10).

Horn inoperative, or unsatisfactory in operation

Horn operates all the time

- ☐ Horn push either earthed or stuck down (Chapter 12 Section 21).
- ☐ Horn cable-to-horn push earthed (Chapter 12 Section 2).

Horn fails to operate

- ☐ Blown fuse (Chapter 12 Section 3).
- ☐ Cable or cable connections loose, broken or disconnected (Chapter 12 Section 2).
- ☐ Faulty horn (Chapter 12 Section 12).

Horn emits intermittent or unsatisfactory sound

- ☐ Cable connections loose (Chapter 12 Section 2).
- ☐ Horn mountings loose (Chapter 12 Section 12).
- ☐ Faulty horn (Chapter 12 Section 12).

Windscreen/tailgate wipers failed, or unsatisfactory in operation

Wipers fail to operate, or operate very slowly

- ☐ Wiper blades stuck to screen, or linkage seized or binding (Chapter 12 Section 14).
- ☐ Blown fuse (Chapter 12 Section 3).
- ☐ Cable or cable connections loose, broken or disconnected (Chapter 12 Section 2).
- ☐ Faulty built-in system interface (BSI) unit (Chapter 12 Section 22).
- ☐ Faulty wiper motor (Chapter 12 Section 14 or Chapter 12 Section 15).

Wiper blades sweep over too large or too small an area of the glass

- ☐ Wiper arms incorrectly positioned on spindles (Chapter 12 Section 13).
- ☐ Excessive wear of wiper linkage (Chapter 12 Section 14).
- ☐ Wiper motor or linkage mountings loose or insecure (Chapter 12 Section 14).

Wiper blades fail to clean the glass effectively

- ☐ Wiper blade rubbers worn or perished (Weekly checks).
- ☐ Wiper arm tension springs broken, or arm pivots seized (Chapter 12 Section 13).
- ☐ Insufficient windscreen washer additive to adequately remove road film (Weekly checks).

Windscreen/tailgate washers failed, or unsatisfactory in operation

One or more washer jets inoperative

- ☐ Blocked washer jet (Weekly checks).
- ☐ Disconnected, kinked or restricted fluid hose (Chapter 12 Section 16).
- ☐ Insufficient fluid in washer reservoir (Weekly checks).

Washer pump fails to operate

- ☐ Broken or disconnected wiring or connections (Chapter 12 Section 16).
- ☐ Blown fuse (Chapter 12 Section 3).
- ☐ Faulty washer switch (Chapter 12 Section 5).
- ☐ Faulty washer pump (Chapter 12 Section 16).

Electric windows inoperative, or unsatisfactory in operation

Window glass will only move in one direction

- ☐ Faulty switch (Chapter 12 Section 5).

Window glass slow to move

- ☐ Regulator seized or damaged, or in need of lubricant (Chapter 11 Section 15).
- ☐ Door internal components or trim fouling regulator (Chapter 11 Section 15).
- ☐ Faulty motor (Chapter 11 Section 15).

Window glass fails to move

- ☐ Blown fuse (Chapter 12 Section 3).
- ☐ Broken or disconnected wiring or connections (Chapter 12 Section 2).
- ☐ Faulty motor (Chapter 11 Section 15).
- ☐ Faulty built-in systems interface (BSI) unit (Chapter 12 Section 22).

Central locking system inoperative, or unsatisfactory in operation

Complete system failure

- ☐ Blown fuse (Chapter 12 Section 3).
- ☐ Broken or disconnected wiring or connections (Chapter 12 Section 2).
- ☐ Faulty built-in system interface (BSI) unit (Chapter 12 Section 22).
- ☐ Remote control batteries discharged (Chapter 1 Section 26).

Door/tailgate locks but will not unlock, or unlocks but will not lock

- ☐ Broken or disconnected link rod(s) (Chapter 11 Section 12, 13, 14).
- ☐ Faulty lock motor (Chapter 11 Section 12, 13, 14).

One lock fails to operate

- ☐ Broken or disconnected wiring or connections (Chapter 12 Section 2).
- ☐ Faulty lock motor (Chapter 11 Section 12, 13, 14).
- ☐ Broken, binding or disconnected link rod(s) (Chapter 11 Section 12, 13, 14).

A

ABS (Anti-lock brake system) A system, usually electronically controlled, that senses incipient wheel lockup during braking and relieves hydraulic pressure at wheels that are about to skid.

Air bag An inflatable bag hidden in the steering wheel (driver's side) or the dash or glovebox (passenger side). In a head-on collision, the bags inflate, preventing the driver and front passenger from being thrown forward into the steering wheel or windscreen.

Air cleaner A metal or plastic housing, containing a filter element, which removes dust and dirt from the air being drawn into the engine.

Air filter element The actual filter in an air cleaner system, usually manufactured from pleated paper and requiring renewal at regular intervals.

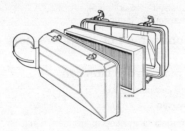

Air filter

Allen key A hexagonal wrench which fits into a recessed hexagonal hole.

Alligator clip A long-nosed spring-loaded metal clip with meshing teeth. Used to make temporary electrical connections.

Alternator A component in the electrical system which converts mechanical energy from a drivebelt into electrical energy to charge the battery and to operate the starting system, ignition system and electrical accessories.

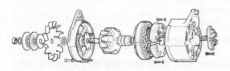

Alternator (exploded view)

Ampere (amp) A unit of measurement for the flow of electric current. One amp is the amount of current produced by one volt acting through a resistance of one ohm.

Anaerobic sealer A substance used to prevent bolts and screws from loosening. Anaerobic means that it does not require oxygen for activation. The Loctite brand is widely used.

Antifreeze A substance (usually ethylene glycol) mixed with water, and added to a vehicle's cooling system, to prevent freezing of the coolant in winter. Antifreeze also contains chemicals to inhibit corrosion and the formation of rust and other deposits that would tend to clog the radiator and coolant passages and reduce cooling efficiency.

Anti-seize compound A coating that reduces the risk of seizing on fasteners that are subjected to high temperatures, such as exhaust manifold bolts and nuts.

Anti-seize compound

Asbestos A natural fibrous mineral with great heat resistance, commonly used in the composition of brake friction materials. Asbestos is a health hazard and the dust created by brake systems should never be inhaled or ingested.

Axle A shaft on which a wheel revolves, or which revolves with a wheel. Also, a solid beam that connects the two wheels at one end of the vehicle. An axle which also transmits power to the wheels is known as a live axle.

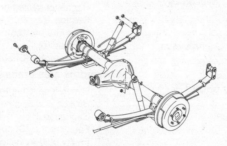

Axle assembly

Axleshaft A single rotating shaft, on either side of the differential, which delivers power from the final drive assembly to the drive wheels. Also called a driveshaft or a halfshaft.

B

Ball bearing An anti-friction bearing consisting of a hardened inner and outer race with hardened steel balls between two races.

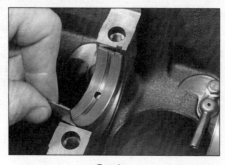

Bearing

Bearing The curved surface on a shaft or in a bore, or the part assembled into either, that permits relative motion between them with minimum wear and friction.

Big-end bearing The bearing in the end of the connecting rod that's attached to the crankshaft.

Bleed nipple A valve on a brake wheel cylinder, caliper or other hydraulic component that is opened to purge the hydraulic system of air. Also called a bleed screw.

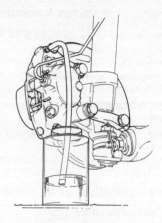

Brake bleeding

Brake bleeding Procedure for removing air from lines of a hydraulic brake system.

Brake disc The component of a disc brake that rotates with the wheels.

Brake drum The component of a drum brake that rotates with the wheels.

Brake linings The friction material which contacts the brake disc or drum to retard the vehicle's speed. The linings are bonded or riveted to the brake pads or shoes.

Brake pads The replaceable friction pads that pinch the brake disc when the brakes are applied. Brake pads consist of a friction material bonded or riveted to a rigid backing plate.

Brake shoe The crescent-shaped carrier to which the brake linings are mounted and which forces the lining against the rotating drum during braking.

Braking systems For more information on braking systems, consult the *Haynes Automotive Brake Manual*.

Breaker bar A long socket wrench handle providing greater leverage.

Bulkhead The insulated partition between the engine and the passenger compartment.

C

Caliper The non-rotating part of a disc-brake assembly that straddles the disc and carries the brake pads. The caliper also contains the hydraulic components that cause the pads to pinch the disc when the brakes are applied. A caliper is also a measuring tool that can be set to measure inside or outside dimensions of an object.

Camshaft A rotating shaft on which a series of cam lobes operate the valve mechanisms. The camshaft may be driven by gears, by sprockets and chain or by sprockets and a belt.

Canister A container in an evaporative emission control system; contains activated charcoal granules to trap vapours from the fuel system.

Canister

Carburettor A device which mixes fuel with air in the proper proportions to provide a desired power output from a spark ignition internal combustion engine.

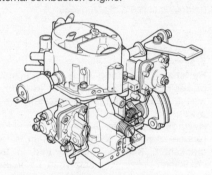

Carburettor

Castellated Resembling the parapets along the top of a castle wall. For example, a castellated balljoint stud nut.

Castellated nut

Castor In wheel alignment, the backward or forward tilt of the steering axis. Castor is positive when the steering axis is inclined rearward at the top.

Catalytic converter A silencer-like device in the exhaust system which converts certain pollutants in the exhaust gases into less harmful substances.

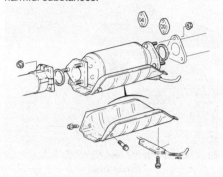

Catalytic converter

Circlip A ring-shaped clip used to prevent endwise movement of cylindrical parts and shafts. An internal circlip is installed in a groove in a housing; an external circlip fits into a groove on the outside of a cylindrical piece such as a shaft.

Clearance The amount of space between two parts. For example, between a piston and a cylinder, between a bearing and a journal, etc.

Coil spring A spiral of elastic steel found in various sizes throughout a vehicle, for example as a springing medium in the suspension and in the valve train.

Compression Reduction in volume, and increase in pressure and temperature, of a gas, caused by squeezing it into a smaller space.

Compression ratio The relationship between cylinder volume when the piston is at top dead centre and cylinder volume when the piston is at bottom dead centre.

Constant velocity (CV) joint A type of universal joint that cancels out vibrations caused by driving power being transmitted through an angle.

Core plug A disc or cup-shaped metal device inserted in a hole in a casting through which core was removed when the casting was formed. Also known as a freeze plug or expansion plug.

Crankcase The lower part of the engine block in which the crankshaft rotates.

Crankshaft The main rotating member, or shaft, running the length of the crankcase, with offset "throws" to which the connecting rods are attached.

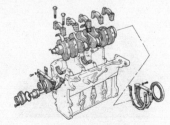

Crankshaft assembly

Crocodile clip See Alligator clip

D

Diagnostic code Code numbers obtained by accessing the diagnostic mode of an engine management computer. This code can be used to determine the area in the system where a malfunction may be located.

Disc brake A brake design incorporating a rotating disc onto which brake pads are squeezed. The resulting friction converts the energy of a moving vehicle into heat.

Double-overhead cam (DOHC) An engine that uses two overhead camshafts, usually one for the intake valves and one for the exhaust valves.

Drivebelt(s) The belt(s) used to drive accessories such as the alternator, water pump, power steering pump, air conditioning compressor, etc. off the crankshaft pulley.

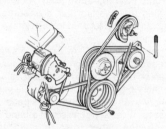

Accessory drivebelts

Driveshaft Any shaft used to transmit motion. Commonly used when referring to the axleshafts on a front wheel drive vehicle.

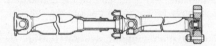

Driveshaft

Drum brake A type of brake using a drum-shaped metal cylinder attached to the inner surface of the wheel. When the brake pedal is pressed, curved brake shoes with friction linings press against the inside of the drum to slow or stop the vehicle.

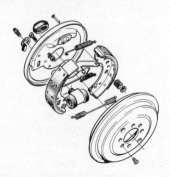

Drum brake assembly

E

EGR valve A valve used to introduce exhaust gases into the intake air stream.

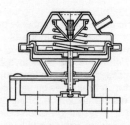

EGR valve

Electronic control unit (ECU) A computer which controls (for instance) ignition and fuel injection systems, or an anti-lock braking system. For more information refer to the *Haynes Automotive Electrical and Electronic Systems Manual*.

Electronic Fuel Injection (EFI) A computer controlled fuel system that distributes fuel through an injector located in each intake port of the engine.

Emergency brake A braking system, independent of the main hydraulic system, that can be used to slow or stop the vehicle if the primary brakes fail, or to hold the vehicle stationary even though the brake pedal isn't depressed. It usually consists of a hand lever that actuates either front or rear brakes mechanically through a series of cables and linkages. Also known as a handbrake or parking brake.

Endfloat The amount of lengthwise movement between two parts. As applied to a crankshaft, the distance that the crankshaft can move forward and back in the cylinder block.

Engine management system (EMS) A computer controlled system which manages the fuel injection and the ignition systems in an integrated fashion.

Exhaust manifold A part with several passages through which exhaust gases leave the engine combustion chambers and enter the exhaust pipe.

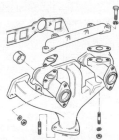

Exhaust manifold

F

Fan clutch A viscous (fluid) drive coupling device which permits variable engine fan speeds in relation to engine speeds.

Feeler blade A thin strip or blade of hardened steel, ground to an exact thickness, used to check or measure clearances between parts.

Feeler blade

Firing order The order in which the engine cylinders fire, or deliver their power strokes, beginning with the number one cylinder.

Flywheel A heavy spinning wheel in which energy is absorbed and stored by means of momentum. On cars, the flywheel is attached to the crankshaft to smooth out firing impulses.

Free play The amount of travel before any action takes place. The "looseness" in a linkage, or an assembly of parts, between the initial application of force and actual movement. For example, the distance the brake pedal moves before the pistons in the master cylinder are actuated.

Fuse An electrical device which protects a circuit against accidental overload. The typical fuse contains a soft piece of metal which is calibrated to melt at a predetermined current flow (expressed as amps) and break the circuit.

Fusible link A circuit protection device consisting of a conductor surrounded by heat-resistant insulation. The conductor is smaller than the wire it protects, so it acts as the weakest link in the circuit. Unlike a blown fuse, a failed fusible link must frequently be cut from the wire for replacement.

G

Gap The distance the spark must travel in jumping from the centre electrode to the side

Adjusting spark plug gap

electrode in a spark plug. Also refers to the spacing between the points in a contact breaker assembly in a conventional points-type ignition, or to the distance between the reluctor or rotor and the pickup coil in an electronic ignition.

Gasket Any thin, soft material - usually cork, cardboard, asbestos or soft metal - installed between two metal surfaces to ensure a good seal. For instance, the cylinder head gasket seals the joint between the block and the cylinder head.

Gasket

Gauge An instrument panel display used to monitor engine conditions. A gauge with a movable pointer on a dial or a fixed scale is an analogue gauge. A gauge with a numerical readout is called a digital gauge.

H

Halfshaft A rotating shaft that transmits power from the final drive unit to a drive wheel, usually when referring to a live rear axle.

Harmonic balancer A device designed to reduce torsion or twisting vibration in the crankshaft. May be incorporated in the crankshaft pulley. Also known as a vibration damper.

Hone An abrasive tool for correcting small irregularities or differences in diameter in an engine cylinder, brake cylinder, etc.

Hydraulic tappet A tappet that utilises hydraulic pressure from the engine's lubrication system to maintain zero clearance (constant contact with both camshaft and valve stem). Automatically adjusts to variation in valve stem length. Hydraulic tappets also reduce valve noise.

I

Ignition timing The moment at which the spark plug fires, usually expressed in the number of crankshaft degrees before the piston reaches the top of its stroke.

Inlet manifold A tube or housing with passages through which flows the air-fuel mixture (carburettor vehicles and vehicles with throttle body injection) or air only (port fuel-injected vehicles) to the port openings in the cylinder head.

J

Jump start Starting the engine of a vehicle with a discharged or weak battery by attaching jump leads from the weak battery to a charged or helper battery.

L

Load Sensing Proportioning Valve (LSPV) A brake hydraulic system control valve that works like a proportioning valve, but also takes into consideration the amount of weight carried by the rear axle.

Locknut A nut used to lock an adjustment nut, or other threaded component, in place. For example, a locknut is employed to keep the adjusting nut on the rocker arm in position.

Lockwasher A form of washer designed to prevent an attaching nut from working loose.

M

MacPherson strut A type of front suspension system devised by Earle MacPherson at Ford of England. In its original form, a simple lateral link with the anti-roll bar creates the lower control arm. A long strut - an integral coil spring and shock absorber - is mounted between the body and the steering knuckle. Many modern so-called MacPherson strut systems use a conventional lower A-arm and don't rely on the anti-roll bar for location.

Multimeter An electrical test instrument with the capability to measure voltage, current and resistance.

N

NOx Oxides of Nitrogen. A common toxic pollutant emitted by petrol and diesel engines at higher temperatures.

O

Ohm The unit of electrical resistance. One volt applied to a resistance of one ohm will produce a current of one amp.

Ohmmeter An instrument for measuring electrical resistance.

O-ring A type of sealing ring made of a special rubber-like material; in use, the O-ring is compressed into a groove to provide the sealing action.

O-ring

Overhead cam (ohc) engine An engine with the camshaft(s) located on top of the cylinder head(s).

Overhead valve (ohv) engine An engine with the valves located in the cylinder head, but with the camshaft located in the engine block.

Oxygen sensor A device installed in the engine exhaust manifold, which senses the oxygen content in the exhaust and converts this information into an electric current. Also called a Lambda sensor.

P

Phillips screw A type of screw head having a cross instead of a slot for a corresponding type of screwdriver.

Plastigage A thin strip of plastic thread, available in different sizes, used for measuring clearances. For example, a strip of Plastigage is laid across a bearing journal. The parts are assembled and dismantled; the width of the crushed strip indicates the clearance between journal and bearing.

Plastigage

Propeller shaft The long hollow tube with universal joints at both ends that carries power from the transmission to the differential on front-engined rear wheel drive vehicles.

Proportioning valve A hydraulic control valve which limits the amount of pressure to the rear brakes during panic stops to prevent wheel lock-up.

R

Rack-and-pinion steering A steering system with a pinion gear on the end of the steering shaft that mates with a rack (think of a geared wheel opened up and laid flat). When the steering wheel is turned, the pinion turns, moving the rack to the left or right. This movement is transmitted through the track rods to the steering arms at the wheels.

Radiator A liquid-to-air heat transfer device designed to reduce the temperature of the coolant in an internal combustion engine cooling system.

Refrigerant Any substance used as a heat transfer agent in an air-conditioning system. R-12 has been the principle refrigerant for many years; recently, however, manufacturers have begun using R-134a, a non-CFC substance that is considered less harmful to the ozone in the upper atmosphere.

Rocker arm A lever arm that rocks on a shaft or pivots on a stud. In an overhead valve engine, the rocker arm converts the upward movement of the pushrod into a downward movement to open a valve.

Rotor In a distributor, the rotating device inside the cap that connects the centre electrode and the outer terminals as it turns, distributing the high voltage from the coil secondary winding to the proper spark plug. Also, that part of an alternator which rotates inside the stator. Also, the rotating assembly of a turbocharger, including the compressor wheel, shaft and turbine wheel.

Runout The amount of wobble (in-and-out movement) of a gear or wheel as it's rotated. The amount a shaft rotates "out-of-true." The out-of-round condition of a rotating part.

S

Sealant A liquid or paste used to prevent leakage at a joint. Sometimes used in conjunction with a gasket.

Sealed beam lamp An older headlight design which integrates the reflector, lens and filaments into a hermetically-sealed one-piece unit. When a filament burns out or the lens cracks, the entire unit is simply replaced.

Serpentine drivebelt A single, long, wide accessory drivebelt that's used on some newer vehicles to drive all the accessories, instead of a series of smaller, shorter belts. Serpentine drivebelts are usually tensioned by an automatic tensioner.

Serpentine drivebelt

Shim Thin spacer, commonly used to adjust the clearance or relative positions between two parts. For example, shims inserted into or under bucket tappets control valve clearances. Clearance is adjusted by changing the thickness of the shim.

Slide hammer A special puller that screws into or hooks onto a component such as a shaft or bearing; a heavy sliding handle on the shaft bottoms against the end of the shaft to knock the component free.

Sprocket A tooth or projection on the periphery of a wheel, shaped to engage with a chain or drivebelt. Commonly used to refer to the sprocket wheel itself.

Starter inhibitor switch On vehicles with an automatic transmission, a switch that prevents starting if the vehicle is not in Neutral or Park.

Strut See MacPherson strut.

T

Tappet A cylindrical component which transmits motion from the cam to the valve stem, either directly or via a pushrod and rocker arm. Also called a cam follower.

Thermostat A heat-controlled valve that regulates the flow of coolant between the cylinder block and the radiator, so maintaining optimum engine operating temperature. A thermostat is also used in some air cleaners in which the temperature is regulated.

Thrust bearing The bearing in the clutch assembly that is moved in to the release levers by clutch pedal action to disengage the clutch. Also referred to as a release bearing.

Timing belt A toothed belt which drives the camshaft. Serious engine damage may result if it breaks in service.

Timing chain A chain which drives the camshaft.

Toe-in The amount the front wheels are closer together at the front than at the rear. On rear wheel drive vehicles, a slight amount of toe-in is usually specified to keep the front wheels running parallel on the road by offsetting other forces that tend to spread the wheels apart.

Toe-out The amount the front wheels are closer together at the rear than at the front. On front wheel drive vehicles, a slight amount of toe-out is usually specified.

Tools For full information on choosing and using tools, refer to the *Haynes Automotive Tools Manual*.

Tracer A stripe of a second colour applied to a wire insulator to distinguish that wire from another one with the same colour insulator.

Tune-up A process of accurate and careful adjustments and parts replacement to obtain the best possible engine performance.

Turbocharger A centrifugal device, driven by exhaust gases, that pressurises the intake air. Normally used to increase the power output from a given engine displacement, but can also be used primarily to reduce exhaust emissions (as on VW's "Umwelt" Diesel engine).

U

Universal joint or U-joint A double-pivoted connection for transmitting power from a driving to a driven shaft through an angle. A U-joint consists of two Y-shaped yokes and a cross-shaped member called the spider.

V

Valve A device through which the flow of liquid, gas, vacuum, or loose material in bulk may be started, stopped, or regulated by a movable part that opens, shuts, or partially obstructs one or more ports or passageways. A valve is also the movable part of such a device.

Valve clearance The clearance between the valve tip (the end of the valve stem) and the rocker arm or tappet. The valve clearance is measured when the valve is closed.

Vernier caliper A precision measuring instrument that measures inside and outside dimensions. Not quite as accurate as a micrometer, but more convenient.

Viscosity The thickness of a liquid or its resistance to flow.

Volt A unit for expressing electrical "pressure" in a circuit. One volt that will produce a current of one ampere through a resistance of one ohm.

W

Welding Various processes used to join metal items by heating the areas to be joined to a molten state and fusing them together. For more information refer to the *Haynes Automotive Welding Manual*.

Wiring diagram A drawing portraying the components and wires in a vehicle's electrical system, using standardised symbols. For more information refer to the *Haynes Automotive Electrical and Electronic Systems Manual*.

Note: *References throughout this index are in the form* "**Chapter number**" • "**Page number**". *So, for example, 2C•15 refers to page 15 of Chapter 2C.*

Note: *References throughout this index are in the form "Chapter number" • "Page number". So, for example, 2C•15 refers to page 15 of Chapter 2C.*

Note: *References throughout this index are in the form "Chapter number" • "Page number". So, for example, 2C•15 refers to page 15 of Chapter 2C.*

Preserving Our Motoring Heritage

< The Model J Duesenberg Derham Tourster. Only eight of these magnificent cars were ever built – this is the only example to be found outside the United States of America

Almost every car you've ever loved, loathed or desired is gathered under one roof at the Haynes Motor Museum. Over 300 immaculately presented cars and motorbikes represent every aspect of our motoring heritage, from elegant reminders of bygone days, such as the superb Model J Duesenberg to curiosities like the bug-eyed BMW Isetta. There are also many old friends and flames. Perhaps you remember the 1959 Ford Popular that you did your courting in? The magnificent 'Red Collection' is a spectacle of classic sports cars including AC, Alfa Romeo, Austin Healey, Ferrari, Lamborghini, Maserati, MG, Riley, Porsche and Triumph.

A Perfect Day Out

Each and every vehicle at the Haynes Motor Museum has played its part in the history and culture of Motoring. Today, they make a wonderful spectacle and a great day out for all the family. Bring the kids, bring Mum and Dad, but above all bring your camera to capture those golden memories for ever. You will also find an impressive array of motoring memorabilia, a comfortable 70 seat video cinema and one of the most extensive transport book shops in Britain. The Pit Stop Cafe serves everything from a cup of tea to wholesome, home-made meals or, if you prefer, you can enjoy the large picnic area nestled in the beautiful rural surroundings of Somerset.

> John Haynes O.B.E., Founder and Chairman of the museum at the wheel of a Haynes Light 12.

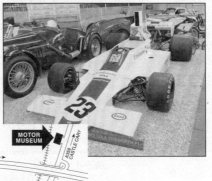

< Graham Hill's Lola Cosworth Formula 1 car next to a 1934 Riley Sports.

The Museum is situated on the A359 Yeovil to Frome road at Sparkford, just off the A303 in Somerset. It is about 40 miles south of Bristol, and 25 minutes drive from the M5 intersection at Taunton.

Open 9.30am - 5.30pm (10.00am - 4.00pm Winter) 7 days a week, *except Christmas Day, Boxing Day and New Years Day*

Special rates available for schools, coach parties and outings Charitable Trust No. 292048